Scottish
Photography

THE FIRST THIRTY YEARS

Sara Stevenson and A. D. Morrison-Low

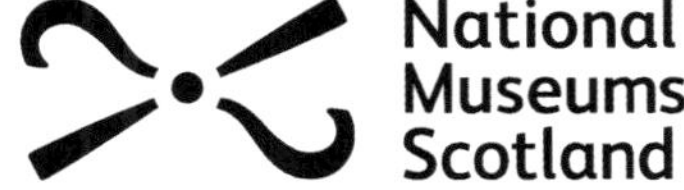

National Museums Scotland

This edition published in 2015 by
NMS Enterprises Limited – Publishing
a division of NMS Enterprises Limited
National Museums Scotland
Chambers Street
Edinburgh EH1 1JF

www.nms.ac.uk

British Library Cataloguing in Publication Data
A catalogue record of this book is available from the British
Library.

ISBN (CASED): 978 1 905267 97 2
ISBN (PAPER): 978 1 905267 99 6

Book design and cover by Mark Blackadder.
Printed and bound in the United Kingdom by Bell & Bain
  Limited, Glasgow.

Front cover and page 1: Ross & Thomson, unknown girl hold-
  ing a framed portrait of a man, perhaps her father, ninth-
  plate daguerreotype. (Howarth-Loomes Collection at
  National Museums Scotland, IL.2003.44.2.90).
Back cover: Robert Macpherson, 'Via Sugherari, the Theatre
  of Marcellus, Rome', c.1858, albumen print. (Scottish
  National Portrait Gallery, PGP 32.3).
Page IV: 'Interior of Fingal's Cave, Staffa', 1863, by George
  Washington Wilson, Aberdeen, stereo albumen prints
  from a wet collodion negative. (Howarth-Loomes
  Collection at National Museums Scotland, IL.2003.44.6.
  1.75)

For a full listing of NMS Enterprises Limited – Publishing
titles and related merchandise visit:

www.nms.ac.uk/books

National Museums Scotland would like to thank the following for their
assistance in the publication of this volume:

Bernard Quaritch Ltd
The Paul Mellon Centre for Studies in British Art

Contents

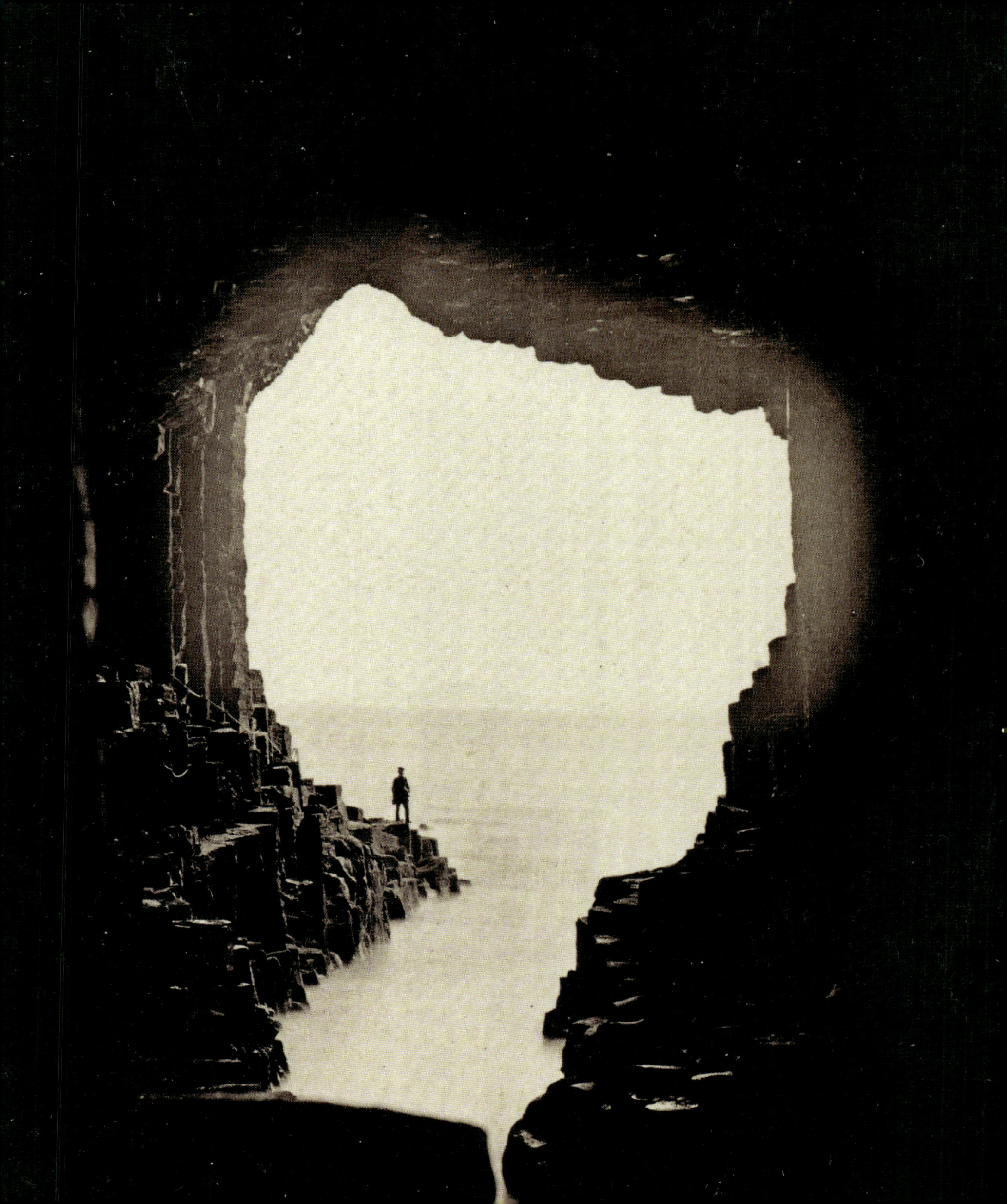

Acknowledgements

Over the years that it has taken this book to appear in print, many people – interested friends, archivists, librarians and curators – have provided help and critical input into this project. First and foremost, we must thank the kindness of Professor Emeritus Graham Smith, of the University of St Andrews, who read this work when it was in an unvarnished condition. Committee members of the Scottish Society for the History of Photography have provided support and, through their publication, the *Bulletin* (subsequently *Studies in Photography*, a space to air thoughts about the development of a particularly Scottish form of the art. Here, individually, we must thank Alex Boyd, David Bruce, Ray McKenzie, Monica and Nigel Thorp, Julie Lawson, Roddy Simpson and Sheila Masson. Among colleagues, past and present, we are grateful to Janis Adams, James Berry, Chris Claxton, Duncan Forbes, Imogen Gibbon, Graeme Gollan, Valerie Hunter, the late Robin Hutchison, Sarah Jeffcott, Anne Lyden, Simon Manfield, Fiona Pearson, Sheila Perry, James Simpson, Helen Smailes, Lis Smith, Christine Thompson, Helen Watson and other staff at the National Galleries of Scotland; Jane Carmichael, Henrietta Lidchi, Jim Tate, Kirke Kooke, Chelsea Clarke, Malcolm Shanks, Neil McLean, Joyce Smith, Graeme Yule, Julie Orford, Victoria Adams, Sarah Teale, Kate Blackadder, Lynne Reilly, Margaret Wilson and Lesley Taylor, the Library and other staff of National Museums Scotland.

Generous benefactors to the collections that we have looked after include Bernard and Alma Howarth-Loomes, Janet Notman, Mrs Ann Riddell and her family and Sir Alan Muir Wood and his family.

During the period leading up to writing, our researches intensified, and we must thank:

– Staff at the Houghton Library, Harvard University
– Kathy Eremin, Straus Center, Harvard University
– Sara Schechner, David P. Wheatland, Curator of the Collection of Historical Scientific Instruments, Harvard University
– Julie L. Melby, Firestone Library, Princeton University
– Malcolm Daniel and Meredith Friedman, Metropolitan Museum of Fine Art
– Peter Galassi, formerly Museum of Modern Art, New York
– Karen Moran, Royal Observatory Edinburgh
– Hil Williamson, formerly Central Library, Edinburgh
– Kevin Maclean, Central Library, Edinburgh
– Staff at the National Library of Scotland
– Alison Rosie and Linda Ramsay, National Archives of Scotland
– Joanna Soden and Sandy Wood, Royal Scottish Academy
– Marianne Smith, Royal College of Surgeons of Edinburgh
– Norman Reid, Tom Normand, Luke Gartlan, Marc Boulay and Rachel Nordstrom, University of St Andrews
– Staff at the Mitchell Library, Glasgow
– Judith Keller, Amanda Maddox and Linda Briscoe Myers, Department of Photographs, Getty Museum
– Jessica S. McDonald, Miriam Katz, Bridget Gayle Ground, Betsy Nitsch and Roy Flukinger, Harry Ransom Center, University of Texas, Austin
– Colin Harding, Karen Hellman, Rebecca Smith, Philippa Wright and Brian Liddy, National Media Museum, Bradford

---

Opposite: 'Interior of Fingal's Cave, Staffa', 1863, by George Washington Wilson, Aberdeen.

– John Ward, formerly Science Museum, London
– John Falconer, British Library
– Richard Ovenden and Francesca Galligan, Bodleian Library, Oxford
– Hilary Roberts, Imperial War Museum, London
– Hope Kingsley and Polly Fleury, Wilson Photography Centre, London
– William Schupbach, Wellcome Institute, London
– Lilly Koltun, formerly Portrait Gallery, Canada
– Louise Désy, Canadian Centre for Architecture, Montreal
– Gael Newton, National Gallery Australia, Canberra
– Nissan Perez, The Shpilman Institute for Photography
– Nicole Ensing and Joan M. Schwartz, Queen's University, Canada
– Emma Baudy, Bank of America, London
– Staff of Orkney Public Library
– Bodo Von Dewitz, formerly Museum Ludwig, Cologne
– Michael Pritchard, Royal Photographic Society, Bath
– Elizabeth Edwards and Kelley Wilder, De Montfort University
– Paul Adair and Robin Rodger, Perth Museum and Art Gallery
– Yupin Chung, Burrell Collection, Glasgow
– Alan Davies, State Library of New South Wales
– Howard and Jane Ricketts
– David Weston and Sarah Hepworth, Special Collections, University of Glasgow
– Joe Struble, Alison Nordstrom and Mark Osterman, George Eastman House, Rochester, NY
– Judy Annear, Art Gallery of New South Wales
– Lorna Mitchell and Leonie Paterson, Royal Botanic Gardens, Edinburgh
– Jennifer A. Watts, The Huntington Library, San Marino
– Bridget Henisch and the late Heinz Henisch
– The late Murray Johnston
– Terry Pepper, National Portrait Gallery, London
– Sophie Gordon, Royal Archives, Windsor
– Martin Barnes, Suhashini Shinha, Marta Weiss, Victoria and Albert Museum
– François Reynaud, Musée Carnavalet, Paris
– Fani Constantinou, Aliki Tsirgialou and their colleagues at the Benaki Museum, Athens

Besides these individuals and organisations, a number of independent scholars have provided us with invaluable assistance with particular problems: these include Hans Christian Adam, William Brock, Robin Gillanders, Michael Gray, Denis Pellerin, Joe Rock, Larry Schaaf, Lindsey Stewart, Gareth Syvret, Roger Taylor, Mike Ware and Paul Muir Wood.

To undertake study for this project, Sara Stevenson was the recipient of British Academy research funding (Sir Ernest Cassell Educational Trust Fund) to visit George Eastman House in 2003; she was a J. Paul Getty Museum Scholar in 2012; and David Douglas Duncan Fellow, Harry Ransom Humanities Research Center, University of Texas, in 2013. We thank all of these foundations for their generosity.

This work could not have been produced without the kindness of an anonymous sponsor, and Bernard Quaritch Ltd and The Paul Mellon Centre for Studies in British Art; and our referees.

Sara Stevenson and Alison Morrison-Low
Edinburgh, June 2015

Foreword

Since the early 1980s, Sara Stevenson and Alison Morrison-Low have been pivotal in developing awareness at home and abroad of the exceptional role played by Scotland in the introduction, development and practice of photography. Individually and collectively, their contributions have been multifaceted, ranging from the generation of superb exhibitions to the publication of exemplary and accessible scholarship.

As founding Curator of Photography and then Principal Curator at the Scottish National Portrait Gallery, Stevenson performed her curatorial functions beyond all realistic expectations, nurturing donations, making astute acquisitions, and writing – always writing – with scholarly conviction and evangelical fervour.

Likewise, Morrison-Low has combined a distinguished career as Curator and now Principal Curator of Scientific Instruments and Photography at National Museums Scotland with astonishingly diverse and productive activity as a scholar. Co-existing with magisterial studies ranging from the manufacture of scientific instruments to weights and measures and Scottish lighthouses are her highly significant publications in the history of photography, especially groundbreaking studies concerning Sir David Brewster and the origins of photography at the University of St Andrews.

Modesty is a Scottish characteristic and so it is not surprising that Stevenson and Morrison-Low have gone about their work without fuss or fanfare. Had they lived elsewhere, they would have been designated living national treasures long before now. As it is, Morrison-Low's *Making Scientific Instruments in the Industrial Revolution* was awarded Germany's Paul Bunge prize in 2008, and in 2003 Stevenson won the International Center for Photography's highly prestigious Infinity Award for her *Personal Art of David Octavius Hill*.

The present volume distils the knowledge the authors have amassed over many years of engagement with the subject, enriched by the immense labour involved in the preparation and writing of the present book. In the tradition of David Octavius Hill, who had a talent for amity and collaboration, Stevenson and Morrison-Low have brought to the subject a long, fruitful and inimitable friendship that is reflected in their shared passion for Scottish photography and is made stronger by mutual respect, tireless labour and great wit – in all senses of the word.

The foundations of this book lie in Morrison-Low's expertise in the science of photography, especially its beginnings in Scotland in the circle of Sir David Brewster; and in Stevenson's profound understanding of the art of David Octavius Hill and Robert Adamson, and the entire spectrum of Scottish photography. But the scope of this book is global, extending from modest communities in Scotland to Africa, Australasia, India, North America, Russia and elsewhere.

Morrison-Low and Stevenson's imposing learning is enlivened by human observations gleaned from contemporary records. It was pleasing to learn that Scots abroad, far from being po-faced in adversity, handled photographic disasters with self-deprecating humour, determination to succeed next time and great inventiveness. It was also intriguing to learn that the salubrious atmosphere of Pau, in the Pyrenees, made sitters' hair curl naturally and gave subjects 'a certain degree of self-satisfied dreaminess'. As observed in this book, an early life spent in Scotland provided excellent training for any rigours that photographers might encounter in the tropical jungles of Africa or in the frigid wastes of Canada.

In the rectorial address that he delivered at the University of St Andrews in 1869, James Anthony Froude no doubt intended to flatter his audience when he proclaimed of the Scots that 'no people so few in number have scored so deep a mark in the world's history'. More recently, in *How the Scots Invented the Modern World*, Arthur Herman has made this case more dispassionately. Neither Froude nor Herman mentioned photography, however. With *Scottish Photography: The First Thirty Years*, Sara Stevenson and Alison Morrison-Low have addressed this lacuna, for they have written a rich, lively and passionate history of the Scottish diaspora as seen through the camera's lens.

Graham Smith

Emeritus Professor of the History of Photography
University of St Andrews

Preface

National Museums Scotland is delighted to have supported and seen to fruition this important publication which celebrates photography: the harnessing of light through technology in the service of documentation and art. It is a fitting and timely record of the role that Scotland has played in the development of photography, and the capacity of two national institutions to lay bare this intricate narrative. This is a meticulously researched chronicle of those individuals whose thrilling discoveries advanced in a social and economic context underpinned by social and political changes, most notably the Industrial Revolution. Here the rich social history of Scotland as a place of photographic experimentation and enquiry is built up in layers.

The publication begins with an anterior view, an exposition of the links between the aims and the sensibility of painting with photography, visually signalled by David Octavius Hill's 'The Market Place, Ayr' (1835). This is a foretelling taken up in a later chapter of Hill's well known, influential and successful collaboration with Robert Adamson evidenced in part through the evocatively captured though slightly blurred scene taken in 1846 at Edinburgh Castle of the 92nd Gordon Highlanders (a calotype) where a singular face emerges with clarity, and also in D. O. Hill's shorter-lived working relationship with Alexander McGlashon that yielded photographs in 1860 (albumen prints) of a different aesthetic and greater precision.

The tracing of Hill's career, briefly here and more fully in the publication, shows the care with which the authors have charted the progress of interest in advancing photographic technology through the life of a pioneer. It is a vivid representation of the tangled and subtle networks that were the foundations for the development of photography throughout Scotland, as seen through the clubs, associations, exhibitions, newspaper advertisements and reports.

To be found in this publication are the chemists and doctors, the scientific instrument makers, the modest experimenters and the landed gentry, those men and women who photographed for interest, for art and for profit, whose acknowledged and unacknowledged careers have contributed to our contemporary ability to photograph the world. Their work adorns the pages, their biographies are meticulously drawn. This is a map of Scotland's national and international influence, the latter encapsulated in the career of Alexander Gardner, whose work undertaken in inauspicious conditions served to bring the horrors of the American Civil War and its major battles to public attention. Photography gave certain licence, and the authors guide us to this. They have also delicately excavated the contribution of women as photographers and photographic assistants. They have satisfyingly brought to our attention the symbolically laden work of Lady Alice Kerr whose dramatic and sultry portrait of Wilfrid Scawen Blunt is enduringly contemporary.

These innovators, though engaged in artistic and scientific pursuits, were not at all times serious. There is humour. To my eye a pair of photographs from the album of Sir James Young Simpson, currently held by the Royal College of Surgeons, clearly conveys the attribute of joyous conviviality. It is not clear what drove James Mathews, James Young Simpson and William Walker to smile at the camera and then turn their back to it with their arms folded, but the gesture transports us to them. This is the front and back of eminent men; they are amused and we with them.

This is an account of photography performed prior to the elaborate 20th century discussion of photography's relationship with the real, its indexicality, the term lastingly assigned to photography by French cultural theorist Roland

Barthes. Indexicality describes photography's shaky relationship with reality and truth, derived physically and chemically from the impact of light and dark on a photosensitive material.

Photographs can of course be purposefully deceitful, yet it is the photographic image's connection with a place, a past or a person that was real that fascinates as time passes. In the context of this publication, of all the photographs featured – beyond the beautifully set up social document of women in a Glasgow close by Thomas Annan, the crisp exactitude of William Donaldson Clark's print of the National Gallery of Scotland, or the tender portrait of mutual clutching of Elia Filleul with his great, great granddaughter by William Collie – the image that makes me pause is the standing portrait of George Wilson. It is a revelatory image because it shows the founding Director of what is now the National Museum of Scotland in a way that I believe to be true. Standing and looking slightly to the side, he wears an academic gown, his right hand gently laid on a glass bottle presumably of chemicals (there is a label) and his left hand more heavily placed on books. This is a man many of us feel has been too little considered as a figure of influence and vision. George Wilson died young before the Museum was a physical fact and his writings leave us wondering what a longer custodianship would have meant. He is more regularly photographed sitting in three quarter length, maybe because his foot was amputated in 1842 after some illness and without the benefit of anaesthetic, a matter he subsequently took up with Young Simpson advocating the patient's point of view. His physiognomy in this unfamiliar photograph seems to confirm his sister's memoir of him as a man of thoughtful intellect, gentle with a genial humour and sparkling eyes. A chemist by training Wilson gave lectures on photography and demonstrated photographic techniques, though he did not to our knowledge take photographs. By the late 1850s Wilson wrote and spoke of museums as laboratories and exchanges where ideas and technology could be discussed, understood and put on view, a place where the fusion of beauty and utility could be properly understood and made publicly accessible. Beauty and utility fittingly describe the processes at the heart of early photography, including the ideas that drove them, the tangible products and instruments made to facilitate these.

This publication details lives and works and is the recognisable product of exhaustive research by its authors over many years and among national archives and collections. It is a testament to the passionate desire to understand and set out in writing the experimental science and art of photography as it unfolded in Scotland. In this endeavour the authors have enjoyed the support of many individuals, institutions and foundations, and National Museums Scotland is particularly thankful to Bernard Quaritch Ltd and the Paul Mellon Centre for Studies in British Art. The Museum is also very grateful to Mrs Alma Howarth-Loomes for access given to the B. E. C Howarth-Loomes Collection.

If photography is about memory, the authors have restored ours by prompting us to recall the beauty of early photographs, as well as the excitement and energy underlying their production. Happily this publication is published at the same time as a special exhibition at the National Museum of Scotland that will allow a wider public to enjoy and witness for themselves what the authors have over many years uncovered and discovered in the field of Scottish photography.

Henrietta Lidchi
Keeper of World Cultures
National Museums Scotland

Introduction

Around 1980, as young curators, we often wondered aloud to each other (and anyone else who might listen) why there was no 'history of Scottish photography': why had no one at least sketched out the outline of who had been the towering figures, what were the landmark moments, the important photographs of 19th-century Scotland. At that time, history of photography was itself a young discipline, more practised and appreciated across the Atlantic than in Europe, and not much at all in Scotland. Thirty-five years later, there are many more interested people working in this rewarding area.

Nationalist histories are often found to be protesting too much. Do we need a history of Scottish photography? Do we need one now? This book has been written in the run up to the 2014 independence referendum, which has provided a critical backdrop to our academic labours. Our justification is this: Scotland's position as a host to the new practice of photography was unusual in some respects: the ground for the science and the art had been laid by the thinkers and practitioners of the Scottish Enlightenment. Inheritors of that great movement – effectively over by 1839 – can be seen in the multidisciplinary figures of Sir David Brewster, based in St Andrews and Edinburgh, or Dr John Pringle Nichol, who was Professor of Astronomy at the University of Glasgow. Broader initiatives, progress through physical investigation of new areas of science, and new discoveries at home and abroad, coupled with the technological and industrial booms of the time, gave a new vigour to explorations in both science and the arts.

The energetic cross-referencing of the early period flowed naturally into the early years of photographic practice: the new 'Victorian' art had its natural roots in the Georgian period. 'Scottish photography' crossed national borders: the Scots have always been on the move, and with the invention of photography they took their cameras with them. This book is therefore designed to address the Scottish photographers in a wide sense: people born here and people working both here and elsewhere. The practice we are describing is thus both local and international in its scope and impact.

To date, only two books have attempted to cover similar ground: and each has done this in rather different ways.[1] The foundation for our work has been laid by *Studies in Photography* (formerly *SSHoP Bulletin*), the journal of the Scottish Society for the History of Photography, formed in 1983; the Festival exhibition, by the Scottish National Portrait Gallery, shown at the Royal Scottish Academy in 1995, 'Light From The Dark Room'; and, of course, the national collections that it has been our great privilege to care for over the past thirty years or so. Our text has been led by contemporary documents and publications, and by the surviving photographs. This has dictated the approach and character of the book and the different chapters.

The first three decades of photographic practice were set in a context of movement and change: religious, political, demographic, aesthetic and intellectual. However, this was undercut both by the individual initiative and the sociable drive behind the explorations of photography. Especially in these early years, the great advantage of a democratic practice lay in private determinations, crossed wires and periodic chaos/confusion; there is no overly-evident chronology or line that can be followed marking progress. The status of the individuals – from itinerant photographers, anxious to make a living and devising splendid self-advertisements, to university professors, playing with the processes in their spare time – has largely determined the written material and photographs they have left us. It was a period of great literacy and, for parts of this story, the words are apt to overtake the pictures. And there are indeed serious gaps in the visual knowledge, particularly with the early daguerreotypes. As museum curators, we very much hope that readers will be prompted to look in the attic and make new discoveries.

Many great and intriguing photographs are now to be found in collections all over the world; but we were delighted to find there are many more in collections within Scotland and Britain as a whole. It has been a pleasure to reacquaint ourselves with images in our own institutions, as well as finding others not so far away.

The first chapter discusses the sympathetic relationship between art, science and technology in Scotland, which laid a fertile ground for photography to flourish. This includes the camera obscura and panorama; the interest in light and atmosphere found in the work of artists, including Henry Raeburn and J. M. W. Turner; interest in the sciences of chemistry and optics; and the industrial approach. The second chapter looks at the crucial period between 1839, with the announcement of photography, and about 1842, when the St Andrews circle of calotypists found success in producing their positive images. Chapter three looks at the professional daguerreotypists, both in the cities, and the itinerants, while the following chapter examines their calotypist counterparts. These include David Octavius Hill, Robert Adamson and Miss Mann; W. H. F. Talbot; the Cundell family and John Muir Wood; William Collie in Jersey; and the early years of James Ross and John Thomson. The fifth chapter looks at professional photographers from about 1851, examining some prominent figures – the later work of Ross and Thomson, Thomas Rodger, James Valentine and George Washington Wilson, among others – as well as the supply of chemicals and equipment. Chapter six looks at photographic societies, the circle of doctors, including Dr Thomas Keith; the 'Upper Ten Thousand', including Lady Alice Kerr, Ronald Leslie Melville, Lady Hawarden and Julia Margaret Cameron's encounter with Scotland; and the criminal element in photography. The following chapter examines radical photographers: Alexander Gardner in the United States, Thomas Annan in Glasgow, William Carrick in Russia, and John Thomson in the Far East. By the eighth chapter, we are able to look at photographers, their patrons and their critics, including the debacle over the showing, or non-showing, of Rejlander's 'Two Ways of Life' to an Edinburgh audience. Chapter nine discusses photographers visiting Europe and the Near East, while the final chapter examines those whose journeys were longer and undertaken in the service of empire.

Scottish photography's first thirty years was a fascinating and productive time; and we are aware that more research will uncover more intriguing stories – and possibly more first-class photographers. We look forward to welcoming further work in this intriguing and rewarding area of research.

We now know of nearly 1500 photographers who operated within the first thirty years and do not attempt to engage with them all here. The University of St Andrews is simultaneously publishing a listing of these photographers with the basic data, which is designed to support this work, and extend the raw material for further research.

Sara Stevenson and Alison Morrison-Low

Note 1.   Normand 2007; Simpson 2012.

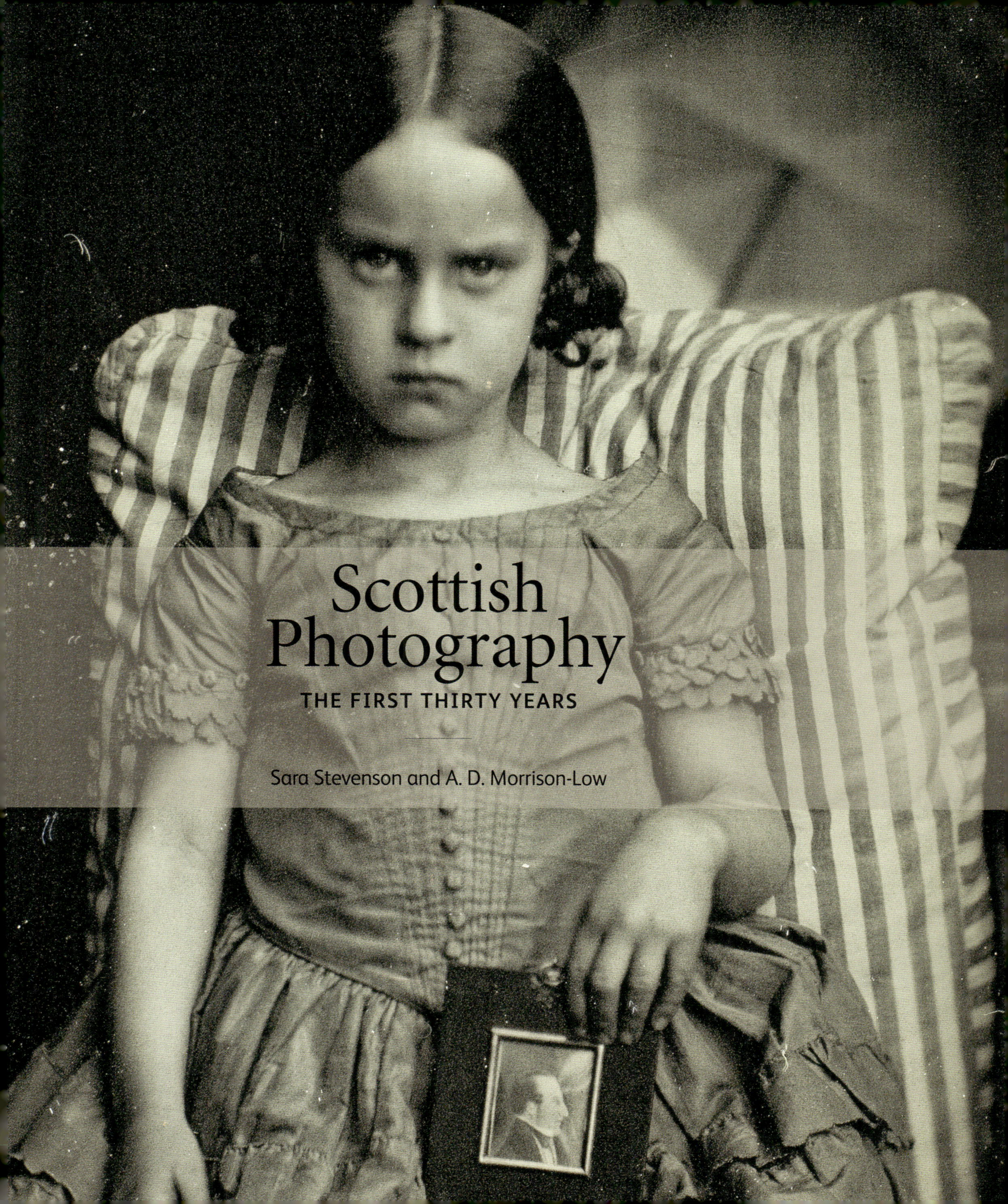

Scottish Photography
THE FIRST THIRTY YEARS
Sara Stevenson and A. D. Morrison-Low

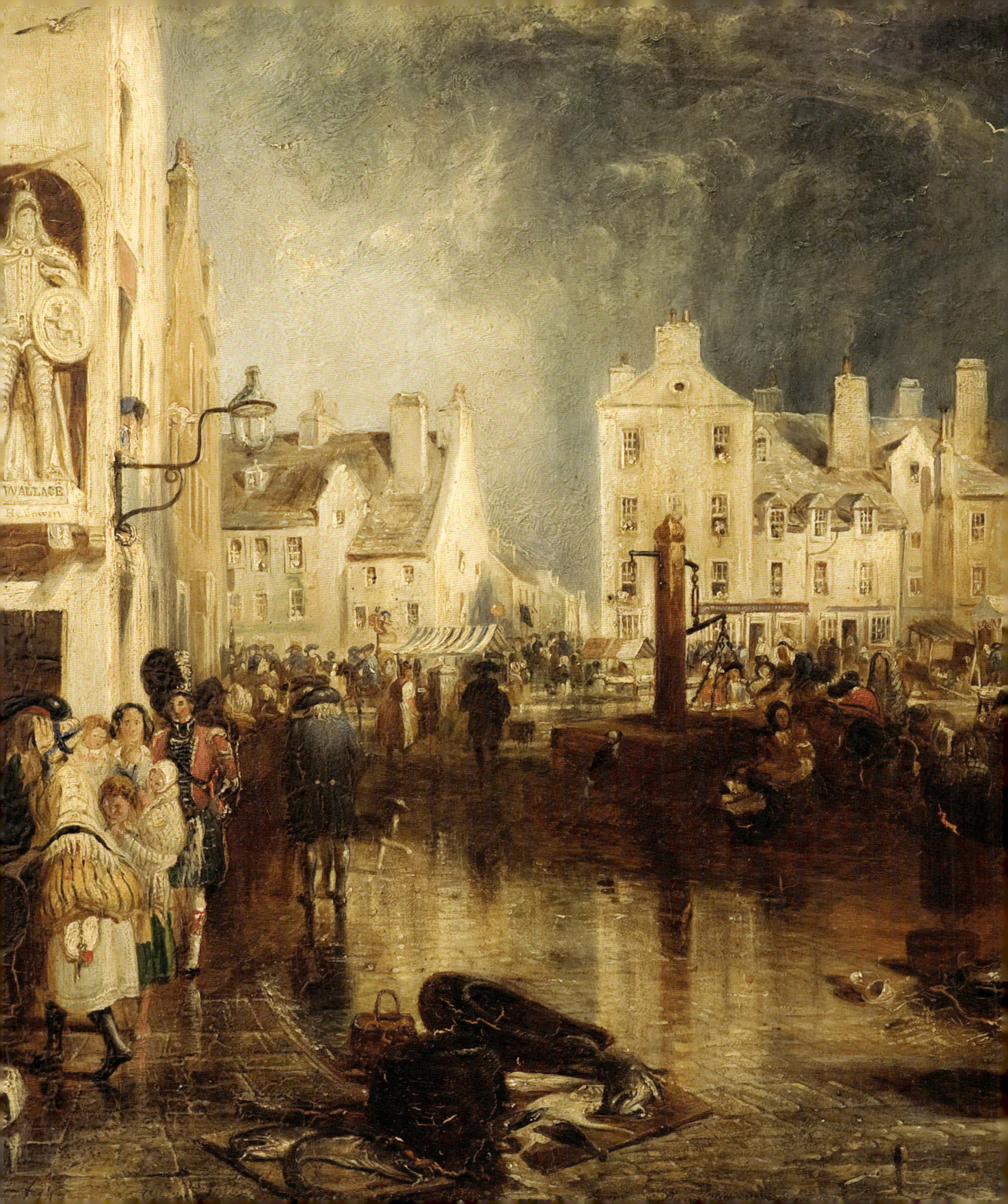

WALLACE

CHAPTER ONE

The Background to Scottish Photography

That which strikes the eye is a kind of Camera Obscura effect,
and from those pictures which seem to be his best, I shd. conclude
He has looked very much at Nature, reflected in the Camera.

✴

Joseph Farington's *Diary,*
on visiting Henry Raeburn's studio, 1801

There were several components required for the invention of the photographic art: the hardware or device (the camera); the light-sensitive chemistry that would make an image of the real world inside that camera; and the ability to stop that sensitivity and save the image. The oldest of these discoveries was the camera. The word 'camera' is simply the Latin for room or box – a space enclosed by six walls.[1] The closed box has proved a fascinating idea over centuries and across the world's cultures – a dominating image of not-knowing, used as a metaphor to explain great issues (Pandora's box, containing all the evil of the world, opened and loosed through curiosity; Schroedinger's cat, trapped in an imaginary box to explain the mysteries of quantum physics).

The painters' interest in the box resulted in the peepshow – a view of the outside world or even another room created within a box [Fig. 1.1], and seen through a little hole in the side. The peepshow became popular street entertainment, and led by natural extension to the much enlarged versions, the panorama and diorama, where the audience itself was inside the box [Fig. 1.2]. In both cases, the way the audience saw was controlled, and the resulting experience was an engaging illusion.

When the walls of the enclosed box are breached with a small hole which lets in the bright light from outdoors, the 'camera obscura' offers magical possibilities. The hole takes in the world as a brightly-coloured image of the view, projected onto the opposite wall, upside down.[2] The idea emerges in antiquity, and was described both in China and Greece. It was exploited to create mystery and examined as a natural phenomenon.

By the 16th century, the camera was familiar in Europe. The 17th-century development of the lens focussed the image, and the camera obscura became a practical device [Figs 1.3 and 1.4].[3] The portable camera was invaluable for

Opposite, Fig. 1.10 (detail): David Octavius Hill, 'The Market Place, Ayr', 1835.

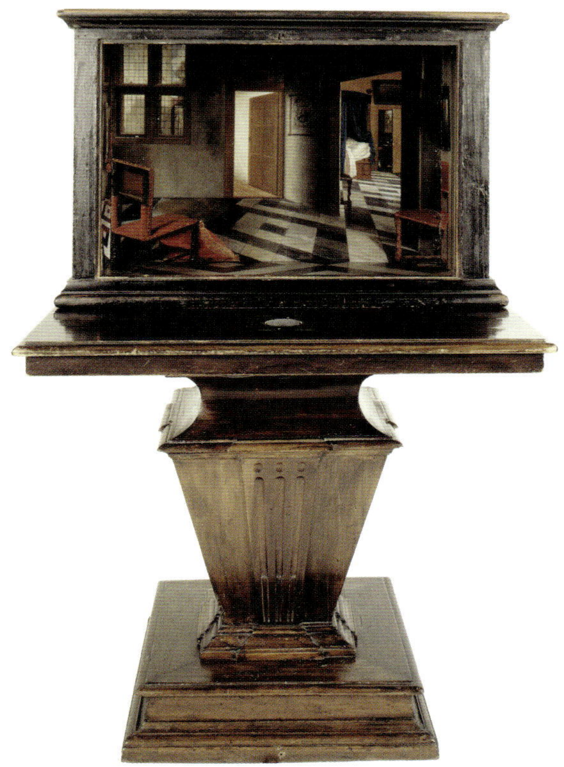

Fig. 1.1 (left): Samuel van Hoogstraten, peepshow with the interior of a Dutch house, *c*.1655–60. (National Gallery, London, NG3832)

Fig. 1.2 (below): David Octavius Hill, 'The Twa brigs, Ayr', 1840, showing a portable peepshow, engraving. (Howarth-Loomes Collection at National Museums Scotland, IL.2003.44.8.48)

the technical draughtsman and the topographic artist, who could sketch a spread of landscape from the image projected on a flat surface. This visual note-taking would speed up the preliminary drawing, as well as offer a reasonably accurate sense of the view within a short time, when the light and the atmosphere might be stable. This, most obviously, would be remarkably attractive for travellers and the British plein-air painters, subjected to the British weather. It was used by surveyors and architects in Scotland, one of whom may have been the army officer and draughtsman, John Slezer (d.1717). He produced the first extended series of Scottish landscape drawings in the late 17th century, which was published as *Theatrum Scotiae* [Fig. 1.5].[4]

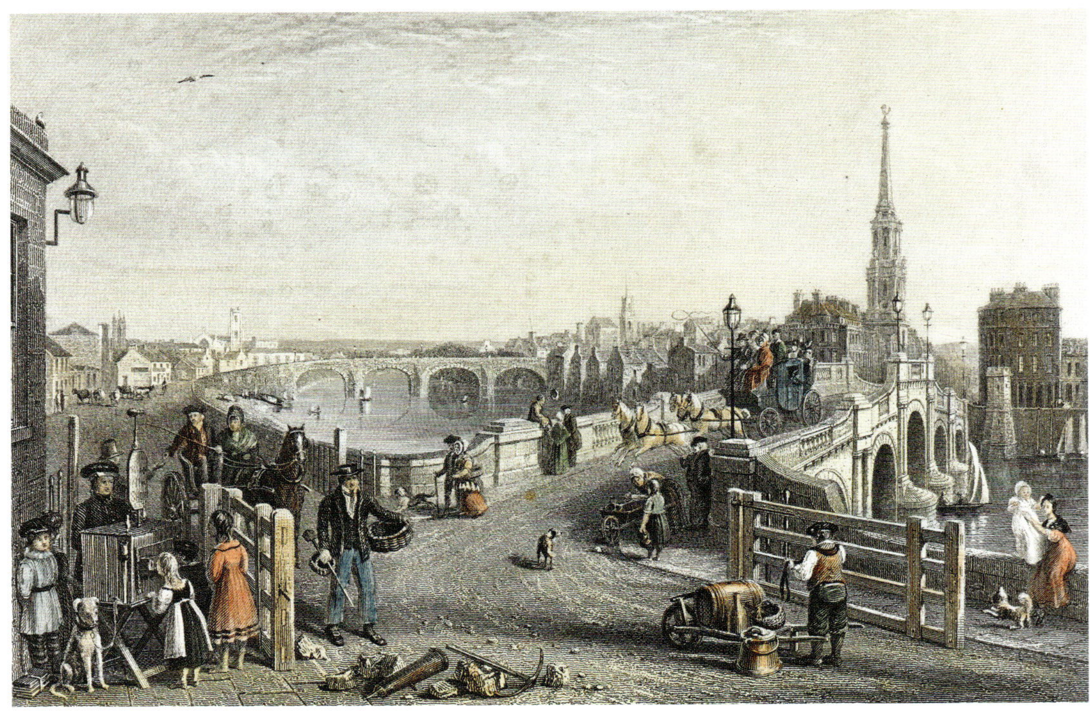

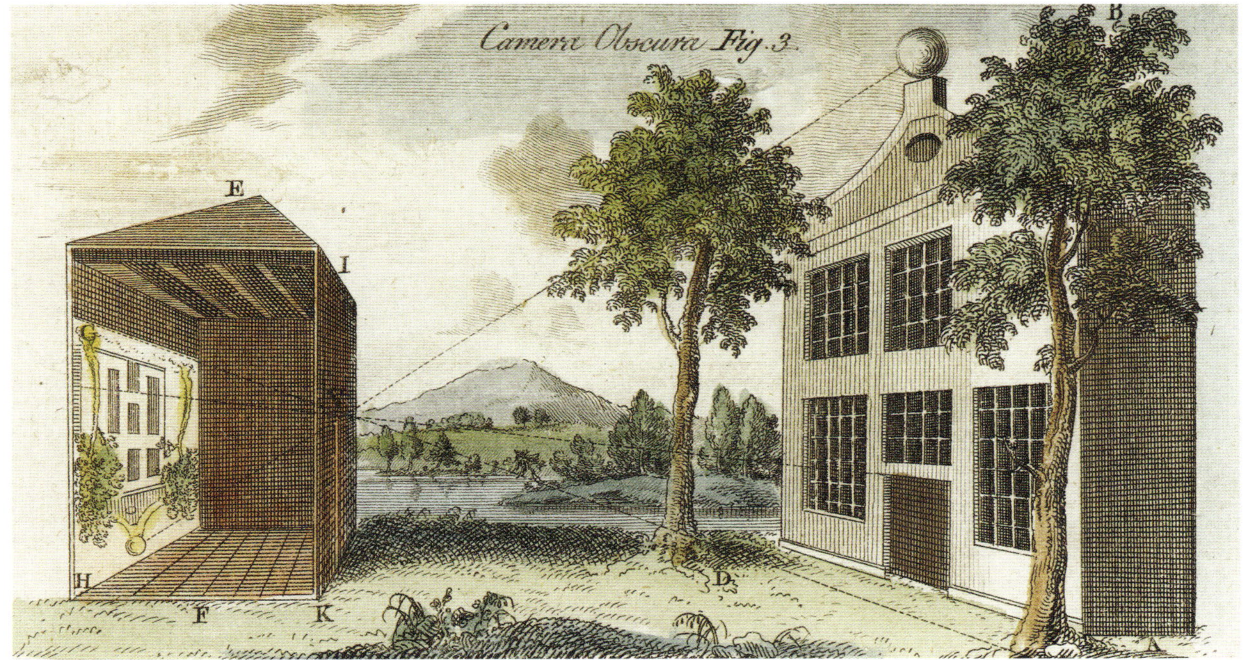

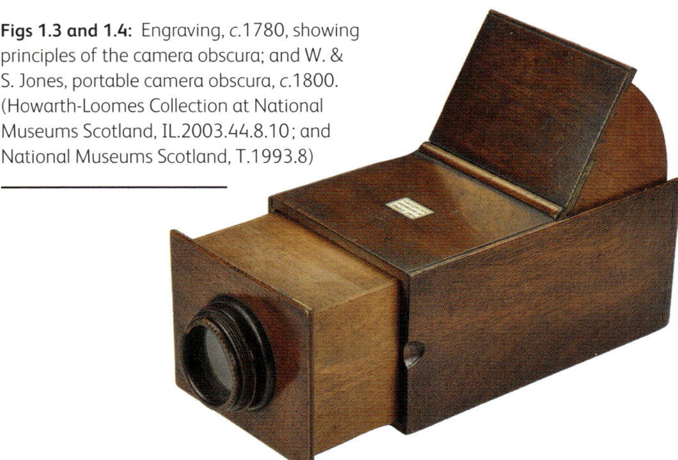

Figs 1.3 and 1.4: Engraving, *c.*1780, showing principles of the camera obscura; and W. & S. Jones, portable camera obscura, *c.*1800. (Howarth-Loomes Collection at National Museums Scotland, IL.2003.44.8.10; and National Museums Scotland, T.1993.8)

When Paul Sandby (1731–1809) toured Scotland in the mid-18th century, as part of the English army of occupation, he was primarily concerned with surveying and mapping the country in the aftermath of the 1745 Jacobite rebellion.[5] He found the camera useful for rapid topographical sketches. Between 1760 and 1774, the Scotsman James Bruce (1730–94) was using a camera obscura on his travels in Abyssinia. As an Enlightenment explorer, Bruce took with him the scientific accoutrements required to map and sketch the flora, fauna, ruins and antiquities, with Luigi Balugani, a skilled architectural draughtsman, to assist him. Despite these accurate records, Bruce's ground-breaking discoveries, including his identification of the source of the Blue Nile, were widely disbelieved. The account of his travels, which filled five volumes, was greeted more as fiction than as fact – the camera was not yet regarded as a purveyor of truth.[6]

The camera worked with direct and indirect light, or reflected and dispersed. It is, for example, reasonable that some of the most pleasing experiments, conducted by Johannes Vermeer (1632–75) with the camera, can be placed in the city of Ghent, threaded with reflecting canals.[7]

Generally speaking, it is not known which painters used the camera, and it is far from evident in their finished work. We tend to consider the impact of the camera on painting, primarily when pictures are precise and visually fixed – the kind of elaborated cityscape in Canaletto's painting. This is not necessarily true. The visual stability of built structures could be captured by slower means – by a fixed method of marking the place between one day's work and the next.

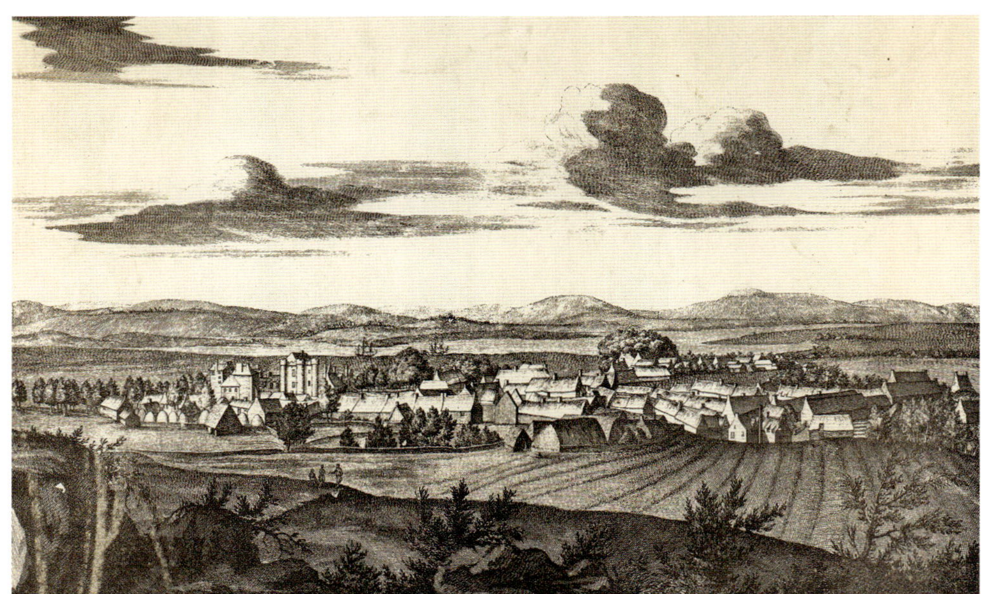

The advanced fascination of the camera obscura, beyond its topographic use, was expressed by British painters in Rome in the 1840s, in rejecting the precise daguerreotype process of photography in favour of the non-photographic camera. Francis Sylvester Mahony, the Irish journalist, wrote to Charles Dickens from there in January 1846:

> You have passed too rapidly amongst us …. As you passed along, you have simply *daguerreotyped* the glorious landscape, the towered cities, and the motley groups; but your countrymen, the landscape painters here, at whose mess-table I am an occasional guest, have stigmatised that new-fangled process … by the opprobrious term of *dog-trapping*. The old method of the *camera obscura*, which they still cling to, allows a more patient study of details, and involves a more laborious investigation of varying appearances.[8]

The camera framed and reduced the world outside and could bring it within the focus of the eye for contemplation; it reduced the distractions of the reality; it gave an intriguing sense of intimate possession (the landscape could be clasped by the hands). The foreign artists in Rome preferred the camera image to the captured photographic image.

What is *seen* in the camera is, most importantly, not fixed – it is framed by the edge of the lens, but it constantly relates to passing time, showing movement, the shifting of light and alterations in the atmosphere. In practice, it is the predecessor of the movie camera, not the still camera. The image is upside down, it is more often blurred than precise, and the colour is apt to be intense, with an apparent internal glow.

In the 18th century, the Swiss mathematician Leonhard Euler described just one variation, which illuminates the painters' study. He wrote of a 'very singular phenomenon … when the aperture made in the window-shutter of the dark chamber is very small'; without a lens, single rays of incoming light fell on the opposite surface as a pair of smaller, dancing spots.[9] The magical picture of the camera obscura was subtly outside the experience of the real world; it was a translation of reality rather than a direct transcription. When Paul Sandy worked in Scotland, he extended his interest from the topographic into a study of atmosphere; a picture of Leith shows him combining an interest in the light with the tangible details of the view [FIG. 1.6]. When he painted Roslin Glen in 1775, he drew Lady Frances Scott (1750–1817) in the foreground working with a camera. Tellingly, her camera is pointed into the low setting sun; she was painting the light [FIG. 1.7].[10]

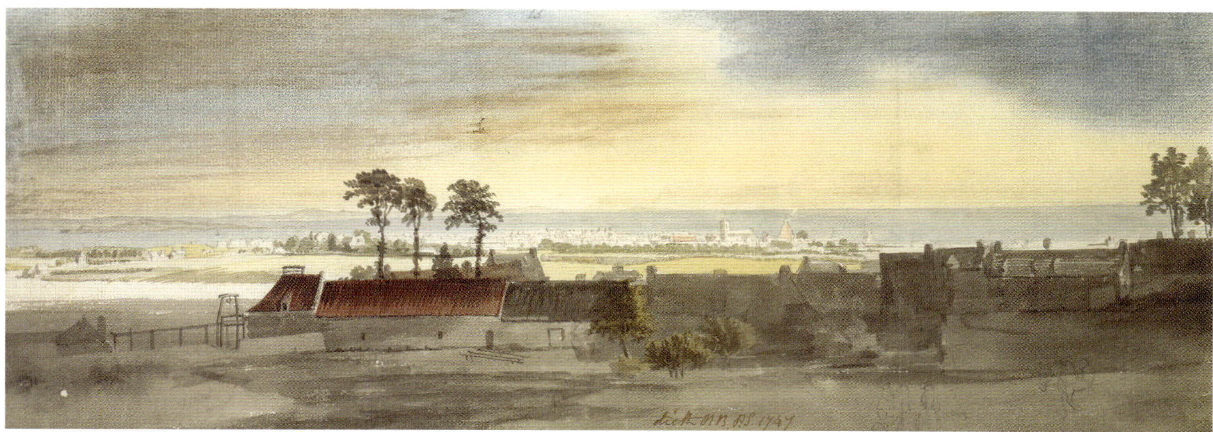

Fig. 1.6 (above): Paul Sandby, 'A distant View of Leith from the south-east', 1747, chalk and watercolour over graphite. (Ashmolean Museum, Oxford, WA.B.I.IV.240.131)

Fig. 1.7 (right): Paul Sandby, Roslin Castle, Midlothian, showing Lady Frances Scott sketching with a camera obscura, c.1780, opaque watercolour. (Yale Center for British Art, Paul Mellon Collection, B1975. 4.1877)

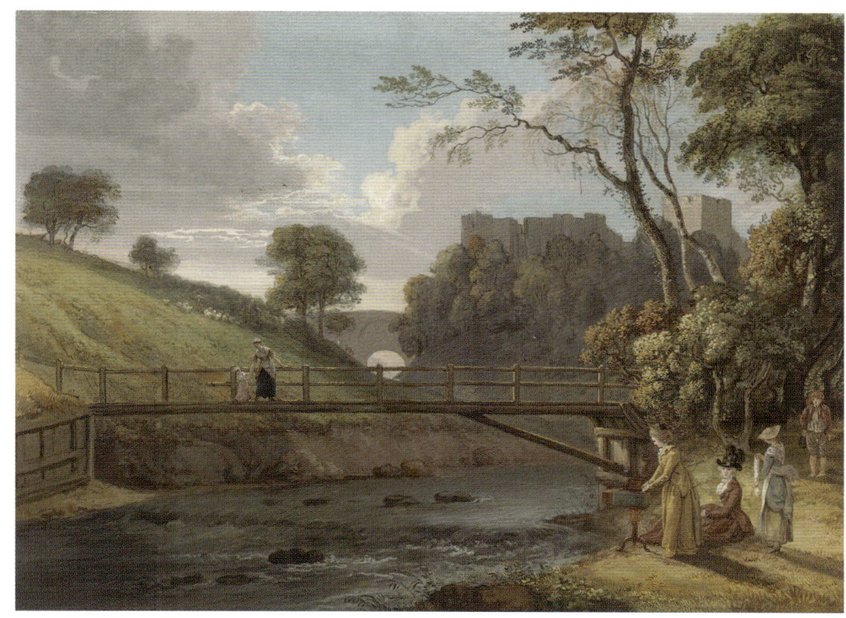

The suggestion that Scottish painters were using the camera obscura to study the effects of light and atmosphere is reinforced by the English landscape painter, Joseph Farington. He visited the Edinburgh studio of the portrait painter, Henry Raeburn, in 1801, and wrote in his diary:

Some of Mr. Raeburn's portraits have an uncommonly true appearance of Nature and are painted with much firmness, – but there is great inequality in his works.'– That which strikes the eye is a kind of Camera Obscura effect, and from those pictures which seem to be his best, I shd. conclude He has looked very much at Nature, reflected in the Camera.[11]

Raeburn did not make preparatory drawings for his painting, so Farington's comment should be taken to imply study rather than copying, and that study is likely to relate to light. His portraits are often notable for their specific use of outdoor light.[12] However, in common with the generality of painters, Raeburn had a north-facing studio, giving him a stable and even light. His house in York Place in

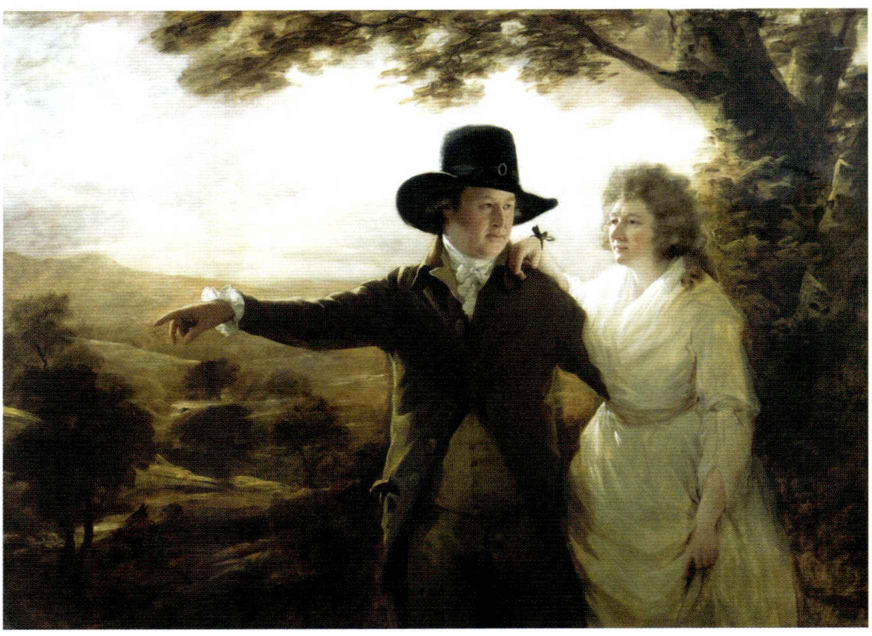

Fig. 1.8: Sir Henry Raeburn, 'Sir John Clerk and Lady Clerk of Penicuik', 1791, oil painting. (National Gallery of Ireland, NGI.4530)

Edinburgh incorporated a tall room with a large window, cut into the ceiling. He increased the light flooding the room by angling the stone surround of the window, and controlled it with a set of shutters, which could both block the light out and give it direction. By adding what he had observed of sunlight to what he could control of north light, Raeburn achieved the appearance of portraits painted in the shifting sun. One of his most extraordinary portrait groups, *Sir John Clerk and Lady Clerk of Penicuik*, painted about 1791 [FIG. 1.8], is an exceptional observation of light, both direct and reflected, which demonstrates the intensity of his study.

Raeburn was 'one of the most intimate friends and companions' of the landscape painter Alexander Nasmyth (1758–1840).[13] Nasmyth was overtly technological in his interests: his son described his workroom as 'crowded with a multitude of artistic and ingenious mechanical objects', and his sketchbooks illustrate such inventions as a mowing machine and a method of breathing underwater.[14] His studio served as the locale for a sociable (intellectually and practically) wide-ranging group of individuals, including the poet, Robert Burns (1759–76); the geologist and architectural historian, Sir James Hall (1761–1832); John Playfair (1748–1819) and John Leslie (1766–1832), professors

of mathematics and natural philosophy; Sir David Brewster (1781–1868), the optical scientist; and naturally the artists of the time, including the cleric, the Rev. John Thomson of Duddingston (1778–1840). With his daughters, who were also professional painters, Nasmyth taught oil painting to young ladies and their mothers, adding to the breadth of their knowledge: Mary Somerville(1780–1872), who was to be an important mathematician, was first recommended to read Euclid's *Geometry* by Alexander Nasmyth 'as the foundation not only of perspective but of astronomy and all mechanical science'.[15] This mingling and cross-referencing of subjects, which would prove so effective and providential in the advancement of photography, was highly-characteristic of the period and the Edinburgh circle.

Alexander Nasmyth and his son James, the engineer, are known to have made and used cameras [FIG. 1.9]. Rev. John Thomson, a landscape painter as well as a minister, invented one in the form of an umbrella, much approved by David Brewster.[16] In 1835, Maria Short, from a family of optical instrument makers, set up a large-scale camera obscura, with other instruments, in a Popular Observatory on Calton Hill, which the Edinburgh artists used. Her subscribers included James Skene, Alexander Nasmyth

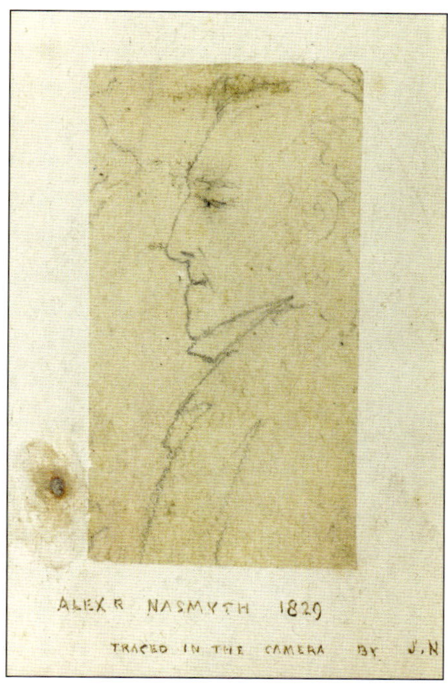

Fig. 1.9: James Nasmyth, 'Alexander Nasmyth', 1829, pencil sketch made with the camera obscura. (Private collection)

and the lawyer as well as photographic inventor, Mungo Ponton.[17] Second-hand cameras obscura were not infrequently offered for sale;[18] the major astronomical observatories also owned examples. The much-regretted sale of equipment from Glasgow's Garnethill Observatory in the January of 1823 included a fine camera obscura.[19]

Thomas Morton, who had devised the barrel loom for weaving patterned carpets, was the owner of an astronomical observatory, with a 'huge telescope … its speculum being 9 and a half inches, and its focal length 9 feet 2 inches' and 'a very fine Camera Obscura also made by the gifted proprietor'.[20] He installed these in Kilmarnock in 1818.[21] Morton also made a telescope and the camera obscura for Dumfries in 1836, for the purpose of observing sun-spots. This is both the oldest and the last-remaining astronomical camera obscura in Scotland.[22]

Poetry and the real

The poets James Thomson (1700–48), Robert Burns, and Walter Scott (1771–1832), all carried a theme which spoke directly of Scotland as a real place, and connected their writing to natural philosophy. Thomson's 'The Seasons', for example, made a rich lyrical address to Spring as an experience, brought to life by the weather and the light, and proclaiming Isaac Newton's scientific eminence against a background of sensual poetry:

> … refracted from yon eastern cloud,
> Bestriding earth, the grand ethereal bow
> Shoots up immense; and every hue unfolds,
> In fair proportion running from the red,
> To where the violet fades into the sky.[23]

Walter Scott was recorded as saying: '… whoever copied truly what was before his eyes, would possess the same variety in his descriptions, and exhibit apparently an imagination as boundless as the range of nature in the scenes he recorded; whereas whoever trusted to imagination, would soon find his own mind circumscribed, and contracted to a few favourite images …'.[24]

This rotating interconnection between the poetic and the physical – the understanding that reality was, in Scott's words, the very source of inventive originality – gives the Scottish arts of the time a dynamic force, and later allows the possibility of a Romantic vision in photography.

The idea of poetic landscape painting in Scotland is attached to the volatile weather – arguably, the solid reality of hills, trees and buildings was topographic and could be approached with surveying instruments; the emotional force rested in the moving, evanescent immediacy found in the effects of colour, cloud, light, moisture and so forth. It is work responsive to rapid change and theatrical shifts in light and mood – connected to an idea of the moment claimed later by photography. It also relates to the specific and local, rather than generalised proposals of the classical ideal, though the distinction is not as neat as we are making it; the later 18th- and early 19th-century artists still worked from the specific details of nature up to a generalised ideal.

The view of Scotland as compounded of atmospheric effects – storm, mist and different lights illuminating wild nature – was merged with a Romantic vision of the country, half-known, dramatic and melancholy, in which the ancient poetry of Ossian was added to the tragic history of Mary, Queen of Scots and the failure of the Jacobite cause. The emotional density of this idea of Scotland was embroidered and expanded through the poetry of Thomson, Burns and Scott, and inspired international interest – Schiller and Goethe; Schubert, Mendelssohn and Rossini; Ingres (commissioned by Napoleon) and Delacroix, among many others.

Joseph Farington toured Scotland between 1801 and 1803. There was an established convention of picturesque tourism encouraged by the landowners, providing viewing platforms and paths, *before* the Walter Scott impact on tourism. The picturesque and the sublime had their own literature laying down what should be admired; it was essentially a tourism dependent on looking.

Travelling by carriage from Killin to Tyndrum, Farington noted the distance as:

> … 21 miles but it was made short to me as my attention was engaged in watching the effects of light & shade on the Mountains. The day was cloudy, but the rain which fell was so slight as to cause no inconvenience, while the effects caused by it were often of the finest kind, so as to render the 'Landscape of the Desert' sublime.[25]

His attention was clearly fixed on the window of the vehicle – in a broad sense, he might be said to be travelling in a camera. He was accustomed to the use of a camera obscura, so the idea would not have been strange to him.

The astonishing impact of the Scottish atmosphere affected the key landscape painter of the earlier 19th century, J. M. W. Turner (1775–1851). His shift, from a comparatively straightforward view of the landscape to one dominated by ideas of light and colour, is generally thought to date from his work in Scotland in 1801. His sketching at that point displayed a 'novel freedom and rapidity'.[26] John Gibson Lockhart, the son-in-law and biographer of Walter Scott, commented on the progress of landscape painting in Scotland in 1819, and added:

> With regard to landscape painting, it is very true that she has not yet equalled the glories of the sister kingdom; but then the world has only one TURNER, and Scotland comes far nearer to the country which has had the honour of producing that great genius than any other country in Europe.[27]

Turner's biographer, Walter Thornbury, gave an account of Turner's friendship with John Thomson and the local 'clique of artists and painters':

> At the meetings of the clique Turner would constantly battle with them upon the subject of light, trying to gain from Brewster and other *savans* something upon that subject. It is supposed that in this discussion … he formed a theory which enabled him to create the varied effects that he has displayed in his works.[28]

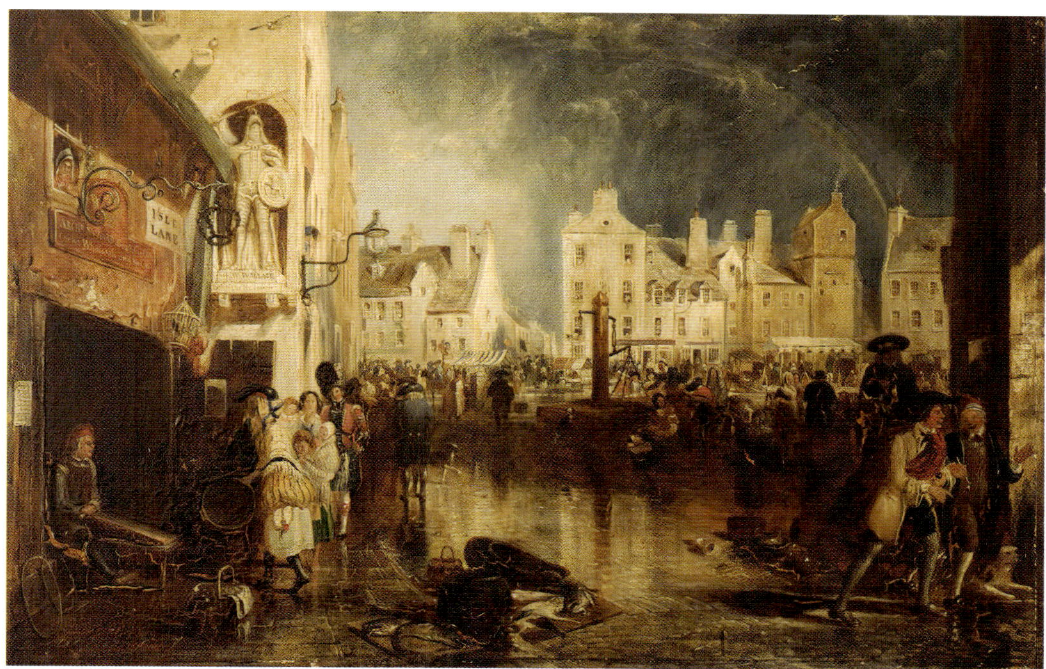

It seems likely that these discussions, which may have happened in 1822, when Turner was working on Walter Scott's *Provincial Antiquities and Picturesque Scenery of Scotland*, engaged James Skene of Rubislaw (1775–1864), rather than the optical scientist, David Brewster. Brewster regarded Skene as possessing 'a great general knowledge of science',[29] and there are letters from Brewster to Skene, written in 1824, on the photometer and the illuminating power of gas, suggesting Skene should study the measurement of light.[30]

Skene was both a knowledgeable and prolific amateur painter and, in 1823, he contributed the article on painting to Brewster's *Edinburgh Encyclopaedia*.[31] He extolled landscape painting as the British art. He was the first critic to recognise Turner's interest in optics, praising his work in these terms:

One of the greatest landscape painters of the present age, Mr Turner, seems to have grappled so vigorously with this important desideratum in the art, that much may be expected from his system of study and acute observation aided by the discoveries daily making in the mysteries of light, his scrutinizing genius seems to tremble on the verge of some new discovery in colour, which may prove of the first importance to the art.[32]

Probably the Scottish landscape artist most impressed by Turner at this time was David Octavius Hill (1802–70), who was to be a key figure in the history of photography. He followed Turner's model in painting the landscapes associated with the literature of Scott, by making a series of landscapes relating to Robert Burns.[33] Hill, who referred to Turner as a 'most glorious artist',[34] made his paintings consciously in terms of weather and light [Fig. 1.10].[35]

It is ironic that both Hill and Turner, in taking an interest in photography in the 1840s, appreciated the new art's inability to capture the fragile effects of the atmosphere, and used it for a study of the figure and light itself. The London daguerreotypist, J. J. E. Mayall, wrote of Turner's visits to his studio between 1847 and 1849:

At first he was very desirous of trying curious effects of light let in on the figure from a high position, and he himself sat for the studies …. However it happened to be a November fog, and I could not work. He stayed with me some three hours, talking about light and its curious effects on films of prepared silver. He expressed a wish to see the spectral image [i.e. spectrum] copied. … He came again and again, always with something new about light.[36]

The panorama

Hill was also affected by an idea of the poetry of geology in his landscape painting, from the influence of his friend, journalist and geologist Hugh Miller (1802–56). The scientific-aesthetic was fuelled by the rise in geological discovery from the later 18th century, which was particularly important in Edinburgh as a major, albeit dormant, volcanic site. The city had been the focus of research, which shockingly demonstrated that the earth's history had 'no vestige of a beginning, no prospect of an end'.[37]

The Romantic character of the city was thus derived from a physical base and the need for a strong defensible position in times of war. In the late 18th century, with the establishment of peace, it overflowed, with the developments of the neo-classical New Town to the north and the later suburbs to the south. As a result, from the later 18th century the city offered an extraordinary stage set of contrasting styles of architecture and different levels and viewpoints. The city was evidently a theatre – and it was a theatre for viewing and seeing, for surprising distances and close views in immediate proximity.[38] It is therefore no coincidence that the idea of the panorama, as a public spectacle, was first devised on Calton Hill (nor indeed, that the first important photographic studio was set up there).[39]

In 1787, the painter Robert Barker (1739–1806) made his way up to the top of the hill, and walked about, viewing the old city to the south, the hills, the beginnings of the New Town and the sea to the north. The idea of the panorama, 'La Nature à Coup d'Oeuil', came to him as 'an entire view of any country or situation, as it appears to an observer turning quite round'.[40] It appealed, for good reason, to Lord Elcho, a military strategist, who gave Barker 'pecuniary assistance' in the work. Barker succeeded in patenting this idea, and built on it a theatrical industry of extended paintings seen inside purpose-built structures, with controlled lighting and the potential for additional entertainments. In the first half of the 19th century, the Scottish cities saw the regular presentation of panoramas [FIG. 1.11], and the painting of these views was undertaken by several Scottish painters, including John Knox who painted a panorama of Glasgow [FIG. 1.12] and a sweeping view from Ben Lomond.

One of the most interesting connections between Scotland and the development of the panorama saw the country itself as the inspiration. The French inventor of the diorama, L. J. M. Daguerre (1787–1851), who later devised the first publicly announced method of photography, made four dioramas from Scotland early in his career: 'The Ruins of Holyrood Chapel, Edinburgh, by Moonlight'; 'Roslyn Chapel near Edinburgh, Effect of Sun'; 'The Effect of Snow and Fog Seen through a Ruined Gothic Colonnade'; and 'The Fire in the High Street, Edinburgh'. The diorama differed from the panorama with the skilful manipulation of lighting, as can be deduced from these titles. The first in particular was immensely successful [FIG 1.13], and shown in Paris, London and Liverpool between 1823 and 1827. It was reviewed with enthusiasm:

Fig. 1.11 (above): Charles Halkerston, 'The rotunda on the Mound, Edinburgh', 1843, oil on panel. (Edinburgh City Art Centre, CAC7/1982)

Fig. 1.12 (below): John Knox, 'Old Glasgow Bridge', c.1817. (Glasgow Museums, OG.1955.119)

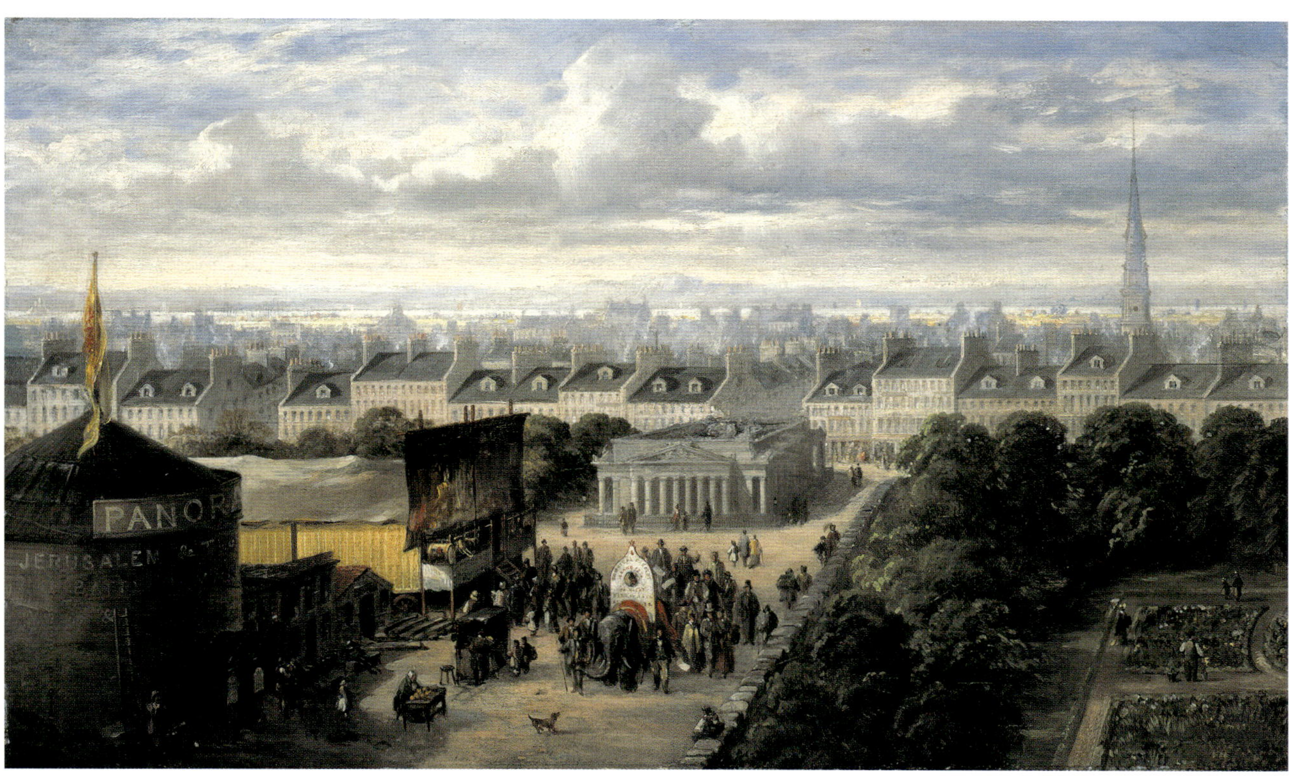

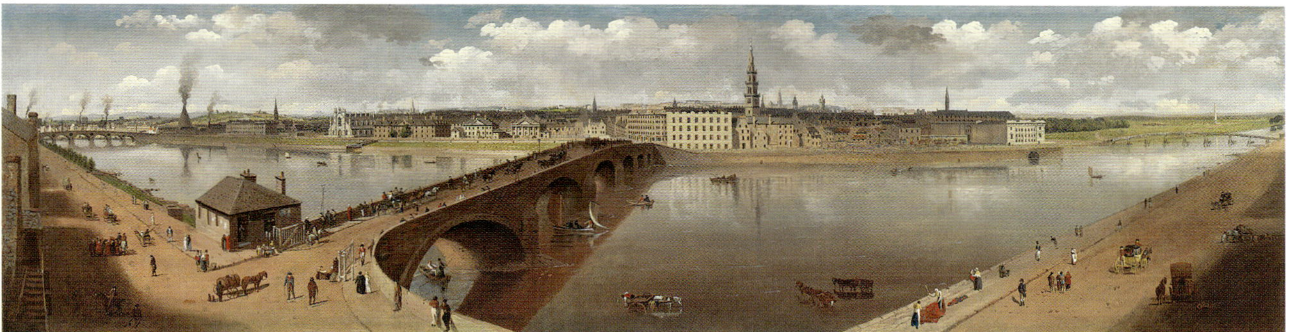

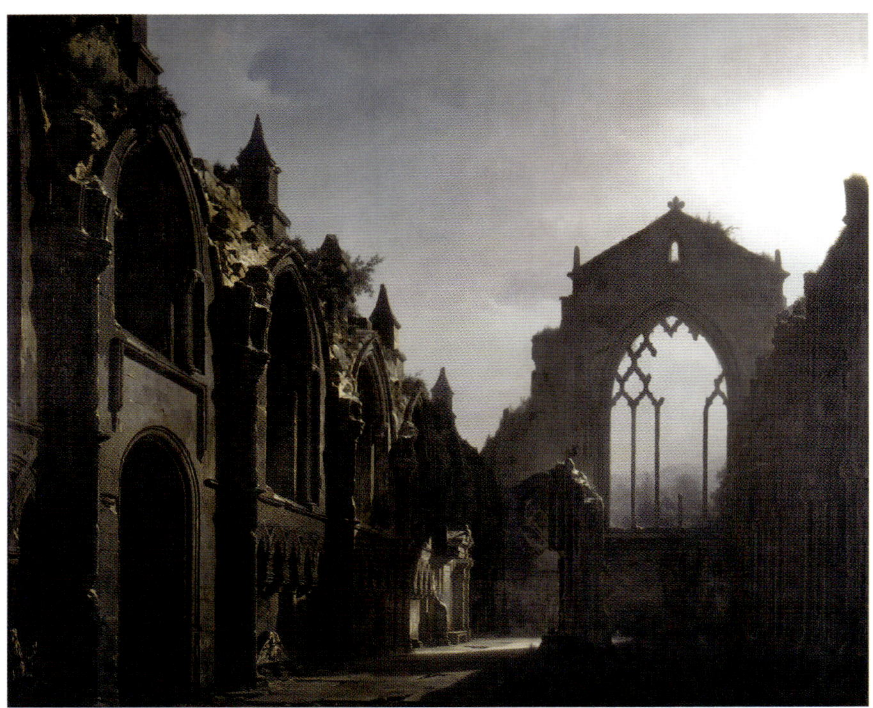

The view of Holyrood chapel, just opened to the public at the Diorama, appears to us to surpass in beauty and gloomy grandeur any of the preceding paintings in this matchless exhibition. There is an apparent reality about this view, which makes us almost suspect that we are under some magical illusion which has brought before us distant objects …. The whole picture is, perhaps, the greatest triumph ever achieved in the pictorial art.[41]

The diorama was a constructed mixture of illusion. While the lights and mist were not actual stars and fog, there were nevertheless real lights showing through a translucent surface. The skill was based on Daguerre's ability as a painter, but also derived from his ability as a showman – such effects were familiar in the theatre. In making his dioramas, Daguerre succeeded in capturing the camera obscura image – the impact of actual moving light and physical effects on the landscape, in an extended expression of time. It was remarkably clever.

We have no evidence that Daguerre came to Scotland. He may have employed a Scottish painter to make the original drawings. However, three of the Scottish dioramas are sufficiently convincing to propose that they were done from the life (*The Effect of Fog* is an imaginary cloister with a Highland figure). The subtlety of effect in the picture of Rosslyn, seen in sunlight and natural shadow, suggests a direct realism.[42] The easel paintings which remain to us are worked up from the diorama effect and are unmoving. If Daguerre did come to Scotland to draw from the actuality, there is one occasion when he might have stood next to D. O. Hill, who also sketched the fire in the High Street of Edinburgh in 1824; this melancholy event – the destruction of a swathe of the tall medieval buildings and the Tron Kirk – drew a number of artists.[43]

Basil Hall (1788–1844) published a book of drawings made with the camera lucida, a device based on a prism patented by William Hyde Wollaston in 1806, which could be used like the camera obscura for rapid sketching. Hall's drawings were made in North America between 1827 and 1828 and, significantly, he wrote in the preface of the book: 'If Dr Wollaston has not actually discovered a Royal Road to Drawing, he has at least succeeded in Macadamising the

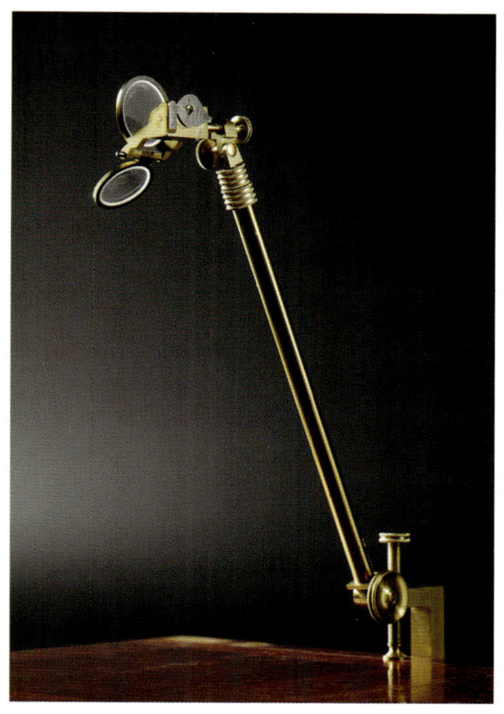

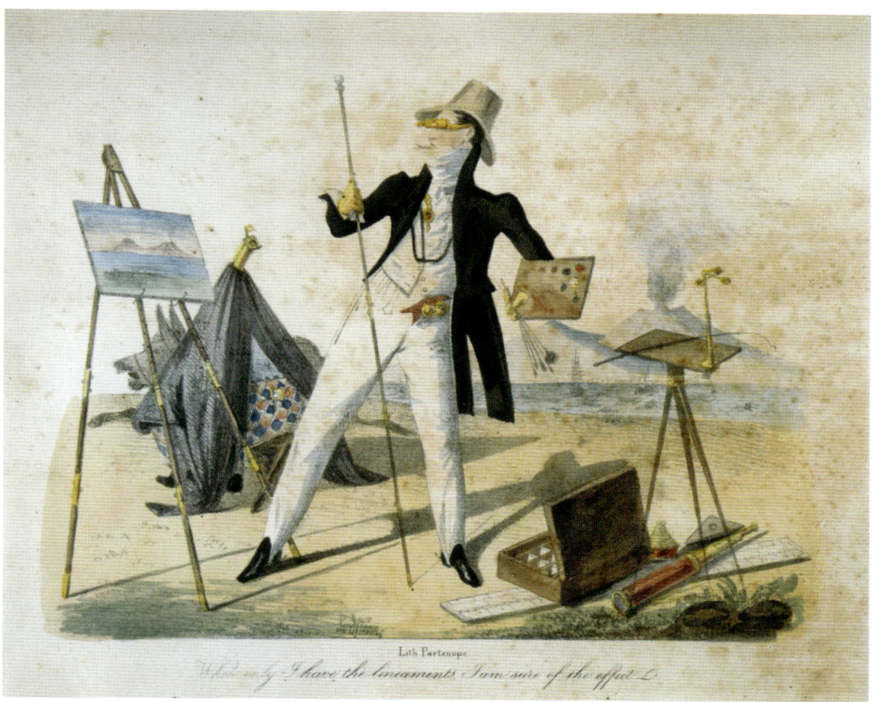

way already known'.[44] The camera lucida was difficult to use; W. H. F. Talbot's account of his invention of photography begins with his attempts to draw first with the camera lucida [FIG 1.14], and then with the camera obscura, only to find 'that the faithless pencil had only left traces on the paper melancholy to behold'.[45] He was prompted by this to search for chemical means of catching the image; and there is an undoubtedly proud echo of triumph over the earlier technology in his statement that photography was 'assuredly, a royal road to *Drawing*'.[46]

James Skene was also an enthusiastic, fluent sketcher and watercolourist, and familiar with the camera lucida. In his article on painting, he wrote of its use:

> The illusions of vision are in every respect remarkable, and in none more than in the misconceptions of landscape. We seem to see colours because we know them to exist. Forms are definite, and lines are straight, which the eye unconsciously sees far otherwise … the degradation of distance is at constant variance with our pre-existing knowledge of the real magnitude of objects; and it comes to be a question of some difficulty, to determine whether a painter ought to be guided by the real size and nature of objects, as geometry proves them to be, and as we see them represented by the camera lucida; or to represent nature as we seem to see it, modified by our habits, by the influencing circumstances of light and vapour, and by all the delusions of vision.[47]

When the Swedish artist Carl Jakob Lindström published a set of caricatures of French, German, Italian and British painters in the early 1830s, he showed the 'Englishman' surrounded by optical equipment. He intended an acid comment on the British obsession with technological aid in seeing the real landscape [FIG 1.15].[48] However, this fascination encouraged both a distinctive vision and an interest in visual exploration, which meant that the British would approach photography in its early years with considerable knowledge.

Fixing the image

It is one thing to view the world through the camera obscura; quite another to capture that ephemeral image. The straightforward method – as practised by many artists and surveyors – was to trace it, and then work it up: and many more artists may have used some form of the device, especially for landscape. For instance, the 18th-century artist Giovanni Battista Lusieri, employed by Thomas Bruce, 7th Earl of Elgin, produced wonderful perspective drawings and views, but there has been no discussion of how he achieved this, perhaps because today's art historians regard the use of such optical aids as somehow 'cheating'.[49] The silence by the practitioners about such usage was perhaps due more to convention than to this modern moral judgment.[50] Nonetheless, various people were attempting to register the views seen through the camera obscura by other, more permanent, methods.

The first attempts to fix pictures or patterns through the agency of light were made by individuals connected to industrial advance. Thomas Wedgwood (1771–1805), son of the distinguished Staffordshire potter, Josiah Wedgwood, studied in Edinburgh and may have attended lectures by the internationally-renowned teacher of chemistry, Joseph Black. With his friend, the chemist and inventor Humphry Davy, Wedgwood later worked on methods of direct printing with silver nitrate on paper and white leather, and in 1802 their results were published.[51] Although some of their images which had been kept in the dark could still be seen in the 1880s, they were concerned by the problem of fixing. Wedgwood's early death may well have prevented him from following through on the idea.

Mrs Elizabeth Fulhame, probably the wife of an Irish-man named Thomas Fulhame, published a remarkable book, *An Essay on Combustion with a View to a New Art of Dying and Painting, wherein the Phlogistic and Antiphlogistic Hypotheses are Proved Erroneous,* in 1794.[52] The book was presumably researched and written in Edinburgh, where her husband – who became a doctor – was a student of chemistry taught by Joseph Black. Her intention has come to be seen as photographic, in the sense that she sought a way of staining cloth with metal compounds exposed in sunlight:

> The possibility of making cloths of gold, silver, and other metals, by chymical processes, occurred to me in the year 1780: the project being mentioned to Doctor Fulhame, and some friends, was deemed improbable. However, after some time, I had the satisfaction of realizing the idea, in some degree, by experiment.[53]

Mrs Fulhame succeeded in precipitating gold and silver salts to colour patterns on cloth and to make maps, with rivers in silver and cities in gold. Her book drew considerable attention in its time, but more for her theories on combustion than for this highly-interesting proposal. Neither of these early experiments went further.

At the beginning of the 19th century, education in Scotland offered some theoretical training in chemistry but extremely limited encouragement to experiment. Practical science, generally, was not taught, even at university level, where lecture-demonstration was the main method of teaching, while reading by the student supplemented the notes he took during the lectures (or cribbed from another student). The Edinburgh scandal of the Burke and Hare murders in 1828, leading to the Anatomy Act of 1832, highlights the difficulties encountered by the medical fraternity in their efforts to understand the workings of the human body.[54] However, scientific information exchange generally was beginning to gather momentum in the years of peace following the end of the Napoleonic Wars in 1815. More periodicals devoted to scientific and technological development were produced; these were often replicated in the press, or in other journals across Europe. Edinburgh became the focus of a publishing boom, helped by a growing middle class with its thirst for knowledge. For example, the Chambers brothers, William and Robert, began publishing their weekly *Chambers's Edinburgh Journal* in 1832, leading to a long-standing business in publishing. The first edition sold 25,000 copies in Scotland alone; two months later the demand had risen to 30,000.[55]

It was not solely periodicals that provided knowledge. The encyclopaedia, originally a French idea, had been adopted by Enlightenment Scotland with great success. The *Encyclopaedia Britannica* was first produced in Edinburgh in three volumes published between 1768 and 1771; by the time the fifth edition (20 volumes, 1815–17) had to be sold on to a new publisher, there was a need for a six-volume supplement, appearing over the next decade. This used famous contributors, such as Sir Walter Scott and Sir Humphry Davy. In the meantime, similar works appeared: the young David Brewster, having turned to scientific journalism as a career, edited the *Edinburgh Encyclopaedia* between 1808 and 1830. In due course he too was recruited to write for later editions of *Britannica*.[56]

Brewster's long and busy life – aside from his own practical investigations into optics and the science of light – concerned various aspects of scientific communication, not just through his extensive journalism and editing. His role in setting up the new forum of the British Association for the Advancement of Science was inspired – he deliberately held it first in York in 1831 as being geographically central to the British Isles and home to a flourishing philosophical society and museum. However, a group of younger scientists (including his own protégé, James David Forbes), outmanoeuvred him politically; in later years, as a grand old man of science, he was welcomed back.[57] The Association proved to be a vibrant peripatetic annual meeting place for new ideas, and it still exists to this day.

Despite her comparatively small population, by the beginning of the 19th century, Scotland could boast four universities, or six colleges, all of which taught some form of science as a part of the undergraduate arts curriculum. These were based in the major centres of population – Glasgow, Edinburgh and Aberdeen, with that at St Andrews going through a period of eclipse by the mid-19th century. The universities provided places for a fairly broad-based education for their students, although without any real emphasis on science and technology. That had to wait for later 19th-century reform.[58]

While chemistry within the Scottish universities was taught exclusively by lecture-demonstration until the middle of the 19th century, individual figures in the manufacturing interest began to take a lead in an analytical concern for materials. Glasgow cotton manufacturer, Walter Crum (1796–1867), may be taken as a significant example. In his youth, he was fortunate to be taught by the eminent practical chemist, Thomas Thomson.[59] Crum also spent two years in Asia Minor and Turkey. His working life began effectively when he took over the calico printing and dyeing business at Thornliebank, south of Glasgow. His scientific explorations continued there, and 'he may be said to have done more than any other manufacturer of his

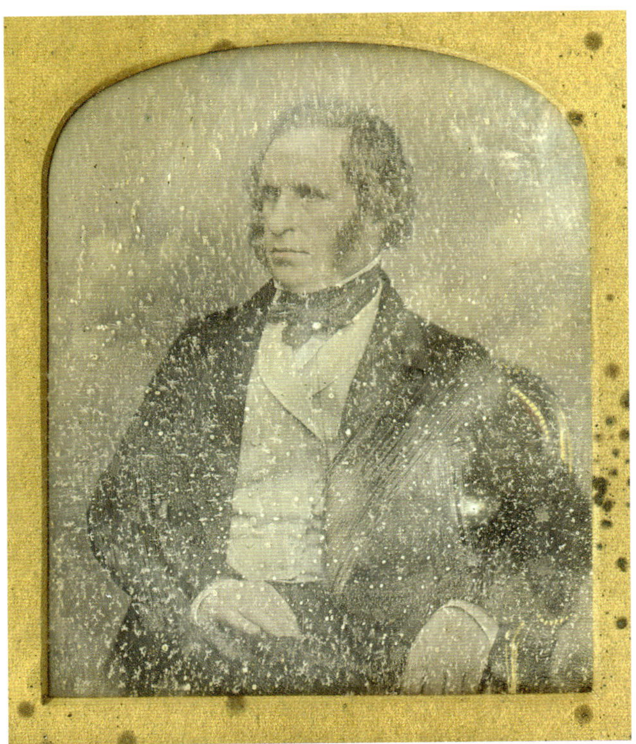

Fig. 1.16: William Edward Kilburn, Walter Crum, *c.*1850, quarter-plate daguerreotype. (The Mitchell Library, Glasgow, TD 1073 14/5, 6)

time to elevate a trade, which had hitherto been practised empirically, into something of a science, based upon exact principles, and though mainly on subjects connected with his own business, Mr Crum's investigations had a scientific interest and value beyond that which belonged to their mere practical application'.[60] He first published on the dye, indigo, in 1823, making his reputation as a man of science.[61] Crum had a wide circle of friends who numbered in the first rank of eminent scientists of the day, including Alexander Humboldt, Justus Liebig, Thomas Thomson, Michael Faraday and Thomas Graham. In 1844 he was elected a Fellow of the Royal Society of London. His interest generously overflowed into education, and he was a leading promoter of the Andersonian Institute in Glasgow.[62]

Crum was daguerreotyped in London at some point in the 1840s – there are two photographs of him by William Kilburn [Fig 1.16] and a stereo-daguerreotype with his daughter taken by Antoine Claudet. He was evidently one of Thomas Annan's first customers in 1855 or 1856, when Annan was in partnership with George Berwick.[63] He also owned a photograph album, which has survived and which contains photographs from the 1850s, including work by Annan and Franz Haenfstangel. He may have taken some of the family photographs himself.

Crum's concerns connected to his profession but provided insights relevant to photography. The paper used by photographers was made from cotton rags; the basis of another photographic medium, collodion, was also cotton. Two of the papers mentioned in his obituary – the dyeing of cotton fibre and nature of gun-cotton (collodion) – may connect to his interest in photography. In his researches into dyes and rationale behind the successful and failed attempts to dye the fabric, Crum makes a number of valuable points – one is the impressive stability of cotton:

It is one of the most inert of vegetable bodies. In the textile fabric it is capable of having incorporated with it, in all proportions, a multitude of different substances, without changing its own or their physical or chemical characters, except by holding them against mechanical attempts to wash away or otherwise to separate them, but yielding them up to their proper solvents as readily as they could be taken from a surface of glass – itself remaining unchanged.[64]

This text also addressed a problem experienced by photographers using cotton rag paper – the presence of arbitrary blank spaces, where the dyes fail to register. Using a powerful microscope, Crum was able to confirm that these patches were caused by unripe, impermeable cotton seeds.

Walter Crum was later credited by the chemist and museum director, George Wilson, with a discovery which relates to the conservation of photography. Wilson wrote:

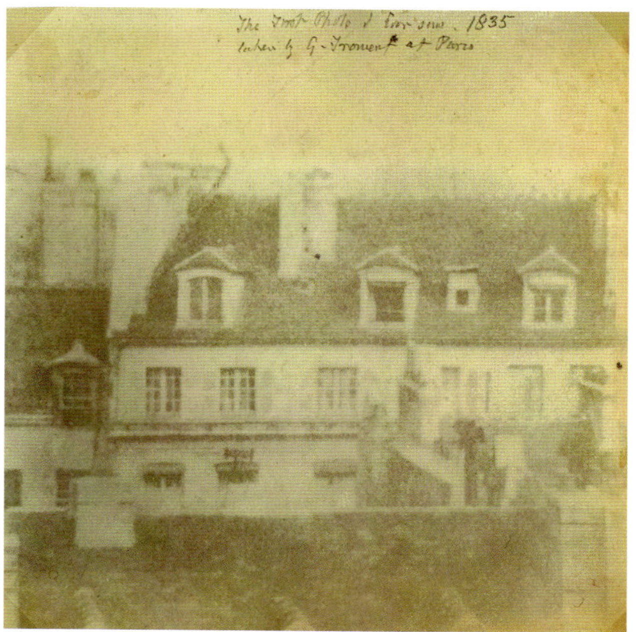

Fig. 1.17: Paul Gustave Froment, 'Paris roof-tops', c.1835, photograph on paper. (National Library of Scotland, Ms 3241 [214])

The acceleration of chemical change by heat is familiar to all. As a fresh illustration of the fact, may I call the attention of the Society to a well-known process in calico-printing called '*aging*,' which consists in exposing to the air cottons charged with salts of iron or alumina, till these are chemically altered and combined with the textile tissue. The *aging* has hitherto occupied a week or thereabouts; but Mr Walter Crum, of Glasgow, who is as remarkable for his knowledge of chemical science as for his ingenuity and success in applying it to practice, recently showed me the process of *aging* completed in *one* day. This striking acceleration of chemical change is brought about simply by substituting *hot moist* air for that which was cold and dry. Conversely, coldness adds to dryness and darkness an additional element of conservation.[65]

This passage makes Crum and Wilson 'the first photographic conservators', and the technique of accelerated ageing is thus a Scottish invention.[66]

The engineer, James Nasmyth (1808–1890), was also involved in industry. He developed heavy machinery – in particular, the steam hammer and the pile driver for massive engineering projects. But he engaged with the impressive cross-cultural energy of the time and was interested in the practice of art. He established his foundry in Manchester and it was probably there that he first encountered photography in the mid-1830s, four years before the official announcement of the art in 1839. He owned a paper photograph of Paris, a view taken from a high window where the photographer could leave his open camera for a time, undisturbed [FIG 1.17]. Nasmyth wrote on the print: 'The First Photo I Ever saw – 1835 taken by G. Froment at Paris.'[67] This was the work of Paul Gustave Froment (1815–65), a highly inventive man who was notably successful in the use of electro-motive power and experimented with photography.[68] Froment spent time in Manchester between 1837 and 1839, studying the engineering workshops, presumably including Nasmyth's Bridgewater Foundry.[69]

Froment's photogenic drawings were shown to the Lyons Society for agriculture, science and industry in June 1839; they included the predictable images of lace and of leaves. The report says he had shown his pictures to the Manchester Literary and Philosophical Society in 1838, where they were thought to be better than Talbot's work.[70] It added that Froment had succeeded in taking camera pictures of interiors, landscape, buildings and sculpture. The evidence of Nasmyth's print makes this likely.[71]

The photograph is a remarkable survival; it provides physical evidence of an important connection between France and Britain. Nasmyth will assuredly have carried this little paper picture with him to Scotland to show there; indeed, this may be the first photograph seen by any number of people in Britain, including Nasmyth's friend, D. O. Hill. Photography may have arrived in Scotland in James Nasmyth's pocket.

Notes

1. The extended literature for this subject includes Scharf 1968; Galassi 1981; Schwarz 1985; Crary 1990; Hockney 2001; Stafford and Terpak 2002.
2. See Hammond 1981.
3. Dupré 2005: 125–339.
4. See Cavers 1993: 8.
5. Bonehill and Daniels (eds) 2009. See also Hewison 2011: 28–30.
6. Bruce 1790. See also Bredon 2001: 41.
7. See Steadman 2001.
8. [Mahony] 1847: 18.
9. Brewster (ed.) 1823, vol. 2: 285–6.
10. Rosslyn and Maggi 2002: 35–6.
11. Garlick and MacIntyre (eds) 1979, entry for 23 September 1801, vol. 5: 1631.
12. See Thomson et al. 1997.
13. Smiles (ed.) 1891: 50.
14. *Ibid.*, 45.
15. Quoted in Neeley 2001: 58.
16. Brewster (ed.) 1806, 2: 488.
17. See Wallace 1992: 101–9.
18. *Caledonian Mercury*, 7 May, 1804; 20 June 1812; 6 June 1816.
19. *Caledonian Mercury,* 30 December 1822.
20. *Kilmarnock and Riccarton Post Office Directory* 1846–7.
21. See Clarke, Morrison-Low and Simpson 1989: 190–6.
22. See <http://www.dumfriesmuseum.demon.co.uk/dumfstory 14.html>
23. Sambrook 1981: lines 202–6.
24. Quoted in Lockhart 1893: 226.
25. Garlick and MacIntyre (eds) 1979, vol. 5: 1655.
26. Butlin and Wilton 1974: 45, quoting Finberg 1961: 74. See also Gage 1969 and Macdonald 2009.
27. Lockhart 1819, 3: 280.
28. Thornbury 1862, 1: 194.
29. David Brewster, 'Tribute to Skene', *Proceedings of the Royal Society of Edinburgh* 6 (1868–69): 243–68.
30. Brewster wrote two letters on the same day, 15 August 1824: National Library of Scotland, MS 3815, fols 77–9 and 80.
31. Brewster (ed.) 1830, 1: xiv, where Skene's authorship is acknowledged.
32. Skene, in Brewster (ed.) 1830, 15: 226–337, quote on 330.
33. Between 1832 and 1834, Turner's landscapes illustrated an edition of Scott 1833–34. Within four to five years from 1834, Hill made 66 paintings, which were engraved and published as *The Land of Burns, A Series of Landscapes and Portraits, Illustrative of the Life and Writings of the Scottish Poet. The Landscapes from Paintings Made Expressly for the Work, by D. O. Hill Esq., RSA The Literary Department* (1840); see also Ray McKenzie, 'The Pre-photographic Printmaking Work of D. O. Hill', *Studies in Photography* (2002–3): 34–41.
34. Hill to David Roberts, 14 January 1852, National Library of Scotland, Acc. 7723.
35. Discussed in Stevenson 2002a; and Sara Stevenson, 'Painting in Light and Chemistry: D. O. Hill's The Market Cross, Ayr (1835) and its Relation to His Photographic Work with Robert Adamson, 1843–47', *Getty Research Journal* 6 (2014): 29–46.
36. Quoted in Thornbury 1862, vol. 2: 259–60.
37. Hutton, 'Theory of the earth, or, An investigation into the laws observable in the composition, dissolution and restoration of land upon the globe', *Transactions of the Royal Society of Edinburgh* 1 (1788): 304.
38. See Sara Stevenson, 'Seeing in Time. Visual Engagement in Stevenson's idea of Edinburgh, considered in the light of paintings and photographs by David Octavius Hill and Robert Adamson', *Journal of Stevenson Studies* 8 (2011): 264–85.
39. See Hyde 1988; Comment 1999; Onnes-Fruitema et al. 2006; Huhtamo 2003; Sara Stevenson, 'The Hill View; "The eye unsatisfied and dim with gazing"', *History of Photography* 30 (2006): 212–34.
40. George Corner, 'The Panorama: with Memoirs of its Inventor, Robert Barker, and his son, the late Henry Aston Barker', *Art-journal* [New Series] 3 (1857): 46.
41. Anon., 'Diorama – The Ruins of Holyrood Chapel', *Mirror of Literature, Amusement, and Instruction* 4 (26 March 1825): 193–6.
42. Rosslyn and Maggi 2002: 26–31.
43. Sketches by D. O. Hill, in National Gallery of Scotland, D.2464A and B.
44. Hall 1829, Preface.
45. Talbot 1844.
46. *Ibid.*, caption to plate XVII, 'Bust of Patroclus'.
47. Skene, in Brewster (ed.) 1830, 15: 331.

Note: Website addresses checked and correct at the time of going to press.

48. Four of Lindstrom's caricatures – of French, German, Italian and British methods of painting – are illustrated in Conisbee, Faunce and Strick 1996: 18–19.

49. Weston-Lewis et al. 2012.

50. See the discussions in Hockney 2001 and Dupré 2005.

51. Thomas Wedgwood and Humphrey Davy, An Account of a Method of Copying Paintings Upon Glass and Making Profiles by the Agency of Light Upon Nitrate of Silver', *Journal of the Royal Institution of Great Britain* 1 (1802). Reprinted in Newhall (ed.) 1981: 16. A recent assessment is by Geoffrey Batchen, 'Tom Wedgwood and Humphry Davy "An Account of a Method"', *History of Photography* 17 (1993): 172–83.

52. Fulhame 1794; see D. A. Davenport, and K. M. Ireland, 'The Ingenious, Lively and Celebrated Mrs Fulhame and the Dyer's Hand', *Bulletin of the History of Chemistry* 5 (1991): 37–42; Schaaf, in Pritchard (ed.) 1990: 10–12; see also Derek Davenport, 'Fulhame, Elizabeth', <http://www.oxforddnb.com/view/article/ 39778>

53. Fulhame 1794: 3, Preface.

54. See Richardson 1987.

55. Cooney, 'Chambers, Robert (1802–1871)', <http://www.oxforddnb.com/view/article/5079>

56. Brock, in Morrison-Low and Christie (eds) 1984: 36–42.

57. Morrell, *ibid.*, 24–9.

58. Anderson, *ibid.*, 30–4.

59. For Thomas Thomson, see J. B. Morrell, 'Thomas Thomson: professor of chemistry and university reformer', *British Journal for the History of Science* 4 (1968–69): 245–65.

60. *Memoirs and Portraits* 1886, 94.

61. Obituary, *Proceedings of the Royal Society of London* 16 (1868): viii–x.

62. *Glasgow Herald*, 6 May 1867.

63. The Kilburn, Claudet and Berwick and Annan photographs are all in the Mitchell Library collection, TD 1073 14/5, 6.

64. Walter Crum, 'On the Manner in which Cotton unites with colouring matter', paper given to the Philosophical Society of Glasgow, 1 February 1843, *Proceedings of the Royal Philosophical Society of Glasgow* 1 (1842–43): 98–104.

65. George Wilson, 'On dryness, darkness, and colours, and coldness as a means of preserving photographs from fading', *Journal of the Photographic Society* 5 (23 May 1859): 292.

66. We are indebted to Dr Mike Ware for this opinion.

67. See Larry Schaaf, 'The First Photograph James Nasmyth Ever Saw', *Scottish Photography Bulletin* 2 (1990): 15–22.

68. The photograph is a direct positive. The yellow cast to the highlights suggests that Froment used washes of silver nitrate combined with potassium iodide. The exposure would have needed to be at least half an hour in bright sunlight. We are indebted to Michael Gray for this opinion.

69. For a brief biography emphasizing his engineering skills, see Paolo Brenni, 'Nineteenth-century French scientific instrument makers VII: Paul Gustave Froment [1815–1865]', *Bulletin of the Scientific Instrument Society* 45 (1995): 19–24.

70. Since Talbot had not shown his work at this time, this opinion is unlikely.

71. *Annales des sciences physiques et naturelles, d'agriculture et d'industrie. Publiées par la société royale d'agriculture, d'histoire naturelle et arts utile de Lyon* 2 (juillet 1839): 276.

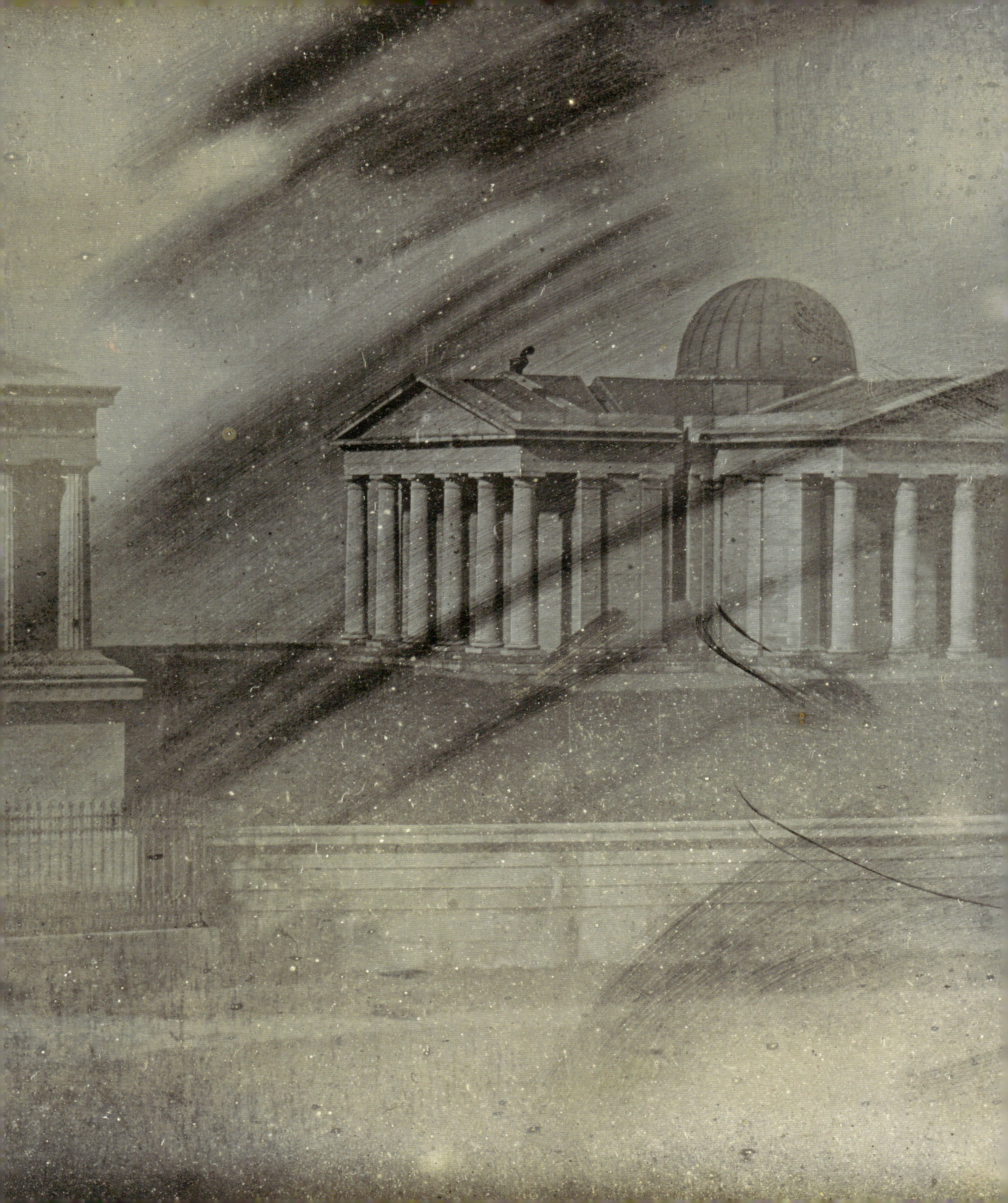

CHAPTER TWO

The Enquiring Mind: 1839 to 1842

Mr Daguerre's method of producing pictures was altogether different from anything I had seen or heard of in England – the pictures were as *perfect as it is possible for pictures to be without colour.*

Anon., *Athenaeum*, 8 January 1839

'Amateur' daguerreotypists

In January 1839, the Parisian showman Louis Jacques Mandé Daguerre (1787–1851) amazed the literate world by announcing his form of photography. He communicated with the scientific and artistic establishments through François Arago, who presented Daguerre's ideas at a meeting of the Académie des Sciences. Arago, the foremost French scientist of his day, concluded that this was of such immense and international importance that he persuaded the French government to intervene. By August, just before the process was published, the French government offered Daguerre a lifetime pension, and gave the process freely to the world. Five days before this, Daguerre had patented his process in England. Subsequently, these rights were bought by an entrepreneur named Richard Beard, who attempted to license all professional practitioners in England.[1] Though the daguerreotype was also protected by patent in Scotland, this was never enforced.[2]

News of Daguerre's discovery tantalised British society, who were not told details of his process for some six months after its announcement.[3] This interest was 'so universal', that the unnamed correspondent of the *Athenaeum*, a leading London literary journal, 'called on M. Daguerre, to possess myself, as far as was permissible, of the facts of his very remarkable discovery, and to add to a report of what has been said on the subject, after a few details of what I had seen'.[4] Great emphasis was made on the long and arduous experiments made by Daguerre, reminding the reader that this was the same man who had produced the diorama, which was then showing in both London and Paris.[5] The correspondent wrote:

Briefly to explain … it enables him [Daguerre] to combine with the *camera obscura* an *engraving* power – that

---

Opposite, Fig. 2.4 (detail): Unsigned [attrib. Thomas Davidson], 'Observatory of Edinburgh and Playfair's Monument from the South East', 1842.

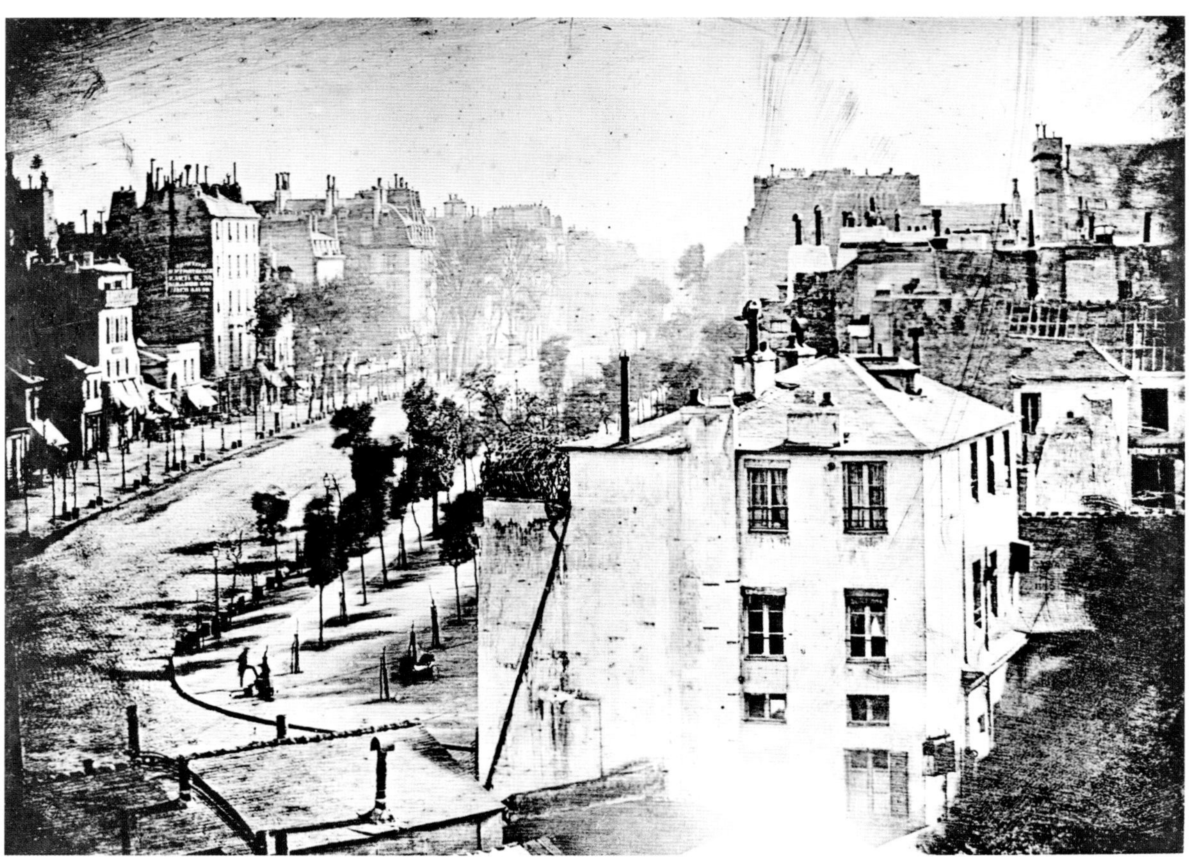

is, by an apparatus, at once to receive a reflection of the scene without, and to fix its forms and tints indelibly on metal in *chiaroscuro* – the rays of the sun standing in the stead of *burin*, or, rather, acid – for the copies thus produced nearly resemble aquatinta engravings exquisitely toned … of course, I can as yet give you no precise details, as M. Daguerre naturally objects to impart them to any one, till he has received some definite answer from the [French] Government, with whom he is in treaty for the sale of his secret ….[6]

At length, the *Athenaeum* was happy to publish a letter by 'one who ranks high in the scientific world', and this makes fascinating reading even today:

It was manifest at once, that M. Daguerre's method of producing pictures was altogether different from any-thing I had seen or heard of in England – the pictures were as *perfect as it is possible for pictures to be without colour* … the truth, distinctness, and fidelity of the minutest details were so exquisite, that colour could have added little to the charm felt in contemplating them; the best idea I can give of the effect produced is, by say-ing, that it is nearly the same as that of views taken by reflection in a black mirror. All the specimens I saw were on hard, plane, polished surfaces; none were on paper, and, in fact, the finest paper is incapable of receiving or conveying the delicate details, which (on examination by the microscope) the pictures are found to contain – the smallest crack, a withered leaf, or a little dust, which a telescope only will detect on a distant building, will be found in M. Daguerre's pictures, when sought for with the aid of a high magnifying glass.[7]

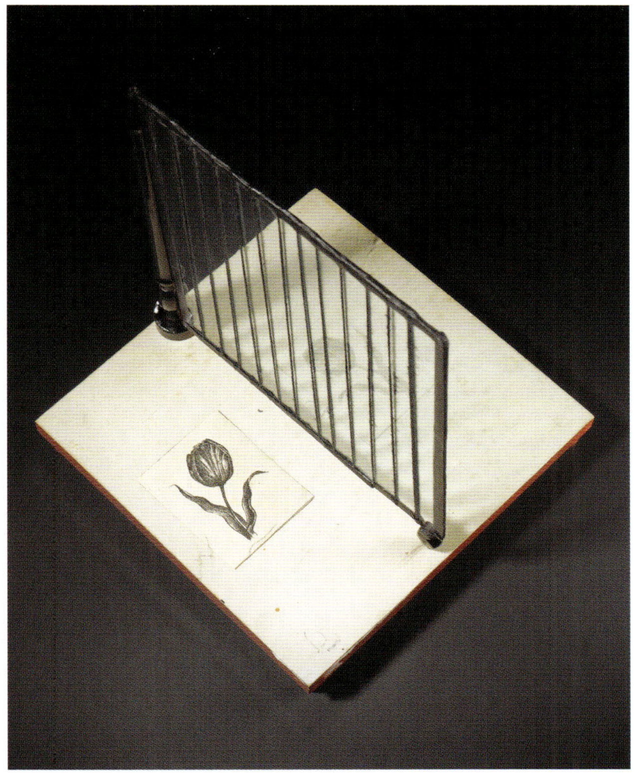

Fig. 2.1 (opposite): L. J. M. Daguerre, 'Boulevard du Temple, Paris, 3', *c.*1838, daguerreotype. (Bayerisches National Museum, Munich, R 6312.1-8)

Fig. 2.2 (left): Camera lucida designed by Sir John Robison, Edinburgh, 1841. (National Museums Scotland, T.2003.142)

I shall conclude by saying, that M. Daguerre's discovery appears to me to be of great value, and directly applicable to useful purposes, as by means of it original pictures of unquestionable fidelity may be obtained from the most intricate objects, as a trifling expense, and by persons otherwise incapable of taking a sketch. Such pictures may then be multiplied by the engraver's art, and the public obtain illustrations of the highest excellence at a moderate cost. A miniature painter, instead of confining his subjects to irksome sittings, may in two minutes take a perfect likeness in light and shade, and may at his leisure transfer this to ivory, with the advantage of colour from his pallet.

I am, &c.   J. R.[10]

Who was this highly-respected scientific figure, 'J. R.'? The likelihood is that he was Sir John Robison (1778–1843), son of a former professor of natural philosophy (or physics) at the University of Edinburgh, also named John Robison. The younger Robison had made a fortune in India, returning home in 1815 a wealthy man and able to marry, enjoy the trappings of a dilettante, but also to dabble in the practical arts.[11] He was interested in the feasibility of reproducing images to the extent of devising a simple camera lucida in 1841 [Fig. 2.2].[12] In 1821 he was involved with David Brewster in setting up the Society for the Promotion of the Useful Arts (known as the 'Society of Arts for Scotland', which after gaining its Royal Charter in 1840 became the Royal Scottish Society of Arts), and it was in the pages of their *Transactions* that he described a visit to Daguerre's studio in a communication dated 1 June 1839: comparison of the text in the *Athenaeum* with this missive shows that they probably came from the same pen.[13]

The correspondent continues, explaining that he had been shown three examples taken outdoors of the same Parisian boulevard – in the morning, at noon and in the evening – and was enchanted to discover the radical differences that the light made.

There is one point in which these pictures have a striking dissemblance from nature, viz., the deserted appearance they give to the busiest thoroughfares – nothing which moves onwards leaves a sensible trace behind .... Waving objects make confused images; but even living objects, if they remain motionless during short periods of exposure, are given with perfect fidelity.[8]

He goes on to describe the two fixed figures in the scene – a shoe-black working on a gentleman's footwear, visible apart from his moving arm, and the gentleman who had moved his head [Fig. 2.1].[9]

A number of interested people in Scotland took up the daguerreotype. Amongst these was a group in Edinburgh loosely connected with the Society of Arts for Scotland, including John Adie (1805–58), second son of the scientific instrument maker, Alexander Adie. The younger Adie 'exhibited a Daguerreotype plate of the Place de Chatelet, Paris, executed (*sans soleil*) by Vincent Chevalier' at a meeting of the Society on 13 November 1839.[14]

The Edinburgh Exhibition of Arts – showing the useful and mechanical arts, and partially sponsored by the Society of Arts – was held during the Christmas period of 1839, when the local press anticipated loans of 'a complete series of illustrations of the Daguerreotype by Mr Adie', and others by Mr Astley.[15] Thomas Astley (1809–50) of the Bonnington Chemical Works was a manufacturing chemist, and he exhibited '3 Specimens of Daguerreotype, being views taken in Edinburgh …'.[16] This is intriguing, as Astley is likely to have visited Daguerre in Paris to have learned the process by this early date. John Adie had obtained a daguerreotype by a Parisian-based optician for exhibition; however, on 26 February 1840, he communicated to the Society of Arts a 'Notice on the use of brass or copper plates, having their surfaces silvered, for producing pictures by the process of daguerreotype', demonstrating that he understood the process.[17] There was also a daguerreotype by Daguerre himself, of a 'View of the Tuilleries', exhibited by John Dunn, an Edinburgh optical and mathematical instrument maker, and Curator of the Society of Arts Museum from 1833; and, as we shall see later, he appears to have tried his hand at the calotype in early 1839.[18] A 'Signior Rampini' lent a 'Specimen of the Daguerreotype from Paris': Rampini was a teacher of Italian, based in Gloucester Place.[19] A 'M. Le Sage' also exhibited 'another French Plate'.[20] He can be identified as Ado Lesage, described as 'from Paris, printseller, frame maker, carver and gilder', based at 21 Hanover Street during 1838 and 1839 – close to John Adie's business as 'Adie & Son' at 58 Princes Street.[21] John Adie proposed his own improvements to the daguerreotype process at a meeting of the Society of Arts for Scotland on 26 February 1840.[22]

A local lecturer named Dr Andrew Fyfe (1792–1861), also connected with the Society of Arts for Scotland, delivered a paper 'On daguerreotype' at their meeting on 15 January 1840.[23] Fyfe was a medical doctor, a Fellow of the Royal College of Surgeons of Edinburgh (he became their president in 1842), a Fellow of the Royal Society of Edinburgh, and of the Society of Antiquaries of Scotland. He had been assistant to the University's Professor of Chemistry, T. C. Hope, and went on to lecture privately in pharmacy and chemistry, before becoming professor of chemistry at King's College in Aberdeen in 1844.[24] The daguerreotype was merely one of a number of photographic processes in which Fyfe concerned himself. His paper on the daguerreotype demonstrates his interest in the hands-on chemistry and practical concerns of someone making a daguerreotype; he was also critical of results.[25] Fyfe went on to discuss the 'rationale' of the process; or how he believed it worked. In the report of the meeting in the Society's proceedings, Fyfe provided examples of his experiments.[26] He investigated, and experimented with, other forms of photography; but none of his daguerreotype experiments is known to survive.

Dr Andrew Douglas Maclagan (1812–1900), who had, like Fyfe, studied medicine at the University of Edinburgh and done further medical training in Berlin, Paris and London, became a member of the Society of Arts for

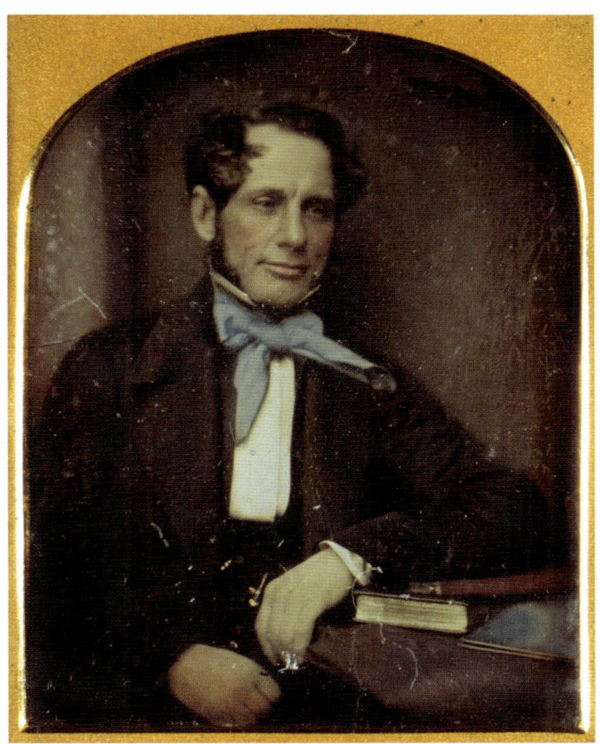

Fig. 2.3: Unknown photographer, Dr Douglas Maclagan, *c.*1840, daguerreotype. (Scottish National Portrait Gallery, PGP 202.48)

Scotland from 1839. At their meeting on 10 April that year, when Andrew Fyfe talked about photographic etching, the report continued that 'Dr Douglas Maclagan also exhibited specimens taken by him'.[27] A collection of daguerreotypes and ambrotypes survives, the subjects of which are Maclagan himself, his family and friends (perhaps also patients), showing him being photographed from an early stage and maintaining an interest into the 1850s [FIG. 2.3]; and there is also a Hill and McGlashon photograph, probably dating from the 1860s, of him with his father and son.[28] It is possible that amongst these earlier examples are images made by Maclagan himself. His interest in chemistry led him to undertake extramural teaching of the subject at the Royal College of Surgeons, Edinburgh, from 1845, and he went on to play a significant role in some famous Scottish murder trials as a forensic advisor: at that of Madeleine Smith in 1859 and of Dr Pritchard in 1865.[29]

Another Edinburgh figure connected with early daguerreotyping was Alexander Bryson (1816–66), who came from a family of watch, clock and scientific instrument makers, with interests embracing horology, meteorology, photography and geology.[30] He challenged the American Alexander S. Wolcott's attempt to patent his daguerreotype camera in Britain on the grounds that he and Thomas Davidson (1798–1878) had already taken photographs by this method, involving the use of a mirror rather than a lens, which reduced the risk of distortion because it had only one reflecting surface rather than the several interfaces of a glass lens.[31] Davidson, like Bryson and Adie, was a professional scientific instrument maker, and also connected with the Society of Arts for Scotland. His role was essentially one of kit supplier to the early practitioners. He constructed cameras for many of the St Andrews circle, Henry Brewster, Hill and Adamson, and Cosmo Innes. Even before the invention of photography, as early as 1834, Davidson was advertising as a 'practical optician', meaning one who actually constructed the instruments he sold, from his premises in Alnwick, Northumberland.[32]

Thomas Davidson's life was recounted by Dr John Nicol (1828–1910), a columnist for the *British Journal of Photography*, who had known him personally. From inauspicious beginnings, Davidson had been employed as a weaver (an occupation well-known for radicalism at this period). He became interested in mechanical matters, attracted local patronage, presented a paper in 1833 before the British Association for the Advancement of Science at Cambridge on improvements to reflecting telescopes, and gave a lecture on optics before the Newcastle Philosophical Society,

> … which attracted the attention of a number of the county magnates, who not only gave him much work to do but raised a subscription by which he was enabled to

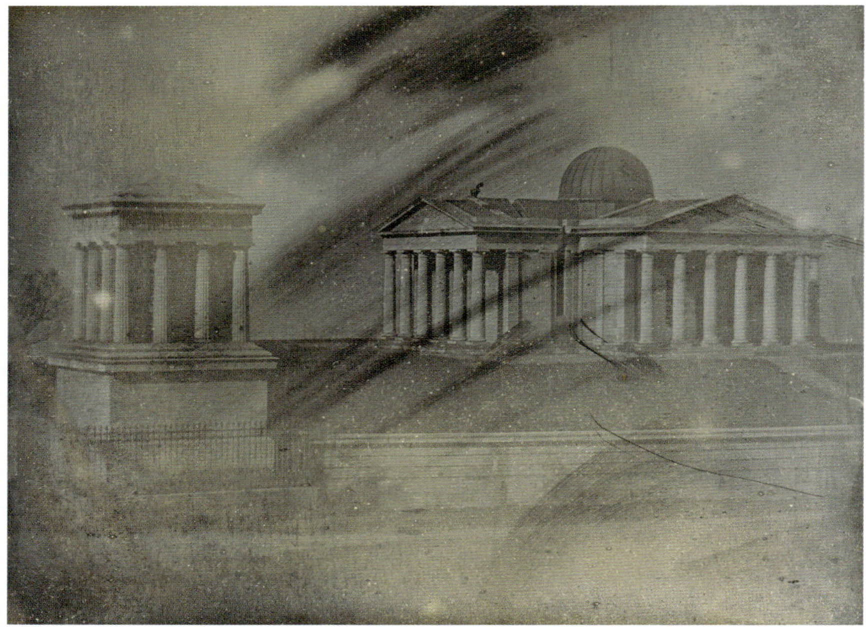

Fig. 2.4: Unsigned [attributed to Thomas Davidson], 'Observatory of Edinburgh and Playfair's Monument from the South East', 1842, whole plate daguerreotype. (On loan from Royal Observatory, Edinburgh, IL.2014.22, National Museums Scotland Photography)

open a shop in Alnwick, under apparently the most favourable circumstances. … But his business capacities were of the most limited kind; and, although there was more than a fair amount of business doing, his affairs gradually got into confusion. He kept no books, never knew exactly how he stood with the world, and at the end of two years gave up the affair in disgust, removing along with his family to Edinburgh, in the hope that in that city of scientific learning his peculiar talents might find profitable employment.[33]

Although a professional purveyor of photographic apparatus, Davidson was not a commercial photographer. His daguerreotypes appear to have been mainly landscape [Fig. 2.4]; and he sold much of his apparatus to non-professionals. Davidson's reputation lies with his lens construction, making a portrait lens from first principles along similar lines to the Viennese optician Joseph Petzval:

Mr Davidson's first experiments were made with a telescope lens, the camera, having been roughly constructed from such boards as were lying about his workshop, and the dark slide a curiosity in the combination of mill-board, sheet iron, and wood. The crucible in which his speculum metal had been melted did duty as a mercury box, and the plates were iodised on a common gallipot, the mouth of which was ground smooth on a flat stone. … the result was the constructing of a lens two and a half inches in diameter and twelve inches focus, and so corrected as to bring both chemical and visual foci on one plane. That such a lens was being made was known to several of his cronies, and, consequently, on its being finished they assembled in the workshop on the eventful day to witness its trial.[34]

This first lens was destroyed in an accident, but

… nothing daunted, Mr Davidson at once set to work, and in a short time had finished another lens – this time of three inches diameter and fifteen inches focus. On trial this lens proved satisfactory in every respect, and being assured that it was capable of giving larger pictures than any that had been hitherto attempted he constructed a large camera, and in a few days was able to show daguerreotypes of exquisite beauty on 8½ x 6½ plates. These pictures commanded a ready sale at good

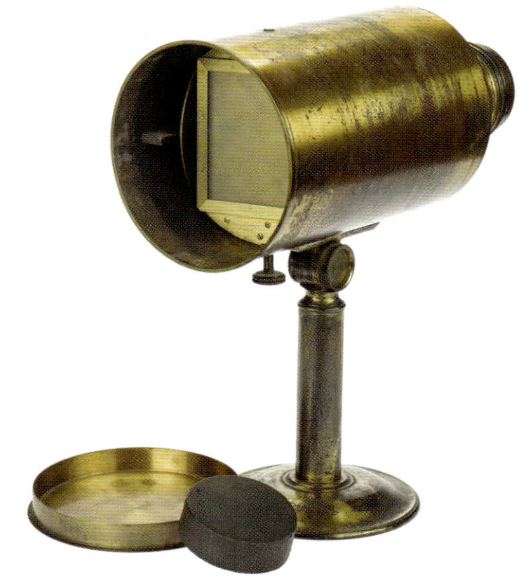

prices, and our friend may at this time be said to have had fame thrust upon him. His humble workshop was thronged by the elite of the city, and lenses and pictures were in such demand that he was forced to seek a larger place and to employ a number of assistants.[35]

Davidson first submitted a communication, 'Description of the process of Daguerreotype', to the Society of Arts for Scotland in November 1840, through another of the Society's Fellows, Mungo Ponton, who was also interested in photography and telegraphy. Andrew Fyfe was in the chair. Davidson described his 'improved apparatus, by which both Landscape and Miniature Portraits may be taken by merely reversing the lenses', and he demonstrated 'his Improved Camera'.[36] Before the Society, in January 1841, Davidson produced an improved camera, and also described a way of producing daguerreotypes by the reflecting camera.[37] In May, Davidson spoke about the optics of reflecting telescopes; and offered another communication about the optics of the magic lantern.[38] At that same meeting, Davidson presented the Society with a copy of his recent publication, *The Art of Daguerreotyping, with Improvements of the Process and Camera*. His communication on the process of daguerreotype was published in the Society's *Transactions*; it included a description of his camera, an example of which has survived [Fig. 2.5].[39] Davidson was awarded the Society's Silver Medal for his three communications.

Among those who used his camera optics was the St Andrews-based optical scientist Sir David Brewster (1781–1868), who became something of a scientific patron for Davidson, and his lenses were used by many of the pioneers of paper photography, as well as for the daguerreotype. Brewster discussed Davidson's work at the Glasgow meeting of the British Association for the Advancement of Science in 1840, demonstrating 'a very perfect apparatus, executed for him by Mr Thomas Davidson of Edinburgh, who has made some essential improvements in the process. Sir David also exhibited several drawings taken by Mr Davidson with that apparatus, of various buildings and scenes in Edinburgh'.[40] In April 1841 Davidson was elected an honorary member of the St Andrews Literary and Philosophical Society; the minutes record that 'the newly elected Honorary Member exhibited Daguerre's apparatus for obtaining impressions of objects, in the Camera Obscura, and explained several improvements he had made, especially for adapting the camera for taking portraits, and at the close of the meeting, exhibited the process itself by taking a view of the New College Buildings'.[41]

In his correspondence with the Wiltshire-based pioneer of the paper process, W. H. F. Talbot (1800–77), Brewster promoted Davidson's cameras on several occasions, as well as mentioning the superb images obtained:

I have got a very fine Camera constructed by Mr Thomas Davi[d]son 12 Royal Exchange Edin[r]., who has executed Daguerreotype pictures far superior, in the estimation of foreigners & others, to those executed by Daguerre. I have two of them of scenes in Edin[r]., that are inexpressibly fine … Mr Davi[d]son took one of the shipping at Glasgow bridge which was much admired.[42]

Amongst others who bought Davidson's cameras, and practised photography outside Scotland, was the Rev. Calvert Jones (1804–77), who informed Talbot that his 'modifications are certainly improvements on Daguerre's system'.[43] Jones had recently made a successful daguerreotype (on 9 March 1841) of Margam Castle, the earliest to be made in Wales, and so was speaking with the voice of experience.[44] Criticism came from the professional London photographer Henry Collen (1797–1879), concerning a Davidson lens: '… it is of too long a focus to be useful for portraiture, and is moreover extremely green, which I cannot but think must very much diminish the photographic effect'.[45] Henry Craigie Brewster (1816–1905), Sir David's youngest son, was able to photograph fellow army officers in Cork with Davidson's apparatus;[46] Kit Talbot (1803–90), cousin to the inventor, based in South Wales, was supplied with 'two capital lenses by Davidson' by the London-based daguerreotypist Antoine Claudet (1797–1867);[47] and, tellingly, in 1846, Calvert Jones reported to Talbot that

> I have been lately corresponding with Davidson at Edinburgh touching his large Cameras which do pictures double the size of ours: he asks £23, and I tell him I shd be glad to buy one if he will inform me of the method which Mr Hill there uses to do groups with them in 30 seconds, which Davidson assures me he saw done within the last week: if this cd be done as to portraiture in London on such a scale, a large fortune might be speedily made.[48]

In 1856, shortly after the formation of the Photographic Society of Scotland, Cosmo Innes (1798–1874), advocate, antiquary, historian, and member of the Edinburgh Calotype Club, delivered a paper recounting his recent travels abroad, in search of recuperation and photographic opportunities:

> I made my preparations for paper after the old Talbot manner, only somewhat weaker in preparation, as used by Dr Diamond. My Camera is one of Davidson's, of Edinburgh. It has a double lens with a long focus, and is a slow worker. I have it in a stout leather case, which saves it from any casual knocking about on Steamers or Railways. The stand I chose for its lightness (having the fear of French railway charges before my eyes) was somewhat too slight for my Camera; and yet it stood firm enough to give me a steady picture when planted in the shallow rapid of the river above the Pont du Gard.[49]

Nicol's account continues with Davidson's determined attempts to improve the daguerreotype process:

> From the Royal Exchange he [Davidson] removed to the Canongate, and set up his lathes and benches in one of the old, historical mansions … . There his business continued in a flourishing state for some time, orders coming in faster than they could be executed by those whom he employed; while he himself was devoting his attention to improving the daguerreotype process, and adapting the oxyhydrogen light to the solar microscope for the purpose of producing pictures of microscopic objects. The results of these labours were from time to time brought before the Royal Scottish Society of Arts;

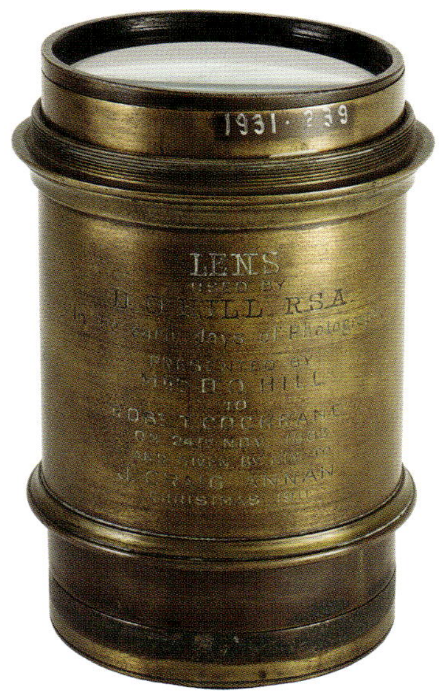

Fig. 2.6: Unsymmetrical doublet lens, unsigned [attributed to Thomas Davidson], *c.*1845. (Royal Photographic Society / Science & Society Picture Library, 2003-5001_0001_0046)

and we find that in January, 1841, he communicated a method by which the pictures might be taken by reflection, so as to get rid of the reversal of the image, which even then had become objectionable.[50]

He also discusses what was probably Davidson's most important contribution to photography: his independent discovery of the doublet, or portrait, lens:

The invention of this lens was the one thing needful to make portrait photography popular, and the inventor, second only to the discoverer of the process itself, is worthy of the highest niche in the temple of photographic fame. Whether this be M. Petzval or Mr Davidson I will not at present venture to say, as I cannot lay my hands on any account of the introduction of the lens by Voigtländer. It is quite certain that the latter finished his first instrument in 1840, and had made and sold a number in the course of 1841. But, whether before or after Petzval, there is no doubt that they wrought independently of each other, or that the Davidson lens was superior to that of Petzval in so far as the chemical and visual foci of the former were coincident, while those of the latter were not.[51]

The 20th-century authority on the photographic lens, Rudolf Kingslake, observed that a symmetrically-constructed lens built around a central stop in which the second element mirrored the first, would cancel the distortions. Davidson, claimed Kingslake, had experimentally used two Chevalier achromatic components in this way in 1841.[52] One of the Davidson lenses used by D. O. Hill and Robert Adamson has survived in the collection of the Royal Photo-

graphic Society. Although unsigned, it has been described as 'an unsymmetrical doublet lens of about 17" focal length and maximum aperture of about f/10' [FIG. 2.6].[53]

Although there is no demonstrable link with Davidson or his workshop, there were others who took up the daguerreotype process. In 1875, on the occasion of the annual outing of the Edinburgh Photographic Society to the garden of Edward Burton (1810–99), living in Colinton, Edinburgh, members found that 'the celebrated engraver … had worked the daguerreotype process in the early days of photography, and he showed his visitors a fine collection of specimens of that style – the most beautiful of all the processes – as well as his collection of pictures and curiosities …'.[54]

As early as 1841, another daguerreotypist, described as 'D. Montreal' – presumably a Frenchman – displayed his work in Edinburgh, at the Royal Scottish Academy. He showed two daguerreotypes of views of Paris, as well as one each of Holyrood and Heriot's Hospital in Edinburgh; the Holyrood daguerreotype is listed with a group as 'The Property of his Grace the Duke of Buccleuch'.[55]

Across the country, in Glasgow, the daguerreotype was first shown in early December 1839, displayed by a frame-maker named John Finlay, in his gallery at 49 Buchanan Street.[56] Finlay announced this in an advertisement in the *Glasgow Herald*: '… just received direct from Paris a selection of the newest engravings …. Also, a beautiful specimen of DAGUERREOTYPE made by Mons. Daguerre himself.'[57] It is possible that this was the same daguerreotype by Daguerre, mentioned earlier in this chapter, exhibited later on in December in the Edinburgh Exhibition of Arts as a 'View of the Tuilleries'.

A long-standing photographer, and member of the Glasgow Photographic Association, Andrew Mactear, recalled some forty years later that: 'One of our members, Mr Samuel R. Brown, being in Paris in 1839, received from M. Daguerre one of his pictures, which on his arrival in Glasgow he exhibited in Royal Exchange Square, and which I recollect seeing.'[58] This example was described in some detail, and in its convoluted vocabulary it shows the difficulty of describing something that is outside the journalist's experience:

> *Daguerreotype Drawing* – To the courtesy of Messrs Willis, we owe the sight of a drawing by the Daguerreotype, which lies at their shop in Exchange Square. The drawing, at first sight, resembles an elaborate drawing in Indian ink; but a moment's examination shows that you are looking at reality, not imitation. Gerard Douw himself could not have hit that sharpness and *fortuitousness* which makes the accidents of nature so exactly transferred to paper in the drawing. The scene is the corner of some artist's studio, with a bust or so, and a bas-relief, or two. A counterpane is hung up by way of a screen. On first looking at it, the counterpane does not seem more minutely imitated than we have seen in the works of Douw or Mieria, but the magnifying glass exhibits new wonders in the drawing, the frayed threads of the counterpane, the scratches and castmarks of the plaster, invisible to the naked eye, are made plain under the magnifier. It is evident that you have before you as it were, a *cast* taken in light and shade from nature. And all these wonders lie within the space of a dozen square inches. Many of our readers may realise the wonderful accounts which they have had of the Daguerreotype, by stepping into the shop of Messrs. Willis, whom they will find ready to oblige.[59]

The image sounds similar to one by Daguerre that still survives from 1837, 'L'atelier de l'artiste'. Ten years later, possibly the same *Glasgow Herald* journalist recalled that first daguerreotype in an editorial column:

> That picture gave the exact representation of M. Daguerre's own studio. There was a piece of figured tapestry, a table on which stood a bust of William Shakspere [*sic*], and some philosophical apparatus, there were also some chairs in the apartment. That picture struck all who saw it with surprise. It was dim, grey, and dreamy. Still the discovery, at hundreds of miles distant from where it was made, was shown to be visible truth.[60]

Even after nearly a decade, recounting the experience of seeing his first photograph caused this professional wordsmith some difficulty.

Mactear's reminiscences continue:

> Dr [Thomas] Paterson (to whom the photographers in Glasgow are largely indebted), as usual with him in anything new and worthy, set to work at it [the daguerreotype] at once. Mr Brown himself and another member,

Mr Hugh Wilson, were also engaged in it, but who has the precedence I cannot determine.[61]

Hugh Wilson, as a member of the council of the City of Glasgow and West of Scotland Photographic Society in 1860, 'showed and described the working of the first daguerreotype apparatus used in Glasgow'.[62] At a meeting of the Glasgow Photographic Association in November 1863, Wilson 'said his first experiments in Daguerreotype were in 1830 [sic], and he had some of his first experiments remaining yet. He had one picture, a view of some cottages on Loch Lomond, which had remained perfect since it was done.'[63]

In 1846, Dr Thomas Paterson, who was an anatomical modeller, working in St Enoch's Square in Glasgow, sent 'some beautiful Casts in copper from Daguerréotypes, and impressions from these casts … by means of the Electrotype' to a friend in London, who showed them and his letter to *The Builder*.[64] Many people experimented with methods to try to duplicate the one-off positive image of the daguerreotype, some with moderate success. Paterson's attempts were well-received.[65]

Another Glasgow amateur, who may have been connected with Paterson, was named George Thomson, and his daguerreotype apparatus dating from 1849 was lent to the Glasgow Photographic Exhibition of 1886 by John Urie. He may have been the same George Thomson who wrote to the editor of *Photographic Notes* from 22 Glassford Street, Glasgow, describing his design of a stereoscopic camera in 1856.[66] John Urie (1820–1910), who later became a commercial photographer, began professional life as a wood engraver, but was inspired by the daguerreotypes he saw at the Great Exhibition of 1851 to see if he 'could manage to daguerreotype the picture I was engraving on to the wooden

block, and then go over it with the graving tool, it would be a much quicker and cheaper process than having each sketch drawn by hand on the block before being engraved'. However, despite his experiments with photography, and reading all he could, 'the daguerreotype process did not prove a practical success so far as my work was concerned, but when the collodion process was introduced I at once applied it with success'.[67]

Allan Alexander Maconochie (1806–85) came from a Scottish legal family and practised law himself from 1829 until his appointment as Regius Professor of Roman and Scots Law at the University of Glasgow in 1842. His interests in chemistry made him an enthusiastic experimenter with the various forms of photography as they appeared. He was mentioned in Lady Trevelyan's diary on 1 May 1839, when she and her husband Sir Walter called on him in Edinburgh and he 'shewed us some specimens he has done of the photogenic drawing. There are both the light image on dark ground & the reverse. They were mostly fern leaves & small plants [...] very clear sharp & pretty some of them were. He had also succeeded in producing, but *not in fixing* the image from the camera'. They met again in Rome, in December 1841, where they 'called at the Allan Maconochies [...] he has taken a great many Daguerotype [sic] views this summer in the Pyrenees but it is an expensive amusement, buying the instrument and all the costly preparations & ingredients it has cost him above £100 – he takes great delight in it'.[68]

Another Glasgow University figure who 'procured Daguerreotype apparatus, and in 1839 initiated the brothers James and William Thomson [subsequently Lord Kelvin] into the mysteries of taking Daguerreotype photographs', was Dr John Pringle Nichol (1804–59), Regius Professor of

Natural Philosophy.[69] He was characterised by Kelvin's biographer as 'a most accomplished man, of quick parts, with a keen eye for recent advances in science, and a poetical imagination'. On reading Sir John Robison's description of Daguerre's process, Nichol excitedly wrote to the *Scotsman* with his ideas for applying the new process to scientific ends. He outlined three possible uses, all obviating the need for human observers, who might introduce error into readings: first, in recording meteorological observations; second, in recording the magnetic variations of the dip-circle, an instrument that responded to the Earth's magnetic field; and third, in astronomical applications, especially in recording the enigma of sunspots and in furthering knowledge of the Moon. He concluded by reminding the readers that the new Glasgow Observatory would be ready by the following spring, and that its equipment would be as good as any elsewhere in Europe.[70]

The photographic journalist Dr John Nicol – not to be confused with John Pringle Nichol, who wrote extensively in the *British Journal of Photography* about pioneering Scots photographers – reminisced about his own youthful attempts at daguerreotyping in Forfar, north of Dundee:

> From a book of 'general jottings' that I have kept with more or less regularity for nearly sixty years, I find that on May 9, 1841, which I remember was a Sunday, by the aid of a smooth, flat stone and sand and water, I ground the mouth of a gallipot until it was airtight when covered with a plate of glass, to be employed as an *iodizing* box. I was then an apprenticed chemist, and was taken into photographic colleagueship by Dr Murray, a then eminent surgeon, in consequence of a supposed acquaintance with the chemicals employed in daguerreotyping.

On May 23d, after, as I well remember, many failures, a recognizable head and shoulders of myself was produced with a sitting, or rather leaning against the door of a summer-house, of four minutes, the doctor being the operator; I, in my turn, making a similar picture of him; and both were for some time on exhibition in the chemist and druggist establishment of W. Law, Forfar.

Subsequent entries show that, prohibited from experimenting with the doctor by the powers which it was my duty to obey, because of his proclivity to Sabbath-breaking, I was taken up by the Rev. Mr Low, pastor of the Congregational Church, and that together we used many plates and much material with what we then thought a wonderful degree of success.[71]

In his 1898 instruction manual, he wrote: 'I confidently dedicate "The Right Road to Photography" to the memory of Dr David Murray with whom, considerably over half a century ago, I first entered into the mysteries of the Daguerreotype.'[72] Partly because the invention of photography was given such wide coverage in the newspapers, there is a combination, in the early response, of intellectual thought alongside a comparatively naïve desire to take pictures. John Nicol was thirteen. Two older men worked with him. This was a pattern throughout photography's first decade. The episode has the additional quirk that the minister, who must have been instrumental in preventing Nicol from working with the infidel doctor, was happy to work with the boy instead. For most people, Sunday was the only day of leisure, but, in Scotland, Sabbath-breaking was strictly frowned upon.

Another photographic journalist who attempted the

daguerreotype was John Traill Taylor (1827–95). He was notable as the respected editor of the *British Journal of Photography* between 1864 and 1895, apart from the years 1880 until 1885, when he crossed the Atlantic to edit the *Photographic Times* of New York. Born in Kirkwall, Orkney Islands, he moved to Edinburgh at the age of eighteen:

> Established in business as a practical watchmaker and optician at Edinburgh in the early forties, his attention was attracted to photography by the appearance of the daguerreotype. During his leisure hours, together with a few other young men similarly interested, Mr Taylor began his first experiments in photography.[73]

He moved to Dumfries in 1851, as a professional watchmaker and retail jeweller, but continued with his photographic interests. In a review paper of processes to the Photographic Society of Scotland in early 1859, his discussion of the daguerreotype was as nostalgic and lyrical as that of the commercial photographer James Ross:

> Daguerre's process quite took the scientific world by surprise. The extreme minuteness, fidelity and beauty of his pictures, excited the most unbounded admiration. Nor is this to be wondered at; for even at the present day, when the eye is accustomed to all that is beautiful in the art, the well-executed daguerreotype never fails to evoke sentiments of the most pleasing kind. Pity it is that the process of Daguerre meets with so few adherents now-a-days! … Veteran photographers still look back to this, their first love, with feelings of deep fondness. If I mistake not, the gentleman who presided at the last meeting of this Society [Horatio Ross, whose work is discussed below] must be one of this class, for at the close of the meeting, in a desultory conversation, he asked me by what door I entered photography; and on my replying that I had been an amateur photographer in 1845, he replied, 'Then, Sir, you must be one of the right sort, for I hold no man a thorough scientific photographer who has not mastered the details of this process'.[74]

In the south-west of Scotland, James Blackwood (1823–93) was a successful carpet manufacturer in Kilmarnock, whose hobbies focussed primarily on geology. It is known, however, that he constructed scientific instruments for himself, including a camera obscura, a microscope and a telescope.[75] 'Stands, tubes, and lenses were all fashioned by himself. He was one of the earliest makers of daguerreotype in Scotland', claimed his obituary.[76] It appears that Blackwood did not continue with this form of photography, and was working in some isolation.

Another practitioner, Dr George Skene Keith (1819–1910), surgeon and elder brother of another famous Scottish photographer, Thomas Keith, took some extremely competent daguerreotype views in the Holy Land during 1844. His father, the theologian Alexander Keith, wrote in the preface to the 36th edition of his massively popular book, *Evidence of the Truth of the Christian Religion*, published in 1849:

> As soon as photography began to take its place among the wonderful arts or inventions of the present day, he [the author] anticipated … the rays of the sun would thus depict what the prophets saw. With this intent, on his first visit to the East, he took with him some calotype paper, &c, the mode of preparing which was then secret;

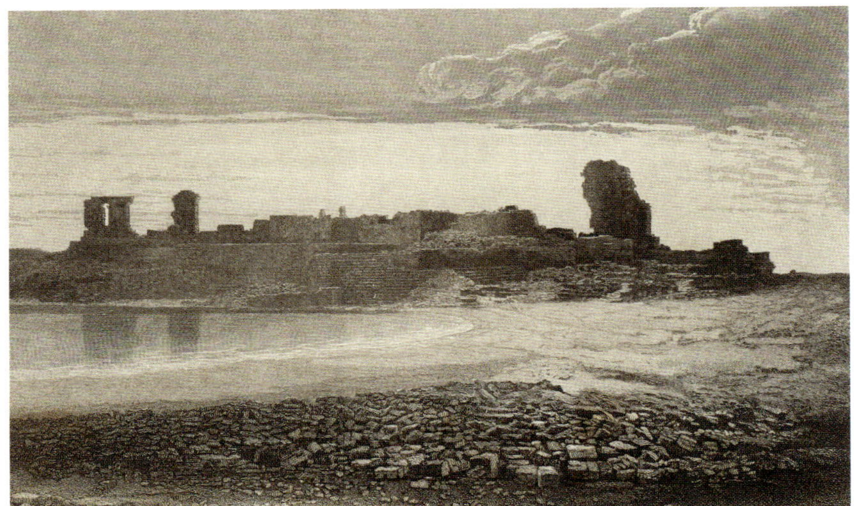

but on reaching Syria it was wholly useless. ... A second visit to Syria, accompanied by one of his sons, Dr G. S. Keith, Edinburgh, by whom the daguerreotype views were taken, enables him now to adduce such proof ....[77]

George Skene Keith's daguerreotypes were among the earliest to be taken in Palestine. Judging from the resulting engravings [FIG. 2.7] (also sold as sets without the text), he was no beginner, and must have learned the art before he set out. Unfortunately his autobiography concentrates on the medical aspects of his life, rather than the photographic side.[78] On his way back home he encountered the colourful entrepreneur, Vincent Nolte, who met him in Trieste:

He [Keith] had travelled through Asia Minor, discovered some ancient cities and mines, and published his travels. His predecessor [Sir Charles] Fellowes [*sic*], and other travellers, doubted the existence of these mines, since they had not themselves been able to find them. Therefore Keith resolved on another voyage, in which he determined to daguerreotype the scenes. He was now returning to England with full and incontestable proofs of his truthfulness; and he gloried in his anticipated victory.[79]

These daguerreotypes were last seen in 1877.[80]

Surrounding Sir David Brewster and the St Andrews group of calotype experimenters were further people interested, briefly, in the daguerreotype. Brewster, of course, was enmeshed in a web of correspondents across scientific Europe, and the advent of the penny post, inaugurated in May 1840, enabled him to receive and send paper images (and instructions on how to make them) to fortunate recipients. The daguerreotype was less easy to disseminate. However, it is clear that the process was known and practised in St Andrews: 'Dr Adamson', Brewster informed Talbot in July 1841, 'is a good Chemist, & successful with the Daguerreotype ...'.[81] Despite this, and the example made by Thomas Davidson mentioned above, no daguerreotypes taken in St Andrews have apparently survived.

Another of Brewster's correspondents, based just outside of Perth, was Lord Gray of Kinfauns (1765–1842), who took a keen interest in the new photographic processes. He was mentioned by Brewster in a letter to Talbot in early 1839:

The account of Daguerre's results had excited great interest here, and I was therefore delighted beyond measure, both from personal and national feelings that you had anticipated the French Artist in his beautiful process. I had a letter a few days ago from Lord Gray of Kinfauns begging me to let him know any thing I might learn of the French process, but I little thought I shd be able to tell him that the first Inventor of it was a Friend of my own.[82]

Gray was also enthusiastic about Talbot's process, and just over a year later Brewster wrote to Talbot:

When on a visit to Lord Gray of Kinfauns I shewed him the specimens referred to, and tho' he had one of Daguerre's which had newly arrived from Paris, yet yours on Paper excited a greater Interest. … When in Edin[r] lately I assisted in executing some views by Daguerre's method, and have ordered a Camera Obscura for the purpose of working myself.[83]

Brewster reported an experiment in daguerreotyping at Kinfauns, to Talbot in August 1841: 'Mr Gray and I tried the effect of Electricity [in accelerating the process] yesterday at Kinfauns in producing a Daguerreotype Copy of a Bust in common day light; but without the least success.'[84]

Major (later Sir) Hugh Lyon Playfair (1786–1861), who had retired to St Andrews after serving in India, was a neighbour of Sir David Brewster. He took photographs by the daguerreotype, calotype and the collodion processes. In a talk about his 'compound achromatic camera' given before the Royal Scottish Society of Arts in June of 1843, Thomas Davidson said that 'it is now two years since I formed instruments on this principle, the first of which is in the possession of Major Playfair. The specimens now before you were taken with this instrument which the Major still uses with success and prefers to all others, though he has Cameras of German, French & also of London manufactures.'[85] Playfair's obituary stated that 'the Major was never

known to try anything which he did not accomplish. In his individuality he was proficient in all kinds of manly sports – a good mechanic, with a special leaning towards photography, which he was the first (being initiated by his friend Claudet) to introduce into St Andrews, now celebrated as a chief home of the art.'[86]

There is a caustic note that Playfair penned to Brewster to pass on to Talbot during those frustrating days in mid-1842 when the St Andrews circle seemed to have hit a brick wall over mastering the calotype:

If your friend Mr Talbot will condescend to peruse these notes [above] & give us any new light on the Subject – we may go on … But with the <u>present light</u> we cannot advance one step & I Regret to say that the Daguerreotype must have infinitely the ascendency unless this Art is more easily attainable – With the other I never have a single failure – with this I never have anything else.[87]

Playfair, along with Brewster, became firm friends with the London photographer Antoine Claudet (1797–1867). He exhibited 'some beautiful specimens of Daguerreotype Portraits, executed by M. Claudet, at the Adelaide Gallery, London, by the refracting Camera' to the Royal Scottish Society of Arts, in Edinburgh, in February 1842.[88]

Antoine François Jean Claudet's links with the non-professional photographers based in Scotland, especially in St Andrews and Edinburgh, mean that he deserves a mention here. Born in Lyons, he moved to London during the 1820s, where he was involved with the import of glass. When he heard of the new invention of photography, he went back to Paris immediately, where he learned (and more

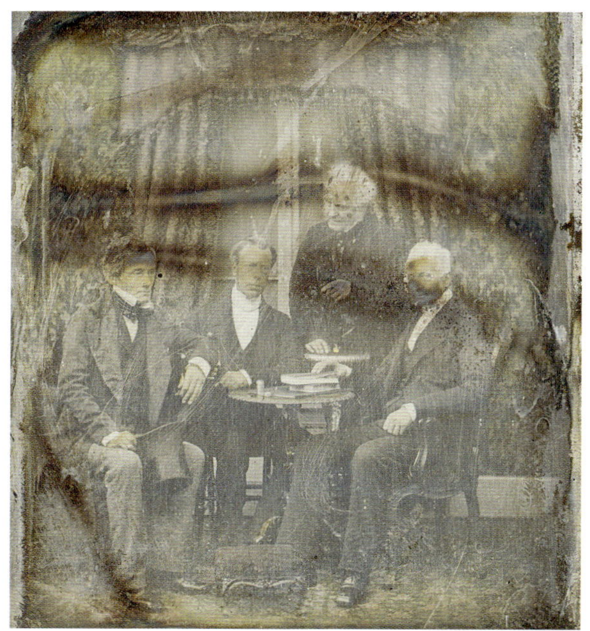

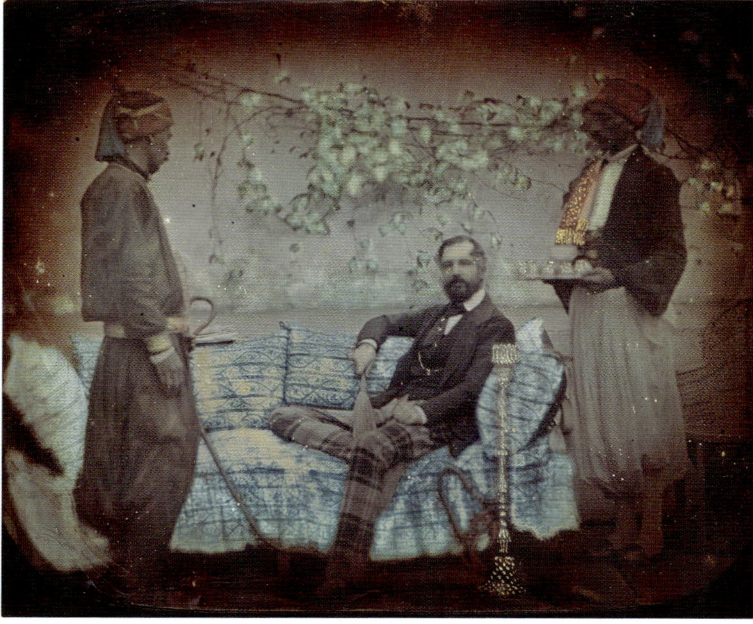

importantly, obtained a licence to practice) the daguerreotype from Daguerre himself.[89] He was thus the second professional photographer (after Richard Beard) to open a studio in London, and by the end of his life this had extended to three premises.[90] His work was certainly appreciated in Scotland; for instance, an advertisement placed in the press in 1850 by D. O. Hill's brother, the publisher and print-seller Alexander Hill, read:

> Mr Claudet's Daguerreotypes. Mr Hill begs to intimate to the Members of the Association for the Advancement of Science, that during their stay in Edinburgh, he will have for Exhibition a large Collection of Mr Claudet's Daguerreotypes, perhaps the most interesting and perfect specimens of this beautiful Art which have been seen in this country.[91]

Hill's gallery was at 67 Princes Street, in the fashionable shopping centre of town.

Claudet visited St Andrews in 1855 for the British Association meeting in Dundee that year. He took a stereo daguerreotype of a group of friends, Professor J. D. Forbes, Rev. William Brown, Hugh Lyon Playfair and Dr George Buist[92] [FIG. 2.8]. However, it is probably true to say that most identified daguerreotypes taken by Claudet of Scots were taken when the Scottish upper classes visited London[93] [FIG. 2.9]. Claudet's great rival, Richard Beard – who probably never came to Scotland himself – had placed in Scottish newspapers an advertisement intended to be noticed by 'Persons Visiting London [;] Portraits, Landscapes, Copies of Paintings, &c., by the Agency of Light [.] Mr Beard's recent improvements in the Daguerreotype invention have been honoured with the following, among a variety of other notices, by the leading public journals …' – quoting high praise from a number of sources.[94]

Claudet was also a friend of the renowned sportsman and amateur photographer, Horatio Ross (1801–86), who proposed the Frenchman for membership of the Photographic Society of Scotland in 10 January 1860.[95] A daguerreotype of Horatio Ross by Claudet was exhibited in the Art Treasures of the United Kingdom exhibition at Manchester in 1857.[96] Ross, too, was a daguerreotype practitioner; he recalled: 'I have devoted much time and attention to this most fascinating pursuit; and it is no great exaggeration to say that for the last thirty years very few days have passed without finding me occupied with some branch of photography.' He stated that he 'began with daguerreotypes in, I think, 1843 or 1844. I have tried most of the processes which since have been brought out – Talbotype, calotype, wax paper, wet collodion, and dry plates'.[97] His daguerreotypes – a group of which have survived – show family members, some of whom are adventurously presented as shooting or fishing [FIG. 2.10], and were taken at his family estate of Rossie Castle in Forfarshire [FIG. 2.11].[98]

Ross had married Justine Henrietta Macrae in 1833 and the couple had five sons; Henrietta was also interested in both field sports and photography, leading to harmony

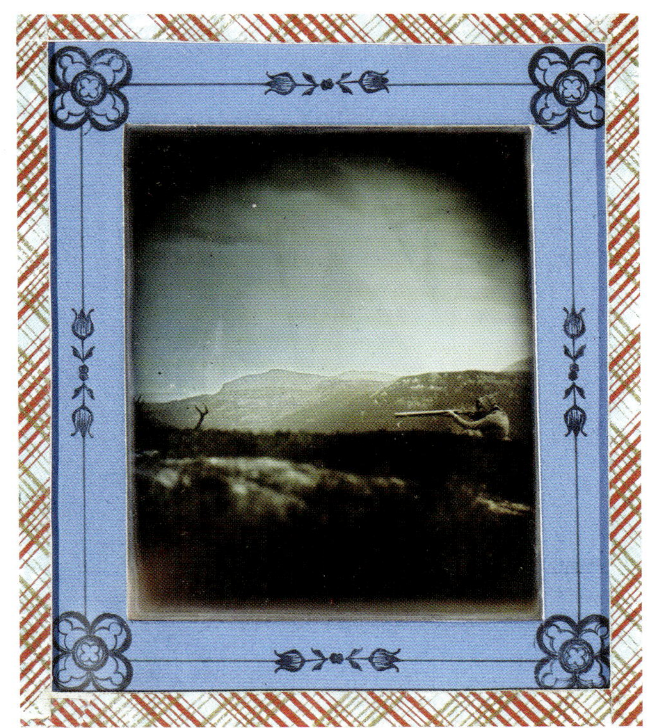

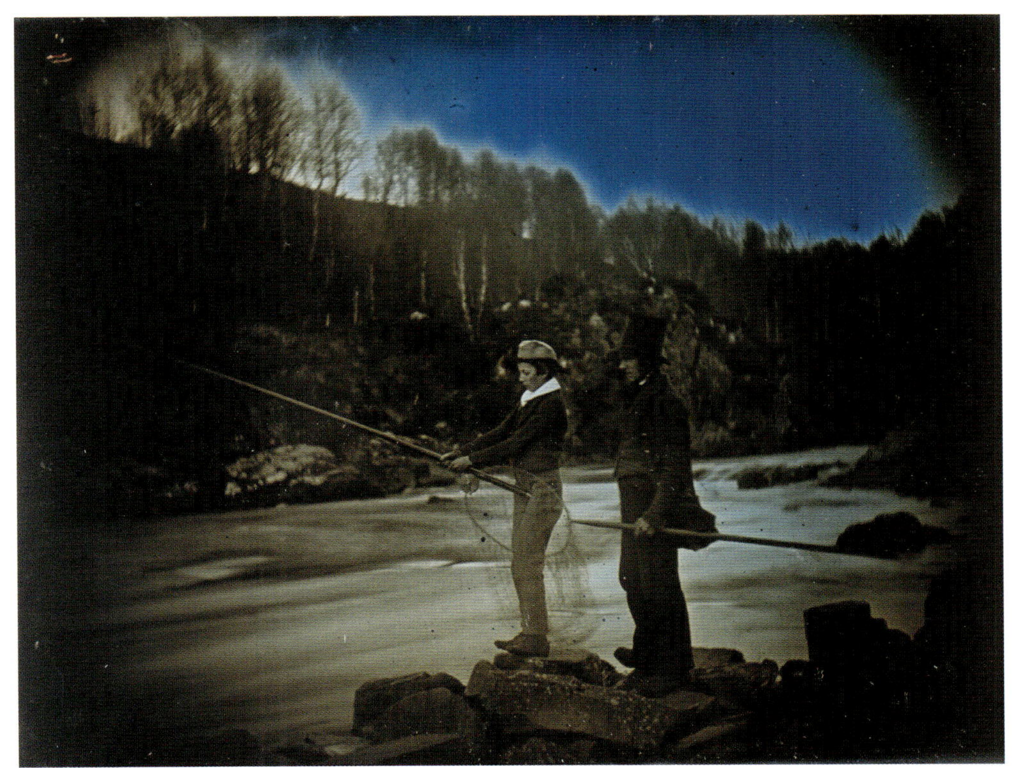

Fig. 2.8 (opposite left): Antoine Claudet, 'J. D. Forbes, William Brown, Hugh Lyon Playfair and George Buist', half a stereo daguerreotype. (St Andrews University Library, Special Collections, J. D. Forbes Collection, ms38081/1)

Fig. 2.9 (opposite right): Antoine Claudet, 'Sir Charles Augustus Murray with two Egyptian servants', c.1851, whole plate daguerreotype. (Scottish National Portrait Gallery, PGP 275.1)

Fig. 2.10 (above): Horatio Ross, 'Craigdacourt', showing Mrs Ross shooting, 1848, daguerreotype. (Victoria and Albert Museum, 246-1946)

Fig. 2.11 (right): Horatio Ross, 'Hoddy and John Munro Fishing at Flaipool', daguerreotype, 1847. (Victoria and Albert Museum, 244-1946)

in the marriage. Pascal Downs notes that for an amateur to use the daguerreotype for landscapes was unusual, as the process had distinct drawbacks; and by 1849 Horatio Ross had turned his attention to the calotype, receiving instruction from the professional Edinburgh photographer, James Ross.[99]

Three ostensibly amateur photographers based in the North East exhibited daguerreotypes at the Aberdeen Mechanics' Institute in 1853.[100] One was listed as 'D. McDonald, Of Aberdeen', showing a frame of eight daguerreotypes; another as 'Mr Petrie of Glenkindie', also exhibiting eight daguerreotype portraits. A third was Alexander Rae (1811–97) whose display included a frame containing a further eight daguerreotypes, four calotypes of a gentleman, and six collodion portraits and groups on glass. Rae had begun life as a pharmacist, and later became a dentist: but he nonetheless produced photographs in a commercial capacity for a time.[101]

It would seem that with the news of Daguerre's 'magic mirror', those with a scientific bent and interest in creativity, took up the instructions, the chemicals, and anything remotely resembling a box camera obscura, and tried their luck – some with more success than others. As Dr John Nicol was to write, some forty years later:

> … the discovery of Daguerre took the world of science by storm. Those only who were connected with science at that time, or had the entrée to scientific circles, can fairly understand the excitement the discovery produced, or appreciate the difficulties with which the would-be-photographers had to contend. Edinburgh, like other university cities, included then, as now, amongst its citizens many professional scientists and many more dabblers in science, who almost without exception took up the *amusement* with a zeal and energy they had never before experienced. Led off by the professors of chemistry and natural philosophy, the process was eagerly prosecuted by the more scientifically-inclined clergymen, physicians, writers to the signet, and even a few leading artists, although by and by, when the cry of 'the craft in danger!' began to be raised, most of the latter fell off. The wonderful pictures, and still more wonderful method of their production, became almost the only subject of dining- and drawing-room conversation. In a comparatively short period of time the whole of what may be called the intellectual portion of society was seized with what an amateur friend, during the later days of wet collodion, not inaptly called 'the black fever;' and if we remember that cameras and lenses least most of the operators had to work with such apparatus as their imperfect knowledge enabled them to construct for themselves, the wonder is not that they did not succeed better, but that they succeeded at all.[102]

The arrival and spread of paper processes

The short period from early 1839 until May 1843, when Robert Adamson (1820–48) first went to Edinburgh, forms a busy and productive time in the history of paper photography in Scotland. The end of this time was announced by Sir David Brewster who wrote to William Henry Fox Talbot:

> Mr Adamson, of whom I have previously written to you, goes tomorrow to Edin[r] to prosecute, as a Profession,

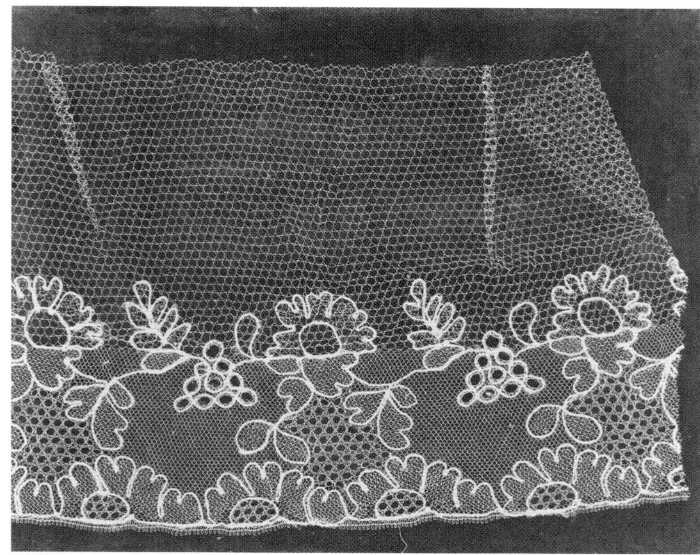

Fig. 2.12: W. H. F. Talbot, 'Lace', photogenic drawing, 1844–46, plate XX from the *Pencil of Nature.* (National Museums Scotland, T.1937.92.20)

the Calotype. He has made brilliant progress, and done some of the very finest things both in Portrait and Land-scape. His Risk & outlay are considerable; & he is there-fore anxious to make a good beginning.[103]

He was the first professional calotypist in the capital.

Talbot had managed to produce positive images on paper from negatives as early as 1835, but had then been distracted by other work. He was galvanised into publica-tion as articles began to appear in the London press in January 1839, describing the excitement generated in Paris by Arago in his address concerning the daguerreotype before the Académie des Sciences. The process was not yet described – Daguerre's method produced a single, reversed and extremely vulnerable positive image on a metal plate, while Talbot's paper-based photography was more robust and, theoretically, infinitely reproducible.[104]

Early the following month, a note appeared in the *Athenaeum*, under the column headed 'Our Weekly Gossip', in which the editor directed the reader's attention to the report elsewhere in the journal of the proceedings at the Royal Society the previous Thursday:

… it appears that the highly curious invention of M. Daguerre, described in a letter of our Paris correspon-dent, is almost identical with a discovery made five years ago by Mr Fox Talbot, and which he has been ever since engaged in perfecting …. One obvious difference, as it appears to us, between the process of M. Daguerre and that of Mr Talbot, is, that the former employs metal plates, whereas the latter uses prepared paper. There can be no question as to the superior advantages of the latter; for it would be most inconvenient, if not wholly

impracticable, for the traveller to carry about with him several hundred metal plates …[105]

Accordingly, on 9 February, the *Athenaeum* published Talbot's paper, 'Some Account of the Art of Photogenic Drawing, or the Process by which Natural Objects may be made to delineate themselves without the aid of the Artist's Pencil'.[106] In their editorial, they pointed out that careful comparisons were taking place in Paris between the two processes; and though various commentators had rushed into print to state how simply such images were to be obtained, the point was that only Talbot and Daguerre had managed to 'fix' their images [FIG. 2.12]. This was followed a fortnight later by an extensive report of the letter sent by Talbot to the Royal Society, a measure of the public interest in this matter.[107] By early March, the *Athenaeum* felt able to comment: '… the question of priority, as between England and France, is settled beyond all dispute: at the same time, we must observe, that the processes of M. Daguerre and Mr Talbot are manifestly different.'[108]

By the following month the *Athenaeum* had made up its mind about 'the new art':

… we may observe that some of our contemporaries continue to argue respecting the discoveries of Mr Fox

Talbot and M. Daguerre, as if a doubt yet existed as to priority. There can be no doubt on the subject. Mr Talbot himself states that for four or five years his attention has been directed to the subject; whereas there is abundant proof that M. Daguerre had made great progress in his discovery – had indeed produced many drawings, more than a dozen years since. But we repeat, that the processes are entirely different, and the results different; and having seen specimens of all, including among the best those of Mr Talbot [and others], we distinctly state that those of M. Daguerre far excel any which have been produced in this country.[109]

But though Talbot had explained and demonstrated his paper process at the Royal Society, no one as yet knew how Daguerre had produced his metal plates. It was to be mid-August 1839 before his process was revealed to the public.

Talbot's paper on the art of photogenic drawing was republished in the *Mechanics' Journal* for 16 and 23 February, in the *Literary Gazette* for 23 February, and in the March editions of the *London & Edinburgh Philosophical Magazine* (one of whose editors was Sir David Brewster).[110] In Scotland, the public was as eager as that in London to find out more about these methods of capturing a shadow.

In Edinburgh, Dr Andrew Fyfe (1792–1861) reported to the Society of Arts for Scotland at their meeting in March, on Talbot's process of photogenic drawing, samples of which he had produced using the oxy-hydrogen light; however, he had used a different salt:

The compound used by Mr Talbot is the *Chlorid* [*sic*], but Dr Fyfe stated that he preferred the *Phosphate*, not only because it is extremely sensible to light, but also because it is applied more easily and uniformly to the paper. It gives a pale yellow tinge, so that it is thus easily known when the paper is equally spread over with it.

Fyfe had found great difficulty in fixing the images by Talbot's recommended methods, and had tried some improvements of his own:

… the light of the oxy-hydrogen blowpipe was sufficiently intense to produce impressions, and after finishing his remarks, he showed the method of doing so. A small dried leaf of the wild geranium was used, by which, in seven minutes a distinct representation of the leaf was produced.

Fyfe then read a letter from the scientific instrument maker and Curator of the Museum of the Society of Arts for Scotland, John Dunn (*c.*1791–1841), who had managed to produce an image of 'a section of a piece of cane, by means of the solar microscope. The impression, which was made on phosphate paper was exhibited.'[111] The use of the solar microscope had been known for a long time as an early form of optical projector that magnified the specimen placed within it into a darkened room; the unfixed images of Humphry Davy and Thomas Wedgwood had been produced in such a device.[112]

The Society of Arts for Scotland next met on 10 April, and the meeting was reported in the press in detail. Andrew Fyfe again spoke 'On Photographic Etching', stating:

… that since the last meeting of the Society he had succeeded in preserving the Photographic impressions done with the phosphate of silver. … He then made some remarks on the process of etching in the common way, and afterwards on another mode of etching, by using a transparent varnish, by which he was enabled to take copies from engravings and oil-paintings, and also to take etchings from the images given by the camera-obscura. Specimens of the etchings were shown. … He also explained an important practical application of the Photographic process to lithography, by which lithographers were not put to the trouble of tracing the object to be taken on the transfer paper. Lithographic specimens made in this way were exhibited.[113]

In Edinburgh, competent chemists were following Talbot's widely-publicised instructions with such success that by 17 April Dr Andrew Fyfe was advertising a 'Popular Lecture in Photographic Drawing and Etching' at the request of the President and Council of the Society of Arts for Scotland, in the Assembly Rooms; tickets were two shillings each. The *Scotsman* commented in an editorial that the lecture was intended 'for those who have not had an opportunity of hearing the results of the experiments in the interesting art of photography, or mode of obtaining impressions of objects by the chemical action of light, without the intervention of brush or pencil; and we doubt not that the public, especially ladies, will avail themselves of the opportunity they will have of becoming acquainted with the photographic process …'.[114] After this, Fyfe gave a demonstration of 'The New Art'; and the *Scotsman* commented that the subject 'is now exciting general interest'. The reporter felt that 'the process was described by the lecturer with great perspicacity …. The uses to which this discovery might be turned were then pointed out, and the

various methods for preserving the tints when taken, which appears not to be advanced to the same perfect state with the other parts of the process.' However, 'the audience was numerous and fashionable, and frequently cheered the lecturer as he proceeded.'[115]

Later that same day the Society of Arts met again; Dr Fyfe gave a further paper, 'Notice of recent improvements effected by him in Photographic Drawing &c. whereby the lights and shadows are not reversed'. On this occasion:

> An impression on paper, taken by Mr Wm. Forrester, lithographer, was shewn. In this the lights and shadows of the originals were preserved as in the original, by covering the light parts of the drawing from which it was taken with a dark ground, and leaving the darker parts lighter, so as to allow the greater transmission of light through what, in the original, was the darkest. A lithographic stone was likewise shewn, on which an impression was taken by Mr Nichol, lithographer, by covering the stone with phosphate of silver, and then, after putting an engraving on it, exposing it to light in the usual way. … Several specimens of impressions from dried leaves were shewn, in which the different parts seem to be as nicely delineated, as in the other processes, where the reverse is given.

These images appeared to be fixed, although Dr Fyfe said that as they had been made only a few days previously, he could not positively assert this. Apparently the weather had been so poor that he had been able to use his method only once in the camera obscura, and was waiting for sunshine to provide better impressions.[116] At the Society's meeting on 15 May, William Forrester presented a 'Specimen of

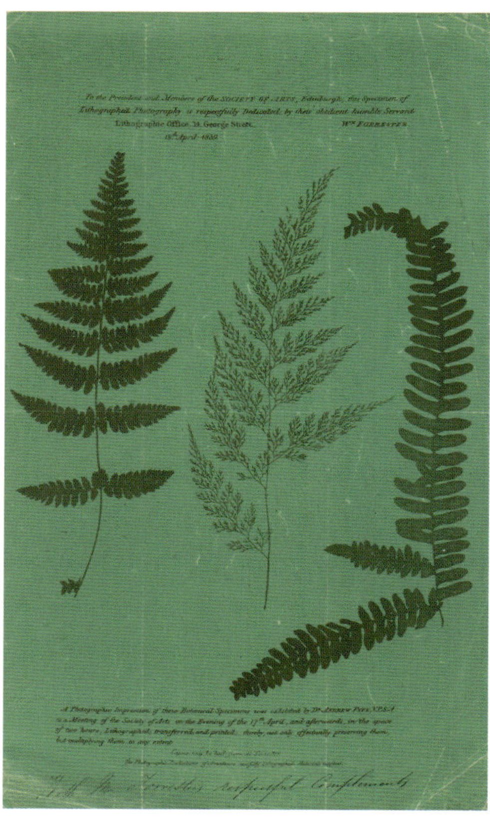

Fig. 2.13: William Forrester, 'Specimen of Lithographed Photography', 18 April 1839. (St Andrews University Library, Special Collection, MS Deposit 69 f9)

Lithographed Photography: which was lithographed, transferred and printed within two hours after the Photographic impressions were exhibited to the Society, at the meeting of 17th April 1839.'[117] An example of this, dated 18 April 1839 and signed by Forrester, has survived in a commonplace book that once belonged to Sir John Robison [Fig. 2.13].[118] Fyfe subsequently made 'Additional Verbal Remarks on Photography' to the Society at their meeting on 3 July, and was invited to produce a written version of all four of his talks 'On Photography' for publication; and this was duly awarded the Society of Arts for Scotland's Silver Medal.[119]

William Forrester and William Nichol were lithographic printers, in partnership between 1832 and 1839. In 1833, Forrester and Nichol jointly published with John Dunn a number of discs for the phenakistoscope, or 'magic disc', a device which uses persistence of vision to show apparently 'moving pictures' and was an early precursor of cinematic apparatus.[120]

Andrew Fyfe's experiments with Talbot's process were not the sole attempt at paper photography to be shown in Edinburgh in 1839. At the meeting of the Society of Arts for Scotland on 29 May, Mungo Ponton (1802–80) delivered the paper, 'Notice of a Cheap and Simple Method of Preparing Paper for Photographic Drawing, in which the Use of any Salt of Silver is Dispensed with', the first publication to discuss a photographic process which used no silver salts in its chemistry.[121]

The discovery that sunlight renders potassium dichromate insoluble forms the basis of almost all photo-mechanical processes, although it is unclear whether Mungo Ponton realised that the solution he was using was combining with the gelatine used to size the paper carrier. He did not patent his process, and the wide dissemination of the method meant that it was available to be experimented upon: a number of pioneers, including Talbot, did so.[122] Used increasingly towards the end of the 19th century, it formed the basis of the carbon process and photo-mechanical processes. It has continued in use, in various silver-free applications, which includes manufacture of printed circuit boards.

Ponton was trained as a lawyer, and involved as legal agent to the National Bank of Scotland, one of the many Edinburgh-based banks of the time. He had been attracted to scientific matters from his youth, being elected a Fellow of the Royal Society of Edinburgh in 1834. Among other interests, he devised improvements to the electric telegraph. However, he became unwell by the early 1840s and retired to Bristol.[123] In 1840, aged 17, M. Carey Lea (1823–97), who became one of America's leading photographic scientists, used Ponton's process to produce a series of photogenic drawings. In the absence of any surviving

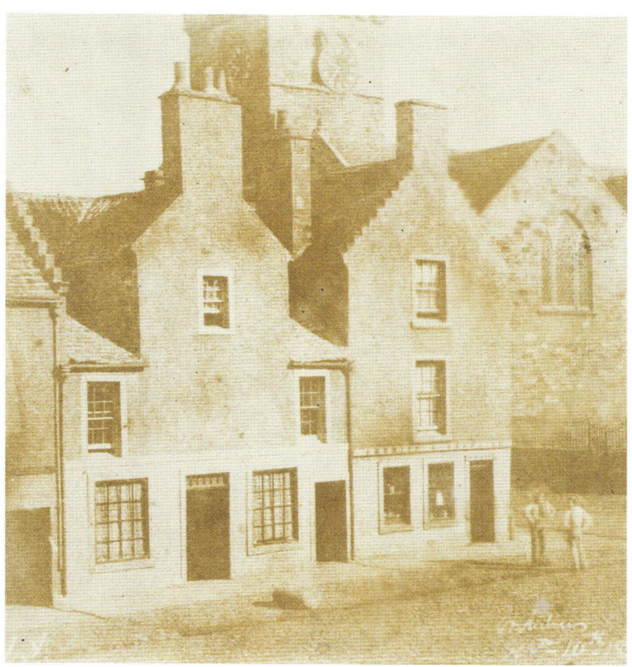

Fig. 2.14: John Adamson, Govan and Smith chemist's shop, St Andrews, calotype, 1842, inscribed in the negative lower left 'JA', and lower right 'St Andrews Sept 10th 1842'. (National Museums Scotland, T.1942.1.2.87.1)

images made by Ponton himself, these must serve as a guide to what his early process looked like.[124]

Ponton went on to devise a photographic method for recording thermometer readings automatically on paper, a process that had been foreseen by Professor J. P. Nichol of Glasgow University as early as July 1839; the Royal Scottish Society of Arts was sufficiently impressed by this technique that it awarded Ponton their silver medal. 'The process is a modification of that discovered by [Robert] Hunt, and to which he has given the name of Energiatype'. Alexander Bryson, the eminent Edinburgh clockmaker, supplied clockwork, and the Society's Committee reported that 'Mr Ponton has … conferred a boon on science'.[125]

Surprisingly, perhaps, it was not in Scotland's capital city but one of the smaller of the ancient university towns, St Andrews on the Fife coast, where W. H. F. Talbot's new art-form was first to be practised. The reason was a group of scientifically-interested people surrounding Talbot's Scottish correspondent, Sir David Brewster, and he – busy with his journalism – passed on details of the new paper process to be attempted in a practical sense. Amongst this group were members of the local Literary and Philosophical Society, including its curator, Dr John Adamson (1809–70), and subsequently his younger brother, Robert Adamson; local pharmacist Alexander Govan [Fig. 2.14]; retired Indian civil servant Sir Hugh Lyon Playfair; and others, including visitors to the town: Brewster's son, Henry Craigie Brewster, an army officer; W. H. Furlong, a young student from Dublin, who acted as an assistant to the professor of chemistry; and a Mrs Dalgleish.[126]

St Andrews society at the beginning of the 1840s was extremely small. Not everyone was attracted to the eminent scientist who had taken up the non-teaching position of the Principal of the United Colleges of St Salvator and St Leonards in 1838:

> Sir David Brewster! He lives in St Andrews and presides over its principal college, yet no-one speaks to him! With a beautiful taste for science, he has a stronger taste for making enemies of friends. Amiable and agreeable in society, try him with a piece of business, or with opposition, and he is instantly, and obstinately, fractious to the extent of something like insanity. With all arms extended to receive a man of whom they were proud a few years ago, there is scarcely a hand that he can now shake.[127]

Thus wrote the eminent Edinburgh lawyer, Henry Cockburn, in 1844. Yet Brewster and Talbot were very much in tune with one another. Talbot's wife Constance wrote to her mother-in-law, Lady Elisabeth Feilding, in August 1835:

> You are perfectly right in supposing Sir D. B. to pass his time pleasantly here. He wants nothing beyond the pleasure of conversing with Henry discussing their respective discoveries & various subjects connected with

science. I am quite amazed to find that scarcely a momentary pause occurs in their conversation. Henry seems to possess new life … when I see the effect produced in Henry by Sir D.B.'s society I feel most acutely how dull must our ordinary way of life be to a mind like that! And yet he shuts himself up from choice ….[128]

Brewster's correspondence with Talbot allowed the St Andrews circle of calotypists to experiment and practice, free from patent restrictions, and far from the bustle of the city. It was perhaps this very distance – from the inventor of the process, and from interference from would-be experts – that enabled the Adamson brothers to find their way towards a chemical and technical expertise that still remains mysterious.

Despite Talbot's letters and the examples of photographs, which he sent north, the St Andrews circle had considerable difficulty with his process, especially in making positive prints, as late as 1842. Initially Talbot had been startled into presenting his photogenic drawing process whilst it was still a fairly simple proposition – it was primarily used for making contact prints because the exposure times were excessively long for camera pictures. It was only on 28 September 1840 that he discovered the implausible concept of the latent image – an image which could not yet been seen by the eye, but which could be developed out chemically. This could reduce exposure times to a few minutes or even seconds, which made portraiture a reasonable proposition, and this is the process which Talbot christened the calotype [or beautiful print]. However he did not send instructions to Brewster until July 1841. For much of the next year, Brewster's colleagues failed to make the calotype work.

It was difficult to secure pure chemicals and good paper. The cotton rag paper and arbitrary faults it might display in contact with the chemistry was one of the prevailing problems of photography in the early decades. W. H. Furlong was still in pursuit of good paper for the calotype in 1856, and was frustrated to find that even the best supplies and quality varied radically, and that, strangely, an occasional batch of nondescript paper would prove good:

I may mention, as an example, several years ago, when perfectly *au désespoir*, on account of bad paper … I selected from the warehouse of Mr Cowan of Edinburgh, a quire of each of a dozen varieties of his papers, and amongst them I found one which was the best Calotype paper I ever met before or since. It was a common scrawl paper, worth 4d. or 5d. per quire, called pott, and weighing 14lbs to the ream. It was very thin and hard, and proved to be perfectly free from spots and blemishes of every kind. Unfortunately I did not return to Edinburgh for some weeks afterwards, and when I called to secure the whole of the parcel, I found it had been sold, and upon trying another lot of exactly the same description, it proved to be completely worthless, and I never could get another quire of the same sort of paper that was of the slightest use.[129]

In experimenting, members of the St Andrews group were able to add their own methods and refinements; John Adamson, for example, made the unlikely discovery that in the first stage of preparation, iodising the paper, it could be much improved by exposing it briefly to sunlight.[130]

A perceptive picture was drawn of Robert Adamson's boyhood, at the end of the 19th century:

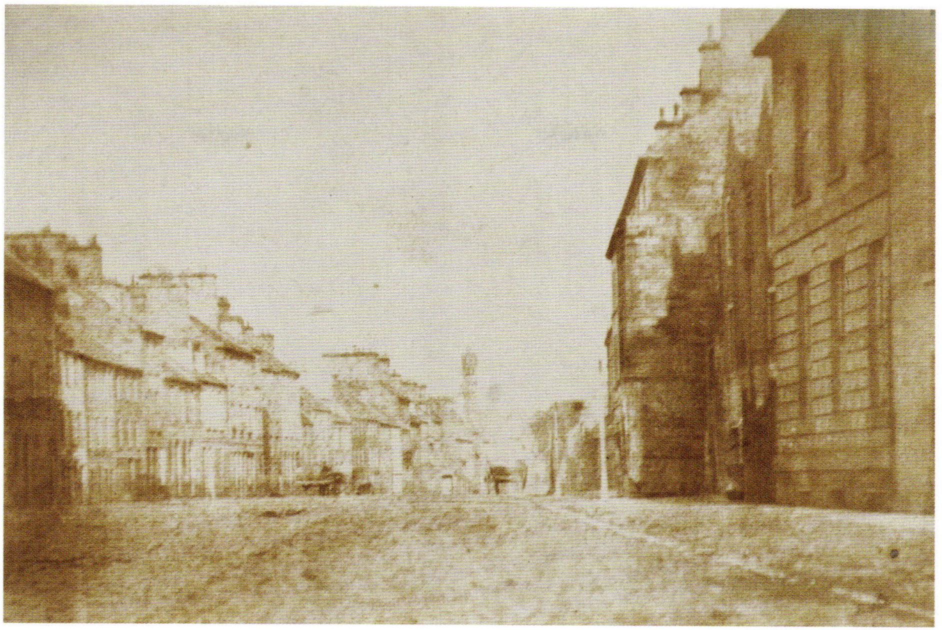

As a boy he was delicate in health and retiring in disposition, with a strong turn for the natural sciences, and an especial aptitude for mechanics; devoting all his spare time to the construction of various models, steam-engines, wheelbarrows and small schooners which he sailed on the burn that ran beside his father's house, and sometimes even building larger rowing-boats, to the no small danger, as we are informed, of those who ventured their persons therein upon the deep. At one time it seemed probable that he would adopt mechanics as a profession; and, indeed, with this in view, he worked for a year or two in a mill-wright and engineer's shop in Cupar, but his frame was hardly muscular enough, his health scarcely sufficiently robust to bear the severe physical strain involved in such a calling.[131]

By August 1842 Robert Adamson was considering calo-type photography as a profession, and Brewster could say he 'has been well drilled in the art by his brother'.[132] The Adamsons worked closely together to ensure that Robert's skill reached a reliable standard, and were able to send an album of small photographs to Talbot in Wiltshire in November. They probably acquired a larger camera to practise landscape photography over the winter [FIG. 2.15]. This early amateur phase ended when Robert Adamson moved to Edinburgh in early May 1843, to pursue photography as a living, leaving his elder brother in Fife where he became increasingly involved in his burgeoning medical practice.

After his brother's death in 1848, John Adamson continued intermittently to pursue the photographic art. He sponsored Thomas Rodger (1832–83), enabling him to attend courses in chemistry at the university, and also in Glasgow, and assisted him to become St Andrews's first professional studio photographer – and there is evidence in Adamson's later photographs that he used Rodger's studios for some of his fine portrait work.[133]

Another figure, who connected with both Daguerre and Talbot at the time of the announcements of their rival processes, was the Scottish scientist James David Forbes (1809–68). Younger than David Brewster by 28 years, and from a wealthy background, Forbes was initially Brewster's protégé (proposed by the older man for Fellowship of the Royal Society of Edinburgh), but the two fell out over a number of issues, including Forbes's successful candidature (against Brewster) for the chair of natural philosophy at Edinburgh University in 1833.[134] Forbes became – even as

Brewster was – involved in a European-wide web of corresponding scientists: these included Talbot and Arago.[135]

Forbes was sent a photograph and two pieces of sensitised paper by Talbot in February 1839 and he responded temperately:

I was extremely much pleased with the Lace specimen of Photogeny which you sent me – & still more gratified to be possessed of some of your paper. I used one piece in the Camera Obscura & spoiled it having left it until it became uniformly dark, and I am preserving the second & last piece until a bright day shall favour the experiment which seems not a very likely event. Dr Fyfe a Chemist here has been making some good experiments with the phosphate of silver, but he finds extreme difficulty in fixing his results. They are chiefly leaves of plants, very delicate & pretty. He has succeeded with the oxy-hydrogen light. Many other persons have of course tried it. I have rather avoided attempting any experiments myself, since everybody seems busy with it & I have no doubt the thing will be thoroughly sifted without my aid. When we consider the quantity of time irretrievably lost in acquiring manual dexterity in matters of this kind & bringing oneself up to the actual state of advancement of the subject before we can hope to add anything new, one sees the folly of prosecuting every new experiment, tempting though it be. I should like very much to know whether you have been led to any important modifications of your process.[136]

When he visited Daguerre in Paris in May, he expressed the same excitement as other commentators and added: 'As to Messrs Talbot & Co. they had better shut up shop at once.'[137]

Notes

1. Gernsheim and Gernsheim 1968: 48–97; Heathcote and Heathcote 2002: 3–10, 25–35.
2. *Ibid.*
3. John Hannavy, 'Richard Beard's Scottish and Irish Patents, and the Development of the Daguerreotype in Those Countries', *Daguerreian Annual* (2007): 88–101.
4. 'Important Discovery in Science and in the Fine Arts', *Caledonian Mercury*, 4 February 1839.
5. *Athenaeum* 587, 26 January 1839; John Plunkett, 'Athenaeum', in Hannavy (ed.) 2008, vol. 1., 92–3.
6. Altick 1978: 163–72.
7. *Athenaeum* 587 (26 January 1839): 69.
8. *Athenaeum* 606 (8 June 1839): 435.
9. *Ibid.*
10. These three daguerreotypes were sent by Daguerre to Ludwig I of Bavaria: see Daniel (ed.) 2003: cat. 14–6.
11. *Athenaeum* 606 (8 June 1839): 435–6; <http://www.oxforddnb.com/view/article/23895?docPos=2>
12. Sir John Robison, 'Notice regarding a cheap and easily used camera lucida, applicable to the delineation of Flowers and other small objects', *Transactions of the Royal Scottish Society of Arts* 2 (1844): 85–6; an example held by National Museums Scotland, T.2003.142.
13. Sir John Robison, 'Notes on Daguerre's Photography', *Edinburgh New Philosophical Journal* 27 (1839): 155–7; the article also appeared in a number of other journals and newspapers, including the *Scotsman*, 3 July 1839.
14. *Proceedings of the Royal Scottish Society of Arts* 1, 1840: 46, Appendix; *Edinburgh New Philosophical Journal* 29, 1840: 391. Vincent Chevalier (d.1841) was part of a group of Parisian opticians, supplying equipment to Daguerre and training a number of daguerreotypists, including his son, Charles. See Buerger 1989: 95, 203.
15. *Caledonian Mercury*, 14 December 1839. Astley had earlier reported on 'the Manufacture of Common Salt' in the *New Monthly Magazine* 24 (1828): 268; and the *Literary Gazette* 12 (1828): 269.
16. <http://peib.dmu.ac.uk/detailphotographer.php?photogNo=126&inum=0&listLength=3&orderBy=coverage>
17. *Edinburgh New Philosophical Journal* 29 (1840): 401.
18. <http://peib.dmu.ac.uk/detailprocess.php?theproc=Daguerreotype&inum=2&listLength=144&orderBy=coverage> For Dunn, see Clarke et al. 1989: 89–95.
19. Catalogue 1840: 40.
20. *Edinburgh New Philosophical Journal* 29 (1840): 391.
21. *Edinburgh Post Office Annual Directory* 1838–39.
22. John Adie, 'The use of brass or copper plates having their surfaces silvered, for producing pictures by the process of daguerreotype', *Edinburgh New Philosophical Journal* 29 (1840): 401.
23. Andrew Fyfe, 'On Daguerreotype', *Transactions of the Royal Scottish Society of Arts* 1 (1840): 415–20; *Edinburgh New Philosophical Journal* 28 (1840): 205–10.
24. See <http://www.oxforddnb.com/view/article/10257?docPos=2> A. D. Morrison-Low, 'Photography in Edinburgh in 1839: The Royal Scottish Society of Arts, Andrew Fyfe and Mungo Ponton', *Scottish Photography Bulletin* 2 (1990): 26–35.
25. Andrew Fyfe, 'On Daguerreotype', *Transactions of the Royal Scottish Society of Arts* 1 (1840): 415.
26. Report of meeting of the Society of Arts for Scotland for 15 January 1840: Andrew Fyfe, 'Verbal Exposition of Daguerreotype', *Edinburgh New Philosophical Journal* 29 (1840): 397.
27. Report of meeting of the Society of Arts for Scotland, 10 April 1839 *Edinburgh New Philosophical Journal* 27 (1839): 421.
28. Scottish National Portrait Gallery, inv. nos PGP 202–48, 52; Hill and MacGlashon inv. no. PGP 46.5 and 6; Stevenson and Forbes 2009: 13.
29. <http://www.oxforddnb.com/view/article/59857?docPos=1>
30. Clarke et al. 1989: 112–22.
31. *Scotsman*, 9 September 1840.
32. *Newcastle Courant*, 14 June 1834.
33. John Nicol, 'Reminiscences of Thomas Davidson, a Weaver Lad', *British Journal of Photography* 26 (15 August 1879): 390–1.
34. *British Journal of Photography* 26 (22 August 1879): 399–401.
35. *Ibid.*
36. Report of meeting of the Society of Arts for Scotland, 23 November 1840, *Edinburgh New Philosophical Journal* 31 (1841): 410–11. Davidson was elected a Fellow in February 1841. Davidson had also lent the camera to the George Street exhibition: see Catalogue 1840: 19: 25.
37. Report of meeting of the Society of Arts for Scotland, 11 January

Note: Website addresses checked and correct at the time of going to press.

1841, 'Description and Drawing of a simple but important improvement in the Camera Obscura, in taking portraits and other objects' and 'Description and Diagram of a Method of taking views by Reflection, in the Daguerreotype, or in the common Camera Obscura', both by Thomas Davidson, *Edinburgh New Philosophical Journal* 31 (1841): 413.

38. Report of meeting of the Society of Arts for Scotland, 31 May 1841: 'On some erroneous statements lately made in a paper before the Royal Irish Academy by Dr Robinson of Armagh, regarding the Reflecting Telescopes made by the late James Short and Sir William Herschell [*sic*]' and 'On an Improved Method of Illumination, by a different arrangement of the Lenses, for the Oxyhydrogen Microscope and Magic Lantern', both by Thomas Davidson, *Edinburgh New Philosophical Journal* 31 (1841): 421.

39. A copy of Davidson 1841 is held in Edinburgh University Library; Thomas Davidson, 'Description of the Process of Daguerreotype, and Remarks on the Action of Light in that process, both in respect to Landscape and Miniature Portraits', *Transactions of the Royal Scottish Society of Arts* 2 (1844): 21–5; the camera is held by National Museum Scotland, T.1925.16.

40. Sir David Brewster, 'A Brief Account of the Camera Obscura, and other Apparatus, used in making Daguerreotype Drawings', *Report of the Tenth Meeting of the British Association for the Advancement of Science* (1841): 9. Brewster was reimbursed for this camera, no longer to be found in the collections at St Andrews University, on 9 July 1841: see A. D. Morrison-Low, 'Brewster and Scientific Instruments', in Morrison-Low and Christie (eds) 1984: 58–65 (65 n.40).

41. St Andrews, University Library, UYUY8525/1, MS Minutes of the Literary and Philosophical Society, 5 April 1841.

42. Document 4151, Brewster to Talbot, 23 October 1840, <http://foxtalbot.dmu.ac.uk/letters/letters.html>

43. Document 4264, Jones to Talbot, 29 May 1841, <http://foxtalbot.dmu.ac.uk/letters/letters.html>

44. See <www.llgc.org.uk/fga/fga_s04.htm>
The whole plate daguerreotype is held by the National Library of Wales PG 00726.

45. Document 4550, Collen to Talbot, 20 July 1842, <http://foxtalbot.dmu.ac.uk/letters/letters.html>

46. Document 4628, Brewster to Talbot, 22 October 1842, <http://foxtalbot.dmu.ac.uk/letters/letters.html>
For more about Henry Brewster's photographic work, see Graham Smith, 'A Group of Early Scottish Calotypes', *Princeton University Library Chronicle* 46 (1984): 81–94; Smith 1990a: 62–8 and Graham Smith, 'Captain Brewster, Calotypist', in Smith 1990b: 71–82.

47. Document 5402, Jones to Talbot, 1 October 1845, <http://foxtalbot.dmu.ac.uk/letters/letters.html>

48. See Document 5704, Jones to Talbot, 12 August 1846, <http://foxtalbot.dmu.ac.uk/letters/letters.html>
'Mr Hill' is the artist and photographer David Octavius Hill.

49. Cosmo Innes, 'Paper read by Mr Cosmo Innes …', *Photographic Notes* (15 September 1856): 169. For Innes, see Marsden 2014: 239–95.

50. John Nicol, 'Reminiscences of Thomas Davidson, a Weaver Lad', *British Journal of Photography* 26 (22 August 1879): 399–401. This is further discussed in the light of the work that Davidson did with Hill and Adamson, see Stevenson 2002a: 40–2.

51. John Nicol, 'Reminiscences of Thomas Davidson, a Weaver Lad', *British Journal of Photography* 26 (22 August 1879): 399–401.

52. Kingslake 1989: 49; [J. Traill Taylor], 'The Optics of Photography and Photographic Lenses. Chapter IX Wide-angle, Non-distorting Lenses', *British Journal of Photography* 30 (20 June 1883): 370; Taylor 1892: 70.

53. Thomas 1969: 27.

54. 'Account of the annual outing of the Edinburgh Photographic Society to Colinton, and their visit to Burton's garden, on 1 Oct. 1875', *British Journal of Photography* 22 (8 October 1875): 491.

55. See <http://peib.dmu.ac.uk/itemexhibition.php?exbtnid=1004&orderBy=exhibitnum&exhibitionTitle=&exhibitionTitle=1841%2C+Edinburgh%2C+Royal+Scottish+Academy>

56. For more about the Finlay business and family, see <www.npg.org.uk/research/conservation/directory-of-british-framemakers/f.php>

57. *Glasgow Herald*, 2 December 1839.

58. Andrew Mactear, 'History of Photography in Glasgow, by Andrew Mactear', *British Journal of Photography* 31 (28 March 1884): 202.

59. *Glasgow Herald*, 13 December 1839, quoting the *Argus*. The *Glasgow Post Office Directory* 1839–40 gives James Willis as 'carver, gilder and printseller, 13 Royal Exchange Square'.

60. *Glasgow Herald*, 24 September 1849. The editor of the newspaper at this point was George Outram (1805–56): see Rosemary Scott, 'Outram, George (1805–1856)', <http://www.oxforddnb.com/view/article/20961>

61. Andrew Mactear, 'History of Photography in Glasgow, by

Andrew Mactear', *British Journal of Photography* 31 (28 March 1884): 202.

62. *Photographic News* 3 (16 March 1860): 341 and (20 April 1860): 399.

63. *British Journal of Photography* 10 (1 December 1863): 472.

64. Quoted from *The Builder* no. 188, in Timbs 1847: 156.

65. Napier 1851, 14: 60, in series *Encylopaedia Metropolitana*.

66. Catalogue 1886, historical section 29; *Photographic Notes* 1 (8 November 1856): 157.

67. Urie 1908: 108 and 110.

68. Taylor and Schaaf 2007: 344; Lady Trevelyan's diary quoted in Larry J. Schaaf, '"Splendid Calotypes" and "Hideous Men": Photography in the Diaries of Lady Pauline Trevelyan', *History of Photography* 34 (2010): 329, 332.

69. Thompson 1910, I:13; for Nichol, see <http://www.oxforddnb.com/view/article/20084>

70. Sir John Robison, 'Notes on Daguerre's Photography', *Scotsman*, 3 July 1839; also *Edinburgh New Philosophical Journal* 27 (1839): 155–7; and *Transactions of the Royal Scottish Society of Arts* 1 (1840): 330–2; J. P. Nichol, 'Photography – Proposed New Applications', *Scotsman*, 13 July 1839. Discussed by A. D. Morrison-Low, 'Photography in Edinburgh in 1839: The Royal Scottish Society of Arts, Andrew Fyfe and Mungo Ponton', *Scottish Photography Bulletin* 2 (1990): 26–35.

71. John Nicol, '"Which is Older" and "Who of our Readers is Veteran Enough to take up this challenge?"', *Wilson's Photographic Magazine* [New York] 33, 470 (February 1896): 81–3.

72. Nicol 1898, Introductory: 4.

73. 'Obituary', *Wilson's Photographic Magazine* [New York], 32 (1895): 570–1.

74. John Traill Taylor, 'Discoveries and Rediscoveries in Photo-graphy; with an account of the Alabastrine Process', *Journal of the Photographic Society* 5 (1859): 151–4.

75. 'James Blackwood, FGS., &c.', *Kilmarnock Glenfield Ramblers* 1, 1894: 29, quoted in Clarke et al. 1989: 193. A telescope with Blackwood's signature was offered for sale by Sotheby's (18 June 1986), lot 205.

76. Abridged from a notice of Mr Blackwood by the Rev. D. Lands-borough, and quoted in Smith 1899: 19.

77. Keith 1849, Preface to the 36th edition.

78. *Scotsman*, 7 August 1850: 'Daguerreotype Illustrations Of Prophecy. Evidence of Prophecy. By the Rev Dr Keith. Thirty-sixth Edition, Second Thousand, in 8vo, 20s. Enlarged above

One Hundred Pages, with Eighteen Daguerreotype Views on Steel, and other Engravings. Set of proofs of the Daguerreotype Views, on India Paper, imperial 4to, price 20s.'

79. Nolte 1854: 473. Also quoted by B. N[ewhall] and R. D[oty], 'The Value of Photography to the Artist, 1839', *Image: The Bulletin of the George Eastman House of Photography* 11, 6 (1962): 25–8.

80. 'Edinburgh Photographic Exhibition [Final Notice]', *British Journal of Photography* 24 (9 February 1877): 63.

81. See document 4315, Brewster to Talbot, 26 July 1841, <http://foxtalbot.dmu.ac.uk/letters/letters.html>

82. See document 3789, Brewster to Talbot, 4 February 1839, <http://foxtalbot.dmu.ac.uk/letters/letters.html>

83. See document 4095, Brewster to Talbot, 18 June 1840, <http://foxtalbot.dmu.ac.uk/letters/letters.html>

84. See document 4319, Brewster to Talbot, 7 August 1841, <http://foxtalbot.dmu.ac.uk/letters/letters.html>

85. Presentation by Thomas Davidson, 'Description and Diagrams of a compound Achromatic Camera', 12 June 1843, *Transactions of the Royal Scottish Society of Arts* 2 (1844): 53 (Appendix); also in National Library of Scotland, Mss Acc 4535, RSSA lecture series, 12 June 1844, T. Davidson, 'Description & Diagram of a Compound Achromatic Camera', paper received on 23 May and read on 12 June.

86. Conolly 1866: 365; this sentence is largely copied from his obituary in the *Gentleman's Magazine* [New Series] 10 (1861): 333–6, which in turn acknowledged that it came from the *Edinburgh Courant*.

87. See document 4577, Playfair to Talbot, 15 August 1842, <http://foxtalbot.dmu.ac.uk/letters/letters.html>

88. *Proceedings of the Royal Scottish Society of Arts* 2 (1844): 15 (Appendix). In the manuscripts relating to this meeting of 14 February 1842, NLS MssAcc 4534, Playfair has written: 'Major Playfair has the pleasure of submitting to the Inspection the following specimens of the Daguerreotype Art executed by Monsr. Claudet at the Adelaide Gallery by the Refracting Camera – 2" – 1st A Portrait of Monsr. Gaudin at the French Institute 30" 2d A Do. of Mr Bodelin 3d A Copy of a Portrait of Monsr. Claudet taken from a Daguerreotype plate by the Electrotype 50" 4 A likeness of Mr Edwards taken by Gas light at the Adelaide Gallery 5 A View of St Martin's Church taken instantaneously in Novr. in London in a dark cloudy morning @ 9 am.'

89. Larry Schaaf, 'Claudet, Antoine', <http://www.oxforddnb.com/

view/article/5548>; and Laura Claudet, 'Claudet, Antoine Francois Jean', in Hannavy (ed.) 2008: 302–4.

90. Stephen Monteiro, 'Veiling the Mechanical Eye: Antoine Claudet and the Spectacle of Photography in Victorian London', 19: *Interdisciplinary Studies in the Long Nineteenth Century* 7 (2008); <www.19.bbk.ac.uk>

91. *Scotsman*, 3 August 1850.

92. St Andrews University Library, Special Collections, J. D. Forbes Collection, ms38081/1.

93. For instance, that of Sir Charles Augustus Murray with two Egyptian servants: Scottish National Portrait Gallery, PGP 275.1; also daguerreotypes by William Kilburn of Walter Crum (1796–1867), Glasgow chemist; and a stereo daguerreotype by Antoine Claudet of Crum and his daughter: Mitchell Library, Glasgow, TD 1073 14/5, 6.

94. For example, in the *Fife Herald*, 6 July 1846.

95. Ordinary Meeting of the Photographic Society of Scotland, *Journal of the Photographic Society* 6 (1860): 129.

96. See <http://peib.dmu.ac.uk/detailphotographer.php?photog No=73&inum=67&listLength=230&orderBy=exhibid>

97. Horatio Ross, 'On Fading', *British Journal of Photography* 22 (1875): 29–30.

98. These survive as a group of eight images, presented to the Victoria and Albert Museum: inv. nos 240–1946 to 247–1946.

99. Pascal Downs OSB, '"The delight of their existence": the photography of Horatio Ross of Rossie (1801–86)', *Studies in Photography* (2006) 35–43; James Ross [not a relation of Horatio Ross], 'A Few Extracts from a Photographer's Old Ledge', *British Journal of Photography* 20 (14 February 1873): 75–7.

100. See <http://peib.dmu.ac.uk/itemexhibition.php?exbtnid=1010 &orderBy=exhibitnum&exhibitionTitle=1853%2C+Aberdeen 2C+Mechanics'+Institution>

101. *Ibid.*, and Taylor and Schaaf 2007: 359–60.

102. John Nicol, 'Reminiscences of Thomas Davidson, a Weaver Lad', *British Journal of Photography* 26 (15 August 1879): 390.

103. See document 4819, Brewster to Talbot, 9 May 1843, <http://foxtalbot.dmu.ac.uk/letters/letters.html>

104. Newhall 1967.

105. *Athenaeum* 588 (2 February 1839): 96.

106. *Athenaeum* 589 (9 February 1839): 114–7.

107. *Athenaeum* 591 (23 February 1839): 156.

108. *Athenaeum* 593 (9 March 1839): 187.

109. *Athenaeum* 597 (6 April 1839): 259.

110. Gernsheim 1984: 137; Gernsheim points out (86) that the paper was also privately printed by Talbot and sent to editors and friends in February 1839 and thus 'constitutes the first separate publication on photography in the world'.

111. *Scotsman*, 6 April 1839; and *Edinburgh New Philosophical Journal* 27 (1839): 418–9.

112. See Schaaf 1996: 73, where Davy and Wedgwood's work (no longer extant) is discussed in relation to Talbot's early photo-micrographs. Also Geoffrey Batchen, 'Tom Wedgwood and Humphry Davy, "An Account of a Method"', *History of Photography* 17 (1993): 172–83.

113. *Scotsman*, 17 April 1839.

114. *Ibid.*

115. *Scotsman*, 20 April 1839.

116. *Edinburgh New Philosophical Journal* 27 (1839): 421–3.

117. *Ibid.*, 425.

118. James David Forbes's papers, University of St Andrews Library, Special Collections, MS Deposit 69f9.

119. *Edinburgh New Philosophical Journal* 27 (1839): 427; award of medal: *Edinburgh New Philosophical Journal* 29 (1840): 393; also *Scotsman*, 1 January 1840; published paper, Andrew Fyfe, 'On Photography', *Transactions of the Royal Scottish Society of Arts* 1 (1840): 319–30; and *Edinburgh New Philosophical Journal* 27 (1839): 144–55.

120. Examples of these discs are held by National Museums Scotland, T.1979.1; Science Museum, London (1990-5036/7183) and 1934-141; and eleven are held by the Beineke Library, Yale University; an advertisement for these appeared in the *Scotsman*, 28 September and 12 October 1833; and *Caledonian Mercury* on 26, 28 September and 5 October 1839. See also: <http://www.stephenherbert.co.uk/phenakPartTwo.htm# fn7>

121. Reported in *Edinburgh New Philosophical Journal* 27 (1839): 425; the published paper *Transactions of the Royal Scottish Society of Arts* 1 (1840): 336–8; and *Edinburgh New Philosophical Journal* 27 (1839): 169–71.

122. Roddy Simpson, 'Ponton, Mungo', in Hannavy (ed.) 2008, vol. 2: 1146–7.

123. See <http://heritagearchives.rbs.com/people/list/mungo ponton.html> for an account of Ponton's professional career; and in addition, see A. D. Morrison-Low, 'Photography in Edinburgh in 1839: The Royal Scottish Society of Arts, Andrew Fyfe and Mungo Ponton', *Scottish Photography Bulletin* 2 (1990): 26–35.

124. See 'Stated Meeting, February 6 [1840]', *Proceedings of the American Philosophical Society* 1 (1840): 170–1. His album is now in the Franklin Institute, Philadelphia.

125. Mungo Ponton, 'On the Registry of the Hourly Variations of the Thermometer, by means of Photographic Papers', *Transactions of the Royal Scottish Society of Arts* 3 (1851): 45–52; also *Edinburgh New Philosophical Journal* 39 (1845): 270–6, read before the Society on 10 March and 12 May 1845.

126. Much of this has been discussed in material published in the past 25 years or so: see, for instance, A. D. Morrison-Low, 'Sir David Brewster and Photography', *Review of Scottish Culture* 4 (1988): 63–73; Morrison-Low, 'Brewster, Talbot and the Adamsons', *History of Photography* 25 (2001): 130–41; Smith 1989; Smith 1990a and 'Captain Brewster, Calotypist', in Smith 1990b.

127. Cockburn 1889: 234.

128. Letter, Constance Talbot to Lady Elisabeth Feilding, 15 August 1835, LA36-58; quoted by A. D. Morrison-Low, '"Tripping the Light Fantastic": Henry Talbot and David Brewster', *Studies in Photography* (2002–3): 83–8, see quote on 85.

129. W. Holland Furlonge [*sic*], 'On the Calotype Process', *Photographic Notes* 1 (1856): 13–16.

130. John Adamson, 'Photography', in Chambers and Chambers (eds) 1857: 777–84.

131. John M. Gray, 'Robert Adamson', in Elliot 1928: 11. John Miller Gray was born two years after Adamson's death, and his information probably came from Dr John Brown who, as a friend of Hill, could have heard it from him rather than from the Adamson family. Gray wrote Brown's obituary, in which he said that Brown was, at the time of his death, 'writing a Preface to a series of calotype portraits to be shortly published – a task for which he was specially qualified by his interest in art and his comprehensive knowledge of the Scottish society of the last generation'. See Gray 1895, 1: 149.

132. See document 4573, Brewster to Talbot, 15 August 1842, <http://foxtalbot.dmu.ac.uk/letters/letters.html>

133. See A. D. Morrison-Low, 'Dr John Adamson and Thomas Rodger: later photography in St Andrews', in Lawson and McKenzie (eds) 1993: 19–37.

134. Steven Shapin, 'Brewster and the Edinburgh Career in Science', in Morrison-Low and Christie (eds) 1984: 17–23.

135. Graham Smith, 'James David Forbes and the Early History of Photography', in Collins (ed.) 1990: 9–13.

136. See document 3854, Forbes to Talbot, 2 April 1839, <http://foxtalbot.dmu.ac.uk/letters/letters.html>

137. Forbes to his sister, Lyons, 20 May 1839, letter in St Andrews University Library msdep7/incoming letters 1856/93, quoted by Graham Smith in Collins (ed.) 1990, p. 11.

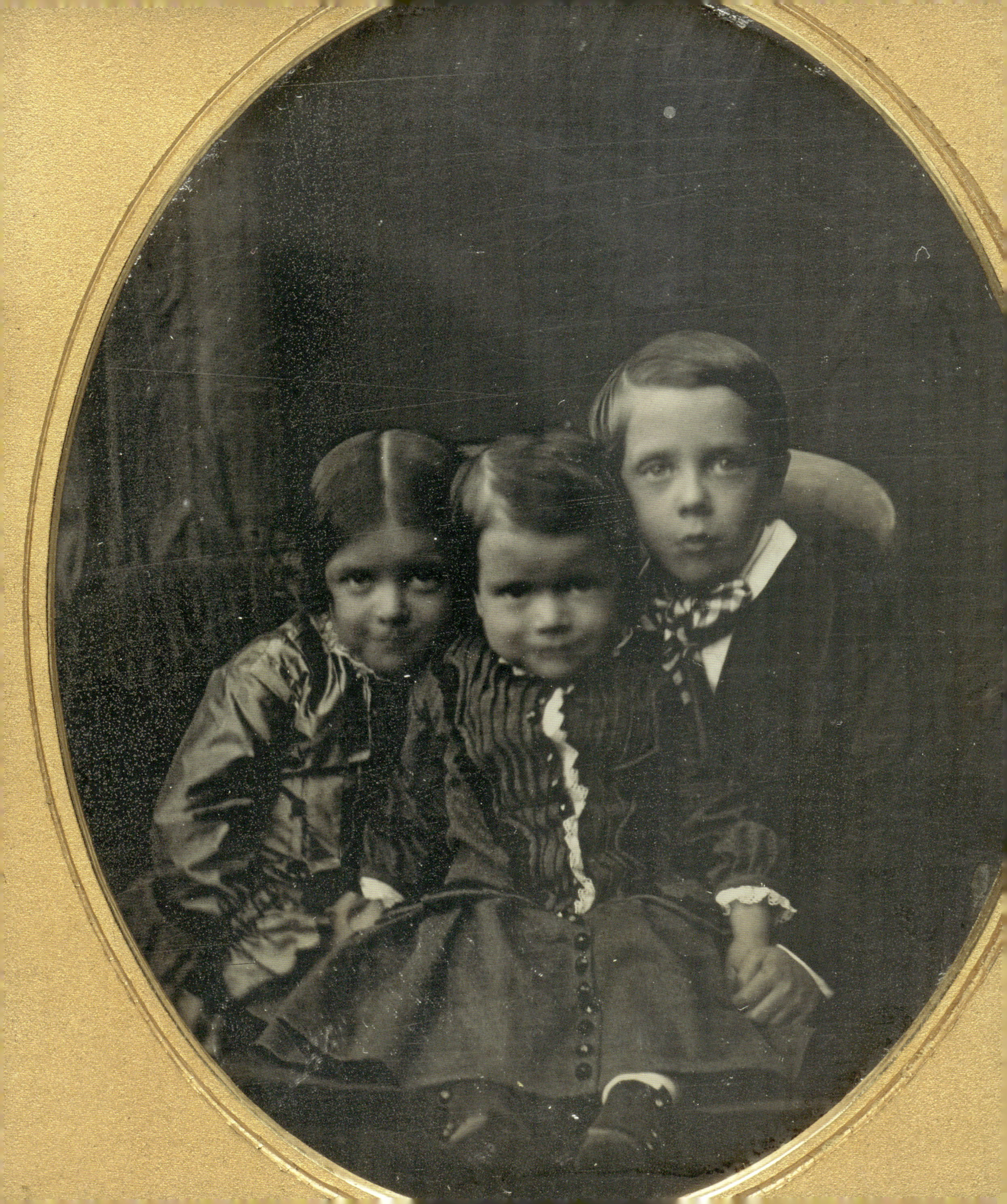

CHAPTER THREE

The Beginnings
of Professional Photography

The posing chair, with something in the shape of a headrest fixed
to its back, was placed against the gable of the adjoining building,
and the operator used to take the sitter by the shoulders and press him
down with the observation – 'There! Now sit as still as death!'

John Nicol, 'Reminiscences of Thomas Davidson, a weaver lad',
British Journal of Photography, p. 400

The daguerreotype in Scotland during the 1840s and 1850s

All over the United Kingdom – including Scotland, where neither Daguerre's nor Talbot's patent held sway[1] – the press was full of discussions about the new process from the time of the announcement in Paris, throughout 1839 and 1840. The well-attended Exhibition of Practical Science, held in the Assembly Rooms, George Street, Edinburgh, from December 1839, displayed 'Specimens of the Daguerreotype' and 'Twenty Photogenic Drawings, made by H. F. Talbot, Esq.', alongside electro-magnetic apparatus, telegraphy and other optical wonders.[2] The exhibition attracted widespread comment in the press.

Much of the emphasis of the literature about early Scottish photography has, with good reason, stressed the role of the amateur and his – it was nearly always a man – input to the new scientific art form. However, there is another side to this particular coin. There was also an economic imperative, and in all the major centres of population portrait studios were set up so that daguerreotype images could be made and sold to an appreciative audience of the growing middle classes – the same audiences who enjoyed purchasing miniatures and silhouettes of loved ones.

Who were these practitioners of the new art? Some of their movements and activities can be traced in contemporary newspapers, but their origins remain obscure and their working lives are difficult to uncover. Sometimes all that survives is a signed daguerreotype; but more often than not the images are anonymous, and the sitters are by now unknown. After the experimental stage, commercial daguerreotypists advertised locally from the early 1840s onwards. While some amateur photographers preferred the daguerreotype, most – perhaps because of the multiplicity of copies that could be produced from one negative –

Opposite, Fig. 3.13 (detail): Ross & Thomson, group of three unknown children, quarter-plate daguerreotype.

practised some form of paper photography. In the main, the daguerreotype was a professional undertaking in Scotland.

Edinburgh: commercial beginnings

In August 1839, Daguerre finally published the process of Daguerreotype. The text was, almost immediately, translated into English by John Smith Memes (1795–1858), the rector of Ayr Academy, who was a Francophile – author of biographies of the Empress Josephine and Napoleon, and of works on art. This had reached its third edition by September.[3] By November, the journalist Robert Chambers was able to report to his avid readers in a second article on 'The Daguerreotype' (the first had been a re-telling of Sir John Robison's account of his visit to Daguerre's studio)[4] the full explanation of the Parisians' method:

> In consequence of an agreement with the French government, by the terms of which M. Daguerre and his partner M. Niepce receive a divided annuity of ten thousand francs (£416 13s 4d), the true and prefect method of Photogenic Drawing, upon the principles of the Daguerréotype, has now been made public by the inventor. The pamphlet in which the stipulated disclosures appear, has been excellently translated by Dr J. S. Memes ….[5]

A full description of the method of making a daguerreotype follows, drawn from Memes's translation – after which, Chambers goes on to say:

> We have seen one [a daguerreotype] brought from Paris, and now in the possession of a gentleman in Edinburgh, which gives a representation of a portion of the streets of the French capital, and in a manner so minute, so delicate, and so wonderfully perfect in shading, as to give one a striking idea of what this invention will yet do for the fine arts. The plate seems to be eight inches by six, and is set in pasteboard, glazed, and framed. The windows of the houses, blinds, sign-boards, stones of the pavement, and other points in the view are brought out with great force. At this time, this specimen is the only one, we believe, yet brought from Paris; but ere long, multiplied specimens will doubtless be in the hands of our countrymen, and these not the production of Parisian, but of native men of science.[6]

As early as October 1839, portrait and animal painter James Howie senior (1791–1858), based at 64 Princes Street Edinburgh, announced 'he has succeeded in producing some beautiful specimens in the above NEW ART on SILVER, the First Public Exhibition of its kind in Scotland'.[7] In April 1841, Lady Trevelyan, wife of the geologist Sir Walter Trevelyan, visited 'Howies who makes daguerreotypes [and] saw some very good ones – one of the Institution on the mound with snow very good – one of Holyrood with colours of sky & building – bought it for £1.1. – saw some portraits not very good.'[8] Howie made professional visits to take daguerreotype portraits to Kirkcaldy in April 1847, Cupar in May 1847, and Duns in the Scottish Borders in 1850.[9] According to the Glasgow photographer John Urie, Howie had 'a bill at his door announcing, in all seasons – summer and winter – "a good light today for taking portraits," so that a blank day never occurred'.[10] Howie was one of a family

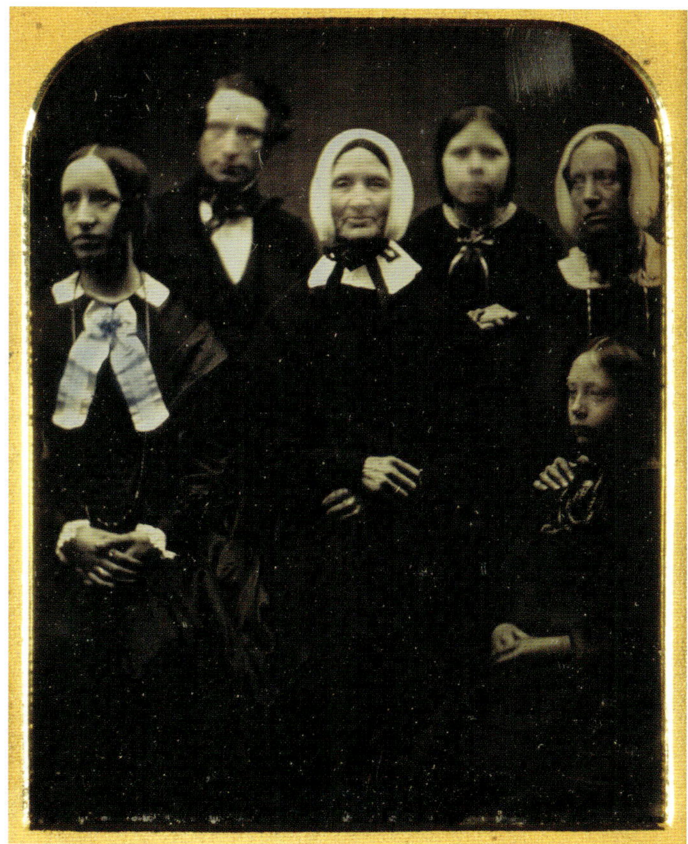

Fig. 3.1: James Howie, unknown family, half-plate daguerreotype. (Riddell Collection, Scottish National Portrait Gallery, PGP R 21)

who had made their living from art, and at least one silhouette portrait by him is known.[11]

The elder Howie was born in Brechin in 1792, and died at the family's business premises at 45 Princes Street, on 27 December 1858.[12] He had practised as an artist in Edinburgh from the early 1820s, and married Mary Winter there on 30 August 1811. They had three children – Ann (born *c.*1827), Julia (born *c.*1833) and James junior (1820–55) – who all practised photography, the daughters working with their father until his death, when they became independent. The son had set up another studio a few doors away.[13]

James Howie senior was remembered as a strong personality [Fig. 3.1]. In 1869, another Edinburgh professional, James Good Tunny (d.1887), wrote:

[James Howie was] the first who made the work of the Daguerreotype a profession in Edinburgh. Mr Howie was a great character as many of you no doubt will remember, especially those who have been *thumbed* round his room when he was in the act of enforcing his photographic propositions.

I remember my old friend Thomas Davidson having constructed a new lens. Sir David Brewster and two other scientific friends were at the testing of it, when it was resolved that they should adjourn to the space of ground now occupied by East Prince's [*sic*] Street Gardens. Mr Howie's camera stand was rather ricketty, so a large window or clock weight always accompanied it. One of Sir David's friends was placed on a chair in the best light – in fact, with the full blaze of the sun in his face. Mr Howie got his camera focussed, and the clock weight laid on top of his camera to keep it steady, and was just about to draw up his slide when his sitter began to mutter about his hat going to be blown away, when old Howie at once satisfied him that there would be little danger of it moving far, as he, with the rough exclamation of '--- your hat,' at once transfixed it with the clock weight. The exposure being over, the gentleman found his hat thoroughly ventilated, as the clock weight had passed right through the crown![14]

The engraving by Joseph Ebsworth of part of his panorama taken from the top of the Scott Monument shows Howie's rooftop studio in 1845, four floors above his Princes Street premises [Fig. 3.2 and detail]. This was the first professional photographic studio in Edinburgh, established in 1841:

Mr Howie's arrangements were at first of the simplest

Fig. 3.2 (below and detail opposite left): Joseph Ebsworth, 'North View of Edinburgh, from the Upper Gallery of the Scott Monument … [at 2.45pm on September, 15, 1845]', 1848, engraving and detail showing James Howie's roof-top studio. (Howarth-Loomes Collection at National Museums Scotland, IL.2003.44.8.91)

Fig. 3.3 (opposite right): James Howie, George Combe, 1846, sixth-plate daguerreotype. (Scottish National Portrait Gallery, PGP 91.4)

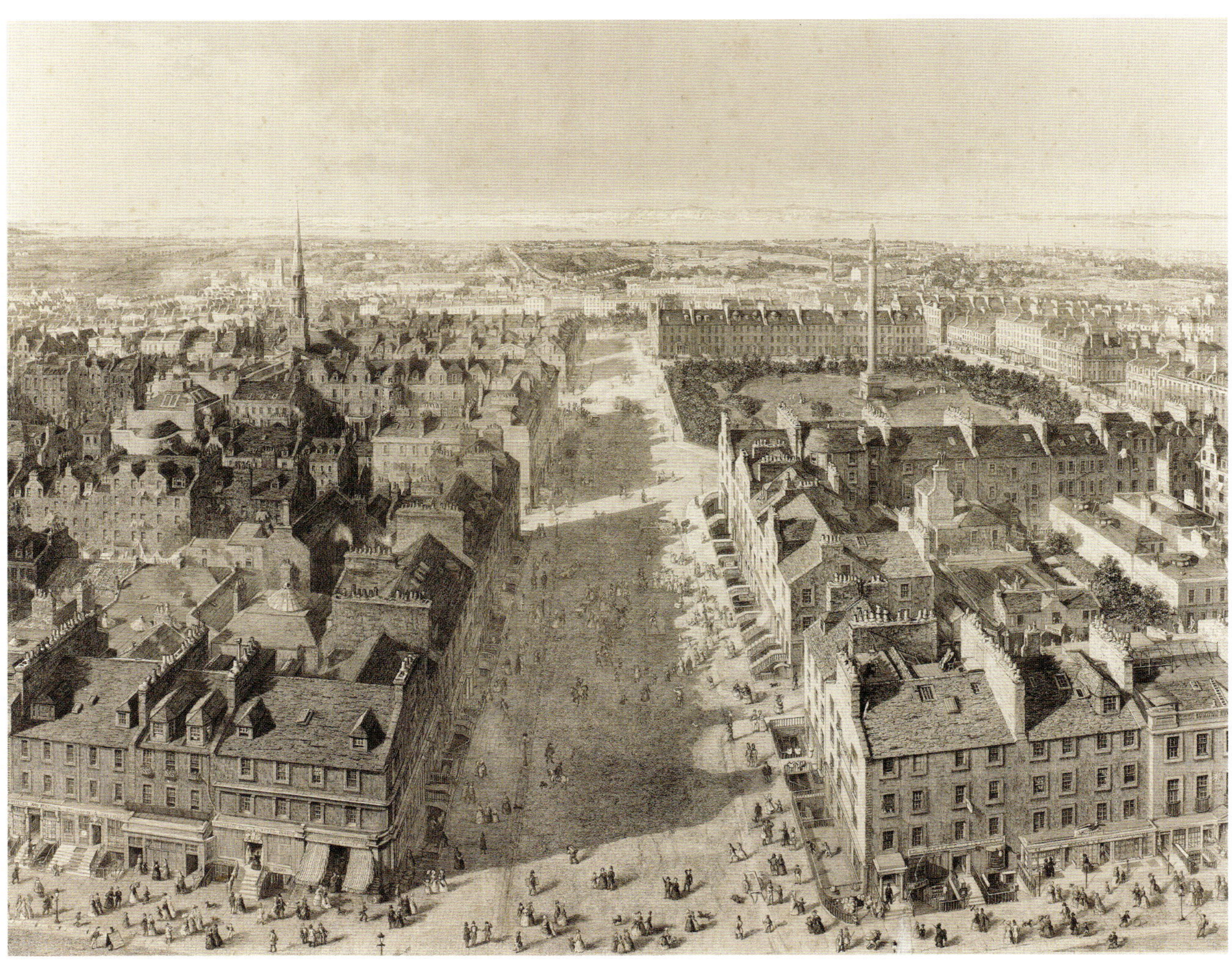

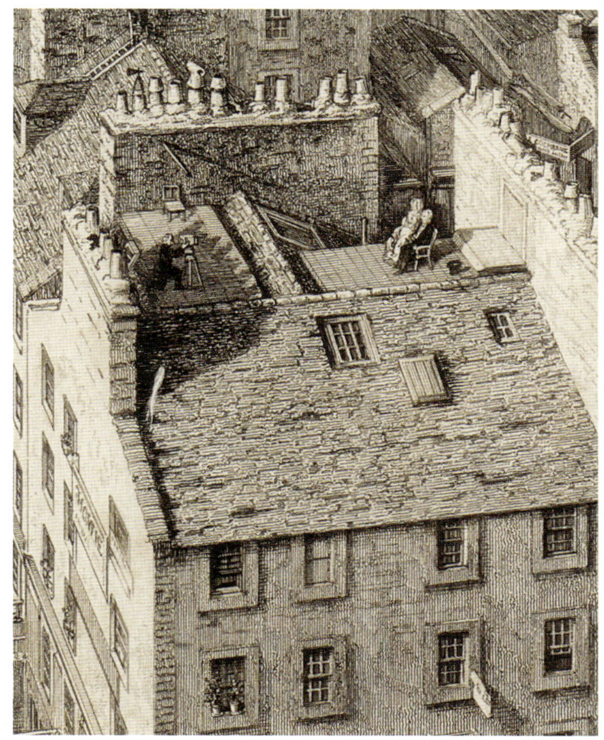

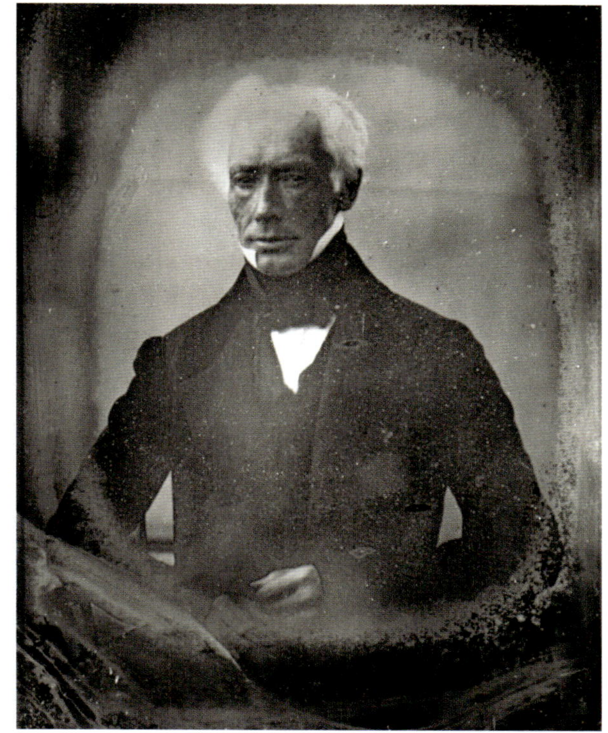

kind. His sitters had to climb three flights of stairs, and then by a kind of ladder reached a skylight through which they got access to the roof of the house. The posing chair, with something in the shape of a head-rest fixed to its back, was placed against the gable of the adjoining building, and the operator used to take the sitter by the shoulders and press him down with the observation – 'There! Now sit as still as death!' Of course, under such circumstances, with the sun shining brilliantly and the exposure counted by minutes, artistic portraiture was not to be expected; but Mr Howie did very well, notwithstanding, and gathered about him large numbers of those interested in the new art from all parts of the country.[15]

A number of daguerreotypes identified as being taken by Howie – possibly even on that daunting roof-top studio – have survived in public collections [Fig. 3.3].[16]

The other prominent early professional figure in the capital was Thomas Davidson (1798–1878). Unlike Howie,

Davidson was interested in all technical aspects of photography and started out as a scientific instrument maker: he did not run a portrait studio. A native of Northumberland, he came to Edinburgh to work in 1836.[17] By 1843 the *Edinburgh Post Office Directory* was carrying an advertisement for Thomas Davidson of 63 Princes Street, offering 'Dissolving Lanterns and Phantasmagoria, daguerreotype and calotype apparatus with the latest improvements'.

In his retrospective of Davidson's photographic career, journalist Dr John Nicol recalled that daguerreotyping

… took possession of his mind with all the force of a mania, and, laying aside everything else for the time being, he stuck to it night and day, bringing both his optical knowledge and mechanical ingenuity into play, until he succeeded not only in producing results equal to anything previously shown by the inventor and discoverer, but until he had out stripped him both in size and quality. … Those acquainted with Edinburgh know that the Royal Exchange Buildings are amongst the

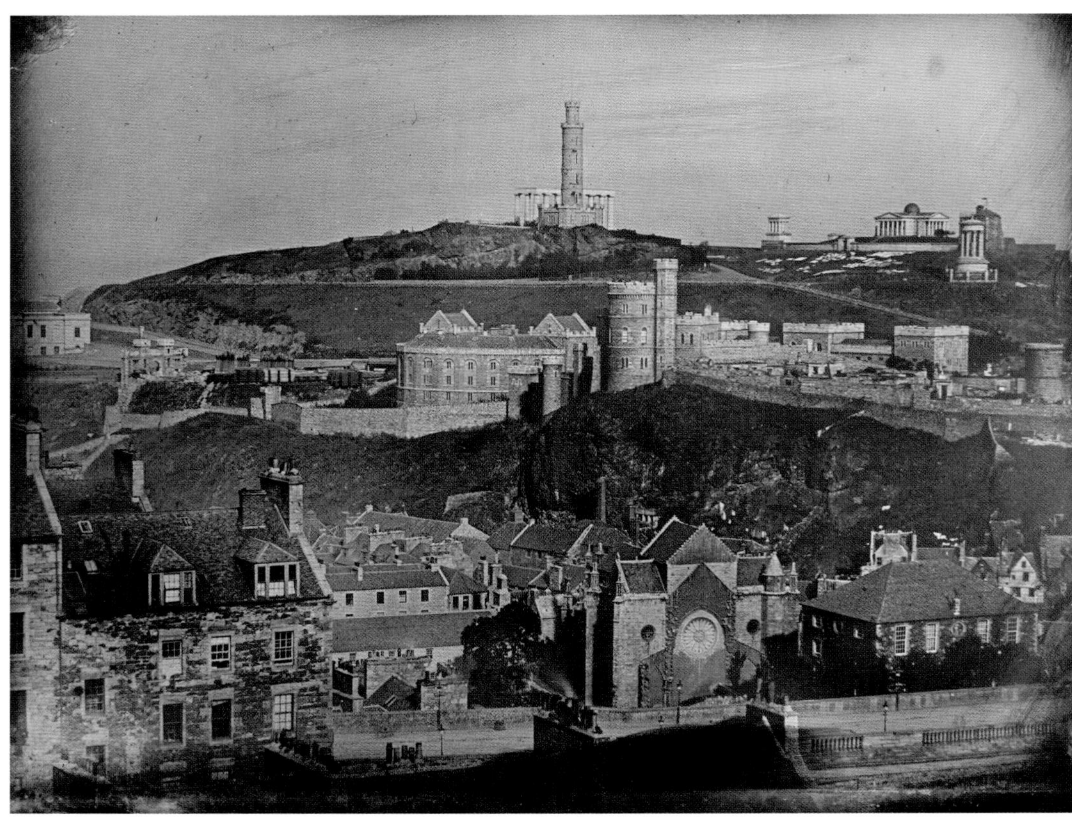

highest of the High-Street houses, and Mr Davidson was at this time located there, nine stories from the ground. The windows commanded a magnificent view of the new town, including the Calton Hill and its surroundings, and on this the lens, roughly stuck into the camera, was turned. In the excusable excitement under the circumstances sufficient care had not been taken to see that the lens was properly fixed, and so, while the company were one by one examining the brilliant image on the focussing-glass, and turning the camera round to bring the various parts of the landscape into view, it slipped out and went down with a crash a depth of nearly a hundred and fifty feet, and was, of course, smashed into a thousand pieces … nothing daunted, Mr Davidson at once set to work, and in a short time had finished another lens – this time of three inches diameter and fifteen inches focus.[18]

Remarkably few of Davidson's landscape images seem to have survived; those that do are unsigned [Fig. 3.4].[19]

Most of the early professional daguerreotypists in Scotland were trained in Paris or in the licensed English studios – their movement into Scotland came a couple of years afterwards. In March 1842, there was notification 'that on Tuesday next the 5th of April', another photographic studio would 'commence taking portraits' at the Portrait Rooms, 19 Princes Street.[20] 'Instantaneous Daguerreotype or Photographic Portraits by Messrs Edwards & Co.'s new patented improved process' were offered by the practitioners, who came from the Royal Adelaide Gallery, London.[21] This establishment was run by Antoine Claudet, who had taken out a licence for the daguerreotype in 1840, before the English patent rights came on the market.[22] However, Edwards was being pursued through the courts by Richard Beard (1801–85), the entrepreneur, who had the licensing of the daguerreotype patent in England.[23]

By early May 1842 Edwards had joined forces with two others, and advertised the studio as 'Edwards, Counsell & Miles … From the Royal Adelaide Gallery, London, and the Photographic Institution, Brighton'.[24] The *Caledonian Mercury* published an editorial comment (or possibly a well placed paid-for puff):

We have seen a considerable number of those of well known citizens, which are exceedingly graphic, striking, and life-like. Even on Saturday, when the weather was very dull, several excellent likenesses were taken, each in the course of a minute. As we before remarked, the verisimilitude of the portrait depends a good deal upon the steadiness of the sitter, and on his presenting his natural face to the reflector – for whatever features are presented, will be most accurately portrayed on the plate.[25]

In June the business was being run by Counsell and Miles, Edwards having left for neighbouring Glasgow: 'MR COUNSELL Artist in Photography to Prince Albert, from Brighton, and Mr MILES, from the Royal Adelaide Gallery, London, are now taking Portraits … . Admission to view the Pictures free. Open from Ten to Five.'[26] Counsell had worked for William Constable, the pioneering Brighton photographer, and his Edinburgh advertisements claimed the patronage of the Queen and Prince Albert there.[27] There had been, so far, no mention of the price of the procedure. But they were trying hard to obtain clients:

Messrs Counsell and Miles continue to take most faithful and striking miniatures of all who choose to sit to their, what may almost be called, magic glass. They are fast multiplying portraits of our citizens and others by

this extraordinary invention … to all who sit to the Daguerreotype we would, as a caution, repeat the anecdote of the lady sitting to a miniature painter, and who, provided by nature with a large mouth, was continually employed in primming it in, to the great annoyance of the limner, whose patience being at length worn out, exclaimed – 'Oh, Ma'am, you need not give yourself all that trouble; for I can give you no mouth at all if you please'.[28]

By the end of June, 'Messrs Counsell & Miles beg to intimate, that in order to meet the applications of numerous Families in Town, they have Reduced their charge for Likenesses to 10s 6d. As Messrs C & M will only remain a very short time longer, an early visit is requested.'[29] In order to beat up business, they were threatening to leave town, as well as cutting costs. The accompanying text was more persuasive:

It will be seen that Messrs Counsell and Miles, have been induced to reduce the price of their beautifully faithful photographic miniatures; and we think they are well advised in so doing, as the original charge rendered the possession of them too exclusive. The art by which these living likenesses are taken is new, and their accuracy and beauty of finish can only be imagined or believed by the evidence of the ocular sense. One or two minutes suffice for a sitting; and in two or three more, by means of a chemical process, the exact physiognomy, and bust of the individual is brought out with all the beauty of the finest mezzotint engraving, which though wanting in colour, possesses the most exquisite lines of light and shade … .[30]

By August 1842, Counsell was working alone at 19 Princes Street, still charging the reduced rate of 10 shillings and sixpence for a portrait: 'These beautiful portraits are finished by this artist in a few minutes, and presented to sitters in an elegant case, at a very moderate price indeed; and we would strongly recommend the numerous strangers now visiting our city to avail themselves of the opportunity of possessing an elegant and accurate portrait.'[31] In early November an announcement appeared in the 'Marriages' column of the newspaper, revealing that John Counsell was a native of New York: he married 'Rebecca, second daughter of Mr George Baker, Upper Clapton, Middlesex' at the studio, which presumably had living quarters attached to it.[32] Two days later, another sort of daguerreotype was on offer from his premises:

Mr Counsell … is now taking portraits at his gallery in Prince's Street, so small as to go into a locket or brooch of the size from a fourpenny to a half-crown piece. These very *minute* portraits, of which we have seen several specimens, are brought out with the same striking fidelity of likeness, and graphic expression, as the common sized miniatures ….[33]

Counsell's advertisement for 'LIKENESSES by the "DAGUERREOTYPE" as good in this weather as in Summer', continued through December and into January 1843.[34] On Christmas Eve, he had further news to entice would-be sitters:

Mr Counsell has recently fixed up a new apartment in his premises … Having been now enabled to bring the light to bear on his instrument directly from the sky,

the portraits are taken almost in a minute, and the glass of his new studio being tinted blue, the sitter does not feel any fatigue, as formerly, from a glare of light. Besides, the portraits can by this new improvement be taken with equal certainty, and within a less space of time, in any state of the atmosphere, whether clear or hazy.[35]

With a note of desperation, perhaps, Counsell also produced a seasonal advertisement:

MINIATURES – CHRISTMAS PRESENTS

MR COUNSELL respectfully informs the Public, that he continues to take LIKENESSES by the 'DAGUERREO-TYPE' as good in this weather as in Summer under his new improvements. As his stay in Edinburgh is now drawing to a close, he requests an early visit.

Pictures from the size of a fourpenny piece, for Rings and Brooches, up to 3 inches by 5.[36]

The last the public heard of Mr Counsell and his new Edinburgh studio was in January 1843, when presumably it closed.

'Mr Counsell's' story may not be straightforward. After he left Edinburgh in early 1843, he seems first to have trav-elled northwards.[37] In April, transformed as 'J. C. Stephens & Co.', he made a brief appearance in the Dundee press.[38] By May, an advertisement in the *Fife Herald* announced 'Novelty to the Inhabitants of Cupar, for a few days only … Photographic Portraiture, or the Daguerreotype. Messrs Stephens & Co., from the Royal Institutions, London and Brighton, respectfully announce to the Public their arrival in Cupar …'.[39] Within a few weeks, 'Messrs Stephens & Co.,' announced that they were leaving: 'Positively the last week …'.[40] It is unclear what had caused this name change.

Between 1847 and 1876, John Counsell Stephens was located in Cornwall, geographically remote from Scotland. Here he continued to practise as a photographer, first as a daguerreotypist, and subsequently with other processes as they came into fashion.[41] He displayed a number of 'daguerreotype likenesses – some by Mr Stephens of Killigrew street, Falmouth', at the Royal Cornwall Polytechnic Society's Annual Meeting and Exhibition in 1849, winning third prize for a 'Frame of Daguerreotypes' in 1851; while his reward was £1 for 'eight daguerreotypes' the following year, when his address was noted in Redruth.[42] He subsequently emigrated to New Zealand, where he died at the age of 72.[43]

Glasgow: the arrival of the daguerreotype

Meanwhile, in Glasgow, Edwards had found himself in immediate competition with a Mr Treffry, whose first daguerreotype rooms had opened in Dublin in November 1841, a few weeks after the pioneering Rotunda Studio; however, Treffry seems to have abandoned Ireland for Scotland fairly rapidly.[44] J. Edwards & Co.'s advertisement appeared in the same newspaper, directly above that of Treffry, in late June 1842, offering 'Instantaneous Photographic or Daguerreotype Portraits'. They were based at the Dilettante Rooms, Buchanan Street, and invited inspection of their results.[45] Treffry stated that by 'a process peculiar to himself, Mr Treffry is enabled to tint the faces of his portraits, so as to give them their natural colours, a pleasing brightness and prominence are thus given to the *tout*

ensemble of the picture'. He charged, for portrait and frame, £1 1s; and if tinted, 5s extra.[46]

Over the next few weeks, Edwards & Co.'s advertisement appeared regularly, but Treffry's more intermittently.[47] In mid-July 1842, as reported in an editorial comment in the *Glasgow Herald*, the two photographers were locked in combat:

Mr Edwards, a cadet of the Adelaide Gallery in London – which has turned out some of the very finest specimens of the art – has established his painting-rooms (to speak in old phrase) in a little temporary erection on the very roof of the Dilettanti Rooms, so that the light of day, which acts to him the part of the pencil, may have free and uninterrupted access. There he has produced some very beautiful living portraits, in the short space of a few seconds, and has even transferred prints and celebrated oil paintings. … We observe that Mr Edwards has commenced to take likenesses of parties or families in groups.

Mr Treffry … appears to be so far independent of sunlight, that instead of going to the roof of a building, he has established himself in the front floor of No 6, Union Street; he has had a good deal of successful experience, and produced some excellent portraits. There is a difference in the style of Mr Treffry's works, and those of the gentleman already named …. There is a lightness about the portraits of Mr Treffry which we much like; and he has fallen upon a plan of tinting, which though liable to be overdone, sometimes lends great beauty to the picture.

Though their styles are different, and their interests not the same, we recommend these artists to the judgement of the public, which will patronize according to its taste.[48]

Yet before the end of the year, both men had left Glasgow.[49] Years later, Andrew Mactear, then a lithographer and subsequently a photo-lithographer, recalled that

In 1841 [1842] the first professional photographer who came to Glasgow was Mr Edwards, who opened in Buchanan-street (opposite the Arcade), and who in dull weather used to secure the loan of my camera. The glass of his place was entirely blue, as was then the custom. In the same year Mr Treffray [*sic*] also began at the corner of Union-street and Argyle-street ....[50]

Edwards and Treffry were peripatetic, like so many of the early daguerreotypists. The tendency was encouraged by a number of factors. Expenses would be less on the road than in a leased town apartment; Scotland in particular was not unduly wealthy and, by moving about, the photographers could pick up trade.

In March 1843, Edwards advertised his arrival in Dumfries, 'where he purposes remaining a few days, in the exercise of a profession which is altogether new in the South of Scotland'. He was available for a few days, but 'NB As Mr Edwards has pressing engagements in Russia, Prussia, &c., this may be the only opportunity of his being in Dumfries again, if ever, for a lengthened period of years'.[51] Rather than moving on to these exotic parts, by September Edwards was advertising in Stirling where 'he has erected his Apparatus for a few days … Charge for Portrait 10s 6d'.[52]

Treffry, almost as mysteriously, wrote to W. H. F. Talbot, the inventor of positive-negative photography, from a London address, to ask for advice about a camera he had constructed.[53] From his Glasgow premises, he wrote again in August 1842, to enquire on what terms Talbot might grant him a licence to practise the calotype in London.[54] While in Glasgow, Treffry had an undated flyer printed to advertise his 'improved daguerreotype portraits', which was produced by the *Glasgow Constitutional* Office, and contains approving quotations from a number of Dublin and Glasgow newspapers.[55]

At the same time that Treffry and Edwards were competing so fiercely, a third daguerreotypist appeared – briefly – on the Glasgow scene. He announced himself as Mr G. Goddard, and may have been a relative of John Frederick Goddard (1795–1866), the chemist who worked with Richard Beard in London, and helped to speed up the daguerreotype process. G. Goddard came from the Polytechnic Institution, Regent Street, London, and claimed that he came with Beard's permission to practise 'this interesting art in Glasgow'. Boasting of the 'patronage of nearly the whole of the court and nobility of the United Kingdom', Goddard had available and on display daguerreotypes of Prince Nicholas Esterhazy, Duke of Argyll, Marquess of Douglas, Marquess of Westminster, Earl Spencer, Baron Parke, Sir W. Molesworth, Professor Daniels, and others. Nevertheless, his advertisement appeared only once.[56]

Andrew Mactear's recollection of photography in Glasgow continued:

Now came Mr Pickering, and in 1846 Mr Bernard commenced; then the art made a rapid advance – in fact, his pictures were splendid. Messrs Borthwick and Stanley next came, and in 1849 Mr Hughes succeeded Mr Bernard. Then Mr Gardner, Mr Young (1850), and Mr

White successively came forward, the daguerreotype process alone being worked by all the above.[57]

Edward Pickering (1827–84) was a Londoner who had worked for Claudet and then set out on his own in Glasgow.[58] He came north for two years in 1844, where his daguerreotypes were much admired: 'We have seen some very beautiful and faithfully executed Daguerreotype portraits, which have been taken by Mr Pickering, at his rooms in the Andersonian University, George Street. One of these, the portrait of a friend of our own, executed in two seconds on Wednesday last, is the most exquisite specimen of the art which we have ever seen …'.[59] He advertised 'Portraits 10s 6d. Frames from 2s 6d upwards'.[60] In early 1845, he claimed that he had been 'three years operator for Mons. Claudet at the Royal Adelaide Gallery in London where he had the honour of taking portraits of his Grace the Duke of Wellington and several of the Royal Family'.[61]

Pickering returned to work with Claudet in London. He was noted in Knightsbridge in 1852 offering stereoscopic daguerreotype portraits for Messrs Voigtländer and Evans, at 3 Lowndes Terrace: 'When viewed through the stereoscope [these wonderful productions] are no longer pictures, but perfect models, and must be seen to be properly appreciated. Plain, coloured, and non-inverted daguerreotype portraits at half the usual charge. The trade supplied with improved stereoscopes. Artist, E. J. Pickering, eight years operator for Mons. Claudet.'[62] Pickering reappeared in Glasgow, probably during 1856, working at 67 Buchanan Street with John Werge for over four years, before briefly branching out on his own account in 1860.[63] By then, the days of the daguerreotype were well over.

J. B. Bernard first appeared in newspaper advertisements during 1846.[64] By April 1847, he advertised that he was 'recently of Paris', and was based at 112 West George Street.[65] It emerged in a 'puff' in the *Glasgow Herald* a few weeks later that he was an American, proposing a shortish visit to Glasgow:

We have had the pleasure of seeing several of the daguerreotypes taken by Mr Bernard, a young American …. His works are of the highest order of merit, and decidedly superior to those of any professor of the daguerreotype who has visited us since the discovery of the art. The fidelity of the likeness cannot be questioned – for it is painted with the pencil of light; but the early specimens of the art presented too often a cold and death-like hue which the perfect accuracy of the portrait failed to atone for. The process employed by the gentleman referred to has wholly obviated these defects; for, by an improved means of regulating the light on the plate, and by more successful combinations of chemical ingredients, the portrait comes forth superior in distinctness of detail, and with a warmth and delicacy of colouring, formerly unknown to the art. In fact, the majority of those portraits we have seen in Mr Bernard's rooms, present all the freshness and beauty – with more than the fidelity – of the most exquisite miniatures.[66]

It is unclear whether Bernard was a genuine American – another contemporary, J. J. E. Mayall, born in Yorkshire, used the 'American' tag in advertising, perhaps because it seemed exotic.[67] After the Great Exhibition of 1851, it was widely recognised that American daguerreotypes were in many ways superior to those made in the British Isles. There was, in any case, a two-way traffic in photographers crossing the Atlantic – both C. J. Hughes and John Werge, who practised the daguerreotype in Glasgow's Monteith Rooms, spent time in the United States.

A further advertisement in June 1847, with Bernard's studio now at 109 West George Street, comprised approving comments from a variety of voices amongst the press: the *Glasgow Herald*, the *Courier*, the *Argus*, the *Glasgow Post*, the *Constitutional*, the *Examiner*, the *Scottish Guardian* and the *North British Mail*. Bernard's process was 'Price complete, with Gold-gilt Frame and Morocco Case, 15s'.[68] In April 1849, advertising his 'coloured photographic portraits', Bernard announced 'his return from the Continent', quoting approval from both the *Herald* and *Courier* for his 'entire new process'. By now, he was based at 67 Buchanan Street, in the Monteith Rooms, where he remained until 1850. This studio housed a number of Glasgow photographers over the next few years.[69]

Members of the Borthwick family migrated to Glasgow from Liverpool in the early 1840s, where John Borthwick practised as a portrait painter. Looking at family sources, he appears to have begun life in Drumelzier, Peebles, moved to Edinburgh where he married his wife Isabella Chisholm in 1822, and there they christened their daughter May Chisholm Borthwick, born 24 April 1823.[70] Father and daughter appear together in the 1846 *Glasgow Post Office Directory*, 48 Holmhead Street; he, as a 'portrait painter', while 'Miss Borthwick' was 'daguerreotypist'. By 1848, she was working alone at 'Pavilion, Buchanan Street, at the foot of Bath Street', with a house in Renfrew Road. Possibly her father had died in the interim. She advertised in the *Glasgow Examiner* in August 1849 that her 'Daguerreotype Portraits! [were] Cheapest in Town … reduced to 4s. 0d.', and stated that as she 'will shortly be giving up business, she

is desirous of having her pavilion let to a daguerreotypist who may purchase the apparatus'. By late October she felt entitled to call her premises the 'Oldest Establishment in Town'.[71] The following month, the *Glasgow Herald* added:

MISS BORTHWICK begs most respectfully to intimate to the Public in general, that she has let her Portrait Pavilion to first-rate Daguerreotype Artists from Paris, to whom she hopes the liberal patronage she has hitherto enjoyed will be kindly extended.

Miss BORTHWICK continues at her Pavilion until 3d December, and hopes all parties wishing their Likenesses from her will visit her during that period.

Immediately below this statement comes:

DAGUERREOTYPE PORTRAITS
BELLETIE & HENDERSON beg to inform the Inhabitants of Glasgow and its vicinity, that they have engaged Miss Borthwick's Portrait Pavilion, which will be Opened by them on the 4th December, where they hope, by giving correct and pleasing Likenesses, to enjoy a liberal share of public patronage.[72]

Presumably, this was the point where Miss Borthwick retired from business, married Francis Lauder, a surveyor in Coatbridge, and also a dyer in a tweed mill; she died at Maxwelltown, 12 July 1893, aged 64.[73] Miss Borthwick was one of the earliest female professional photographers, and certainly the first in Scotland to run a business under her own name.[74]

Belletie & Co. had worked in Paris; by June 1850 their

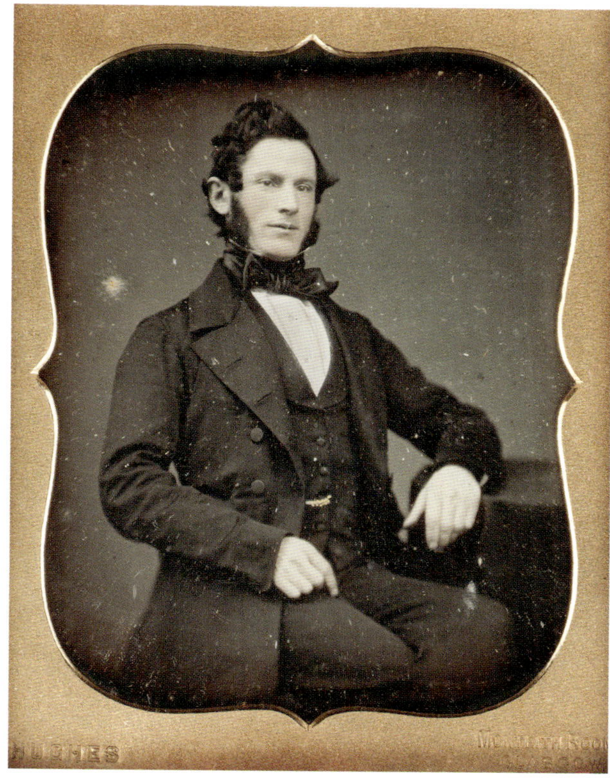

Fig. 3.5: Cornelius Jabez Hughes, unknown seated gentleman, *c*.1850–56, quarter-plate daguerreotype. (Howarth-Loomes Collection at National Museums Scotland, IL.2003.44. 2.15)

premises were at 1 Cathedral Street in Glasgow; by October, they were offering 'a correct likeness for 2s 6d (and upwards)' at '212 Buchanan Street (Corner of Cathedral Street)'; and they offered lessons: 'Daguerreotype Taught on Moderate Terms'.[75] Belletie then moved to London, where he was in partnership with a photographer named James Henderson between 1851 and 1853 (possibly the same Mr Henderson with whom he worked in Glasgow).[76]

Of the Glasgow daguerreotypists enumerated by Andrew Mactear, we know most about Cornelius Jabez Hughes (1819–84), who had learnt photography from J. J. E. Mayall in London [Fig. 3.5].[77]

After remaining two or three years with Mr Mayall, Mr Hughes in 1849 established himself as a daguerreotypist in Glasgow, purchasing the business of Mr Barnard [*sic*], in Buchanan-street, which he raised to the front rank in that city. Though strictly a daguerreotypist during his sojourn in Glasgow, he adopted and worked the collo-

dion process to a small extent soon after its introduction. In 1855 he returned to London.

In London Hughes's attempt to set up in business in the Strand was eventually unsuccessful. In 1859, he turned to wholesaling photographic materials and equipment from a warehouse in Oxford Street, but moved in 1861 to the Isle of Wight, again as a photographer.[78] Examples of his Glasgow daguerreotypes are to be found in a number of public collections, all portraits.[79]

The other practitioners identified by Mactear were less prominent figures: Stanley, Gardner, Young and White. Taking these in turn: a 'Mr Stanley' advertised at the Photographic Institution, 75 Princes Street, Edinburgh, in the *Scotsman* between July 1848 and April 1850. He emphasised that 'Mr Stanley's stay in Edinburgh is limited'.[80] A lengthy paragraph in a theological and literary journal trumpeted Stanley's abilities at his Princes Street studio: '… being a talented artist, he is enabled literally to paint on [all the unpleasant defects], and the result is a highly pleasing and life-like miniature, embellished with a background of country, mountain, and sky, as full of nature as the miniature itself, and imparting to it the warmth and finish so long desired in the best Photographic portraiture.'[81] He also advertised in Glasgow in 1849 as 'Stanley & Co.' at 140 Buchanan Street. He formed a partnership in Dublin with John Barratt in 1850, but the pair had relocated to London by 1852 [Fig. 3.6].[82]

By July 1845, William Gardner (*c*.1809–71) was promoting three sizes of daguerreotype portrait at 8s., 15s., and 21s., including case, as well as offering a price list for photographic apparatus and tuition.[83] In June 1848, he advertised 'Portraits by the daguerreotype, taken daily, from 9am to

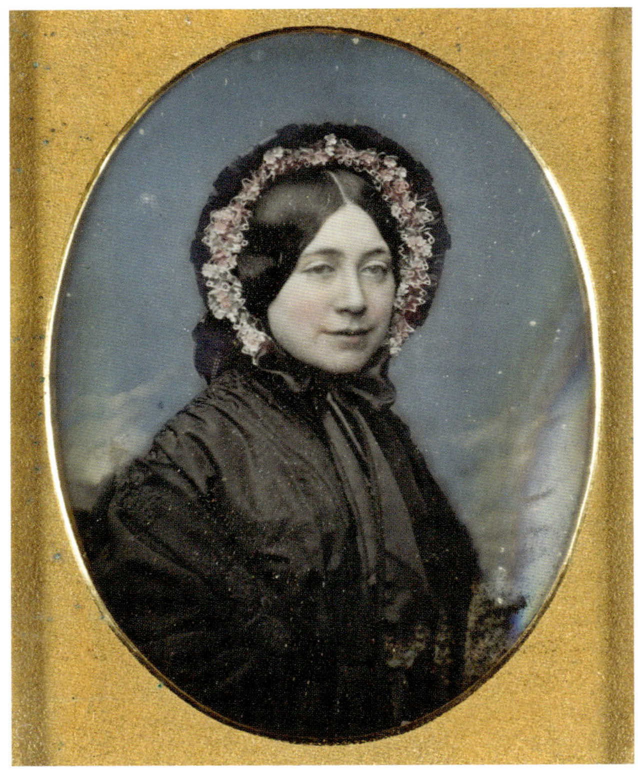

6pm, at the Daguerreotype Portrait Rooms, 110 Buchanan Street, where, by means of a glass-enclosed sitting room' better images were obtained than ever before, but with 'prices greatly reduced – 1st, 2d and 3d size, 7s, 9s, and 12s': these are not conventional descriptions of daguerreotype plate sizes but, ominously, their price had dropped in the intervening time. Gardner had earlier formed a partnership within his family firm of scientific instrument makers, whose founders had been in business with the great entrepreneur and engineer James Watt (1736–1819), but who were collectively destined to fail in business in each generation. By 1848, William Gardner described himself as an 'optician, 3 Royal Bank Place, Glasgow'; and there was a short approving paragraph in the same newspaper: 'We beg to direct attention to the advertisement of Mr Gardner, who has obtained very considerable proficiency in the daguerreotype art. We have seen several admired likenesses which have been taken by him.'[84] Nevertheless, Gardner appeared to be trying a number of different livelihoods in

an attempt to stay solvent: he was listed in the *Glasgow Post Office Directory* between 1856 and 1861 as a 'Photographer, Chemical and Philosophical Instrument Maker', at 56 Gordon Street, Glasgow. He petitioned for bankruptcy in 1864.[85]

In his account of early photography in Glasgow, John Urie (1820–1910) – apparently inspired to take up photography as a profession after seeing daguerreotypes in the Great Exhibition of 1851 – wrote: 'Then we had Mr Young, who would keep advertising "Come to Young and Sun, and see yourself as others see you." Though I don't think he ever had a son, yet the same sun is the sole partner of our artistic existence' [Fig. 3.7].[86]

Stephen A. McLeod Young was born in Paisley in about 1819, and had set up his daguerreotype studio in late summer 1849.[87] His business continued well into the 1870s. J. P. White was listed as an 'artist' in 1851, but as a photographer from 1852.[88] Urie commented: 'Mr White, and also Mr Hughes, produced excellent daguerreotypes, the former sending out high-class paper pictures taken on plain salted paper, and toned by the hypo-gold bath.'[89] There is an example of a daguerreotype by White in a public collection, as well as a later image elsewhere [Fig. 3.8].[90] Urie himself took up photography in 1852, and his first advertisement began with the statement that 'the immense superiority of Collodionized Glass Pictures, in comparison with ordinary Daguerreotypes or Calotypes, whether for portraits or still life, has already been acknowledged by the most eminent scientific men'; however, '2 daguerreotypes of Mr Haldane and Dr John Thomson lent by John Urie', presumably from

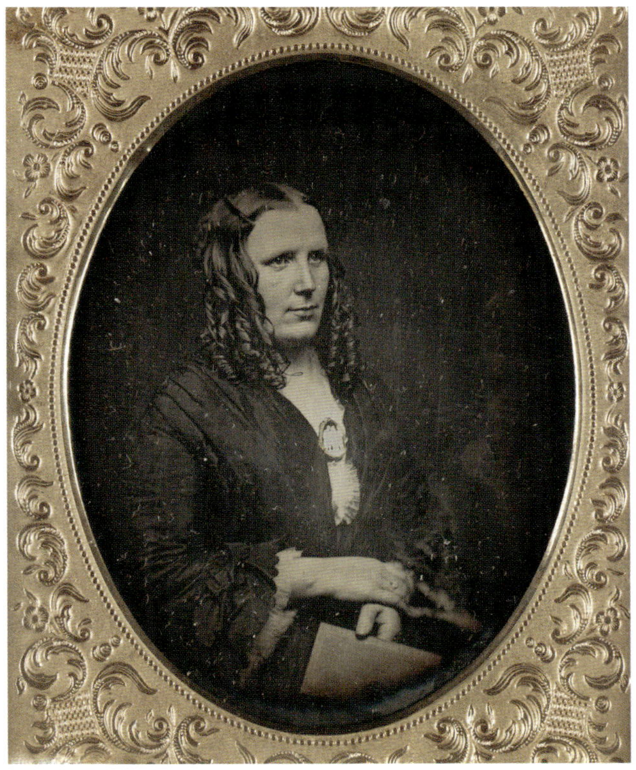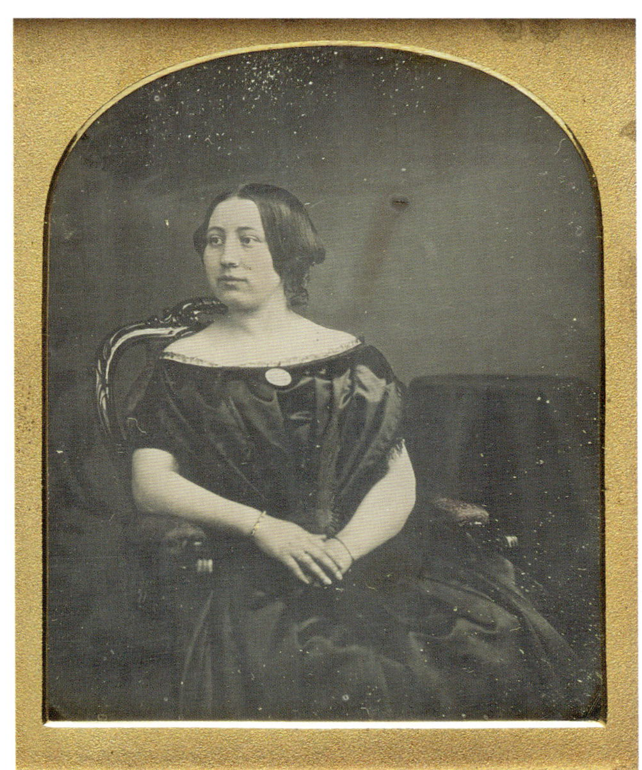

Urie's collection, were displayed at the Glasgow Photographic Exhibition of 1886.[91]

Urie's own account of the earliest days of photography in Glasgow tallies with that of Mactear:

I think the first place daguerreotypes were taken or shown in Glasgow was at the Zoological Gardens in the New City Road, and the next by a Mr Picken [Pickering], at the Andersonian Institute, in George street; then came Messrs William Gardner, Bernard, Young, White and Miss Descerne [*sic*]. I remember having my patience sorely tried when sitting on the top of a house in Buchanan-street with the full glare of sunshine beating on my face for a quarter of an hour. The operator told me not to move till he came back, as there was somebody in the shop requiring attention. I will never forget what I suffered during that terrible sitting ....[92]

Technologies do not disappear overnight when new processes – faster, cheaper, easier, less dangerous – surpass them: instead, there is a transition period, when customers (perhaps traditional, perhaps those who loved the shiny, pin-sharp look of the daguerreotype) could still acquire their images, done the old-fashioned way, alongside the new wet collodion process with its resultant multiple paper prints. This process could also be produced to resemble daguerreotypes: by backing the wet collodion negative with a piece of black paper, or painting the back with black paint, a single, sharp positive image could be put into a small case. There was clearly a demand.

In June 1853, John Urie – by now producing 'photographic portraits on glass' – announced: 'Truthful Likenesses by A. Litch, the celebrated American Photographist. J. Urie … has made arrangements with Mr Litch, whose daguerreotype portraits and views have been the theme of so many American publications, and who is now prepared to execute portraits with the highest degree of artistic finish at a moderate charge. Urie's American Photographic Rooms (portraits on silver or glass) 33 Buchanan Street, Glasgow.'[93] By now the 'American' soubriquet meant something to the newspaper-reading public; and Albert Litch (1814–93) was a genuine American. First noted in Boston, Massachusetts, between 1845 and 1847, in partnership with John Whipple (1822–91), famous for his astronomical photography, by 1850 Litch was based in New Haven, Connecticut. A year later he was to be found in New York city: in March 1853, *Humphrey's Journal* (one of the pre-eminent photographic journals in the United States) reported that Litch was travelling in Europe, and was about to open a daguerreotype studio in London or Liverpool. But Albert Litch did not remain long in Britain and by the end of the year he was back in the United States.[94] Perhaps he had observed that the profession of daguerreotypist was not to have the same longevity in Scotland as it was to find in the United States.

Daguerreotype studios in Aberdeen and the North

Daguerreotype photography arrived in Aberdeen in 1842, with an announcement from a duo named Watson and Fannin in mid-July: '69, UNION STREET, ABERDEEN, … MESSRS. WATSON & FANNIN, in announcing their Opening of their PHOTOGRAPHIC GALLERY, fitted up at considerable expense, on MONDAY 25th inst.'. Stressing that their up-to-date process had ironed out any problems, they quoted from a number of London journals, implying quality: their prices were 'Single Miniature, in a neat Case or Frame, £1 1s; two of the same sitter, £1 11s 6d; full length Portraits, large size, £2 2s; Kit-cat [half-length] £2 2s'.[95] The firm advertised intermittently, announcing in early Octo-ber that they would be closing their Aberdeen studio 'for a short period, during their visit to Inverness'.[96] On their return, they proclaimed they would recommence photography from 1 December, 'but that their stay in Aberdeen will, from arrangements they have entered into in the North, be necessarily short'.[97] In the New Year, the shortness of their stay was reiterated, along with a reduction of their prices: 'SINGLE PORTRAITS may be had now for 10s 6d; FRAMES or CASES, 5s', along with a variety of shops where their wares could be inspected.[98] On 29 March 1843 it was advertised that the dissolution of the co-partnery of 'W. Watson and J. Nickle Fannin' had been signed the previous day 'in Aberdeen, Dingwall, and Inverness'. W. Watson stated that he would continue at the gallery in Union Street for no more than three weeks.[99]

In September 1846 the 'Daguerreotype Portrait Gallery' opened for business in Aberdeen.[100] It was run by a 'Mr Blackwood, a young gentleman from Paisley, whose great success while prosecuting the art as an amateur' had encouraged him to turn to professional photography. He rented a room on the roof of the Aberdeen Mechanics' Institute New Buildings in Market Street.[101] By December, Blackwood advertised that his establishment would open for shortened hours.[102] Further advertisements appeared for the Daguerreotype Portrait Rooms from June 1847, explaining that these were to be 'reopened, with the addition of a splendid New Apparatus, for taking the largest size of Portraits hitherto attempted, and by the newest and most approved processes for fixing and colouring'. But this was to be 'only for a very limited period'; although tuition was offered, as were 'apparatus and chemicals supplied to order'.[103] An editorial puff was placed on 28 July 1847: 'We have several times had an opportunity of witnessing the

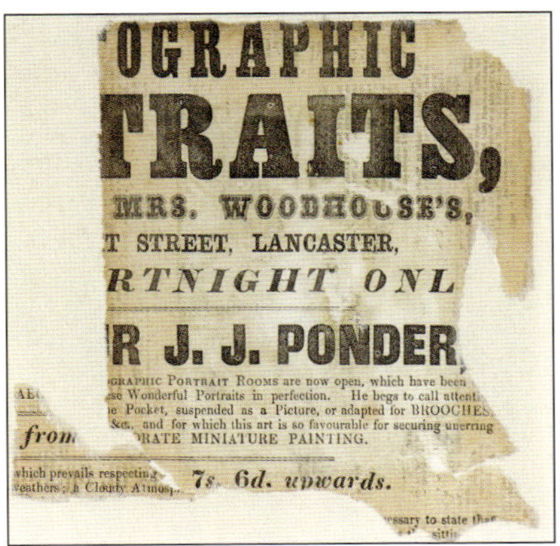

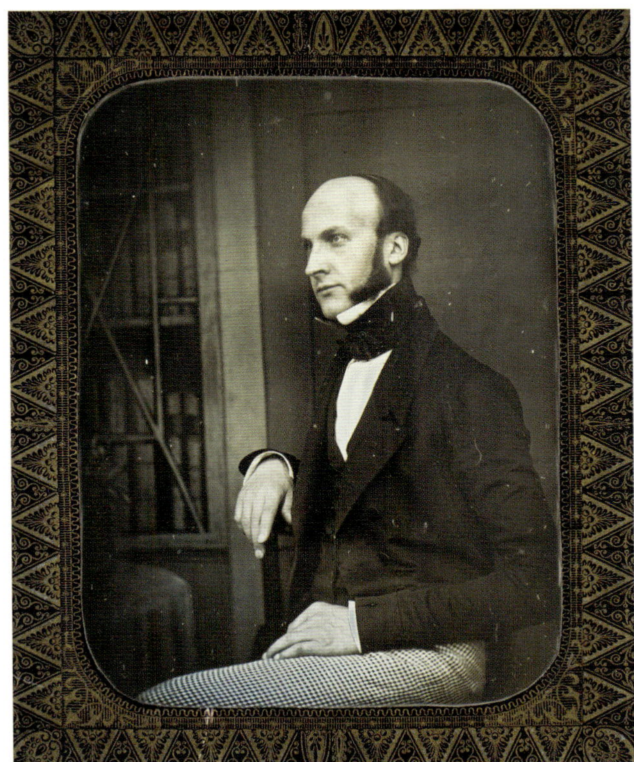

celerity, and beauty, and fidelity, with which this art is practised by Mr Blackwood, at his studio in the Mechanics' Institution …'.[104] The 'LAST NOTICE' for the studio proclaimed that it 'Will Finally Close on SATURDAY 14th August'.[105] Mr Blackwood was to be found in Inverness later that month.[106] An editorial in the *Inverness Courier* commented that, 'Mr Blackwood also favoured us by taking a view of High Street, Inverness. It was done in a second, and presented a most interesting street view. The steeple formed the most prominent object, and the post office, and Union Hotel gave the sketch a massive and substantial appearance, which was well relieved by the picturesque declension and bend in Bridge Street.'[107]

Joseph J. Ponder appeared briefly in the *Edinburgh Post Office Directory* for 1848, at Greenside Place, but also visited Aberdeen that year, advertising in the local press. He was based at the Mechanics' Institute in Market Street during August [FIG. 3.9]. The following year he advertised activity in Newcastle-upon-Tyne and Carlisle, and by 1855 he was the proprietor of a studio in London.[108] Another daguerreotypist, who also advertised briefly the following month, was Francis Craigmyle (or Craigmile), whose main profession as a teacher of writing and drawing was based at the new public school between 1841 and 1854.[109] 'Portraits on silver taken *in a few seconds*, by F. Craigmile, 71, Bon-Accord Street, where Specimens may be seen, and Instructions given in the Art', were undertaken from his home.[110] He rapidly moved on to newer forms of photography, exhibiting a 'collodion portrait floated from glass' and a collec-

tion of collodion portraits on glass in the 1853 exhibition at the Aberdeen Mechanics' Institute.[111]

In July 1849, 'photographic portraits' were advertised in Inverness by 'Messrs. J. Durward Clarke & Co., from Edinburgh'. They were keen to provide 'superior daguerreotype portraits during any weather … plain from 8s. 6d., coloured from 13s.6d'.[112] Although no trace of this partnership has been uncovered in the capital, J. Durward Clarke by himself advertised his intention of visiting Wick, in Caithness, to take daguerreotypes from July to early October 1850. In November, he went on to neighbouring Thurso, and then is seen no more.[113]

Unusually, a local Huntly man, Alexander Mackie, a painter and house decorator by trade, announced an attempt to spend part of his working week as a daguerreotypist:

The Subscriber's success in the above Art [Daguerreotype Portraits], and the constantly increasing patronage he is receiving, have rendered it necessary that he should state publicly his intention of devoting the greater part of his time to Portrait taking in the above line for Three or Four Weeks from this date, after which only One Day in the Week – viz. Monday – will be appropriated to this department of his Business. … In House Painting and Paper-Hanging, he will be obliged by the order of his friends as formerly. Alex. Mackie, Painter etc.[114]

However, his advertisement appeared only in early March 1851, and he was presumably unable to continue with this diversification of trades.

An advertisement was placed in an Elgin newspaper in August 1849 for daguerreotype portraits taken by a William Clark. This stated that his daguerreotypes

> … are so completely gilded with a strong solution of Chloride of Gold, as to prevent any atmospheric influence from producing the slightest effect or deterioration. The Establishment is so fitted up that these Portraits are all taken in an elegantly-lighted parlour, entirely away from public notice.[115]

Clark may have been the same man who appeared later that year in Forres, advertising that he had been previously employed in Edinburgh.[116]

Brief visits were paid to the north by other daguerreotypists, including a M. Alphonse, to Inverness in April 1851; A. & J. Smith, to the same city in early 1854 ('A. Smith begs to intimate that he continues to carry on his business as hairdresser and perfumer …. He also continues to practise as a chiropodist, and has for many years successfully devoted his attention to the eradication of corns, bunions, deformed nails etc.'); and a Mr B. E. Pearce, in Inverness during September 1855, who combined his skill as a travelling silhouette artist with those of the daguerreotypist from 1851.[117] He had visited Aberdeen the previous year, and went on to Edinburgh and Whitehaven: he may well have been the Benjamin Pearce who had a studio in Torquay in the early 1860s.[118]

Another itinerant daguerreotypist who settled in Aberdeen went by the name of Herr Frederick. First recorded in Dumfries in March 1850, he appeared in Aberdeen about a year later, with an editorial puff stating 'the portraits taken by Herr Frederick are superior to any which have ever before been seen in this city'. His advertisement revealed that Herr Frederick was 'from Bavaria' and based at '64, Union Street'.[119] By March 1851, Herr Frederick was established in more permanent premises, when he advertised: 'Superior coloured daguerreotype portraits … in order to enable him to take Groups and Miniatures for Lockets and Brooches, he has, at considerable expense, fitted up that Building, No 21, Market Street … where he flatters himself that he will be able to produce, in a few seconds, Likenesses far surpassing, in brilliancy and general delineation, anything hitherto produced in the art in this quarter. Prices, from 5s 6d upwards.' Frederick continued: 'All kinds of Fancy Hair Work, viz Ladies' Bracelets, Necklaces, Guards, &c. &c. made up from parties' own Hair, by Madame Frederick and Madame Hubel.'[120] Hair work was the woven or plaited hair of the subject of the daguerreotype, incorporated into lockets or bracelets as jewellery [FIG. 3.10].

In January 1854, there was an interesting paragraph in the Aberdeen press, headed:

> TESTIMONIAL – A number of the friends of Herr Frederick, Daguerreotype Artist, Market Street, met, on

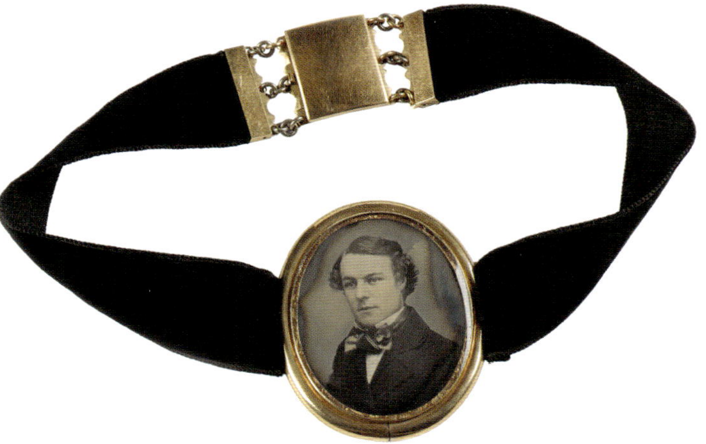

Tuesday evening, the 17th inst., in Miller's Star Hotel, George Street, for the purpose of presenting to Mr Frederick a handsome Silver Snuff-box, as a token of their regard, to mark their appreciation of his superior talents in the art of Photography, and as a small expression of their very general feelings of sympathy towards him, which was shared in by many of the visitors of the late Photographic Exhibition. The party spent a pleasant evening, and were unanimous in expressing their conviction, that while there was no wish to detract from the merits of those who had been awarded prizes in the several departments of Calotype, Colodeotype [*sic*], &c., the Daguerreotype department had been apparently overlooked, and Mr F's abilities in that branch scarcely done justice to by the judges.

In the same newspaper, photographers Wilson & Hay and John Lamb, separately advertised that they had won medals for their paper photography at the recent exhibition of photographs at the Aberdeen Mechanics' Institute.[121] Herr Frederick had exhibited '29 daguerreotypes and collodion portraits' at this exhibition.[122] The judges remarked that, 'Although the specimens [of daguerreotype portraits] exhibited were creditable to the exhibition, they did not in any instance appear to us to exhibit such degree of advancement in the art as would warrant us in awarding a prize.'[123]

Frederick advertised again in Inverness, in September and October 1854, returning to Aberdeen after this visit: 'Herr Frederick … will resume his Professional Duties as Daguerreotype and Calotype Artist, at his Rooms, 21, Market Street [Aberdeen], on and after Monday the 2d October next … Madam Frederick will attend to the Hair-

Work Department, in which she is allowed to be unequalled in Aberdeen.'[124]

The Fredericks were listed in the street directories between 1857 and 1866, showing that they were no longer itinerant. An advertisement appeared there from 1858:

Photographic Rooms, 173 Union Street, West End of Union Bridge.
Herr Frederick Begs to acquaint the Public that he has removed from 21, Market Street to the above New and more convenient Premises. Having had Fourteen years' experience, H. F. flatters himself that he can produce Portraits equal to any other in the Profession, and at Moderate Price.
Hours, from Nine, A.M., to Dusk.
Mrs Frederick will attend to the Ornamental Hair Department as usual.[125]

Presumably by this time, Herr Frederick was using the wet collodion process.

The daguerreotype in Dundee

Dundee was briefly visited by its first professional photographers in April 1843: J. C. Stephens & Co., trading as 'Messrs. Stephens from London'.[126] They claimed to be 'from the Royal Institutions, London and Brighton, daguerreotypists', visiting Cupar, the main market-town in the neighbouring county, Fife, in May and June 1843.[127] Mr Holmes opened his 'Daguerreotype Portrait Rooms' during August 1847 'at Mrs Anderson's Albert Court, No. 39 Nethergate'. There 'Daguerreotype Portraits [were] taken in a few Seconds!' and the prices stipulated at small size 10s, intermediate size 15s, large size £1, and an extra charge for colouring at 5s. In an editorial article the photographer is described thus: '… an artist, of whose merits fame speaks very highly, has come to our town for the purpose of executing photographic portraits. Mr Holmes succeeds in completely removing from his likenesses the uneasy disagreeable expression of the eye, communicated by the strong light in which the sitter has generally been placed.'[128] Mr Holmes has been identified as Edward Holmes, born about 1808 in Lincoln, who became a daguerreotypist in Hull in October 1843.[129]

Mr Holmes was followed by a Mr Wrench, another itinerant photographer, who visited Dundee in 1849 and 1850.[130] His prices were 'from 5s 6d and upwards' and he was based at 59 Renfrew Street; he cautioned would-be customers that he 'advises an early application, as his stay here will be for a short time only'. By July 1849 this had become 'The Last Week But One', and he announced 'A LARGE CAMERA OBSCURA FOR SALE. The Purchaser will have ample instructions how to use it'.[131] Wrench had not abandoned photography, but by the time he returned 'for

a short season' in March 1850, he found himself in competition with a 'Mr Brown, late of London and Antwerp', who first made an appearance at his rooms, anonymously, at 30 Union Street in September 1849.[132] Brown can be identified with John Cormack Brown, who figures in the 1850 *Dundee Post Office Directory* as a 'Daguerreotypist and teacher of drawing and painting'. He advertised fairly regularly in the local press, and encouraged editorial comment:

> During the short time Mr Brown has been among us, he has had numerous sitters; and many of them, we believe, not content with a portrait for their friends at home, have been induced by the facilities afforded, to send correct likenesses of themselves to their relatives at a distance.[133]

By 5 December 1849 he was advertising, 'the Inhabitants of BLAIRGOWRIE are respectfully informed that, at the urgent request of a number of families, Mr B. has taken the TOWN HALL FOR DAGUERREOTYPE PURPOSES, And will COMMENCE OPERATIONS there about the 12th instant'.[134] In the New Year he had returned to Dundee, where he had dreamed up a way of tempting even shy customers:

> At the request of a number of Families, Mr B. has made arrangements for one day in the week for Ladies only, beginning with Wednesday 13th, and continuing every Wednesday during the season, – on which days he will endeavour to have some fruit and flowers, with a painted Balcony, to assist in forming a fine background.

By now, the pricing of portraits was described as moderate: smallest 5s; medium size 8s 6d and largest size 15s, with 'no extra charge for Colouring Portraits'.[135] Brown also visited Cupar in May.[136]

Later in May, Brown dropped his prices, but only for a month – smallest size 4s 6d; medium size 7s 6d, with the largest reduced to 10s 6d.[137] By early June, again looking to appeal to the female portion of his potential customer-base, he extended his advertisement with:

HINTS TO SITTERS

The early part of the day is the best to obtain a good Photographic Portrait. Dresses of a light kind (though not white) are preferable to dark ones. The contrast of the colours ought not to be too great, as it is apt to produce a harsh and cutting effect. Above all it is necessary that the sitters have a pleasant expression: for this purpose a friend should always be with them, to talk and keep them in good humour. It is much better to have one spoiled with laughing than its being sad or cross-looking.[138]

Mr Brown vanished from Dundee, and the following month a single advertisement for 'Coloured Daguerreotype Portraits' by a Mr Neil at 119 Murraygate appeared.[139] Possibly the same man, though spelling his name as 'Neill', worked in Forfar almost two years later.[140]

Another daguerreotypist outside the major Scottish towns was based in Kirriemuir by August 1850, just to the west: '… we observe that Mr James Gibb, from Dundee, has been doing rather a respectable business in the Daguerreotype Portrait line here, for some weeks past.'[141] Gibb went on to exhibit a daguerreotype of a crying child for the Dundee Royal Infirmary Fund in 1854, and subsequently became a carte-de-visite photographer.[142]

Hot on Mr Neil's heels, another daguerreotypist, this time based at 67 Reform Street, advertised in the local press. Better than coming from London, Monsieur André Orange (1811–63) came 'FROM PARIS … [and] in consequence of numerous solicitations, he has been induced to prolong his Visit for a longer period; and trusts that his extensive practice in Paris, and the universal satisfaction he has given to his numerous patrons in this town, will be deemed sufficient for those requiring his services'. He stressed that he was unconnected with 'any other Firm in Town or Country'.[143] By December 1850 he announced 'his return from Paris with a Complete Set of New Apparatus for CALOTYPE and DAGUERREOTYPE, with all the recent improvements. He has also fitted up a Studio …'. Apparently this had perfect lighting for Scottish winter conditions; and he was able to offer lessons in both the calotype and daguerreotype, as well as having 'several SETS of APPARATUS FOR SALE, which he has recently brought from Paris'.[144]

By 1852, André Orange had moved to Edinburgh, where he opened his photographic studio at 63 George Street, and 'for the convenience of Ladies and others who may dislike the public room, Mr A. O. has Private Apartments suitably fitted up'.[145] He also photographed street scenes: 'A fine engraving of the Wellington statue, from a very beautiful Daguerreotype by M. Orange … Price, on large enamelled cards of plate paper, 6d.; Proofs, 1s.'[146] By 1860 he was at 11 Nicolson Square, where he ran 'the Edinburgh School of Photography, under the Distinguished Patronage of Sir David Brewster', and he taught 'ladies and gentlemen the art of photography in all its branches'.[147] When he died in 1863, his brief obituary in the photographic press read:

M. Andre Orange, a photographer well known in Edinburgh circles, died in that city on the 18th ult., after a lengthened illness, aged 51 years. Originally a watchmaker, Mr Orange had, almost since the introduction of photography, devoted himself exclusively to the latter art.[148]

Later daguerreotyping in Edinburgh

Earlier in this chapter, we left daguerreotypists in Edinburgh in January 1843. Subsequently, a Mr Mullins advertised that the instruction-book of 'Beard's process of manipulating', was available for two guineas, and 'maybe had of Mr Mullins, at the Photographic Institution, No. 19 Princes Street, Edinburgh, where Specimens of the views and Portraits may be seen. A Course of Lessons, five guineas. An early application is requested, as Mr Mullins has other engagements'.[149] By the following year, a number of practitioners were to be found in the *Edinburgh Post Office Directory*, among them being Charles Gray, who briefly ran the same Photographic Portrait Institution in 1844, premises afterwards taken on by McMillan and Thomson in 1845.[150] Based at this same address was the firm of McMillan and Rutherford, pocketbook makers – so it appears that McMillan made the cases and Thomson took the daguerreotypes [Fig. 3.11]. Daniel McMillan (1805–81) was born in Glasgow and died in Hackney. He subsequently became a dressing case manufacturer at 132 Fleet Street, London, between 1848 and 1851,

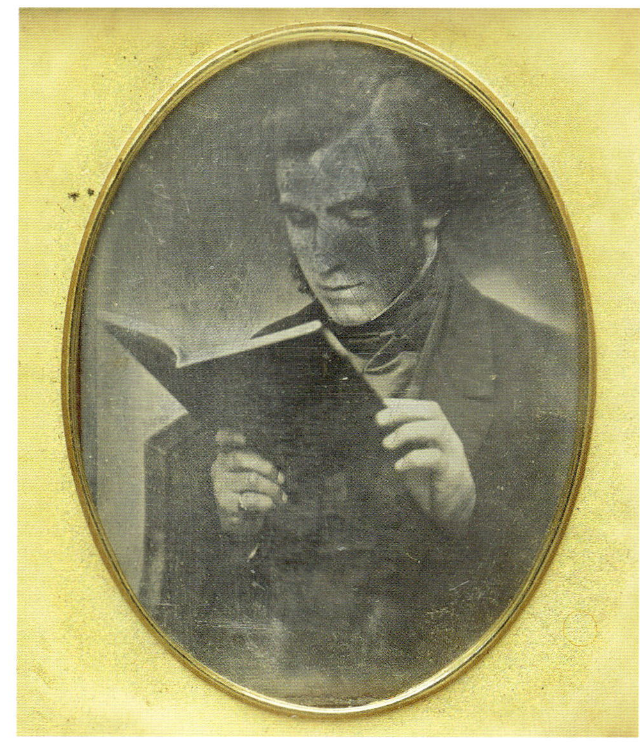

with a photographic studio at same address from 1851 until 1853, and is listed as a dealer in photographic materials from 1853 until 1867.[151]

John Thomson (1804–81) was born in Leith, a vintner's son. An obituary, written by the photographic journalist Dr John Nicol, who would have known Thomson personally, was later to record:

Mr Thomson was of a quiet, retiring disposition, and the materials for a biography are consequently very limited …. At the time that Daguerre's discovery was given to the world Mr Thomson was a clerk in his father's office, who was a wine merchant in Leith, and before any definite information regarding it had reached this country he was visited by a friend who had just returned from Paris, from whom he got sufficient information as to the *modus operandi* to induce him to attempt a repetition of the Frenchman's experiments; and having previously been a somewhat diligent student of chemistry, he met with success sufficient to rouse enthusiasm and encour-

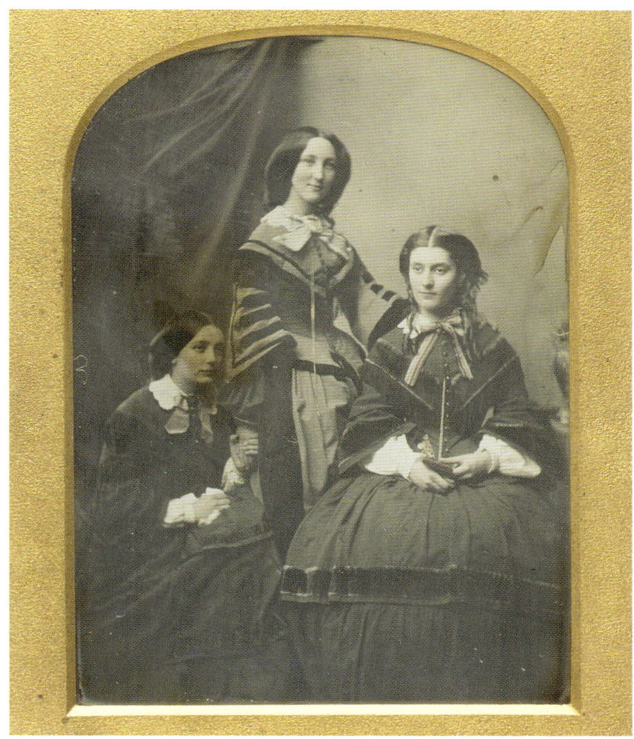 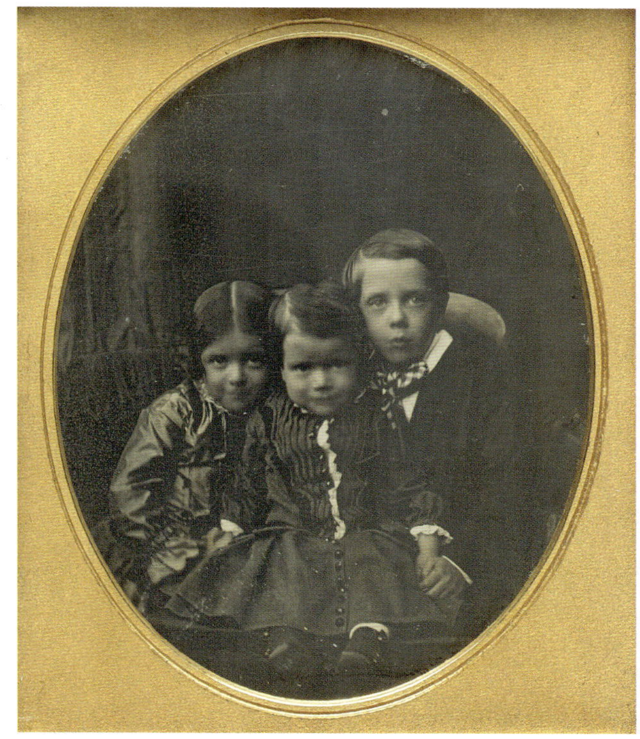

age perseverance. … Being of a practical turn of mind, Mr Thomson soon saw that the new art could be turned to profitable account, and, as the daguerreotype picture required, for protection, to be enclosed in a case – which, till it became an article of ordinary trade, was a some-what expensive affair – he entered into partnership with a jewel-case manufacturer, and thus was formed … Macmillan and Thomson …. the partnership was dis-solved within a year or two; and in about twelve months afterwards …. Mr Thomson became acquainted with Mr James Ross, at that time a professional artist, the out-come of which was the formation of the well-known firm of Ross and Thomson – a firm, which in virtue of the happy union of the great artistic taste and ability of Mr Ross with the technical skill and chemical know-ledge of Mr Thomson, rapidly attained a popularity that has continued to the present time.[152]

Thomson is thus confirmed as one of the partners of the short-lived firm of McMillan & Thomson, Daguer-

reotypists, 19 Princes Street, Edinburgh, whose 1845 busi-ness was superseded by that of Ross & Thomson in 1847. James Ross (1816–95) began professionally as a 'calotypist' with a studio at the National Monument on Calton Hill in 1846 [Fig. 3.12].[153] The name Ross & Thomson was strongly associated with portrait daguerreotypes from Edinburgh, though they also won prizes for their paper photography.[154]

James Ross's account of the firm's beginnings, pub-lished as 'A Few Extracts from a Photographer's Old Ledger', offers details of their daguerreotype trade. For example:

June 17, 1848. – A gentleman paid for a daguerreotype in case 10s. 6d. – the first entry for a likeness by that most beautiful and most lasting process. It was almost a pity that the public taste ever fell so entirely away from pictures upon silver. No other kind of photography whatever can give the same degree of delicacy and power. One would as soon think of adding colour to the 'red, red rose, that's newly sprung in June,' as of retouching a daguerreotype. … [Fig. 3.13]

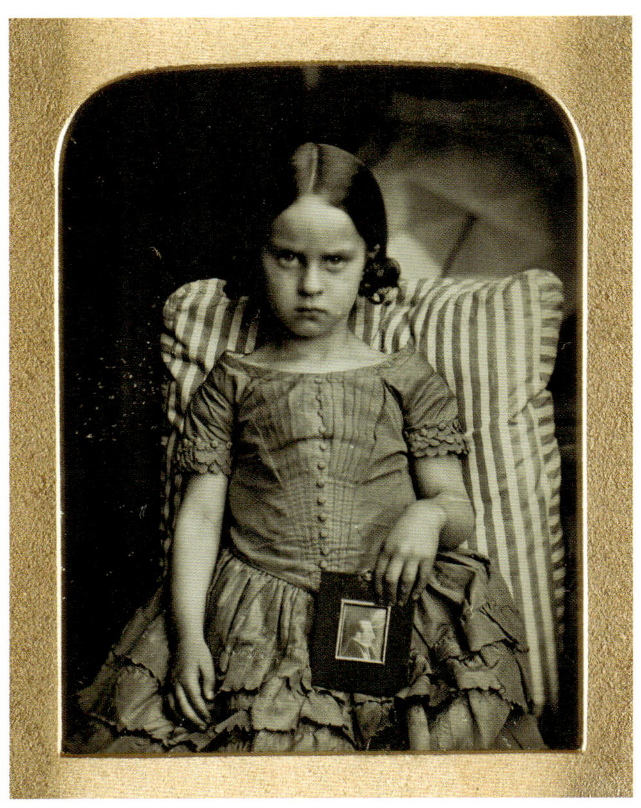

Fig. 3.14: Ross & Thomson, unknown girl holding a framed portrait of a man, perhaps her father, 1847–60, ninth-plate daguerreotype. (Howarth-Loomes Collection at National Museums Scotland, IL.2003.44.2.90)

June 26, 1849. – Received from Le Prince Adam Saphiha [*sic*, see ref. [155]] for daguerreotype apparatus, &c., £15. The patronage of this royal pupil is memorable from the fact that he delivered to us from Sir David Brewster one of the very first lenticular stereoscopes that ever left St Andrews.[156]

In March 1850 the firm bought a four-inch lens for £30 and a three-inch lens for £14 from the eminent opticians Voigtländer and Sons of Brunswick. They found the full plate lens, with a short focal length 'was more rapid in action than any of the lenses we had hitherto been working with. With it we succeeded in taking by the daguerreotype process some groups of a rather sensational character. These brought great crowds about our show case, and one or two were sold for high prices. These were our earliest and, perhaps, our best attempts at figures in lifelike action'. Having taken a series of albumen prints to the Great Exhibition in 1851, and won a Council medal for these, Ross then went to the metropolis to retrieve them:

October 15, 1851. – Mr Ross's expenses to London, £5 10s. In the great city I found that daguerreotype was almost the only style of photographic portraiture practised. … During 1852 the most notable thing regarding ourselves was the great and increasing demand for daguerreotype portraits.

He refers briefly to the technical side of daguerreotyping:

February 5, 1853. – Smith's work for repairing wheel – a revolving machine for polishing daguerreotype plates. It required three men to work it and one to keep on the plates, but the surface it produced upon the plate was most perfect.

By 1854, they had rented new premises, so they could keep the calotype and daguerreotype processes entirely separate [Fig. 3.14].[157]

Around 1862 Thomson, having made enough money from his foray into photography, decided to retire from Edinburgh, and became factor to the fourth Earl of Rosslyn, and Curator of Roslin Chapel, for the next thirty years.[158] He took and sold photographs to tourists there.[159] Ross continued the firm under both their names until he himself retired in 1878, when his assistant (with whom he had been running the business), Thomas Pringle (1832–94), changed the name to 'Ross & Pringle'.[160] Ross outlived his successor by a year, dying at the age of eighty.[161]

At the 1853 meeting of the British Association for the Advancement of Science in Hull, London photographer

Antoine Claudet gave two papers about daguerreotype improvements; the second session was a 'morning devoted to Photography' and paper, glass and daguerreotypes were explained and demonstrated. 'A great number of very beautiful specimens of the art were exhibited. Two views in particular, executed by Messrs Ross and Thomson of Edinburgh, of an unusually large size, were most remarkable for the perfection of every part.'[162] In late 1853, a photographic exhibition organised by the London-based Society of Arts and the Photographic Society of London was held at the Mechanics' Institute in Aberdeen.[163] Ross and Thomson exhibited four daguerreotypes, of a 'Beggar Lassie', three children from life, a portrait of a lady and a portrait of the Rev. Dr Guthrie.[164] Their portrait of the Rev. Dr Thomas Guthrie (1803–73), Free Church minister, was engraved and advertised in 1856: 'Robert R. Nelson respectfully invites inspection of the unfinished proof of the above portrait, from the *inimitable Daguerreotype* by Messrs Ross & Thomson, which he has on view for a short time at 27 Hanover Street.'[165] Ross himself was to say:

May 13, 1851 – One large daguerreotype of Dr Guthrie, in frame, £1 1s. As a general rule, the successful picture of a great beauty brought more grist to the mill than the portrait of a great man; but this right reverend philanthropist was an exception to the rule. Sir D. Brewster, by his great influence in high places, laid the foundation of our house; but Dr Guthrie, by his example, did more to rear its walls than any other man, great or small, who ever honoured us with his patronage. The number of that great orator's admirers who followed him to buy copies of his picture, and to sit for their own, may truly be said to have been legion – for they *were* many.[166]

The firm continued to exhibit daguerreotypes: at the Photographic Society of Scotland in 1856, these included portraits of the author W. M. Thackeray and artist George Harvey.[167]

There was another short-lived daguerreotyping studio in Edinburgh, in February 1845. This advertised: 'Royal Daguerreotype Portraits, with all the latest Parisian and London improvements, are now taken at 39 South Bridge. Price 3s 6d each …'.[168]

The Howie family had been involved with photography from the beginning. By December 1850, James Howie Junior (1819–55) offered 'Photographic Portraits at Half-Price. On New Year's Day, and three following days, these portraits will be taken at half-price, by Mr Jas. Howie, Jun., at his photographic Saloon … Observe Prices: 1st Class, 1s 6d; 2nd, 2s 6d; 3d, 4s; 4th, 7s 6d … '.[169] In the later 1840s, Britain, along with other European countries, had encountered a severe economic slump, exacerbated in the Highlands of Scotland and Ireland by the devastating potato famine. This shows in the price of a daguerreotype, noted here, falling from one guinea to 7s 6d [Fig. 3.15].

In an 1851 article, probably written by David Brewster for *Hogg's Instructor*, an Edinburgh publication for family consumption, the work of both James Howie and Thomas Davidson was recommended: '… a good camera is essential to success in photographic experiments: those lenses manufactured by Mr Davidson of Edinburgh have never been surpassed in taking views of landscapes … Some of the finest Daguerreotypes we have lately seen, were taken by Howie, junior, Edinburgh.'[170] In August and September of 1853, Howie advertised: 'Mr J Howie, Junior's, photographic or daguerreotype portraits taken daily in any weather at 71 Princes Street …'.[171] By November 1854, he

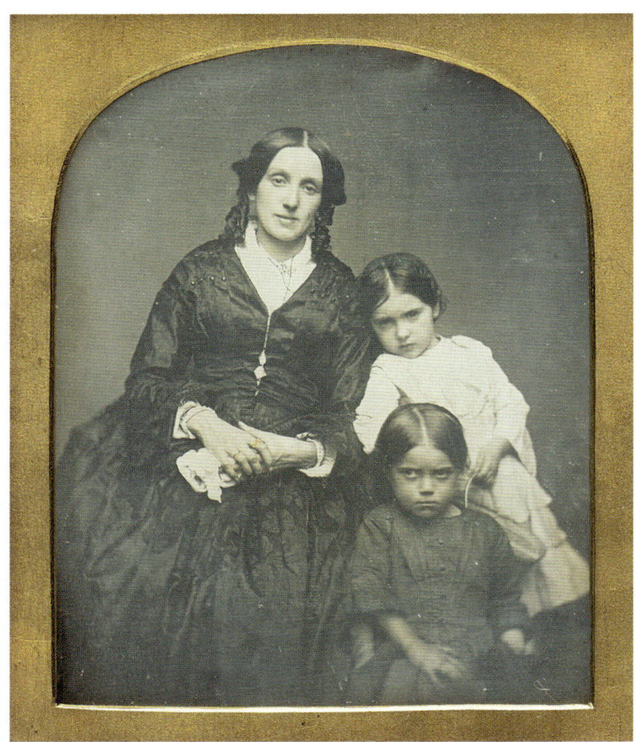

proclaimed the 'Overwhelming Success of the cheap prices at Howie Junior's American Photographic Gallery, 71 Princes Street. Portraits taken in Daguerreotype, Collodion and Calotype. Prices from 1s. First Class Assistants, Two Glass Pavilions, and splendid Apparatus, advantages unsurpassed by any establishment in Britain.'[172] In February 1855, just after Howie Junior's death, this studio and its activities were described less ambitiously as: 'Photographic portraits taken daily, by the daguerreotype and collodion processes, at Howie Junior's American Photographic Gallery, 71 Princes Street. Prices from one shilling'; this would by then have been the elder Mr Howie's grandson, keeping on the family business.[173] By April, the 'Overwhelming Success …' was being trumpeted anew.[174]

Professional daguerreotype photography after 1851

It is unclear whether many daguerreotype studios in Scotland were producing stereo daguerreotypes; but enough of them – as with single daguerreotypes – are unsigned for it to be a possibility. Ross & Thomson provided daguerreotypes for the stereoscope; in 1852 they advertised:

> Photography: The finest daguerreotype likenesses are taken by Messrs Ross & Thomson, Photographers to the Queen, who had the honour of being awarded the Council Medal at the Great Exhibition, for 'great improvements to Photography.' Pictures applicable for the Lenticular Stereoscope, the beautiful Invention and Discovery of Sir David Brewster, may be had on application; as also the instruments of the most approved pattern. 90 Princes Street, Edinburgh, 1852.[175]

James Ross confirmed this in his reminiscences:

> *January* 15, 1853. Paid Mr J. Pearce £6 10s, for thirteen stereoscopes, showing that this magical instrument must have been working its way into public favour. Once or twice we took instantaneous views of the city on silver plates, which in delicacy surpassed the finest glass pictures we ever saw for the stereoscope.[176]

An advertisement in the *Dumbarton Herald* in July 1852 for the 'American Daguerreotype Portrait Rooms at 110 Buchanan Street [Glasgow]', extolled the success of the 'superior character' of the American daguerreotype. A 'Mr Brewster', having learned their 'improved mode of manipulation', announced that he had set up in business there, and 'portraits taken for the stereoscope' were on offer.[177] For a time, he was in partnership with James White, with branches in Ayr and Edinburgh.[178]

C. Jabez Hughes (1819–84) produced stereo daguerreotypes in Glasgow. He advertised in May 1852:

Stereo Portraits or Solid Photographic Likenesses
Mr Hughes begs to call the attention of the Public to these new and extraordinary productions which are exciting so much interest at present in the scientific world. These Portraits require to be personally examined to appreciate their remarkable character, for instead of the flat appearance of the ordinary Daguerreotype, they stand out in all the relief and roundness of life itself.[179]

Hughes's successor in the Glasgow studio was John Werge (1824–1911), originally from the north of England, and who wrote his reminiscences:

I learnt that Mr Jabez Hughes, then in business in Glasgow, was in want of an assistant, a colourist especially. Having met Mr Hughes in Glasgow in 1852, and knowing what kind of man he was, I wrote to him, and was engaged in a few days. I went to Glasgow in January, 1855, and then commenced business relations and friendship with Mr Hughes that lasted unbroken until his death in 1884. My chief occupation was to colour the Daguerreotypes taken by Mr Hughes, and occasionally take sitters, when Mr Hughes was busy, in another studio. I had not, however, been long in Glasgow, when Mr Hughes determined to return to London. At first he

wished me to accompany him, but it was ultimately arranged that I should purchase the business, and remain in Glasgow. … While Mr Hughes was in Glasgow he was very popular, not only as a Daguerreotypist, but as a lecturer. He delivered a lecture on photography at the Literary and Philosophical Society, became an active member of the Glasgow Photographic Society, and an enthusiastic member of the St Mark's Lodge of Freemasons. Only a day or two before he left Glasgow, he occupied the chair at a meeting of photographers, comprising Daguerreotypists and collodion workers, to consider what means could be adopted to check the downward tendency of prices even in those early days. I was present, and remember seeing a lady Daguerreotypist among the company, and she expressed her opinion quite decidedly. Efforts were made to enter into a compact to maintain good prices, but nothing came of it. Like all such bandings together, the band was quickly and easily broken.[180]

'In 1857 I abandoned the Daguerreotype process entirely,' wrote Werge, 'and took to collodion solely; and, strangely enough, that was the year that Frederick Scott Archer, the inventor, died'.[181] A number of Werge's daguerreotypes, stamped 'J. WERGE' and 'MONTEITH ROOMS, GLASGOW' are known to have survived [FIG. 3.16].[182] For many of his professional contemporaries this change of process was to be a natural progression during the later 1850s.

For instance, John Adamson (*c*.1822–1912) – not to be confused with Dr John Adamson of St Andrews – took up commercial photography in Glasgow in 1850:

The … photographer of that date moved in an atmos-

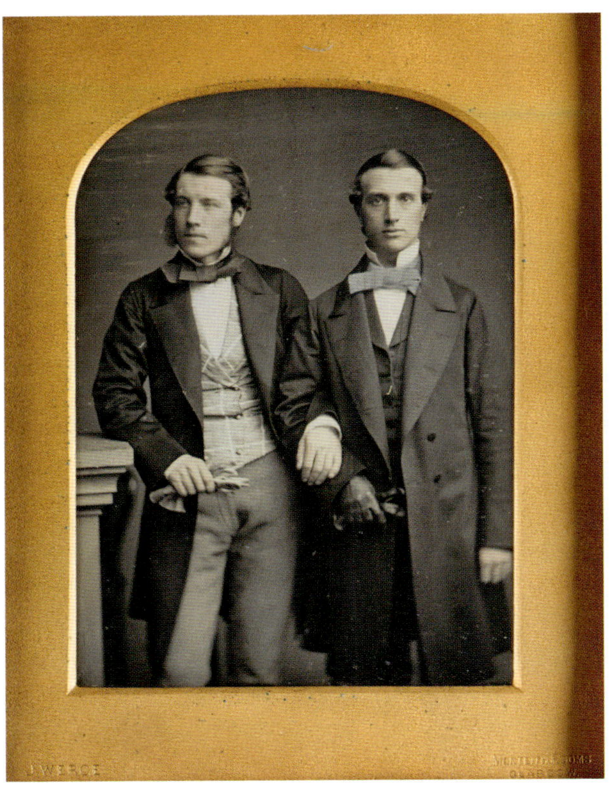

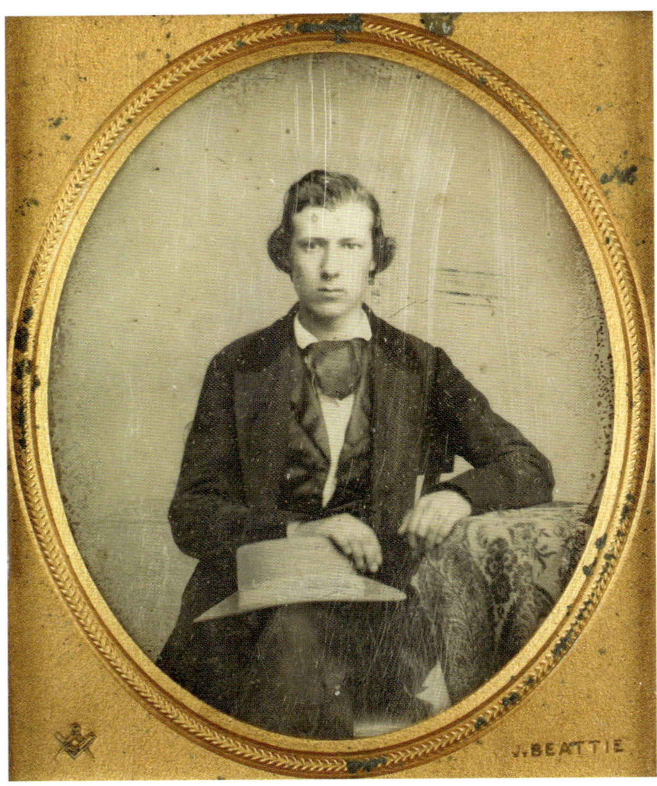

phere saturated with chemical vapours by no means conducive to a superabundance of health. Mr Adamson, in brief, found it necessary, on hygienic grounds, to leave Glasgow in 1854, selecting Rothesay, famed for the salubrity of its climate, as his future residence. The change had the happiest effect in every way; and what might have been regarded as unfortunate, became responsible for the production of a marine photographer, *par excellence*, who, otherwise, amidst the smoke and grime of Glasgow, might have remained a mere 'taker' of excellent photos.[183]

This description suggests that he followed the daguerreotype process.[184] A colleague later recounted that 'Mr John Adamson … a joiner to trade, finding himself in bad health in Glasgow, migrated to Rothesay …'. Like so many others, he abandoned the daguerreotype for wet collodion: '… many a time have I listened to Mr Adamson, snr., recounting his early days in wet-plate work'.[185] At the time

of his death, in September 1912, he was believed to be the oldest professional photographer in the United Kingdom, although by that date the firm was trading in Adamson's name by Robert Whiteford.[186]

The career path of John Beattie, who was born in Abernethy, Perthshire, but who died in 1883 in Clifton, near Bristol, was very different. According to his obituarist, he began as a lecturer in phrenology and electricity. In 1850, he met Oliver Sarony (1820–79), an itinerant photographer ('on the road'), and in early 1851 the pair became partners [Fig. 3.17]. Calling themselves 'The American Daguerreotype Gallery', they took photographs during daylight hours, and Beattie lectured on photography during the evenings. This was financially successful, but nevertheless their partnership was dissolved after a few months and 'Mr Beattie entered into business on his own account, travelling, as before, from place to place, and employing several assistants as artists. He eventually settled in Clifton, where he conducted a high-class business up to 1869, when he retired'.[187]

Fig. 3.16 (opposite left): John Werge, two unknown young men, 1856–59, half-plate daguerreotype. (Howarth-Loomes Collection at National Museums Scotland, IL.2003.44.2.87)

Fig. 3.17 (opposite right): John Beattie, unknown young man, 1851–60, daguerreotype, stamped on the mount 'J. Beattie'. (Rijksmuseum, Amsterdam, RP-F-F14509)

Fig. 3.18 (right): George Popowitz, James Coutts Crawford (1817–89), quarter-plate daguerreotype, 1849–60. (Alexander Turnbull Library, Wellington, New Zealand, 1/2-081410-F)

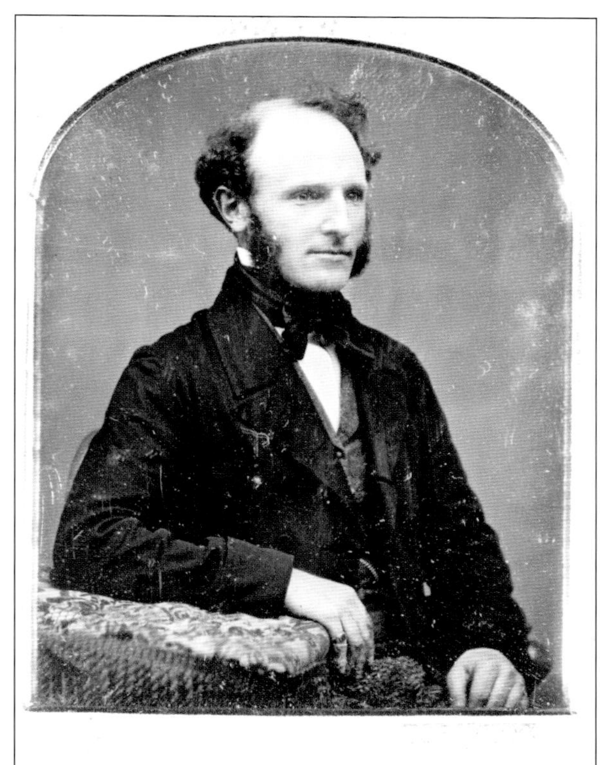

According to another source, while working as a daguerreotypist in August 1851, Beattie met Frederick Scott Archer, who introduced him to his method of wet plate photography on glass.[188]

Another commercial photographer, later known for his wet plate work, was James Cramb, who in 1854 advertised daguerreotype portraits at Victoria Square, 43 Nethergate. Cramb announced his return to Dundee after visiting London and principal provincial towns. His prices ranged from 3s. 6d., and he offered instruction in photography; in a subsequent advertisement he promoted himself as 'The only Establishment where Portraits are done by the Daguerreotype process'. Calling them 'unrivalled Miniatures at Prices little higher than is charged for the most imperfect Photographic Caricatures', he went on to exhort his would-be customers:

> Remember! a bad likeness is worse than useless, and one that leaves but a shadow behind in a heartless delusion. When loved ones have passed from among us, how invaluable does a good Portrait become! And how bitter is the feeling if we have neglected the opportunity of obtaining a correct remembrancer of the familiar features, or only such as increases the mortification and regret![189]

Cramb exhibited 'an excellent case of portraits' by an unspecified process at the Photographic Exhibition held in Dundee.[190] He was based in premises in Victoria Square between 1856 and 1859, and then presumably moved with his

brother, John Cramb, to Glasgow, where they also advanced their photographic techniques into wet collodion.[191]

George Popowitz may have been the circus clown noted in Tourniaires's Royal Olympic Arena of Arts, Dock Green, Hull in May 1843; the circus put on a benefit for 'Monsieur Popowitz, the unrivalled clown' in Manchester in November that year; and again in Liverpool in February 1844.[192] When he registered the birth of his son, Leon Ellias George Popowitz, in Liverpool in December 1843, he gave his profession as 'horse rider'.[193] Popowitz purchased daguerreotype patent rights from Richard Beard and set up the 'Daguerreotype and Photographic Portrait Establishment' in the attic of the subscription library, Bromley House, Nottingham. In December 1845, he announced his arrival 'from Paris', where he may have learned the daguerreotype (or where he thought his would-be customers would be impressed to hear of it). On 27 March 1846, he offered a reward of ten pounds in the *Nottingham Mercury* for information leading to detection of the unauthorised use of the daguerreotype in his territory. Apparently, he left the Midlands in early 1847 [FIG. 3.18]. He first established himself in Edinburgh on the Mound and moved to 60 Princes Street during the December of 1849.[194] In 1851 he was recorded in the Census, with three children, as 'George Popowitz aged 50, "Photographic Artist master" residence at 3 East Register Street. Native of Hungary'.[195] A later memoir (1908) stated:

> Previous to [Tunny], the only photographer in Edinburgh was Popowitz, a Pole, who established himself in a wooden sentry box on the Mound, then a wilderness; the photos were on glass, and we still have those of us three brothers. My brother John is in a jacket with a turn-down collar, and at the age of fifteen I am in a coloured vest, and with the stiff black stock of the period.[196]

This contradicts the contemporary evidence that while Popowitz was based on the Mound, he exclusively used the daguerreotype process; but it is also incorrect about the photographer's nationality. Popowitz's daguerreotypes were stamped with his name in capitals on the matt, but do not give their place of origin: thus, it is unclear whether they were taken in Nottingham or Edinburgh.[197]

Possibly the last professional in Edinburgh to advertise the daguerreotype was the exotically-named Sotires Georgiades (1810–90) who, according to the inscription on his Edinburgh tombstone, was born in Argos, Greece.[198] One of his first Edinburgh advertisements claimed he was 'late of Paris' and based in 'his Photographic Establishment, No 4 Mound, First Door below the Panorama', he apparently took over the premises recently vacated by Popowitz. He stated that 'the sitters have all the privacy they may wish, and their general comfort is secured by the accommodation afforded', reassurance necessary for women who possibly still found the photographic procedure uncomfortable. His prices were, he stated, 'moderate, being 5s 6d for the smallest size Portrait; 8s 6d for the middle size; and 15s for the largest size. Family Groups are taken at a small advance from these charges'.[199]

By late August he had moved to new premises at No. 75 Princes Street, 'which contains apartments, elegantly fitted up, for the accommodation of Ladies and others who may desire privacy'. More importantly, 'correct and pleasing Likenesses are produced in every state of the weather, as the Photographic operation is carried on in a Glass Chamber! that secures it from the unfavourable influence of bad weather'.[200] Prices remained the same. He continued to advertise his 'Superior Daguerreotype Portraits' into 1854, and appeared in the street directories at the Princes Street address and 58 Queen Street until 1862.[201]

According to Alexandros Rangavis, Greek diplomat and man of letters, on 3 August 1850:

> I was returning to my own residence when I saw over the door of a house the legend 'Photographic Studios of Sotires Georgiades'. Without a moment's hesitation I went straight up and found that the man was in fact a Greek, though with nothing else of interest about him apart from his nationality.[202]

With Sotires Georgiades's daguerreotype work, the commercial initiation of this process appears to come to an end. By 1857 the daguerreotype process had been superseded by newer, paper processes, but at a meeting of the Photographic Society of Scotland James Ross looked back on the process with affection, and sadness at its passing:

I was in hopes that the Daguerreotype would have been the subject of this night's consideration, and as France was the place of its birth, a French Photographer I thought was to sing its *requiem* in this, the place of its burial. In no part – in this country at least – has it lived for so long as in our own cold climate, and for my part I think it should 'have died hereafter,' when perchance its place might have been filled, if that were possible by something more lovely still. Not only was it the first-born but far the most beautiful of the many branches of the Photographic family. It was indeed both 'a thing of beauty and a joy forever.' Whether this can at some future time be said of the hybrid style of Photography that has succeeded it time alone can tell.[203]

Numbers of professional daguerreotypists in Scotland

It is difficult to assess how many daguerreotypists were practising in Scotland in the twenty years of the process's greatest popularity. It appears from the newspaper sources that many of these were itinerant, and thus not noted in street directories. To take at random the particulars of 'Mr Brown, from the Photographic Institution, Dundee', on his 'short visit to Cupar' in May 1850; he was described – no doubt, from information he supplied to the newspaper editor – by the *Fife Herald*, as 'a young gentleman of very high promise as a general artist – for we know that in Edinburgh, where we had the pleasure of his acquaintance, his paintings in oil were much admired. He intends to devote himself for a few months to the execution of likenesses by photography.'[204] Presumably, if this was not a success, Mr Brown would return to the capital and oil painting.

Unusually, John Cormack Brown, 'daguerreotypist and teacher of drawing and painting', is noted at 30 Union Street, Dundee, in 1850; and a 'John C. Brown, landscape painter' is to be found at Viewforth Cottage, Leith, in 1851, so that – despite 'Brown' being a popular name – this is probably the same individual.[205] The histories of photography tend to assume that photography undermined and replaced the trade of painting – especially in miniature. But, as John C. Brown's story indicates, the traffic continued both ways and the professions could be combined.

The early history of professional photography in Scotland, and especially that conducted by the daguerreotypists, tended to follow tracks laid down by the itinerant painters – specifically, the portrait artists who worked on a smaller scale than the oil painters, in miniature, water-colour, chalk or silhouette. They moved seasonally out from the cities in the wake of the wealthy and in search of the reasonably prosperous. Like the daguerreotypists, these artists advertised to drum up excitement in the few weeks they worked in one place. Some of the advertisements in the 1840s are indeed ambiguous – it is not clear if the operator is offering photography or painting, and in some cases he or she may have undertaken both.

One of John Muir Wood's paper negatives, of St Giles Cathedral in Edinburgh, shows a travelling van in the street, painted with the words 'Eliza Cook. Dispatch Portrait Company' [FIG. 3.19].[206] It is a comment on the ephemeral nature of her trade that this picture is the only knowledge we have of her. Speed was one of the selling points of photography, because a miniature required several sittings of some hours. Eliza Cook's sign may mean that she was a silhouettist. A note in *Chambers's Edinburgh Journal* in 1844 makes the point:

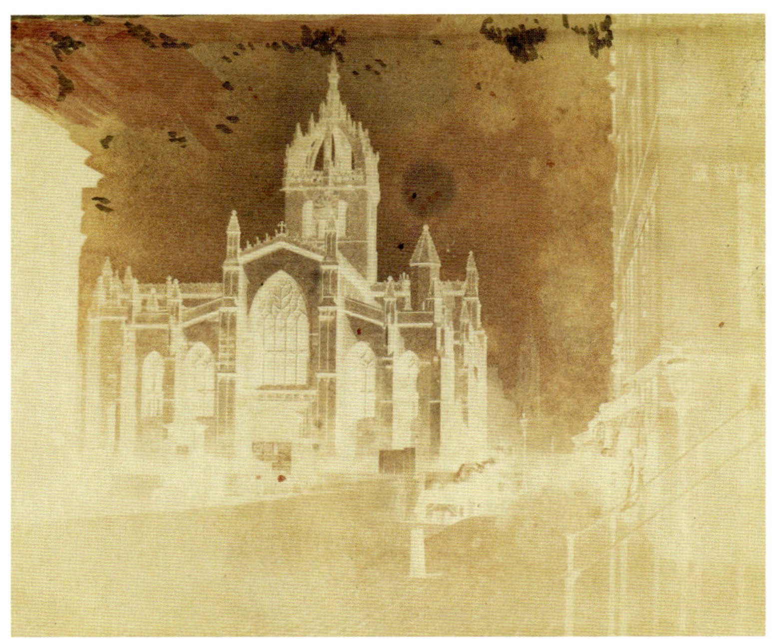 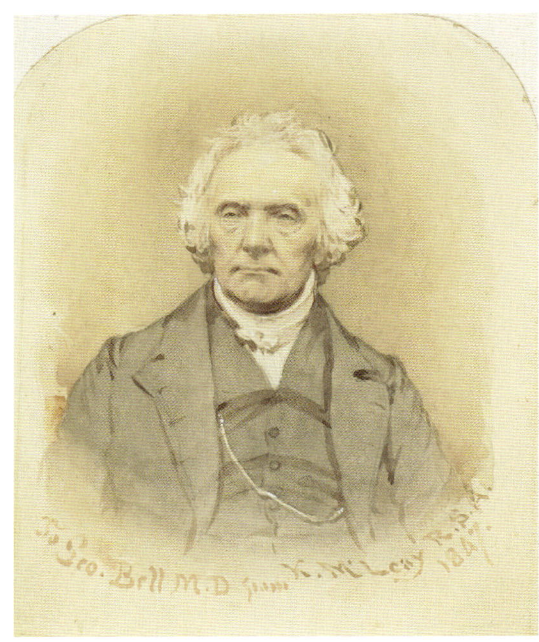

The process is so simple, and the subject executed so rapidly, that provided the artist be constantly employed, he may earn a respectable living. A sheet of blackened paper and a pair of scissors are all the implements he requires. His sitters turn their profiles in the best point of view, and he copies their visages as he cuts his way into the black sheet. The head when completed, is stuck on some white card by way of contrast, and the subject is finished. [These were the cheapest portraits and generally there was attached] in this country an equally black advertisement, announcing that the likenesses are taken 'in this style at 6d.' – nay, we have sometimes seen the price temptingly reduced to the small charge of 3d.[207]

In the 1840s, the silhouettists worked faster and considerably more cheaply than the daguerreotypists (at the guinea rate for a daguerreotype, the sixpenny charge for the silhouette was 42 times less expensive than the photograph). The daguerreotype was aimed at the luxury market – the miniature painter's trade – enclosed in a little frame or hinged box, with the photographer's name embossed tastefully in gold or even omitted altogether.

In less than twenty years the business of the miniature painters was overtaken by photography. Some painters, such as Theresa Dessurne, a 'photographic miniature painter' in Glasgow from 1855, took on the colouring of photographs – requiring a delicate skill on the fragile surface of daguerreotypes, but no original talent. James Howie and James Ross in the 1840s, and John Moffat and James Valentine in the 1850s, were trained as painters and turned to photography.[208] The established and highly-skilled miniaturist Kenneth MacLeay (1802–78) found his business severely undercut by photography. Between 1849–59, his annual income halved from £500 to £250. He addressed this problem by taking on Iván Szabó's photographic studio based in Newington, south Edinburgh, and devised a hybrid approach between photography and watercolour [Fig. 3.20]. He was fortuitously rescued by royal patronage of his watercolour practice in the 1860s.

Notes

1. Talbot was advised by Brewster not to take out a patent in Scotland (before reform in 1858, patents had to be taken out separately, and expensively, in all three kingdoms): see document 4190, Brewster to Talbot, 4 February 1841 <http://foxtalbot. dmu.ac.uk/letters/letters.html>: 'I am glad you have taken out a Patent. To extend it to Scotland wd be unprofitable.' For the daguerreotype: see John Hannavy, 'Richard Beard's Scottish and Irish Patents, and the Development of the Daguerreotype in Those Countries', in *Daguerreian Annual* (2007): 88–101: though Daguerre took out a patent, it was never applied in Scotland.
2. *Caledonian Mercury*, 21 March 1840; Catalogue 1840: 26, 40, 49.
3. Daguerre (Memes, trans.) 1839.
4. 'The Daguerreotype', *Chambers's Edinburgh Journal* (29 August 1839): 243–4; Robison, 'Notes on Daguerre's Photography [1 June 1839]', *Edinburgh Philosophical Journal* 27 (1839): 155–7; *Transactions of the Royal Scottish Society of Arts* 1 (1841): 330–2.
5. *Chambers's Edinburgh Journal* 8 (2 November 1839): 327.
6. *Ibid.*, 328. For John Smythe Memes, see Scott (ed.) 1915–16, *Fasti Ecclesiae Scoticanae* III: 263.
7. *Scotsman*, 16 October 1839.
8. Quoted by Schaaf, '"Splendid Calotypes" and "Hideous Men": Photography in the Diaries of Lady Pauline Trevelyan', *History of Photography* 34 (2010): 332.
9. *Fife Herald*, 8 April 1847 and 20 May 1847; *Berwick and Kelso Warder*, 15 March 1850.
10. John Urie, 'Pictures from Life, From the Scrapbook of a Photographer', *British Journal of Photography* 24 (5 and 12 October 1877): 474.
11. Victoria & Albert Museum, P.5–1926.
12. The family gravestone in Warriston Cemetery, Edinburgh, is shown at <http://www.edinphoto.org.uk/pp_d/pp_howie_ james_1820_ gravestone.htm#detail_from_gravestone> See death notice *Caledonian Mercury*, 29 December 1858.
13. Torrance 2011: 357–61.
14. James Tunny, 'Early Reminiscences of Photography', *British Journal of Photography* 16 (12 November 1869): 546.

15. John Nicol, 'Reminiscences of Thomas Davidson, a Weaver Lad', *British Journal of Photography* 26 (15 August 1879): 390–1, 26 (22 August 1879): 399–401.
16. In the Howarth-Loomes Collection at National Museums Scotland, IL.2003.44.2.12, 38, 247 and 248, all unidentified sitters; Scottish National Portrait Gallery PGP 426, of 'G. Thompson'; PGP 91-1, an unidentified woman with two children; PGP 91-3, 'Professor James Pillans (1778–1864); PGP 91-4, 'George Combe, 1788–1858'; from The Riddell Collection, PGP R21, unidentified family of six; Prentenkabinet Universiteit Leiden, 72.287, an unknown woman, and RP-F-F14442, an unknown man. One daguerreotype that has not apparently survived, is that of the poet Thomas de Quincey (1785–1859), taken in 1850.
17. John Nicol, 'Reminiscences of Thomas Davidson, a Weaver Lad', *British Journal of Photography* 26 (15 August 1879): 390–1.
18. John Nicol, 'Reminiscences of Thomas Davidson, a Weaver Lad', *British Journal of Photography* 26 (22 August 1879): 399–401.
19. NMS T.1938.104; and Royal Observatory, Edinburgh.
20. *Caledonian Mercury*, 31 March and 4 April 1842.
21. *Caledonian Mercury*, 9 April 1842; *Scotsman*, 9 and 11 April 1842.
22. R. Derek Wood, 'The Dageurreotype Patent, the British Government, and the Royal Society', in *History of Photography* 4 (1980): 53–9.
23. Heathcote and Heathcote 2002: 74; also R. Derek Wood 1979, 'The dageurreotype in England, Some primary material relating to Beard's lawsuits', *History of Photography* 3 (1979): 305–9.
24. *Caledonian Mercury*, 9 May 1842; *Scotsman*, 9 and 11 May 1842.
25. *Caledonian Mercury*, 9 May 1842.
26. *Caledonian Mercury*, 4 June 1842.
27. *Ibid.*, and also <http://spartacus-educational.com/DShistory index.htm>
28. *Caledonian Mercury*, 4 June 1842.
29. *Caledonian Mercury*, 30 June 1842.
30. *Ibid.*
31. *Caledonian Mercury*, 1 August 1842. A further advertisement, with editorial comment, appeared on 1 September.
32. *Caledonian Mercury*, 3 November 1842.
33. *Caledonian Mercury*, 5 November 1842.
34. *Caledonian Mercury*, 24, 26, 29 and 31 December 1842; 2 and 4 January 1843.
35. *Caledonian Mercury*, 24 December 1842.
36. *Caledonian Mercury*, 26, 29 and 31 December 1842; 2 and 5

January 1843; *Edinburgh Evening Courant*, 2, 5 and 7 January 1843.

37. Some of his activities can be pursued on the website: <http://records.ancestry.co.uk/john_stephens_records.ashx?pi =67738628>
These show that he was born in Edmonton, Middlesex, in 1818, learned the daguerreotypist's trade acting as assistant to William Constable, Brighton's earliest photographer, before travelling to Edinburgh to join Messrs Miles and Edwards. It is possible his troubles began with his marriage to Rebecca Baker, who later died in London in 1846, with Counsell remarrying the following year, this time in Sheffield, to a woman named Sarah Herring.
38. *Dundee Advertiser*, 21 April 1843, quoted by Heathcote and Heathcote 2002: 115.
39. *Fife Herald*, 25 May 1843.
40. *Fife Herald*, 1 June 1843.
41. See <http://www.edinphoto.org.uk/pp/pp_counsell_stephens_ cornwall.htm>
42. *Royal Cornwall Gazette, Falmouth Packet and General Advertiser*, 28 September 1849, 10 October 1851 and 1 October 1852. See also Thomas 1988.
43. *Otago Daily Times*, 6 August 1890; *Otago Witness*, 7 August 1890.
44. See Chandler 2003: 17.
45. *Glasgow Argus*, 30 June 1842, quoted by Heathcote and Heathcote [n.d.]: 152; also *Glasgow Herald*, 1 July 1842.
46. Heathcote and Heathcote [n.d.]: 152; also *Glasgow Herald*, 8 July 1842.
47. Edwards & Co.'s advertisements appeared in the *Glasgow Herald* for 11, 15, 22, 25, 29 July and 1 August 1842; Treffry's advertisements in 11, 25 July and 1 and 5 August 1842. More advertisements from the *Glasgow Argus* are quoted by Heathcote and Heathcote [n.d.]: 152–3.
48. *Glasgow Herald*, 18 July 1842.
49. Heathcote and Heathcote [n.d.]: 153; note Edwards' final advertisement in the *Glasgow Argus*, 1 September 1842, and that of Treffry, 28 July 1842.
50. Andrew Mactear 1884, 'History of Photography in Glasgow, by Andrew Mactear', *British Journal of Photography* 31 (28 March 1884): 202 (written in 1864; re-read before the Glasgow Photographic Association on 6 March 1884).
51. *Dumfries and Galloway Courier*, 27 March 1843, quoted by John Hannavy 2007, 'Richard Beard's Scottish and Irish Patents, and the Development of the Daguerreotype in Those Countries',

Daguerreian Annual (2007): 88–101, see quote on page 96.
52. Advertisement quoted in full by Simpson: 2012: 16.
53. Document 4321, Treffry to Talbot, 19 August 1841, <http://foxtalbot.dmu.ac.uk/letters/letters.html>
54. Larry Schaaf has observed that the London partnership of William Treffry, William Henry Treffry, and Samuel Bevan, engineers and iron founders, was dissolved in June 1842. The daguerreotypist may have been a relative. Document 4587, Treffry to Talbot, 23 August 1842, <http://foxtalbot.dmu.ac.uk/letters/letters.html>
55. Glasgow University Library Eph. D/204.
56. *Glasgow Herald*, 25 July 1842.
57. Andrew Mactear, 'History of Photography in Glasgow', *British Journal of Photography* 31 (28 March 1884): 202.
58. <http://www.photolondon.org.uk/pages/details.asp?pid=6104>
59. *Glasgow Herald*, 28 June 1844.
60. *Glasgow Herald*, 8 July 1844.
61. *Glasgow Examiner*, 4 January 1845, also 1 March, 12 and 19 April, 3 May 1845: quoted by Heathcote and Heathcote [n.d.]: 153; see also Batchen, 'Beauties and Deformities Alike: Beard, Claudet, and the Business of Photography', in Batchen (ed.) forthcoming; see also <www.simeonsolomon.com/abraham solomons-portrait-of-wellington.html>
62. *Daily News*, 17 April 1852.
63. *Glasgow Herald*, 3 and 27 February, 5 March and 13 July 1860.
64. According to the *Photographic News* 27 (21 March 1884): 186, quoted by Heathcote and Heathcote 2002: 74.
65. *Glasgow Herald*, 2 April 1847.
66. *Glasgow Herald*, 26 April 1847.
67. Hannavy 2008, 'Photographic retailing', in Hannavy (ed.) 2008, 2: 1093.
68. *Glasgow Herald*, 25 June 1847.
69. *Glasgow Herald*, 26 January, 20 April, 3 April 1849.
70. <http://freepages.genealogy.rootsweb.ancestry.com/ ~anncarson/Borthwick/jbliverpool.htm>
71. *Glasgow Examiner*, 4 August and 20 October 1849, quoted in Heathcote and Heathcote [n.d.]: 155, 156.
72. *Glasgow Herald*, 26 November 1849.
73. <http://genforum.genealogy.com/lauder/messages/143.html>
74. Bernard V. Heathcote and Pauline F. Heathcote 1988, 'The Feminine Influence: Aspects of the Role of Women in the Evolution of Photography in the British Isles', *History of Photography* 12 (1988): 259–73 – mention of Miss Borthwick on page 271.

75. *Glasgow Advertiser*, 1 June 1850; *Glasgow Post Office Directory*, 1850–51; *Glasgow Herald*, 18 October 1850.

76. <http://www.photolondon.org.uk/pages/details.asp?pid=582> and <http://www.photolondon.org.uk/pages/details.asp?pid=3715>

77. Turley 2008, 'Hughes, Cornelius Jabez', in Hannavy (ed.) 2008, 1: 719–20. Advertisements noted in the *Glasgow Examiner* for 10, 17 January, 7 February, 13, 20 and 27 March by Heathcote and Heathcote [n.d.]: 156.

78. 'The Late Mr C. Jabez Hughes', *British Journal of Photography* 31 (29 August 1884): 548–9, quotation on p. 548.

79. For example, J. Paul Getty Museum, inv. no. 84.XT.1566.2, quarter-plate tinted daguerreotype of a man in uniform of the Lanarkshire Yeomanry regiment, *c*.1853; 84.XT.266.15, half-plate tinted daguerreotype of married couple; 84.XT. 835.18, quarter-plate tinted daguerreotype of a seated woman, with book and glasses; John Hannavy Collection: daguerreotype of man, taken at Monteith Rooms; Howarth-Loomes Collection at National Museums Scotland, IL.2003.44.2.13, quarter-plate daguerreo-type of a middle-aged woman in a white bonnet, with stamp 'Hughes / Monteith Rooms / Glasgow'; IL.2003.44.2.14, quarter-plate daguerreotype of a painting of a middle-aged seated man, stamped in mount 'HUGHES / MONTEITH ROOMS / GLASGOW', and stamped into case: 'MONTEITH / ROOMS / C.J. HUGHES / 67 BUCHANAN ST. / GLASGOW'; IL.2003.44.2.14: sixth-plate tinted daguerreotype of seated gentleman, stamped in mount 'HUGHES / MONTEITH ROOMS / GLASGOW'.

80. *Scotsman*, 8 July 1848; 16 May 1849; 30 Jan. 1850; 20 March 1850.

81. 'Photography – As applied to the Production of Likenesses', *Macphail's Edinburgh Ecclesiastical Journal and Literary* Review, 7 (1849): 294.

82. *Glasgow Examiner*, 11 August 1849, quoted by Heathcote and Heathcote 2002: 114; *Glasgow Herald*, 28 September, 12 and 19 October 1849; with Barratt in Dublin, *Freeman's Journal*, 30 July 1850. The pair were together in London from May 1852 until at least 1858, see <http://www.photolondon.org.uk/pages/details.asp?pid=420> A daguerreotype of a young girl is in the Howarth-Loomes Collection at National Museums Scotland, IL.2003.44.2.91; another is in the Cavan County Museum, CCMF2012011, <http://ccmfariscollection.blogspot.co.uk/2012/08/barratt-stanley-daguerreotypehtml#!/2012/08/barratt-stanley-daguerreotype.html>

83. *Glasgow Examiner*, 5 July 1845, as quoted by Heathcote and Heathcote [n.d.]: 153.

84. *Glasgow Herald*, 19 June 1848.

85. Clarke, Morrison-Low and Simpson 1989: 170–3.

86. Urie 1877, 'Pictures from Life,' *British Journal of Photography* 24 (5 and 12 October 1877): 474–5, 486–7, quote on 474.

87. *Glasgow Examiner*, 29 September 1849, quoted by Heathcote and Heathcote [n.d.]: 156: also 6, 13, 20, 27 October and 10 and 17 November 1849. An example of his work is at NMeM Kodak Collection DC/40, quarter-plate daguerreotype of a seated young woman, stamped on the back of the case 'YOUNG'S / PHOTO-GRAPHIC ROOMS / 15 BUCHANAN ST'.

88. *Glasgow Post Office Directory*, 1851–56: he was listed at 34 Paterson Street, Kingston, Glasgow, in 1851; as a photographer, at 3 and 110 Buchanan Street, with his house at 34 Paterson Street, in 1852; and based at 14 Buchanan Street between 1853 and 1854, before becoming White & Co. in 1855; the following year the firm was based at 16 St Enoch Street, Glasgow 1856.

89. John Urie, 'Pictures from Life,' *British Journal of Photography* 24 (5 and 12 October 1877): 474–5, 486–7, quote on p. 474.

90. SNPG PGP R 38, quarter-plate tinted daguerreotype of a lady; Howarth-Loomes Collection at National Museums Scotland IL.2003.44.1.30, positive collodion portrait of young man, with stereo-viewer and bunch of snowdrops, taken outside, embossed on case: 'White Photographist 14 Buchanan St Glasgow'.

91. *Glasgow Herald*, 27 August 1852; Catalogue 1886: historical section, no. 26.

92. Urie 1877, 'Pictures from Life,' *British Journal of Photography* 27 (5 October 1877): 474. Mark Dessurne (1825–85) has been noted as a London artist who came to Glasgow and practised portrait photography 'on glass' in 1852, and 1857–60, as well as in Dumfries between 1854 and 1855, before returning to London. Theresa Dessurne, working as a photographic miniature painter from 1855, may have been a sister or daughter: see *Glasgow Herald*, 3 September 1852; Heathcote and Heathcote 2002: 72. See also Wright et al. (eds) 2006: 297.

93. *Glasgow Herald*, 27 August 1852; *Glasgow Examiner*, 4, 11, 18, 25 June 1853, quoted by Heathcote and Heathcote [n.d.]: 158.

94. See <http://craigcamera.com/dag/li_table.htm#Litch,Albert> and also Hughes 2013: 360, n. 9.

95. *Aberdeen Journal*, 13, 20 and 27 July 1842.

96. *Aberdeen Journal*, 24 August, 5 October 1842; *Inverness Journal*, 30 September and 14 October 1842.

97. *Aberdeen Journal*, 7 December 1842.

98. *Aberdeen Journal*, 4, 11, 18 January; 1, 15 and 22 February 1843.

99. *Aberdeen Journal*, 29 March 1843.

100. *Aberdeen Journal*, 12 September 1846, quoted by Heathcote and Heathcote [n.d.]: 2.

101. *Aberdeen Journal*, 16 September 1846; *Aberdeen Herald*, 12 and 19 September, 3, 17 and 31 October 1846.

102. *Aberdeen Journal*, 2 December 1846.

103. *Aberdeen Journal*, 2, 9, 16, 23, 30 June; 7, 14, 21, 28 July 1847.

104. *Aberdeen Journal*, 28 July 1847.

105. *Aberdeen Journal*, 11 August 1847.

106. *Inverness Courier*, 31 August 1847, quoted by Heathcote and Heathcote 2002: 60; his 'Daguerreotype Portrait Rooms' remained in Inverness for the month of September: *Inverness Courier*, 14 and 21 September 1847.

107. *Inverness Courier*, 31 August 1847, quoted by Heathcote and Heathcote [n.d.]: 190–1.

108. *Aberdeen Herald*, 12 August 1848, quoted by Heathcote and Heathcote 2002: 104. See also Howarth-Loomes 1973: 33 – associated with daguerreotype IL.2003.44.2.103.

109. *Aberdeen Herald*, 9 September 1848, quoted by Heathcote and Heathcote 2002: 70.

110. *Aberdeen Journal*, 6 September 1848.

111. See <http://peib.dmu.ac.uk/itemphotographer.php?photogNo=486&orderby=coverage&photogName=Craigmyle%2C+F>

112. *Inverness Courier*, 12 and 26 July, 9, 16 and 30 August 1849, quoted by Heathcote and Heathcote [n.d.]: 190; also *Inverness Advertiser*, 3 July 1849.

113. *John O'Groat Journal*, 5, 12, 19 and 26 July, 2 and 9 August, 6 September, 4 October and 15 November 1850.

114. *Aberdeen Journal*, 5 March 1851.

115. *Elgin Courier*, 24 and 31 August, 7 September 1849.

116. *Forres, Elgin and Nairn Gazette*, 8 December 1849, quoted by Heathcote and Heathcote 2002: 66.

117. *Inverness Courier*, 24 April 1851; *Inverness Courier & General Advertiser*, 2 and 16 March, 4 and 18 May 1854; *Inverness Courier*, 15 and 29 September 1855, quoted by Heathcote and Heathcote [n.d.]: 191.

118. *Aberdeen Herald*, 25 February 1854, quoted by Heathcote and Heathcote 2002: 102–3.

119. *Dumfries & Galloway Courier*, 19 March 1850, quoted by Heathcote and Heathcote 2002: 77; *Aberdeen Journal*, 23 October 1851.

120. *Aberdeen Journal*, 5 March 1851.

121. *Aberdeen Journal*, 25 January 1854.

122. See <http://peib.dmu.ac.uk/detailexhibition.php?exbtnid=1010&inum=3&listLength=63&orderBy=exhibid>

123. *Aberdeen Journal*, 7 December 1853.

124. *Inverness Courier*, 5 October 1854, quoted by Heathcote and Heathcote 2002: 77; *Aberdeen Journal*, 27 September 1851.

125. Advertisement in *Aberdeen Post Office Directory*, 1858–61.

126. *Dundee Advertiser*, 21 April 1843, quoted by Heathcote and Heathcote 2002: 115.

127. *Fife Herald*, 25 May and 1 June 1843.

128. *Dundee Courier*, 3 August 1847.

129. Heathcote and Heathcote 2002: 84.

130. *Dundee Courier*, 4 August 1847 for Edward Holmes; 20 and 27 June, 11 July 1849, and 6 March 1850 for Mr Wrench.

131. *Dundee Courier*, 1 July 1849.

132. *Dundee Courier*, 6 March 1850 for Wrench; *Dundee, Perth, and Cupar Advertiser*, 18 September 1849; *Dundee Courier*, 12, 19 and 26 September, 10, 24 and 31 October 1849 for Mr Brown.

133. *Dundee Courier*, 17 October 1849.

134. *Dundee Courier*, 5 December 1849.

135. *Dundee Courier*, 27 February, 6, 13 and 20 March 1850.

136. *Dundee Courier*, advertised in 8 May 1850; and the *Fife Herald*, 16 May 1850; this last quoted in the editorial columns of the *Dundee Courier*, 29 May 1850.

137. *Dundee Courier*, 29 May 1850.

138. *Dundee Courier*, 5 and 26 June 1850.

139. *Dundee Courier*, 10 July 1850.

140. *Dundee Courier*, 24 March 1852.

141. *Dundee Courier*, 21 August 1850.

142. See <http://peib.dmu.ac.uk/itemphotographer.php?photog No=571&orderby=coverage&photogName=Gibb%2C+J>

143. *Dundee Courier*, 24 July 1850; Torrance 2011, 2: 130–1.

144. *Dundee Courier*, 4 and 18 December 1850.

145. *Scotsman*, 24 July and 7 August 1852.

146. *Scotsman*, 14 August 1852.

147. *Scotsman*, 9 May and 2 July 1860 and 10 April 1861.

148. *British Journal of Photography* 10 (16 March 1863): 129.

149. *Scotsman*, 4 November 1843. Mullins may have been the Henry Mullins, who had worked for Richard Beard and settled in Jersey, in July 1848: see 'Old Photo', 'Photography in the Channel Islands', *The Illustrated Photographer* 1 (1868): 456.

150. *Scotsman*, 15, 22 and 29 March and 5 April 1845. Examples of

McMillan & Thomson's work are to be found in SNPG: PGP 91.2 and PGP R 37, both sitters unidentified.

151. See <http://www.photolondon.org.uk/pages/details.asp?pid=4985>

152. John Nicol, 'Notes from the North', *British Journal of Photography* 28 (25 March 1881): 148.

153. *Edinburgh Post Office Directory*, 1846–47.

154. Examples of daguerreotypes in public collections are to be found in SNPG: PGP 171.4, 424, PGP EPS 414, 415, 420, 427, 428; PGP R 10, 12, 13, 26 and 30; and PGPL 15.5; NMS M.1948.81.2 daguerreotype of 2nd Lieutenant J. S. Baird, Royal Artillery; M.1961.141, tinted daguerreotype of Commander Edward Hay, R.N.; NMS T.1981.25, 65, 66 and 67; private collection on loan to NMS IL.2003.44. 2. 39, 62 and 90; NMeM Science Museum Collection: 1900-432, 1965-425, 1965-426; Prentenkabinet Universiteit Leiden, 66.0203: a daguerreotype of Marion Forbes (*née* Campbell) and her son; Rijksmuseum, Amsterdam, RP-F-F14362: daguerreotype of an unknown couple.

155. Gordon 1870: 194 describes Prince Adam de Sapiéha (1828–1903) as a 'foreigner'; his family was originally from Lithuania, but by the mid-19th century they were considered Polish nobility.

156. James Ross, 'A Few Extracts from a Photographer's Old Ledger', *British Journal of Photography* 20 (14 February 1873): 75–7.

157. *Ibid.*

158. Information from archival material, gifted to the Scottish National Portrait Gallery with photographs, by Iain and Sandy Clark in memory of Mrs Catherine Clark, PGP 403.

159. 'Cuthbert Bede', *The Visitors' Handbook to Rosslyn and Hawthornden* (Edinburgh: R. Grant, n.d., but *c.*1864): 19, note.

160. John Nicol, 'Notes from the North', *British Journal of Photography* 25 (27 December 1878): 617.

161. 'The Late Thomas Pringle', *British Journal of Photography* 41 (16 March 1894): 169; 'Death of Mr James Ross', *British Journal of Photography* 42 (29 March 1895): 194.

162. A, Claudet, 'On the Practice of the Daguerreotype', *British Association for the Advancement of Science (London): Report Part II* (1854): 4–5.

163. 'Photographic Exhibition', *Aberdeen Journal*, 7 December 1853.

164. See <http://peib.dmu.ac.uk/itemexhibition.php?exbtnid=1010&orderBy=exhibitnum&exhibitionTitle=&exhibitionTitle=185%2C+Aberdeen%2C+Mechanics%27+Institution>

165. *Scotsman*, 27 December 1856; an example of this print is held in the National Portrait Gallery in London, NPG D35080.

166. James Ross, 'A Few Extracts from a Photographer's Old Ledger', *British Journal of Photography* 20 (14 February 1873): 75–7.

167. See <http://peib.dmu.ac.uk/itemexhibition.php?exbtnid=1025&orderBy=exhibitnum&exhibitionTitle=&exhibitionTitle=185 6%2C+Edinburgh%2C+Photographic+Society+of+Scotland>

168. *Scotsman*, 1 February 1845.

169. *Scotsman*, 28 December 1850.

170. [David Brewster] 1851, 'Photography', *Hogg's Weekly Instructor*, new series 6, 1851: 57–9; Brewster is known to have contributed to this journal from his daughter's biography: Gordon 1870: 286.

171. *Scotsman*, 20, 27 and 31 August and 7 September 1853.

172. *Scotsman*, 8 November 1854.

173. *Scotsman*, 21 February 1855. Death notice in the *Caledonian Mercury*, 15 January 1855.

174. *Scotsman*, 28 April 1855.

175. *Scotsman*, 26 May 1852; also *Caledonian Mercury*, 3 June 1852 and a version of this appeared in the *Aberdeen Journal*, 5 May 1852.

176. James Ross, 'A Few Extracts from a Photographer's Old Ledger', *British Journal of Photography* (14 February 1873): 75–7.

177. *Dumbarton Herald*, 1 and 8 July 1852, quoted by Heathcote and Heathcote [n.d.]: 157–8. This man does not appear to have been related to Sir David Brewster.

178. Torrance 2011, 1: 109; 2: 371–2.

179. *Glasgow Herald*, 7 May and 27 August 1852.

180. Werge 1890: 36.

181. *Ibid.*, 38.

182. Examples are to be found in the Scottish National Portrait Gallery, PGP R 31, an unidentified couple; Howarth Loomes Collection at National Museums Scotland: IL.2003.44.2.87, two unidentified young men, linked arms; Rijksmuseum Amsterdam: RP-F-F14514, sixth plate of an unknown woman; J. Paul Getty Museum: inv. no. 84.XT.1566.1, quarter-plate tinted daguerreotype of a man standing facing the camera.

183. Stratten 1891, 'Messrs. J. Adamson & Son, Photographers, Rothesay': 252.

184. An example is in the Howarth-Loomes Collection at NMS IL.2003.44.2.102, daguerreotype portrait of an unidentified woman, framed for hanging on wall, with label on back, 'JOHN ADAMSON / Photographic Artist / No. 3, Windsor Place / Sauchiehall Street, / Glasgow' dated 1855; he appeared in the

Fig. 3.19: John Muir Wood, St Giles Cathedral showing the van of 'Eliza Cook', 1840s, calotype negative.

Glasgow Post Office Directory, as 'John Adamson, photographic artist, 87 Sauchiehall street', in 1855, but not thereafter.

185. Lundie 1912, 'Correspondence: The Oldest Studio', *British Journal of Photography* 59 (6 December 1912): 947.

186. 'Obituary', *British Journal of Photography* 59 (20 December 1912): 985.

187. *Ibid.*, 677–8.

188. Heathcote and Heathcote 2002: 59. See Audrey Linkman, 'A Roving Scot: Itinerant Photography in the Heart of England in the 1850s', *Scottish Photography Bulletin* 1 (1992): 3–15, using Beattie's own reminiscences published as 'Scintilla'. An example of a daguerreotype of a young man, stamped with 'J. BEATTIE' and a Masonic symbol, is in the Rijksmuseum, Amsterdam, inv. no. RP-F-F14509.

189. *Dundee Courier*, 5 September 1855.

190. *Dundee Courier*, 19 April 1854.

191. *Dundee, Perth and Cupar Advertiser*, 28 April 1854; *Dundee Post Office Directory* 1856–59. Professional photographers at 57 West Nile Street, Glasgow 1859–76, *Glasgow Post Office Directory*.

192. *Hull Packet and East Riding Times*, 12 May 1843; *Manchester Times & Gazette*, 4 November 1843; *Liverpool Mercury*, 9 February 1844.

193. Heathcote 1991, 'The Photographic Studio', in Coope and Corbett (eds) 1991: 101–30, particularly 112–3.

194. *Scotsman*, 1 and 5 December 1849.

195. 1851 Census record, Torrance (transcribed) 2011, I: 287–9.

196. Letter from Dr David Christison, 18 January 1908, quoted in Chiene 1908: 56.

197. There is a daguerreotype of an unknown woman by Popowitz in the Scottish National Portrait Gallery, PGP 109; one by him of James Coutts Crawford (1817–89), quarter-plate daguerreo-type Ref: 1/2-081410-F. Alexander Turnbull Library, Wellington, New Zealand <http://natlib.govt.nz/records/23106957> inv. no. PA10-029; and another of an unknown seated woman wearing a flowered bonnet, fur cuffs and stole, in Harvard University, Houghton Library, Department of Printing and Graphic Arts, part of the Harrison D. Horblit Collection of Early Photography, TypDAG3175.

198. See <http://www.edinphoto.org.uk/0_a/0_around_edinburgh_calton_new_graveyard_georgiades_2212.htm>

199. *Scotsman*, 9 January 1850.

200. *Scotsman*, 28 August, 11 September 1850.

201. *Scotsman*, 11 January, 1, 8 and 22 February 1854; *Caledonian Mercury*, 16 January 1854; *Edinburgh Post Office Directories* 1852–62.

202. Alexander Rangavis, *Memoirs*, for 3 August 1850, quoted by Xanthakēs (Solman and Cox, trans.) 1988: 64.

203. James Ross, 'On Taking and Printing Stereoscopic Pictures', *Photographic Notes* 2 (1857): 258.

204. *Dundee Courier*, 29 May 1850.

205. *Dundee Post Office Directory*, 1850–51; *Edinburgh Post Office Directory*, 1851–52.

206. There was a prominent Eliza Cook (1818–89) who was a poet and journalist. She published two articles on the daguerreotype in her journal in 1850, but they do not suggest any connection with the practice of the art, see Anon., 'Daguerre and his Predecessors', *Eliza Cook's Journal* 2 (May 1850): 390–2; *Eliza Cook's Journal* 3 (October 1850): 93–5.

207. Anon., 'Popular French Songs. No. V.- Portraits à la mode', *Chambers's Edinburgh Journal* [New Series] 2 (17 August 1844): 111.

208. See Smailes 1992.

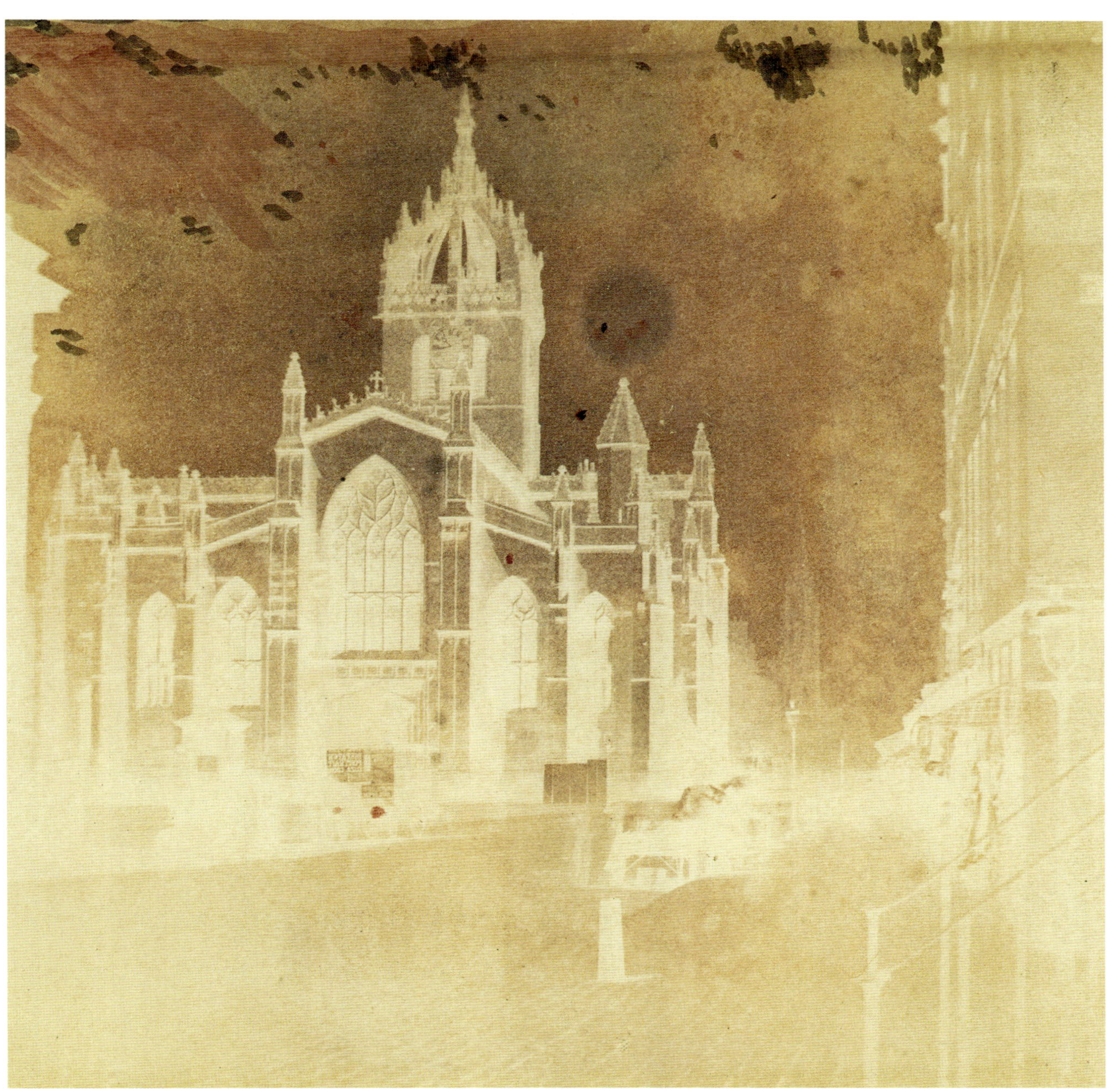

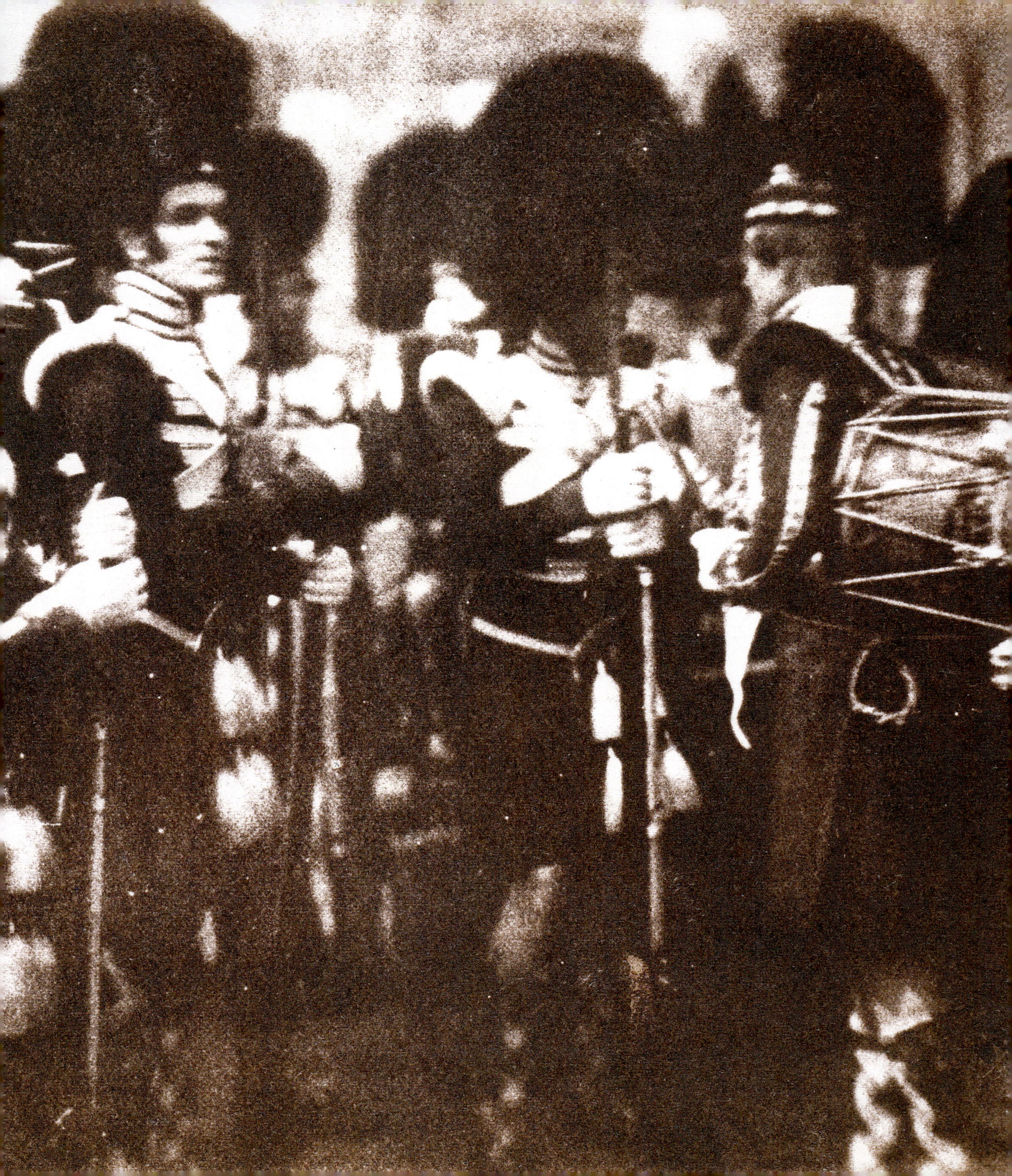

CHAPTER FOUR

The Practical Calotype

I think you will find that we have, in Scotland, found out
the value of your invention not before yourself, but before
those to whom you have given the privilege of using it.

✳

Sir David Brewster, letter to W. H. F. Talbot, 3 July 1843

In the early days, public unfamiliarity with the photographic art and its protagonists meant that newspaper advertisements were verbal loudhailers. The claims were extravagant – of technical and aesthetic improvement, of novelty, of foreign skill. They were backed by the often innocent press. Our problem of understanding their actual achievement in photography is appreciable – photographs have disappeared over time; those we have may not be identified.

Robert Adamson and the Hill-Adamson partnership

This reverse is true in the work of the calotype partnership of David Octavius Hill (1802–77) and Robert Adamson (1821–48).[1] Adamson was the first professional calotypist in the capital. He had leased the highest house on Calton Hill, in a position just below the magnificent viewing platform for the city found by Walter Scott and J. M. W. Turner, amongst others. The roof of his house is seen in Turner's watercolour, 'Edinburgh from the Calton Hill', c.1819.[2] While other city photographers set up studios precariously on rooftops, and generally glassed them over, Adamson had a south-facing garden roughly a thousand feet above sea level and elevated above the worst of the city's pollution.

Something unexpected then happened.

Silence.

Adamson, who had expended a considerable sum of money in his new profession, did not advertise at this point or, independently, at all within the next four years. Hill and Adamson's partnership shared the collaborative character, which advanced photography in the early years, but it was also distinguished by Adamson's reticence [FIGS 4.1, 4.2]. He

Opposite, Fig. 4.5 (detail): D. O. Hill and Robert Adamson, 92nd Gordon Highlanders at Edinburgh Castle, April 1846.

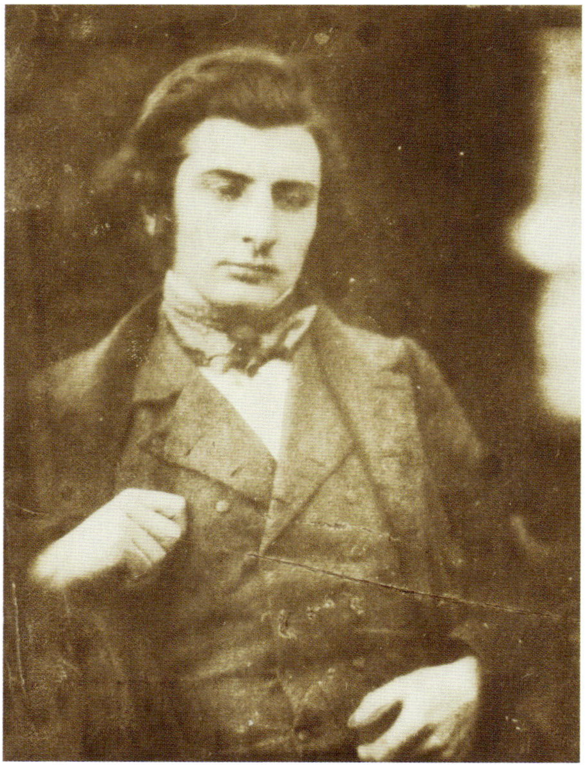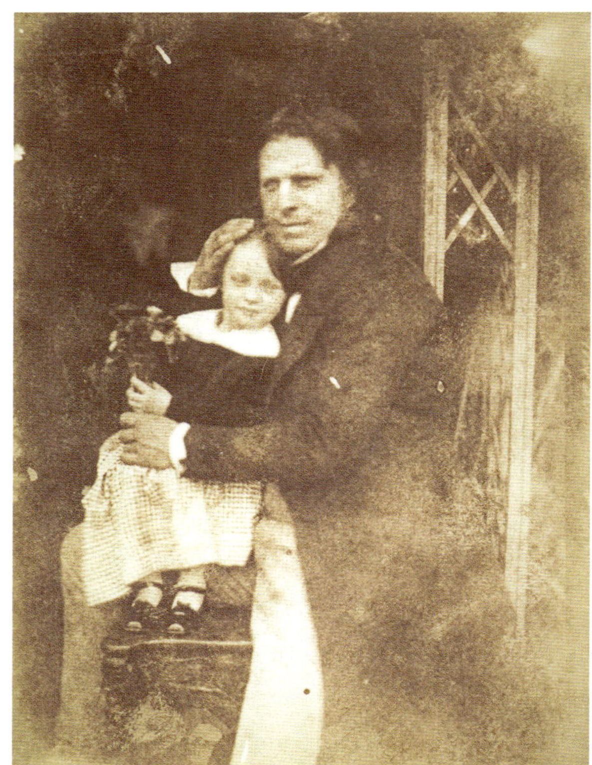

and his brother, Dr John Adamson in St Andrews, continued to experiment together in the course of the partnership, but neither communicated his expert knowledge to
the public while Robert was in business. John Adamson
published their improvements of the calotype only after
Robert had died.[3] Hill spoke for them in 1845:

About three years ago this said process was chemically
and artistically speaking a very miserable affair. … I say
entre nous that I believe Dr Adamson & his brother to be
the fathers of many of those parts of the process which
make it a valuable and practical art. I believe also from
all I have seen that Robert Adamson is the most successful manipulator the art has yet seen, and his steady
industry and knowledge of chemistry, is such that both
from him and his brother much new improvements
may yet be expected ….[4]

The scientific author and geologist Hugh Miller (1802–56),
in introducing his extended review of Hill and Adamson's
work, noted Adamson's quietude in a moral argument:

There are some two or three slight advantages which
real merit has, that fictitious merit has not; among
the rest, an especial advantage, which, we think, should
recommend it to at least the quieter members of
society – the advantage of being unobtrusive and
modest. It presses itself much less on public notice
than its vagabond antagonist, and makes much less
noise; it walks, for a time at least, as if slippered in felt.

Tactfully, Miller did not set up a contrast between the
practice of the calotype and the daguerreotype, but took
the opportunity to attack the then fashionable performance of phreno-mesmerism (a combination of hypnosis
and feeling the bumps on the head):

Phreno-mesmerism and the calotype have been introduced to the Edinburgh public about much the same time; but how differently have they fared hitherto! A real invention, which bids fair to produce some of the greatest revolutions in the fine arts of which they have ever been the subject, has as yet attracted comparatively little notice; an invention which serves but to demonstrate that the present age, with all its boasted enlightenment, may yet not be very unfitted for the reception of superstitions the most irrational and gross, is largely occupying the attention of the community, and filling column after column in our public prints. We shall venture to take up the quieter invention of the two as the genuine one, – as the invention which will occupy the most space a century hence ... .[5]

Miller was the editor of the newspaper, the *Witness*, which was established to support the Free Church movement. Adamson had arrived in Edinburgh at a critical moment. On 18 May about a third of the ministers of the Church of Scotland broke away from the General Assembly in protest at the method of patronage then exercised by landowners, and founded the Free Church. The ministers thus lost their means of livelihood for a principle. D. O. Hill was deeply impressed by the event and started a great historical painting at the meetings of the new church. David Brewster observed him sketching and suggested Hill come to Adamson's studio, with a view to using calotype photography as an aid. The two men made trials and set to work. Brewster reported to Talbot on 21 July:

They have succeeded beyond their most sanguine expectations. – They have taken, on a small scale, Groups of <u>25</u> persons in the same picture all placed in attitudes which the Painter desired, and very large Pictures besides have been taken of each individual to assist the Painter in the completion of his Picture.

Mr D. O. Hill the Painter is in the act of entering into Partnership with Mr Adamson, and proposes to apply the Calotype to many other general purposes of a very popular kind, & especially to the execution of large pictures representing different bodies & classes of individuals.

I think you will find that we have, in Scotland, found out the value of your invention not before yourself, but before those to whom you have given the privilege of using it.[6]

It is a mark of how impressed Hill was by the beauty of Adamson's prints and the aesthetic potential of the medium that this partnership was already determined to go beyond sketching portraits for one ambitious painting. They were considering other large paintings and encompassing 'many other general purposes of a very popular kind'. Hill, who had succeeded in a publishing venture before, was evidently thinking of publication on an impressive scale.

They held their first exhibition of the drawings and photographs for the Free Church painting in the week beginning 12 July.[7] While Hill could make drawings during the Free Church sessions, the groups and individual portraits of the ministers and other key figures, including Hugh Miller, required him to bring the sitters to the studio by appointment – at a time when they were phenomenally busy. The studio organisation must have crested on the same wave of excitement that created the Free Church itself.

So far as we know, Hill and Adamson had one assistant, Jessie Mann (d.1867). Since she, like Hill, originally came from Perth, it may be assumed that Hill introduced her to the studio.[8] She is of importance as one of a mere handful of identifiable women working so early in photography. James Nasmyth, in a letter to Hill, expressed the energy and devotion of the trio:

> … how goes on the divine solar art? and how does that worthy artist Mr Adamson the authentic contriver & manipulator in the art of light and darkness? and thrice worthy Miss Mann that most skillfull and zealous of assistants you must excuse me bothering you with so many questions of that kind as I have the remembrance of All on Em so clearly calotyped in my minds Eye as last I saw them in full manipulation of the divine art of light.[9]

Nasmyth was visually and technically sophisticated, so his high opinion of Robert Adamson and Jessie Mann is important. He was the only visitor to the studio to mention Miss Mann.[10] Jessie Mann wrote to Hill in May 1856, in the hope of borrowing photographic equipment for Rev. Thomas Smith, a Free Church missionary just home from Calcutta and who was 'very fond of that amusement (of taking views and portraits)'.[11] From the letter, we can deduce a close and merry relationship within the studio – Miss Mann addresses Hill:

> Dear D. O.
> Isabelle thinks I should say *Darling D. O.* because you are *her darling*; so you can read it any way you like best.[12]

Within the first year of the partnership, Hill and Adamson followed the Free Church to their meeting in Glasgow in September, took photographs in Greyfriars' Churchyard and commenced work in the fishing village of Newhaven. In the spring of 1844 the partnership took on a new dynamic. Hill moved in with Adamson and they commissioned a large-scale camera from Thomas Davidson, which was designed to take architectural or landscape photographs up to 16 x 13 inches, or smaller groups and single portraits. They planned to make photographs which would offer a direct challenge to the excellent contemporary print makers.

In the summer, they advertised the publication of no less than six volumes of calotypes at five guineas each: *The Fishermen and Women of the Firth of Forth, Highland Character and Costume, The Architectural Structures of Edinburgh, The Architectural Structures of Glasgow, Old Castles, Abbeys &c in Scotland,* and *Portraits of Distinguished Scotchmen.*[13] Although many of the photographs were taken for these projects, with the sad exception of the structures of Glasgow, the albums were not published.

In late September 1844, they travelled south to York at Brewster's suggestion to take photographs during the meeting of the British Association for the Advancement of Science – their only excursion into England. Hill and Adamson took some fine photographs, including architectural calotypes of York Minster [Fig. 4.3] and Durham Cathedral, which demonstrate the excellence of their large camera.

While in York they met Talbot for the first time, but despite Hill's sending him a formal invitation to sit, they did not photograph him. It was an unexpectedly stressful occasion. Talbot had been asked to give a report on photography, but had made the tactical error of saying (rather

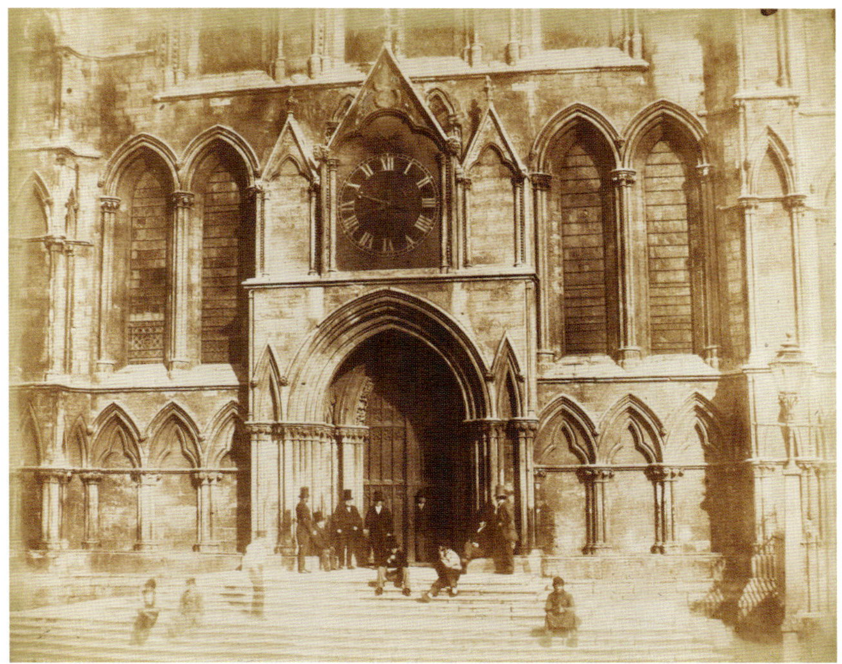

Fig. 4.3: D. O. Hill and Robert Adamson, York Minster, south door, September 1844, calotype. (National Museums Scotland, T.1977.4.3)

late in the day): 'Beyond the branch which I myself cultivate, I have but little knowledge of the photographic processes which have been devised; and as it would be peculiarly necessary for me to do full justice to the discoveries of others this would require an amount of reading and research on my part to which my time is inadequate.'[14] He added that he intended to be in Belgium at the time of the meeting, but then decided to come. There were a number of photographic methods aired in the meetings, by authorities in the field such as John Herschel, Robert Hunt and Professor William Grove. Talbot was then left in the invidious position of challenging the papers – objecting to the new names for processes and claiming priority in his own research. This generated bad feeling and Talbot came away from the meeting feeling ill – possibly from anxiety. Hill and Adamson, working with Talbot's process, also encountered critical hostility. Hill was still discouraged five months later, when he wrote to David Roberts:

His Lordship [Lord Northampton, a notable patron] I had the honour to Calotype at York, and succeeded in making what I think a singularly Rembrantish & very

fine study. I did a few other things at York – which by the Yorkites have since been considered beastly affairs (though a few of them were among the best things I have tried) but one Yorkites opinion consoles me – for Etty saw in them revivals of Rembrant Titian and Spagnoletto. A little more of the Calotype in the Spring months & in all probability I will then leave it to be worked out by less occupied hands.[15]

After the British Association meeting, Talbot went north to Scotland with Nicolaas Henneman. There they toured with the intention of taking calotypes of architecture and landscape relating to the life and writings of Sir Walter Scott.[16] The following year they produced albums of twenty-three of the photographs as *Sun Pictures in Scotland*, the first photographic publication concerning one subject.

Talbot, like most of his contemporaries, saw Scotland largely in Walter Scott's terms. The landscape of Scott's novels and poetry was familiar – people recognised the real places from the words; the land presented a stage for his fiction, and the photographs in turn would conjure up the words. Talbot spent three weeks in Scotland, first in the

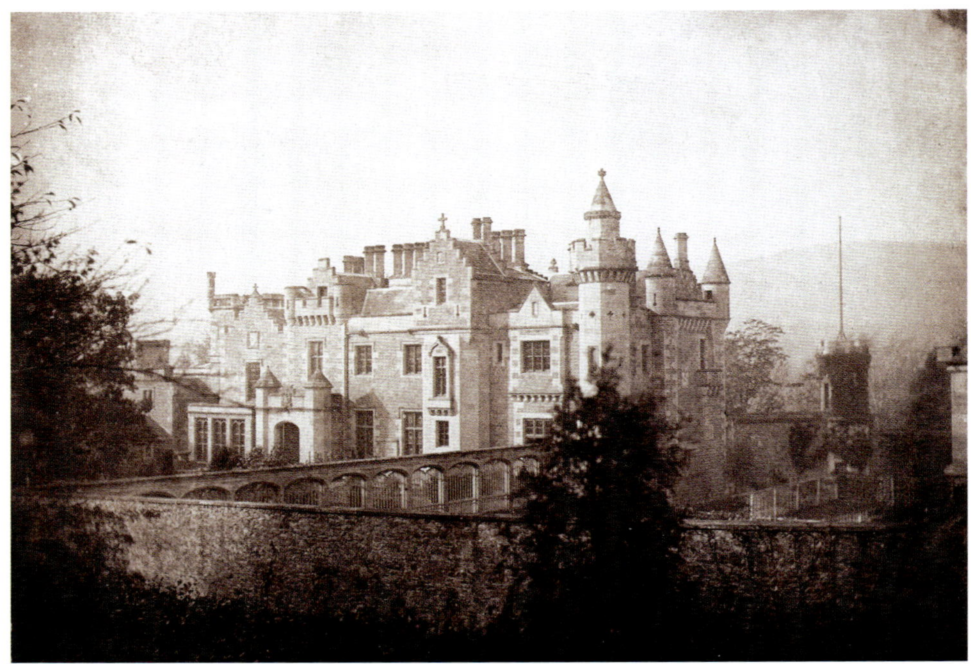

Borders taking the Abbeys, though frustrated by 'extremely dark weather' in the two days he spent at Jedburgh. Making photographs while travelling was particularly difficult as the negatives were at their best soon after processing and preferably slightly damp. While they could not control the autumn light levels, the cooler and wetter weather made the calotype more sensitive; they prepared the paper in advance and sandwiched it between sheets of glass. They then moved to Edinburgh, west to Hamilton and Lanark, then up to Loch Katrine – the most resonant and romantic of Walter Scott's settings, for the poem, 'The Lady of the Lake'. Talbot returned south via Melrose Abbey, Abbotsford and Dryburgh, where Scott is buried [Fig. 4.4].

This suggests something of a role reversal, with Hill and Adamson photographing a scientific meeting and Talbot proposing to calotype the poetic landscape; Hill may have been disconcerted to find Talbot tackling a subject so close to his own heart. They do not seem to have conversed, even when Talbot was in Edinburgh, staying in a hotel at the foot of Calton Hill.[17] Talbot had made the critical move in connecting photography to the tourist industry, but his motivation seems a little doubtful – he had planned to go to Belgium, and the decision to substitute Scotland may have been spontaneous or even have an element of accident. It is possible that he was responding to the challenge of Hill and Adamson's work in England by moving into their territory.

In 1845, Hill was pursuing another ambitious idea, the publishing of albums containing a hundred calotypes:

I say that this first book of English Calotype *pictures*, for really Talbot's examples in his *Pencil of Nature* are not intended to be such, should be such as to make the French look only second best in their Sun Painting efforts. It should almost be a book worthy of the [tables] of sovereigns and of the highest cognoscenti. Now there is my naked bosom in the matter, which I hope will not make you rate me as absolute and arragant as Petruccio, making you exclaim, 'Why! This gallant will command the sun'.[18]

Some of these albums were constructed, and one was sent down to London to be shown at the gallery of the art dealer Dominic Colnaghi. The landscape painter David

Fig. 4.4 (opposite): William Henry Fox Talbot, 'Abbotsford', 1844, calotype from *Sun Pictures in Scotland*, plate IV. (National Media Museum/Science & Society Picture Library, 1937-1345-0001)

Fig. 4.5 (right): D. O. Hill and Robert Adamson, 92nd Gordon Highlanders at Edinburgh Castle, April 1846, calotype. (National Museums Scotland, T.1977.4.7)

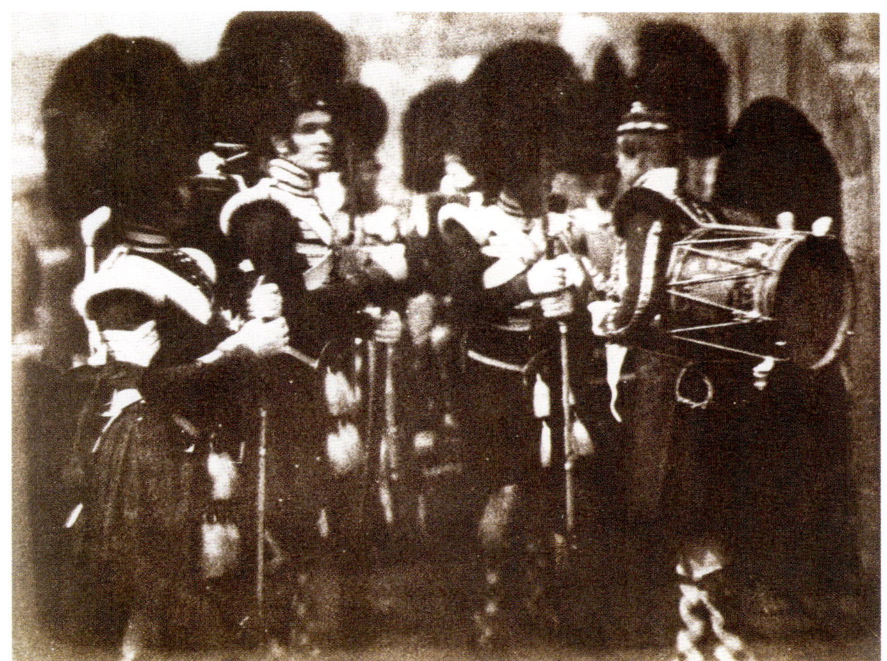

Roberts reported that Colnaghi had concealed it under his counter. The essential problem was undoubtedly that Hill never succeeded in negotiating with Talbot, who had sold the patent rights to other photographers in London and who set up Nicolaas Henneman in business in Reading. Hill and Adamson's activity in Edinburgh did not conflict with the patent; but selling in the lucrative London market would have done, and doubtless Colnaghi was nervously aware of the fact.

Ironically, the original motive for the Hill and Adamson partnership, the great Free Church painting, was hindered by photography – they took hundreds of portraits and the painting was not finished for more than twenty years. In 1846, Hill followed up on the intention expressed by Brewster in 1843, using photography to inform paintings, 'representing different bodies & classes of individuals', in painting a large-scale picture of Edinburgh from the Castle, for which they took panoramic studies and photographs of soldiers on duty at the Castle [Fig. 4.5]. This painting shows the city in its extraordinary uprearing, volcanic perspective, crowded with many people drawn from the calotypes.[19]

Hill's primary motivation in working with photo-graphy was not an interest in making money. The Hill and Adamson partnership did not set up a portrait studio and wait for customers to turn up and be photographed. Hill specifically said:

> I have sunk some hundreds of pounds and a huge cantle of my time in these Calotype freaks. I think the art may be nobly applied – much money could be made of it as a means of cheap likeness making – but this my soul loathes; and if I do not succeed in doing something by it worthy of being mentioned by Artists with honor – I will very likely soon have done with it.[20]

This is not an immediately obvious point, because the main body of their work lies in single portraits and groups. These portraits, from the pictures of the Scottish ministers to photographs of small children, have both the clarity of direct human communication, and the articulacy of the beautiful prints which present that communication without barrier to a modern world.

The range of people, exotic figures like Rev. Peter Jones or Kahkewaquonaby of the Mississauga/Ojibway tribes

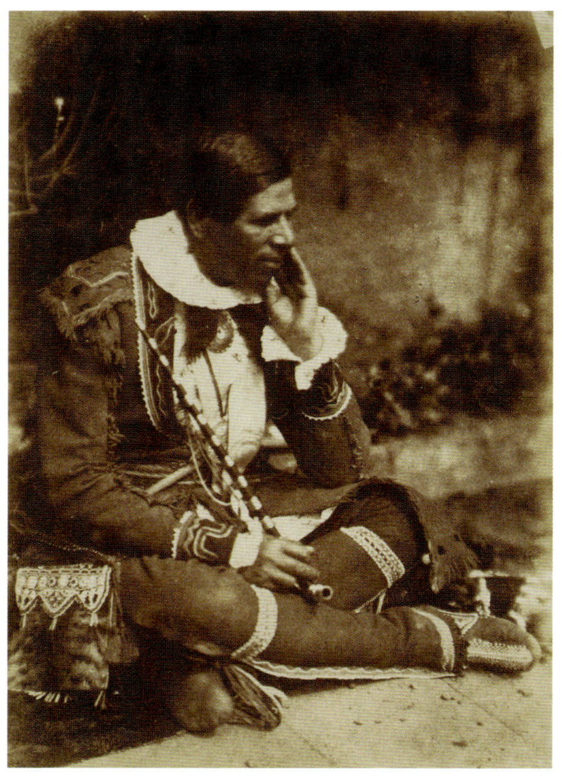

in North America [FIG. 4.6], to artists such as James Drummond, or authoritative writers such as Mrs Jameson, is very impressive. They explored character and they constructed groups. They built their compositions from a sophisticated understanding of light and atmosphere.

Both men, working with Miss Mann, were engaged in exploring and pushing the calotype process, chemically and aesthetically. It has been shown that as late as October 1846, Adamson was experimenting with the chemistry of his work – in one portrait session he used three different formulae for three photographs; Hill rearranged the portrait for each photograph.[21] They compounded the risk in the cause of experiment. Their effective partnership lasted somewhere between three to four years in all. The dated negatives end in the summer of 1846, although they are known to have taken important photographs afterwards. It may be that Adamson's health deteriorated then. At the end of 1847, he returned home to St Andrews. There, in January 1848, Robert Adamson died.

On 18 January, Hill wrote in distress:

… I have today assisted in consigning to the cold earth all that was earthly of my amiable true & affectionate Robert Adamson. He died in the full hope of a blessed resurrection. His truehearted family are mourning sadly especially his brother the Doctor – who has watched [?] him as a child during his long illness – I have seldom seen such a deep & manly sorrow. Poor Adamson has not left his like in his art of which he was so modest.[22]

The Cundell Brothers and James Nasmyth

John and Robert Adamson were highly-skilled experimental chemists. Their success with the calotype process in 1842 was a personal achievement. For most people the process remained intractable. In February 1844, the London-based George Smith Cundell (*c.*1798–1882) published an account of the calotype, which was credited with making Talbot's idea comprehensible and workable. His article began by comparing the success of the daguerreotype and the calotype process: '… while the Daguerreotype was at once understood and successfully practised, over the whole civilized world, most of the few persons who have attempted the sister art, after failing of success, have given it up in disappointment.'

He did not conceal his impatience:

Had Mr Talbot thought fit to publish directions for the details and refinement of his process, as minute and explicit as those given by M. Daguerre, his invention, it is probable, would now have stood in a very different position. … it is with the hope of promoting its improvement, by removing some of the difficulties left at the threshold … that I have been tempted to offer this little treatise to the public … with every respect for the distinguished author of the calotype, I hope I may without impropriety do that which he has omitted to do, by furnishing plain directions, from my own experience, by which calotype pictures may be produced, without much difficulty and with tolerable certainty and success.[23]

His work was pointedly quoted during the dispute with Talbot over his patent, which hindered experiment and development and, equally pointedly, is one of the publications listed in Lady Eastlake's 1857 article on the progress of photography. She told the history in this way:

In the execution of a process so delicate and at the best so capricious as that of photography, the experience of numbers, such as only free-trade can secure, is required to define the more or less practical methods. Mr. F. Talbot's directions, though sufficient for his own pre-instructed hand, were too vague for the tyro; and an enlistment into the ranks of the 'Pilgrims of the Sun' seldom led to any result but that of disappointment. Thus, with impediments of this serious nature, photography made but slow way in England; and the first knowledge to many even of her existence came back to us from across the Border. It was in Edinburgh where the first earnest, professional practice of the art began, and the calotypes of Messrs. Hill and Adamson remain to this day the most picturesque specimens of the new discovery.

It was at this crisis that a paper published in the 'Philosophical Transactions' [*sic*] of May, 1844, by Mr. George Cundell, gave in great measure the fresh stimulus that was needed. The world was full of the praise of the daguerreotype, but Mr. Cundell stood forth as the advocate of the calotype or paper process, pointed out its greater simplicity and inexpensiveness of apparatus, its infinite superiority in the power of multiplying its productions, and then proceeded to give those careful directions for the practice, which, though containing no absolutely new element, yet suggested many a minute correction where every minutia is important.[24]

Cundell followed his explanation of the calotype with an article on 'Combination of Lenses for the Camera', designed to correct lens distortion by mounting two Wollaston lenses about a central stop. This came after Davidson's similar proposal in 1841 for a 'Combination Lens or Symmetrical Doublet'. Amongst other advantages, such a combination reduced the evident curves given to straight lines in architectural photographs.[25] Cundell's camera design, provided with a focussing scale, the lens shielded by a hood and with internal baffles to minimise reflections inside, was made and sold by George Knight and Sons in Cheapside in 1845.[26] He published another article in 1846, on 'Gallo-Nitrate of Silver'.[27]

Cundell showed photographs at the Graphic Society meeting in London in 1844, and the critical reception was most gratifying:

The principal attractions among the contributions towards the evening's artistic gratification were the always interesting sketches of Roberts in the Holy Land,

&c.; a portfolio of drawings by Sir David Wilkie; and a series of representations of figures and landscape produced by the agency of the sun. These were contributed, we believe, by Mr Cundell, and not only manifested considerable skill in the arrangement as regards the production of light and shade, but were justly considered perfect curiosities when regarded as the immediate offspring of the solar rays …. Two specimens particularly struck us: one as coming so near to the deeply-marked productions of Rembrandt – a head coming out brightly from a mass of deep shadow; the other a group of persons reposing in the sunshine in the garden-front of a house. The bricks, the roses, and the pleasant party ranged themselves before the eye with a brilliancy and an exactitude that, from the admirable look of nature, paid the highest compliment to the Dutch painters, by reminding every spectator of them. A book of well-collected Rembrandt etchings also lay on the table ….[28]

Both Roberts and David Wilkie were Scottish artists, and the context may not have been coincidental. The commentary is of interest partly because it implies that the members were still unfamiliar with the calotype.

Cundell was to be found later showing calotypes in a different, scientific, setting. The surgeon Alfred Smee was a neighbour in Finsbury Circus in London and had himself published an article detailing the chemical manipulations of photogenic drawing in 1839.[29] In 1847, Smee held a soirée to address the terrible question of the potato famine, presently devastating Ireland and the Highlands. He served variations of bread, which might help to alleviate the problem, to two to three hundred of 'the most distinguished professional and literary men' of London.[30] The newspapers reported that 'The room also held various tables showing examples of the use of gutta percha, beautiful examples of electro statues, electro plating, gilding, &c. There were also fine specimens of Daguerreotype and Calotype exhibited by M. Gassiot and Mr Cundell.'[31]

It may be no coincidence that Smee, like Cundell, was engaged with the photographic suppliers, Horne and Thornthwaite. A portrait of G. S. Cundell appears in an album which belonged to the firm. They were amongst the earliest suppliers of photographic equipment and chemicals in London and, in the 1850s, they sold Cundell's camera design.[32]

In 1848, Cundell was recorded as making photographs on the principle of Wheatstone's version of stereoscopic imagery, using mirrors:

> Professor Wheatstone, in his researches into light and optics, discovered a property in optics, previous to the perfecting of calotype pictures, to which Mr Cundell has since successfully applied it, and which, while most extraordinary, in an optical point of view, will probably lead to discoveries in the delicate arts of obtaining sunlight pictures … of very considerable importance. On placing two calotype pictures of the same object in the grooves against the uprights – such, for instance, as a jug vase, a piece of statuary, geometrical figures, &c, each eye of course sees the reflection in the corresponding mirror ….[33]

Finsbury Circus was also home to the London Institution, which was established to provide a fine library, reading rooms and a lecture theatre, predominantly for scientific issues. By 1852 Smee, Gassiot and Cundell were all advisors.

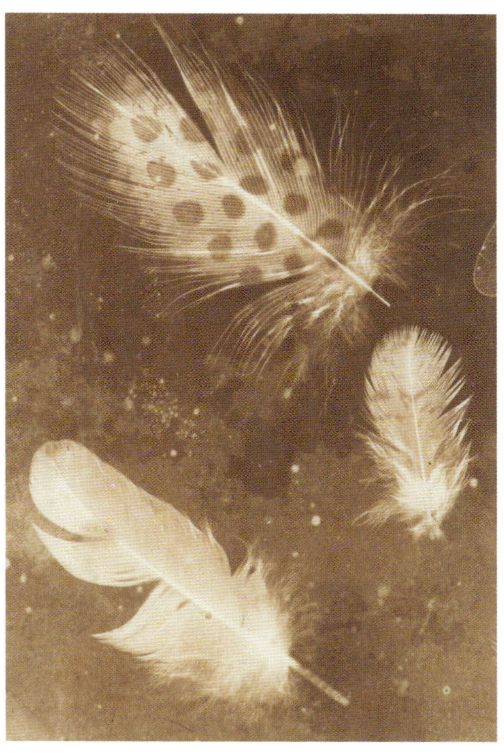

Fig. 4.7: A member of the Cundell family, 'Feathers', c.1845, photogenic drawing. (Gernsheim Collection, Harry Ransom Center, University of Texas at Austin, fTR655.11.39)

The catalogue published then included a copy of Cundell's 1844 article and a set of 'Fourteen Calotype Pictures, executed by the Author', illustrative of the paper.[34] Cundell could not have published calotypes for sale, so presumably this was done only for the Institution's library, where they could have been seen by large numbers of people.

The Cundell brothers were the children of a brewer based in Leith, and Joseph Cundell (c.1802–1907) stayed there as the agent of the British Linen Bank. At least three of them were involved in photography, and they evidently travelled at intervals from the south to the north, via York.[35] They were a sociable group and generous in distributing their photographs. They took a number of calotypes in the environs of London, on familiar walks which James Nasmyth, a close friend of George, described.[36] Their early landscape photographs are engaging, small-scale pieces of their territory. Three photographs taken on the estates at Traquair, in the Scottish borders, imply that George, who was factor to the Earl of Traquair for his estates in the West Indies, visited on professional business, and stayed long enough to enjoy photography.[37] Henry Cundell (1810–86), who was an amateur painter, is the only one who exhibited in the 1850s, and he figured in touring exhibitions set up by the London Society of Arts between 1852 and 1854. His photographs ranged from pictures taken in North Wales, to Perthshire, Durham and Kensington. The Cundell album of photographs held in George Eastman House refers to him as 'the artist', and this may mean that he took most of the pictures in that particular book.[38] Their work remained comparatively small in scale, but displays a wide, exploratory range of interest [Fig. 4.7].

In the albums and collections that contain examples of their work, it is not easy to allocate work to individuals. But from these groups of material, we can connect the Cundells to a number of people. Photographs in the Texas album are ascribed to 'G. Munby' in 1842.[39] He was presumably the Edinburgh-born botanist, Giles Munby, brother-in-law of the Cundells; two of the brothers married Munby sisters. The Edinburgh Central Library album belonged to the painter, James Eckford Lauder, and includes work by Hill and Adamson.[40] James Nasmyth, who was a close friend of G. S. Cundell, whom he addressed admiringly as 'the worthy master', and also of D. O. Hill, may have acted as a conduit between Manchester, London and Edinburgh. He was photographed by the Cundells and by Hill and Adamson, and took an encouraging interest in photography in the 1840s.

When he retired from his highly successful engineering business in 1856, Nasmyth was only forty-eight. He turned his mind to astronomy, but also to photography:

I had an earnest desire to acquire the art and mystery of practical photography. I bought the necessary apparatus,

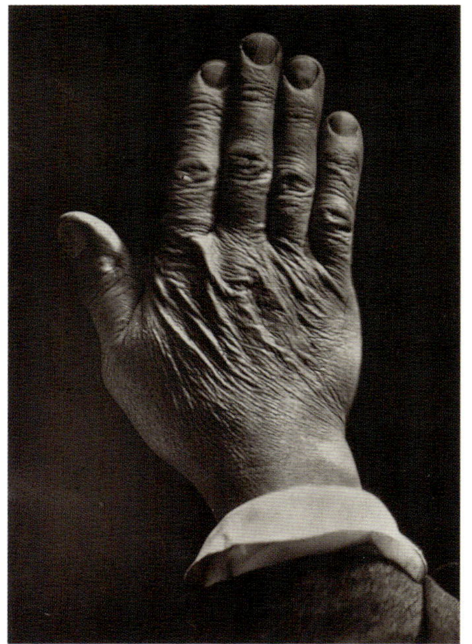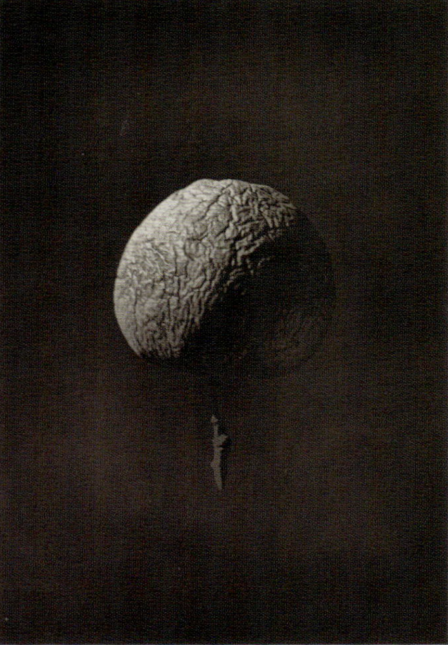

Figs 4.8: James Nasmyth, 'Back of Hand & Wrinkled Apple', Woodbury-type, from James Nasmyth and James Carpenter, *The Moon, Considered as a Planet a World and a Satellite*, 1874. (The Riddell Collection, Scottish National Portrait Gallery, PGP R 830.1 and 2)

together with the chemicals; and before long I became an expert in the use of the positive and negative collodion process, including the printing from negatives, in all the details of that wonderful and delightful art. To anyone who has some artistic taste, photography, both in its interesting processes and glorious results, becomes a most attractive and almost engrossing pursuit. It is a delightful means of educating the eye for artistic feeling, as well as educating the hands in delicate manipulation.[41]

He combined his two enthusiasms in making a study of the moon, producing a book. This included a pleasing analogy between the surface of the moon, a wrinkled hand (his own) and a shrivelled apple, to express his understanding that the surface of the moon might have dried in the wrinkles characteristic of age [Figs 4.8].[42] There is a significant element of his character and his professional knowledge contained in the image; Nasmyth strongly believed in the tactile sense:

The truth is that the eyes and fingers – *the bare fingers* – are the two principal inlets to sound practical instruction. They are the chief sources of trustworthy knowledge in all the materials and operations with which an engineer has to deal. No *book* knowledge can avail for that purpose. The nature and properties of the materials must come in through the finger ends.[43]

The argument holds well for the photography of his contemporaries.

John Muir Wood

The leading Scottish figure amongst the photographers whose work appears in the albums associated with the Cundells, was the musician John Muir Wood (1805–92).[44] His father was a successful piano maker, with a factory at Calton Hill in Edinburgh. By profession, Wood himself was a pianist, who trained in Paris with Pixis in 1826 and with Carl Czerny in Vienna in 1827. By this time, the family firm was in difficulties, so he initially worked as a teacher. He became an entrepreneur, setting up performances for Franz Liszt and Charles Hallé, and at least one literary event, for William Makepeace Thackeray. In 1848 Wood arranged the concerts for Frédéric Chopin held in Glasgow. Julius

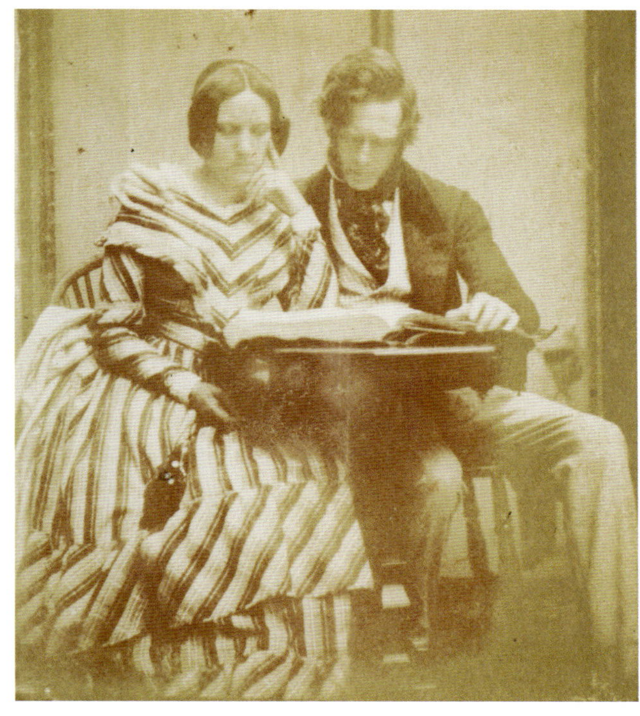

Fig. 4.9: J. M. Wood, 'Henry and Lucy Cundell', 1840s, calotype. (John Muir Wood Collection, Scottish National Portrait Gallery, PGP W 50)

Seligmann remembered Muir Wood telling him that 'he had never had so much difficulty in arranging a concert as on this occasion. Chopin constantly changed his mind …'.[45] It is perhaps unsurprising that Wood has not left us a photograph of Chopin, but sadly he does not seem to have taken pictures of any of the famous people for whom he arranged performances in Scotland.

In 1853 to 1854, Wood organised the first season of international opera in Edinburgh and Glasgow, a programme of no less than twelve different productions. A notice of the operas, published in the *Glasgow Herald* in January 1854, declared that they comprised

> … some of the most popular, newest and most excellent operas in the entire range of the musical drama, we think that there can be no doubt that Mr Wood, as *entrepreneur*, will find his bold and onerous speculation will redound as much to his profit as it will speak for his mercantile daring and artistic taste.[46]

Wood was a European, regularly visiting London and the Continent to market pianos, and to stay in touch with contemporary music. His photographs show him to have visited Ireland, Belgium, France and Germany. His Scottish photography was more evidently related to his leisure time.

With John Muir Wood we have the photographs, but only an uncertain knowledge of his photographic training or practice. Through the care and the generosity of his family he has left us a body of work of between 800 and 900 images – both negative and positive. The first certain date for his photography, which comes from Wood's diary of a trip abroad, is 1847, but the pictures from this group are successful, which argues that he began work earlier. His photography carries through into the 1860s. Wood was evidently connected to Joseph Cundell in Leith, and to Charles Edward Cundell, who was in Edinburgh in the 1840s, apparently as a wine merchant, and he also took (or owned) a photograph of Henry and Lucy Cundell, who married in 1842 [FIG. 4.9]. His collection contained Cundell work taken in London and includes photographs by Hugh Owen of Bristol, among others.[47] The Wood music-selling business was in Waterloo Place in Edinburgh, which runs from Princes Street to just below Calton Hill, where Hill and Adamson operated. Hill would have walked past the shop every day he worked at the Academy. Since Hill and his family were musical, and indeed attended Wood's first opera season, it is probable that he and Wood were acquainted, and the latter is likely to have seen the Hill and Adamson calotypes on exhibition.[48]

Wood's aesthetic approach may also have involved the artist James Eckford Lauder, who accompanied him on a sketching tour of the west coast in 1841. Lauder's album of photographs by the Cundells included work by Wood.[49] His photography shows a talent for group pictures [FIG.

4.10] and a sensitivity to portraiture. Since Lauder was a genre painter, he may have arranged some of Wood's group photographs or used them as studies; the unusual subject of 'The Wishing Bone' appears in both a Wood photograph of Mr Purdie and his friends and in one of Lauder's exhibited paintings in 1854.[50]

The origins of Wood's technical understanding may be equally diffuse. As he travelled widely and spoke a number of languages, he could have come by photographic knowledge not just in Edinburgh and London, but across Europe. As early as 1827, when in Vienna, he showed an interest in optics. In a letter home, he wrote:

I went to the University to hear a lecture on Optics, & although from my confined knowledge of the language I understood but a small portion of it, still it did not fail to interest me; when it was finished the Professor showed me his collection of Instruments, pointed out their different uses, and even performed experiments on some of them that I might better understand what he meant.[51]

One of the people he photographed was an Irish eye-surgeon, Dr James Jasper MacAldin, who lectured on electricity, chemistry and light, and who may have stimulated Wood's interest [Fig. 4.11]. In the photograph, MacAldin is shown with a little 'Thunder House' for one of the demonstrations, thought amusing in parlour demonstrations of science as well as public lectures: a charge of electricity was sent through the house from the battery and the house fell down. The skull is present to demonstrate the deadly implications of this force.

Wood was open to experiment. When in Ghent in 1847, he encountered '3 *agreeable* Englishmen, Snell, Charles and Wm H Barry, all architects apparently'. Charles Barry was taking calotypes, and Wood noted that he 'got detail of his process & showed mine; his w[or]k sharp but bad in colour & would not print out well.' Despite this opinion, when he was taking views a few days later in Mechelen, he tried Barry's process.[52]

When he and his brother George set up a new business in Glasgow selling music and pianos in 1848, Wood was able to connect more readily to photographers there. In 1850, he joined the Glasgow Philosophical Society, whose Vice President was Walter Crum. It may be that Wood's particular interest in the printing of photographs using different metallic compounds, which give his pictures a rich variation of colour, relates to C. J. Burnett's experiments, which were published with enthusiasm in the mid- to later 1850s.[53] Around 1860, he was one of the earliest experimenters with the carbon process, before it was made practicable.

Wood's originality and the pleasure of his landscape photographs undoubtedly connect to his music and to his sense of nationalism. He travelled extensively throughout Scotland on foot and by water, and knew it well. One of Wood's appealing landscapes, taken on the Island of Staffa in relation to Fingal's Cave, offers us the balance of great geological violence and history with the posed figure of modern man in a top hat [Fig. 4.12]. Wood, whose taste in music was both national and Romantic, may have heard 'the song that the sea waves sing on the great basalt organ pipes of Staffa', and Mendelssohn's great Hebridean overture, in his head, while taking this photograph.[54] The stone resemblance to organ pipes, the reference to Mendelssohn, and even at a stretch the possibility that the figure saw himself here as seated at a great organ, make an unsubtle reference between the photograph and music. But it seems

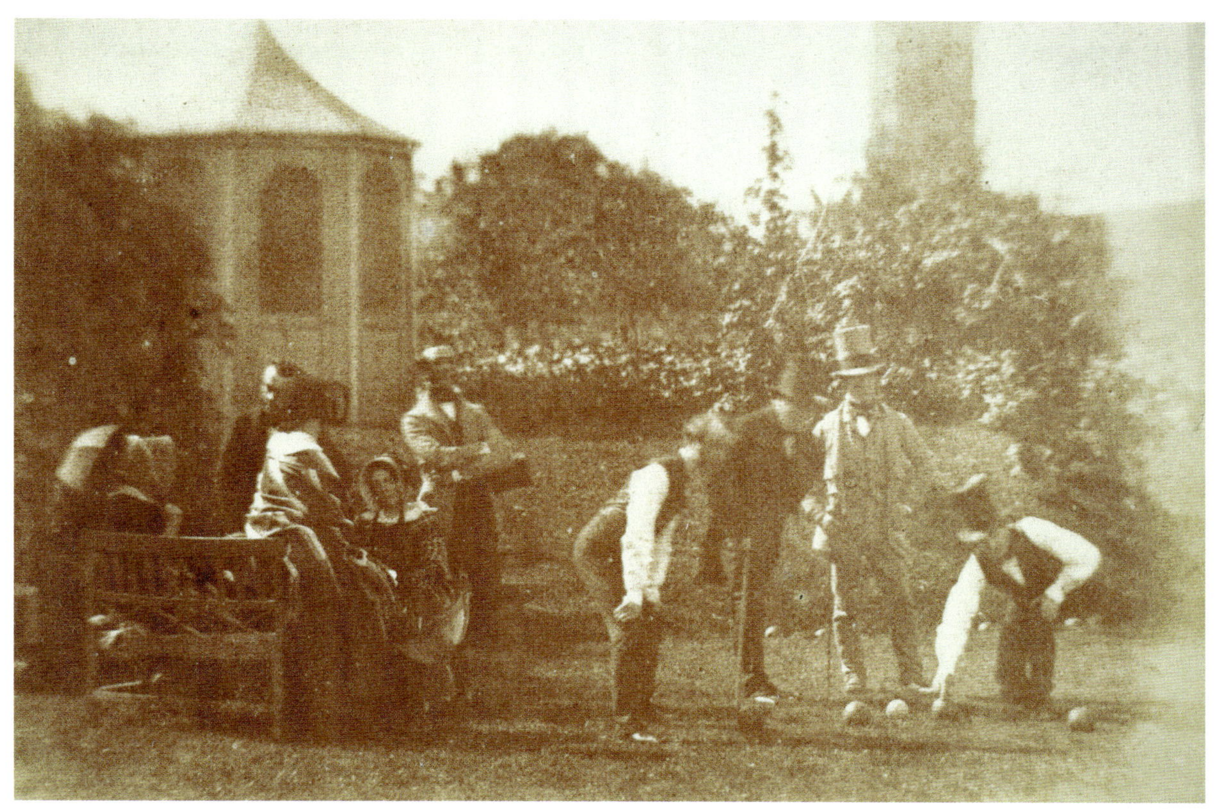

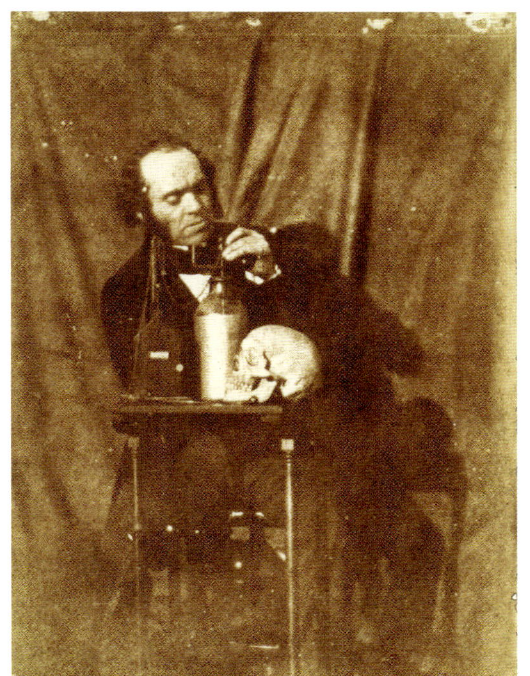

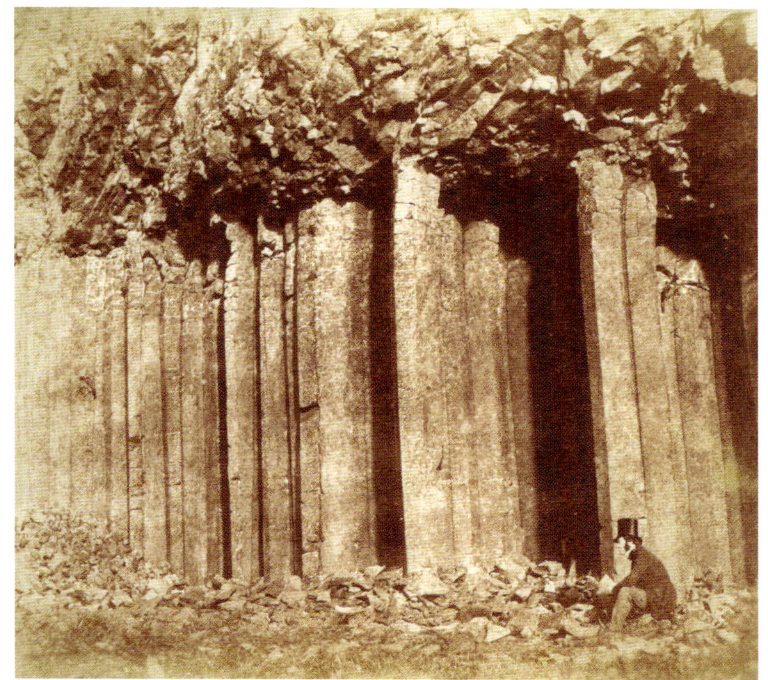

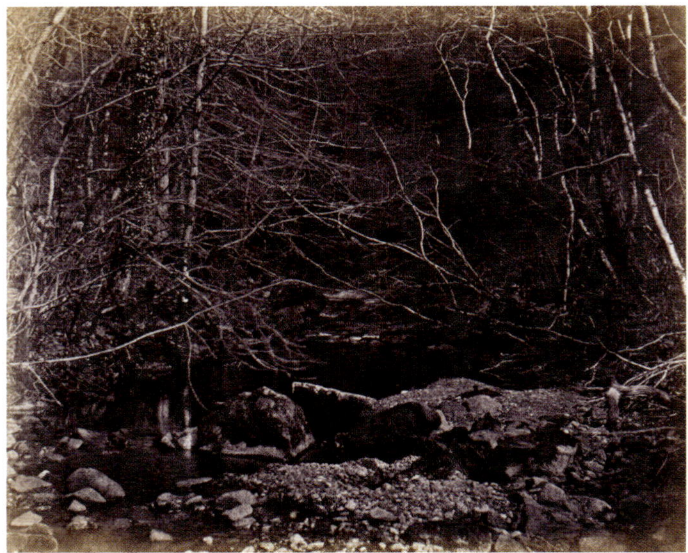

likely that Wood's knowledge of music gave his visual work an additional dimension. The Romantic element in the contemporary music he admired, and in the history of Scotland expressed in its landscape, appears particularly in his woodland photographs. Wood wrote and published work on Scottish music and song. He referred to ancient Gaelic music in these terms: 'The Ossianic chants are short and wild … formless and uninteresting as mere music. From these emerge airs still wild and irregular, but with a certain sublimity arising from their very vagueness.'[55] This is a difficult thought, but can be related to his small, dense pictures of pathless tangle; we are not invited in but the pictures are fascinating [FIG. 4.13].

William Collie

At the other end of the United Kingdom, William Collie (1810–96) had established himself on the island of Jersey by the early 1840s.[56] He was born in Skene, Aberdeenshire. He appears as a portrait painter in the Aberdeen street directory between 1831 and 1837, which may be the point at which he migrated.[57] He figured in the 1841 Census record for Jersey, living in St Helier, as a portrait painter and professor of drawing.

Collie took up photography in the spring of 1847 and engaged in portraiture and studies of the market women [FIG. 4.14]. Indeed he sent a set of his photographs of Jersey market women to the *Art-union* journal in June, where they were favourably reviewed:

Mr W. Collie of Belmont-House, Jersey, an artist of repute, has forwarded to us some examples of 'Calotypes' taken from life. They are copies chiefly of the market women of the island, whose expressions, countenances, & picturesque costumes, are well suited for the purpose. We have seen nothing at all comparable to them, except those of Mr D. O. Hill, of Edinburgh; in both cases we have proofs how greatly this interesting art may be improved in the hands of artists. The calotypes of Mr Collie are wonderfully accurate: each may be indeed a model for a painter: proving how emphatically Art may be assisted by Nature. Some of those before us are likenesses; and we may be justified in describing them as even in this respect highly satisfactory; for a degree of refinement has been obtained of which the art has seemed incapable.[58]

Daguerreotypists had come to the island earlier in the 1840s, but Collie may have been the first to work seriously with the calotype process there.[59]

Collie was joined in his photography by his neighbour, John Brodie (d.1849), who was a distiller, importing Irish whiskey to the island, treating it with an unspecified procedure and re-exporting it to England.[60] Brodie may have connected Collie to the London firm of R. and T. Willats, who supplied photographic equipment and published an instruction manual for the calotype in 1845.[61] An album

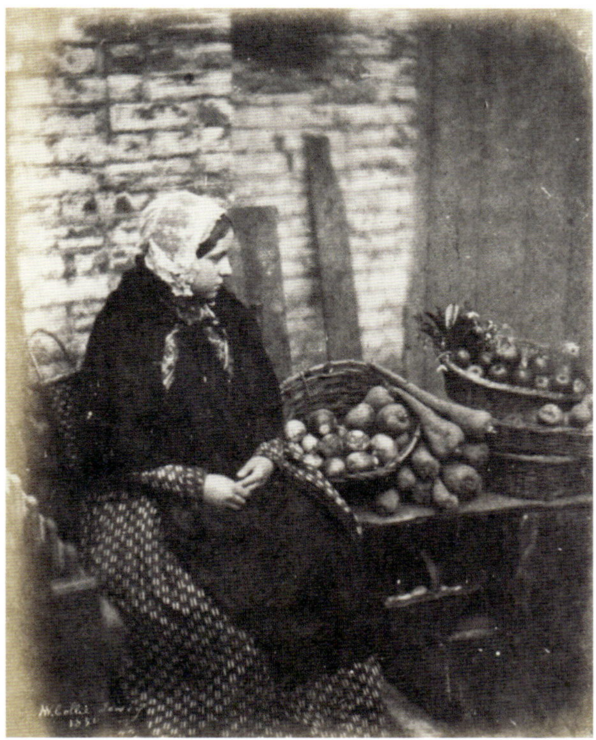

containing work attributed to Brodie, but including images that appear in the Collie album, was assembled by Richard Willats.[62] The social circle shown in these pictures has a distinctly Scottish appearance, as both Collie and Brodie wear Highland bonnets and plaids. Collie himself was engaged as a trustee with the Free Church of Scotland, which built a church in St Helier in 1856.[63]

Collie exhibited at the Great Exhibition in 1851. Perhaps disconcertingly, his work was shown in the Channel Islands context, and the photographs appeared amongst other products of Jersey and Guernsey, including specimens of shells, winter wheat and a 'Pair of Socks, knit without glasses by the contributor (Mrs Bertrams), aged 93'. He exhibited 'Calotype Pictures from Life – "French and Jersey Market-women".'[64] The jury reported, depressingly, that his frame contained '… several calotype pictures, chiefly portraits and domestic scenes. These are not all equally good; many of them are blotty and wanting in depth'.[65]

William Collie wrote of his disappointment in 1860, when he presented a set of photographs to the Photo-graphic Society of London, 'as showing the object I had in their production – namely, the application of our beautiful art to the interesting object of portraying scenes of more general interest than mere portraits …. I have every reason to believe that they were among the first of the kind then attempted ….'[66] But he had been delighted by the review in the *Art-journal* (formerly *Art-union* journal).

> I would have been glad to have turned them to some account, but the patentee, Mr Talbot, interfered with the sale of them in England; I had therefore to content myself with a little fame and less fortune.[67]

I sent a frame containing twenty Calotypes to the Exhibition of 1851, which are mentioned in the Reports of the Juries … only as mere Calotypes, without the slightest reference to the novelty of the application of the Calotype process to living subjects …. The omission could only have been the result of ignorance of the difficulties we had to encounter in getting up those subjects …. The description I appended to my pictures they had the audacity to cover over, and to add one of their own ….

Collie suffered from isolation in his practice, and it may be assumed that he did not connect effectively with D. O. Hill, despite the *Art-journal*'s reference. His pictures have some similarity to Hill and Adamson's Newhaven series because the market women were distinguished by their dress; they were French and a socially different group. He was, like Hill interested in a broad art market and equally frustrated. However, Collie was concerned with making attractive, individual pictures, rather than an interconnected series.

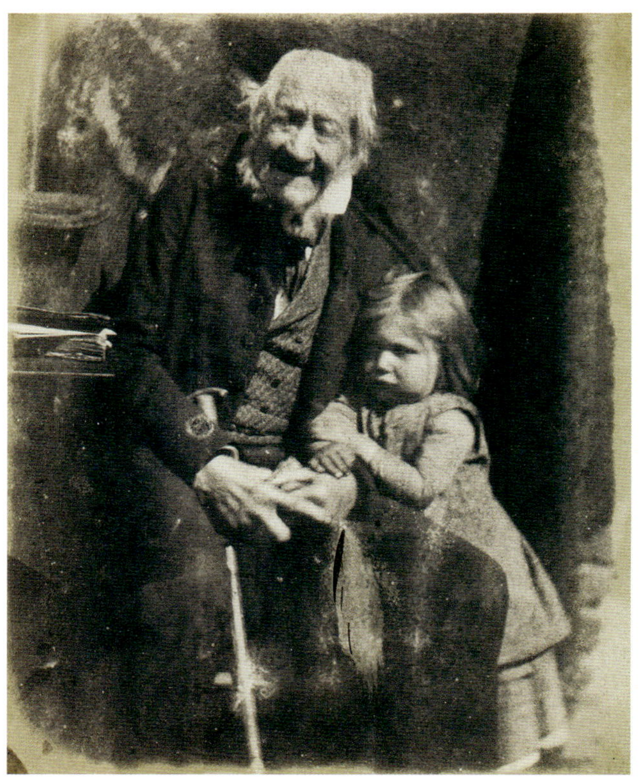

His portraits generally have the relaxed appearance of familiar neighbours and friends. In the picture he made of Elia Filleul 'age 102 with great, great grandchild', the composition is given strength and tenderness by the manner in which the hands connect and the sense that they are holding on to each other, not just physically but in the truly extraordinary sense of the time they encompass [Fig. 4.15].

Collie continued his photographic practice into the 1860s, taking up the collodion process, and attempting landscape photography. He photographed the eclipse of the sun in 1860. It does not seem that he had a wide professional practice in photography, and in Jersey this opportunity was taken up more effectively by others.

Ross and Thomson's early years

James Ross (1816–95) first attempted the calotype process around 1843. He told the story in April 1857:

My attention was first drawn to this subject [of fading] from the circumstances of the very first calotype I ever had in my hand vanishing from my sight while admiring it. It had been merely washed, probably in common salt. This took place some fourteen or fifteen years ago, when in conjunction with Mr Bishop, a very able chemist, I made my first experiments in the art. We soon, or rather I should say my fellow worker soon, mastered the negatives completely, but for some eighteen months or more we entirely failed in fixing the positive proofs.

This chimes well with the experience of the St Andrews circle, in their early attempts to print positives. Robert Bishop, a wood engraver, appears in the Edinburgh street directory for one year in 1844, at 23 Lauriston Place, sharing premises with Ross, a 'portrait and landscape painter'.[68] They persevered with paper photography:

… and it was with no small pride that at the end of six weeks we found a positive unchanged which had been all that time exposed uncovered in the open air to weather of every kind. The cause of our failure had all along been too short a time in the hypo, and too little washing after; but this one … was washed most thoroughly in many changes of boiling water, a mode which Mr Thomson and I still pursue. … the oldest pictures we have are all printed upon Whatman's highly glazed Turkey Mill Paper. Here … is one positive printed by Mr Thomson in 1841, sixteen years ago, without the least appearance of change.[69]

Ross began his profession as a calotypist on Calton Hill in 1845. In September he applied to the Directors of the

National Monument (the uncompleted structure in memory of the fallen during the Napoleonic Wars on the blustery top of the Hill) to rent an area within the fencing, 'to take Calotype portraits'.[70] In April 1847, he was given permission to use small structures designed to house sculpture by Robert Forrest, one as a waiting room and the other to colour the calotypes.

Ross formed a partnership with the daguerreotypist John Thomson (1804–81) in 1847, and the duo set up shop in Princes Street. Their partnership initially offered both calotype and daguerreotype images, with Thomson named as daguerreotypist and Ross as the calotypist. Ross later reminisced:

August 21, 1847. – Mr Keith, printseller, Hanover-street, paid to account 10s. for various calotypes of Holyrood Palace, John Knox's House, Canongate, Tolbooth, High Church, and other old buildings of historical interest. The negatives were all generally taken as early in the day as possible, and printed during the afternoon. The evenings were devoted to the most wearisome part of our labour, viz., preparing the iodised paper, my own working hours being from 5 o'clock in the morning till 10 o'clock at night. … the humble individual now addressing you was in those days rather a public character, never appearing in the street laden with camera, tripod, and plate boards, without being immediately surrounded by a very numerous but not very select crowd of idlers, who were sometimes apt to give vent to their feelings of disappointment, at not seeing the result of my labour, in language far more forcible than polite.

Their prestige and reputation as photographers was assured by the entry made in their ledger on '*May* 12, 1849. – Paid Mr Seaton for binding calotypes for London, £1. 10s. These were specimens sent to Windsor Castle for inspection previous to our being appointed photographers to the Queen – a small investment which soon gave large returns.'[71] This album of calotypes remains in the Royal Collection, as evidence of Ross's ability at this stage[72] [Fig. 4.16]. On 14 June 1849, the firm was granted the Royal Warrant as Photographers at Edinburgh to Her Majesty and advertised itself as 'Photographers to the Queen'.[73]

Possibly because of the premature death of Robert Adamson, Ross and Thomson were commissioned to record a historic building. As Ross recalled:

August 14, 1848. – Mr Bryce, architect, George-street, paid £24 7s. 6d. for some seventy or eighty calotypes, these being various portions of the Old College Kirk, every stone of which was numbered with white paint for the purpose of having it rebuilt exactly as it then stood. Strange to say, these stones, after lying twenty-five years heaped up in the corner of a neighbouring field, are at this very time being rebuilt – to a certain extent, at least – precisely as they originally stood.[74]

This was reported in Dundee:

This venerable edifice, as viewed from the North Bridge, has assumed at the present moment, a curious appearance, every stone of the building being numbered with white paint. … in order to facilitate the labour of reconstructing a similar edifice, the contractors have had Messrs Ross and Thomson, photographers, Princes' Street, busily engaged for some weeks past taking

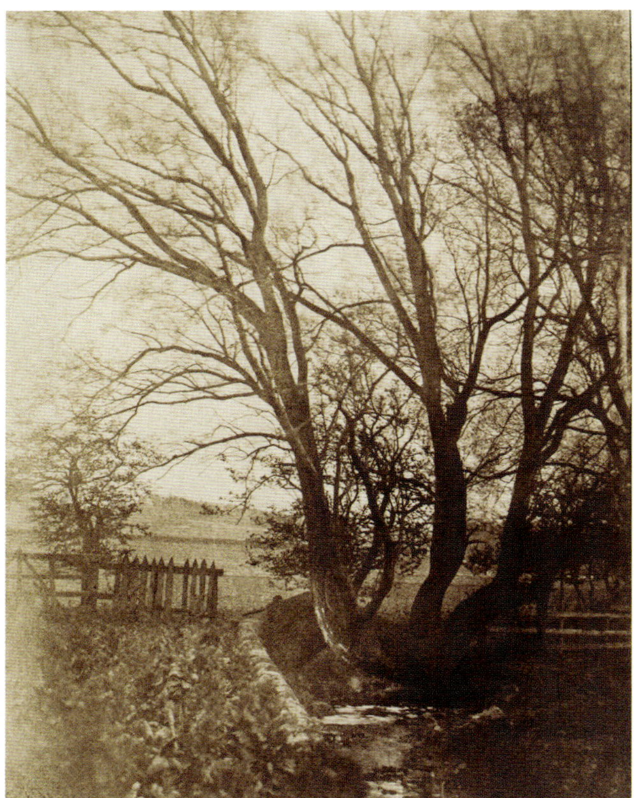

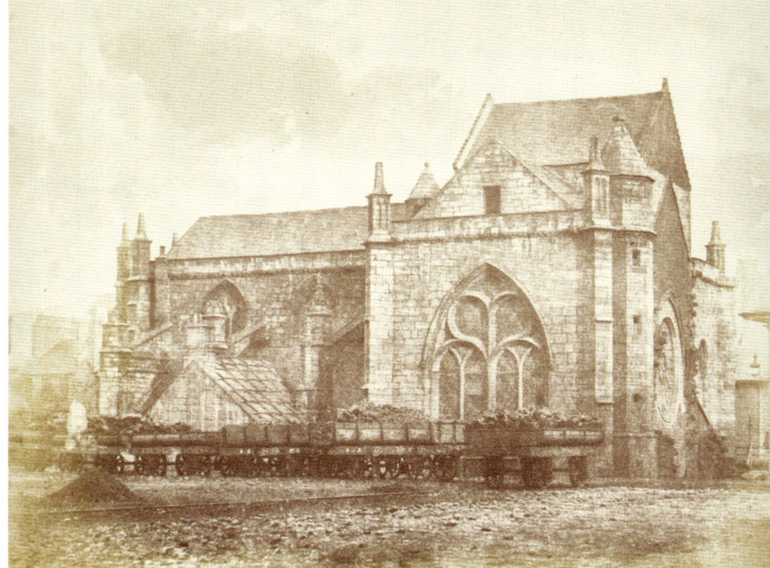

calotype views of every part of the building, both external and internal. No mistake, therefore, can possibly occur in securing a perfect *facsimile* of the ancient church. Having been favoured with a sight of the calotype views (of which there are a great number) we can speak confidently of the excellence of execution; every peculiarity of the building being indicated with exquisite precision in the calotypes. The labours, delicate and difficult they have been, of the artists are now approaching a termination, and in a short time the venerable building will be wholly removed from its present site.[75]

The shameful tale of how this ancient church was demolished, to make way for a goods yard behind Waverley Station, has been recounted by Graham Smith [FIG. 4.17].[76] It is a notable example of the sweeping damage done by the railway companies during the great railway boom of the decade. This impressive record of the building was to prove

fruitless. The stones lay piled up on Calton Hill for some years, and the building was only ever partly reconstructed.

That the firm had the unstinting support of Sir David Brewster must have helped; at the twentieth meeting of the British Association for the Advancement of Science held in Edinburgh in the summer of 1850, Brewster as President summed up the advancement of photography thus:

The superiority of the Talbotype [calotype] to the Daguerreotype is well known. In the latter, the pictures are reversed and incapable of being multiplied, while in the Talbotype there is no reversion, and a single negative will supply a thousand copies, so that books may be illustrated with pictures drawn by the sun. The difficulty of procuring good paper for the negative is so great, that a better material has been eagerly sought for; and M. Niepce, an accomplished officer in the French service, has successfully substituted for paper a film of albumen, or the white of an egg, spread upon glass. This new process has been brought to such perfection in this city by Messrs. Ross and Thomson, that Talbotypes taken by them, and lately exhibited by myself to the National Institute of France, and to M. Niepce, were universally regarded as the finest that had yet been executed.[77]

In the business part of the meeting, Brewster displayed prints from paper processes by Hill and Adamson, Samuel Buckle of Peterborough, and Ross and Thomson, 'by the process in albumen invented by M. Niepce of Paris. They were the specimens referred to in the President's Address, and consisted chiefly of views of Edinburgh, and copies of pictures and statues. They were considered by all who saw them superior to any photographs that had been produced either in this country or on the continent.'[78] Certainly, those images that have been identified as by Ross and Thomson are worth noting, because of their striking composition.[79]

Ross and Thomson submitted 'Frames containing Talbotype pictures from negatives on albuminised glass' to Class XXX of the Great Exhibition of all Nations at the Crystal Palace in London, in 1851. They were awarded a Council Medal for both technical and aesthetic excellence, the citation of which read:

> Ross and Thomson (Class XXX., No. 299, p. 839) have exhibited several beautiful Talbotype pictures, consisting of views from nature, interiors, groups, &c., and they are the only exhibitors, in the British section, of photographs by the albuminous process …. In addition to the extreme clearness observable in the details of their landscape scenery, and the great delicacy of their delin-

eation of objects in general, we may take notice of the excessive beauty of the tints which their works exhibit. Not only are the shadows deep and Rembrandt-looking, where suitable to the effect required, but the middle distances display a beauty of colour nowhere equalled, excepting in the very superior works by M. Martens, in the French Department.

> … The coating of the glass with albumen is a difficult operation; the method adopted by Ross and Thomson differs from the French process … and consists in pouring a quantity of the albumen on the plate and revolving it over a slow heat, for the purpose of ensuring its even distribution. As shown in the practice of these exhibitors, this method would seem to be perfectly successful; and indeed the most beautiful and extreme delicacy and variety of tint, the aerial perspective by which the background is made to recede by imperceptible gradations into the horizon, all amply attest the powers of Messrs. Ross and Thomson.

> A number of Talbotypes, also exhibited, display equal variety of tint, and a depth and richness of tone without any straining for effect.[80]

Ross remarked upon their success in his cheerful manner:

> *March* 29, 1851. – our pictures for the Great Exhibition … consisted principally of Edinburgh Views, and *Alnwick Castle*; one, of *Donaldson's Hospital* [Fig. 4.18], was printed upon albumenised glass, backed up with plaster of Paris, which gave every particle of detail in the negative. A faintly-developed negative of a group of

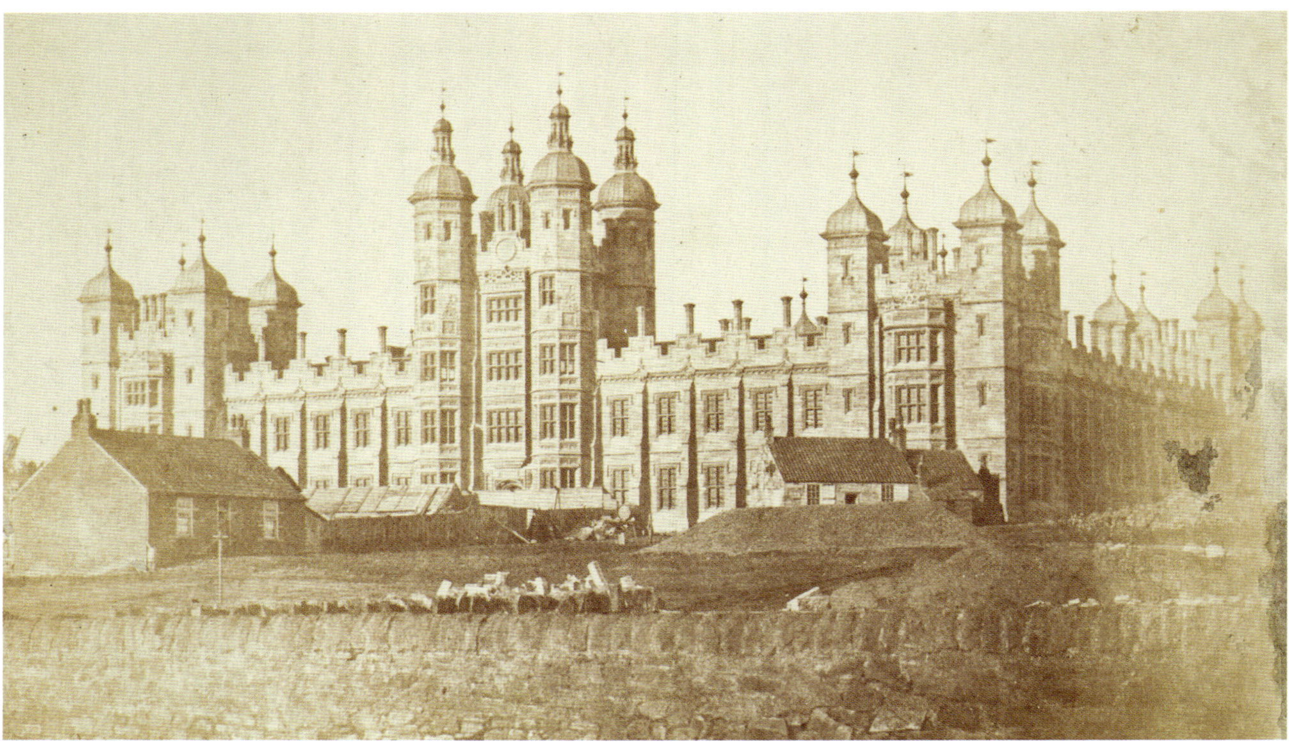

statuary, which was neither more nor less than a positive on glass blackened on the back, puzzled the jurors completely as to how it was produced. Nevertheless these learned gentlemen awarded us the Council medal, and a most flattering critique appeared in that comprehensive volume, the Jurors' Report. Immediately on receipt of this good news we exhibited a large placard in our show case, announcing that we had gained the first prize in the world's exhibition, &c., &c., headed with the words 'Scotland for Ever!' printed in large capitals. No one need inquire who did that foolish thing, but a sense of justice prompts me to say that it was not Mr Thomson.[81]

Interestingly, Ross commented that 'during 1852 the most notable thing regarding ourselves was the great and increasing demand for daguerreotype portraits'. This was against the expected trend; but the advent of new technologies does not entail the instant demise of those that are apparently superseded.

Notes

1. See Morrison-Low, 'Robert Adamson 1821–1848', *Studies in Photography* (1998): 2–4; and Stevenson 2002a.

2. National Galleries of Scotland; and see Stevenson 2002a: 146–7.

3. Adamson, 'Photography,' *Chambers's Information for the People* 2 (1857): 780–1.

4. Letter from D. O. Hill to David Roberts, 12 March 1845, manuscript in National Library of Scotland, Acc. 7723.

5. Hugh Miller, 'The Calotype', *Scotsman*, 12 July 1843.

6. See document 4839, Brewster to Talbot, 3 July 1843, <http://foxtalbot.dmu.ac.uk/letters/letters.html>

7. Advertised in the *Scotsman*, 8 July 1843: 'Mr D. O. Hill's Picture of the First General Assembly of the Free Protesting Church of Scotland' went on to proclaim that 'A Large Number of the Preliminary Studies and Sketches for the above National Picture … comprising nearly the whole of the Calotype Pictures executed jointly by Mr Adamson and Mr Hill, will be exhibited privately at Mr A. Hill's Galleries, 67 Princes' Street, on Wednesday the 12th inst. and following week.'

8. Roddy Simpson, 'Exposing Miss Mann', *Studies in Photography* (2010): 42–8.

9. James Nasmyth to D. O. Hill, March 1847, manuscript in Royal Observatory, Edinburgh.

10. Roddy Simpson, 'Exposing Miss Mann', *Studies in Photography* (2010): 42–8. I have assumed in Stevenson 2002a: 13–4, that she was the assistant who took the photographs of the King of Saxony and his entourage, but subsequent research has shown that the misnamed 'assistant' on this occasion was Adamson himself: *Caledonian Mercury*, 5 August 1844.

11. Jessie Mann letter to D. O. Hill, 26 May 1856, Royal Scottish Academy archive.

12. Isabelle was six years old.

13. Advertised in the *Scotsman* and *Edinburgh Evening Courant*, 3 August 1844.

14. See document 4328, Talbot to John Phillips, 11 September 1844 and document 5063, Lady Elisabeth Feilding [Talbot's mother] to Talbot, 12 September 1844, <http://foxtalbot.dmu.ac.uk/letters/letters.html>

15. D. O. Hill to David Roberts, 25 February 1845, National Library of Scotland, Acc. 7723.

16. Graham Smith, 'H. Fox Talbot's "Scotch Views" for *Sun Pictures in Scotland* (1845)', in Di Bello, Wilson and Zamir (eds) 2012: 17–34.

17. Talbot's letters home are no longer extant and may only be guessed at from the replies made by his wife and mother.

18. Letter from D. O. Hill to David Roberts, 12 March 1845, National Library of Scotland, Acc. 7723.

19. D. O. Hill painting, 'Edinburgh, Old and New' (1846–47), in the collection of the Scottish National Gallery, NG 1964.

20. Letter from D. O. Hill to David Roberts, 14 March 1845, National Library of Scotland, Acc. 7723.

21. K. Eremin, J. Tate and J. Berry, 'On the Chemistry of John and Robert Adamson's Salted Paper Prints and Calotype Negatives', *Studies in Photography* (2002–3): 67–74.

22. Letter from D. O. Hill to Joseph Noel Paton, 18 January 1848, National Library of Scotland, Ms Acc. 11315.

23. George Cundell, 'On the practice of the Calotype Process of Photography', *London, Edinburgh and Dublin Philosophical Magazine and Journal of Science* [3rd series], 24 (1844): 321–2.

24. Lady Eastlake (Elizabeth Rigby), 'Photography', *Quarterly Review* 101 (April 1857): 442–68.

25. Kingslake 1989: 49. The Wollaston lens is shaped to prevent the worst effects of blurring around the edges of an image.

26. Smith 1975: 32–3. An example of Cundell's camera (Acc. no. 2003-5001/1/4158, The Royal Photographic Society Collection at the National Media Museum) is discussed by Harding 2009: 24–5.

27. George Cundell, 'Gallo-Nitrate of Silver and its Action on Iodised Paper', written in London, July 7 1846, *London, Edinburgh and Dublin Philosophical Magazine and Journal of Science* [3rd series], 29 (1846): 101–3.

28. Anon., 'Societies in Connexion with Art', *Art-union* 5 (January 1844): 19.

29. Alfred Smee, 'Photogenic Drawing', *Literary Gazette* 12 (18 May 1839), republished in Odling 1878: 157–64.

30. Odling 1878: 33. His small daughter, who sidled in to take an interest in the food, noted that the Iceland moss bread was nauseous, but the hay bread and biscuit were very sweet and palatable.

31. Anon., 'Potato Disease and Famine Bread', *London Standard*, 9 February 1847, and *Glasgow Herald*, 12 February 1847.

Note: Website addresses checked and correct at the time of going to press.

32. Richard Willats (b.1820), a London optician taking an early interest in photography, and also based in Cheapside, had two of the Cundell London calotypes in his album (The Firestone Library, Princeton University: GA 2005.00262) and acknowledged his debt to G. S. Cundell in his own manual in 1845, see Croucher (ed.) 1845.

33. Anon., 'Optical Illusion', *Manchester Courier*, 14 June 1848; *Newcastle Journal*, 15 July 1848; *Exeter and Plymouth Gazette*, 5 August 1848.

34. Catalogue 1852: 136.

35. The brothers were: Charles Edward (1805–80), also a banker; Joseph (b.1802), agent for the British Linen Bank; Henry (1810–86), a landscape painter, and George Smith (1791–1882): see Stevenson, Lawson and Gray 1988: 9; Taylor and Schaaf 2007: 305, discusses G. S. Cundell and Henry Cundell.

36. Smiles (ed.) 1891: 149–50.

37. The James Eckford Lauder/John Muir Wood album in the Edinburgh Central Library [YTR 140 W89] has two Traquair landscapes, and the Wood collection in the Scottish National Portrait Gallery has a photograph of the Bear Gates at Traquair.

38. George Eastman House , Rochester, NY.

39. University of Texas, Harry Ransom Center, Gernsheim Collection.

40. Edinburgh Central Library, YTR 140 W89.

41. Smiles (ed.) 1891: 369.

42. Nasmyth and Carpenter 1885.

43. Smiles (ed.) 1891: 95.

44. Stevenson, Lawson and Gray 1988; we are also indebted to Paul Muir Wood for sharing his recent, unpublished research with us.

45. Huneker 1900 (reprinted Auckland, NZ, 2008): 69.

46. *Glasgow Herald*, 30 January 1854.

47. For Owen, see Taylor and Schaaf 2007: 355–6.

48. In a letter from Hill to Noel Paton, 23 January 1854, Hill wrote: 'The opera has been bewitching all of us – tho the art of Der Freischutz is all the enchantment I have had of it. What [do you think] of Chatty [his daughter] being three nights running – that is the Oratoria – and two opera nights': National Library of Scotland Acc. 11315.

49. Edinburgh Central Library, YTR 140 W89.

50. SNPG PGP W54; the painting was exhibited in the Royal Scottish Academy in 1854: see McKay and Rinder 1917: 202 n.

51. From a letter in the collection of Paul Muir Wood.

52. From Wood's diary in the collection of Paul Muir Wood.

53. See Mike Ware, 'Burnett, Charles John', in Hannavy (ed.) 2008, vol. 1: 230–1.

54. The quotation, which is a comment on a watercolour by Copley Fielding, comes from Handbook 1858: 17.

55. Wood 1879–90, vol. 3: 448.

56. We are indebted to Gareth Syvret for generously sharing his unpublished PhD thesis, 'Les Îles de la Manche: Photography in the Channel Islands 1840–1870', in preparation for De Montfort University.

57. He may have been related to the William Collie, a bookseller who owned a circulating library in Aberdeen between 1821 and 1847: see National Library of Scotland, Scottish Book Trade Index.

58. Review in *Art-union* (June 1847): 231.

59. See Heathcote and Heathcote 2002: 175–6.

60. The case was investigated by the English Customs and Excise in 1845, The National Archives, Cust. 119/113.

61. Croucher (ed.) 1845.

62. Collie's own album is now in the National Media Museum, Bradford and the Willats album is in the Firestone Library, University of Princeton, ref. GA 2005.00262.

63. Jersey Archive J/H/F4/1. He raised a 'clameur de haro' when the church was transferred to the English Presbyterian church in 1871, J/H/F4/12.

64. Catalogue 1851: vol. IV: 941–2.

65. Reports 1852: 279.

66. William Collie, 'Early Calotypes', Letter to the Editor, *Photographic Journal*, 15 February 1860: 166.

67. The Channel Islands shared with Scotland a certain legal independence; patents applied in England had no authority there. This had the advantage that Collie could practise the calotype process without reference to Talbot. But, of course, once he crossed into England with his photographs, the patent would apply.

68. Taylor and Schaaf 2007: 292.

69. James Ross, 'On the fading of positives', *Photographic Notes* 2 (1857): 361.

70. Quoted by Joe Rock, 'James Ross and hand coloured calotypes', <https://sites.google.com/site/joerocksresearchpages/home/james-ross-and-hand-coloured-calotypes> Genealogical details for Ross can be found in Torrance 2011: 215–6.

71. James Ross, 'A Few Extracts from a Photographer's Old Ledger',

British Journal of Photography 20 (14 February 1873): 75–7.

72. These can be seen online at: <http://www.royalcollection.org.uk/search/site/Ross%20an%20Thomson>
Also, Joe Rock, 'James Ross and hand coloured calotypes', at: <https://sites.google.com/site/joerocksresearchpages/home/james-ross-and-hand-coloured-calotypes>
Other examples are held by the Scottish National Portrait Gallery.

73. Roger Taylor, 'Photographers to Her Majesty', in Dimond and Taylor 1987, pp. 211–3.

74. James Ross, 'A Few Extracts from a Photographer's Old Ledger', *British Journal of Photography* 20 (14 February 1873): 75–7.

75. 'Trinity College Church, Edinburgh', *Dundee Courier*, 16 August 1848.

76. Graham Smith, 'A calotype view of Trinity College Church, Edinburgh, by David Octavius Hill and Robert Adamson', *Burlington Magazine* 126, no. 981 (December 1984): 781–2, 786.

The fate of the church after this date is discussed by Holmes 1988.

77. David Brewster, 'The President's Address', *Report of the … British Association for the Advancement of Science; … 1850* (1851): xxxvi–xxxvii.

78. David Brewster, 'Notice regarding the recent improvements in photography', *Report of the … British Association for the Advancement of Science; … 1850* (1851), Part II, *Transactions*: 6.

79. Scottish National Portrait Gallery, 'Edinburgh from the Castle', PGP R 201; the J. Paul Getty Museum, 'Edinburgh from Salisbury Crags', inv. no. 85.XP.355.74; the Gernsheim Collection at the Harry Ransom Center, University of Texas at Austin, the 'Lake Price Album', fTR 655.11 P853 HRC-P, pp 48 and 50, both salt prints of trees in a wood.

80. Reports 1852: 278.

81. James Ross, 'A Few Extracts from a Photographer's Old Ledger', *British Journal of Photography* 20 (14 February 1873): 76.

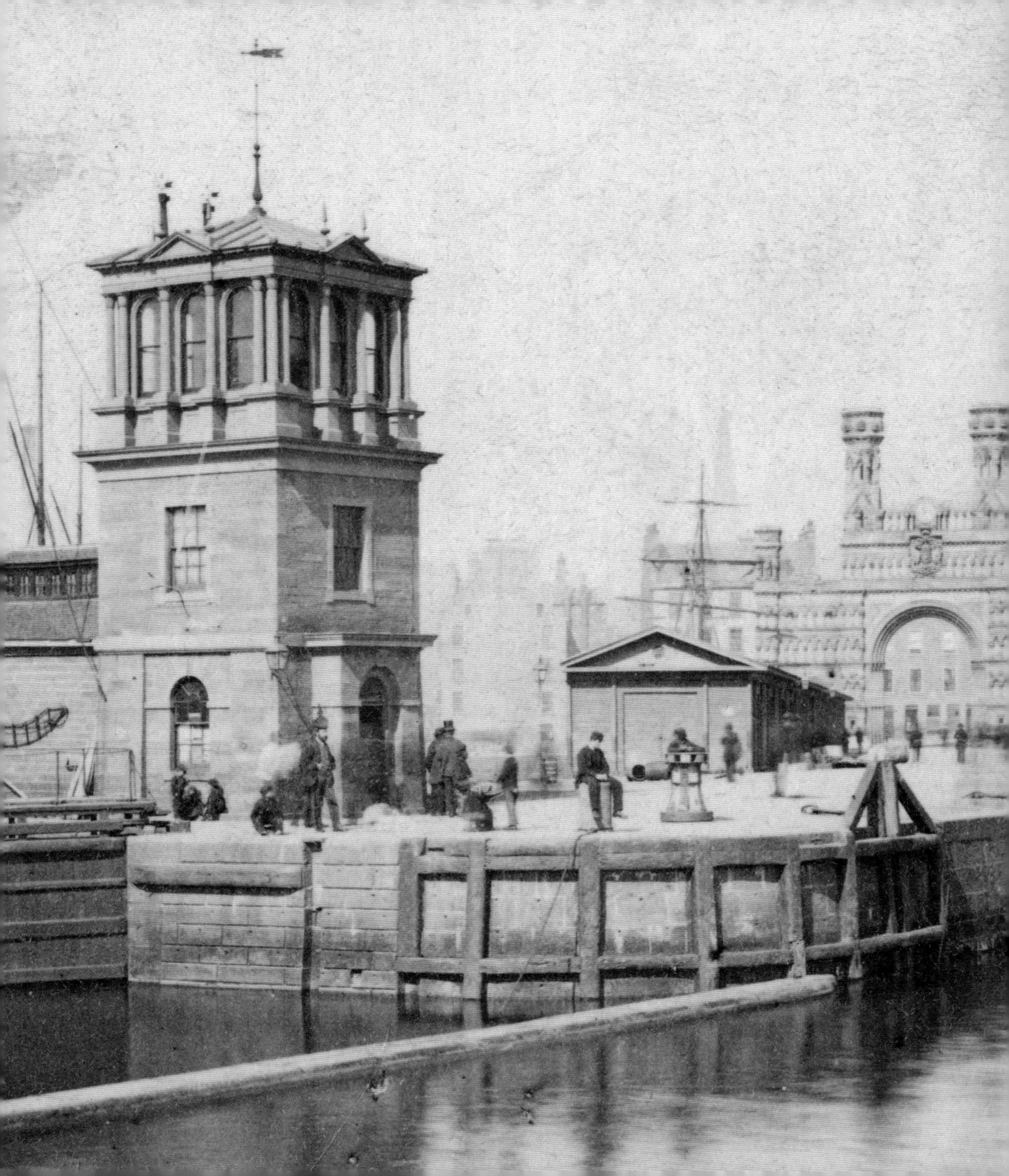

CHAPTER FIVE

Professional Photography comes of Age

The sale of photographs, but more particularly of Stereoscopic subjects,
in Edinburgh, Glasgow and other Scottish towns, is considerable.
In the last letter from our Scottish agent, (Mr J. Spencer), he mentions
that he has disposed of no less than eight or nine thousand
Stereoscopic Slides within the last three months ….

★

Thomas Sutton, Editorial, *Photographic Notes*, March 1857

The year 1851 saw a series of landmarks for photography: the introduction of stereo photography, the wet plate process, the Great Exhibition in London, and the death of Daguerre. Commercial photography had made its tentative start with the daguerreotype process, but the peripatetic nature of its practitioners – even those with urban studios – meant that numbers are difficult to trace. Often, photographers had other trades, such as miniature painter or drawing master. As demand rose, so commercial photographers settled in fashionable parts of town to catch passing trade. By 1860, at a meeting of the short-lived Caledonian Photographic Club in Edinburgh, it was reported with some exaggeration that:

Princes Street would soon be one great photographic

establishment from end to end, as … several photographers of standing were about migrating thither: Tunny of Clerk Street; Rodgers [*sic*] of St Andrews; Duboscq of Paris; together with two eminent London photographers … Ross and Thompson [*sic*] … were leaving their present place in favour of more suitable premises.[1]

The decade after the Great Exhibition saw a rise in demand, supplied by photographers using the newer forms of the art. Prominent professionals working north of the Border included the above-mentioned James G. Tunny, Thomas Rodger of St Andrews, and the partnership of Ross & Thomson. Sadly, Jules Duboscq never opened a branch in Edinburgh, but other names from around Scotland made their mark: among them George Washington Wilson of Aberdeen, Thomas Annan of Glasgow, James Valentine of Dundee, and Magnus Jackson of Perth. They worked with a number of processes, from the calotype through to

Opposite, Fig. 5.5 (detail): James Valentine, 'Dundee Docks from West Protection Wall', *c*.1860.

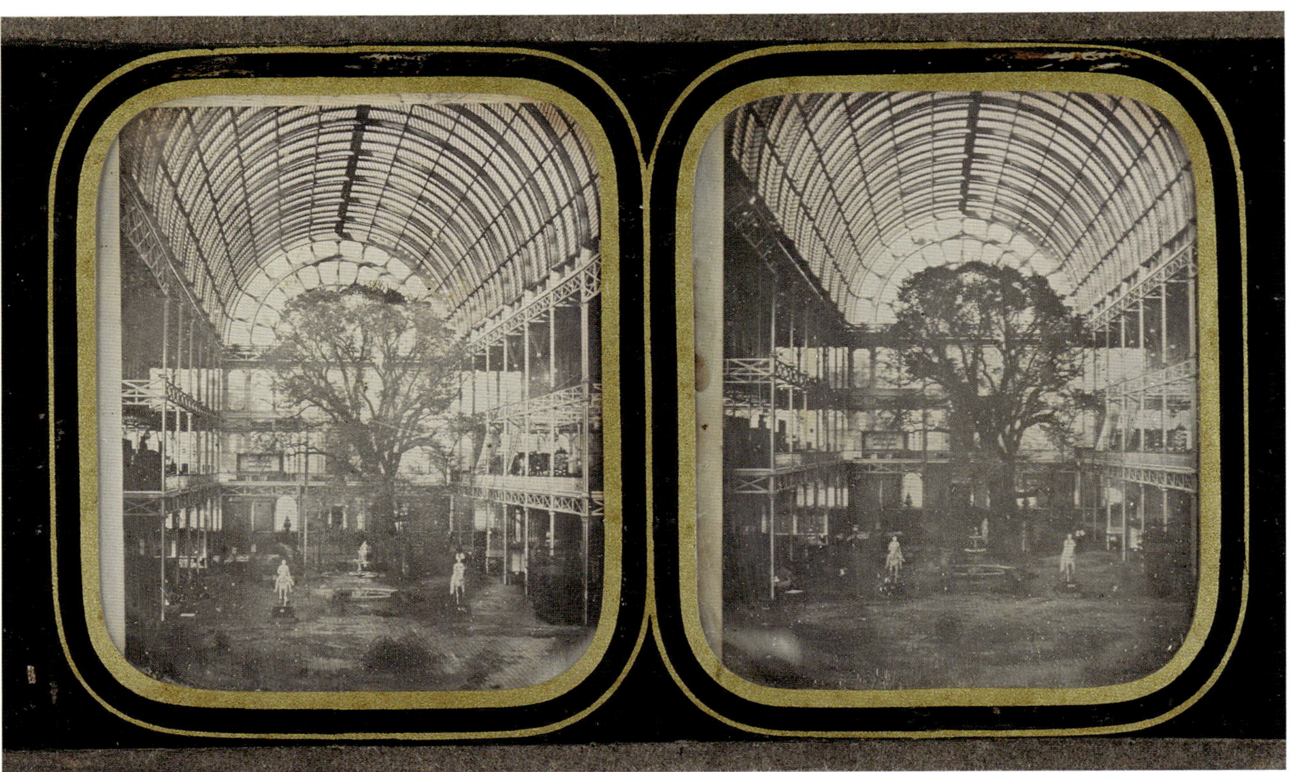

the wet collodion process, and the variations of these: wet collodion positives (or ambrotypes), tintypes, cartes-de-visite and stereo photography.

The stereo image in Scotland

The introduction of the wet collodion process in late 1851, without licensing implications for commercial use, increased demand for photography. With cheaper materials, image-taking became available to a larger audience, pushing down the social scale. Yet the daguerreotype remained popular with many, and on offer as one of many forms of photograph for which a customer might ask.[2]

At the Great Exhibition in London in 1851, when the lenticular stereoscope and its images were first publicly appreciated, the stereo daguerreotype made its public debut. Stereo images were taken with a camera that mimicked the two slightly-different views seen simultaneously by the left and right eye, and then recombined them in a viewer persuading the brain to think it was seeing in three dimensions. Despite some assertions that no daguerreotypes were taken of the Crystal Palace in its original Hyde Park venue, this is not the case. There are stereo daguerreotypes of the inside of the glasshouse structure, looking north [Fig. 5.1]; and on the back of one example, there is a monogram 'DS' in red.[3] This monogram shows that the item originated in the photographic studio of Jules Duboscq (1817–86). He was the Parisian optical instrument maker contacted by Sir David Brewster in 1850 to make his lenticular stereoscope.[4] Duboscq was in partnership with his father-in-law, Jean Baptiste François Soleil, hence the monogram for 'Duboscq-Soleil'.[5] He was one of a number of photographers that were given permission to take daguerreotypes inside the Crystal Palace, along with the London photographers Antoine Claudet, J. J. E. Mayall and T. R. Williams.[6]

Stereo daguerreotypes were first shown to the extensive public at the Great Exhibition, and their introduction,

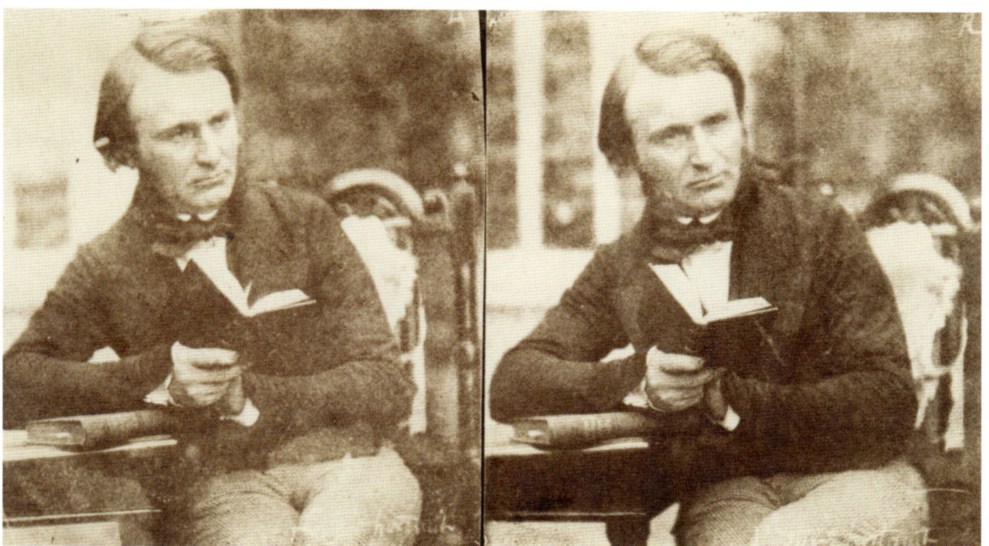

with the distinguished optical scientist Sir David Brewster as midwife, to royal approbation and subsequent universal acclaim, has been rehearsed in every history of photography.[7] But is this story true? The received history is this: with the opening of the Crystal Palace, the relatively new science of photography and stereoscopy found a perch amongst the longer-established instruments for astronomy, microscopy, surveying, weighing and measuring, telegraphy, chemistry and meteorology, in Class 10, 'Philosophical, Musical, Horological, and Surgical Instruments'. 'Brewster's Stereoscope' was to be found in the French section, with other scientific instruments displayed by Duboscq-Soleil.[8] The jury for Class 10 comprised fifteen leading figures from Britain, United States and Europe, under Sir David Brewster's chairmanship.[9]

The stereoscope had already been demonstrated by Professor Charles Wheatstone (1802–75) at a meeting of the Royal Society in 1838, using a pair of drawings of a single object made from slightly different points of view (left and right).[10] Wheatstone's viewer was a large and cumbersome instrument, owing more to science than domestic entertainment, but the optical theory demonstrated sparked a lively debate about the principles of binocular vision.[11]

One of Wheatstone's chief rivals was Brewster, whose numerous scientific papers on optics, the nature of light,

and the physiology of human vision, placed him at the very forefront of his field. During the course of these investigations in the 1840s, Brewster later claimed to have found Wheatstone's viewer to be 'of little service, and ill-fitted, not only for popular use, but for the application of the instrument to various useful purposes'.[12] After experimenting with alternative designs, he produced a simpler hand-held viewer which he called a 'lenticular stereoscope'. This was made for him by George Lowden of Dundee. Brewster published his design in an Edinburgh journal, and encouraged experimentation in St Andrews, where Dr John Adamson appears to have taken an early stereoscopic image [FIG. 5.2].[13] However, disheartened by an indifferent reception in Britain, Brewster offered his design to the eminent Parisian instrument maker, Jules Duboscq, in 1850.[14] In the words of one scientific commentator, the Abbé Moigno, Duboscq created a viewer of such beauty that it attracted 'a spontaneous and unanimous cry of admiration' (Brewster's translation) from all who saw it.[15]

This sequence of events could not have been improved upon; Duboscq included Brewster's new stereoscope among his displays in the French Courts of the Great Exhibition, where the excellence of his scientific instruments ensured him a Council Medal.[16] According to Brewster's account of events, it was here, at the Great Exhibition, that his viewer

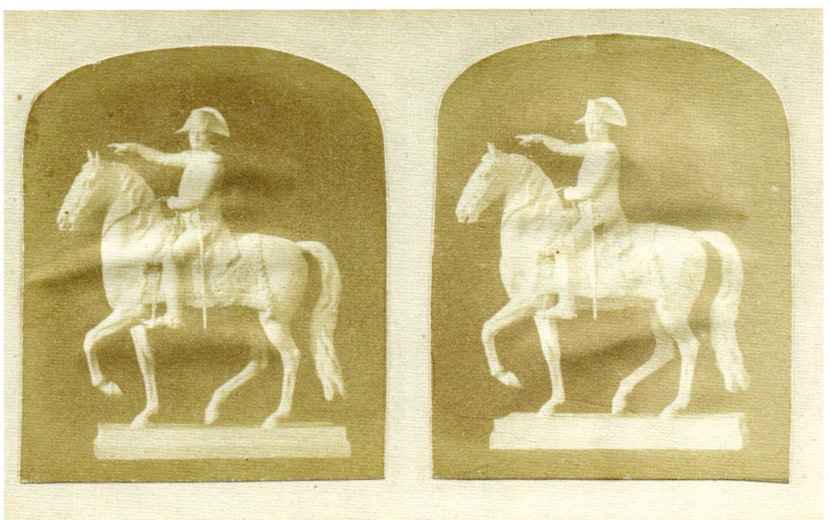
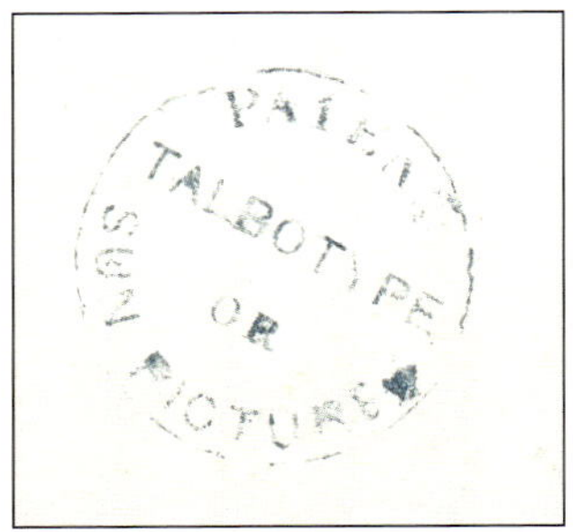

Fig. 5.3, with detail: Unknown photographer, ceramic statue of Napoleon on horseback, stereoscopic calotypes, stamped on reverse: 'Patent / Talbotype / or Sun Pictures', *c*.1845. (Howarth-Loomes Collection at National Museums Scotland, IL.2003.44.6.14.421)

caught the 'particular attention of the Queen, and before the closing of the Crystal Palace, M. Duboscq executed a beautiful stereoscope, which I presented to Her Majesty in his name'.[17] Roger Taylor comments, 'Queen Victoria makes no mention of seeing the stereoscope during her visits to the French displays, despite reporting in some detail on the embroidery, clocks and candelabra. She does refer to photographs, but only in passing. The gift of the stereoscope goes unrecorded in the Royal Archives.'[18] Brewster's tale of royal approval has been widely quoted as the principal reason why stereoscopy found such immediate and universal favour in the years immediately following the Great Exhibition. But the history of how stereoscopy transformed itself from the realms of science into one of the more notable marketing successes of the mid-19th century is far more convoluted. Attempts to reconstruct how this may have been developed have been heavily overwritten by David Brewster's fury at Charles Wheatstone's undoubted priority in what he regarded as his own field, and his own increasingly acrimonious attempts to distinguish between the two forms of stereoscope.

With the daguerreotype, the Brewster stereoscope became extremely popular. The clear detail of the process enhanced the three-dimensional illusion; the blur of the calotype would undermine it [Fig. 5.3].[19]

The timing was crucial. The exhibiting of the lenticular stereoscope coincided with the publication of another, improved, photographic method: the wet collodion process. Here a light-sensitive emulsion was spread on a glass plate (thus countering the lack of rigidity in a paper-based process). This proved to be more rapid and provided finer detail than the calotype negative. The positive used thin paper coated with a layer of egg white containing salt, and this coating could vary from very thin to a thick gloss. The albumenised paper was sensitised with silver nitrate solution before use, and printing was done by daylight under a negative. It was faster, cheaper, more detailed, almost infinitely reproducible, and free from patent restrictions – the days of the daguerreotype and calotype were numbered.

With Brewster's promotional work, *The Stereoscope: its History, Theory and Construction, with its Application to the Fine and Useful Arts and to Education*, published in 1856, it comes as no surprise to learn who was sponsoring its publication. It was the recently-formed London Stereoscopic Company, whose 16-page advertising supplement was bound into the back of Brewster's book. In 1854, George Swan Nottage (1823–85) had started what became one of the largest photographic publishing companies in the world. By the 1860s the company had branches around the world, including New York and Sydney. By 1884, Nottage had amassed a fortune and was elected Lord Mayor of London. Hundreds of thousands of stereoscopic images were sold by

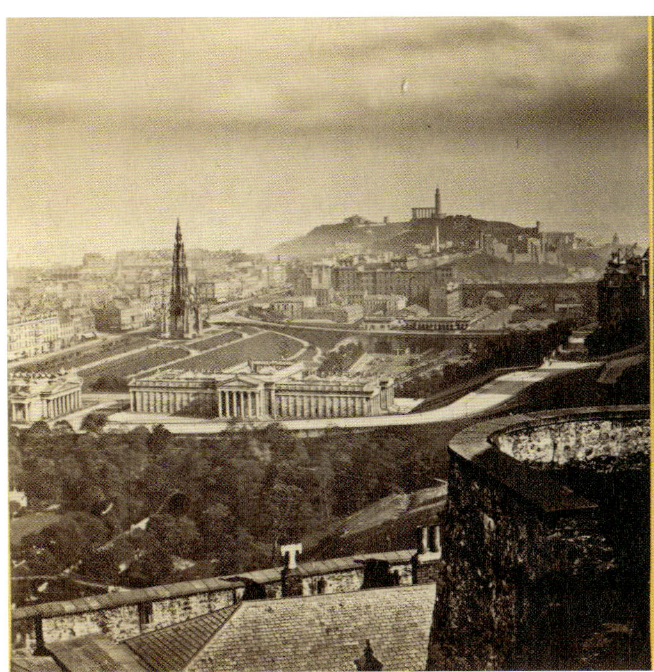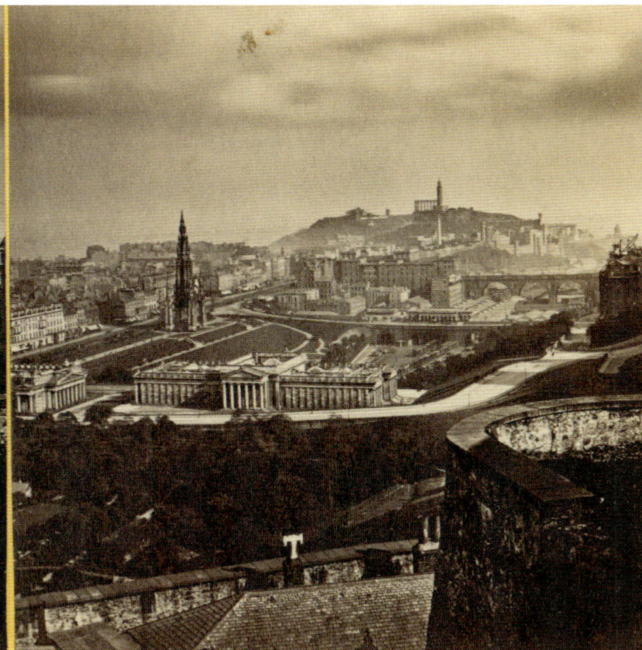

the company in a major craze.[20] While the role of Brewster in this great success is equivocal – he was not the first to devise a stereoscope – his role in developing an instrument which could be widely used, his skill in the art of promotion, and his public enthusiasm, were integral to stereoscopy's success. Sir David Brewster's emphatic insistence on his role has paid off: he continues to be regarded as the true inventor of the stereoscopic viewer, and the instigator of the post-1851 stereo craze.

Stereo daguerreotypes were produced by at least two Scottish-based photographers; and the wet collodion process was rapidly popularised by a number of commercial firms north of the Border. Among them was Archibald Burns (1831–80), based in the Rock House studio in Edinburgh formerly occupied by D. O. Hill and Robert Adamson [Fig. 5.4]. Burns showed stereo views at the Photographic Society of Scotland's 1858 exhibition, using a dry plate method (this took longer exposure times than the wet plate method, but for landscape work this did not matter as much as for portraiture).[21] Others were Cramb Brothers of Glasgow, James Valentine of Dundee [5.5], and especially George Washington Wilson of Aberdeen [Fig. 5.6]. These and other businesses turned out industrial quantities of stereo images for the burgeoning middle-class drawing rooms of Victorian Britain. As Thomas Sutton commented in 1857:

> The sale of photographs, but more particularly of Stereoscopic subjects, in Edinburgh, Glasgow and other Scottish towns, is considerable. In the last letter from our Scottish agent, (Mr J. Spencer), he mentions that he has disposed of no less than eight or nine thousand Stereoscopic Slides within the last three months; an amount really extraordinary. But the Stereoscope has already become a piece of household furniture, and like the Kaleidoscope, another of the popular inventions of Sir David Brewster, we may expect soon to see it at every fair, bazaar, and toy shop in the Kingdom. Photographers who work with an eye to profit will do well to bear this in mind.[22]

Fig. 5.4: Archibald Burns, Edinburgh from the Castle, *c*.1860, stereoscopic albumen prints. (Howarth-Loomes Collection at National Museums Scotland, IL.2003.44.6.2.227)

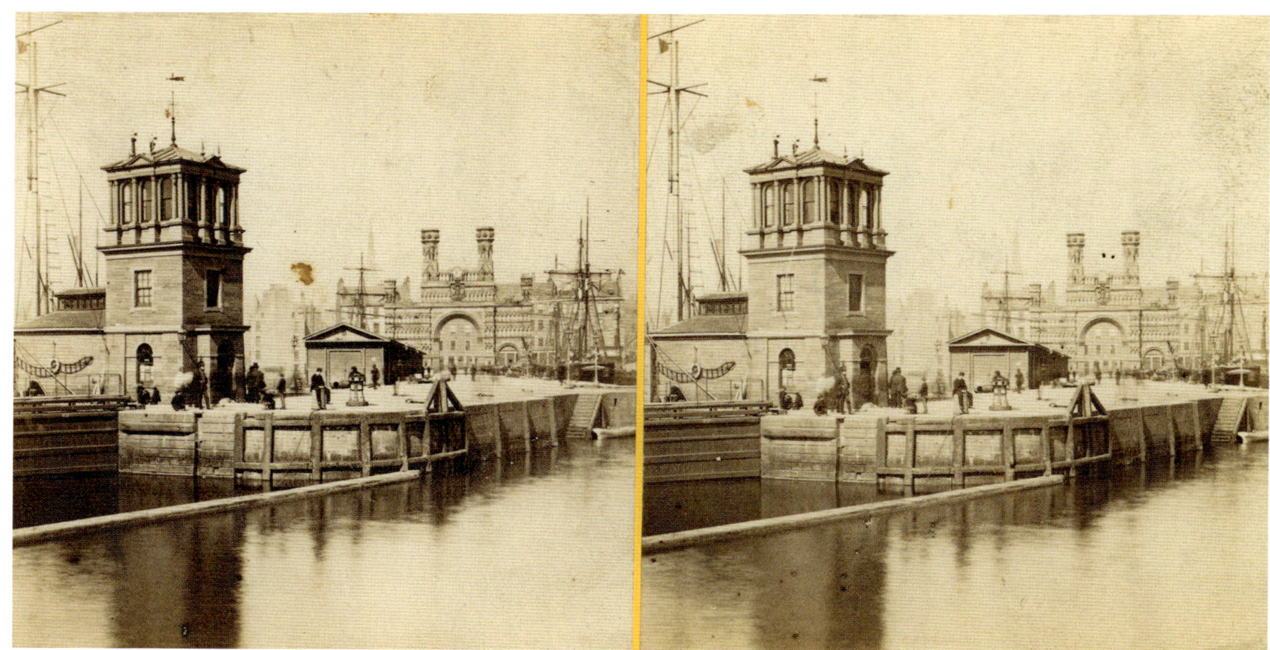

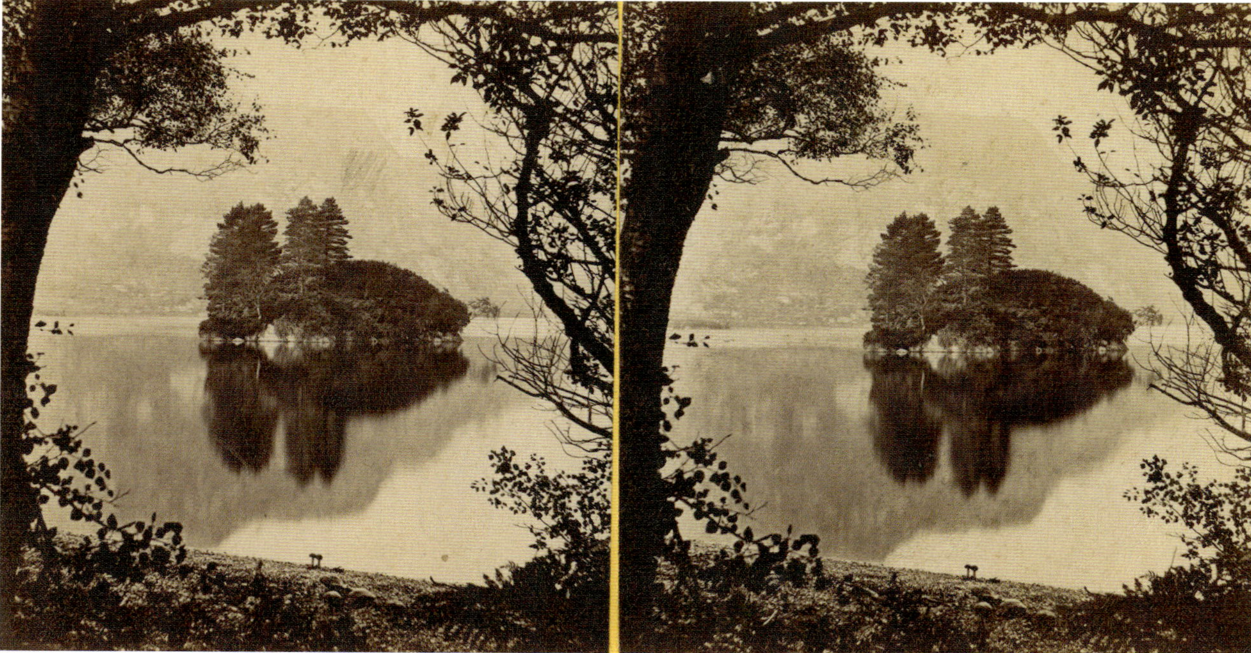

Fig. 5.5 (above): James Valentine, 'Dundee Docks from West Protection Wall', *c.*1860, stereoscopic albumen prints. (Howarth-Loomes Collection at National Museums Scotland, IL.2003.44.6.2.454)

Fig. 5.6 (below): George Washington Wilson, 'Otter Island, Loch Katrine', *c.*1865, stereoscopic albumen prints. (Howarth-Loomes Collection at National Museums Scotland, IL.2003.44.6.1.77)

Fig. 5.7 (opposite): James Ross and John Thomson, 'Punch', 1864, modern copy of an albumen print from an album once belonging to David Brewster. (Private collection)

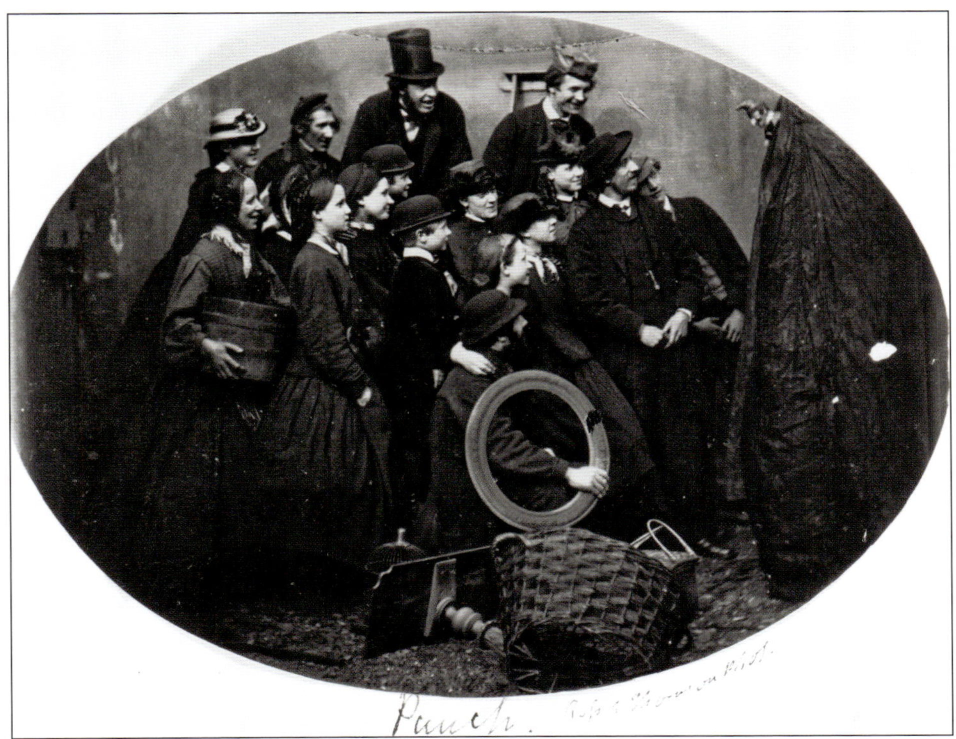

Commercial photographers in Scotland after 1851

This enormous flourishing industry blossomed from apparently small shoots. Ross and Thomson, whose beginnings were rooted in the daguerreotype and the calotype, advertised infrequently. From this, it can be assumed that their Royal Warrant and prestigious premises in Princes Street in central Edinburgh, as well as reports of the quality of their work, spread by word-of-mouth, ensured that they were well-known. In May 1853, Ross noted that the business had laid out £1 5s for a photographic trip for the partners and their assistants, 'by way of inaugurating a Saturday half-holiday'. At this point, the norm was to work every day except Sunday, which in Scotland was taken very seriously. 'This was at the time found to be impracticable,' remarks Ross, 'none of the other photographers in the city showing any desire or willingness to assist in such a laudable movement. From that time forward we invariably closed our premises at four o'clock on Saturdays.'[23] Towards the end of his life, Ross was regarded as an enlightened employer;

he was also a canny capitalist, investing in property, so that his savings ensured a comfortable retirement.[24]

Ross mentions acquiring a Voigtländer lens in April 1854 (he and Thomson bought one before, in 1850), costing the princely sum of £23 [modern equivalent £13,000]. In due course this was sent for reconditioning to the makers, based in Brunswick, and 'returned greatly improved; we now [1873] use it daily for taking the portraits of children' [Fig. 5.7].[25] Reviewing the Paris Universal Exhibition 1867, the *British Journal of Photography* critic wrote, somewhat hotly:

Mr James Ross, of Edinburgh … exhibits a very large number of card portraits – about 200 if I remember rightly – and some fifteen artistic studies, about 8 x 6 inches. … Mr Ross is evidently an excellent photographer and an artist of a high order of merit. His portraits of children are unapproached as pictures by any in the Exhibition. … Mr Ross succeeds in his artistic studies fairly. He produces pictures which tell the story well, and, without saying they are faultless in composition,

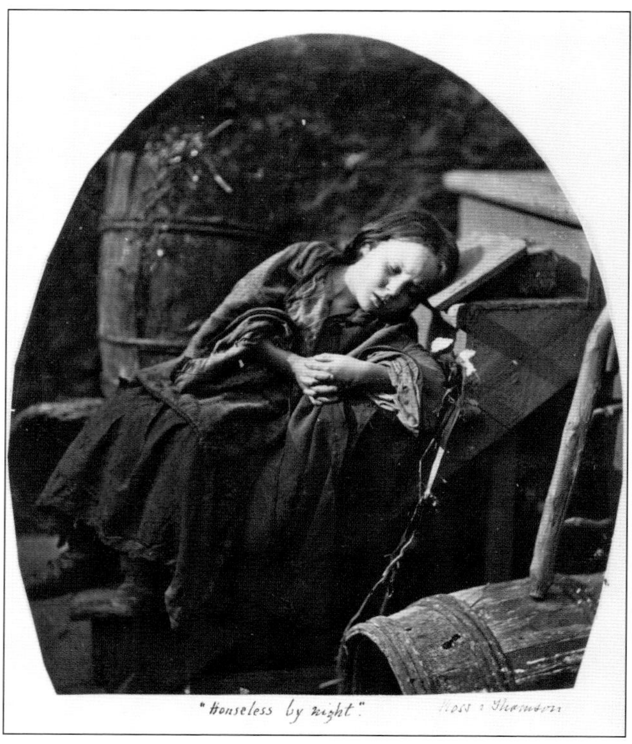

Fig. 5.8: Ross and Thomson, 'Houseless by Night', *c.*1865, modern copy of an albumen print from an album once belonging to David Brewster. (Private collection)

or that his models are all that can be desired, yet the result is a success which few have equalled, and … I wonder it never occurred to somebody that the head of the table must be where the lord of the feast is seated. The firm of Ross and Thomson received only honourable mention at the Exhibitions of 1855 and 1862, while in 1851, at the first Great Exhibition, they were awarded the Council medal – equal to a gold medal or the grand prize at Paris.[26]

The photography of children was one of the firm's strong suits.

In December 1853, the Mechanics' Institution based in Aberdeen showed a touring exhibition from the Society of Arts in London, at which Ross and Thomson exhibited 54 photographs. They showed calotypes, albumen prints and daguerreotypes. Two identified daguerreotypes pictured a 'Beggar Lassie' and 'Rev Dr Guthrie'.[27] Thomas Guthrie was a notable preacher and philanthropist. He was responsible, in 1849, for establishing a 'ragged school' in Edinburgh to bring destitute children in from the streets, to feed and educate them for a better life. Guthrie used an engraving, 'From Photograph of a Boy on entering the School, now a respectable Tradesman', as the frontispiece of the third edition of his *Seed-time and Harvest of Ragged Schools*.[28]

The *Children's Friend*, on 1 February 1865, illustrated two engravings of photographs: 'Lost, or a day before entering Dr Guthrie's Ragged School', showing a boy in handed-down clothes looking wistfully into a breadshop window, and 'Found; or, six months after entering Dr Guthrie's Ragged School', a happy boy with food in his hand and books beside him, wearing clothes that fit.[29] The pictures occupy a page each with text rousing the sympathy of the young to send contributions.[30] A photograph by Ross and Thomson entitled 'Houseless by Night', showing a girl, again in over-large handed-down clothes, sleeping on a stair between beer barrels, shows a strong compositional and emotional relation to these two images [FIG. 5.8]. It may reasonably be assumed that they took the other two images, thus associating themselves directly with one of the most important humanitarian movements of the time.

In October 1849, Ross and Thomson made a technological advance which gave them an immense advantage in the field and opened the way to the great commercial expansion of the 1850s. Ross's memories included a landmark purchase:

October 5, 1849. – Paid for half-dozen eggs, 6d.; the day after for three plates of glass, 2s. This marks the exact date of our commencing the then newly-published albumen process, discovered by M. Niepce. With but comparatively few failures we succeeded so well that paper negatives were abandoned for ever. Thanks to the praise Sir David Brewster bestowed upon our handi-work (in a lecture given in the Music Hall by that great, good, and influential man), public attention was drawn towards our firm in a more marked and profitable manner than it had been previously. For a time our Edinburgh views (full plate) sold for 7s. 6d. each, as fast as we could print them. Copies from one large negative brought £1 1s. each.[31]

The new albumen process enabled sharper images carried on a sturdier negative: and the photograph-buying public liked them. Ross's 'Old Ledger' noted that in April 1850 the firm paid 8s 6d to *The Times* for 'an advertise-ment that Ross and Thomson were the only photographers on this side of the channel who had succeeded with the albumen process': 'Photography on glass – Messrs Ross and Thomson, photographers to the Queen for Scotland, are the only professional practice in the United Kingdom who have succeeded with this wonderful improvement in the art.'[32]

In July 1854, Ross noted 'Rent of Lauriston, £10. This was for a piece of ground upon which we erected a small building, at the expense of £100, for the purpose of copying large pictures and separating entirely the calotype process from the manipulation of the daguerreotype.'[33] Business on both these technical fronts continued to grow. The ensuing two entries in Ross's 'Old Ledger' are accounts of trips taken out of town: one to the Highlands, where the weather was far from ideal, the other across to Fife to take photographs for a court case. Another interesting commission was under-taken in 1855, when the photographers went to Falkirk:

During the Crimean war there were nearly 3000 men employed at this place, forming cannon, shot, and shell. The proprietor wished to have pictures of the men while engaged in these warlike operations. This was impos-sible. But our people managed to get some very fair stereoscopic groups in the open air.[34]

In the autumn of 1856, Ross remarked on

… two stereoscopic slides of trees – the first pictures taken at Powder Hall, then, and for long after, the most picturesque corner to be found in the neighbourhood of Edinburgh. Within the space of a few acres were to be seen very fine specimens of the beech, birch, elm, ash, willow, poplar, lime, and larch, all growing in beauty side by side, while under their shadows flourished the fox-glove, coltsfoot, tassiligo [tussilago, or coltsfoot], dock, burdock, moonwort, the creeping bramble, and the towering thistle, broken pailings [*sic*], hingeless gates, dilapidated walls, a house old enough to look, and in-deed was reported to be, haunted gave contrast of col-our and variety of form to a scene worthy of Gaspar Poussin.[35]

That Ross spent his time well in this derelict but rather beautiful part of Edinburgh can be measured by the photo-graphs of plant life the firm submitted for exhibition over the next few years [Fig. 5.9]: among items exhibited at the Photographic Society of Scotland in 1856 was 'View near Powderhall, Edinburgh'; and 'Stereoscope, with View near Powderhall'; in 1858, at the Photographic Society of London, a frame containing 'Lime Trees, Powderhall', 'Beech Stems', 'Avenue, Powderhall', 'Dock-Leaves', 'Nettles', 'Pathway, Powderhall', 'Ferns and Brambles'; at the British Association, meeting in Aberdeen in 1859, 'Thistle', 'Coltsfoot', 'Dock-

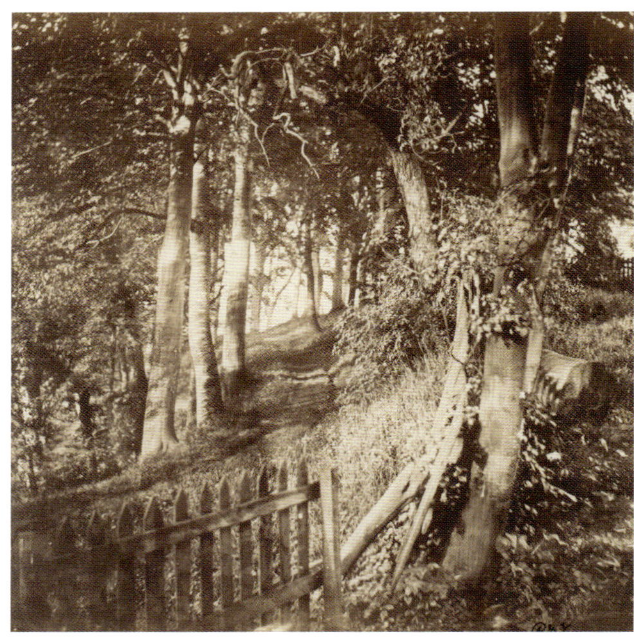

Leaf', 'Tussilago and Fox Glove', 'Nettles', 'Brambles', and more; and that same year to the Photographic Society of Glasgow, 'Avenue, Powderhall' 'Ferns', 'Nettles', 'Plane Tree, Powder Hall', 'Beech Wood, Powder Hall', and others. All of these were collodion prints.[36] The London prints were viewed 'with admiration' by the reviewer at the *Athenaeum*, who wrote that it was like

> … reading Keats and Tennyson to look at the soft, white, velvet mass of the poisonous, veined nettle-leaves, green and rank, huddling up in a dark guilty mass to hide where the murdered child was buried, while the bee sings round the white diadems of their beguiling flowers as if nothing was wrong and earth was still a Paradise. How the wild hops – vine-like cling and twine – how the ferns spread and arch their palm-leaf fronds – how the hooked bramble with its square red stalk trails and spreads.[37]

John Thomson left the firm in about 1862 [FIG. 5.10]; and James Ross continued under the same name. He went into partnership with Thomas Pringle in 1867, and he himself retired in 1878. John Nicol wrote:

> Mr Ross, who had the advantage of being trained as an artist, was one of the fortunate few, who, having taken up the new art enthusiastically, soon adopted it as a profession, and he is one of the still fewer whose career as a professional photographer has been in every way an unqualified and unbroken success.[38]

This eulogy continued for several fulsome paragraphs. At the time of his death, at 'the ripe old age of eighty-one' in

May 1895, less was said, although the firm was commended 'for singular excellence of their views taken on albumen plates'.[39]

As a young man during the 1840s, James Good Tunny (1820–87) would stand above the Calton Hill studio, hopefully watching D. O. Hill and Robert Adamson at work:

> Time after time have I gone and stood on the projecting rock below Playfair's monument on Calton Hill, and drawn inspiration from viewing Mr Adamson placing a large square box upon a stand, covering his head with a focusing-cloth, introducing the slide, counting the seconds by his watch, putting the cap on the lens, and retiring to what we now know to be the dark room. Oh! If only I could have got an introduction to these men, it would have been the consummation of my happiness![40]

The son of an Irish handloom weaver, Tunny was born in Edinburgh in 1820. He became a shoemaker, a profession renowned for its radicalism. His 'Early Reminiscences of Photography', given before the Edinburgh Photographic Society in 1869, explains how he first heard about Talbot's experiments through the press: inspired by this, he dis-

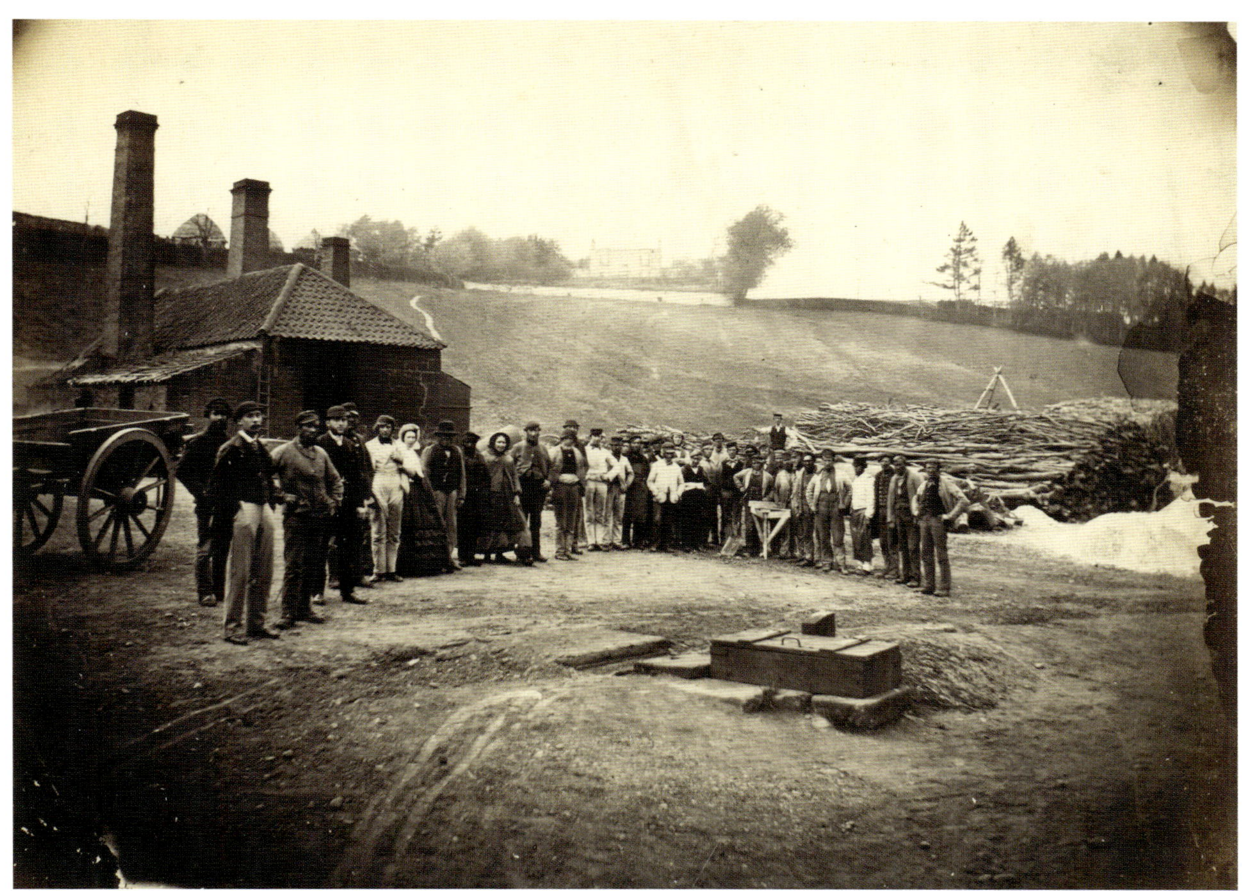

solved a sixpence in nitric acid in an attempt to make a photogenic drawing:

> The enthusiasm with which I returned to repeat my experiment can only be appreciated by those who have just soiled their fingers for the first time, in the development of their first negative. Day after day, leaves, bits of lace, and grasses were laid on the sensitive prepared sheets of paper, and pressed in contact by a sheet of glass laid over them with weights at the corners. Such was the simplicity of our early printing-frame.[41]

Tunny took up professional photography only in 1851, and though a little can be gleaned from his reminiscences, much of how he mastered the early forms of photography remains opaque. Tunny mentions the names that might be expected: Hill and Adamson, 'the late Mr Howie', 'my old friend Thomas Davidson', and 'Messrs Ross and Thomson, of this city'. In his lecture, Tunny managed to enrage contemporaries about his understanding of the priority of two inventions: the wet collodion method and the process of photography on porcelain.[42] A recent biography has described how he amassed the capital to set himself up in business as a photographer, and put his savings into property, which provided extra income. His family life appears to have been busy, and was probably extremely noisy: he married, successively, three wives, and fathered eleven children, six of whom (including all four sons) predeceased him.

Tunny's third wife, Margaret Wilson Tunny (1841–77), was actively involved in the studio. Her work was mentioned in an affectionate obituary by Dr John Nicol:

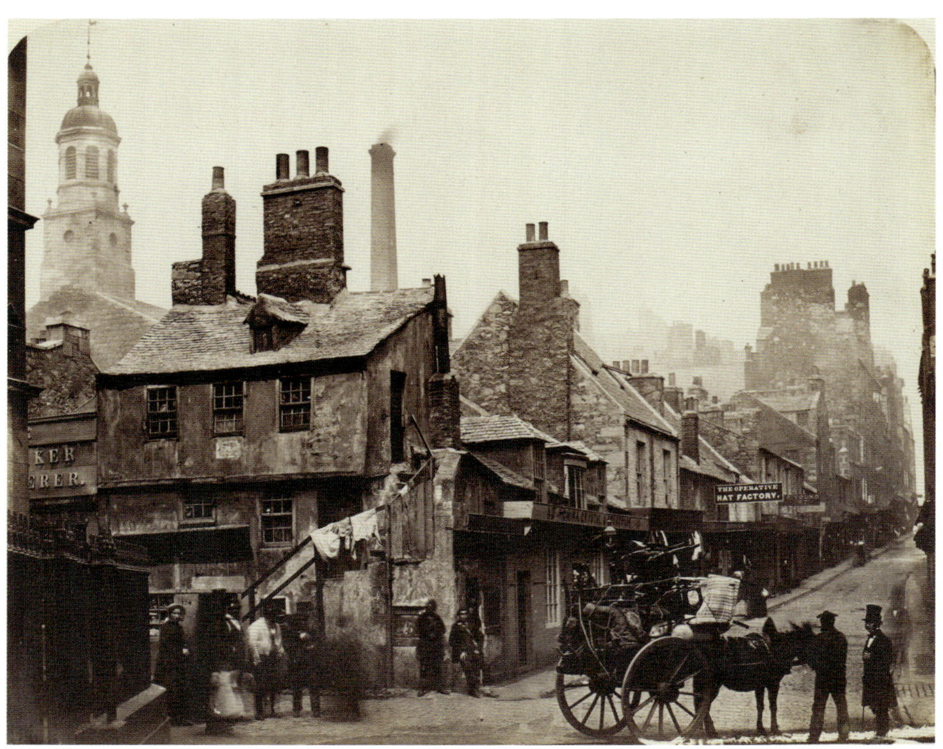

She was a 'helpmeet' to Mr Tunny in the true sense of the term, an enthusiastic lover of the art, and one of the most artistic photographers that ever laid paper on a negative. Mrs Tunny possessed a refined and cultivated taste, and a thorough knowledge of the requirements of photography – a lasting memorial of which may be seen in the recently-erected establishment in Maitland-street, which is one of the most elegant and perfect in the country, and which we hope we are committing no breach of confidence in saying was principally the work of the deceased lady. Mrs Tunny, while ever diligent in business, displayed at all times an open-handed friend-ship, and gave a hearty welcome to all connected with the art. She never seemed so happy as when exercising a genuine hospitality to the numerous strangers who came 'within her gates'.[43]

In 1856, Tunny extended his studio at 78 South Clerk Street, grandly called 'the Newington Photographic Rooms'. One of his studio cameras survives from this address. He advertised 'the Glass Saloon … on the Ground Floor, and thus readily accessible, even to invalids. It admits of being largely thrown open to the air, so as to secure the beneficial influence of the free reception of light, without the discom-fort of exposure in ungenial weather.'[44] Four years later, he rented premises in the centre of the main shopping thor-oughfare, at 93 Princes Street, in competition with Ross & Thomson, G. &. D. Hay, James Howie, John Moffat and Peter Truefitt, all successful professional photographers.[45] By the following year, the 1861 Census states he employed two men and three women, demonstrating that the business was growing.[46] By 1866, he abandoned the South Clerk Street premises, which he had rented initially to a former assistant. In 1870, he moved from central Edinburgh back to the suburbs with his growing family, and built a work-shop and studio in the garden of a house in Salisbury Place.[47] In the autumn of 1874 Tunny went on a six-month tour of the United States, visiting photographic establish-ments, and although not exactly industrial espionage, it clearly made an impact on his own business; he gave up

Fig. 5.11 (opposite): J. G. Tunny, 'Foot of Cowgate, & St Mary Wynd', Edinburgh, *c.*1854, calotype. (James Drummond album, Royal Scottish Academy, 1995.040.37)

Fig. 5.12 (right): J. G. Tunny, 'The Game Bag', *c.*1854, calotype. (Prentenkabinett, Universiteit Leiden, 61.0935.48)

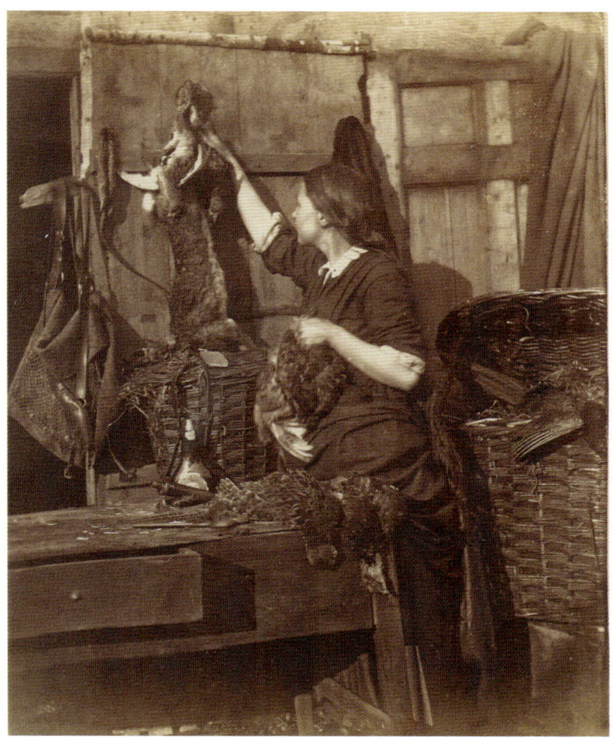

the subsidiary Princes Street studio and bought two large properties in Edinburgh's West End. There he built, from scratch, an impressive photographic establishment.[48]

Tunny was a politically-active radical, and used some of the more boisterous techniques from this side of his life in his dealings with other photographers. He had major quarrels with William McCraw and Thomas Rodger of St Andrews over priorities of invention; and other disagreements in his professional life were not uncommon. His photographs, shown at many exhibitions held in Scotland over the period of his professional career, were greeted with enthusiasm by contemporaries [Figs 5.11 and 5.12]. Tunny taught a number of photographers and exhibited their work as 'Early paper negatives taken by amateurs between 1844 and 1855, some printed on Talbotype, others on wax paper' to the Glasgow Photographic Exhibition in 1886. Tunny's portraits and landscapes found considerable praise.[49]

Another notable photographer, based in Scotland, whose portraits were well-received was Iván Szabó (1822–58). One of the results of Europe's 'Year of Revolution' in 1848 was the arrival on British shores of a large number of political refugees: and this Hungarian had a great impact on the Scottish photography scene.[50] Initially, he arrived in St Andrews, where he supported himself by teaching European languages at the secondary school. He was taught the art by Thomas Rodger (1832–83), the town's talented first professional photographer. In mid-July 1856, Iván Szabó removed to the capital, where Sir David Brewster advised Professor James David Forbes:

> If you know of any friends who wish to have a good Photograph of any of their family, I would recommend to them, as a first rate artist, Mr Szabo, a Hungarian who

was one of the Hungarian army that surrendered at Komoran [*sic*]. He has since that time taught French and German in this Country, but having taken a liking to Photography his friends advised him to follow it as a profession. He is quite a Gentleman and a most sensible fellow.

> He has taken a house at No. 4 Salisbury Place, Newington.[51]

Brewster had been flattered by the portrait taken by Szabó, and subsequently used in a micro-photograph retailed by the Manchester optician, J. B. Dancer [Figs 5.13 a and b].

Before long, in the eyes of local critics reviewing the annual Photographic Society of Scotland's exhibition, Szabó had equalled his tutor:

> Nothing can exceed Mr Rodger's power of catching a characteristic expression or attitude, and the tints are soft and delicate, though sufficiently decided. Some portraits by Ivan Szabo, of Salisbury Place, Newington,

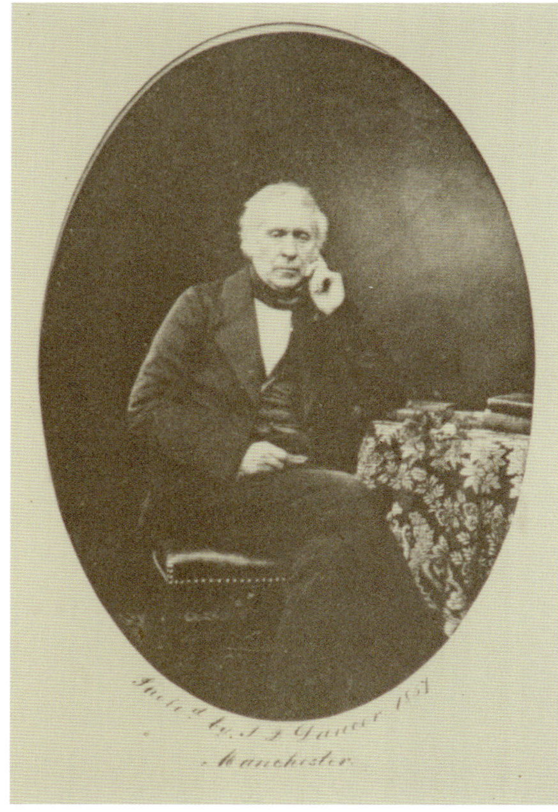

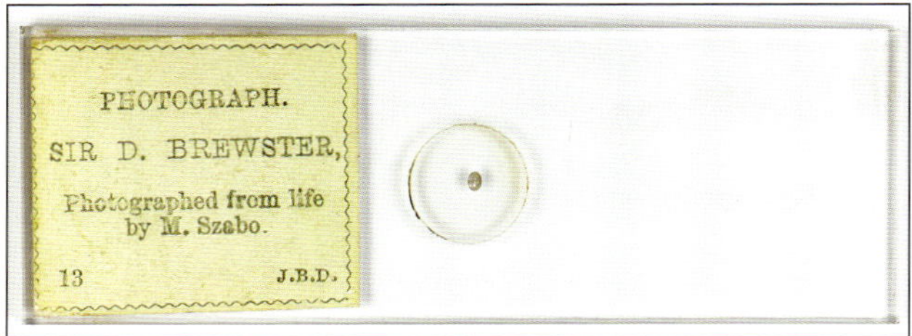

Figs 5.13 a (left) and b (above): (a) Iván Szabó, 'Sir D. Brewster photographed from life by M. Szabo', albumen print enlarged from (b) micro-photograph, *c*.1855. (Howarth-Loomes Collection at National Museums Scotland, IL.2003.44.9.405.23)

a pupil, if we remember rightly, of Mr Rodger's, are in many respects equal to those exhibited by his instructor, and are decidedly superior to any others in the exhibition.[52]

Another was to state:

Messrs Rodger, Tunny, Szabo and Adamson, … all exhibit works of varied excellence and unquestionable ability. … The gentleman whose portraits next claim attention is, I understand, a Hungarian, who, until the recent disturbances in his own country, held a commission in the Hungarian army. The gain is ours that he has exchanged arms for art, the sword for the camera. Considering the limited time which Mr Szabo has as yet devoted to the cultivation of photography, his success is not only remarkable in itself, but holds out the promise that he will ere long attain the very highest position among photographers. Mr Szabo is particularly happy in the natural and pleasing pose of his figures, his works being worthy of admiration equally as pictures and as likenesses.[53]

Iván Szabó [FIG. 5.14] subsequently won a medal at the Brussels Exhibition for his portrait of 'Mrs Finlay'. However, his health was frail and he died suddenly of apoplexy in November 1858. His studio and business was taken on by the former miniaturist, Kenneth MacLeay.[54]

Thomas Rodger (1832–83), Szabó's instructor, was the son of a house painter in St Andrews, and is listed in the 1851 Census as a 'druggist', at the age of 18. He had apparently attended the university's chemistry class for the session 1849/50, where he was taught by Dr John Adamson as the university professor was terminally ill. Rodger began working with Adamson as an assistant, and then he was apprenticed to a local pharmacist named Dr Thomas Malcolm, along with George Berwick.[55] Rodger and Berwick became great friends, to the extent that one of Rodger's sons was named after George [FIG. 5.15].

Dr Adamson's interest in Rodger continued, while his

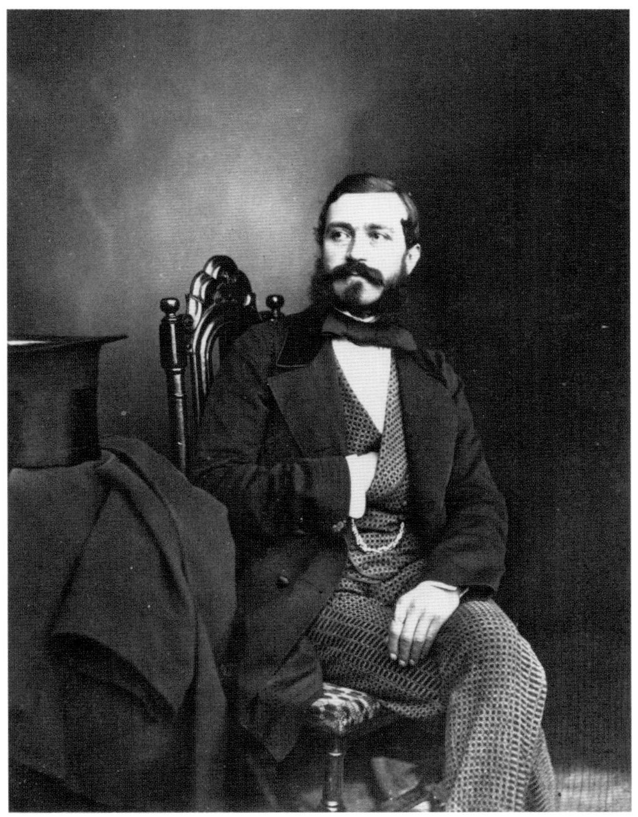

Fig. 5.14: Iván Szabó, self-portrait, *c.*1855, modern copy of an albumen print from an album once belonging to David Brewster. (Private collection)

burgh between 1856 and 1864, the Photographic Society's exhibition in London in 1858, and the Photographic Society of Glasgow in 1859.[58] His work was evidently highly thought of, as shown by a critic of the Edinburgh exhibition in 1856:

> Nothing can excel Mr Rodger's power of catching a characteristic expression or attitude, and the tints are soft and delicate, though sufficiently decided.[59]

Rodger was awarded a silver medal for his calotype portraits exhibited at Aberdeen in 1853; and the following year the Royal Scottish Society of Arts also awarded him a medal for his paper 'On Collodion Calotype'.[60] After this his exhibits were all in collodion. He won further medals from the Photographic Society of Scotland in 1859 and 1864.[61] Rodger constructed a purpose-built studio in St Andrews, and thanks to the ongoing interest of John Adamson, who may well have used this space for some of his own photographic portraiture, Rodger's work was not entirely commercial, although numbers of the popular cartes-de-visite have been noted with his address.[62]

After F. S. Archer's publication of his wet collodion process in late 1851, the number of professional photographers increased in Scottish cities. Among them was Aberdeen-born John Moffat (1819–94):

> An engraver by profession, he was also a competent crayon and chalk artist, and at the advent of the Daguerreotype process naturally set himself to the reading up and studying the new art that was then taking the world by storm. It was not, however, till the publication of the collodion process in 1850 [*sic*] that he resolutely set himself to master the practice of it.[63]

own burgeoning medical practice prevented him from spending much time with photography. It seems likely that Adamson trained him as thoroughly as his own brother – his early work has a rich density of colour which gives it great distinction. Rodger may have begun work as St Andrews's first professional photographer as early as 1849, probably with financial and practical assistance from his father. The influential friendship of John Adamson meant that Rodger was introduced to a wide circle of prominent people [Fig. 5.16], both locally and beyond, such as Sir Coutts Lindsay, painter and aesthete, which helped establish the young man in his business. He was involved in helping Lord Kinnaird catalogue his art collection photographically in the 1850s.[56] His involvement with Rossie Priory continued into the 1860s.[57] He exhibited at the Aberdeen Mechanics' Institute in 1853, at the London Photographic Institution in 1854, the British Association Meeting in Glasgow in 1855, the Photographic Society of Scotland's exhibitions in Edin-

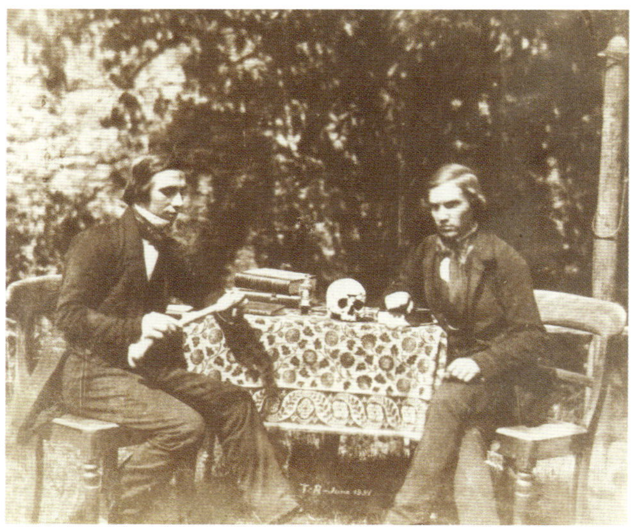

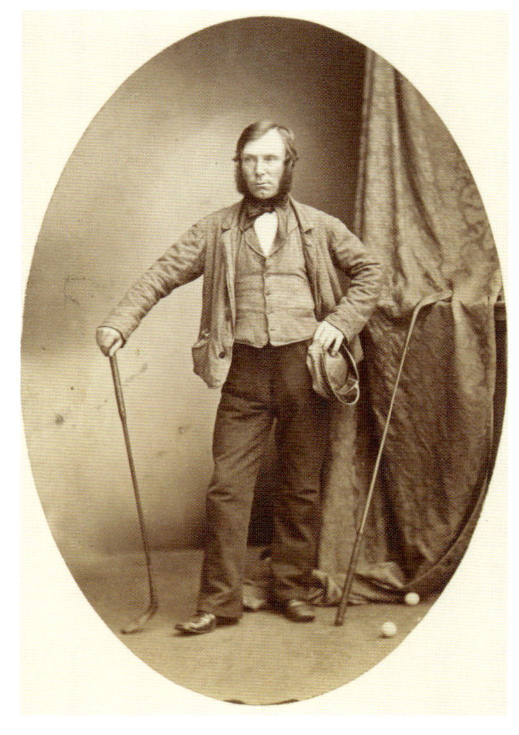

Fig. 5.15 (above): Thomas Rodger, 'Dr George Berwick and Mr Rodger', 1851, calotype. (St Andrews University Library Special Collections, ALB-6-33[1])

Fig. 5.16 (right): Thomas Rodger, 'Allan Robertson (1815–59), golf champion 1850–51', 1855, albumen print. (St Andrews University Library, Special Collections, ALB-1-3)

Moving to Nicolson Square in Edinburgh's Old Town in 1854, where he first worked as a photographer, Moffat was initially recorded in the street directory as an engraver. That same year he opened a branch in Dundee, run by J. A. Walker 'who will have the entire management of the business here, and conduct it on Mr Moffat's principle'.[64] Moffat joined the Photographic Society of Scotland, and exhibited in their shows from 1858, his portraits receiving critical acclaim. He moved in 1856 from Nicolson Square to the east end of Princes Street, and a central location at no. 60 from 1859. Subsequent moves westwards were to 103 in 1861, then 125 Princes Street in 1875.[65] A day-book covering the period 30 June 1856 to 31 May 1858, which lists customers, charges and expenses, is an unusual and historically rewarding survival. His profit for the second half of 1856 was £600, showing his success in his business.[66]

Moffat is probably best remembered now for two sessions, specifically using the carte-de-visite format – the first on 8 March 1864, at a meeting of the Photographic Society of Scotland [Figs 5.17 a and b]:

The President [Sir David Brewster] then read two communications 'On the Use of the Light of Magnesium Wire in Combustion, as a Photographic Agent' [by Henry Roscoe, who had previously read them before the Manchester Literary and Philosophical Society] …

Some interesting experiments followed these communications. The first of these was photographing a bust, which was illuminated by light from the combustion of magnesium, which had been forwarded to the President from Manchester. … A second experiment was made, the sitters being Sir David Brewster and Mr Talbot. When the picture was developed and submitted for inspection, it was found to be very satisfactory, the likenesses of each of the eminent sitters being excellent. The time of exposure was 42 seconds.[67]

Moffat wrote to Talbot suggesting a further meeting:

I am very anxious to do you justice in the proposed sitting and hope to produce such a portrait that will

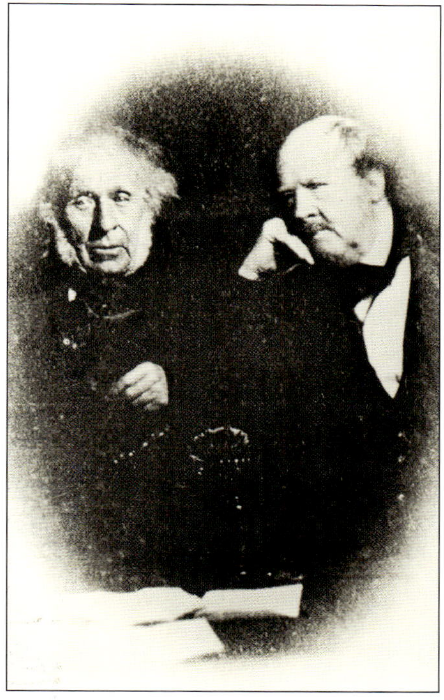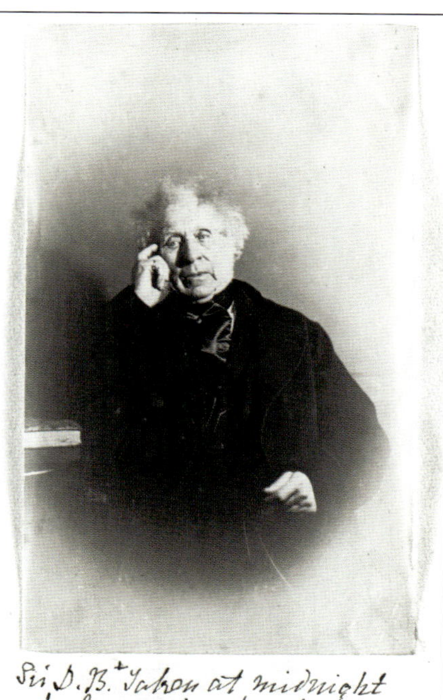

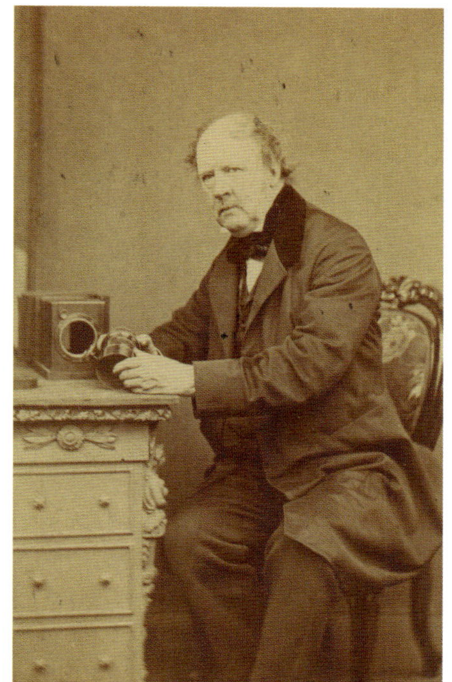

at least bear comparison with any I have yet produced.

The little thing with the light of the magnesium wire was very well as far as the experiment went, but many more experiments would have to be undertaken before we could make the pictures presentable as portraits.[68]

So in May 1864, Moffat photographed William Henry Fox Talbot, sitting with a camera lens in his hands, at his premises at 103 Princes Street [FIG. 5.17 c].[69] Two further accounts of Moffat's business are recorded by contemporaries, one in 1876, and another in 1887.[70] The firm survived well into the 20th century.

The carte-de-visite was the second form of photogra-

phy that, after the stereo image, allowed commercial practitioners to reach eager customers. One or more small portraits were produced in the studio rapidly on a single negative, and the customer was asked to choose which image he or she thought worthy of reproduction. Invented by the Parisian photographer, A. A. E. Disdéri, who observed that an entire culture had grown up around the leaving of visiting cards by the leisured new middle classes, these cartes-de-visite were slightly larger than the visiting card. Once one had exchanged cartes with one's nearest family and friends, one could begin to collect portraits of the famous, or infamous; and once Queen Victoria had been encouraged to have her image released in this format, collecting became the fashion.[71]

The photographers' metier divided between portraiture and landscape. Archibald Burns (1831–80), for instance, was mostly interested in landscape. He started life in the publishing trade and specialised in producing photographic views for the new class of tourists who travelled to Scotland to see 'Edinburgh and its neighbourhood' and the scenery conjured up by Sir Walter Scott's fiction. As well as

Fig. 5.17 a (left) and b (middle): (a) John Moffat, 'Sir David Brewster and W. H. F. Talbot taken by magnesium light', 1864, carte-de-visite. (National Museums Scotland); and (b) 'Sir D.B. Taken at midnight by Magnesium Light', 1864, modern print of a carte-de-visite from an album once belonging to David Brewster. (Private collection)

Fig. 5.17 c (right): John Moffat, 'W. H. F. Talbot', 1864, carte-de-visite. (Royal Photographic Society / Science & Society Picture Library, 2003-5001/2/24052)

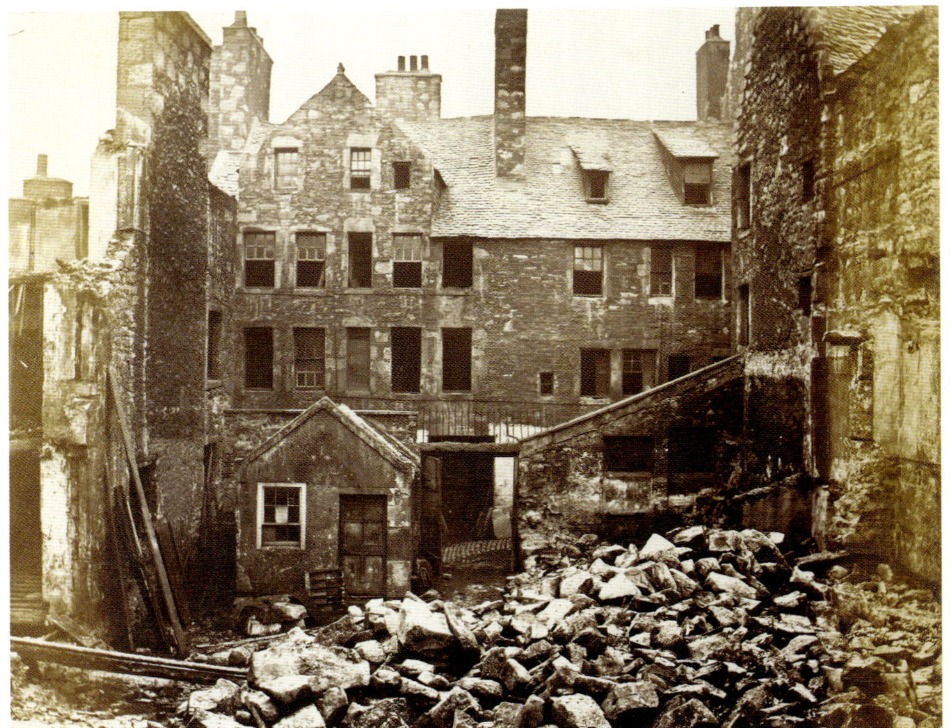

stereo images he produced from 1858, Burns made albumen prints, to be tipped into books, most notably Thomas Henderson's *Picturesque 'Bits' of Old Edinburgh*, published in 1868.[72] Burns was subsequently hired to photograph part of this area of Edinburgh which was swept away and redeveloped a few years later. With the passing of the Edinburgh Improvement Act in 1867, ancient and decaying properties around the High Street were bought up and demolition began in November 1870 [FIG. 5.18]. Roddy Simpson observes that Burns may have been motivated by his awareness of the documentary photography that Thomas Annan was undertaking for the Glasgow Improvement Trust.[73] Burns produced twenty-six images of vanished medieval Edinburgh, one set using a salted print technique. Simpson suggests this may have been to emphasise the historical nature of the content; or possibly as homage to the recently-deceased D. O. Hill.[74] Burns also produced his landscape images in carte-de-visite format [FIG. 5.19].

Magnus Jackson (1831–1891) was originally apprenticed to his father, Thomas, a carver and gilder and print-

seller.[75] In the 1850s he moved to London, where he learnt photography in the course of a three-year stay. He returned to Perth and by 1860 set up a small studio in Marshall Place. He used this as a base and undertook extended outside work. Jackson wrote in 1881:

The variety of work a photographer, who devotes his time to subjects outside the studio, is called upon to do in the course of a season is what no one would believe unless they saw the work performed. … the tent I have been using for the last fifteen years … is an ordinary trunk three feet long, eighteen inches deep, and of the same width as depth. I have it so arranged that three small wheels can be attached. The cloth or covering is supported by four wooden rods fitting into the corner of the trunk. The inside is fitted so as to hold all that is necessary for a week's work on 10 x 12 plates; the divisions help to support the bath while working. My reasons for holding on for so many years to the same primitive-looking vehicle or tent is that it is very

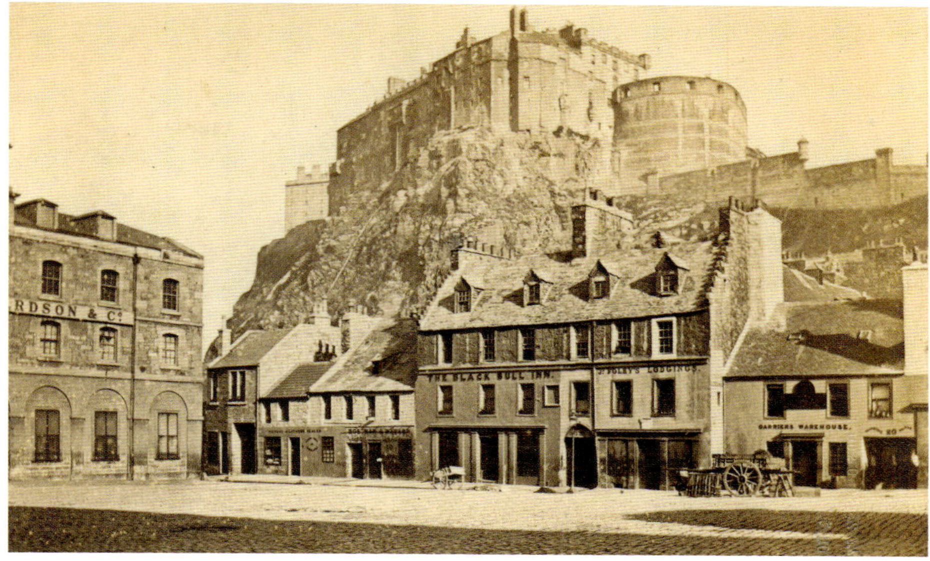

Fig. 5.19: Archibald Burns, 'The Grass-market and Edinburgh Castle', carte-de-visite. (Howarth-Loomes Collection at National Museums Scotland, IL.2003. 44.4.2165)

convenient for getting into woods through which run narrow paths, and along the footpaths adjoining the policies of mansion houses in the country. It can also be put into the luggage van if going per rail, and the wheels fit very nicely on the back seat of an ordinary dog cart, having sometimes to go very long distances into the country to photograph I do not think that anything better could be devised …. It has only one fault; when packed ready for a journey the weight is something terrible ….[76]

Jackson took impressive photographs of animals from 1856, when he learnt the salutary lesson that it was no use making pictures where the quality was good 'but not one was a good picture of any of the animals'.[77] His excellent advice on the subject takes in the psychology of the cattle-men and grooms as well as the animals themselves.

One of Jackson's most extraordinary pictures was taken in the Perth slaughter house – for which he became responsible as a Town Councillor from 1878 [FIG. 5.20]. His role as a public figure connects to the evident interest in people and events seen in his photography – often an unexpected view or grouping. He was perhaps most famous in his time for tackling the difficult question of photographing trees, dealing with the awkward question of the green which

defeated so many earlier photographers, and expressing the patience needed, in waiting for the wind to drop: 'Trees', he wrote, 'need very careful watching' [FIG. 5.21].[78]

John Urie (1820–1910) became one of Glasgow's most prolific commercial photographers. Born in Paisley, the son of a handloom weaver, he set up in business in the Gallow-gate as a woodblock printer, moving to Buchanan Street in 1849. Like so many others, he was keen to see the latest technologies in his line at the Great Exhibition. He spent three weeks in London, visiting the Crystal Palace

… almost every day, and was greatly impressed by the vastness of the building, the greatness of the crowds that thronged it, and the wonderful variety of the products … to be seen there. The machinery and the pictures, especially the daguerreotypes, were the principal sources of attraction to me.[79]

The daguerreotypes fascinated Urie, who 'thought it might be a good thing if I could work it in connection with my wood engraving business'.[80] Fortunately for Urie, this was the moment when the wet collodion process was announced, and he found its use in his business saved time and money; he built a large glass house on the roof of his premises, which won the praise of the Glasgow press.[81] Portrait

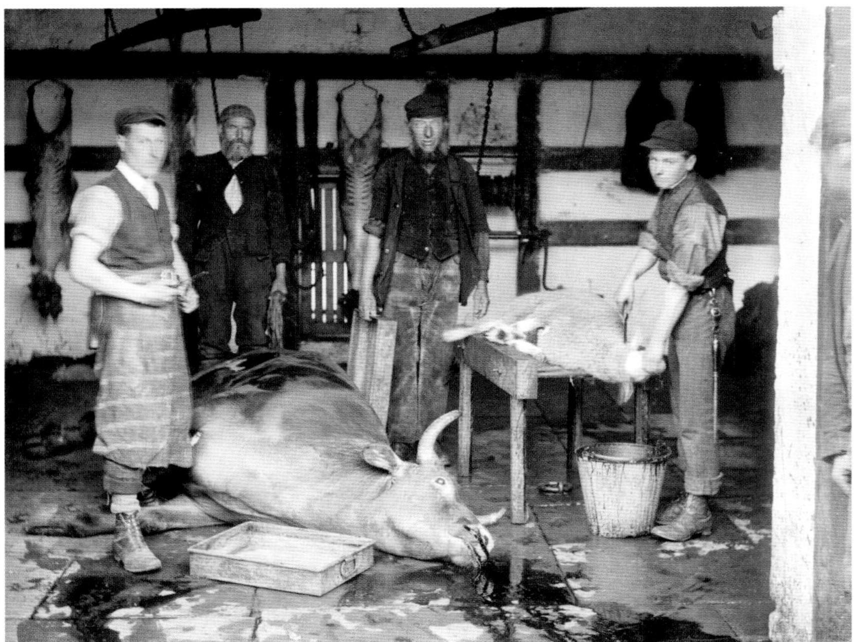

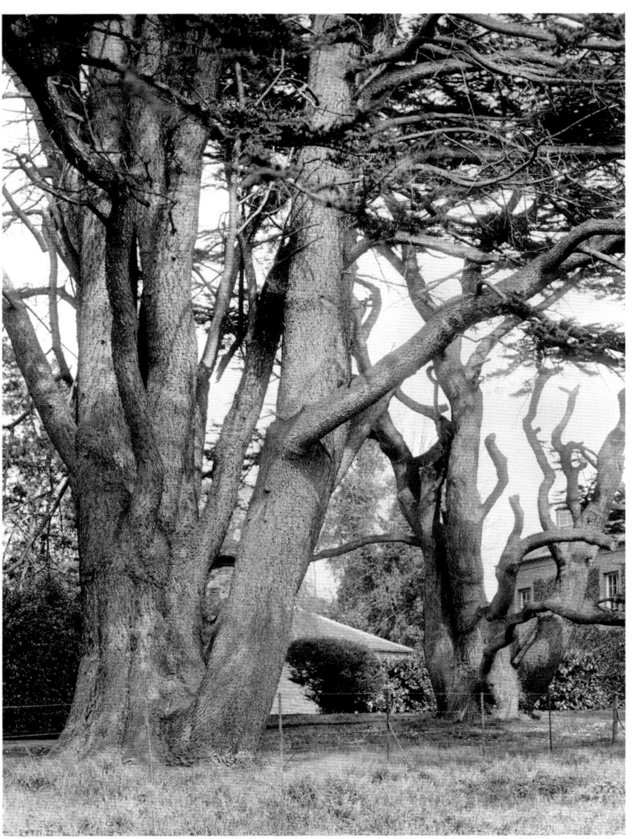

photography became the mainstay of his business, and he also contributed to inventions to help with the application of photography to printing.[82]

Urie discovered that 'the financial returns which photography brought me were very great, but they were a small consideration compared with the interest of the study of the art itself'; this statement may be taken as true of many commercial photographers at this period.[83]

In 1857, Urie photographed

a young lady of good birth and breeding whose deeds were soon to startle the world. Madeline [*sic*] Smith came twice to my studio to be photographed – once along with her father and mother and the other members of the family to be taken in the customary family group [Fig. 5.22], and on another occasion she came alone. She was a strikingly beautiful girl of about twenty, and though there was then nothing but her personality to attract attention, I could not help remembering her ....[84]

Within months she was the central figure in a celebrated trial at the Crown Court in Edinburgh and famously

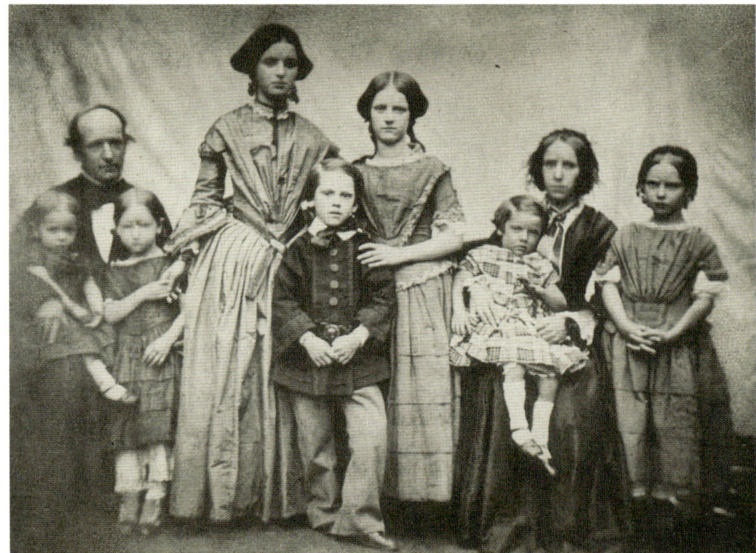

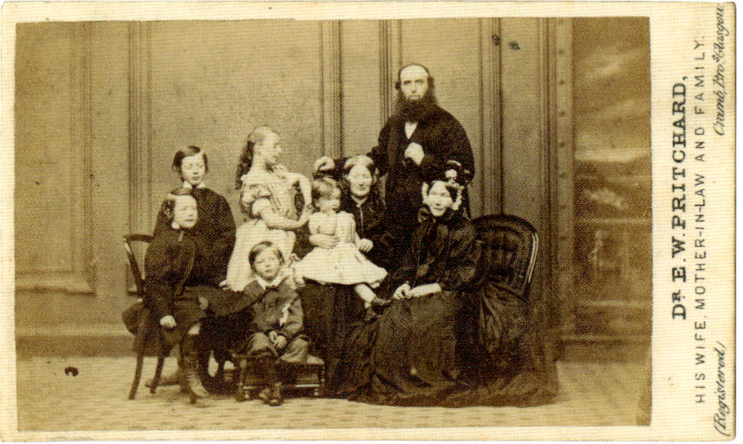

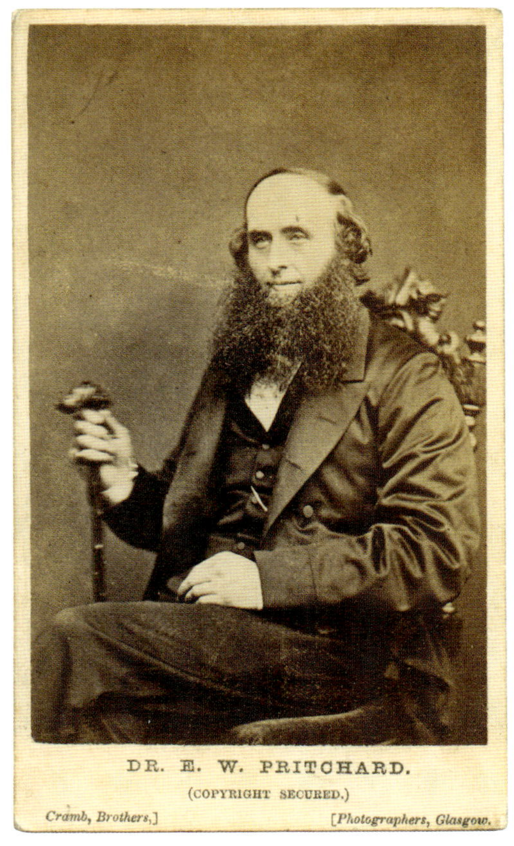

Figs 5.23 (above and left): Cramb Brothers, 'Dr Edward Pritchard' and 'The Pritchard Family'. (Howarth-Loomes Collection at National Museums Scotland, IL.2003.44.4. 518 and 517)

acquitted with a 'Not Proven' verdict of poisoning her French lover. Urie placed a large photograph of Madeleine Smith in his window that caused such crowds that the police requested that he remove it. He declined. Urie also knew Dr Pritchard ('the Poisoner') 'whose name has since become a synonym for baseness, cruelty and hypocrisy'; and John Henry Greatrex, photographer and forger of bank notes, a 'sanctimonious hypocrite'.[85]

After he left Dundee in 1859, James Cramb joined photographic forces with his brother John (d.1894) in Glasgow. The Crambs were photographers of some standing in the city. Like Urie, they were able to play to public voyeurism.

In the early 1860s a local doctor and his family came into the studio to have their portraits taken in carte-de-visite form. Imagine their excitement when the Crambs realised that not only was the doctor convicted of a horrible murder; but that they had photographed two of his victims as well. This was Dr Edward Pritchard (1825–65), regarded as something of a quack, who murdered his mother-in-law and his wife.[86] As the *Glasgow Herald* reported on the final days of the last man to be publicly executed in the city, its newspaper advertising columns were warning off would-be pirates of the Cramb Brothers' good fortune [FIGS 5.23]:

Fig. 5.24 (right): Attributed to Thomas Rodger, James Valentine, 1850, calotype. (St Andrews University Library, Special Collections, ALB-6-81)

Fig. 5.25 (opposite): George Washington Wilson, 'Balmoral Castle from the north-west', stereoscopic photographs, 1863, albumen prints. (Howarth-Loomes Collection at National Museums Scotland, IL.2003.44.6.1.132)

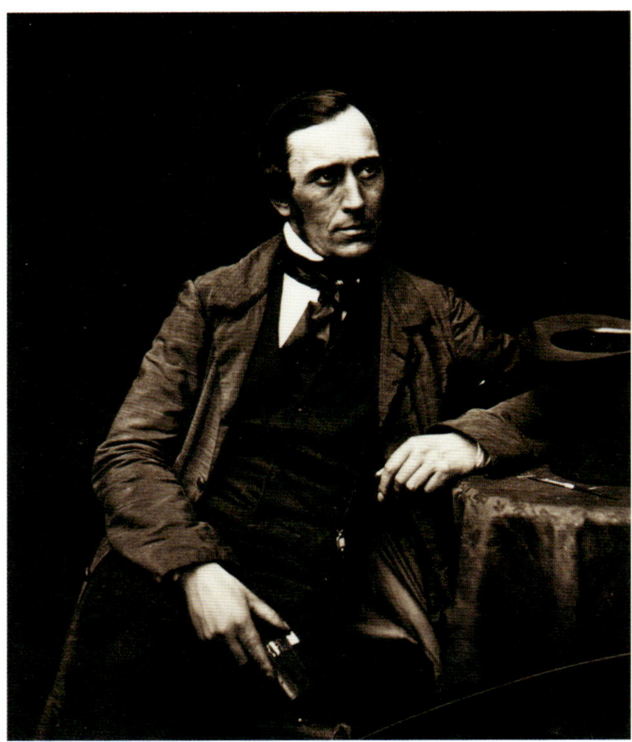

Portrait of Dr E. W. Pritchard
Cramb Brothers, 67 West Nile Street, Glasgow, have published Several Fine Carte Portraits of Dr Pritchard – Price 1s each or by post for 13 Stamps. Terms to the Trade liberal. These Portraits are all Copyright, and bear the Publishers' Names. Legal Proceedings will be taken against any one offering Pirated Copies for Sale.[87]

Above this advertisement, J. H. Greatrex was offering 'a single sitting, one shilling', John Urie advertised cartes-de-visite at 'five shillings per dozen', while J. Howie's Glasgow studio offered '4s per dozen', and the Glasgow Photographic Company's rates were '5s per dozen'. Cramb Brothers were maximising their profit from crime.

The two most prolific photographers in Scotland at this period were Aberdeen-based George Washington Wilson (1823–93) and Dundee-born James Valentine (1815–79). Valentine was ten years older than Wilson, but he followed in the footsteps of the Aberdonian. Both were successful businessmen, and happily large sections of their working archives have survived to the present.[88]

James Valentine was a linen weaver's son sent to Edinburgh to study art. Returning home in 1832 he set up in a linen block printing business with his father. In 1838, he formed his own business in engraving and printing, particularly in stationery. By 1851, Valentine employed fourteen workers and decided to add portrait photography to the firm's business: apparently, he first took himself to Paris to learn the daguerreotype.[89] By 1855 he claimed to be building one of the largest glasshouses in the country, and his portrait photography proved successful [FIG. 5.24]. Valentine (observing what was happening in Aberdeen) added landscape photography to his portfolio, with such success that

Queen Victoria commissioned forty views of Highland landscape from the firm in 1867, rewarding him with a Royal Warrant.[90] Valentine, like Annan in Glasgow and Burns in Edinburgh, also took photographs of decaying Dundee before its demolition at about this time.[91]

After instruction at Francis Frith's studio in Surrey, William Valentine (1844–1907) joined his father's firm in 1863, becoming a skilled landscape photographer; his younger brother, George Dobson Valentine (1852–1890), specialised in portraiture – his poor health took him to New Zealand in 1884. An elder brother, from James Valentine's first marriage, John Valentine (1841–68) was a pioneering photographer in Hawaii, dying in California aged only 26.[92] The firm's greatest commercial success, however, came after the death of the founder with the popularity of the picture postcard towards the end of the 19th century.

The most prolific and acclaimed commercial Scottish photographer of the 19th century was, without a doubt, George Washington Wilson (1823–93). He was much emulated. One of his obituaries stated:

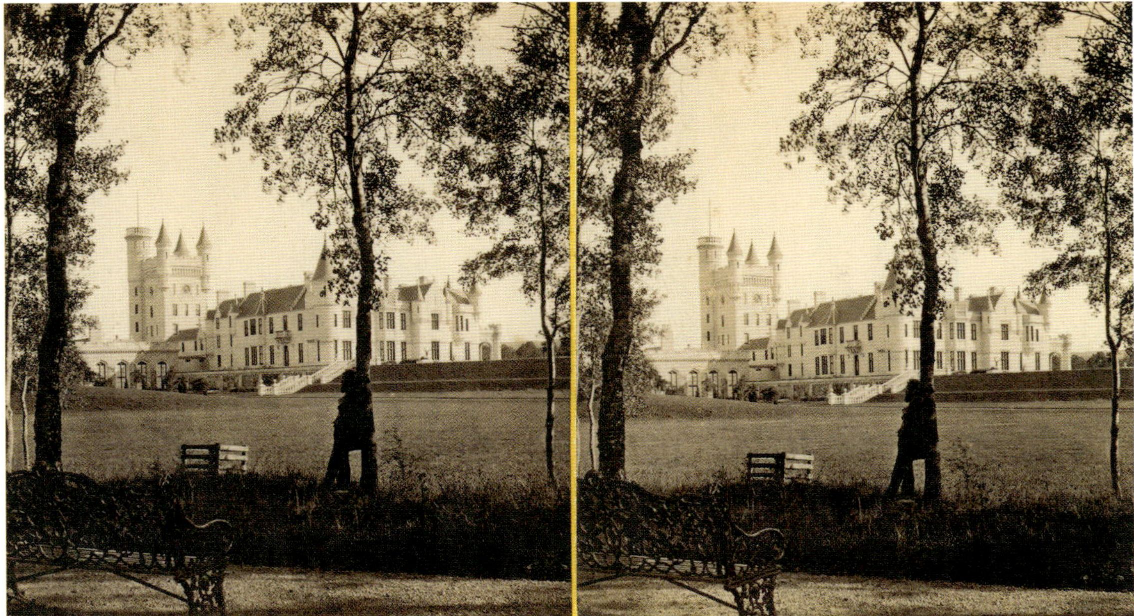

There is no one whose name has ever been associated with all that is excellent in the art of photography that stands so high as that of George Washington Wilson, of Aberdeen. When he first issued his singularly beautiful stereoscopic views, it was at once universally felt that a real artist had arisen, one who would aid in elevating landscape photography from the somewhat low state of mediocrity in which it existed. In his pictures were concentrated the highest development of artistic beauty and technical skill, and they became models for imitation. … we know of some who did not disdain to follow Mr Wilson's footsteps in such a literal fashion as, having one of his views in hand, and observing the relation of one portion of scenery to the other, to eventually by this means discover the identical spot where his camera had been planted, and there also plant their own tripods.[93]

Wilson was born in rural obscurity. After completing an apprenticeship as a carpenter in 1846, aged 23, he decided to train as an artist in Edinburgh and became a miniaturist. Roger Taylor suggests that Wilson left the capital in late 1848 to be with his dying father; and chose to settle, after a period in London, in Aberdeen.[94] Here he continued portrait painting, supplemented by drawing and painting classes, close to where his friend, John Hay junior, ran his photographic business.[95] In 1853 they became partners as Wilson & Hay. Another obituary recounts how 'a year later, the new firm had the distinction of being summoned to Balmoral to take views under the guidance of the Prince Consort, for the Royal album – a practice which was afterwards followed by Mr Wilson every three years' [FIG. 5.25].[96] Wilson and Hay dissolved their partnership after two years – John Hay's father was in financial difficulties – and Wilson carried on alone.[97] He proved to be a very successful businessman, as well as a fine photographer, but the seal of royal approval at the outset of his photographic career may have given him the impetus he needed.

Wilson won medals for his photography from the outset: his first was obtained (with Hay) at the photographic exhibition held at the Aberdeen Mechanics' Institute in 1853, but he went on to win recognition internationally in London in 1862, and Paris in 1867, the latter for work in stereoscopy.[98] He then turned from portrait photography to that of the landscape:

He had a keen eye for scenic beauty, and he thoroughly

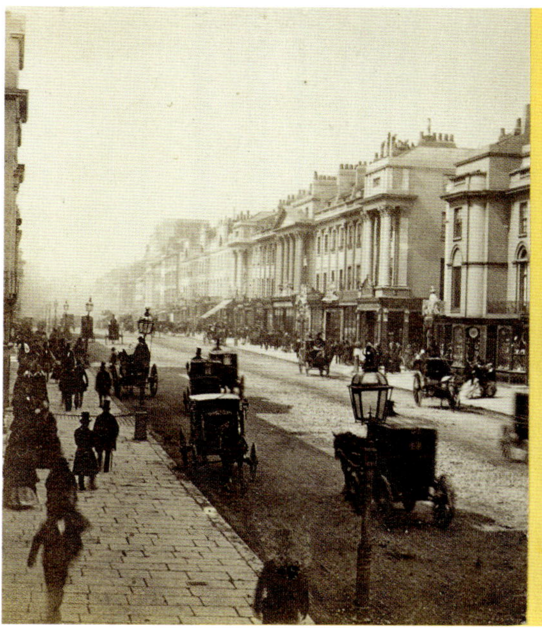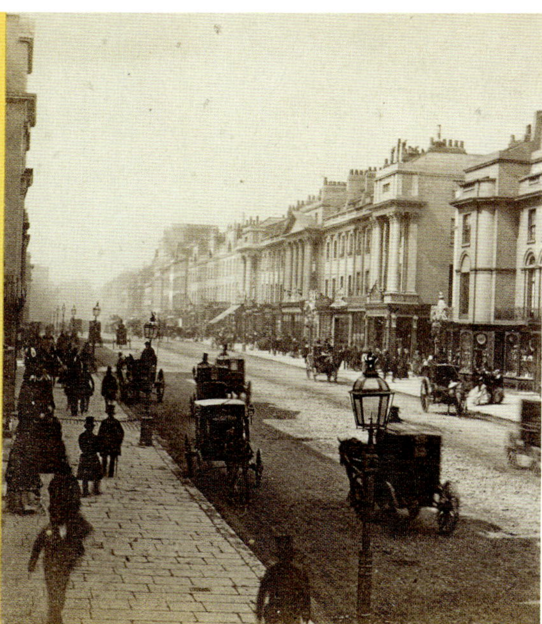

explored his native land searching for the picturesque. When he found it, he skilfully brought his camera to bear, thus producing vivid representations of the many charming and romantic scenes which are so abundant in North Britain. What he thus accomplished has been aptly and justly summed up in a single sentence – 'Sir Walter Scott discovered Scotland with his pen, and George Washington Wilson rediscovered it with his camera.'[99]

At a period when the tourist industry was gathering impetus, Wilson enabled his customers to see the sites described by Scott in their own drawing rooms; many were thus encouraged to visit and take home pictures of the places they had seen for themselves. It was the beginning of 'Bonnie Scotland'.

By 1860, the local press was happy to expend column inches on Wilson's art:

His views … attracted much and just attention on their appearance, as being equal, if not superior to any land-scape views which had been then issued by any native artist; and the publication of his latest instantaneous views of the Loch of Park and the Breaking Wave, last year, was generally recognised as a new era in stereo-scopic photography …. These views at once secured Mr Wilson a name second to none in the kingdom.[100]

The 'instantaneous' photographs were also a great success with his public. Later examples show people moving thorough busy streets [FIG. 5.26], or gun-fire from ships' cannon. This was in contrast with earlier photographs which were mostly unable to register movement, making streets appear empty.

Wilson's premises in Aberdeen expanded, and in 1864 alone the business sold over half a million prints.[101] By 1872, he was employing 'thirty assistants who are constantly occupied in printing, toning, mounting, and filling his numerous orders';[102] by the Census of 1881 there were 15 men, 21 women, two boys and two girls.[103] On his trips, first around Scotland, and subsequently around the United Kingdom, he was accompanied by an assistant, William Gellie, whose help is acknowledged in a number of papers published by Wilson in the photographic press.[104]

Wilson also formed a fruitful relationship with the London optical instrument maker J. H. Dallmeyer, who provided him with his cameras, both stereoscopic and for cabinet views. Dallmeyer, once apprenticed to the famous optical instrument maker Andrew Ross, reportedly said

> … that Mr Wilson had been using a single lens, which he had recently made for him, for instantaneous stereoscopic work: its peculiarity being, that it might be worked with a very large aperture. In the ordinary stereoscope, with a lens of six inches focus, in which these views were intended to be inspected, the slight curvature of lines would be corrected, as it had a tendency to produce the opposite kind of distortion to that exhibited in these pictures, and thus, in the stereoscope, the lines would appear straight. … and for larger pictures, Mr Wilson used the triple achromatic lens; and he had just been making him a camera with a swing back, which, permitting the plane of delineation and the object always to be parallel, prevented convergence of the lines when it was necessary to tilt the camera.[105]

Not all photographers, amateur or commercial, had such a happy relationship with the suppliers of the tools of their trade.

Camera makers and suppliers of chemicals and materials from 1839

Despite the rapid increase in commercial photographers after the introduction of the wet plate process, there was no real corresponding growth of photographic suppliers in Scotland, possibly because materials and apparatus could be obtained easily from south of the Border or abroad. A growing railway network ensured that most photographic

hardware could be supplied from the boom towns of Birmingham and Manchester, where small workshops produced wooden frames for larger camera wholesalers, and optical glass – difficult to come by before the repeal of duty in 1848 – ensured the growth of firms like Chance Brothers of Smethwick, Birmingham.[106] In the early years, photographers emulated W. H. F. Talbot by getting their cameras constructed locally or finding an optical instrument maker who could supply one made in London or Paris; chemicals and paper could similarly be obtained from high street vendors.[107]

A handful of enthusiastic pioneers designed or produced their own apparatus, and we have already seen some of Thomas Davidson's early efforts in this direction. According to Davidson, he supplied a camera to Hill and Adamson in 1844: this could take big images, using glass optics, or be adapted to use a mirror, which produced comparatively smaller images:

> Messrs Adamson and Hill … had also a camera, about two feet square, fitted up for taking portraits as large as life; but the imperfections in it, & difficulty of preparing paper so large, were against it. I also made a speculum of 24" diameter & 30" focus, for the aforesaid, for taking smaller portraits, or to reflect light on the object; but that was never much used.[108]

Davidson had also used a device resembling the solar microscope, to produce 'enlargements' of botanical specimens. He wrote in relation to Woodward's solar camera (a form of photographic enlarger):

> … it is by no means entitled to a patent. It is now more

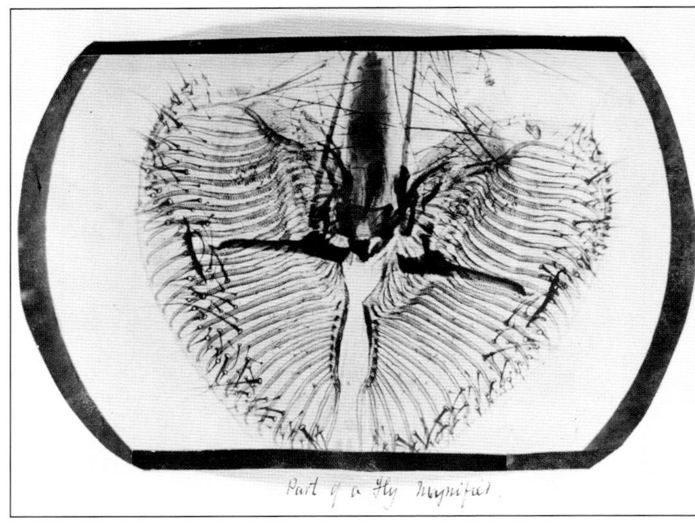

Fig. 5.27: Unknown photographer, 'Part of a fly magnified', *c*.1855, modern copy of an albumen print from an album once belonging to David Brewster. (Private collection)

than sixteen years since I assisted Messrs. Adamson & Hill, photographers, Edinburgh, in taking a few copies of magnified representations of minute objects by an achromatic solar microscope, which I had made for Mr. Octavius David Hill, Calton Stairs, Edinburgh …. The objects I adopted were transverse sections of wood, about 3/8" in diameter. The enlarged copies were … about 18" in diameter. The last time I saw the aforesaid magnified impressions, they were framed & hanging in James Bryson's shop, Princes Street, Edinburgh; & as regards patents, Mr Hill & Mr Adamson had arranged to lodge a *Caveat*, but the premature & lamented death of the latter prevented it.[109]

These photo-micrographs – presumably similar in appearance to those made as early as 1839 by W. H. F. Talbot (which still survive) – demonstrate that though most photography was done by contact printing [Fig. 5.27], so that negatives and positives were almost always the same size, even from the very beginnings there was a method of enlarging the image through magnification, and the power of the sun.[110]

John Urie was inspired by the daguerreotype process after seeing examples at the Crystal Palace in 1851, and in his memoirs he wrote about his experiments:

Having read up all that I could about the [daguerreotype] process, I got hold of a cigar box, and, with the eye of a pair of spectacles for a lens, I made my first camera. This was long before the days of elaborate and beautifully-constructed cameras. We had then to feel our way. The early photographers had to do everything for themselves – design their own cameras, and get them made

by a joiner or cabinet-maker; prepare their own plates and papers; and mix up their own chemicals for development.[111]

He would not have been alone in this do-it-yourself photography.

Photographic chemicals were perhaps easier to obtain, as local pharmacies and chemists could, and did, supply explosive and poisonous materials – such as the gun-cotton dissolved in ether that formed the basis of the collodion process, or the heated mercury that sensitised plates for the daguerreotype – that would make today's health and safety-conscious officials blench with horror.

Edinburgh designers and suppliers of apparatus

After the introduction of the wet plate process, further improvements were made to apparatus by Scottish practitioners. One such camera pioneer was the surgeon and amateur photographer Dr William Walker (d.1885), who was involved in the formation of the Photographic Society of Scotland in March 1856. He read a paper on the calotype process at their meeting on 13 May 1856, and described a portable camera made by Robert Bell. This was subsequently illustrated and shows a convenient folding apparatus with a cloth body over a collapsible wooden frame, which was 'suited to take pictures 8 inches by 7, measures when folded down, with the slide and box with prepared paper inside, 18 inches in length by 10 in breadth, and 2½ in thickness, and weighs only 8¾ lbs.' The description of this apparatus ended: 'The Camera was made by Mr Bell, of 25, Potterrow, Edinburgh, and cost, without Lens or stand, £3 3. 0.'[112]

The following year, Horatio Ross read a paper to the Society about 'the comparative merits of different processes of Photography in taking views in mountainous districts', his stated ambition being to do justice to 'our grand scenery of our own Highlands'. He was at this period using the wet collodion process, and found the amount of apparatus this entailed meant that he had to use a pony and the services of some 'willing fellows', number unspecified. 'My large folding Camera [plates 14 x 12 inches] was packed in a shiny leather cover. It was made by our townsman, Mr Robert Bell, of 25, Potter Row, who indeed fitted me out with all my gear, and I am happy to take this opportunity of doing him justice by stating that his Camera answered admirably, and at the end of all the severe work and exposure it went through, it had not warped, or gone wrong in any way.'[113] Ross appears to have displayed this camera to members of the Photographic Society of Scotland in May 1856.[114]

Charles George Hood Kinnear (1830–94) was an architect, one of the partners in the successful Edinburgh firm of Peddie & Kinnear; one biographer has suggested that his interest in photography was ignited by his former employer, the architect David Bryce. He was able to undertake many of his photographic expeditions through inheritance.[115] In 1857 he made a photographic tour on the Continent with two like-minded friends:

Towards the end of last August, I set out, in company with two other members of this Society, Messrs. Alexander and James Adam, on an Architectural and Photographic Tour through the Northern Provinces of France. My companions had a folding camera, by Ottewill, taking pictures 11 x 9 ins, and I had a flexible-bodied camera, made according to my directions, by Mr Bell, of Potterrow. It is somewhat on the principle of Capt. Fowkes' [*sic*] camera … ; but my camera is stronger than Capt. Fowkes', and so is less liable to be injured by the rough usage to be met with in travelling, and is besides more rigid; and, moreover, it costs only one half the price of the other. It takes pictures 12 ½ x 10 ½ ins., and folds into a compass of 15 ½ x 13 x 3 ½ inches, and weighs 13 lbs., with slide and focusing-glass complete. Both cameras were fitted with Ross's single achromatic lenses.[116]

Kinnear's camera – a design rapidly adopted by many camera makers – was described and illustrated in a further number of the journal, where its characteristics were summarized, and its manufacturer identified as Mr Bell: it 'cost about £4' [FIGS 5.28].[117] The revolutionary aspect of Kinnear's design was that the bellows were tapering, rather than square. The leather bellows nested into each other until almost flat when closed, so the camera could be reduced to a smaller and lighter piece of kit.

The Photographic Society of Scotland held an exhibition of apparatus at their meeting in November 1859. At this, a portable camera was shown by a 'Mr Nelson, Photographic Apparatus Maker, Clyde Street. It was essentially the same as that exhibited to the Society by Mr Kinnear in 1857', modified to fold up without dismantling, and dispensing

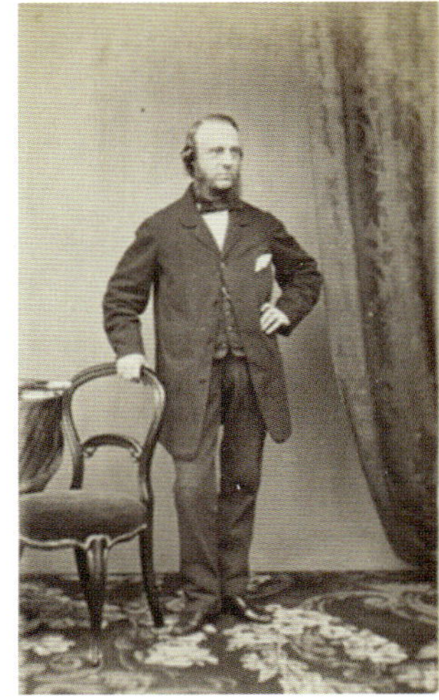
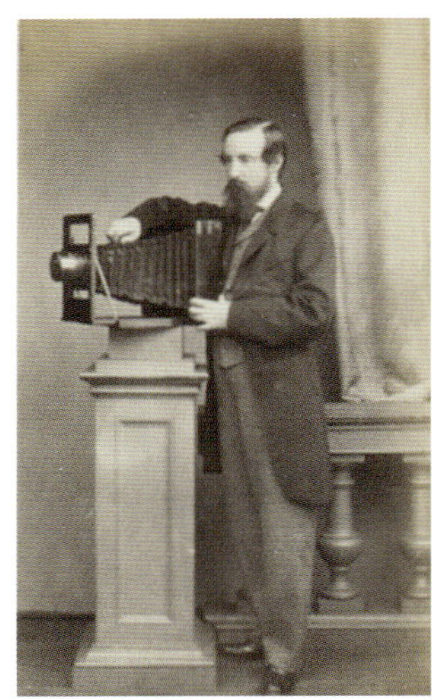
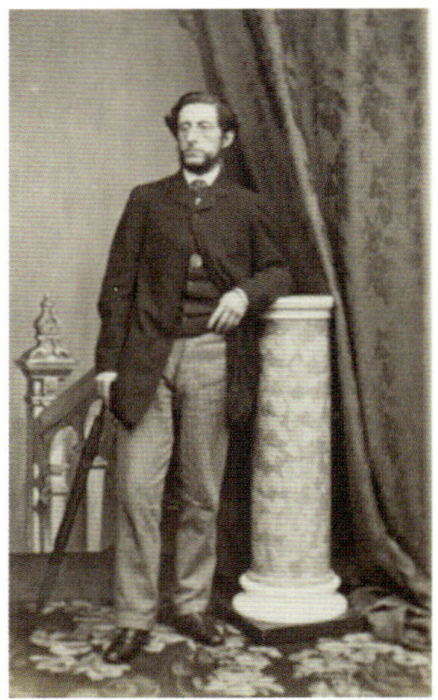
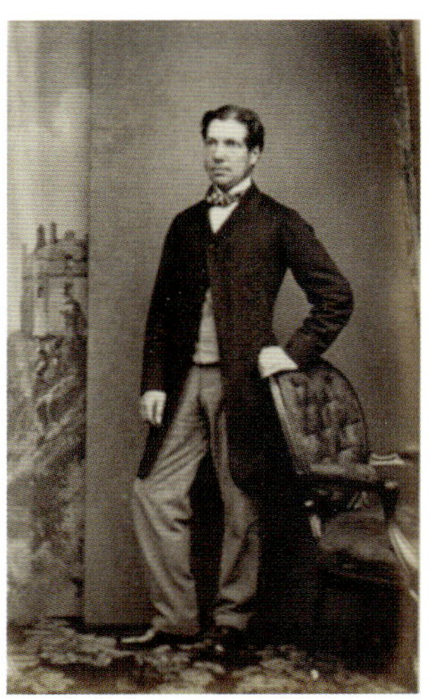

Figs 5.28: Unknown photographers, members of the Edinburgh Photographic Exchange Club, including C. G. H. Kinnear, top right, *c*.1859, carte-de-visite. (Edinburgh Photographic Exchange Club album, National Media Museum/Science & Society Picture Library, 1990-5131-1-46)

with the horizontal movement.[118] Kinnear showed his portable camera again 'possessing a new arrangement of swing-back … Mr Kinnear stated that he had found the swing-back arrangement of the greatest use in taking views of buildings in cases when it was impossible to get sufficiently far away from the building to admit of the whole of it being included in the view, and yet the camera kept horizontal …'. This new modification ensured that the resulting image had parallel perpendicular lines. Once again, the camera was made by Mr Bell.[119]

Bell appears in local street directories between 1856 and 1866 as a 'wright' or joiner, and used his skills for customers eager to improve the simple sliding wooden boxes of the early days.[120] Nelson's camera was mentioned again, this time by W. D. Clark (1813–73), in a paper read before the Photographic Society of Scotland in May 1863. Clark compared Nelson's camera favourably with Kinnear's:

> Everyone knows the distortion got by tilting up the camera in architectural subjects …. I think a very simple way of getting rid of this defect with a Kinnear camera is to have the front part that carries the lens so arranged that it can be turned back and fixed at any angle necessary … A 15 x 12 camera I have, made by Mr Nelson of Edinburgh has this plan carried out ingeniously ….[121]

At an ordinary meeting of the Photographic Society of Scotland in April 1858, a number of pieces of improved apparatus were displayed, both by photographers and instrument makers. Dark tents ('furnished with folding tables; the large tent weighed 15 lbs and the smaller 7 lbs'), a tripod stand and portable stereoscopic camera with nine

dark slides were shown by John Lennie. He was a member of a family of optical instrument makers who opened a shop at 46 Princes Street in 1857, and had been a member of the Society since June 1857.[122] With his brothers William, James and Joseph, he helped their widowed mother, Mrs Eliza Lennie, with the business after the death of their father, James Lennie, in December 1854.[123] Before James Lennie's death, the firm advertised 'Stereoscopes, French and Italian photographs, photographic apparatus' as part of their stock-in-trade.[124] By 1856, Mrs Lennie's 'optical and photographic establishment' was advertising that its 'Photographic Department' could supply 'Portrait Lenses,

Fig. 5.29: *Captain Francis Fowke, bellows camera incomplete, c.1857, made by Ottewill & Co., London. (National Media Museum / Science & Society Picture Library, 1908-134)*

View Lenses, Expanding Cameras, Bellows Cameras, Stereoscopic Cameras, Tripod Stands … at Wholesale Prices.' In addition, the shop was 'Solo Agent in Scotland for the Sale of W. T. Fisher's Positive Collodion, 9d per ounce. Developing Solution, 2d per pint.'[125] Three years later, 'The Edinburgh Photographic Establishment, 46 Princes Street, where every Article required for the Practice of Photography may be obtained' was able to list a considerable variety of kit, including 'Apparatus Manufactured Expressly For India', as well as developing materials and apparatus.[126] The following year, Lennie's offered 'Stereoscopes, Achromatic, Prismatic, Cosmoramic, Dioramic, Portable, and every novelty invented'; while they were also selling 'Stereoscopic Slides of Edinburgh and Scottish scenery, Coloured Groups, Statuary, Illuminations, and Transparencies, the largest choice in Scotland.'[127] It seems clear from surviving stereo images that the firm was selling large numbers bought in from different photographers during the period of immense popular demand of the 1850s and 1860s.

Further apparatus shown at the Photographic Society of Scotland included material from Paris and London: for instance, Captain Fowke's portable camera by Ottewill of London [Fig. 5.29]. James Bryson (1824–94) exhibited a 'microscopic camera' and 'a new form of stereoscope for exhibiting pictures of any kind'. Bryson was from a family of horologists and instrument makers; his elder brother Alexander had 'exhibited and explained his apparatus for micro-photography' at a meeting of the Photographic Society of Scotland in December 1857.[128] J. M. Bryson's shop in Princes Street had shown the photo-micrographs produced by Thomas Davidson's apparatus, and so it is hardly surprising that the brothers were interested in micro-photography. A final piece of apparatus displayed at

this meeting of the Society was 'a new form of stereoscope for large pictures', shown by John Moffat, 'similar in principle' to the example shown by James Bryson.[129]

Bryson's most famous client was the Astronomer Royal for Scotland, C. Piazzi Smyth (1819–1900). He and his wife Jessica Duncan set off for Tenerife in the Canary Islands in 1855. They intended to try the theory expressed by Isaac Newton that the thinner atmosphere in the mountains would enable the viewer to see the heavens with less distortion:

In the month of May, 1856, H.M. Lords Commissioners of the Admiralty, advised by the Astronomer Royal, were pleased to entrust me with a scientific mission to the Peak of Teneriffe [*sic*]. Their Lordships most liberally placed £500 at my disposal for defraying the necessary expenses; and left me, within the bounds of such expenditure, as untrammelled by detailed instructions, as any explorer could desire.[130]

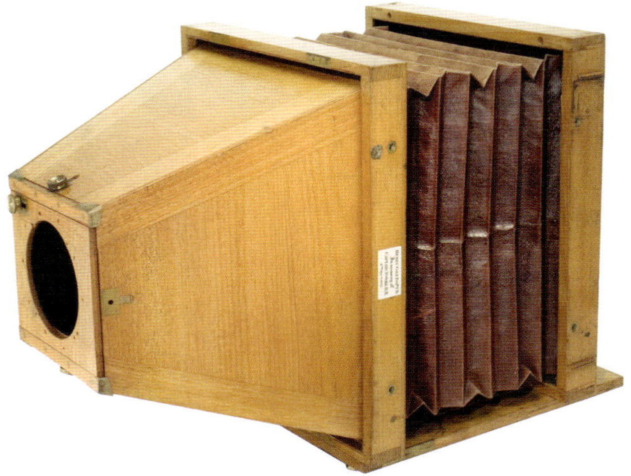

Fig. 5.30: C. Piazzi Smyth, 'Sheepshanks Telescope, First erected on Mount Guajara, the Peak of Teneriffe in the Distance, 1856', stereo albumen prints. (Howarth-Loomes Collection at National Museums Scotland, IL.2003.44.8. 159.5)

Smyth's sarcasm was to lose him many friends over the coming years; but the experience of travelling to the Canaries in a borrowed yacht, with borrowed equipment, to try to do his job – observing the clear heavens from the highest peak on an Atlantic island, instead of through the smog of the aptly-named Auld Reekie – brought on his sharpness of tongue. The consistent underfunding of the Royal Observatory at Calton Hill made Smyth increasingly bitter. He had petitioned the government to pay for the trip. The scientific results were subsequently published in a variety of well-received publications (illustrated by enlargements printed by his wife Jessica, and photoglyphic engravings by the process recently devised by Talbot, from his negatives); and his popular account – illustrated by twenty stereo photographs, taken by Smyth during his expedition, bound into the book – was partially underwritten by his London publisher, Lovell Reeve [Fig. 5.30]. This was the first publication to be illustrated in this way:

> Stereographs have not hitherto been bound up, as plates, in a volume; yet that will be found a most convenient way of keeping them, not incompatible with the use of the ordinary stereoscope open below and well adapted for Mr Reeve's new form of the instrument, – The Book Stereoscope, – constructed by Messrs Negretti and Zambra, to fold up in a case like a map.[131]

Teneriffe: An Astronomer's Experiment was published in an edition of two thousand, which necessitated the attachment of 40,000 stereo pairs on to pre-printed pages.

The photographic equipment Smyth took to Tenerife in 1856 may not have been made in Scotland.[132] For Smyth's next major scientific expedition, in 1865 to Egypt, to survey the Great Pyramid of Giza, he designed a small camera. He had a pair of cameras, each with a Dallmeyer lens, using microscope slides coated with wet collodion. The slides were sensitised, developed and fixed inside the camera. These were used to take (mostly successful) images, while magnesium light was burning, inside the passages of the Pyramid.[133] Only one incomplete camera taken to Egypt now survives; but James Bryson made examples in about 1870, and one of these is in the National Media Museum at Bradford.[134]

Equipment and essentials in the West of Scotland

George Mason (1839–1901) FRPS was best-known by the time of his death as a successful Glasgow photographic supplier. He was born in Alloa in 1839 and in 1863 went to work for John Spencer in Sauchiehall Street, Glasgow. He was a wholesaler whose stock ranged across optical, photographic and chemical wares.[135]

Spencer first advertised in the photographic press in June 1856: 'John Spencer supplies Cameras, Cases, Frames, Passe-partout, Chemicals &C at the lowest possible prices', from 16 Saltmarket Street, Glasgow.[136] He followed this in October with a notice for 'Cameras in Walnut wood, from 12s. Double Achromatic Portrait Lenses, mounted in brass with rack and pinion, for 20s. Collodion, Positive or Negative, 5d per oz; for 12 oz. or upwards, 4½d per oz. Nitrate of Silver 4s per oz.'[137] By January 1857, he had 'made arrangements by which he is enabled to keep a much larger stock than formerly, thus avoiding any delay in the execution of orders. Being the importer of goods from America, France, & Germany, he is able not only to have great variety but to sell them at least as low as any one in the trade.'[138] The

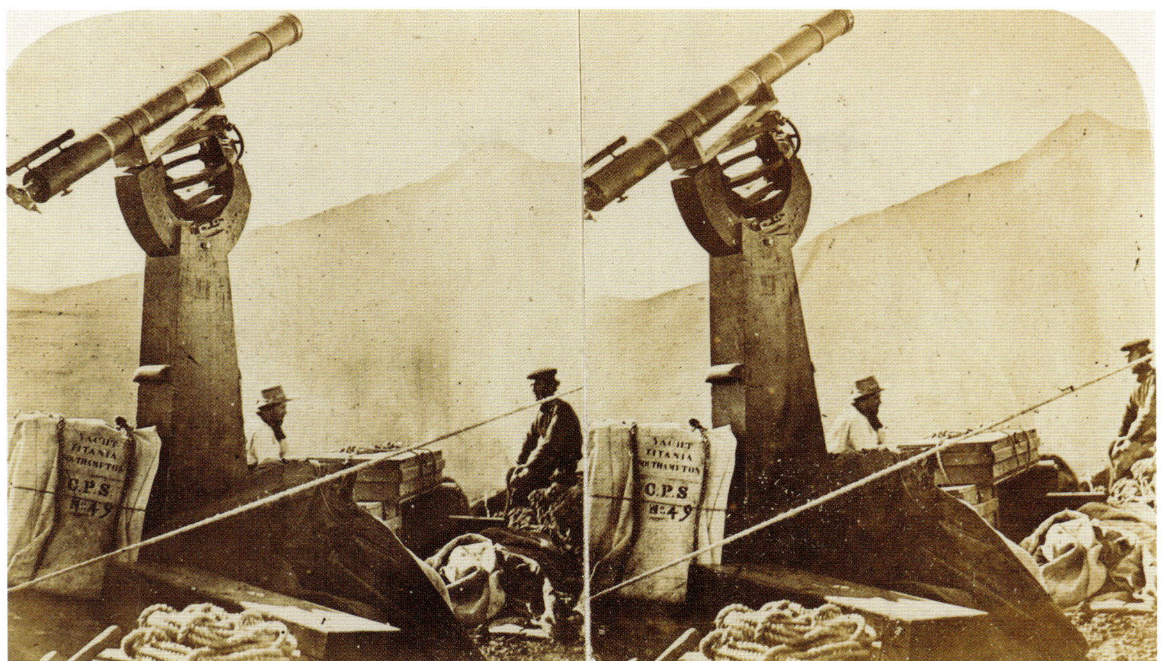

following year, Spencer moved into 'more commodious premises', a 'Photographic Depot' at 30 St Enoch Square.[139] In November 1858 he announced that, along with apparatus, chemicals, and 'every Photographic publication [that is] on Sale', Spencer was also 'Agent for Mr Geo. Wilson's Stereo-scopic Views of Scotland, including Staffa and Iona, the West Highlands, the Falls of Clyde, &c.'[140]

With the rise in demand for albumenised paper as an adjunct of the wet collodion process, John Spencer's obituarist recalled that 'ten years ago [i.e. in 1868], the sole occupation of two girls consisted in breaking the shells of eggs employed in albumenising. In one year alone, Mr Spencer used up 247,000 eggs, selling in twelve months as much as 1200 reams of albumenised paper, which was used not only in this country but exported largely to France, Germany, America and China.'[141] The use of the egg white had led to some discussion about what could be done with the redundant yolks: indeed, as early as 1861, the *British Journal of Photography* had creatively suggested 'The Photographer's Cheesecake'.[142]

John Urie recalled John Spencer as

… one who has done more for the advancement of photography in the west of Scotland than any other man …. I think I can still see his mild and intelligent face, and hear his kindly and attractive voice, while giving instructions to his amateur and professional purchasers of chemicals. All went to him, when in a fix, for counsel and direction, well knowing that his advice would be readily given; and I think I am not wrong in asserting that much of the success of our art in Glasgow is justly due to the warm and earnest interest he took in promoting by every means in his power the well-being of photographic art and artists.[143]

George Mason became Spencer's business partner in 1869, having worked for him for six years. By 1870 he had taken over the concern. At various times, he was a board member of the North British Dry Plate Company, and of G. W. Wilson & Co. Ltd. He took up practical photography in 1853, aged 14, though it is not certain who taught him or where. His subsequent writings under the pen-name 'Mark Oute' first appeared in the *British Journal of Photography* and its *Almanac*, and were subsequently collected as *Pictures in Black and White.* These provided 'studies of photographic life, incident, and character' which were 'held in appreciative remembrance' at the time.[144] John Traill Taylor, editor of the Journal, provided a Preface, in which he admitted that the apparently 'fancy sketches' had, on closer inspection, 'revealed the fact that they were all drawn from life, and drawn too with accuracy'.[145]

Dundee and the North

There was apparently only a small community of photographers, either amateur or commercial, in Scotland's larger northern centres. One man involved in a number of aspects of the photographic art, wrote his autobiography towards the end of his life. This was George Lowden [or Lowdon], junior (1825–1912), whose first advertisement with his father as 'G. Lowden and Son. Opticians and Fancy Mechanics' at 25 Union Street, Dundee, in June 1849, did not mention photography. Lowden re-advertised as 'late G. Lowden & Son' in the *Dundee Courier* in early 1850 with a woodcut of a fly-caught fish, and 'ANGLING' inscribed across it.[146] Dundee, situated on the Firth, or estuary, of the longest river in Scotland, the Tay, was no doubt then (as now) populated with eager fishermen. By July, he was advertising electro-medical coils, in his new profession as 'optician'; his strap-line in March 1851 was:

> Daguerreotype and Calotype Cameras.
> G. Lowden Junr., Optician, would call the attention of Artists, and Amateurs, desirous to prosecute the beautiful art of Photography, to his assortment of Achromatic and other Cameras, fitted for all the processes, which for

general accuracy, will be found equal to those made in London. Cameras, Tripod Stands, Achromatic, Miniscus [*sic*], and Plane Lens, made to order.
> Pure Chemicals Kept.[147]

However, in his 'Reminiscences', Lowden wrote of an earlier interest in photography. He spoke of a lecturer, J. T. Wilson, who gave a series of popular lectures on chemistry:

> In one of the lectures he had occasion to refer to Daguerre's discovery of photography from silver plates, and I procured from Paris and exhibited on the walls of the lecture hall eight Daguerreotypes, taken by Daguerre. They were portraits, clear and bright, but could only be seen by holding them side on to the light. These were the first seen in Dundee.[148]

J. T. Wilson of the Glasgow Mechanics' Institution gave lectures on electricity and optics in Dundee's Watt Institution in May 1844, although there is no mention in the local press of the daguerreotypes. Practitioners of the art had appeared in the town the previous year.[149]

George Lowden claimed to have made the first lenticular stereoscope in 1849 for Sir David Brewster, whom he met through Lord Kinnaird, subsequently devising an improved version of the stereoscope with larger lenses.

> I was taking pictures by the Fox Talbot method process in 1849 (having failed to succeed with it in 1846), and since that period have taken pictures and made many cameras and given instruction to a large number of professionals and amateurs – notably to the late artist-photographer, Mr G. W. Wilson of Aberdeen. I sold him

a camera in 1853, and gave him his first lesson. The camera complete cost him £5 10s, from which out of his artistic hands sprang a considerable fortune.[150]

By 1852, Lowden was advertising his optical instruments, in particular his telescopes, as being 'three-fourth the price charged by English opticians'. His cameras were still fairly prominent:

> … for the Daguerreotype, Calotype, and Glass processes, the Object Glasses of which, both Plain Achromatic, and Double Combination, for large field and correct definition, will be found as good as those of Foreign manufacture, and at a lower figure. The Object Glasses can be separate to give any size of picture. …[151]

A half-plate folding camera survives, with an engraved ivory plate: 'LOWDON / MAKER / DUNDEE' [FIG. 5.31].[152] None of his camera lenses has been noted in the literature, or are known to survive, but these perhaps were unsigned. Lowden exhibited fifteen of his own photographs to the Dundee Royal Infirmary Fund exhibition in 1854.[153] The local press concluded: 'Mr Lowden gives promise of standing in the first class of landscape photographists.'[154]

In Aberdeen, cameras were advertised initially by a scientific instrument maker called William Duncan, among 'Camera Obscuras, Camera Lucidas, Photographic and Daguerreotype Cameras, with Apparatus'.[155] Second-hand items were advertised in the local press from October 1845, when a 'Gentleman about to leave Aberdeen' was eager to divest himself of an 'Acromatic [*sic*] Camera, with Complete Apparatus for Calotype'.[156] The photographer John Lamb (*c.*1829–99), setting up in business in 1853, advertised:

> … The Glass and Calotype processes taught, and accommodation given to Pupils in the Premises, with the use of Ross's finest Lenses … SALTED, Sensitive, Albumenised, Waxed, and Plain Callotype [*sic*] Papers, and Lenses with or without Cameras, may be had at moderate prices. Parties buying a Camera and Lense [*sic*] will have an opportunity of seeing it tried, and be presented with a Collodion (or Glass) Portrait of themselves, as a guarantee of its quality.

> Negative and Positive Collodion at Tenpence per ounce. From the extensive sale which J.L. has received for his Collodion, and the high terms in which it has been spoken of by disinterested Photographers, he takes this opportunity of soliciting a trial of its merits, in the full

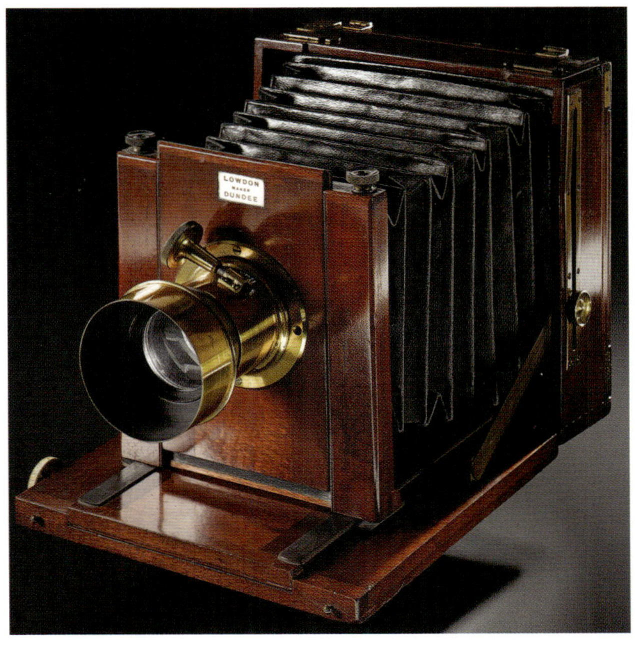

confidence that Artists and Amateurs will find in it an article affording every satisfaction.[157]

When John Hay junior began in the photography business, he advertised that 'cameras, all sizes' could be supplied, as well as 'collodion, 9d per oz'.[158]

In smaller population centres, photography arrived intermittently with travelling practitioners; market towns similar to Hawick, in the Scottish Borders, had to wait until the 1850s before settled professional photographers became a regular part of the high street.[159]

Some conclusions

A rapid tally through the street directories shows that in Scotland's main areas of population there were the following numbers of settled studios during the first thirty years of the profession (below):

This does not take into account the numbers of people who worked in these small, family-run establishments. The few large businesses included that of George Washington Wilson in Aberdeen. Roger Taylor comments that the 1861 Census shows that the town of Aberdeen employed 62 people in the photographic trade, whereas the street directory for that year shows 14 named firms. The same Census shows 644 people employed throughout Scotland.[160] By 1881, there were 953 working photographers listed in the Census for Scotland; though this probably does not account for what Richard Torrance calls 'the ancillary trades' associated with photography. Ranging from 'agent' to 'traveller', he lists some 53 associated trades.[161] Many of these people would be drawn from the photographer's own family, with the women in particular, silently in many cases, doing bookwork or printing. Nevertheless, as demand for photography continued to grow throughout the 19th century, as processes became faster and cheaper, the profession of photographer stabilised and became eminently respectable.

1840	1845	1850	1855	1860	1865	1870
Aberdeen						
0	0	0	1	13	19	24
Dundee						
0	0	1	3	5	9	12
Edinburgh						
0	2	2	13	27	43	41
Glasgow						
0	1	1	13	43	54	41

Notes

1. 'Professional Photography in Edinburgh', *British Journal of Photography* 7 (1 March 1860): 69.
2. See Edgerton 2008.
3. National Museums Scotland, IL.2003.44.2.299. Another similar example, without the annotations on the reverse, is in the Library of Congress, DAG no. 1298; <www.loc.gov/pictures/collection/dag/item/2004664479/>
4. Identified by Lene Grinde, 'Conservation of Stereo Daguer-reotypes', George Eastman House (2005), figs 54 and 65: see <http://notesonphotographs.org/index.php?title=Grinde,_Lene._%22Conservation_of_Stereo_Daguerreotypes.%22>
5. Paolo Brenni, 'Nineteenth-century French scientific instrument makers: XIII: Soleil, Duboscq, and their Successors', *Bulletin of the Scientific Instrument Society* 51 (1996): 7–16.
6. Claudet advertised 'The stereoscopic daguerreotype views of the Great Exhibition, by Mr. Claudet, which have excited the admiration of Her Majesty and Prince Albert, are now exhibited at Mr. Claudet's Photographic Gallery …' in the *London Literary Journal* (1 December 1851): 581; a large single daguerreotype was made by John Jabez Edwin Mayall, now in the Getty Museum (inv. no. 84.XT.955), and he advertised 'Stereoscopic Views of the Great Exhibition' in Measom 1853: 28. Similar images were sold in 1995 by descendants of T. R. Williams, at Bonhams Chelsea (see *An Important Collection of T. R. Williams Daguerreotypes* [6 July 1995], lots 18, 28–31). Examples of these views are identified on the Victoria and Albert Museum's website as being by T. R. Williams (inv. nos 1685-1939 and 1682-1939).
7. Part of this chapter was presented at the 30th Scientific Instrument Commission Symposium at Kassel in 2011.
8. Catalogue 1851, I: 404–78; for Duboscq-Soleil, see vol. III: 1235.
9. Reports 1852: 243.
10. Charles Wheatstone, 'Contributions to the Physiology of Vision: Part the First. On Some Remarkable, and hitherto unobserved Phenomena of Binocular Vision', *Philosophical Transactions of the Royal Society of London* 128 (1838): 371–94; see also Bowers 2001: 45–54.
11. I was helped with my doubts about the veracity of the story of the birth of the stereoscope by an unpublished paper by Professor Roger Taylor, 'The Optical Wonder of the Age', kindly supplied in 2009. This has subsequently been published in Richardson (ed.) 2013: 1–12.
12. Brewster 1856: 28; he goes on to enumerate seven further 'imperfections', see 62–3.
13. 'Dr Adamson of St Andrews, at my request, executed two binocular portraits of himself, which were generally circulated and greatly admired', wrote Brewster in his anonymous review [David Brewster], 'Binocular vision', *North British Review* 17 (1851): 176; and Brewster 1856: 29. These images (inv. no. St Andrews University Library ALB8-88) are discussed by A. D. Morrison-Low, 'A Third Dimension', in Reid et al. (eds) 2010: 104–5.
14. Brewster 1856: 28–30.
15. Brewster 1856: 30, quoting *La Presse*, 28 December 1850: 1550.
16. Reports 1852: 272.
17. Brewster 1856: 31.
18. Taylor 2009. As a historian of photography who has had privileged access to the Royal Archives, Taylor has satisfied himself that Brewster's pleasing vignette cannot be confirmed from the Queen's extensive diaries.
19. A number have survived, but the quality appears poor, possibly because the images had to be attached to card, which may have contributed to their fading. The Talbot Establishment in Reading appears to have produced a quantity, complete with their stamp.
20. Nottage came from a family who owned a foundry, and opened a shop to sell bronze statuary on Oxford Street in 1854. He bought in half a dozen stereo paper tissues and geometric designs from abroad, and these were placed informally in the window, from where they were instantly snapped up. Realising he had a successful product, Nottage continued to sell these, rapidly abandoning the bronzes. See <www.photolondon.org.uk/pages/details.asp?pid=5707> and also Sarah McDonald, 'London Stereoscopic Company', in Hannavy (ed.) (2008), 2: 870–2.
21. Anon., 'Twelve Stereographs by Archibald Burns of Edinburgh', *Photographic Journal* 1 (3 November 1859): 267–8; Anon., 'Critical Notices. Stereograms from Scotland. By Mr Archibald Burns, Edinburgh', *Photographic News* 2 (25 November 1859): 135–6.
22. Editorial, *Photographic Notes* 2 (1 March 1857): 81.

Note: Website addresses checked and correct at the time of going to press.

23. James Ross, 'A Few Extracts from a Photographer's Old Ledger', *British Journal of Photography* 20 (14 February 1873): 76.

24. John Nicol, 'Notes from the North', *British Journal of Photography* 25 (17 December 1878): 617; Pipes 1984: 32–3.

25. James Ross, 'A Few Extracts from a Photographer's Old Ledger', *British Journal of Photography* 20 (14 February 1873): 76.

26. *British Journal of Photography* 14 (6 September 1867): 422–3.

27. Catalogue of the Aberdeen exhibition 1853, nos 203 and 206: <http://peib.dmu.ac.uk/itemexhibition.php?exbtnid=1010&orderBy=exhibid&exhibitionTitle=1853%2C+Aberdeen%2C+Mechanics%27+Institution>

28. Guthrie 1860.

29. *Children's Friend* 5 (1 February 1865): 23–5.

30. This pairing of 'before' and 'after' photographs was later used for fundraising (controversially and on a large public scale) by Dr Barnardo in London. His ragged schools were started in 1866.

31. James Ross, 'A Few Extracts from a Photographer's Old Ledger', *British Journal of Photography* 20 (14 February 1873): 75.

32. *Ibid.*, and in *The Times*, 17 April 1850.

33. James Ross, 'A Few Extracts from a Photographer's Old Ledger', *British Journal of Photography* 20 (14 February 1873): 76.

34. *Ibid.*, 77. Ross lived at East Powderhall from 1859 to 1864.

35. *Ibid.*

36. <http://peib.dmu.ac.uk/itemphotographer.php?photogNo=352&orderby=coverage&photogName=Ross+%26amp%3B+Thomson>

37. Review, *Athenaeum* (29 May 1858): 692.

38. John Nicol, 'Notes from the North', *British Journal of Photography* 25 (17 December 1878): 617.

39. 'James Ross', *British Journal of Photography* 42 (29 May 1895): 194.

40. J. G. Tunny, 'Early Reminiscences of Photography', *British Journal of Photography* 16 (12 November 1869): 545–6.

41. *Ibid.*

42. Tunny's career is given in detail by Bukits 2009; see also Torrance 2011, 2: 323–6.

43. John Nicol, 'Notes from the North', *British Journal of Photography* 24 (29 June 1877): 309.

44. *Caledonian Mercury*, 7 June 1856. The camera is held by National Museums Scotland, T.1953.X.13.

45. Bukits 2009: 45. The Princes Street premises were described in an article, 'In the North', *British Journal of Photography* 17 (10 June 1870): 264–6.

46. Cited by Torrance 2011, 2: 323–6.

47. Bukits 2009: 38–57.

48. John Nicol, 'Notes from the North', *British Journal of Photography* 23 (25 February 1876): 90–1.

49. Catalogue 1886, item 43; for Tunny's exhibits between 1839 and 1865, see <http://peib.dmu.ac.uk/itemphotographer.php?photogNo=408&orderby=coverage&photogName=Tunny%2C+James+Good+%28%3F-1887%29> Also, for example: 'There are none, however, which please us more than those of Mr J. G. Tunny of Edinburgh, whose portraits and landscapes are much to our taste', in a Review of the Photographic Society, London, exhibition, *Art-journal* [New Series] 1 (1855): 85, referring to professional photographers. See also Buckits 2009: 157–80.

50. See Julie Lawson, 'Iván Szabó: A Hungarian Photographer in Scotland', in Collins (ed.) 1990: 17–21; James Downs, 'Out of the Shadows: Iván Szabó (1822–58), a forgotten "photographic luminary"', *Studies in Photography* (2008): 28–38.

51. St Andrews University Library, J. D. Forbes Papers Msdep7/incoming letters/1856/93: Letter from Sir David Brewster to J. D. Forbes (14 October 1856). Brewster sent J. B. Dancer a copy of the Iván Szabó photograph of himself, taken with a small crystal lens according to Brewster's theory of accuracy in portraiture, and Dancer used this, almost ironically, reduced further as a microscopic image. See Michael Hallett, 'Dancer, John Benjamin', in Hannavy (ed.) 2008, 1: 378–80.

52. *Caledonian Mercury*, Review, 29 December 1856.

53. *Edinburgh Evening Courant*, 17 January 1857; and see *The Daily Scotsman*, 4 February 1857.

54. 'Report of the meeting of the Photographic Society of Scotland', *Journal of the Photographic Society of London* 5 (1858): 73; Torrance 2011, 1: 295.

55. 'Dum Spiro Spero', 'Scottish Pioneers in Photography', *British Journal of Photography* 44 (9 July 1897): 444–3. See also Karen A. Johnstone, 'Thomas Rodger, 1832–1883' (unpublished M.Litt dissertation, University of St Andrews, 1997).

56. 'Dum Spiro Spero', 'Scottish Pioneers in Photography', *British Journal of Photography* 44 (9 July 1897): 442.

57. Letter from Rodger to Kinnaird, from St Andrews (25 November 1867) about printing from the negatives and testing two or three lenses, Perth and Kinross County Archives, MS 100/2, Bundle 665, Misc. correspondence 1859–69. St Andrews University has recently acquired photographic material from Rossie Priory, while this book was being written.

58. <http://peib.dmu.ac.uk/itemphotographer.php?photogNo=
349&orderby=coverage&photogName=Rodger%2C+Thomas+
%281833-1883%29>

59. Review of Photographic Society of Scotland exhibition,
Caledonian Mercury, 29 December 1856.

60. For his 'Portrait of Professor Macdonald and Major Playfair',
Aberdeen Journal, 7 December 1853; Thomas Rodger, 'On
Collodion Calotype', *Transactions of the Royal Scottish Society of
Arts* 4 (1856): 292–9; Thomas Rodger, 'The Collodion Process',
British Journal of Photography 3 (1857): 256–7.

61. See announcement in the *Photographic Journal* 6 (15 February
1860): 155; and *Caledonian Mercury*, 10 March 1864.

62. Graham Smith, 'James David Forbes and Thomas Rodger',
Scottish Photography Bulletin (Autumn 1987): 14–19; A. D.
Morrison-Low, 'Dr John Adamson and Thomas Rodger:
Amateur and Professional Photography in Nineteenth-century
St Andrews', in Lawson, McKenzie and Morrison-Low (eds)
1993: 18–37.

63. Obituary, *British Journal of Photography* 38 (16 March 1894):
168–9.

64. *Dundee, Perth and Cupar Advertiser*, 7 July 1854.

65. Moffat 1989: 5, 9, 13.

66. Mentioned in Moffat 1989: 11–13, in a private collection; a
Xerox copy is with the National Library of Scotland.

67. *Photographic Journal* 9 (15 March 1864): 5–6, quoted by Moffat
1989: 17.

68. See document 8809, Moffat to Talbot, 16 March 1864,
<http://foxtalbot.dmu.ac.uk/letters/letters.html>

69. Michael Hallett, 'Early Magnesium Light Portraits', *History of
Photography* 10, 1986: 299–301; Graham Smith, 'Magnesium
Light Portraits', *History of Photography* 12, 1988: 88–9.

70. John Nicol, 'Notes from the North', *British Journal of Photo-
graphy* 23 (25 February 1876): 90–1 and 464; 'A Visit to Mr John
Moffat's Photographic Art Gallery, 125 Princes Street, Edinburgh',
Mercantile Age (9 September 1887): both accounts quoted in
Moffat 1989: 19–25.

71. Howarth-Loomes 1973: 81–91.

72. Roddy Simpson, 'Archibald Burns – photographer of Old Edinburgh', *Studies in Photography* (2009): 68–77.

73. *Ibid.*, 73.

74. *Ibid.*, 76. The salt-print set is held by the National Library of
Scotland.

75. See Susan Payne and Paul Adair, 'Magnus Jackson and the Black

76. Magnus Jackson, 'Photography outside the studio', a communication to the Dundee and East of Scotland Photographic Association, *British Journal of Photography* 28 (4 February 1881): 55.

77. *Ibid.*, 69, quoting the gentleman owner of the cattle.

78. *Ibid.*, 56.

79. Urie 1908: 107.

80. *Ibid.*, 108.

81. *Glasgow Sentinel*, 4 September 1862.

82. Don [Donald] McCoo, 'John Urie Portrait Photographer, 1820–
1910', *Scottish Photography Bulletin* 2 (1989): 3–14.

83. Urie 1908: 116.

84. *Ibid.*, 125.

85. *Ibid.*, 126, 128.

86. A. H. Millar, 'Pritchard, Edward William (1825–1865)', revised
by J. Gilliland:
<http://www.oxforddnb.com/view/article/ 22820>

87. *Glasgow Herald*, 15 July 1865. Reports of the crime and trial are
to be found on 22, 23, 25, 28, 29, 30, 31 March; 1, 4, 5, 26 April;
27 June; 4, 5, 6, 7, 8, 10, 11, 12, 13, 14, 17, 29, 31 July; and 1
August 1865.

88. According to one estimate, the Valentine Archive contains over
120,000 items, in the Special Collections Department of the
University of St Andrews; while there are 45,000 glass plate
negatives, and two manuscript collections held at Aberdeen
University's Special Libraries and Archives: Marc Boulay,
'Scotland's Industrial Photographic Production, Technologies
and Distribution: the Legacy of James Valentine and George
Washington Wilson': <http://www.st-andrews.ac.uk/imu/
imu.php?request=multimedia&irn=164033>

89. Obituary, *Dundee Advertiser*, 20 June 1879, quoted by Robert
Smart, '"Famous throughout the World": Valentine & Sons Ltd.,
Dundee', *Review of Scottish Culture* 4 (1988): 75–87, 76.

90. *Ibid.*, 76–7.

91. See Antonia Laurence-Allen, 'Class, Consumption and
Currency: Commercial Photography in Scotland, 1851–1888'
(unpublished PhD thesis, University of St Andrews, 2012).

92. Robert Smart, '"Famous throughout the World": Valentine &
Sons Ltd., Dundee', *Review of Scottish Culture* 4 (1988): 77–8.
See also Roddy Simpson 2012: 112, 124–8; William Main,
'George Dobson Valentine in New Zealand', *History of Photo-
graphy* 6 (1982): 333–8.

Art: the happy marriage of old and new technology', *Studies in
Photography* (2008): 42–50.

93. 'George Washington Wilson', *British Journal of Photography* 40 (17 March 1893): 165–6.

94. Taylor 1981: 1–15.

95. They both advertised their businesses, sometimes in the same column: Hay at 19 Guestrow and Wilson at 23 Crown Street, *Aberdeen Journal*, 27 July 1853.

96. 'Death of Mr G. W. Wilson', *Aberdeen Journal*, 10 March 1893.

97. *Aberdeen Journal*, 28 February 1855.

98. *Aberdeen Journal*, 7 December 1853, 16 July 1862 and 14 August 1867.

99. 'Death of Mr G. W. Wilson', *Aberdeen Journal*, 10 March 1893.

100. 'Aberdeen Stereoscopic Views', *Aberdeen Journal*, 25 September 1860.

101. Brian Liddy, 'Wilson, George Washington', in Hannavy (ed.) 2008, vol. 2: 1500–1.

102. 'Sketches of Prominent Photographers', *Photographer's Friend* 2 (1872): 49, quoted by Taylor 1981: 132.

103. Quoted by Torrance 2011, 2: 381.

104. For instance, G. W. Wilson, 'A voice from the hills: Mr Wilson at home', *British Journal of Photography* 11 (16 and 30 September, 7 and 21 October 1864): 352–4; 374–5; 388, 410.

105. Report of a meeting of the North London Photographic Association, 21 January 1863, *Photographic News* 8 (30 January 1863): 7. See also Roddy Simpson 2012: 121.

106. It would be some time before Lancaster of Birmingham and Billcliff of Manchester would come to dominate this part of the trade. Joshua Billcliff's business began in 1860; J. Lancaster moved into the photographic industry from optical instruments in about 1870: see Channing and Dunn 1996: 24–5; 69. For Chance Brothers, see Chance 1919.

107. For more detail about this, see A. D. Morrison-Low, 'Instrument making and Early Photography', *Photohistorian* 149 (January 2007): 29–37.

108. Thomas Davidson, 'The Solar Camera', *Photographic Journal* 6 (1859): 264. Discussed by Sara Stevenson, 'Robert Adamson and David Octavius Hill', in Ward and Stevenson 1986: 33.

109. *Ibid*. Discussed by Stevenson 2002a: 41.

110. Ward and Stevenson 1986: 78.

111. Urie 1908: 110.

112. 'Abstract of Mr William Walker's Paper on the Calotype Process', *Photographic Notes* 1 (1856): 76; 'Mr Walker's Portable Camera', *Photographic Notes* 1 (1856): 131–2.

113. Horatio Ross, 'Paper on the comparative merits of different pro-cesses of Photography in taking views in mountainous districts', *Photographic Notes* 2 (1857): 95–7.

114. Meeting of the Photographic Society of Scotland, 8 May 1856: *Journal of the Photographic Society of London* 3 (21 May 1856): 48.

115. <http://www.scottisharchitects.org.uk/architect_full.php?id= 200119>
This leans heavily upon David W. Walker, 'Peddie and Kinnear' (unpublished PhD thesis, University of St Andrews, 2002).

116. C. G. H. Kinnear, 'Abstract of an Account of an Architectural and Photographic Tour in the North of France', *Journal of the Photographic Society of London* 4 (21 December 1857): 116–21. Francis Fowke RE (1823–67) was also an architectural engineer, the designer of the 1862 International Exhibition hall, as well as the National Museum of Scotland (1861–66), and designed a camera in 1856: see
<http://www.nationalmediamuseum.org.uk/collection/ photography/photographictechnology/collectionitem.aspx?id= 1908-134>

117. 'Mr Kinnear's Portable Camera', *Journal of the Photographic Society of London* 4 (1858): 165–6. Rob Niederman, 'Kinnear Cameras: Large Format in a Smaller Size', *Photogram* 34 (2006): 3–7.

118. 'Conversazione', *Journal of the Photographic Society of London* 6 (1859): 75. See the example of Nelson's Kinnear camera at: <http://www.earlyphotography.co.uk/site/entry_C426.html> Perhaps John Nelson, cabinet maker 'at 15 St. James's Square', which Clyde Street adjoins: *Edinburgh Post Office Directories*.

119. 'Conversazione', *Journal of the Photographic Society of London* 6 (1859): 75–6.

120. *Post Office Edinburgh Directory* 1856–67.

121. W. D. Clark, 'Notes on the Collodio-Albumen Process', *Journal of the Photographic Society of London* 8 (1864): 281.

122. 'Photographic Society of Scotland: Ordinary Meeting: April 13th, 1858', *Journal of the Photographic Society of London* 4 (1858): 198.

123. For the Lennie business, see Clarke, Morrison-Low and Simpson 1989: 123–5; William apparently left shortly thereafter for Liverpool, see
<http://www.edinphoto.org.uk/pp_i/pp_lennie_family.htm>

124. *Scotsman*, 26 November 1853.

125. *Scotsman*, 9 July 1856.

126. *Scotsman*, 24 June 1859.

127. *Scotsman*, 30 May 1860.
128. *Journal of the Photographic Society of London* 4 (1858): 116.
129. *Ibid.*, 199.
130. Smyth 1858: vii.
131. *Ibid.*, xi.
132. Larry Schaaf writes: 'Very little is known of his [Piazzi Smyth's] exact method, but the camera was most likely of the type with a sliding lens on the front that had to be moved between exposures for the left half and the right half of the stereo pair': Larry Schaaf, 'Piazzi Smyth at Teneriffe: Part I, The Expedition and the Resulting Book', *History of Photography* 4 (1980): 296.
133. John Nicol, 'Photography in and about the Pyramids: how it was accomplished by Professor C. Piazzi Smyth', *British Journal of Photography* 13 (8 June 1864): 268–70. See also a Report of a meeting of the Glasgow Photographic Association, *British Journal of Photography* 14 (15 February 1867): 78.
134. Thomas 1964: 12; Harding 2009: 48–9. NMSI 2003-5001/1/2975. The camera taken with the Smyths is now at the Royal Observatory, Edinburgh.
135. See Stratten 1891: 94; Clarke, Morrison-Low and Simpson 1989: 293.
136. Advertisement, *Photographic Notes* 1 (17 June 1856): 92.
137. *Photographic Notes* 1 (1 October 1856): 194.
138. Advertisement, *Photographic Notes* 1 (15 January 1857): 35.
139. Advertisement, *Photographic Notes* 3 (1 August 1858): 183.
140. *Photographic Notes* 3 (15 November 1858): 273.
141. Report of the death of J. A. Spencer, manufacturer of albumen and carbon paper, *British Journal of Photography* 25 (1878): 194–5.
142. Henisch 1994: 55–9, quoting the recipe given in the *British Journal of Photography* (2 September 1861): 313.
143. John Urie, 'Pictures from Life. From the Scrap Book of a Photographer,' *British Journal of Photography* 24 (1877): 487.
144. Anon., 'The Late George Mason', *British Journal of Photography* 48 (14 June 1901): 375.
145. Mason n.d. [1888]: v.
146. *Dundee Courier*, 20 June 1849 and 20 February 1850.
147. *Dundee Courier*, 24 July 1850 and 12 March 1851.
148. 'George Lowdon, Optician and Scientist, Dundee. Sketch of his Reminiscences and Career', *Dundee Advertiser*, 3 and 6 February 1906.
149. *Dundee Courier*, 30 April 1844.
150. 'George Lowdon, Optician and Scientist, Dundee. Sketch of his Reminiscences and Career', *Dundee Advertiser*, 3 and 6 February 1906.
151. *Dundee Courier*, 7 April 1852.
152. National Museums Scotland T.1981.41, half-plate folding camera in wood, with a portrait lens designed for use with Waterhouse stops, engraved 'A. Ross, London / 6789'; described in Clarke, Morrison-Low and Simpson 1989: 151. See this chapter for Lowden's/Lowdon's activities as a scientific instrument maker: *ibid.*, 146–9.
153. <http://peib.dmu.ac.uk/itemphotographer.php?photogNo=569&orderby=coverage&photogName=Louden+%5BLowden%5D%2C+George+Jr.++%281825-1912%29>
154. *Dundee Courier*, 19 April 1854.
155. *Aberdeen Journal*, 14, 28 May; 18 June; and 16 July 1845.
156. *Aberdeen Journal*, 29 October 1845.
157. *Aberdeen Journal*, 14, 21, 28 September; and 5 October 1853.
158. *Aberdeen Journal*, 27 July 1853.
159. R. E. Scott, 'Hawick's Photographers since 1854', *Transactions of the Hawick Archaeological Society* (1974): 42–7.
160. Taylor 1981: 29.
161. Torrance 2011, 1: 6–7.

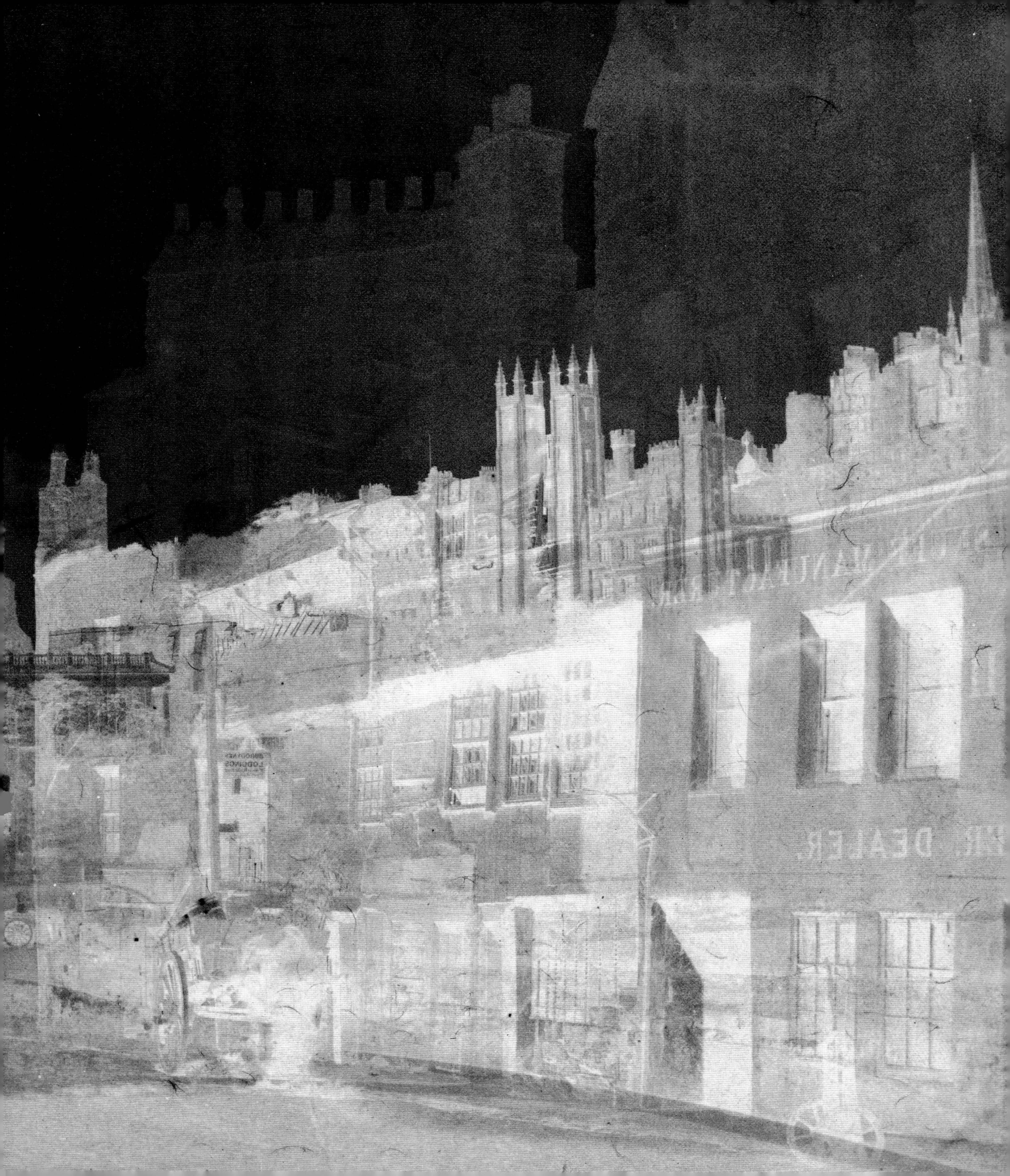

CHAPTER SIX

Photography and Society

… the photograph has filled me with astonishment from
the vast visual angle embraced and the sharp definition
and absence of distortion at the edges.

✳

Sir John Herschel writing to J. H. Dallmeyer
about a W. D. Clark photograph of Melrose Abbey, 1867

The intellectual concentration required to make photographs might suggest that the photographers would be focussed and isolated in their work. Generally, the opposite was true. Most people required discussion, demonstration and teaching through example. The difficulties of the practice found solutions in a sociable approach. It was an attractive pursuit partly for this reason. Photographers were associated in groups interested in photography itself; in professional groupings, like the doctors; and in the wealthier sectors of society.

The Photographic Societies

The first photographic clubs – the Edinburgh Calotype Club and the Calotype Club in London – were composed of friends and small in scale. They did not publicise their meetings and the *Art-journal* refrained from giving information on the London club, to prevent strangers from pestering this knowledgeable group. The Edinburgh club was possibly established as early as 1841:

> Shortly after the first discovery of the Calotype by Talbot, and its communication to Sir David Brewster, a few Edinburgh gentlemen visited the latter, saw his set of Calotypes, and were made aware of the method by which they were produced. On their return they entered eagerly on the study, and formed a little Calotype Club.[1]

The proposal that this was the first photographic society in the world may be optimistic. However, Roddy Simpson suggests that a letter from David Brewster to Talbot in October 1841, which says 'difficulties have been experienced by several persons in Edinburgh', may support the idea.[2] The Club was principally composed of lawyers: John Cay (1790–

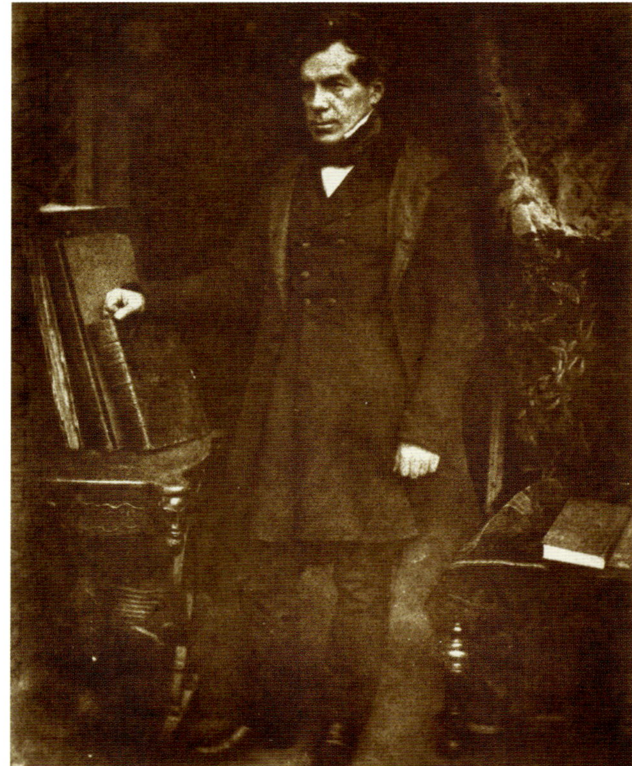

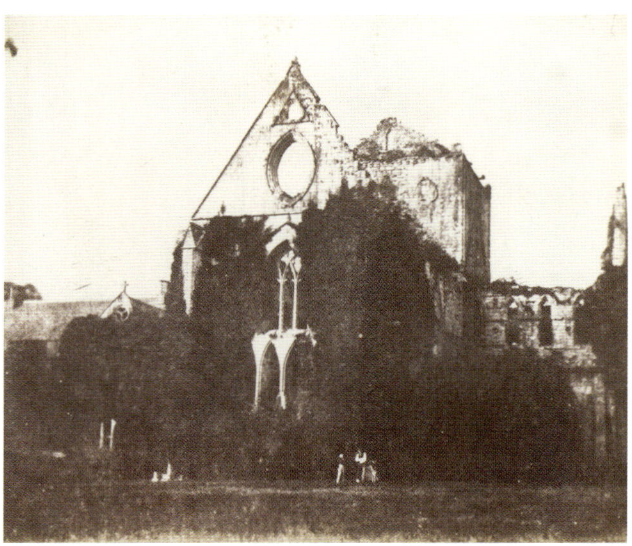

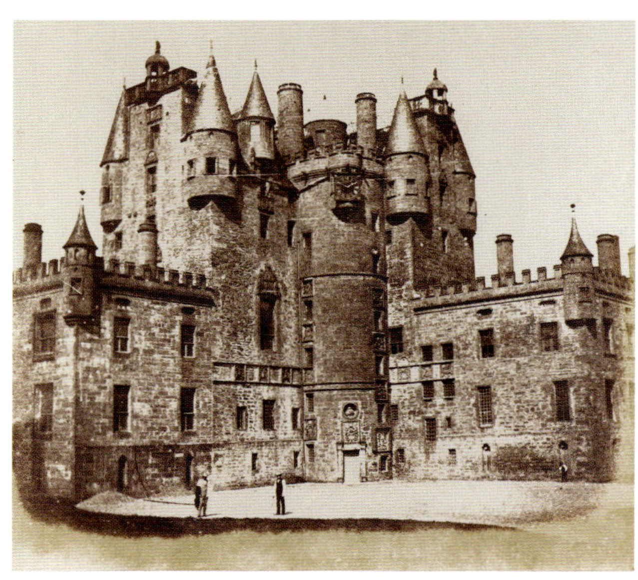

1865), Cosmo Innes (1798–1874), George Moir (1800–70) [FIG. 6.1], James Francis Montgomery (1818–97), Mark Napier (1798–1879), John Stewart of Natley Hall (1813–67), a landowner, and Hugh Lyon Tennent (1817–74). In 1849 Lord Cockburn noted in his journal, when he was on the legal circuit around Scotland addressing serious cases, that the lawyers took the opportunity to visit the ruins of Pluscarden Abbey, near Elgin [FIG. 6.2]: 'We loitered about the ruin for some hours, and had a turf refection, and a good deal of calotyping conducted by my friend Cosmo Innes, the Sheriff of the county.'[3] Calotypes of such subjects by members of the Club appear in an album of the Society of Antiquaries of Scotland [FIG. 6.3].[4] The members 'met at each other's houses, had a friendly meal together, exhibited their productions, and discussed new experiments and their results'.[5] They exchanged photographs and at least two of the members put the calotypes into albums that survive.[6]

In London in 1847, a group of enthusiasts also set up a Calotype Club, and George Smith Cundell was one of the

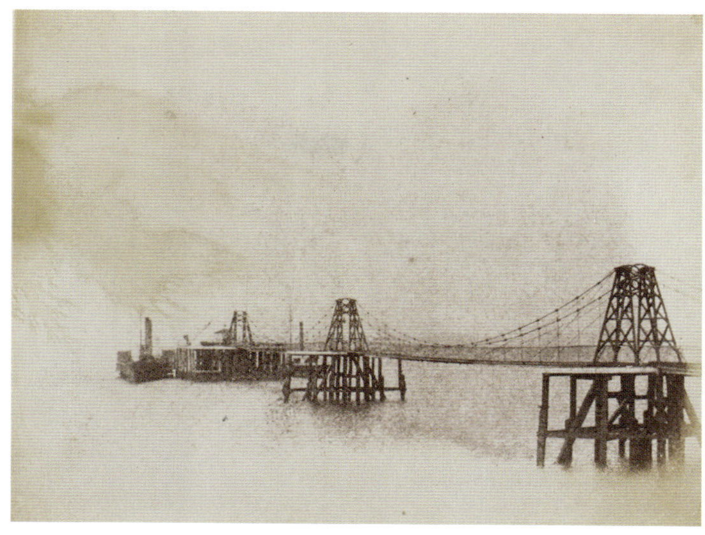

Fig. 6.4: Unknown photographer, 'Newhaven, Chain Pier', early 1840S, salt print from a calotype negative. (National Museums Scotland Library album, D.2014.3.10)

twelve members, along with other experts, Robert Hunt, Frederick Scott Archer, William Newton, Hugh Welch Diamond and Edward Kater.[7] They planned to 'keep up a constant communication with each other, detailing their several improvements and discoveries, and interchanging the repetitions of such sun-pictures as each may have produced' [FIG. 6.4].[8]

The *Art-journal* reported about the club's success in 1848:

> The Club meets once or twice a month at the house of some member, and the labours of each one are submitted to the body, and improvements in manipulation communicated. The result has been most satisfactory, and Photographs produced by the Calotype process by Mr Cundall [*sic*], Mr [Hugh] Owen and other members, are among the most beautiful things we have seen, representing in the utmost perfection all the minute detail, combined with the broad general features of external nature, and the magic beauty of light and shadow.[9]

The wet collodion process, which was announced in 1851 by Frederick Scott Archer, was unrestricted by patent, and photography became widely accessible. Between 1854 and 1870, the formation of photographic societies mirrored the opening up of the practice. The Glasgow Photographic Society and the Photographic Society of London, joined by mobile and London-based Scots, were founded in 1854; the Photographic Society of Scotland, based in Edinburgh, and the Dumfries and Galloway Photographic Society, were launched in 1856.

The announcement of the Glasgow Photographic Society called for those interested to enrol 'at Mr James White's Photographic Instrument Maker, 14 Renfield Street, or with Mr D[uncan] Brown, Government School of Design at Ingram Street'.[10] The first meeting took place in March, in 'Mr [James] McLure's Pictorial Rooms, Buchanan Street'. 'Mr [Cornelius Jabez] Hughes subsequently read a most interesting paper on the rise, progress, and prospects of the science, after which a short discussion took place amongst the members, during which a number of most interesting specimens of the art – many of them done by Glasgow photographers – were displayed.' Robert Hunt, who had made an authoritative study of photography, gave a lecture which was 'loudly applauded by the respectable audience'.[11] It was a lively group.

Duncan Brown (1819–97) was well placed as the janitor at the Government School of Design, with access to the artists and the collections of the School. He was a friend of the lithographer William Simpson, and photographed the portrait painter Daniel MacNee, and the landscape painter Horatio McCulloch; he was also connected to industry and the Bairds of Gartsherrie, ironmasters. His photographs, taken over thirty to forty years, of people and landscape are distinctive and animated [FIG. 6.5]. Brown's paper, 'On the Collodion process: its Pursuit under Difficulties', for the Glasgow Photographic Association in 1861, recounted his early experience:

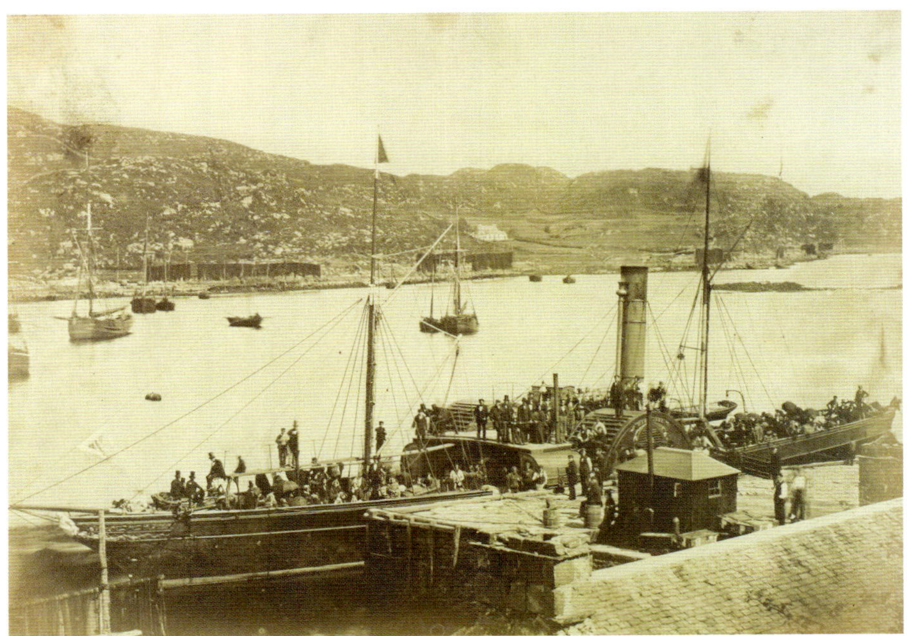

… a young acquaintance of mine had made a box, and we purchased a lens, which cost only a few pence, fitted it to the box with a paper tube, and set to work with great glee. … The first process with which we commenced was the calotype, following the formula given in the Art Union Journal of June, 1846; but, after many trials, and about as many failures, we gave it up in despair ….

I very soon after this procured a quarter plate camera, with a good lens, which had been used by a lady for taking daguerreotypes in this city.[12] I also got some books containing improved formulae, and began again, and arrived at great success (at least I thought so at the time) …. Recollect it was slow work in those days: an exposure of from one to two minutes, in the sun's rays, was then necessary. …

… It was in the latter end of 1851 that persons who had been at the Great Exhibition told me of the collodion pictures shown there ….

You may imagine with what sanguine hopes I prepared to try my hand; but where was I to find materials, especially the collodion? There were no establishments in Glasgow at that time where ready-made materials for the collodion process could be procured, and … I had no knowledge of chemistry. I at last mustered up courage, and consulted Dr [Thomas] Paterson – a gentleman who did more for the art in its early stages than any that I know of. He showed me how to prepare the cotton …. I then set off with a light heart, with the doctor's prescription, procured the different materials, got home, made them up, waited with no small share of patience for a good day. With the first opportunity I set to work – failed over and over again – till at last I got something … which a gentleman of my acquaintance used to characterize as belonging to the coal trade![13]

As late as 1851, taking a photograph was a serious challenge; Brown's enthusiasm for the idea of a society and the company of like-minded photographers may be readily understood.

The Glasgow Photographic Society was founded partly in anticipation of the meeting of the British Association for the Advancement of Science, scheduled for Glasgow in late 1855. It was determined to stage a major exhibition and contributions were invited. Much of the documentation for this exhibition survives.[14]

Dr John Adamson wrote with a list, dated two days

after the exhibition deadline, demonstrating his interest in the chemistry, the scientific uses of photography and aesthetics:

> No. 1 – calotypes taken in 1842 – from negatives by Mr Talbot's original process on paper – fixed by immersion for 5 minutes in water of ammonia
> No. 2 – skeletons of animals from negatives on glass by the ordinary collodion process
> No. 3 Portrait of a gentleman from a collodion negative
> No. 4 & 5 – Companion pictures entitled Light & Shade – from the same individual
> No. 6 A Lady as Katherine in 'The Taming of the Shrew' Act II Scene 1st

> The last three pictures are an attempt to shew [*sic*] that photography is capable of something beyond mere portraiture.[15]

Others sent detailed entries on process. Charles John Burnett (1820–1907), based in Aberdeen, forwarded three frames of characteristically detailed chemistry, including '"Harvest" from one of Ross & Thomson's Albumen glass negatives … paper prepared by Solution of Hydrofluate of Uranic oxide, exposure 1½ hour to light, Development by Ferridcyanuret of Potassium'.[16] Throughout the following decade, Burnett conducted experiments in photographic chemistry, and communicated his results freely. He investigated the use of alternative metals in photography, and had some priority in the carbon process, the use of uranium and palladium.[17]

The American editor of *Humphrey's Magazine* commented in 1857:

> [Burnett] has taken such a prominent part in the proceedings of the principal Photographic Societies of Europe, and has aided so materially, by both voice and pen, in bringing forward and elucidating abstruse questions in the Science of Optics applied to Photography and his name has appeared so frequently in our pages in this connection that it has become almost as familiar to American as to European photographers.[18]

Burnett experimented in photography but had little interest in taking photographs. He wrote, airily: 'The fact is, I cannot well find time for the prosecution of discovery, and for pretty specimen making, and as soon as I see *unmistakeable* indications of what are the real *capabilities* of any process, I am generally off to something else.'[19] Mike Ware has commented that he was

> … an equivocal figure in the history of photographic processes. His publications attest an eclectic interest in photoactive substances of all kinds, but it is sometimes hard to discriminate in his writings between the results of genuine experiment and the speculations of an inventive mind.[20]

His impact is understandably difficult to track, but he certainly impressed his contemporaries.

Some 1200 pictures were shown at the Glasgow exhibition.[21] Most of the photographers operating in Scotland sent work. The exhibition was held in the warehouse of Wylie and Lochhead in Buchanan Street, and the Society paid for splendid decorations, including eighteen paper styles, borders, pilasters, bases, capitals, Elgin marbles and claret crimson glazed calico.[22]

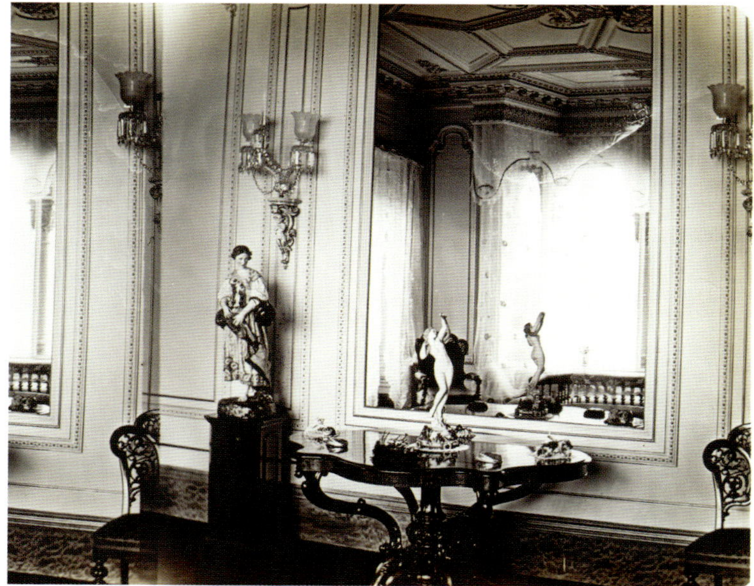

One of the prominent figures at the 1855 exhibition was John Kibble (d.1894), a metal merchant, best known today as the man who built the fine glasshouse known as 'Kibble's Palace' for the City. This and interior views of his house were photographed stereoscopically by John Benjamin Dancer [FIG. 6.6], as elegant exercises in light and glass, showing Kibble's taste for classical statuary.[23]

John Kibble showed thirty-three very large photographs in 1855, principally collodion positives, but four tantalisingly described as 'Exper. Proc.' or experimental process. He had succeeded in making large scale, instantaneous photographs. Alexander McNab (b.*c*.1822), who opened a portrait studio in Glasgow in 1854, wrote to the Editor of *Photographic Notes* in 1857, hoping (unsuccessfully) to correct an error in reporting Kibble's name and augmenting the information on his photographs:

Mr Ross has paid a graceful and well-merited compliment to Mr Ribble's noble and magnificent photographs, but there is a mistake in Mr Ribble's name .... I have thought it might be of interest to your numerous readers to give you a general idea of the magnitude of the preparations required for their production ....
Negative of Millport, 44 x 32 inches

[Negative of] Broomilaw [*sic*], 42 x 30 inches [FIG. 6.7]. Positives from above, 40 x 50, full size of paper. Process. – Taupenot. Exposure: 15 minutes, on 9th day after sensitizing. Lens: 13 ins. Diameter; 6 feet focus. Weight of largest Negative, about 40lbs. Vertical sensitizing bath, contains thirteen gallons of a 30 grain solution Nitrate of Silver.[24]

On 18 January 1861, the Glasgow and West of Scotland Photographic Society held a successful 'soirée and conversazione', despite the hard frost freezing the heating apparatus in the hall. Kibble was President:

The hall and adjoining room were decorated with specimens of our art, contributed by members of the council. Amongst them were prominent the numerous views by the President, one of which, 40 inches by 30 inches, was fitted up as a cosmorama, and seen through the magnificent lens with which it was taken looked truly grand. Mr Kibble's monster camera &c., with which these pictures are done, is much the largest in the world.

... One of them is a glass positive, and is, we believe, the largest on record, and obtained for Mr Kibble the Manchester medal .... The lens with [which] these

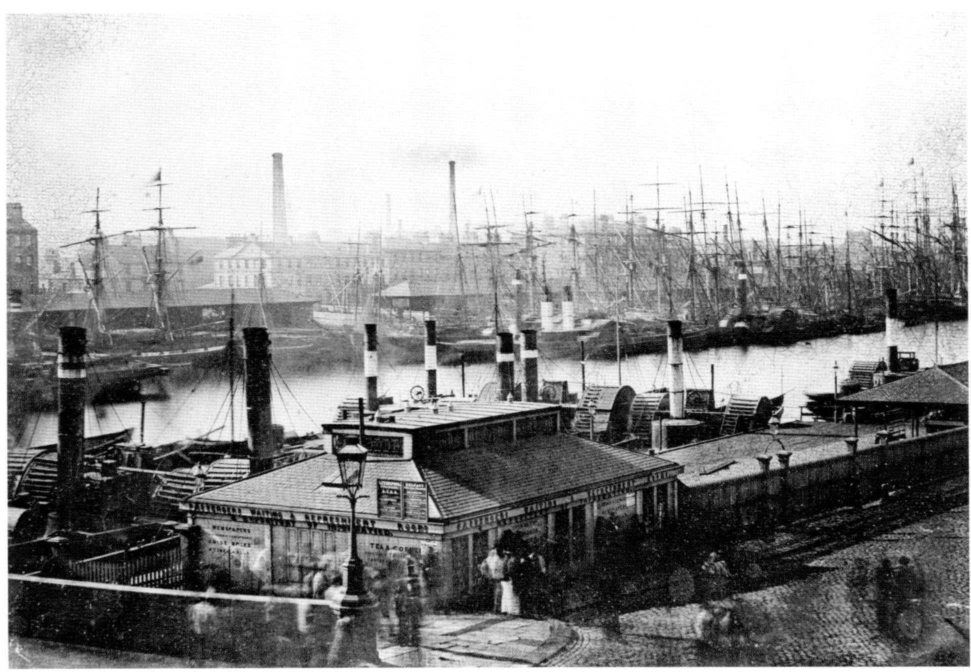

pictures were produced, was made by Ross, and cost £170. The diameter of the lens, clear of mounting, is 13 inches, and its focus, for parallel rays, 6 feet. The camera to which it is attached, was mounted on wheels and drawn by a horse.[25]

The photographic societies spawned the journals of photography, which reported their proceedings in detail. The initially amateurish character of this is seen in the report of the first meeting of the London Photographic Society in 1854. Robert Hunt gave another rousing speech on the work to be done, and used as an example the lack of 'any process sufficiently instantaneous to fix on the Photograph a representation of the movement of waves'. The reporter, evidently badly-placed and hopping up and down to hear, added a footnote on

> … a gentleman just arrived from Scotland, who had brought with him some remarkably fine sea views, obtained upon glass. In these views the foam of the waves is admirably represented, and in the Stereoscope the illusion is complete. The attention of the meeting was drawn most forcibly to this new and important improvement, which excited their interest in the highest degree. Inquiries were naturally made from every one if the collodion employed to obtain such views was the same as that in general use. The exhibitor of these views replied, that he had prepared the collodion himself, and from his remarks, it is inferred that *wheatstraw* entered into the composition. We much regret that we could not obtain the name of the gentleman ….[26]

This was unhelpful reporting. The gentleman was Allan Maconochie, and unlikely to have used wheatstraw in his photography. As early as June 1852, Maconochie took a sequence of photographs

> … of the inauguration of the Duke of Wellington's statue in Edinburgh, and having arranged so as to open and close the operation of the lens instantaneously at the moment of uncovering the statue, I have a view of all the crowd, the statue, and the canvas covering in the *act of falling* down, although there was a thunder-storm at the time, and the rain falling in torrents ….[27]

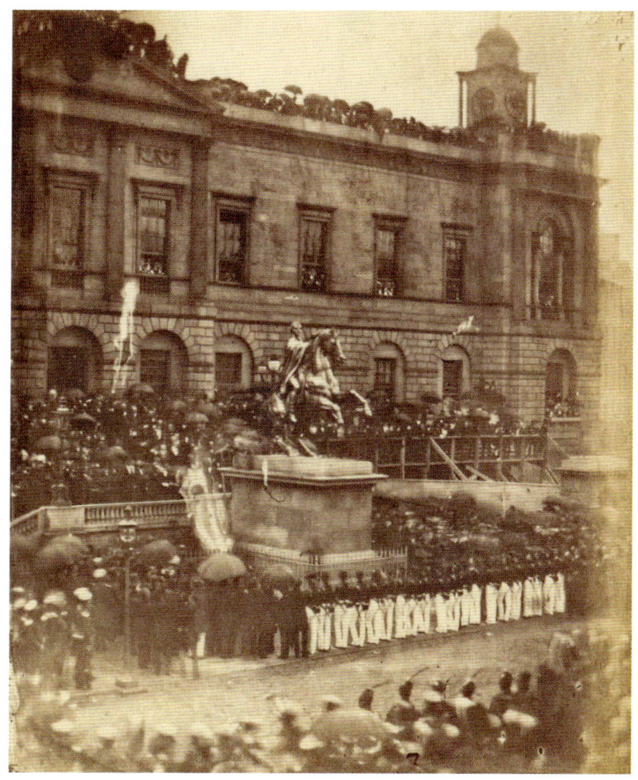

He achieved this by adding iodide of iron, made by a process of 'long cooking', to the collodion, which rendered it '*instantaneously* sensitive' [FIG. 6.8].

In the 1850s, reports of society meetings could be extensive, even verbose. The international sprouting of publications and their need for articles meant that reports of discussions from Paris to Sydney would appear in the British journals; news of Dumfries, Edinburgh or Glasgow would be published worldwide. The societies achieved a splendid, public stage.

The encouragement of the journals may have had an unfortunate effect – an early example of the glamour of the media offering fame for no originality and little effort. In 1863, A. H. Wall presented a sardonic account of photographic societies. He commented:

> It is no very difficult thing to join a photographic society .... Being elected you speak at the society's meetings, and afterwards read your name and utterances in neat black print, conscious the while that your words are travelling into foreign lands, and that your name and fame will be known to men afar off. So it sometimes happens that members who have nothing to say, and are very ambitious of saying it, write it out at great length in more or less elaborate papers, which they are kind enough to read before our photographic societies ....[28]

The Dumfries and Galloway Photographic Society was launched in 1856, with the landowners Patrick Dudgeon (1817–95) of Kailzie and Cargen as President, and Richard Rimmer (1826–1905) of Marchmount as Vice President. Dudgeon presented the Society with a 'magnificent album ... [containing] several exquisite photographs by the celebra-

ted photographer, Mr Stewart of Pau' in 1856.[29] Dudgeon had given examples of his own work, with others by Stewart, to the Royal Scottish Academy in 1853, which were [FIG. 6.9] particularly admired by the Academicians for 'the delicate shadowing of some of them during snow'.[30]

The Secretary and Treasurer was John Traill Taylor (1827–95). He was in Dumfries by 1851, and working with collodion by 1854. Two years later he expressed a preference for albumen, as 'the most accommodating process .... Compared with collodion, its cost was as one to nine. Albumen was easily procured, for one could find fresh eggs in abundance everywhere'.[31] Traill Taylor was an activist, organising the Society and giving papers. He moved back to Edinburgh, joining the Photographic Society of Scotland in 1858.[32]

The Photographic Society of Scotland was launched in March 1856 on the initiative of Horatio Ross. It first met in Ross and Thomson's studio in Princes Street, Edinburgh. Sir David Brewster was elected President with Horatio Ross

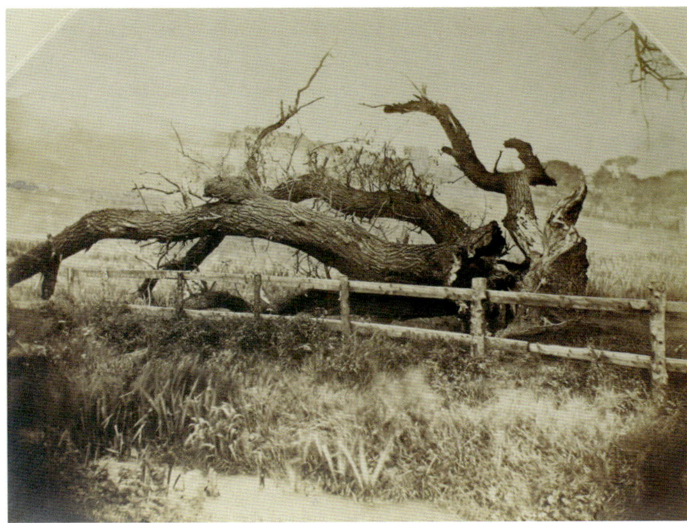

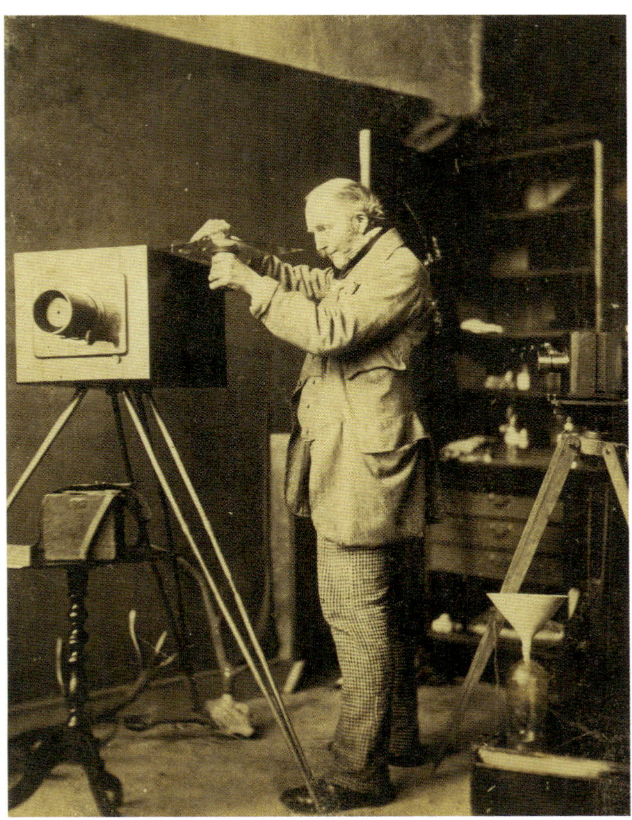

Fig. 6.9 (above): Patrick Dudgeon of Kailzie, 'Old Saugh [willow] Tree, Park of Kailzie', *c.*1852, calotype. (Royal Scottish Academy, 1993.365)

Fig. 6.10 (right): Henrietta Ross, 'Horatio Ross in his studio', *c.*1857, albumen print. (J. Paul Getty Museum, 84.XM.892.1)

and George Moir as Vice Presidents.[33] The only professional photographer on the council was James Ross. In the next two years, the well-organised Society heard a number of important papers on subjects as diverse as the waxed paper process (Thomas Keith), uranium (C. J. Burnett), a photographic tour of France (Cosmo Innes), forgery (T. B. Johnston), photolithography (Robert Macpherson) and 'the production of photographs on fluorescent surfaces, and on the various modes of rendering visible the ultra violet chemical rays' (Professor George Wilson). In these years, the Society held two very successful exhibitions. 'Despite the disadvantages of the situation in the Exhibition Rooms, and the inclemency of the weather', more than 8000 visitors attended, 1050 photographs were exhibited and 'a large number were purchased'.[34] The Society started collecting photographs. The number of members rose to 119 in the first year and 151 in the second.[35]

On 15 September 1857, Thomas Sutton (1819–75), the editor of the journal *Photographic Notes* (official reporter to the Society), expressed the gratifying opinion:

Photography has many zealous followers in Scotland, and much of the enthusiasm and originality of research, which once distinguished the leading men of the London Photographic Society, appears to have migrated northwards. The London Society is rapidly losing its prestige, and yielding the honour of the first place to the Photographic Society of Scotland, at whose meetings, during the past session, many very original and interesting papers have been read.[36]

Horatio Ross was already a photographer of knowledge and standing [Fig. 6.10]. He was regularly employed as the judge in the Society's medal competitions. His fame and authority as a member of Society, meticulous standards of work, and broad sociability, combined with a sense of sporting fairness, suited him for a role of gentlemanly patronage. We know that he took lessons and sought advice from professional photographers: James Ross, James Good Tunny, and the firm of Horne and Thornthwaite in London, who gave him a formula for dry plate photography in 1866 or 1867. His substantial contributions to the exhibitions may indicate that he was seeking helpful criticism for the problems he encountered, as well as showing his best work. After his talk on the difficulty of photographing distance in landscape, the Society set up a committee to investigate.[37] At a meeting of Birmingham Photographic Society, in September 1858, Paul Pretsch exhibited two specimens of the Petzval lens with a large number of photographs 'by Rejlander, Llewellyn, Horatio Ross, and other well-known artists; they speak very highly of the capabilities of these lenses for Landscape purposes …. The distances too, are well preserved and faithfully rendered.'[38] This indicates a professional response to Ross's paper.

It made sense to elect the wealthier enthusiasts to office: they could be generous and have useful connections; they might own sophisticated equipment. But the balance began to shift as the professional photographers became established. James Ross, who was the first to become impatient, was a man of authority; the winner of a medal from the Great Exhibition and Royal Warrant holder, he challenged the Photographic Society of Scotland as early as 1858 in the face of its evident success. With the backing of seven working photographers, a lithographer and bookseller, he proposed a special meeting to consider the motion, 'That, in all time coming, the Council of the Society shall be equally composed of Amateur and of Professional Practical Photographers.'[39] The underlying point here was both the control and the values of the Society – how exhibitions would be hung and who would determine the award of medals, which offered public endorsement to professional studios.

The resentment, brought out by the issue of medals, is illustrated by a letter from Edinburgh in 1859. This was addressed to the Editor of *Photographic News*, commenting on the medals awarded in Edinburgh to

… the Rev. T. M. Raven and Mr. Lyndon Smith, of Leeds. The former has carried away the 'member's medal,' and the latter has received the 'stranger's medal.' … You have in your capacity as a journalist frequently had opportunities of reviewing the works of these gentlemen. Of the productions of the latter you have expressed a high opinion;– while of the former, in your review of the last exhibition, you wonder 'what could have induced him to exhibit his two views – "Pierrefitte," and "View near Luz," as there is not the slightest pretence to anything like detail in them' [Fig. 6.11]. Now, I am not for one moment going to say anything about the photographs, or to say that there were not photographs in our exhibition quite as good as those to whom the awards were made. What I wish to do is simply to state that this prize medal system has been fraught with great evil, and has given a great amount of dissatisfaction.[40]

The issue of the medals – the status they gave – was entangled with the question of photography's status as an art form. James Ross's opposition to the management of the Society was triggered by this question, which surfaced at the meeting in 1856, when Robert Macpherson showed two photolithographs. James Ross asked if a smooth stone would take a better impression. The painter George Harvey responded, '… so far from these stipplings appearing to him to be objectionable, they were a positive merit. They gave vigour and brilliancy to the print.' D. O. Hill agreed.[41]

This was a divide in taste and the definition of excel-

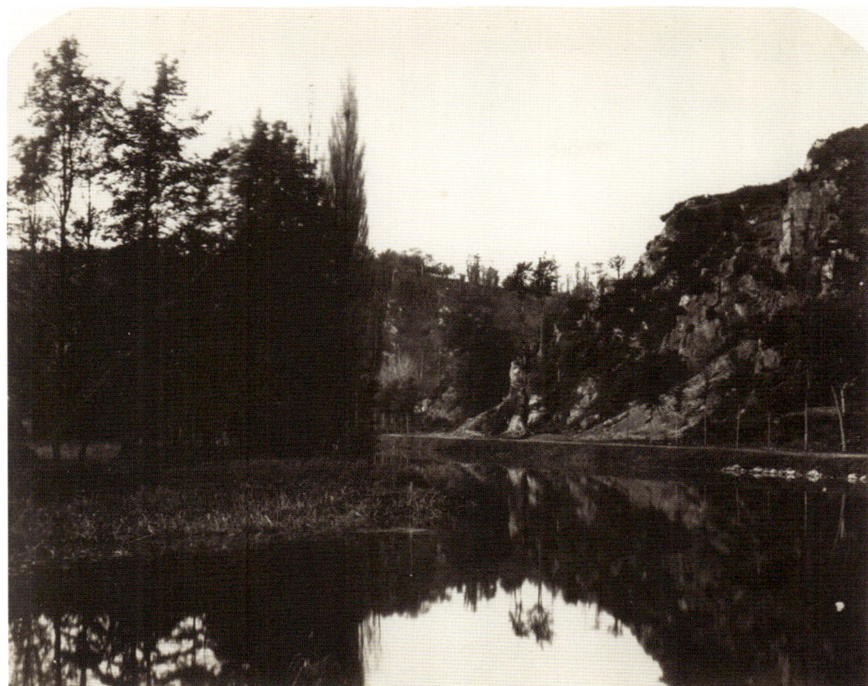

lence. Most professional photographers now used glass negatives, making detailed albumen prints; many amateurs continued to work with the comparative blur of paper negatives. Moreover, the point made obliquely by the painters in discussing Macpherson's work, was the issue of the physical medium itself; the recognition that it was part of the art. The transparent film of collodion glass negatives and albumen prints suggested the medium was a window, an unmediated view of the world, rather than a physically created surface. In the 1860s, when there was growing hostility towards the re-touched or painted photograph, the interest was two-fold: to avoid covering up natural truth, and to resist the correction of chemical and technical faults, as part of the photograph's making and character. The second point was not necessarily appreciated.

The quarrel gained force when O. G. Rejlander's elaborate composite picture, 'The Two Ways of Life', was hung in the 1857 Art Manufactures exhibition in Edinburgh. It was said that the Photographic Society, sensitive to impropriety in a photograph exhibiting nude women, refused to accept the photograph for their exhibition. Thomas Sutton reported in *Photographic Notes* that it was 'a subject intended to teach a high moral lesson, and … certainly the cleverest photograph that has yet been produced. We sincerely hope no such prudery will find its way south of the Tweed'.[42]

D. O. Hill and Alexander McGlashon

In 1856, the Secretary, C. G. H. Kinnear, invited D. O. Hill to give the Photographic Society of Scotland

> … hints on the artistic arrangement & selection of points of view &c of Photographic pictures … the management of light & shade, the adaptation of the tone of the print to the nature of the picture &c &c. On all of these matters there is an excessive amount of ignorance among the majority of photographers & nothing is more likely to advance the Art, as an Art, than a little sound knowledge ….[43]

Hill fell ill and never gave the talk. Instead he sent over

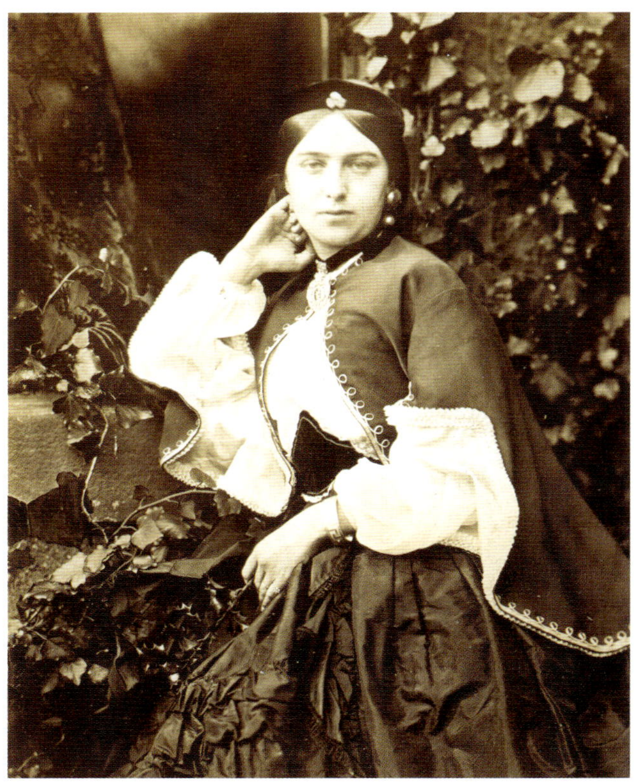

seventy calotypes to the Society's first exhibition in December as 'early efforts of that wonderful art which has since become so great a fact in the world's history'.[44] Hill tried working with Alexander McGlashon (d.1877), around 1860, perhaps in response to the art debate. He persuaded him to work out of his studio, both in Edinburgh and in Polmont in September 1860, taking photographs during a 'Volunteer Fete' organised by Hill's friend and patron, railway engineer John Miller.[45]

In the group of about thirty photographs [FIG. 6.12] Hill and McGlashon took, Hill was attempting emotional and narrative depth – working with people he admired and loved, like the sculptor Amelia Paton, whom he married in 1862. Characteristically, he linked the pictures to history and to literature, with photographs related to Tennyson, Shakespeare and a 16th-century Scottish ballad. The ambition was allusive, infusing 'the artistic and poetic element with photography'.[46] Hill would have liked McGlashon's work for its richness, and his response to the detail of the collodion process is found in the delicacy of the arrangement of hands and material.

They exhibited the photographs in the Photographic Society of Scotland's exhibition in 1861, as 'Contributions to the Fine Art of Photography'. Hill, not McGlashon, was awarded a silver medal.[47] John Traill Taylor objected.[48]

Dr John Brown wrote a review of this exhibition for the *Scotsman*, headed 'Mr Hill's Calotypes', and dismissed other portraitists in the exhibition in sweeping terms, including Claudet, whose work had been awarded a medal:

> … everything is there that the perfection of skill, manipulation, materials, light, and infinite practice can achieve, and what have you? A clever, leaden, flat miniature, with a background as hard and as *blae* as a slate – no spaciousness, no substance, no ease or grace, power or life, or play – nothing but surface, and a poverty of invention … .

From this rhetorical springboard, Brown broke into a paean of praise for Hill and McGlashon's work:

> Did you ever see anything out of Giorgione more subtle and to the life – more a living breathing man? Such a sense of colour as well as of texture! Such a multitude of tones in unity![49]

When another group of the photographs was shown at the International Exhibition in London in 1862, J. T. Taylor wrote, sardonically:

> We are at some loss to understand what is meant by a placard attached to some portrait groups photographed

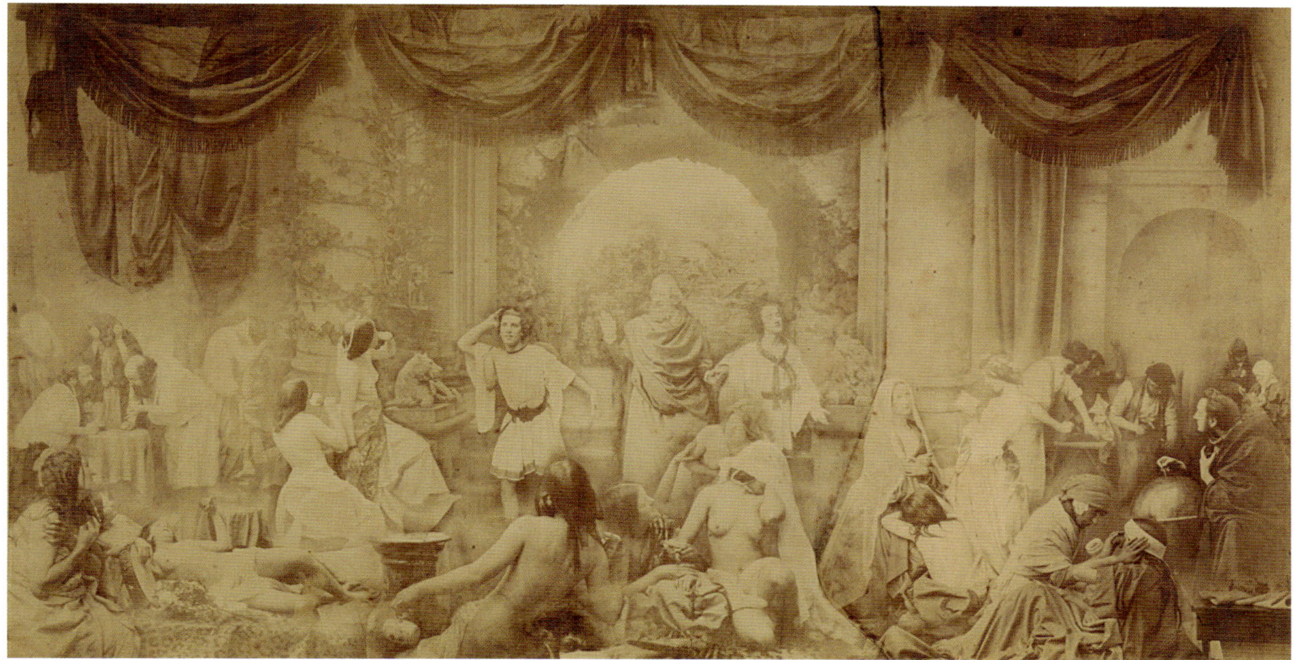

by Mr McGlashon, the announcement being to the effect that they are 'contributions towards *fine art* in photography by D. O. Hill'. We presume that Mr Hill posed the groups which Mr McGlashon photographed but how these are to be regarded as more specially conducive to *fine art* than the groups by several of our artist-photographers who are also portraitists, we cannot make out. We have seen as good, nay better, groups – by which we mean more artistic ones – by Lake Price, Rejlander, Robinson and several others.[50]

Hill and McGlashon were competing with the much-admired professionals, Oscar Rejlander, Henry Peach Robinson and William Lake Price. Prince Albert owned several copies of 'The Two Ways of Life' [FIG. 6.13], and David Brewster admired it: 'The application of photography to historical painting has been finely exhibited in the remarkable compositions of Rejlander and Robinson. The "Two Ways of Life" … (for which we paid ten guineas), and his "Wayfarer" and other compositions, cannot be surpassed, except in colour, by any specimens of ordinary art'.[51] The crucial difference in their photographs was the relation to actuality. Hill and McGlashon's photographs were composed in front of the camera out of doors, showing people in their own character; Rejlander and Robinson constructed their compositions in the studio, using models.

In January 1863, Thomas Sutton sent a paper on art and photography to the Photographic Society of Scotland. Sutton, who took a liberal line in berating the Society in 1858, had reversed his opinion. He now declared that Rejlander's 'Two Ways of Life' was indecent and that his models were prostitutes. He wrote:

> The first chalk-drawings of a schoolboy upon a wall were more admirable, from the human interest they possessed, than the finest view of inanimate natural objects upon the ground-glass of the camera. God had created those objects, and He had also created man, man's works were, therefore, indirectly His works … pictures that were the result of human imagination, observation, and powers of imitation, were more noble than, and belonged to a different class of thing altogether from, the image in a camera.[52]

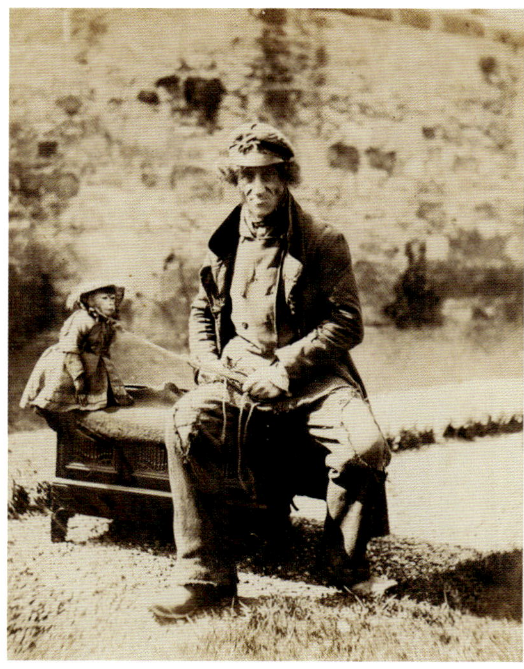

The following discussion was acrimonious and devisive.

It was not a simple debate, nor one that could be resolved satisfactorily. James Ross may be allowed the last word in this case:

> Why is photography judged of wholly by its results in the hands of those who, although clever enough at mere manipulation, are not possessed of what constitutes even the first principles of art? Apply this unfair manner of judgement to painting, and might it not, then, in some cases, be proved to be a very mechanical art indeed?[53]

The question damaged the Society and helped to set the members at odds. There were, however, other problems. One was simply the scale of interest. The membership mounted into the hundreds, partly by encouraging non-photographers to join. The practical exchange of information and demonstration was discarded for lectures or entertainment, and the members became audiences. This was demonstrated by the experience in Glasgow. By 1860 the first two of Glasgow's photographic societies had folded. The new Glasgow Photographic Association held a splendid

Fig. 6.14 (left): Horatio Ross, 'Italian Organ Grinder', 1858, salt print from collodion negative. (National Media Museum / Science & Society Picture Library 1990-5131_1_12)

Fig. 6.15 (opposite left): W. D. Clark, 'The National Gallery of Scotland', c.1858, albumen print. (Riddell Collection, Scottish National Portrait Gallery, PGP R 128)

Fig. 6.16 (opposite right): W. D. Clark, 'View of south transept from the west, Melrose Abbey', c.1866, albumen print. (Royal Commission on the Ancient and Historical Monuments of Scotland, Item DP 149997)

soirée in 1862, entertaining four hundred people with an exhibition, 'a bountiful service of tea and coffee' (and fruit), a band providing popular quadrilles and operatic selections. The entertainment included a Photographic Diorama set up by Dr John Taylor, Professor of Natural Philosophy at the Andersonian University (1846–62).[54] This was followed by a demonstration of electric light, and C. Jabez Hughes sat for his portrait. Referring to himself as representing 'the very dark ages of photography', Hughes said, 'those days are now long gone by, and photography has, like the mustard seed, sprung all at once into a huge tree'.[55]

Some members coped with the over-scaling of the societies by making smaller groups. In Glasgow a 'Practical Society' was proposed in 1858, with no more than forty members, an annual subscription of a guinea, entitling them to the use of a glass-room and other facilities, and meetings for mutual improvement and discussion.[56] The Edinburgh Exchange Photographic Club was an offshoot of the Photographic Society of Scotland, set up with the determination not to exceed thirteen members and restricted to the exchange of photographs and information.[57] This group was composed of amateurs, who included long-standing members of the Edinburgh Calotype Club, George Moir and Cosmo Innes, along with other members of the Society: A. F. Adam, Dr James Duncan, A. Y. Herries, T. B. Johnston, C. G. H. Kinnear, Rev. T. Milville Raven, Horatio Ross, G. M. Tytler, H. G. Watson, William Walker and John Ziegler. Horatio Ross collected his group of these photographs in an album; the calibre of the photographers can be identified, with details of the processes they used [Fig. 6.14].

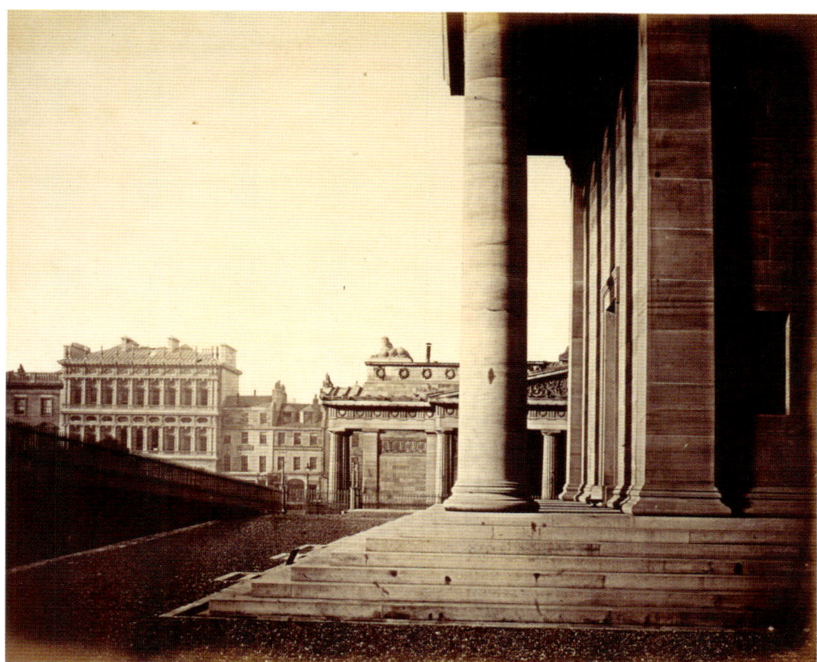
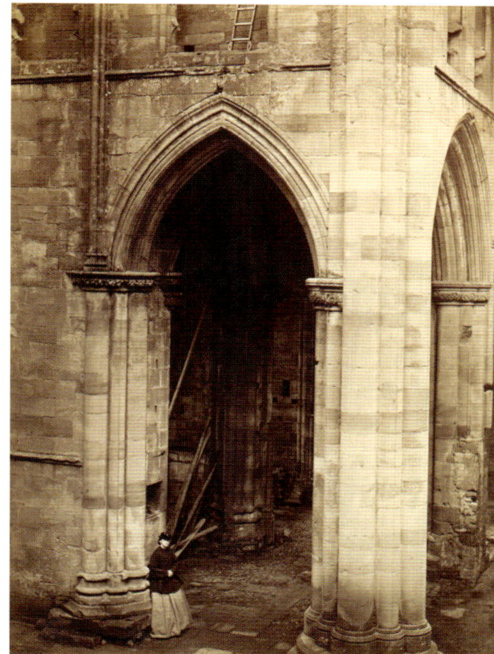

James Ross's bid to make the Photographic Society of Scotland half-professional in 1859 failed. Alongside it there grew the Edinburgh Photographic Society, founded in 1861, 'for the purpose of mutual improvement in the *practical details* of the Photographic Art. It is intended that it shall act as a useful handmaid to the parent Society, by discussing subjects, which might be considered as beneath its notice.'[58]

The amateur was still dominant, but John Traill Taylor was the Secretary of the new society.

The restlessness of the photographic societies here and across the world was possibly just a form of social expression – reorganisation of the personalities and the local balance of power. Certainly, quite a few of the people involved in the one society transferred happily to the other.

The Photographic Society of Scotland continued until 1866, when they held their final exhibition and awarded six medals.[59] They presented 'an extra medal' to the Society's Secretary, William Donaldson Clark (1813–73).[60] Clark was born in Ayr, and employed by the 'Turkey Red' fabric printing works in Dunbartonshire. He established a successful calico printing works near Manchester and retired to Edinburgh around 1865. He had found an interest in photo-graphy as 'one of the Manchester School', and had photo-graphed extensively in Scotland by 1858, when he exhibited 32 landscapes, taken around Edinburgh and in Derbyshire at the Photographic Society of Scotland's exhibition [Fig. 6.15].

Clark was a close friend of landscape painter Horatio McCulloch (1805–67), who advised him in photography. When Clark sent pictures with a paper to the Society, he pointed out, '… those in which the point of view had been selected with care by some members of the Royal Academy of Edinburgh and photographed by himself. In one instance, such a picture had been characterised by a critic as being excellent in its photography but very deficient in its artistic arrangement.'[61] The reporter added, cautiously, 'Without quoting Mr Clark's precise language, his idea seemed to be that a critic who could say that, was not competent for the duties devolving upon him'.

In 1865, Clark worked with the architect, John Smith (1827–69) of Darnick Tower near Melrose, on an elaborated project to photograph Melrose Abbey [Fig. 6.16]. Smith was himself a photographer and was awarded the Photographic Society of Scotland's medal that year, for the best view by

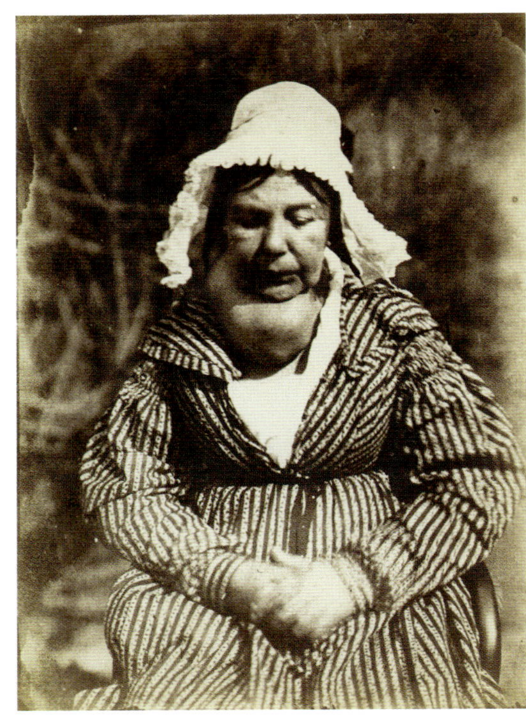

an amateur: a 'beautiful and artistic little picture, "On the Leader Water, near Melrose"'.[62] To photograph the Abbey, they built a mobile scaffold, and worked with three Dallmeyer lenses. Clark brought back '… upwards of a hundred negatives. Though Melrose Abbey is perhaps the most hackneyed subject in Scotland, I may fairly claim that we have produced a series of views distinguished by novelty and originality'. He added:

> The day before I left Melrose, Mr Dallmeyer most kindly sent me the first specimen he had made of a new architectural lens, to include a very wide angle. We found that this lens would enable us to take a new set of subjects that could not be done by any other lens in my possession. As the focus was too short to be conveniently worked by the cameras we were using, I am having the body of a camera made to suit it, and as soon as this is ready we shall again go to work at the Abbey.[63]

The London optician, Dallmeyer, found a fault in this lens.[64] He sent a copy of one photograph to Sir John Herschel for his advice: 'The lens in question … was intended for architectural views in very confined situations. Mr Clark tried the instrument, and kindly sent me the view of Melrose Abbey now before you, and, as you perceive, the picture is perfect in every respect, barring the central spot.' Herschel responded to the quality of the photograph:

> The photograph… has filled me with astonishment, from the vast visual angle embraced, and the sharp definition and absence of distortion at the edges.
> The building itself is a very strange one, and I cannot make out its perspective; but that is obviously the

fault of the building, and not of the photograph. If you will allow me, I will retain it as a curiosity.[65]

There is no doubt that Clark had impressive equipment. It is not surprising that he stepped lightly from the dying Photographic Society to the Edinburgh Photographic Society, and was elected to its Council in 1867.

The Doctors

James Young Simpson

In the early years, the medical profession was prominent in photographic experimentation. Figures like Dr John Adamson or Robert Christison had a major impact – they had the materials to hand and were experimenting with these ingredients for professional reasons. Christison, who taught George Wilson, George Skene Keith and John McCosh, published *A Dispensatory, or Commentary on the Pharmacopoeias of Great Britain: comprising the Natural*

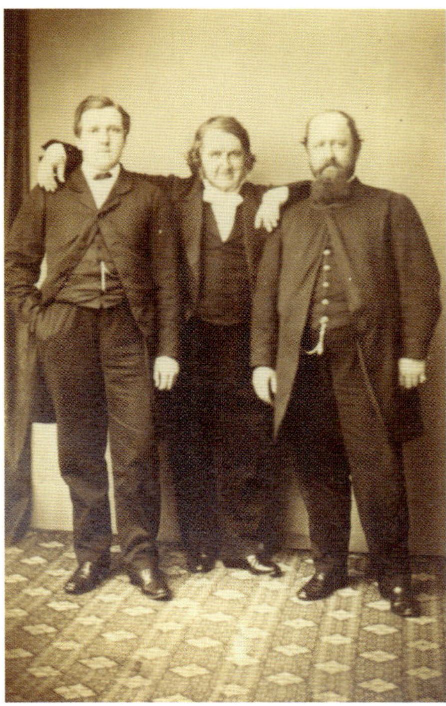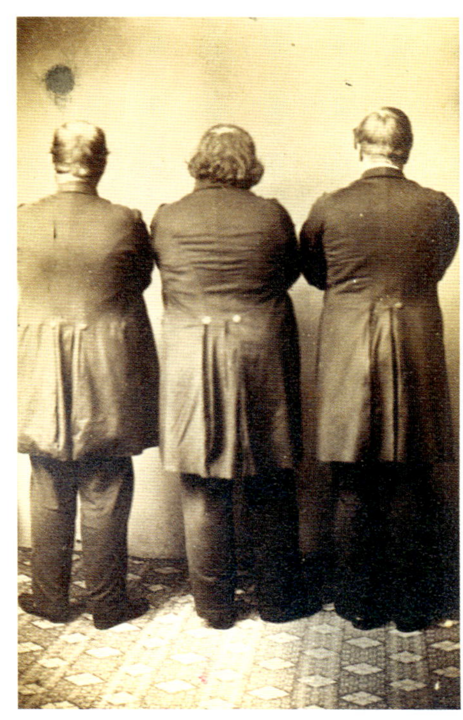

Figs 6.18: Unknown photographer, Dr James Matthews Duncan (left), Dr James Young Simpson (middle) and Dr William Walker (right); undated albumen prints. (J. Y. Simpson album, Royal College of Surgeons of Edinburgh, JYS1870)

History, Description, Chemistry, Pharmacy, Actions, Uses, and Doses of the Articles of the Materia Medica, in 1842. This offered practical and analytical information on medical materials, which would prove interesting to photographers.[66] This cross reference is present in the earliest Scottish medical photograph – a calotype taken by Hill and Adamson of a woman suffering from an exceptionally large goitre [FIG. 6.17].[67] They may have taken this for Dr James Inglis, whom they photographed at the British Association meeting in York in 1844. Inglis was a medical graduate from Edinburgh, whose 'Essay on Iodine and Bromine' and their use in the cure of goitre, won the Hope Prize for chemistry in 1834. It would not have escaped his interest in Hill and Adamson's practice, that these were two key elements of photographic chemistry.

The Edinburgh surgeon, James Young Simpson (1811–70), experimented with the new material, collodion or gun cotton, as a way of covering wounds in 1847 [FIG. 6.18]. The *Chemical Gazette* had published the discovery by Schoenbein and Boettger in April that year, that collodion was best dissolved in ether. By May, Simpson was reporting on his own experiments.[68] Simpson described 'a great variety of trials', and quoted Bigelow as saying the process 'is inert … is impervious to water and can be washed, is colourless and transparent, no heat is necessary in the application and may be made at a trifling cost'. Various journals would reprint discoveries of this importance and such information travelled rapidly. The incidental point here is that collodion was essential to the development of photography within the next decade – a clear, tough, inert film that would carry chemicals and adhere to glass, capturing great detail in the image.

Simpson was not a photographer, but he was a close friend of Dr Douglas Maclagan, one of the earliest to take an interest in the daguerreotype. As a celebrated man, Simpson was much photographed and evidently enjoyed the act. He expressed his opinion of the art in a speech given in 1853:

Amidst the thousand startling discoveries and revolutions accomplished during the last half century by the science of chemistry, no application of that science is perhaps more strange than the fact, that the chemist has taught the artist to convert that sun himself into a marvellous and matchless painter, who can elaborate the most difficult portraits, and the most complex landscapes and figure pictures, with a precision and minuteness unattainable by human art, – and with a rapidity so great, that if properly tasked, he could finish countless galleries of them, in a briefer space of time than is occupied by one single dip and dash of the brush of a mortal artist.[69]

Thomas Keith

The surgeons were engaged in stressful, often lethal work. Photography had the advantage of being an absorbing leisure pursuit. The foremost photographer among the doctors was Thomas Keith (1827–95).[70] Keith was the son of Rev. Alexander Keith of St Cyrus, Kincardineshire, and a brother of Dr George Skene Keith. He attended Aberdeen University and trained in medicine in Edinburgh. He was apprenticed to James Young Simpson in 1845, achieved his MD in 1848, and moved on to work with the surgeon James Syme in the Royal Infirmary, who taught him 'sound principles in the treatment of surgical cases, especially simplicity, painstaking, and absolute cleanliness'.[71]

Keith carried detailed control and experiment from his profession to photography. When the Photographic Society was launched in 1856, he gave an explanation of the waxed paper process, which he used exclusively. He said with customary modesty:

> The manipulation is in almost every respect identical with that of Le Gray …. I have merely this evening to describe a certain modification of his process, which seems to me more satisfactory in its results, and better adapted to our atmosphere.[72]

It is clear that he greatly simplified Gustave Le Gray's process, and the published comment on his paper says:

> … in addition to Dr Keith's own experience of the uselessness, or indeed injurious effect, of many of the substances generally added to that solution, such as cyanide and fluoride of potass, arsenic, alcohol, grape sugar, &c., some of the members who formerly employed the complex iodizing formula containing these, but who have now adopted the simple ingredients and proportions recommended by Dr Keith, have found that … they produce pictures as least as good … with much greater certainty.[73]

Keith emphasised the need for meticulous care. While finding that sensitised paper did not keep well, he also discovered that it did keep when contained in a dark slide – away from light and pollution. He attributed his success

> … entirely to this, that I never expose my paper, unless the light is first-rate. … Consequently I limit the time for taking negatives to a few weeks in the middle of summer. I sensitize my paper overnight, for in the middle of summer I am almost sure of clear mornings soon after sunrise, and most of my negatives have been taken before 7 in the morning, or after 4 in the afternoon. The light then is much softer, the shadows are larger and the half tints in your picture are more perfect, and the lights are more agreeable. If working during the height of the day, I prefer having partly diffused light, partly sunshine.

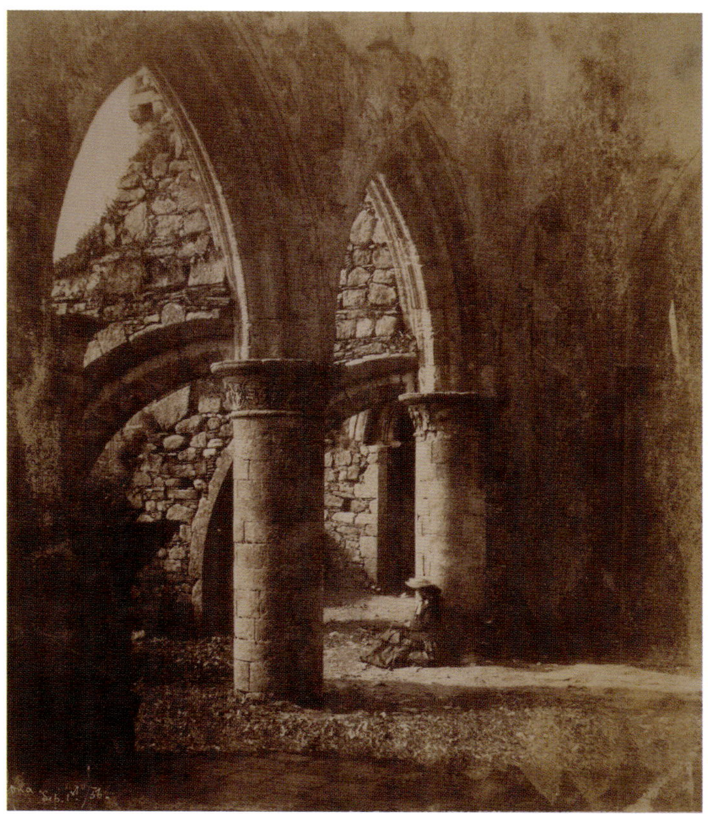

Fig. 6.19: Dr Thomas Keith, 'Iona', with Elizabeth (Johnston) Keith, 1 September 1856, salt print from a waxed paper negative. (Scottish National Portrait Gallery, PGP 58.2)

… I am quite satisfied that the commonest cause of failure arises from the paper being exposed in a bad or indifferent light, especially in town, where the atmosphere is so adulterated with smoke. I never got a good picture when there was the slightest trace of that blue haze which smoke produces between the camera and the object.[74]

C. G. H. Kinnear considered that Keith's negatives were 'the finest that had yet been produced. The dark parts had great intensity, and the whites were perfectly transparent and pure; the middle tints were also well brought out, and shewed all the details with the smoothness and sharpness of glass negatives'.[75] Keith's negatives are unconventional – large and closer to a square than a rectangle, which increases their impact. He apparently exhibited his work only on two occasions. The review in *Photographic Notes* of the Photographic Society's first exhibition singled out his 'Pillars at the Cathedral of Iona', as 'a most vigorous and powerful Picture'.[76] Another, more open and elegantly composed picture of the ruins of the Abbey includes his wife, Elizabeth Johnston [Fig. 6.19]. Most endearingly, the picture has his loving regard at its heart. She is not there simply to provide us with a modern focus, reflecting on history – we know who she is, and she gives a pleasurable balance to the melancholy of the ruin.

The antiquarian interests of the Edinburgh doctors were based on professional familiarity with the place. The re-design of the city in the later 18th century had drawn the prosperous away to the New Town on the north side; the historic heart – a conglomeration of tall 'lands' and narrow closes – degenerated into slums. Visitors would be essentially the religious and charitable and the doctors, who accepted a responsibility to the poor. In much of his work, Keith celebrated the history of the Old Town – the strongly expressed light and shadow on the decaying stone buildings brings out a sense of the past, in dense patina and mystery. The spine of rock between the Castle and Holyrood Palace and the roads leading down and underneath newer buildings were sites of dramatic, sometimes violent history; places lived in by the great and influential and by the quirkily independent characters of the past. The disengaged definition of the Picturesque, seen in passing in a ruinous cottage or a gnarled tree, cannot apply to Keith's approach. The melancholy inherent in the ruins of past greatness was enforced by the misery of the many people living there.

There are figures in his photographs – perhaps people who knew him. His pictures also have a number of signs and posters, which help to reveal the life of the place; the well-painted sign on the side of one of the buildings known as 'Society' [Fig. 6.20], offers us the services of Mrs Cockson:

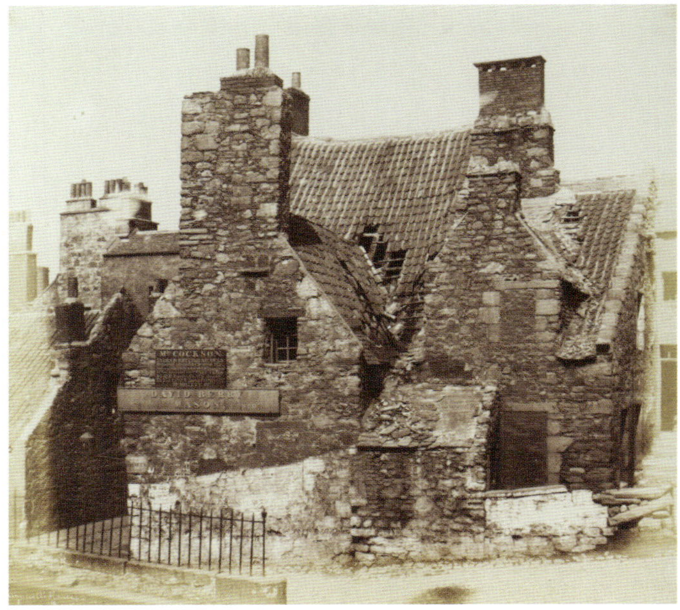

INDIA & BRITISH SHAWLS
Repaired Altered & Cleaned the
Figure of Old INDIA SHAWLS Transferred
To New Grounds CHANTILLY VEILS
& LACE Transferred, LACE Joined.
TABLE LINEN Darned to Pattern.

Mrs Cockson was presumably a widow, with skills devoted to the rescue of past elegance; there is a whole decaying social history in this sign alone. She balances the derelict building with a declaration of survival and restoration.

One of Keith's negatives [FIG. 6.21] is a virtuoso performance, enabled by his control of the exposure times. He said:

> Experience soon taught me … that by increasing or diminishing the strength of the iodizing solution … almost any degree of sensitiveness could be procured, from the rapidity of collodion to the slowness of albumen. I was thus enabled to get equally powerful negatives in one minute as in half an hour …. I accordingly selected for the ordinary purposes of views of buildings and landscapes, such proportions as would require an exposure of from three to five or six minutes … a more sensitive paper than this I found could not be depended upon, unless used within a very short time after preparation.[77]

In this case, it may be assumed that he was using the least sensitive solution, and giving himself time to move around. The negative shows the city of Edinburgh, from positions around the Royal Mile, into the Cowgate on the south side and into Princes Street on the north, uphill and

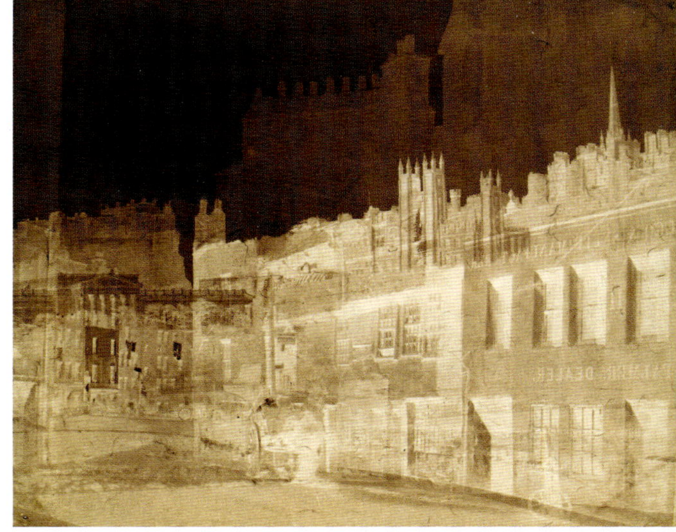

downhill in an area of about half a mile square. There are at least six exposures on the paper. The images are overlaid, and were taken sequentially, leaving the slide with the negative in the camera, and removing the lens cap in different locations, presumably underexposing each time. How far he could see what he was doing is open to discussion, but the result was controlled. Both the calculation involved in this exercise and the skill in making it work are admirable. There seems to be no print – but that is scarcely surprising – it is a fine example of a photographic act performed for its own interest.

Keith stopped taking photographs in 1858 – his practice was more active. It is likely that he and his wife found a more agreeable occupation for his leisure hours than ironing wax into paper (which he generally did at night). But he has left us around two hundred photographs, described by Dr John Brown as 'of quite exceptional beauty and artistic quality'.[78]

Keith may have taught photography to John Forbes White (1831–1904), who became his brother-in-law – he certainly communicated his enthusiasm.[79] The two men engaged in photographic expeditions together in the North East of Scotland, and it can be difficult to determine which man took which photograph. White was the son of an Aberdonian flour miller, who educated his children well. White's mother was a woman of visual knowledge – a collector of antiques and a gardener, which presumably gave him a grounding in aesthetic discrimination. He intended to take up medicine but, on his father's death in 1845, took over the family business. White's first dated negatives belong to 1855. Like Keith he used a large format camera and explored architectural and landscape photography [FIG. 6.22]. He too gave up the practice of photography after a few years, apparently in 1859. His business prospered, and increasing wealth enabled him to become a patron of artists – from the Dutch school, Corot, and the Scottish painters, George Reid and George Paul Chalmers. It is pleasing to consider that he must have been amongst the first connoisseurs of painting who discovered aesthetic appreciation from a practice of photography – learnt from a surgeon. When the photographs were reprinted by the Annan firm at the end

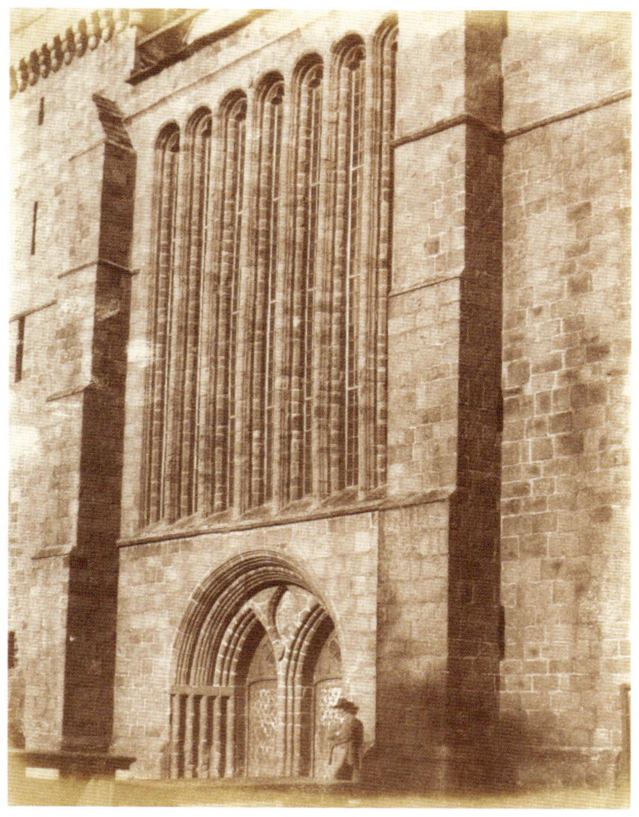

of the century for the Glasgow International Exhibition, he was surprised and said, 'Isn't that beautiful?'[80]

William Walker and others

In 1853, Thomas Keith first appeared as a doctor in the Edinburgh post office directory, living with his brother at 58 Northumberland Street. By happy coincidence, Dr William Walker (*c.*1814–85) lived at number 47, and the scientific instrument maker John Adie (1805–57) lived at number 50. At this favourable time Keith first took up photography. Around the corner, living in Dundas Street, was the history painter, James Drummond (1816–77). Drummond was an early member of the Photographic Society of Scotland, and advised on exhibitions and medals, but it may be that he was an enthusiast for photography rather than a photographer himself. In the sale after his death, the volumes of

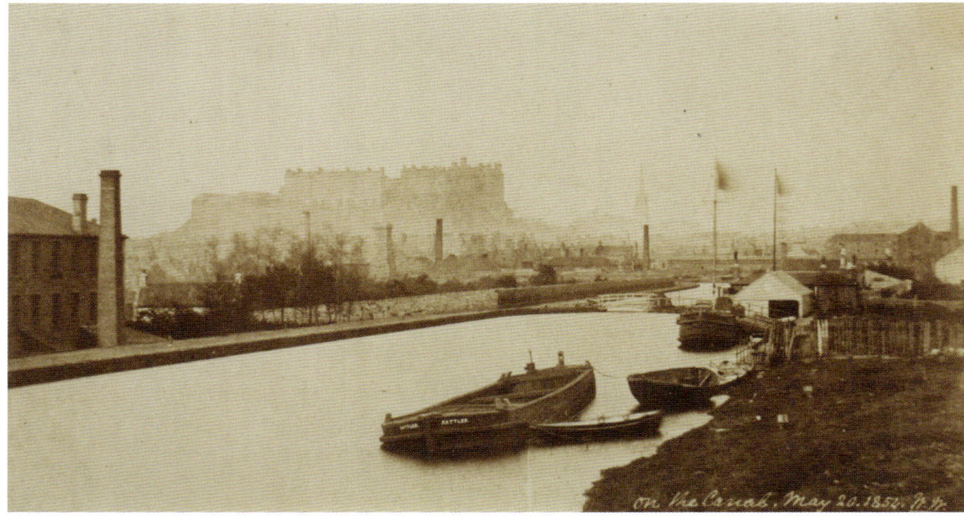

photographs included two by Hill and Adamson, and a folio of 'Calotype views of Old Edinburgh, and 18 others chiefly of Iona'. These were principally taken by Thomas Keith and William Walker [FIG. 6.23], with some of J. G. Tunny's pictures.[81] Keith, Walker and Drummond were all members of the Society of Antiquaries, along with James Young Simpson. Drummond himself painted scenes from Scottish history, principally shown in a theatrical Edinburgh setting. He also made a straightforward drawn record of the old heart of the city, which worked in parallel with the photographs.

William Walker came originally from Dumfriesshire.[82] He was the first eye surgeon at the Royal Infirmary in Edinburgh, and became ophthalmic surgeon to the Queen. His obituary said that he was 'distinguished by his robust common sense .... He was a cool and dexterous operator, and … specially excelled in the after-treatment of his cases, to which he attributed, in great part, his success … [he had] a retiring manner, [and] a warm heart.'[83] In 1871, Walker was made President of the Royal College of Surgeons in Edinburgh, and his portrait was painted for the College: rather than holding a surgical instrument or medical publication, he is holding a photograph.

Walker was wider in his technical approach to photography than Keith. He read a paper on the calotype, specifically Dr Diamond's version, which was concerned with details of care in manipulation and 'the strictest attention to cleanliness in all the different stages'. The abstract contained the following thoughts:

The existence of bromine in the iodizing solution he considered to be of importance, as he had found that when it was present, even in a small quantity, he invariably obtained the half tints and greens of a landscape better than he did without it …. He considered that sufficient exposure in the camera was not generally given, and thought that it should always be long enough to obtain the shadows and darkly illuminated parts of a landscape, leaving the light parts to take care of themselves …. With a 2 inch lens, having a focus of 13 inches, and using a stop of ½ inch, about ten minutes was a good average time …. He thought that the best prints were always obtained from an unwaxed negative, as the shadows were not so transparent, and the half tints much more delicate.[84]

Walker's surviving photographs are mostly pictures of the Old Town and landscapes, around Edinburgh and in his native Dumfries. He exhibited regularly at the exhibitions of the Photographic Society of Scotland. But he had a conveniently portable camera and his pictures are smaller in scale than Keith's – their evenness suggests a search for detail rather than impact.

While Thomas Keith confined his photography to leisure, Walker seems to have considered it also as a professional tool. Botany was essential to medical study and Walker was a member of the Edinburgh Botanical Society from 1836. In 1857 he took a stereo photograph of a plant grown in the Royal Botanic Garden; *Asafoetida*, which came from a dry climate in Persia, was flowering in Edinburgh after fifteen years. The botanist John Hutton Balfour described the erratic progress of the plant, with the assistance of Walker's photograph.[85] The extraordinary care taken in its cultivation was not abstract curiosity [Fig. 6.24]; it was of considerable therapeutic value.[86]

Dr James Matthews Duncan (1826–90) was born in Aberdeen, the son of a merchant, and trained in medicine at Aberdeen, Edinburgh and Paris. He also worked in obstetrics as James Young Simpson's assistant. He was a careful and practical researcher.[87] Like Walker, he was a founder member of the Photographic Society and stayed until 1865. His connection to the Botanical Society is shown in a photograph he took to demonstrate that the Garden's glasshouse was too small and the palm trees were growing out of the roof.

Duncan exhibited landscapes, taken in the Highlands by the waxed paper process, in the Photographic Society's exhibition in 1858 [Fig. 6.25]. He and Walker were both members of the Photographic Exchange Club. In 1859, he donated prints of the village of Onich, from negatives 'taken by Kinnear's formula' with prints made with an 'Alkaline chloride of gold toning Bath'. Walker contributed views of the West Bow, Edinburgh from a calotype negative, printed with an 'Alkaline gold toning Bath', and later 'View on the Water of Leith', 'On the Esk', and 'Water of Leith'.

Walker used photography closely in his work. In 1861, he responded to a paper by Alexander Johnstone Macfarlan (1838–69), 'On the Application of Photography to the Delineation of Diseases …'. Walker expressed the 'opinion, formed on his own experience of it in cases of diseases of the eye which had come before him professionally, of the great value of the applications of photography'.[88]

The Upper Ten Thousand

By the mid-19th century, the population of Britain was substantially based in the cities, and much of the wealth of the country was owned by the new industrialists. Nevertheless, the aristocratic and landed class still held power and authority. This social group was remarkable not just for its wealth and possessions but for its leisure and readiness to relax and play, especially in the countryside.

In 1833 when David Brewster and his colleagues initiated the British Association for the Advancement of Science, they set up the first professionally-led scientific conference. Before that time, much of the patronage of the sciences and the scientific instrument makers lay in the hands of the wealthy, and something of this situation persisted. Brewster first became friends with W. H. F. Talbot at his home, Lacock Abbey. He carried photographs with him when he went to visit grand houses, such as Rossie Priory in Perthshire.

Rossie Priory

According to the Rev. Robert Graham, Talbot no sooner invented the calotype than he communicated with Brewster, then the guest at Rossie, of George, 9th Baron Kinnaird

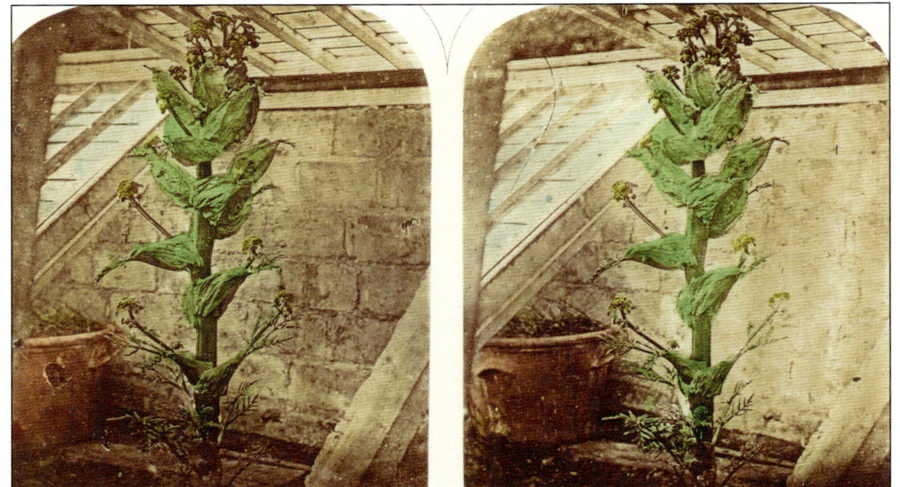

Fig. 6.24: Dr William Walker, *Asafoetida*, 1858, hand-coloured stereoscopic albumen prints. (National Library of Scotland, *Stereoscopic Magazine*, vol. 1, 1858, H.4.b.12–16)

Fig. 6.25: Dr James Matthews Duncan, 'On the Aline Water, Inverness shire', albumen print from waxed paper negative, *c*.1858. (Edinburgh Exchange Photographic Album, National Media Museum / Science & Society Picture Library, 1990-5131_1_21)

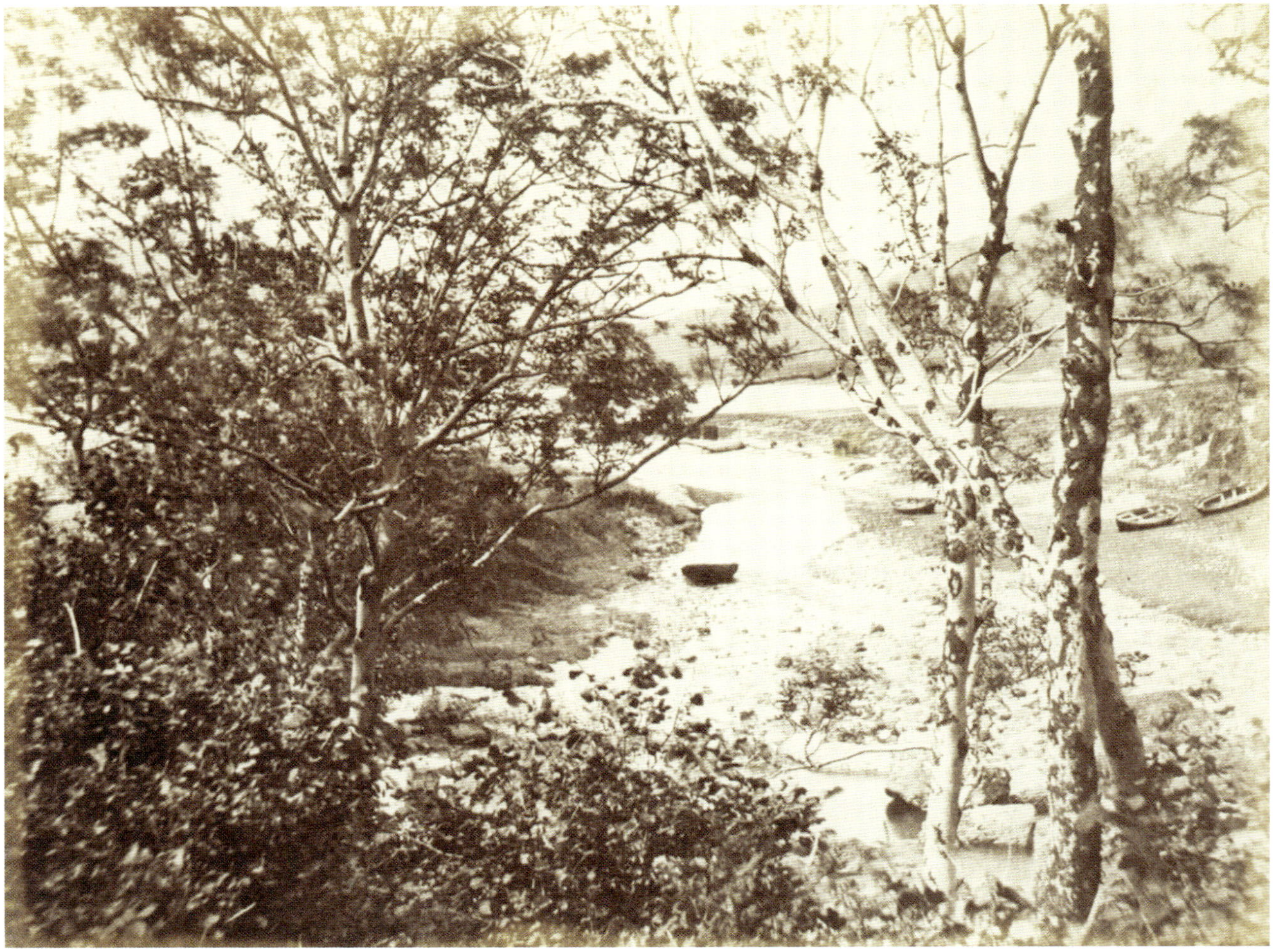

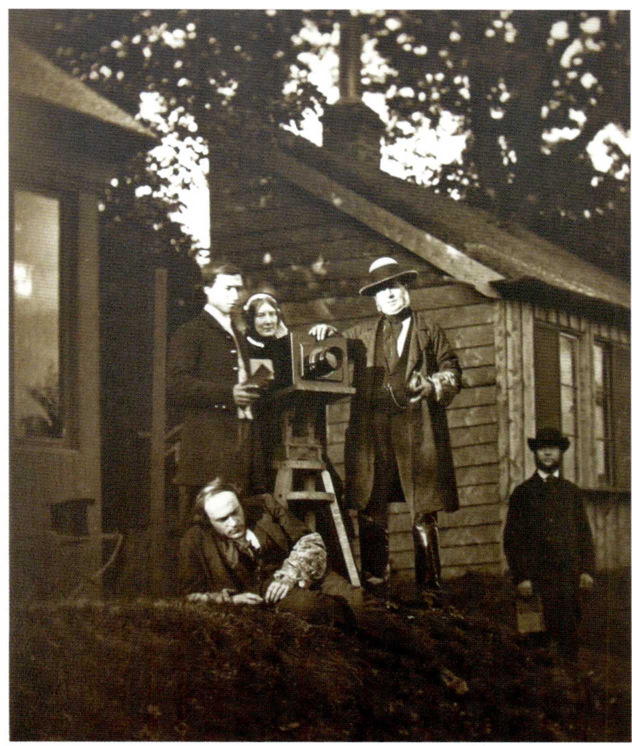

Fig. 6.26: Members of the Rossie Priory circle, group in front of studio and darkroom, including Lord and Lady Kinnaird, *c.*1860, digital print from a stereoscopic negative. (St Andrews University Library, Special Collections, 2014-3-164)

(1807–78) and Lady (Frances Ponsonby) Kinnaird (d.1910). The story goes that Kinnaird was keen to try, Brewster secured the equipment and the chemicals, and an old lady was persuaded to sit for twenty minutes in full sunshine. Disappointingly, only a hazy outline of the lady appeared on the paper. The twenty-minute exposure may suggest an early experiment, perhaps before Talbot had published the key discovery of the latent image in 1841. The Kinnairds' enthusiasm for photography and their link to Brewster are first confirmed in a letter Talbot's mother wrote in April 1845, when Brewster had shown them Talbot's *Sun Pictures in Scotland*. She wrote:

> … they were émerveillés at the beauty of your Scotch views which had been shewn to them by Sir David Brewster. He is a great friend of theirs & they talked a great deal in his praise.[89]

Robert Graham (1818–1900), who joined the Kinnairds in photography, trained at the University of St Andrews. In 1849, he moved from Dundee to Abernyte, and to the parish of Errol in 1858 (within a few miles of the Priory), where he worked for forty-two years. It may be that he was first involved in the Kinnairds' photography from 1849, and probably he was involved with their stereoscopic photography. Graham expresses the original excitement of Rossie in the throes of photography:

> All available tubs, buckets, foot-pails, wash-hand basins, and every sort of vessel which could contain water, were laid hold of for the frequent washings and soakings which were required. Every room which could be darkened was needed for the drying in the dark. The region

of every domestic in a household was invaded, and servants were kept running perpetually with pails of hot and cold water, warm smoothing-irons &c … Rossie Priory is one of the largest houses in Scotland, yet we have often seen it moved from one end to another, and all in it, from its noble owner to the humblest domestic, in a fever of excitement.[90]

The Kinnairds built a studio, with a domed glass roof in the centre, and a separate dark room, in the Priory grounds [FIG. 6.26]. There are extant stereoscopic, carte and half-plate negatives in the collection of the University of St Andrews (which relate to their practice in the 1860s) and there remains an alphabetical listing of their sitters, with a catalogue of the equipment. The latter identifies 13 lenses by Dallmeyer and Ross and six cameras: an enlarging and copying camera, 15 x 12 inches; a folding camera by Otte-will; a 12 x 12 inch bellows camera by J. Spencer; a binocular bellows camera; a carte de visite camera; and a 6 x 6 inch camera. Some of this may have been abandoned when the list was made – the carte camera is annotated 'pinch lost'; and the dark tent is qualified: 'Lining of Tent very much destroyed by mice'. The listing also mentions five carbon printing frames and one of 'the Autotype Co Pattern'.[91] The Kinnairds worked with Thomas Rodger as an assistant, and continued to use his services after he set up his St Andrews studio. In the early 1860s, they employed John Cumming, who probably worked for Ross and Thomson and later owned The Edinburgh Photographic Gallery in Hanover Street, and then John Weeks, who worked for Thomas Rodger from 1866. Cumming was employed in 1861, and his letter of acceptance offers a comment on the status of photographers at the Priory:

My charge for 26 working days would be 25 pounds Your supplying all chemicals &c. during the time engaged in the work. I would have no objections to live in the Stewards room …. PS This charge 25 pounds for one month, is much less than what I mentioned before to Messrs R & T but as the order is for a long period I have made it this.[92]

From the surviving evidence, the Kinnairds photographed their own people and properties, as well as art collections, which were indeed impressive. Kinnaird's father, the 8th Lord, was a collector of fine art. He himself, when on leave from the army as a young man, 'passed much of his time in Rome, making excursions to Pompeii, Etruria, and other celebrated places in that classic land, collecting the many rare objects that adorn the Priory'.[93]

Thomas Rodger's obituary states that he was given responsibility to photograph 'the splendid collection of ancient and modern paintings and statues which adorn the princely halls of Rossie'.[94] The photographers, including the Kinnairds themselves, experienced difficulty with the paintings, but they succeeded in making a set of carbon prints of sixty-three sculptures.[95] The surviving prints from each subject vary between one and sixty, which suggests a private edition of the catalogue. However, the catalogue may only exist in one specimen, reduced in its ambition, and showing only a few photographs.[96]

The British Association for the Advancement of Science met at Dundee in September 1867. Brewster and Kinnaird were Vice-Presidents. Several speakers addressed photographic concerns in the sections on Mathematical and Physical Science, and Chemical Science. James Clerk Maxwell described 'A Real Image Stereoscope' devised by him, with one large lens for the viewer rather than two separate ones for the left and right eye; Antoine Claudet spoke on stereoscopic vision in relation to the illusion of the 'Thaumatrope'; on a mechanical method of equalizing focus; and on portraits taken through rock crystal and topaz lenses; Brewster presented William McCraw's enamel photographs.

A report on the occasion commented on the liberality of the neighbourhood:

Lord Kinnaird has shown especial hospitality to the [chemists]… staying at his seat – Rossie Priory – have been Dr Angus Smith, Mr Crookes, Mr Spiller, and Mr Ansell, the inventor of the fire-damp indicator.[97]

Smith, William Crookes, and John Spiller were actively experimenting with photographic chemistry. By inviting this group to the Priory, the Kinnairds gave themselves privileged access to photo-chemical investigation.

The Association arranged excursions for the members

– one to Rossie Priory, and an encounter with Thomas Rodger:

> No member who … partook of the unbounded hospitality of Lord Kinnaird at his noble mansion, Rossie Priory, will easily forget the unalloyed pleasure …. In front of the Priory, our friend Mr Rodger, of St Andrews, had placed a gigantic camera, and with a noble Voigtlander lens of about five inches diameter he took two groups of the party.[98]

Lady Alice Kerr and Ronald Leslie Melville

Lady Alice Kerr (1836–92) [Figs 6.27 a–d] was the daughter of John Kerr, 7th Marquess of Lothian and his wife, Lady Cecil Chetwynde-Talbot, daughter of the 2nd Earl Talbot. The family circle was intensely involved both in religion and the arts. She, her mother and her siblings converted to Roman Catholicism in the 1850s – her sister, Lady Cecil, became a nun in 1859.[99] The Lothian family were patrons of the arts and, significantly, were part of the Little Holland House circle dominated by admiration for the painter George Frederick Watts and the poet Alfred Tennyson. The prominent photographer, Julia Margaret Cameron (1815–79), was herself part of this circle.[100] The similarity in subject matter between the work of Kerr and Cameron has its roots in this. Both Lady Alice and Cameron regarded Renaissance painting as a source of inspiration [Fig. 6.27 a].

Lady Alice Kerr lived in a society which entertained house parties both in England and Scotland.[101] The visitors engaged in tableaux, inspired by the Bible, by painting and by poetry. Lady Alice photographed Alice Blunt and her brother, Wilfrid, as Judith and Holofernes – one of the most alarming stories of a woman's strength and belief in the Old Testament.[102] Whilst Judith is thoughtfully poised with a sword over the unconscious man, the tableau does not attempt the blood and carnage, which were shown in brutal paintings by Artemisia Gentileschi and Caravaggio among others, but it may have been prompted by these. Perhaps disappointingly, the tableau cannot be regarded as an early feminist declaration of the strength of women; the context of Lady Alice's recent conversion makes it plain that this is an allegory – a heroic defence of the principles of religion. Such subjects were not current in Protestant art, but they would have been familiar to the Kerrs from the Grand Tour and the art galleries of Italy.

By contrast, her photograph of Reginald Talbot, wearing the armour of a Life Guard, with a young woman turned towards him, gives us a picture of some tenderness – his hands lightly touching her hair. Lady Alice succeeded in taking allegorical photographs of children, and her photograph of a young girl, perhaps as a water nymph holding bamboo and waterlilies, is an excellent portrait of the girl and an admirable picture [Figs 6.27 c and d].[103]

Her portrait of Wilfrid Scawen Blunt (1840–1922) [Fig. 6.27 b] has great intensity.[104] Kerr has placed Blunt close. All extraneous detail lies outside the frame. The focus is shallow, solely on his eyes and lips and the forward wave of his hair. His eyes, looking at her, are shadowed, making the pupils larger and more evidently seductive, and she has put two sources of a reflecting, secondary light to enliven them. A similar edge of light touches his lips. The portrait is distinguished from Cameron's male portraits, which expressed an elevated concept of hero-worship. By striking contrast, this is a photograph of a lustful and self-

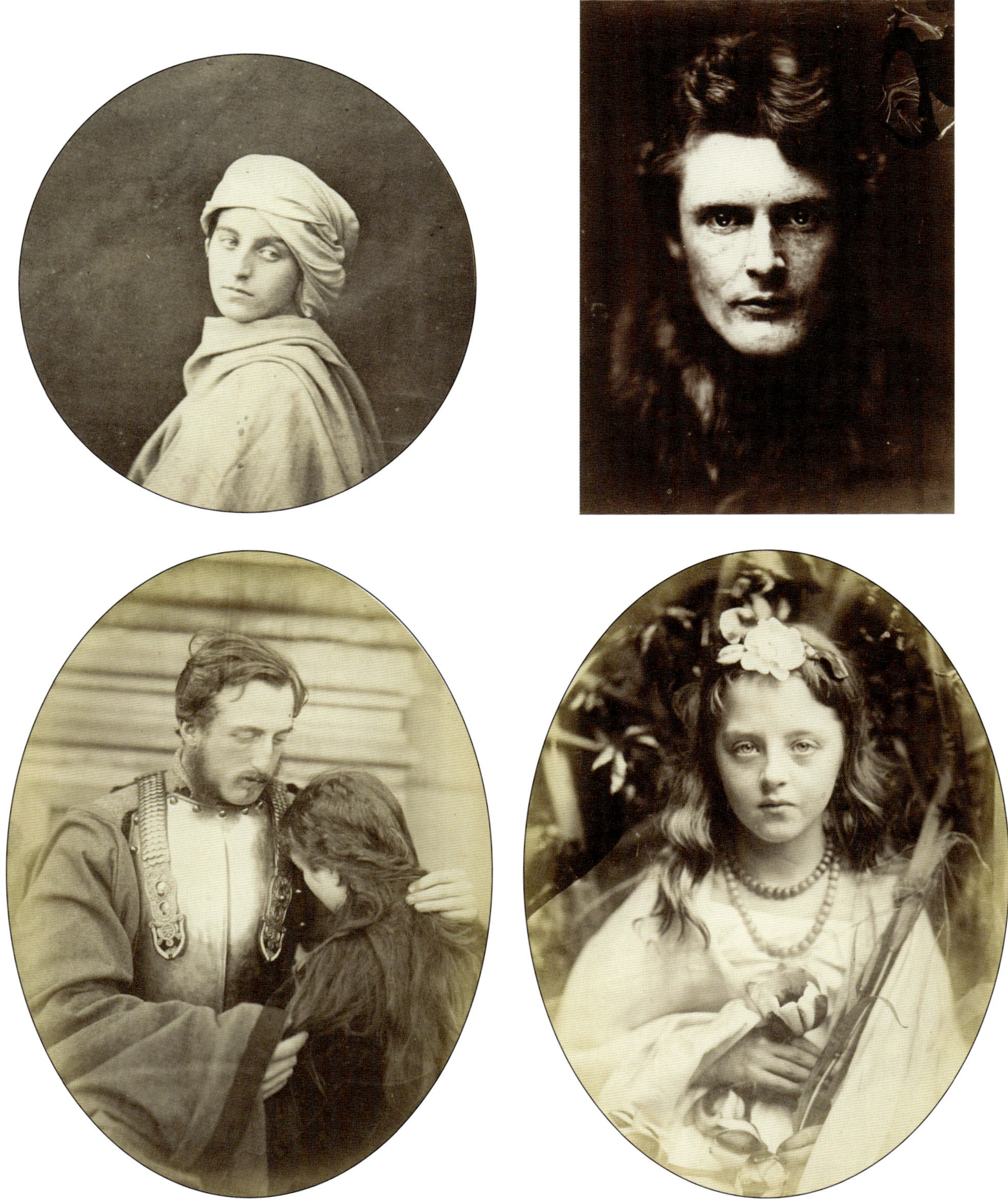

admiring man. Here, the relationship between the subject and the photographer has an emotional charge, directed in part by the sitter's response. The photographer may not have known him too well; she is said also to have photographed him also as Sir Galahad. Here, Blunt is heavily engaged with his own image, but simultaneously looking at the photographer. She is a young woman he was familiar with, and whome he is said to have considered marrying; the picture may relate to their courtship. It is an extraordinary photograph.

Victorian humorists were quick to exploit the possibilities of young ladies flirting through photography. The camera enabled young women to look critically at young men. In this close society, where the young would know each other from childhood, photography could have become a significant method of discovery in the shift from juvenile play to courtship. This raises an additional question that relates to the use of photography in such a personal context; photography, the essentially public art, could be used as a private idea, without reference to its publicity, even when the photographs were subsequently printed in numbers and distributed. This curious public/private form of art could be used by women as a form of overt expression (both as photographers and as performers), which may seem to us to be breaking the conventions of the day.

The most interesting quirk in this situation was acting – the presentation of the individual in another persona. In staging the powerful role of Judith, a biblical heroine preparing to decapitate the Assyrian general, Lady Alice side-stepped the social rules (the concept of feminine subservience and delicacy), offering, moreover, a picture implying the erotic relationship between love and death, explored with such enthusiasm by contemporary poets. She also

photographed Blunt's sister as the Lady of Shallot, who died for love of Lancelot. The breaking of polite convention was justified through religious symbolism, the authority of fine art and the licence of poetry, which enabled the actuality of violence and passion to come through in moral and aesthetic terms.

There was another important element to this. Throughout the 19th century, the tyranny of fashion, its distortion of the female form and its dullness for men, was a constant complaint.[105] The Victorian taste for fancy dress and the grand balls promoted by the Queen among others provided some relief.[106] Victoria and Albert themselves encouraged the performance art of tableau and the photographic picturing of these staged sets, when they asked Roger Fenton to photograph the royal children performing 'The Seasons' from James Thomson's poem in 1854.[107]

In 1863, the Earl and Countess of Fife entertained the Prince and Princess of Wales at Mar Lodge for the Highland Games of the Braemar Gathering. Victor Albert Prout (1835–77) was called on to arrange suitable tableaux and brief plays with the willing guests, with themes symbolic (Faith, Hope and Charity), literary (Elaine) and historic (Mary, Queen of Scots attended by Rizzio). Prout photographed the performers and constructed a book to commemorate the occasion, which noted, most happily, that the tableaux 'delighted all who witnessed them by their dramatic vigour and poetic sentiment [eliciting] applause of the warmest kind, in which the Prince and Princess heartily joined'.[108] The exhausting nature of this aesthetic performance is shown in Prout's photograph of the participants slumped in the drawing room later [FIG. 6.28].

Possessed of wealth and leisure, Society could walk both sides with ease: in high fashion, they were photo-

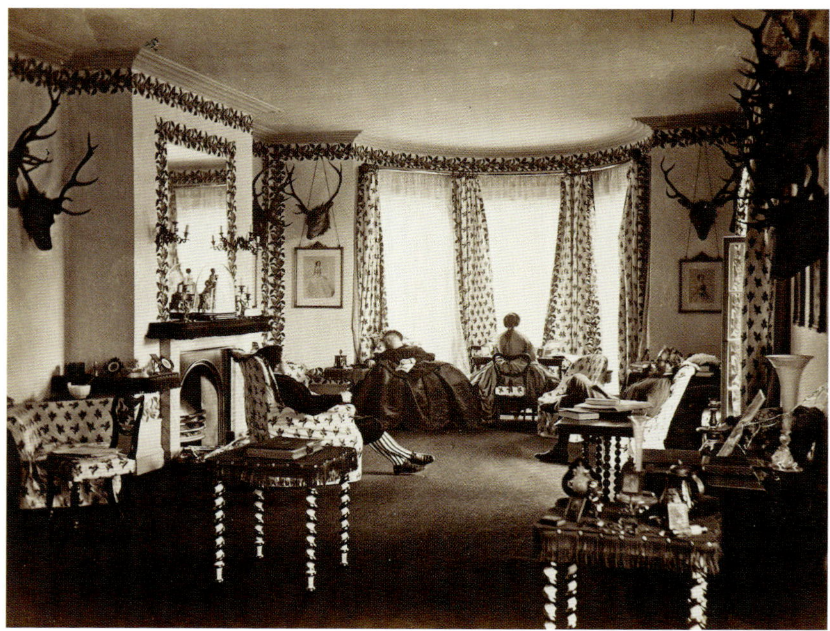

Fig. 6.28 (left): Victor Albert Prout, 'Interior of the Drawing Room, Mar Lodge', August 1863, albumen print. (Mar Lodge album, Scottish National Portrait Gallery, PGP 162.55)

Fig. 6.29 (opposite left): Ronald Leslie Melville, 'Lochiel's Warning', undated, albumen print. (Melville Album, J. Paul Getty Museum, 86.XA.21.68)

Fig. 6.30 (opposite right): Ronald Leslie Melville, '(Lady Middleton)/Juliet/Medea', c.1865, albumen print. (Melville Album, J. Paul Getty Museum, 86.XA.21.74)

graphed by the studios of André Adolphe Eugène Disdéri (1818–89) in Paris or Camille Silvy (1834–1910) in London; in fancy dress they performed at country house parties, and were photographed by their friends.

Ronald Leslie Melville, subsequently 11th Earl of Leven and 10th Earl of Melville (1835–1906), also took photographs principally in the country house context – portraits, sporting pictures and tableaux.[109] His sitters connect with those of Lady Alice, and his photographs share similar subject matter. They combine fiction and reality, sometimes in unexpected ways [FIG. 6.29]. One of his most bizarre studies is 'Lochiel's Warning', from the verse by Thomas Campbell, where a Wizard gave a blood-curdling promise of doom to Cameron of Lochiel before the Battle of Culloden in 1745:

> Life flutters convulsed in his quivering limbs,
> And his blood-streaming nostril in agony swims.
> Accursed be the faggots that blaze at his feet,
> Where his heart shall be thrown, ere it ceases to beat,
> With the smoke of its ashes to poison the gale.[110]

Dr Archibald Cameron, brother of Lochiel, leading supporter of Prince Charles Edward Stuart, was captured and executed after the battle as a traitor. In the photograph, the role was taken by his descendant, chief of Clan Cameron, rejecting the Wizard's advice as cowardice. It is an ambitious scene, and Lochiel's slightly wooden performance expresses the difficulty of re-enactment. Like Alice Kerr's 'Judith and Holofernes', the performance and photograph require that we put intense feeling into viewing the picture.

This photograph is taken outdoors and it uses diffuse available light, but others show a more sophisticated approach. Melville evidently set up a studio where he could control the lighting and work in broad close-up. In his portrait of Lady Middleton [FIG. 6.30], he used strong side lighting and focussed on her profile. He evaded contemporary dress with the use of a drape across her shoulders, and she unpinned her hair. These portraits were inevitably compared with Julia Margaret Cameron's work. The chronological relationship between their productions is unclear, but in 1871 a reviewer admired his work in the International Exhibition at Cameron's expense:

> … while his pictures possess all the artistic peculiarities of this lady's work … they are also good as photographs, possessing both artistic and technical excellence.[111]

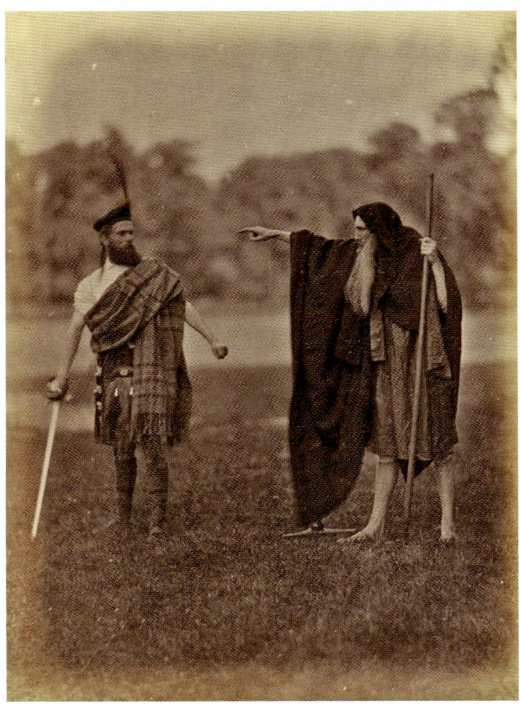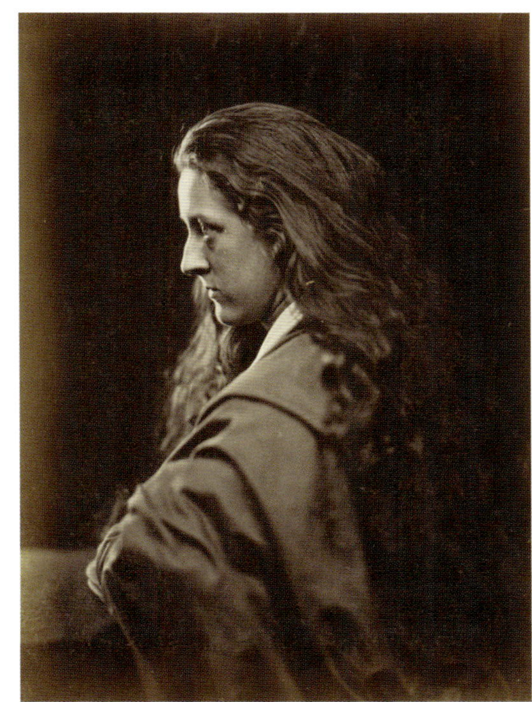

Melville was an accomplished portraitist and a humorous organiser of social groups. In two of these, showing the well-wrapped up party going to a dance in Portree he took the group coming and going [Fig. 6.31]. An idea of both relaxation and exercise lies behind Melville's practice; he went out shooting with the Rosses' expert son, Edward, and took a sequence of photographs of the kill, which indicates that he knew and learnt from Horatio Ross.

Melville's career as a photographer so far suggests the dilettante. He took photographs between his responsibilities in banking and on the family's estates. It is, therefore, disconcerting to find that in January 1868, he set off for the Abyssinian war, to take photographs, make watercolours and write an extended journal. He shot and stuffed game, and brought back live animals and plants for study.[112] His involvement in the war itself was partly blocked by the military, and he reached Magdala after the fall of the citadel. But he had the status of war correspondent, which gave him freedom of movement and official protection.

Melville may have been as much moved by the mysterious character of Abyssinia as by the excitement of the war.

Knowledge of the country had not much increased since James Bruce visited in the 18th century. Melville's journal illustrates his enthusiasm in exploring the country, his sense of its beauty and the need to record information. His drawings are capable illustrations of the landscape and the Ethiopian church, which he visited, and he used photography to copy the drawings.

The seven Royal Engineer photographers in Abyssinia, under Sergeant John Harrold, were principally employed in copying maps for the army. The account of their difficulties, using wet collodion, illuminate Melville's situation. The Engineers had eighteen boxes of equipment, and took materials to make 200 large glass negatives and 1700 prints. The chemicals evaporated in the great heat; the dark tent, 'exceedingly hot and close and very unsteady', was torn apart by strong winds, scattering sand over their work. Water was scarce and full of chlorides, and the officers were not very bright: 'a great deal of useless work was sometimes performed on account of the ignorance of photographic matters on the part of staff officers who gave orders.'[113]

Melville encountered the same conditions, but had

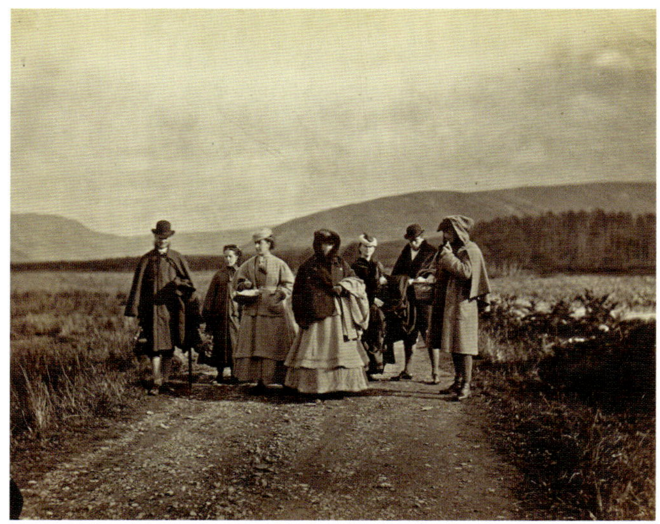 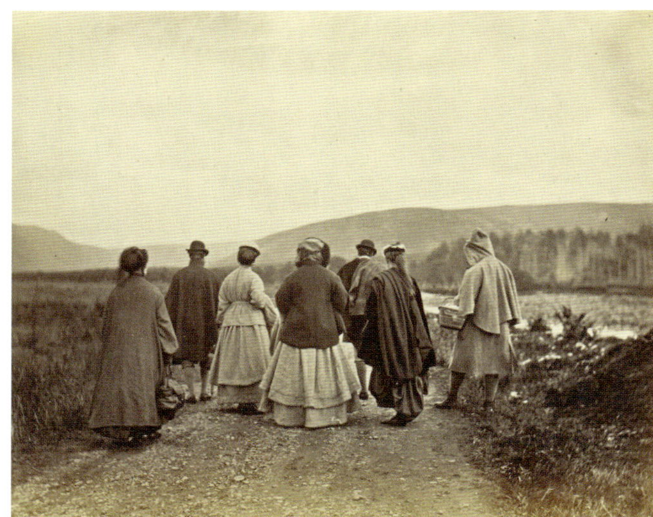

particular difficulty with the dry collodion process. At Senafé, he found a Mr Brown with a convenient dark tent. Mr Brown was 'very civil and we arranged a matinee photographique, beginning with the prisoners in the stocks. His being wet collodion very successful. The brutes moved during my long dry-plate exposure. Did about half a dozen tolerable photos'[114] It is cheering to find the Abyssians, and not just those placed in extreme discomfort in the stocks, lacked respect for the British army. Sergeant Harrold, attempting to photograph a church interior with a dry plate negative, engaged the priest in conversation hoping that the photograph could be exposed unnoticed. The priest, not deluded, kicked over the camera.

The Amateur Photographic Association

The Amateur Photographic Association, based in London, was formed in 1861 in response to the rising tide of professional photographers. Among the Scottish members were Melville and his brother, Alexander, James Sinclair, 14th Earl of Caithness, Robert Murray, Lady Matheson (wife of Sir James Matheson), Alexander Henderson, John Clerk of Penicuik, Captain G. R. Playfair and John Campbell of Islay. The subscription entitled the members to prints made from negatives by other members, arranged qualitatively

in five classes according to size and excellence. By 1863, the Secretary had 3000 negatives in hand, with the prints carefully identified by a number for each photographer and sub-numbers for each image.[115] The Association's role in promoting the exchange of photographs throughout the world was unquestionably impressive.

The Prince of Wales became President of the Association and their glamour was declared by a soirée held in February 1863. Four hundred people crowded into 'Mr Melhuish's spacious rooms' where the principal object of admiration was, rather unexpectedly, a painting by Rosa Bonheur covered by curtains ('For some minutes the attention of the Prince was riveted upon it'). Classical music was performed and 'champagne and ices were provided ad libitum'. Mr P. H. Desvignes displayed a large revolving, dissolving stereoscope run on clockwork, which could go on for some hours. M. Rimmel 'kindly lent the celebrated "Perfume Fountain," which first graced the bridal boudoir of the Princess of Wales at Windsor' and evidently sprayed the room vigorously with scent.[116] But while the Scottish societies also engaged in conversaziones and soirées in the 1860s, sad to say champagne is never mentioned.

The members of the Association were not in effective retreat. They continued to exhibit and to be criticised for their work. James Sinclair, 14th Earl of Caithness (1821–81), was a Fellow of the Royal Society and an ingenious

Figs 6.31 (opposite): R. L. Melville, 'Going to the Ball at Portree', 1860s, albumen prints. (Melville Album, J. Paul Getty Museum, 86.XA.21.102 and 103)

Fig. 6.32 (right): Earl of Caithness, 'Hoar Frost', *c.*1867, albumen print. (George Eastman House, 1977: 0689:0134)

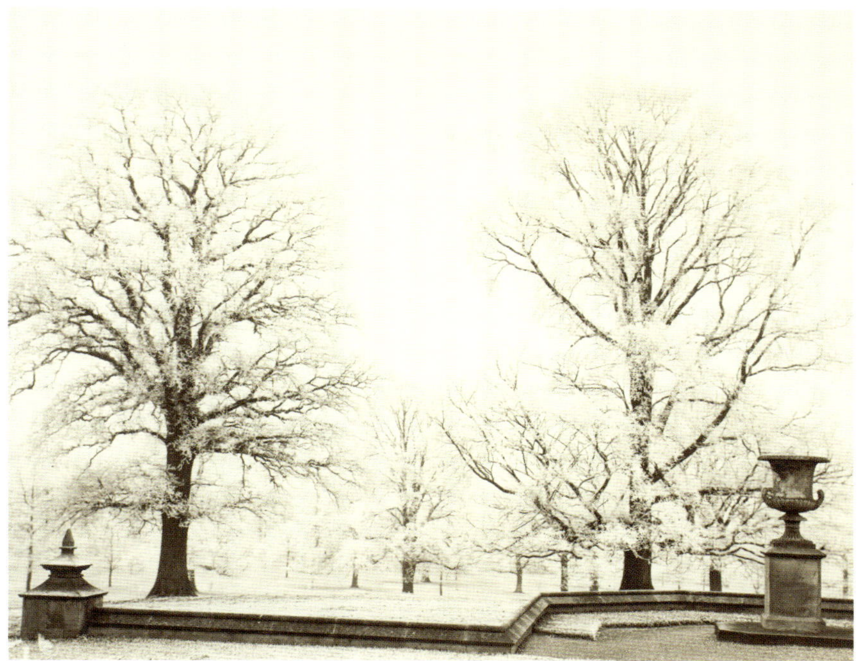

inventor. He commissioned a steam carriage from Thomas Ricketts in 1860, for travelling on macadamised roads, and drove a hundred and forty-six miles around the Highlands. He was a Lord-in-Waiting at the Court; Queen Victoria ambiguously remarked in her private journal that he had 'much to say for himself, as he knows so much'.[117] He exhibited at Aberdeen in 1859; the reviewer noted, with delicate patronage, 'interesting subjects from Orkney by the Earl of Caithness; and although the negatives appear to have been rather thin if anything, still for a Lord they are very creditable productions'.[118] He won a prize for his photograph of 'Hoar Frost' in 1862 [FIG. 6.32], an excellent work, though showed a little too often. A review of the Paris Universal Exhibition in 1867 noted temperately 'a number of passable views, amongst them the well-known *Hoar Frost*'.[119]

In an album once belonging to the Frasers of Lovat, there is a photograph of Alastair Fraser (1831–85), who was a Lieutenant-Colonel in the Scots Fusilier Guards.[120] He is standing by a handsome photographic cart [FIG. 6.33], but we do not know if the photographs in the album were all taken by him. The album contains good portraits [FIG. 6.34]. Fraser, like Melville and the Rosses, had the natural connec-

tion with photography among the landed classes – that of shooting game. One group includes Fraser on the left, holding a gun. He may have set up the photograph and then rushed into position – in the picture, he has shifted in a way that suggests accidental movement. Fraser was a notably accurate shot, and the clear eyesight and steadiness of hand required for this would also be useful for photography. In this album, the decoration of the pages offers a splendid example of a secondary talent associated with photography.

Lady Hawarden and Mrs Cameron

The photographs by Clementina, Lady Hawarden (1822–65) of her daughters are radically different from the generality of the work taken in this country house party circle.[121] She was born Clementina Fleeming at Cumbernauld, near Glasgow, and married Cornwallis Maude, who became 4th Viscount Hawarden in 1856. Her early photographs, including stereo images, were taken on the family estates at Dundrum, Tipperary, and are comparatively ordinary. Her later, more intense photographs were taken indoors in London.

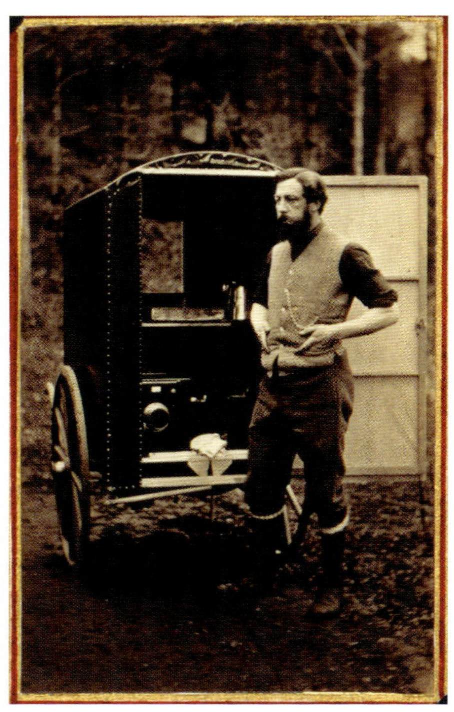

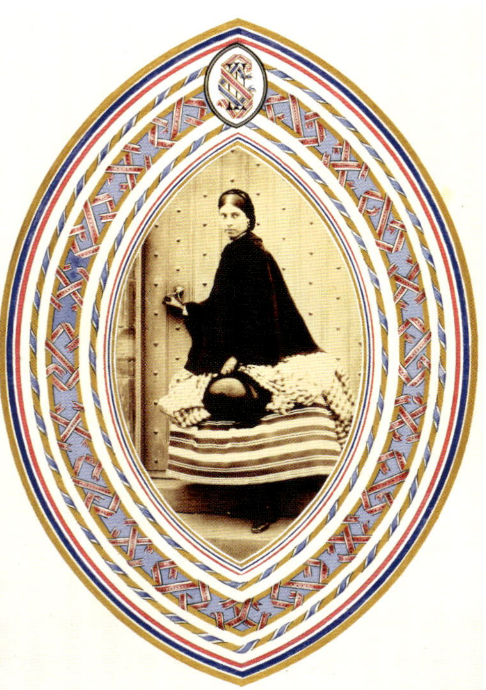

It is significant that she joined the Photographic Society of London in 1863, rather than the socially-fenced Amateur Photographic Association. She wanted the challenge of the professionals; her work was admired both by the professional, O. G. Rejlander, and the amateur, Lewis Carroll, who owned nine of her pictures.[122] How well her contemporaries understood her work is open to question [Fig. 6.35]. When she died at 42, Rejlander wrote her obituary for the *British Journal of Photography*. He appreciated her work, but his definition is inadequate:

> [She] worked honestly, in a good comprehensible style … [aiming at] elegant and, if possible, idealised truth …. She was also in her manner and conversation – fair, straightforward, nay manly, with a feminine grace. She is a loss to photography, for she would have progressed.[123]

Hawarden was evidently serious in her art and interested in the education of women. She bore ten children, and seven were girls, so her household would have been dominated by women. She hired herself out as a photographer at a charity fair for the benefit of the Female Schools of Art in 1864, making over £50 for the funds.[124]

She was technically knowledgeable, informing the *Photographic News* in 1863 that her exhibition photographs were made with 'a highly bromised collodion: a very strong iron developer, sometimes containing as much as fifty grains of iron to the ounce, and with Dallmeyer's No. 1 Triple lens, which secures this wonderful depth of definition'.[125]

Hawarden knew the etcher, Seymour Hayden, and through him James MacNeill Whistler, who was influenced by her in his painting.[126] Her photographs were critically approved, whereas Julia Margaret Cameron's were often attacked for their technical messiness. One reviewer used Hawarden's work as the ladylike model, taking another sideswipe at Cameron, even in a valedictory tribute made after her death:

> With a mastery of light and shade peculiarly her own, combined with a delicacy which contrasts, with wonderful force, with some other attempts at securing light and shade in photography, but without any delicacy at all,

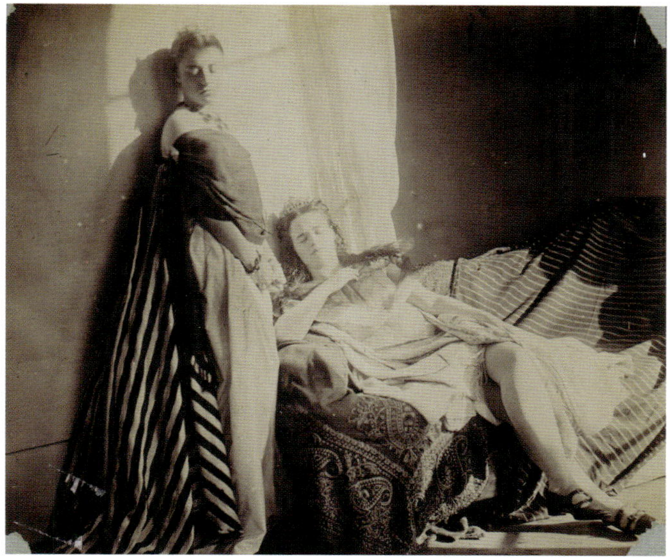

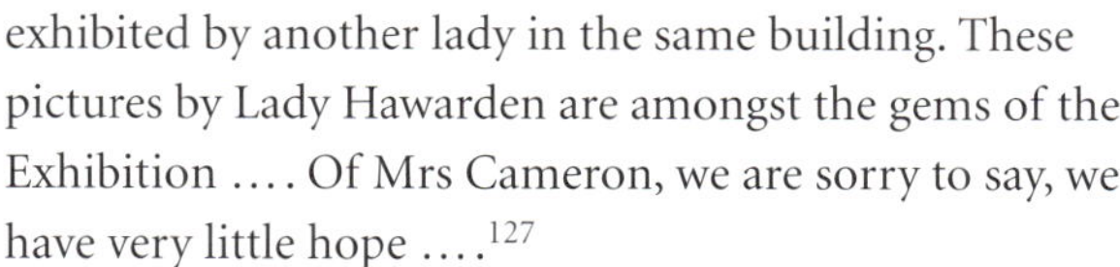

exhibited by another lady in the same building. These pictures by Lady Hawarden are amongst the gems of the Exhibition …. Of Mrs Cameron, we are sorry to say, we have very little hope ….[127]

Another reviewer picked up on the idea of the drawing room, as a ladylike venue of operation, without considering the practicalities of the pictures:

> As examples of chiaroscuro they are wonderful; and, as results, for the most part obtained with the management of light possible in a lady's drawing room, they are a lesson to all photographers. The exquisite taste, fine feeling, and excellent photography, combine to produce an amount of pictorial effect very rare in photography.[128]

The references to delicacy and the drawing room seem calculated to find her a suitably female place, confined indoors and taking up photography as she might have taken up embroidery, with no need to disarrange the furniture. She was more sophisticated than this.

The drawing room in the London house at 5 Prince's Gate had indeed been adopted for photography.[129] It was a first floor room with a balcony and high windows facing south over the garden of the square. She seems to have

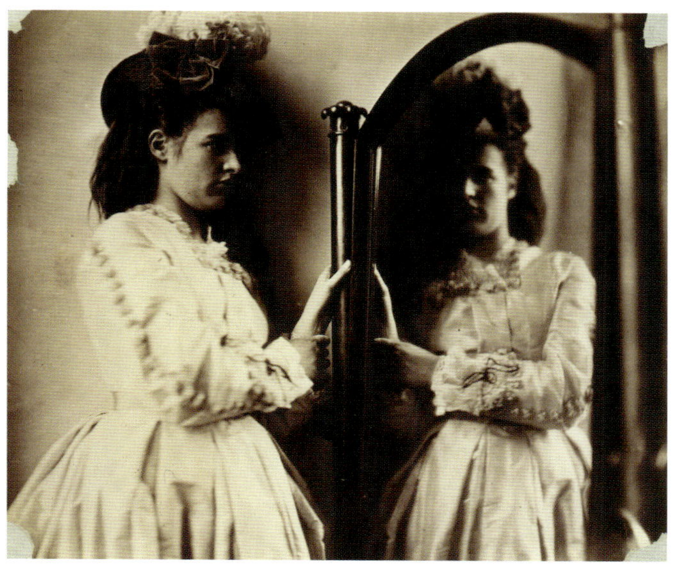

reserved the room largely unfurnished for her studio. Presumably the windows were plate glass, but in the photographs their surface appears scratched; and details of the room, such as the skirting board, appear scuffed or distressed. Only a few props are used, a cheval glass, table and so forth, and she had a moveable screen covered in a blank pale material. She was highly conscious of light, shadow and reflections. In Julie Lawson's words: 'She allows the light to suffuse and dissolve form rather than to disclose it. This is the opposite of what most painters do, with notable exceptions like her near contemporaries, the Impressionists.'[130] The draperies worn by her daughters in some of the pictures are a light gauze, like the curtains, an unstructured form of dress which conceals and captures the light with blurring edges. There are pictures where this sense of passionate dissolve, melting in light and heat, can be seen in the lifted and unfocussed eyes of her sitter. Her figures are often arranged to cast a particular shadow. Many of the pictures are concerned with the confusion and ambiguity of mirrors [Fig. 6.36], and use the glass of the windows for reflection as well as light. She sometimes focussed on the reflection in a mirror rather than the girl's face – the reality is out of focus. And in one photograph, two girls, linked together in close gaze, act as the mirror to each other.

Hawarden avoided titles that gave narrative direction.

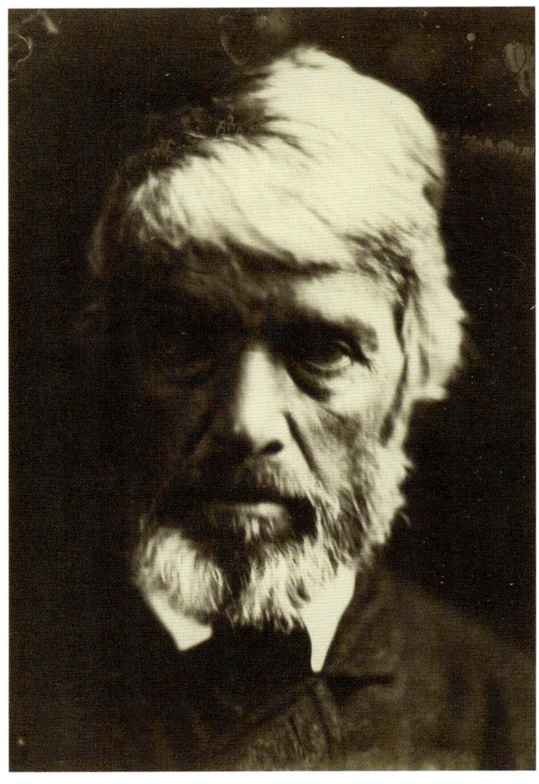

This creates a speculative distance from the passionate, sometimes melancholy strength of the photographs. The use of undress, fancy dress and generalised drapery adds to that ambiguity, complicated by the male historic dress adopted by one young woman. We cannot be sure what is being offered, even in simple terms. They are photographs which need to be approached for their undiluted visual expression.

In November 1864, the Secretary of the Photographic Society of Scotland received the first of a sequence of letters from the Isle of Wight.[131] Mrs Cameron wished to exhibit in Edinburgh and asked to become a member of the Society: '… Regarding my Eligibility as a Member all my Husband's family being of the Errols & Locheils are well known in Scotland.'[132]

She sent twenty-one large-scale photographs, both portraits and allegorical pictures. Characteristically, she described her work as 'very excellent' and 'very beautiful', and added, helpfully: 'Regarding their excellence I can assure you that they are pronounced by the great artists in London "to be among the finest things in existence".'[133] The reviews were generously complimentary. The *Scotsman*, for example, commented that her picture of G. F. Watts – 'admirable for its breadth of effect and artistic treatment … looks like a replica of Rembrandt' and that in her portrait of Henry Taylor, she 'almost reaches the sublime. In its gusto it reminds one of Michael Angelo'.[134] The reviews make it clear that her pictures were hung high; presumably because they were big, both physically and in impact and could be seen better from a distance, but also because they might have overwhelmed the work of others [Fig. 6.37].

However, the prize committee reported:

The beautiful picture by Mr H P Robinson of London, titled 'Brenda,' so artistic in its arrangements and so perfect in its photographic manipulation, was at once selected as the prize portrait.

This selection was all the more creditable to Mr Robinson, as there were many portraits of high quality on the walls; amongst which, the productions of Messrs Nelson, Dallas, Moffat, McGlashan and Walker, Horsburgh and Dr Adamson, may be mentioned; and in this department the Committee would desire to make honourable mention, as regards their grouping and arrangement, of some of the highly artistic picture portraits by Mrs Cameron ….[135]

From Mrs Cameron's point of view, the insult was underlined by a second award, to John Ramsay L'Amy for the best group picture, 'containing sixteen figures'; Mrs Cameron appeared yet again at the end of the also-rans.

She did not renew her membership of the Society.

Notes

1. Gray 1928: 3 [probably working from notes by Dr John Brown]; for a discussion of the Club's history, see Simpson 2012: 47–52.
2. See letter 4339, Brewster to Talbot, 5 October 1841: <http://foxtalbot.dmu.ac.uk/letters/letters.html> See also Simpson 2012: 47
3. Cockburn 1889: 357.
4. Now in the Library of the National Museums Scotland, pressmark ATTIC TR 140 Hil, vol, 2. Presented by James F. Montgomery in 1851.
5. Gray 1928: 3.
6. The albums, in the Edinburgh Central Library and the National Library of Scotland, are discussed by Roddy Simpson on the website: <http://digital.nls.uk/pencilsoflight/> There are also groups of Edinburgh Calotype Club photographs in the Scottish National Portrait Gallery, probably from Sheriff Tennent's collection; and in the National Media Museum.
7. There is confusion in this history between the Cundells and Joseph Cundall (1818–95), a professional photographer. Less helpfully, 'Cundell' is sometimes spelled 'Cundall'. The annual report of the Photographic Society of London for 1861 mentioned the death of Peter Wickens Fry and said: 'Under Mr Fry's auspices a Photographic Club was formed; and Mr Cundall, who did so much towards rendering the Calotype a manageable process, and Mr F. Scott Archer, to whom we owe the use of the iodized collodion, were frequently to be seen at those agreeable gatherings.' 'Cundall' here is unmistakably intended for G. S. Cundell. See 'Photographic Society of London. Annual General Meeting', *Journal of the Photographic Society* 7 (15 February 1861): 99.
8. See Seiberling and Bloore 1986: 8, quoting 'The Calotype Society', *Athenaeum* 1054 (18 December 1847): 1304.
9. Anon., 'Photographic Club', *Art-union* 10 (1 April 1848): 130–1.
10. Advertisement in the *Glasgow Herald*, 30 Jan., 3 Feb. 1854.
11. Report of the meeting on 8 March, *Glasgow Herald,* 10 March 1854.
12. Perhaps Miss Borthwick, in which case the date at this point in his story would be late in 1849 or 1850.
13. Duncan Brown, 'On the Collodion process: its Pursuit under Difficulties', Paper read to the Glasgow and West of Scotland Photographic Society, 4 April 1861, republished from the *British Journal of Photography*, in *Humphrey's Journal* 13 (15 June 1861): 54–6.
14. Mitchell Library, Glasgow, Ms 250.
15. Dr John Adamson, Letter to William Church, 3 September 1855, St Andrews, Mitchell library, Ms 250/4. Adamson wrote a paper for the Association meeting, which was read by Sir David Brewster, but not published in the Report.
16. Charles John Burnett, Letter to William Church, 1 September 1855, Kincardine, Mitchell Library, Ms 250/34.
17. See, for example, Burnett, Letter to the Editor from Old Aberdeen, 'A few Remarks on Printing by Carbon and other Pigments by the aid of bichromates and other metallic salts, along with Gelatine, Gum, or other animal and vegetable substances', *Journal of the Photographic Society* 5 (22 November 1858): 84–6; Mike Ware, 'The Eighth Metal: the Rise of the Platinotype Process', in Lawson, McKenzie and Morrison-Low (eds) 1993: 99–111.
18. Editorial comment (following republishing of Burnett's article on uranium and a letter on blue lenses from *Photographic Notes*), *Humphrey's Journal* 9 (1 August 1857): 111–2.
19. Burnett, Letter to the Editor, *Photographic Notes* 2 (15 September 1857): 345–6.
20. Ware 2014.
21. *Report of the Meeting held in the Council Hall of Glasgow on Thursday 22nd November, 1855, for concluding the transaction connected with the recent Meeting of the British Association in that City,* 1855: 6.
22. Account from Wylie and Lochhead, Mitchell Library Ms 250/159.
23. Dancer, a Manchester-based optical instrument maker, was employed by Sir David Brewster as the first to make a twin-lensed camera for stereoscopic images in 1853. See Hallett, 'Dancer, John Benjamin', in Hannavy 2008, vol. 2: 378–80.
24. Alexander McNab, Glasgow, 19 March 1857, Letter to the Editor, on the previous Report of the Photographic Society of Scotland's meeting, 'Mr Ribble's [sic] Monster Negatives', *Photographic Notes* 2 (15 April 1857): 145.
25. Account of the City of Glasgow and West of Scotland Photographic Society soirée and conversazione, *Photographic News* 4 (18 January 1861): 32; see also A. A. Steward, 'Glasgow's "Broomielaw"', *History of Photography* 10 (1986): 70.

Note: Website addresses checked and correct at the time of going to press.

26.	Report on the 'Inaugural Meeting of the Photographic Society', *Journal of the Photographic Society of London* 1 (3 March 1854): 3. John Stewart had also taken photographs of waves by the spring of 1854, which he exhibited in Edinburgh and at the London Photographic Society.

27.	A. Maconochie, 'Normal Collodion and Iodide of Iron', Extracts from Letters to Roger Fenton, *Journal of Photographic Society* 1 (21 July 1853): 87–8.

28.	A. H. Wall, 'A Few Thoughts About Photographic Societies', Paper read to the South London Photographic Society, October 1863, *British Journal of Photography* 10 (15 October 1863): 407. Wall is described as a 'professional writer' by Edwards 2006: 5.

29.	Report, 'Dumfries and Galloway Photographic Society', *Photographic Notes* 1 (1 November 1856): 217.

30.	Minute book, Royal Scottish Academy, 1853, RSA collection.

31.	John Traill Taylor, Letter to the Editor, *Liverpool Photographic Journal* 12, January (1856): 15; John Traill Taylor, 'On the Albumen Process', Paper given to the Dumfries and Galloway Photographic Society, 8 July 1856, *Journal of the Photographic Society* 3 (21 July 1856): 84.

32.	He appears in the *Edinburgh Post Office Directory* for 1859–60.

33.	The records of the Society are in the collection of the National Archives of Scotland, GD 356/1, 2 and 3.

34.	Report of the first annual general meeting of the Photographic Society, 10 March 1857, National Archives of Scotland, GD 356/1.

35.	Report of the second annual general meeting of the Photographic Society, 9 March 1858, National Archives of Scotland, GD 356/1.

36.	Thomas Sutton, Editorial, *Photographic Notes* 2 (15 July 1857): 257

37.	Horatio Ross, 'On the comparative merits of the different processes of Photography in taking Views in Mountainous Districts, and on the Photographic Exhibitions now open in London and Paris', Paper given to the Photographic Society of Scotland, 10 February 1857, *Photographic Notes* 2 (15 March 1857): 95–6.

38.	Report of a Meeting of the Birmingham Photographic Society, 28 September 1858, *Photographic Notes* 3 (15 October 1858): 237–8.

39.	The photographers were James Ross and John Thomson, D. S. Hay, John Moffat, James Henderson, W. P. Truefitt, George Simson and William McCraw. They were supported by James Ramage, lithographer, and James Wood, bookseller. Printed notice, 1 January 1858, records of the Photographic Society of Scotland, National Archives of Scotland, GD356/3.

40.	'S. J .W. Edinburgh', 'Prize Medals', *Photographic News* 2 (25 March 1859): 32.

41.	Report of the Meeting of the Photographic Society of Scotland, December 1856, *Photographic Notes* 1 (1857): 8.

42.	Editorial comment, *Photographic Notes* 3 (1858): 24.

43.	Letter from C. G. H. Kinnear to D. O. Hill, 12 April 1856, Royal Scottish Academy Archive.

44.	Draft letter from D. O. Hill to C. G. H. Kinnear, 14 December 1856, Royal Scottish Academy Archive. See also <http://peib.dmu.ac.uk/itemphotographer.php?photogNo=194&orderby=coverage&photogName=Hill%2C+David+Octavius+%26amp%3B+Adamson%2C+Robert>

45.	John Miller was Captain of the Edinburgh Volunteer Engineers. See Roddy Simpson, 'The Artist and the Engineer – the friendship of David Octavius Hill and John Miller', *Studies in Photography* (2007): 49–58.

46.	Letter from Hill to the Photographic Society of Scotland, 10 March 1862, National Archives of Scotland, GD 356/12/71.

47.	Hill queried this decision in writing: '… the manipulation being entirely due to my friend Mr A Macglashan … I should be happy if the medal were given to him.' He was assured that the medal was awarded personally. Letters from Hill to the Photographic Society of Scotland, both written on 10 March 1862, National Archives of Scotland, GD 356/12/71.

48.	Taylor was writing for the *British Journal of Photography*, and he became its Editor in 1864. See John Hannavy, 'Taylor, John Traill' in Hannavy 2008, vol. 2: 1382.

49.	Dr John Brown, 'Mr Hill's Calotypes', *Scotsman*, 10 February 1862.

50.	John Traill Taylor, Review of the International Exhibition, *British Journal of Photography* 9 (15 May 1862): 129.

51.	David Brewster 1862: 190.

52.	Anon., Account of the Meeting of the Photographic Society of Scotland, 13 January 1863, *British Journal of Photography* 10 (2 February 1863): 56.

53.	James Ross in a letter defending photography as a fine art, *British Journal of Photography* 11, (28 October 1864): 423

54.	'Our correspondent', 'Glasgow Photographic Association. Grand Soiree, Exhibition and Conversazione', *Photographic News* 7 (27 February 1863): 103.

55.	'Glasgow Photographic Association', *British Journal of Photography* 1 (2 March 1863): 105.

56. Prospectus of the Glasgow Practical Society, published in *Journal of the Photographic Society* 5 (21 October 1858): 50.

57. For the activity of Edinburgh Photograph Exchange Club from 1859, see National Archives of Scotland, Ms GD356/28, and the 'Rules of Edinburgh Photograph Exchange Club' in W. A. K. Johnston Papers, National Library of Scotland, Acc. 5811.

58. Report in the *Photographic Journal* 7 (15 March 1861): 146.

59. The Society was officially wound up in 1871.

60. See Lawson 1990.

61. W. D. Clark, 'Notes on the Collodio-Albumen Process', *British Journal of Photography* 10 (1 May 1863): 194.

62. Report of the Photographic Society's Prize Committee, *Photographic Journal* 9 (15 April 1865): 35.

63. W. D. Clark, 'On Pictorial and Photographic Representations of Melrose Abbey', Paper read to Photographic Society of Scotland, 8 May 1866, *Photographic News* 10 (25 May 1866): 248–50.

64. The spot proved to be the real image of the diaphragm aperture produced by the back lens of the three-element lens.

65. J. H. Dallmeyer, 'On the cause of the Central Spot, or "Flare" in Photographic lenses', *British Journal of Photography* 14 (21 June 1867): 289.

66. See Ware 2014: 31 and footnote 124.

67. See G. M. Wilson, 'Early Photography, Goitre and James Inglis', *British Medical Journal* 4 (May 1973): 104–5; see also Paula Summerly, 'Medical Photography', in Hannavy 2008, vol. 2: 916–9.

68. James Young Simpson, 'On solutions of Gun-Cotton, Gutta Percha, and Caoutchouc, as Dressings for wounds &c.', *Pharmaceutical Journal* 8 (1 August 1848): 84–9; the article was reprinted from the *Edinburgh Monthly Journal* and had already been seen in the *London Medical Gazette*, which reported that Simpson had made the trials known to the Edinburgh Medico-Chirurgical Society 'in May last'. Experiments were also under-way in Boston at this time.

69. Simpson 1856: 78–9.

70. See Minto 1972; Hannavy 1981; *Studies in Photography* (2007), Papers given at a Conference on Thomas Keith in Edinburgh 2006 – Fiona Myles, 'Discovering Thomas Keith's photographs', *Studies in Photography* (2007): 19–20; John Hannavy, 'Thomas Keith (1827–95) – a Scottish master', *Studies in Photography* (2007): 21–30; Fiona Myles,, 'Dr Thomas Keith: a selective bibliography', *Studies in Photography* (2007): 41; Roddy Simpson, 'Stairs and lamp-posts: evidence of location in images by Thomas Keith', *Studies in Photography* (2007): 31–6. Also Hannavy 2015.

71. Obituary, *British Medical Journal* 2 (19 October 1895): 1003.

72. 'Dr Keith's Paper on the Waxed Paper Process', given on 10 June 1856, *Photographic Notes* 1 (17 July 1856): 101–4.

73. *Ibid.*, 101, Report of the meeting of the Photographic Society of Scotland, 10 June 1856.

74. *Ibid.*, 104.

75. *Ibid.*, 101.

76. Anon., Review of the first exhibition of the Photographic Society of Scotland, *Photographic Notes* 2 (15 January 1857): 24.

77. 'Dr Keith's Paper on the Waxed Paper Process', given on 10 June 1856, *Photographic Notes* 1 (17 July 1856): 101.

78. Gray 1928.

79. See Minto and Fyfe 1970.

80. Quoted by Lady Fyfe in Minto and Fyfe: 10.

81. Chapman 1877, lots 633–69.

82. Julie Lawson, 'William Walker: an Early Amateur Photographer,' *Scottish Photography Bulletin* (Autumn 1988): 3–13.

83. Obituary, *Edinburgh Medical Journal* 31 (October 1885): 399–400.

84. 'Abstract of Mr Walker's Paper on the Calotype Process', Paper given to the Photographic Society of Scotland, *Photographic Notes* 1 (1856): 77–8; 'Mr Walker's Portable Camera', *Photographic Notes* 1 (1856): 131–2.

85. J. H. Balfour, 'Description of Nartex Assafoetida, Falconer, at present in flower in the Royal Botanic Garden', *Transactions and Proceedings of the Botanical Society of Edinburgh* 6 (1860): 64–8.

86. The plant died after a severe frost in April 1857. Walker's photograph was published with text by Professor Balfour, in the *Stereoscopic Magazine* 1 (1858), opposite p. 105.

87. See Ornella Moscucci, 'Duncan, James Matthews (1826–1890)', <http://www.oxforddnb.com/view/article/8218>

88. William Walker, vote of thanks to A. J. Macfarlan, at the meeting of Photographic Society of Scotland, 10 December 1861, *Photographic Journal* 7 (16 December 1861): 329.

89. Document 5239, Lady Elisabeth Feilding to Talbot, 25 April 1845: <http://foxtalbot.dmu.ac.uk/letters/letters.html>

90. Rev. Robert Graham, 'The Early History of Photography', *Good Words* 15 (1874): 450–3, reprinted in *History of Photography* 8 (1984): 231–5.

91. Perth and Kinross County Archives, Ms 100/2, Bundle 665.

92. John Cumming to Lord Kinnaird, 17 July 1861, Perth and Kinross County Archives, Ms 100/2, Bundle 668.

93. Anon., 'Death of Lord Kinnaird', [*Dundee*] *Evening Telegraph*, 7 January 1878.

94. 'Dum Spiro Spero', 'Scottish Pioneers in Photography', *British Journal of Photography* 44 (9 July 1897): 442.

95. These are now in the Perth and Kinross County Archives, Kinnaird Papers, Ms 100/2, Bundle 1154.

96. In the collection of Perth Museum and Art Gallery. Kinnaird 1898.

97. 'Our Special Correspondent', 'British Association for the Advancement of Science. Dundee meeting 1867', *Chemical News and Journal of Physical Science* 16 (13 September 1867): 135.

98. Editorial account of the British Association meeting in Dundee, September 1867, *British Journal of Photography* 14 (13 September 1867): 436.

99. See Beard 1997.

100. See Cox and Ford 2003: 18–21.

101. Dakers 1993: 10, 23–4, 265, records an album of Lady Alice's work at Stanway House in Gloucestershire, which belongs to the Earl of Wemyss.

102. While Holofernes, the Assyrian general attacking Israel, lay drunk in his tent, Judith took his sword and cut off his head. The Book of Judith, chapter 13, The King James Bible. This tableau is illustrated in Dakers 1993.

103. These are both in an album which is attributed to R. L. Melville, but more likely to be by Lady Alice Kerr, in the Michael Wilson collection.

104. See Falconer and Hide 2009: 98.

105. For Victorian fashion as seen through its photographs, see Gernsheim 1981 and Ginsberg 1982.

106. See Stevenson and Bennett 1978.

107. Baldwin, Daniel and Greenough 2004: 77.

108. Quoted in Stevenson and Bennett 1978: 48

109. See Helen Smailes [wrongly printed as Smaills], 'A Gentleman's Exercise: Ronald Leslie Melville, 11th Earl of Leven, and the Amateur Photographic Association', *Photographic Collector* 3, no. 3, Winter 1982: 262–93.

110. Campbell 1868, 'Lochiel's Warning'.

111. Anon., Review of the London International Exhibition, *British Journal of Photography* 18 (May 1871): 216.

112. On his return, he gave an Arabian baboon and a *Pelomedusa gehafi* (a turtle) to London Zoo, and a *Haemanthus tenuiflorus coccineus*, with its beautiful ball-shaped scarlet flower, to the Royal Botanic Gardens at Kew, recorded in Sclater 1872: 332, and in *Curtis's Botanical Magazine* 27 (1871): tab. 5881.

113. H. Baden Pritchard, 'Photography in connexion with the Abyssinian Expedition', Paper given to the Photographic Society of London, 8 December 1868, *Photographic Journal* 13 (15 December 1868): 184–8. See also John Falconer, 'Photography and the Royal Engineers', *Photographic Collector* 2 (Autumn 1981): 33–64.

114. Melville's journal for 13 April 1868, quoted by Helen Smailes [wrongly printed as Smaills], 'A Gentleman's Exercise: Ronald Leslie Melville, 11th Earl of Leven, and the Amateur Photographic Association', *Photographic Collector* 3, no. 3, Winter 1982: 292. Melville constructed an album of the Abyssinian photographs, now in the Bodleian Library, which suggests that he did not take many successful photographs.

115. There is a set of loose prints with these numbers, presumably not distributed by the Association, in the collection of George Eastman House.

116. Anon., 'Soirée of the Amateur Photographic Association', *Journal of the Photographic Society of London* 9 (16 March 1865): 16–7.

117. Queen Victoria's journal, 10 January 1860, Royal Archives, quoted by Frances Dimond, 'Catalogue of the exhibition', in Dimond and Taylor 1987:108.

118. Review of the Exhibition, *Liverpool Photographic Journal* 3 (1 October 1859): 243.

119. Review of the Exhibition, *British Journal of Photography* 14 (20 September 1867): 449.

120. Now in the Scottish National Portrait Gallery, PGP 346.

121. See Lawson 1997, and the Victoria and Albert Museum website <http://www.vam.ac.uk/page/l/lady-clementina-hawarden/>

122. Lewis Carroll album, 'Professional and other photographs', Gernsheim Collection, University of Texas, 964:0016:0001-0053.

123. O. G. Rejlander, Obituary, *British Journal of Photography* 12 (27 January 1865): 38.

124. Anon., 'Photography at the Horticultural Gardens', *Photographic Journal* 9 (15 July 1864): 84.

125. Review of the Photographic Society of London's exhibition, *Photographic News* 7 (27 February 1863), quoted on the Victoria and Albert website.

126. Discussed and illustrated by Lawson, 1997: 17–20.

127. Review of the Photographic Society of London exhibition, *Photographic Journal* 12 (15 August 1865): 126.

128. Review of the Photographic Society of London exhibition 1862–63, *Photographic News* 7 (16 January 1863): 25.

129. 'Maude, Clementina, Viscountess Hawarden (1822–1865)', <http://www.oxforddnb.com/view/article/48878> According to Virginia Dodier, Hawarden used the whole of the first floor.

130. Lawson 1997: 7.

131. Roddy Simpson, 'Julia Margaret Cameron and the Photographic Society of Scotland', *History of Photography* 28 (2004): 82–7.

132. Letter from Mrs Cameron to T. B. Johnston, 24 November 1864, National Archives of Scotland, GD 356/15/43, quoted in Roddy Simpson, 'Julia Margaret Cameron and the Photographic Society of Scotland', *History of Photography* 28 (2004): 83.

133. *Ibid*.

134. Quoted in Roddy Simpson, 'Julia Margaret Cameron and the Photographic Society of Scotland', *History of Photography* 28 (2004): 86.

135. Report on the meeting of the Photographic Society of Scotland, 14 March 1865, *Photographic Journal* 10 (15 April 1865): 34.

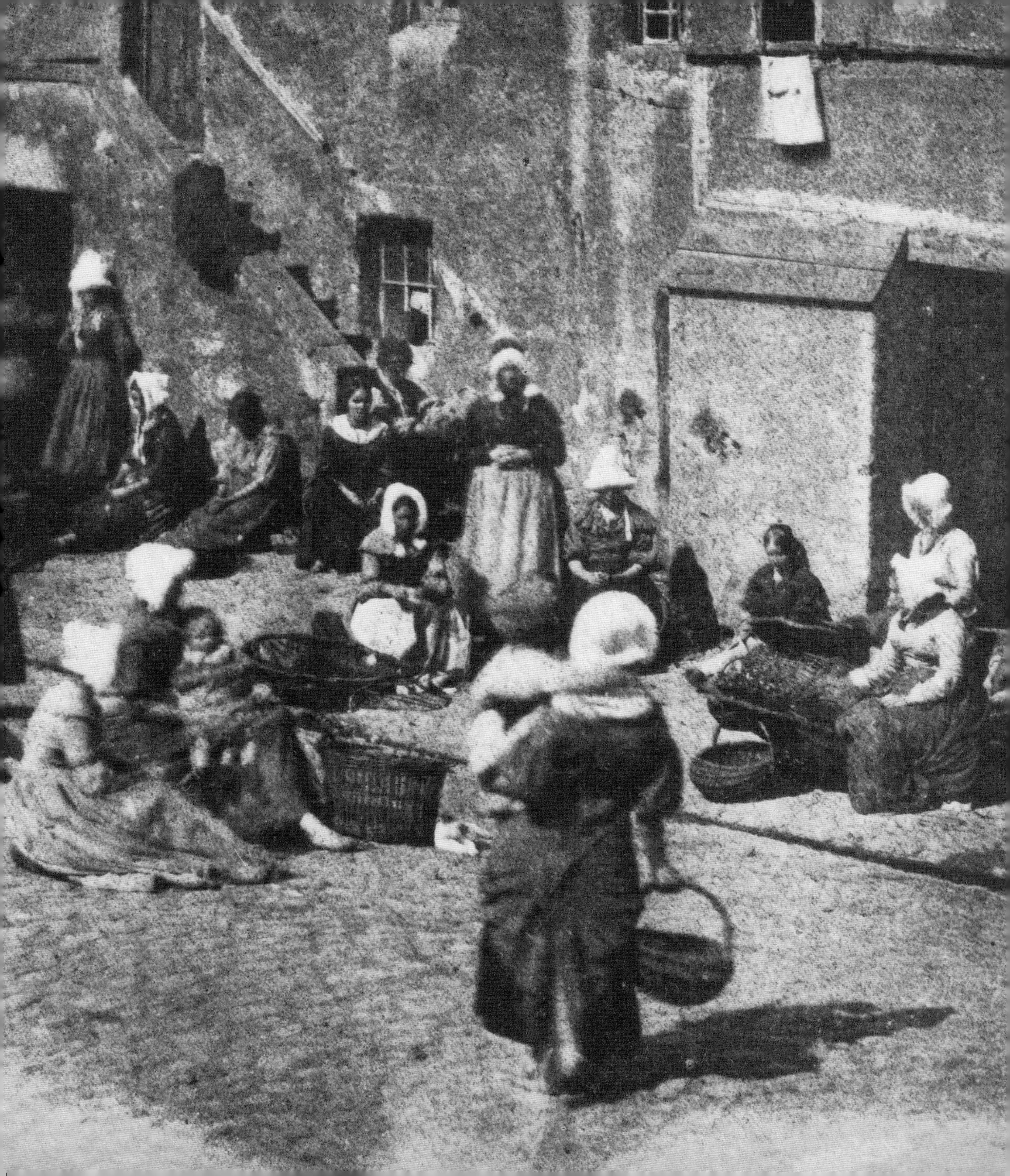

CHAPTER SEVEN

The Radical Photographers

I felt as if some bright and purifying angel had laid a mighty
finger on the squalid and neglected spots. Those open spaces,
those gleams of sunlight, those playing children, seemed earnests
of better things to come and of better days in store.

✶

Octavia Hill on seeing Thomas Annan's photographs
and the improved Glasgow slums, 1873

Photography was essentially an invention of the Industrial Revolution. By the 1840s, the adverse social and economic impact of that revolution had become painfully clear – the economic booms were followed by severe slumps; the astonishing advance and increased wealth of the nation were imbalanced by periodic destitution, by endemic disease and high mortality. The cities were crowded by incomers looking for work, and the centres of the cities were overtaken by slums. Journalists and other deeply concerned writers attempted to analyse and answer these problems.

The first photographic essay addressing such issues in Scottish photography looked at a model of excellence – a cultured and self-determining working community – rather than at the disaster of the slums. In 1844, D. O. Hill and Robert Adamson advertised an album on *The Fishermen and Women of the Firth of Forth*. They took around 130 photo-graphs, principally on site in the fishing village of Newhaven, a mile to the north of Edinburgh, but also on the other side of the estuary in St Andrews [FIG. 7.1]. The organisation and the number of people involved in the exercise is impressive – individual pictures contain up to thirty people, including

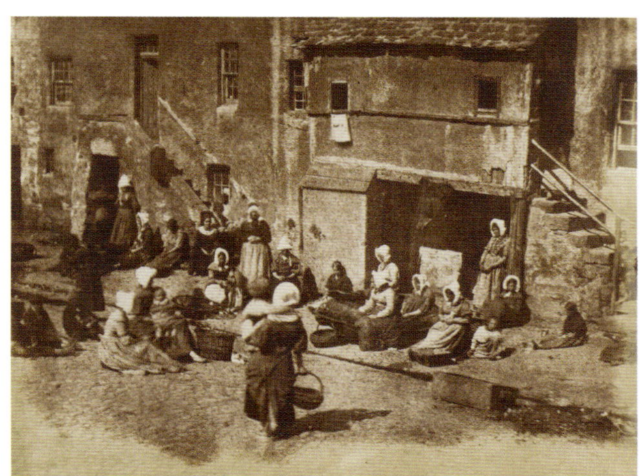

Opposite, Fig. 7.1 (detail) and right: D. O. Hill and Robert Adamson, 'Fisher-gate, St Andrews', 1843–48, calotype. (NMS, T.1942.1.1.53.2)

restless children. The pictures show empathy between the photographers and their subjects, based on admiration for working life. With this series, Hill and Adamson invented social documentary photography, many decades before it became a practical proposition in the photographically-illustrated magazines.[1]

Alexander Gardner in America

The history of Scottish American photography is dominated by the career of Alexander Gardner (1821–82) and his associates. Gardner was born in Paisley. His father died when he was ten and his mother, Jean Glenn Gardner, raised her young family in Glasgow while working as a grocer. At 14, Gardner was apprenticed to a jeweller for seven years. His mother 'executed her trust with sleepless fidelity … recognizing in all its fullness, the value of knowledge. Alexander was a ready scholar, and soon became proficient in the higher class of studies, including astronomy, botany, chemistry and phonography [i.e. shorthand note-taking].'[2] He extended his education at the Gorbals Popular Institution for the Diffusion of Science, which connected him to the early experimenters with photography within the city.[3] In the later 1840s, he edited the radical newspaper, the *Glasgow Sentinel*, where his commentary reveals his strong sense of social justice and concern for the rights of the working man. At this time, some of his family and friends determined to set up an ideal community on Owenite principles at a town called Clydesdale in Iowa, in the United States.

Gardner's interest in photography was evident in the early issues of the *Sentinel*, where it was regularly noticed.[4] When he left the paper, he took up calotype photography professionally between December 1855 and April 1856 in 'Mr Buchanan's Woodyard' by the quayside in Dumbarton, a town west of Glasgow.[5] This was one of the ports for migration to the United States, so Gardner may have placed himself there for departure in 1856. By then the Clydesdale community had failed economically – his sister and his brother-in-law, among others, died of tuberculosis. Gardner and his immediate family moved to New York, where he took employment at Mathew Brady's photographic studio. While there, he introduced more efficient business practice and was involved in the studio's shift from the daguerreotype to the wet collodion process. He brought in the idea of enlargement – copying from daguerreotypes and printing them up to 17 x 21 inches in size. These 'Imperial' pictures, retouched or painted, were popular and fetched the surprisingly large sums of $50 to $750 depending on the work involved.

By 1858, Brady opened a new studio in Washington, with Gardner in charge, and Gardner's brother James and the young Timothy O'Sullivan as assistants. The new studio also promoted the 'Imperial' enlargement. Here, Gardner observed the potential of the opposite proposal – the little carte-de-visite photograph – and in 1859 brought in four-lens cameras to make multiple images for mass sale. When the American Civil War broke out in 1861, he ordered further cameras of this kind in anticipation of the demand for portraits, driven by the forces of soldierly pride and human fear. By making an agreement with E. & H. T. Anthony in New York, Gardner sold thousands of cartes of the major figures of the war and made a considerable profit for Brady.

It would be easy to see Gardner shifting from youthful radicalism to a middle-aged business mentality – absorbed in practicality and profit. But the battles of the Civil War

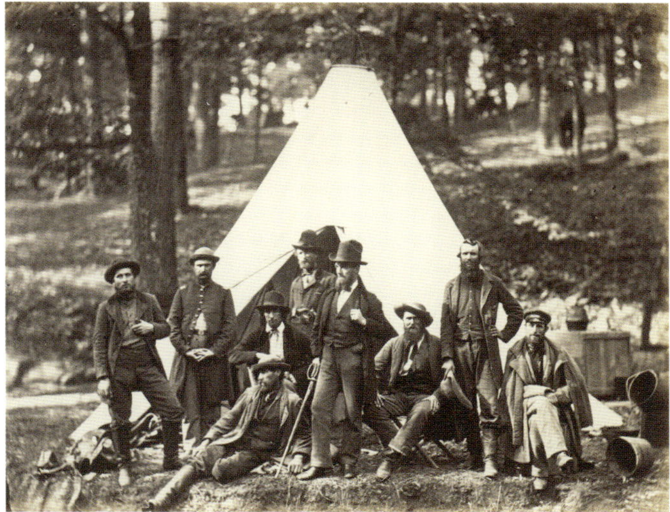

were to be fought, alarmingly, within reach of Washington. Gardner's role changed; he turned to war photography in the field.[6]

John Werge, who experienced the war at first hand, noted:

> I found photography actively engaged in the city, in the camp, and on the field, fulfilling a mission of mercy and consolation in the midst of carnage and tumult – fulfilling such a mission of holy work as never before fell to the lot of any art or art-science to perform.[7]

The power of the individual photograph gained force – as a focus of love and admiration between people separated and in danger. Gardner believed in his new country, and in the justice of the Union (northern states) cause; he saw the Confederate (southern states) desire to split apart from the Union as treachery, destroying the new society. His record of the war, subsequently published as Gardner's *Photographic Sketchbook of the War*, is based on this essential premise.

By November 1861, Gardner was appointed an honorary captain by General George B. McClellan. This gave him full access to the Army of the Potomac. He was attached to the Topographical Engineers, and in effect to the Secret Service under Allan Pinkerton.[8] His official responsibility included copying maps: knowing where they were going and understanding the terrain was an unforeseen difficulty. According to H. Baden Pritchard, of the General Photographic Establishment of the British War Department: 'To so great an extent was photography used in this connexion during the late American war, that within the period of one month during General Grant's advance to the Rapidan, no less than 1200 maps of this kind were circulated.'[9]

Gardner greatly admired Pinkerton's men and wrote:

> The scouts of an army undergo more hardship and brave greater peril than any other class. Secrecy being their only safety, their heroic deeds pass unrecorded, and when the necessity for their services has ceased to exist, with rare exceptions the brave men are altogether forgotten .... Men of iron nerve and indomitable perseverance, they braved the halter [i.e. hanging] with perfect consciousness of their peril, and seldom failed in an undertaking [FIG. 7.2].[10]

Gardner probably equipped the scouts with a cunning device, based on photographic development. In the same caption, he added:

> Each man was provided with a pass from the Commanding General, written with a chemical preparation that only became visible when exposed to solar rays, and on the back of which was penciled some unimportant memoranda, to deceive the enemy, should the scout fall into his hands. If captured, he could drop this paper, apparently by accident, without exciting suspicion; and if successful in his expedition, the pass, after a moment's exposure to the light, enabled the bearer to re-enter our lines, and proceed without delay to headquarters.

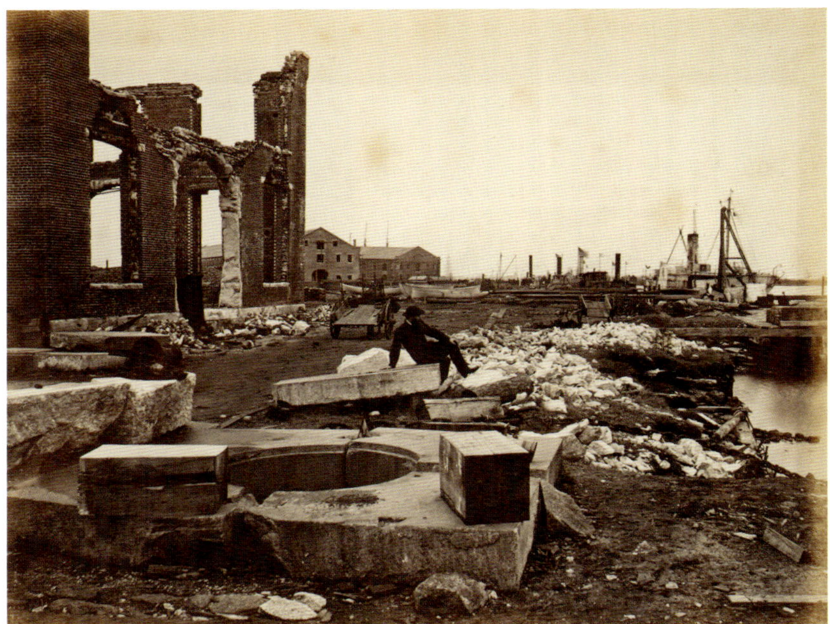

When President Lincoln dismissed General McClellan for refusing to pursue the Confederate army with dispatch in 1862, Gardner resigned from formal service in the army, and worked thereafter with his fellow photographers: his brother James, Timothy O'Sullivan, James F. Gibson, George N. Barnard, David Knox and John Reekie. They worked as an extended team, taking army groups, encampments and sites of battle and destruction. The difficulty of photographing in the field with the wet collodion process demanded continuous, running co-operation between the men. By September 1862, they had refined their skill. When Gardner and Gibson arrived on the battlefield of Antietam, a scene of dreadful carnage, they were able to take photographs of unprecedented honesty and fearfulness. They took seventy photographs – principally stereoscopic – in the course of four days. Brady exhibited these. The people of New York, distanced from the fighting, were able to see in intimate 3-D, just what this war meant, in the bloated and damaged corpses of men who had lost 'all semblance of humanity' to corruption.[11] It has been considered that Gardner took these pictures because 'they commanded the public's attention and translated into sales and profits'.[12] Such abstracted cynicism makes no sense in the context.

Gardner voiced an idea of the heroism of the Union dead in his *Photographic Sketchbook of the War* in 1866:

Localities that would scarcely have been known, and probably never remembered, save in their immediate vicinity, have become celebrated, and will ever be held sacred as memorable fields, where thousands of brave men yielded up their lives a willing sacrifice for the cause they had espoused.[13]

He expressed the hope that the brutal facts revealed by photography would undermine the glamour of war and make it impossible. Gardner wrote, in the caption to O'Sullivan's Gettysburg photograph, 'A Harvest of Death':

It shows the blank horror and reality of war, in opposition to its pageantry. Here are the dreadful details! Let them aid in preventing such another calamity falling upon the nation.[14]

While Gardner wrote this after the war, presumably his motivation was driven by such thoughts at the time. He was distressed by destruction, some immediately evident to our

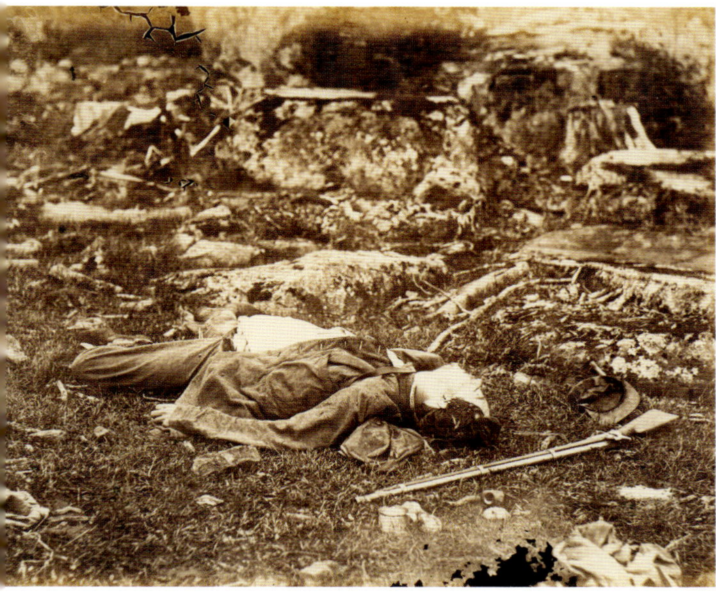 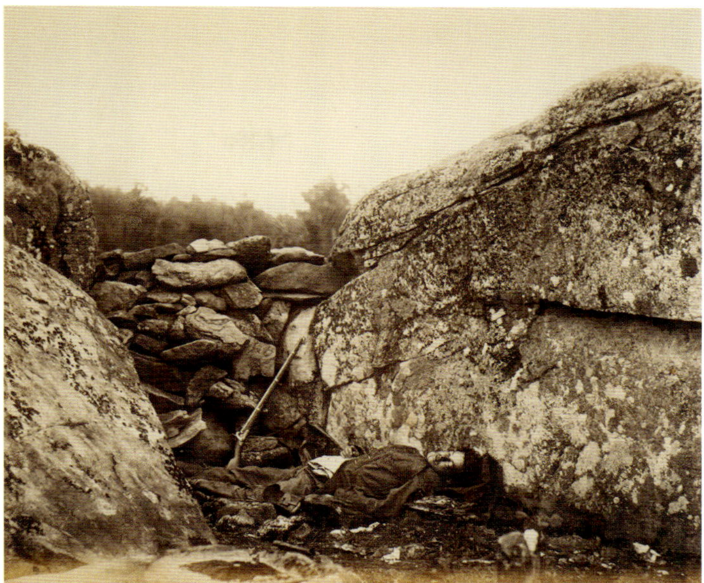

urban eyes, like James Gardner's photograph of the ruined Navy Yard, which achieves a beauty familiar in images of historic ruins. [FIG. 7.3] It was more difficult to express visually the wrecked farmlands, and Gardner conjured up the memory of peace in words. He wrote of the picture showing the Stone Church at Centreville, an established settlement and an archetype of peace:

> Centreville had smiled on many generations … there was always an odor of wild roses and honey-suckle about it, and a genial hospitality to welcome the stranger … war crushed it … and the spot now only interests the visitor because of the wreck that has come upon it.[15]

The generals were apt to stage their battles on the good lands the farmers had laboriously cleared and levelled. Gardner gave the title 'Harvest of Death' to O'Sullivan's terrible photograph. Bloody fighting had turned the land into a mass graveyard, possessed by the acid irony of its harvest.

Graphic artists, especially photographers, have always had this problem,: their work is tied to time, a single view in one direction. Photographing so enormous and scattered a subject as war concentrates the problem and the decision-making. Gardner was a journalist and so was able to expand

on the photographs in words expressing a greater moral issue. They were extraordinarily difficult pictures. But it is here that Gardner has run into subsequent criticism, partly because modern critics have a taste for possessing important pictures in their own terms.[16]

The Civil War photographs are necessarily a focus of profound American interest, explored from a 20th and 21st-century perspective.[17] Certain images have been appropriated in discussions, which shift their meaning. Prominent among these are two photographs that Gardner called 'A Sharpshooter's Last Sleep' and 'Home of a Rebel Sharpshooter', taken on the battlefield after the Battle of Gettysburg (1–3 July 1863) [FIGS 7.4a and b]. According to Gardner, the dead men were gunmen 'who brought their own rifles, and could snuff a candle at a hundred yards', and who could pick off the opposition one at a time from a concealed position.[18] He does not specify which side the first man fought on.

His sense of meaning in these photographs may have developed in the next three years. In the *Photographic Sketchbook of the War*, Gardner placed them out of chronological order, after the photograph of the Union Cemetery at Gettysburg. A contrast is drawn. These men found in 'a secluded spot' and 'a lonely place', were lost – unregarded. In the case of the 'Home of a Rebel Sharpshooter', Gardner says the soldier had built up the wall between the rocks to protect his position, but in the returning fire from the artillery above, he was wounded in the head and 'had lain upon his blanket to await death'. Gardner then questions his thoughts as he lay suffering: '… did death come slowly to his relief, while memories of home grew dearer as the field of carnage faded before him?' He adds that when he returned to Gettysburg on the occasion that Lincoln delivered the Gettysburg Address, at the dedication of the National Cemetery, he went back up the hill and found the skeleton of the soldier undisturbed:

> None of those who went up and down the fields to bury the fallen had found him. 'Missing,' was all that could have been known of him at home, and some mother may yet be patiently watching for the return of her boy, whose bones lie bleaching unrecognized and alone, between the rocks at Gettysburg.[19]

The soldier's 'home' was his tomb; he suffered a lonely and isolated death. During the war many men died without identification – thousands were buried unknown, leaving their families in the dark, unable to mourn. The dignity of the photograph may suggest a tribute to an unknown soldier – but it offers a poignant contrast with the Union cemetery, a place where the dead were honoured, and families and the nation would find a place for their sorrow.

The photograph may have become more familiar in the next century.[20] In 1910 it appeared in the ten-volume *Photographic History of the Civil War*. This was a revisionist history, designed not merely to glorify the war but to sanctify it, as 'an epic in which romance and chivalry is more inspiring than that of the olden knighthood; brother against brother, father against son, men speaking the same language, living under the same flag, offering their lives for that which they believe to be right. No Grecian phalanx or Roman legion ever knew truer manhood …'.[21]

The war, in this telling, rather than doing untold damage to the nation, cemented the Union. 'Home of a Rebel Sharpshooter' was pointedly placed in the volume of poetry, accentuating the emotional character of the image and potentially giving it a heroic, fictional role.[22]

The further argument following this re-writing of the Civil War – that Gardner moved the corpse to stage a picture – was first aired fifty years later, during the Vietnam War, and may have been fuelled by war-weariness. The theory has been much elaborated since.[23] It was proposed that the two photographs, 'A Sharpshooter's Last Sleep' and 'Home of a Rebel Sharpshooter', show the same man in two locations. The idea is based on a visual resemblance between the two bodies, and depends on understanding the photographs as 'sentimental' rather than factual.

Gardner and his colleagues did shift detritus from the pictures. However, this proposal requires that they carried a corrupting corpse seventy yards uphill through one of the hard fought grounds of the battle between Confederate infantry and Union artillery on the heights – the 'Slaughter Pen'. They would be carrying this mortuary load over boulders, through churned mud, broken branches, damaged bodies, broken weaponry and worse. One detail of this story is certainly incorrect: the proposal that there is only one gun in the photographs, appropriated by Gardner and his crew as a prop. Examination of the photographs shows two guns with clearly different cocking mechanisms. Unfortunately, the wet conditions and dim light on the battlefield

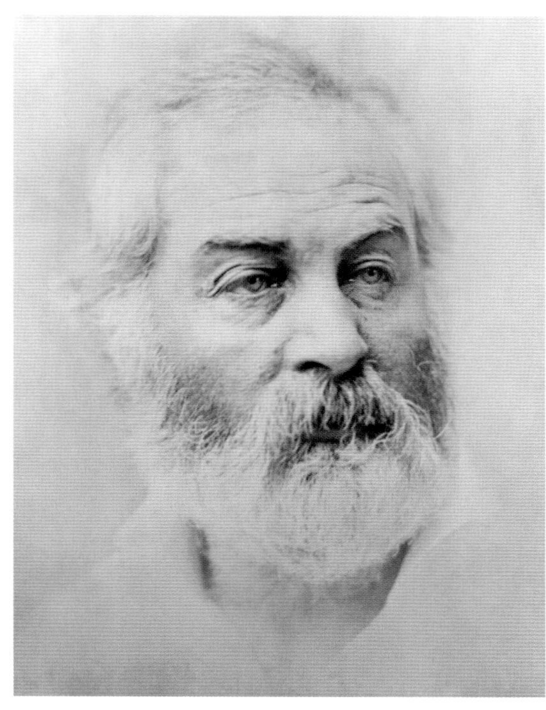

put stress on the photography; the men's, or man's, appearance is far from well-defined. So the visual identification is open to doubt.

Gettysburg claimed the worst casualties in the war – more than 50,000 at a recent estimate. While the great sweep of the battlefield offered scenes of grotesque distress, more than one man must have died with apparent dignity. It is arguable that the modern analysis expresses a view of war as necessarily ugly and disconnected from moral reflection – which curiously enough has not deterred the admiration of war.

During the war, Gardner photographed Walt Whitman, the great American poet. Whitman regarded the picture as his best portrait. He said that Gardner was one of the champions of his first book of poetry, *Leaves of Grass* (published in 1855), which was not immediately popular.[24] Its style was disconcerting; its morality and sexual approach caused some doubt. It presented an admiring sequence of the independent migrants attracted to America: a nation on the move and an inclusive country. This evidently struck a deep chord with Gardner. Whitman commented:

> Gardner was always a mighty good fellow – also mightily my friend: he was always loving .… Gardner was a real artist – had the feel of his work – the inner feel if I may say it so: he was not a workman – only a workman (which God knows is a lot in itself, too!) – but he was also beyond his craft – saw farther than his camera – saw more: his pictures are an evidence of his endowment.[25]

This balances the idea of Gardner as a practical businessman or a facile constructor of fiction [Fig. 7.5].

On a number of occasions, Gardner photographed

Abraham Lincoln, the American President who took the Union into war. Gardner was present when Lincoln delivered the Gettysburg Address in 1863. The assassination of Lincoln on 14 April 1865, days after Robert E. Lee surrendered to Ulysses S. Grant at Appotomax, must have hit Gardner hard. Gardner's involvement in the aftermath of this conspiracy proved as impressive as his photographs of the war. He is said to have photographed the body of John Wilkes Booth, who killed the President, for the Secret Service, but apparently he was instructed to make only one print to avoid the risk of circulating photographs turning the murderer into a martyr. Gardner was the only photographer to take the other conspirators on the prison ship; the photographs are neither humiliating nor monstrous. The strangest are those of Lewis Powell or Payne, a peculiarly violent man who attacked the Secretary of State, William H. Seward. This is a picture, outwith convention, of an uncivilised man [Fig. 7.6]. It is extraordinary for the underlying knowledge of his violence, here brought to an abrupt stop, which will result in his execution. The impact of this photograph caused Roland Barthes to extend his philo-

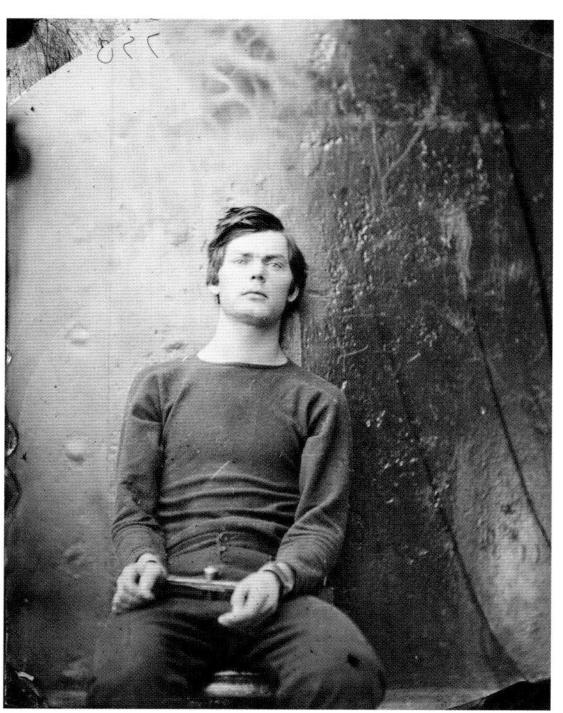
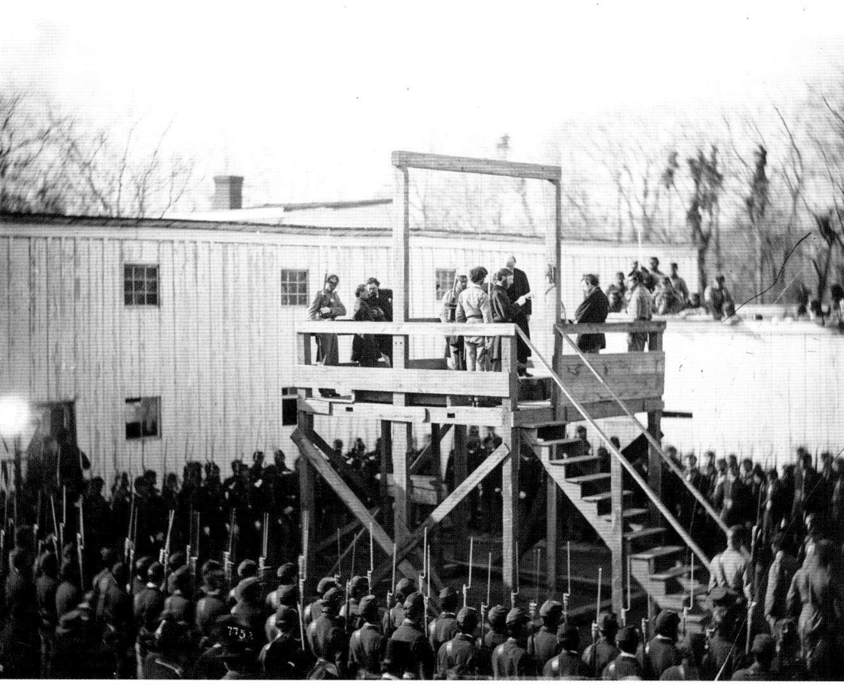

sophical reflections on photography and its relation to his own mortality, to time and death within the photograph; Payne is alive but he is immediately destined to die: 'I read at the same time: *This will be* and *this has been*.'[26]

Gardner and O'Sullivan were employed to photograph the execution of these men and the woman who protected them. This event was not public, but was performed before an army regiment and official spectators. Gardner also photographed the execution of Captain Henry Wirz, condemned of brutality towards Union prisoners [Fig. 7.7]. It took place in the yard of the Capitol prison – soldiers excluded from the yard are there in the pictures, having climbed up the elm trees outside, desperate to see. The photographing was part of the judicial process, a deeply important proof of justice and an unprecedented use of photography.

After photographing the battlefield of Gettysburg in July 1863, Gardner returned to Washington. He had parted company with Brady, and now owned the studio. Working in Washington, the seat of government, Gardner engaged in government affairs – he had photographed the Japanese delegation which came to the United States in 1860 to ratify the treaty established by Commodore Matthew C. Perry. Later he photographed the last occasion when the government treated with the Native Americans as a separate nation – at Fort Laramie in 1868. The impact of this, from the decision taken in Washington to regard the Indian nations as subject to the laws of the United States, adds a particular melancholy to Gardner's photographs which were, paradoxically, 'the earliest surviving record of the Indians of the North Plains taken in their own territory'.[27] Between April and May, he took 200 negatives, some formal groups and portraits, with unstaged photographs of the meetings and the Indian encampments, and produced a portfolio of prints, *Scenes in the Indian Country*.

Gardner was employed to make formal portraits of individual Indians, acting as delegates to Washington, a plan suggested by the Commissioner for Indian Affairs about 1865, on the dismal grounds that

The Indians are passing away so rapidly that but a few years remain within which this can be done and the loss will be irretrievable …. The photographs …

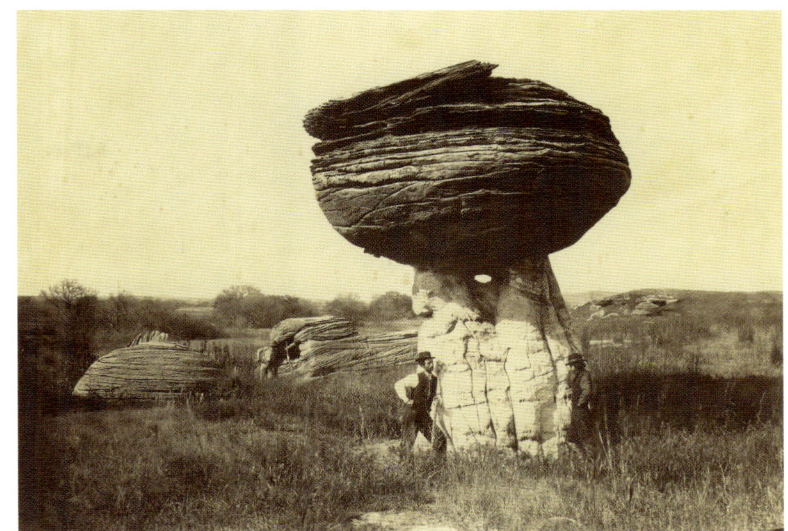

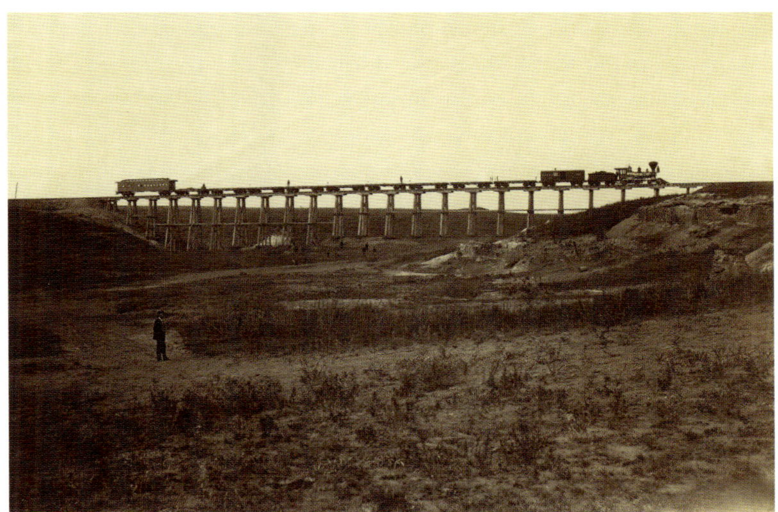

should be single and of what is known as Imperial size … the pictures should be portraits of the men and not of their garments or ornaments.[28]

In the event, this project was funded by an English collector, William Blackmore, and Gardner only became the official photographer for the Office of Indian Affairs in 1872. But he took responsibility for portraits of the Native Americans who came to Washington, and in the controlled conditions of the studio achieved effective portraits.

Gardner photographed the advance of the Union Pacific Railway, the first trans-continental railway, from August 1867 to February 1868 [Figs 7.8 and 7.9].[29] As in his earlier practice, he used the stereo camera to take immediate photographs, showing life; the larger format pictures are more considered. They offer a view of the newly-opened territories appealing to all migrants – sites which showed established townships, complete with banks and churches; sites which had just sprung up along the track. A settlement begun six weeks before, appears as a strange, fragile line of building and tents along the centre of an empty landscape. Gardner presented a land of space and freedom – the 'level ground' offered to a nation damaged by the war.[30] It was a landscape supposedly without history, seen as a future – an 'unlimited horizon … identified with the destiny of the American nation'.[31] It is likely that Gardner himself thought of his family's failure to establish a community and the immense advantage of the railway's path for trade and connection across the country.

The Indian nations are only present in these pictures as they relate to a European concept of settlement or indicated by historic sites. Gardner was promoting the country as a direct opposite of the overcrowded and corrupt cities of Europe – he showed a new, blank canvas, where communities could determine their own lives. The contrast between these photographs and Thomas Annan's of the slums of Glasgow requires no commentary.

Gardner's photographic practice fell within a period of dramatic American history. He was not simply a witness, recording events. He was an energetic actor in the country's affairs, and his photographs are a critical component of the time. We see his world through the eyes of a man concerned with justice and prepared to fight for his beliefs. In the words of the eulogy delivered after his death in 1882, he held photography to be 'one of the fine arts, ranking with painting and sculpture'; he was an active social improver and latterly a philanthropist; 'he believed, and lived as he believed that "a good name was more to be desired than great riches"'.[32]

Thomas Annan in Glasgow

Thomas Annan (1829–87) started life in the village of Dairsie in Fife, son of John and Agnes Annan who owned a flax mill on the River Eden. This was close to the towns of St Andrews and Cupar, where photography had been practised and exhibited from the earliest opportunity. He was first apprenticed as a lithographer in Cupar and moved to Glasgow in 1849 to work for the engraver Joseph Swan.[33] In 1855, he joined a medical student called George Berwick (b. c.1829, d. 1892/3), in a photographic partnership, in Woodlands Road, just a mile outside the centre of Glasgow.

Berwick was connected to St Andrews. He and the young Thomas Rodger were friends and fellow experimenters in chemistry. Berwick, like Rodger, published a working account of the wet collodion process in 1854, and both recommended the use of iron in the developer. It is probable that Berwick was teaching Annan, during his holidays as a student, in the course of their two-year association, and before he graduated as a surgeon. They set up business at the beginning of the commercial boom in photography. The City was expanding exponentially, in population, in access to raw materials, in growing industries and trade, and in communication and transport, both the railway and steam ships connecting Glasgow to the outer world. The ready shifts in enterprise and the breadth of Glasgow's manufactures made it a model of free trade and balance in the face of the severe depressions. Such depressions might be bad for the individual, but the whole community flourished.

This idea of diversity as good business practice appeared immediately in Berwick and Annan's work. They first exhibited when the British Association for the Advancement of Science came to Glasgow in autumn 1855. They signalled their connection to advanced engineering through a photograph of the iron steam ship *Persia*, built by the Clyde shipbuilding firm of Robert Napier for Cunard – the largest and the fastest vessel afloat. As portraits, they showed photo-

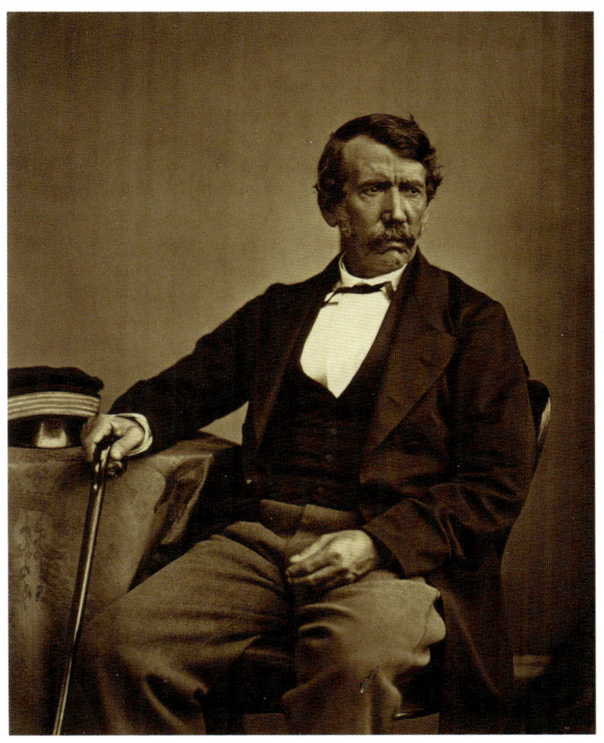

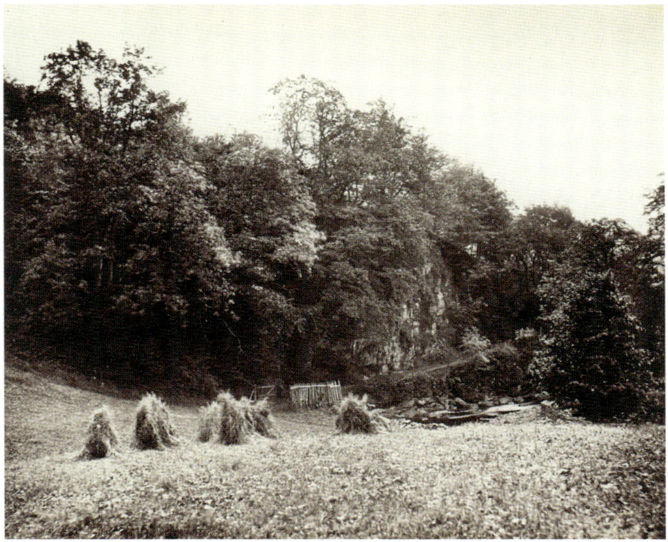

Fig. 7.10 (left): Thomas Annan, 'David Livingstone', 1864, carbon print. (Gift by T. & R. Annan & Sons, 1930, Scottish National Portrait Gallery PGP 74.2)

Fig. 7.11 (above): Thomas Annan, 'The Last Stooks of Harvest', 1864, albumen print. (The Mitchell Library, A117)

graphs of ministers, an expression of Annan's religious admiration; for architectural photography, they showed a picture of the Glasgow Observatory; and they demonstrated their technical and aesthetic skill in a composite picture, 'Portrait of a lady in an avenue'. They gave the first published account of constructed photography in the *Journal of the Photographic Society* on 15 September, and concluded of their own experiment: '… the effect is very fine indeed, the rotundity and relief given to the figure far surpassing that obtained from artificial backgrounds.' They advertised their work as possessing 'fine gradations of light and shade', and they also on this occasion exhibited photographs of two sculpted busts, to demonstrate their interest in the arts and the varied appearance of sculpture in differing lights. All these interests reappeared in the course of Annan's career. He travelled outside the city and he did not pick up the trade of 'cheap-likeness making' that D. O. Hill abhorred. His commercial list of pictures was principally landscapes, with a few portraits, all of people he admired: church ministers, the missionaries David Livingstone and

the South African Tiyo Soga, university professors, and radical members of parliament. His portraits have a strength and close attention, which is most remarkable in the portrait of David Livingstone [FIG. 7.10].

Annan was an excellent landscape photographer. His landscapes are lyrical and imbued with a sense of history and poetry – showing the country of Mary, Queen of Scots or the novels of Walter Scott. His sense of nature as filled with moral and religious meaning appears in such pictures as 'The Last Stooks of Harvest' [FIG. 7.11] – an image of life leading to the mystery of afterlife. He is, however, nowadays known as the photographer of the Glasgow slums – the black side of the Industrial Revolution. Throughout the time he lived there, Annan witnessed the struggles to alleviate poverty, endemic illness and squalid living conditions. As a photographer, he recorded the first great public work, to provide Glasgow with clean water. A phenomenal piece of engineering turned Loch Katrine into a reservoir and piped 50 million gallons of water a day, essentially by the force of gravity, through mountainous districts, thirty-

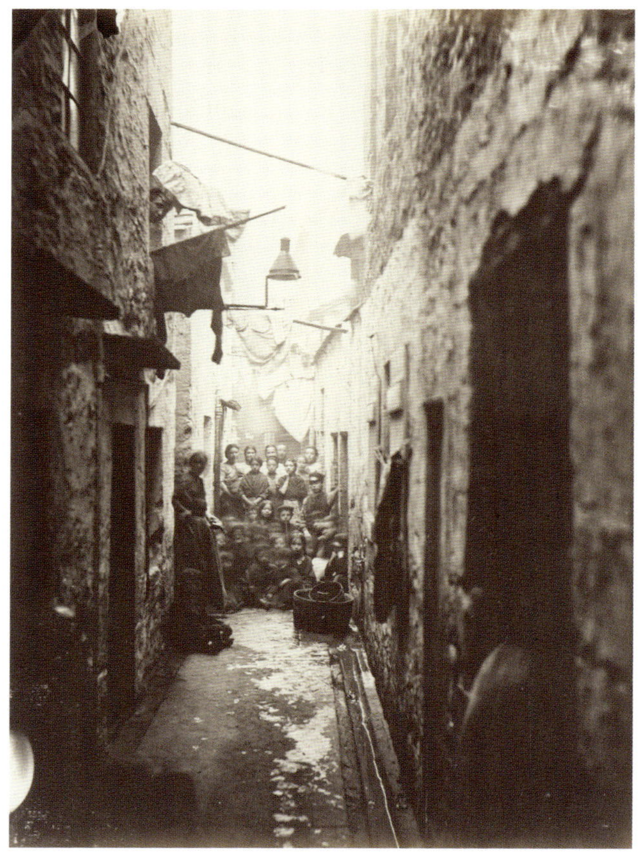

Fig. 7.12: Thomas Annan, 'Close, No 118 High Street Glasgow', 1868–71, albumen print. (Canadian Centre for Architecture, PH1980:0358:015)

five miles to the City.[34] This massive project was completed by 1859, when Queen Victoria ceremonially turned on the tap, watched and photographed by Thomas Annan.

In 1866, the City passed an Act through Parliament – to purchase and clear slums at the heart of the old town. They set up a City Improvement Trust, and it has been assumed that Annan was commissioned by that Trust to record the historic buildings before they were demolished. But Annan began work two years after the Act was passed, and the first mention of the photographs in the official minutes came in 1871. It seems more likely that Annan was employed by the city architect, John Carrick.

The photographs are dated between 1868 and 1871 and there are, in the official set assembled for the committee members in 1871, thirty-two large-scale photographs. The photographs are remarkable, not just for the evidence of grim living conditions but for an unexpected optimism. The closes were notoriously dark – apt places for distress and covert crime. They would be difficult to photograph, and Annan made it yet more difficult: there is washing prominent in some photographs, blocking the light still further; he often pointed his camera into the light along the closes, making the near buildings harder to define. There are evident signs of stress on the chemistry – imperfections in the negatives – and the occasional moving figures and animals blurring the picture.

When Archibald Burns (fl.1858–80) took a similar series of photographs of the clearing of the Edinburgh central slums in 1870, his pictures were radically different. Posters on the walls show that the inhabitants had been given notice to quit and had already left. Employed by the Edinburgh council, he took his pictures within a period of only four weeks in November and December, when the

light would have been at its worst. The pictures, nevertheless, are accomplished, showing the ruins of the historic architecture and the loss of a beleaguered population.[35]

Annan's photographs were neither a comprehensive survey of the neighbourhood, nor a picture of historic remains – most of the buildings were comparatively new. The area Glasgow proposed to clear was large and sprawling; they targeted closes and buildings, not whole streets. They needed to buy the properties before demolition, and they had difficulty in establishing ownership in the interlocked buildings, extended into courts, and divided on stairs. They were obliged by the Act to provide housing for a good proportion of the dispossessed tenants. Added to this, they found themselves responsible for the condition of the buildings they now owned, and were obliged, for example, by a new Police Act, to take street lighting into the closes.

Annan's photographs may have been intended to

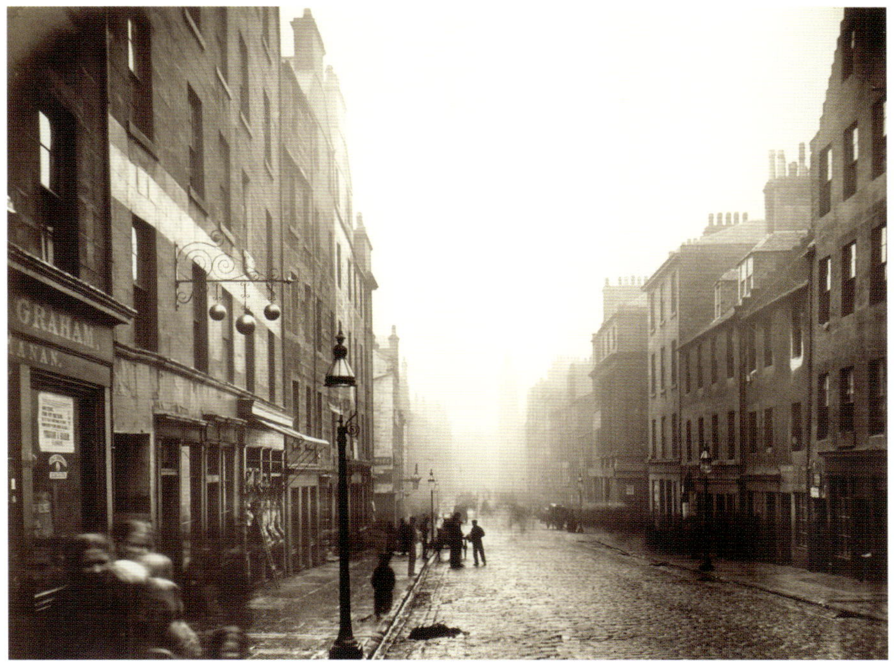

Fig. 7.13: Thomas Annan, 'High Street from College Open', 1868–71, albumen print. (Canadian Centre for Architecture, PH1980: 0358:04)

account for the progress of work, heavily dependent on practicality at any given moment. John Carrick had a staff of three. He was also responsible for the design and erection of the new buildings and facilities, including a neo-classical washhouse and new parkland. The photographs would have served as a demonstration of progress. They show some improvements: gas lighting, the demolition of out-houses, the installing of outside sinks. In 1871, the Trust realised that it needed more time, and the photographs then became part of the case presented to Parliament. The pictures subsequently became evidence of the City's pride, especially when the work was stopped by the crash of the City of Glasgow Bank in 1878. The Trust then framed sets of 'The Old Closes' and of the Glasgow waterworks photographs, to show in the public library and museum, where they would be seen by a predominantly working-class audience.

Annan's view of the project is seen in the pictures themselves. There is a beauty in them, a sense of hope in a place of despair. The light, shining at the end of closes, suggests a way out and a better future. The obtrusive washing lines are emphasized by a pyramid group of the women and children with buckets for washing seen in one photograph – the implication is that these are women of self-determination, who are concerned for their families [Fig. 7.12].

The closes are filled with people – not always immediately seen. The photograph of the open Saltmarket with its audience of interested people shows Annan's readiness to engage with human crowds, while presenting a telling background of public houses and loan companies. The distinctive picture of the High Street [Fig. 7.13], apparently taken in fog and rain, proves his subtle understanding of light (the way light particles may bounce around in fog, and water can cause dark surfaces to reflect). In this picture he has successfully caught the feeling of an occupied and busy street, dominated symbolically by the shining wet pawnbroker's balls.

Annan wanted his photographs to express the evils of the past and indicate a better future. The London improver, Octavia Hill, saw the photographs and the site in 1873. She wrote, in terms that connect with Annan's vision:

I found that here and there a house, here and there whole sides of a close or alley, had been taken down to let in the brightening influence of sun and air. The haggard, wretched population, which usually huddles into dark out-of-the-way places, was swarming over the vacant ground for years unvisited by sun and wind. Children were playing in open spaces who had never, I should think, had space to play in before. I felt as if some bright and purifying angel had laid a mighty finger on the squalid and neglected spots. Those open spaces, those gleams of sunlight, those playing children, seemed earnests of better things to come – of better days in store.[36]

William Carrick (1827–78) and John MacGregor (d.1872) in St Petersburg

William Carrick's family were timber merchants based in the Russian city of St Petersburg. He was born in Edinburgh but educated in Russia, where he studied as an architect at the Imperial Academy of Arts, but discovered that he had little aptitude. He then went to Rome, where he practised watercolour painting for three years. While he was there, the Crimean War broke out, interrupting trade between Russia and Britain and damaging the Carrick firm. Carrick needed to earn a living. In 1857, he returned to Edinburgh to study photography with James Good Tunny, and while there he met John MacGregor, who had recently set up a studio. MacGregor photographed George Carrick, a medical student and William's brother, and he was sufficiently proud of the photograph to exhibit it at the Photographic Society of Scotland in 1858.

When Carrick went back to St Petersburg, John MacGregor followed and joined him in business. In 1859 they opened a portrait studio at 19 Malaya Morskaya, close by The Hermitage, the great Cathedral of St Isaak and River Neva. However, they were not appreciably successful in business. They faced stiff competition, and photographic materials were expensive and difficult to find.[37] Charles Piazzi Smyth, in the city in 1859, explained the situation:

> … there is scarcely a more frequent sign to be met with along all the principal streets than Photographer; and the specimens exhibited outside the studios, chiefly large-sized portraits, were among the finest things we have ever seen in that line; but when we were in want of a mere glass dipper – and carefully eschewing the fashionable Nevski, wormed our way along a side street, until we saw a photographic material-shop in an upper story, and then ascended with our request, – Oh! What a price they wanted! It made us fly downstairs determined to do without.[38]

The atmospheric conditions were also a difficulty. The city stands at 59 degrees north and temperatures were extreme, from bitter cold to exceptionally hot (Edinburgh and Glasgow at almost 56 degrees north are warmed by the Gulf Stream, and are not subject to the extremes of a continental land mass). The sun shone, on average, only 100 days of the year. Smyth found the conditions extraordinary. His outdoor exposures varied from three seconds to three-quarters of an hour: in one place they met heavy rain and gusting winds; in another place:

> In the roadway the dust was deep – There was no wind, and the sun was hot, – bright, we were going to say, but that was not exactly the case … the clay soil of a thousand streets, triturated in a dry atmosphere to impalpable powder, went up like a great smoke to heaven and hanging there immovable, made all the firmament itself

instead of blue, appear a deep yellow, above and all around. Through this hazy, yet sunlit and hotly sun-reflecting medium, every object was now seen.[39]

Even in the studio, these conditions cannot have been easy. Carrick's 'democratic and unmercenary character' generated further difficulties.[40] He wrote to his mother:

Dukes and duchesses, counts and countesses, generals and colonels with their ladies, footmen, chambermaids and cooks, all come to our attic and pose for portraits. First come first served, I am equally polite with everyone and try to do my best for everyone. If I make any difference, I do it, of course, in favour of the lower and poorer class. I give them more attention because they need more than the wealthy and the high-ranking.[41]

In 1861, the Russian serfs were liberated and great social improvements seemed to be promised. This inspired the great liberal movement in Russia, supported by intellectual society and galvanising the painters to engage with realism along with the photographers. Carrick had legal status as a British citizen and was nominally a foreigner in St Petersburg, but it would appear that he was a revolutionary, concerned with social and political change. When he returned from Edinburgh in 1858, he smuggled in three issues of a political journal, *Kolokol* (*The Bell*), published in London by the exile Alexander Herzen, who advocated a form of democratic anarchy and believed educating the people would lead to revolution. The police arrested Carrick; they released him, but sent the man for whom he had brought the journal into internal exile. Presumably William Carrick was committed to the principles held by his wife. Alexandra

Grigoryevna Markelova was a writer, an atheist and a feminist, known as a 'genuine militant Nihilist'. They married in 1868, but he kept the relationship secret from his family for some years. His mother's initial reaction, that he had been 'caught in the talons of the most ungodly set of people that ever existed, for they neither fear God, nor the laws of the times we live in', explains his secrecy, though two years later she was able to say that William believed he had married 'the best and noblest woman' he had ever known.[42]

The series of 'Russian types' by Carrick and MacGregor were originally based on the street life of St Petersburg. Trades that, in other cities, were conducted indoors were followed on the street by individuals coming in from the country, carrying their tools and goods [Figs 7.14]. Engravers and painters had established a tradition of picturing these remarkable people, who were fascinating to strangers and Russians alike. Carrick and MacGregor invited them into the studio and photographed them against a neutral background. The pictures strike an impressive balance of nature – people warmly treated – and a convincing sense of their individuality was achieved.

The studio began with the carte-de-visite size of photograph and then turned to the larger format, the cabinet size. Having photographed the people of the streets, Carrick and MacGregor went out into the country around St Petersburg, to capture individuals and groups there. This expansion of their practice expanded their art. Some of the pictures, particularly the groups, have an aesthetic delicacy and use of outdoor light, which foreshadows the later Pictorialist approach.

In summer 1871, they were invited to travel inland to the Volga by the progressive landowner, Nikolai Mikhailovich Sokovnin, and photographed a wide swathe of the

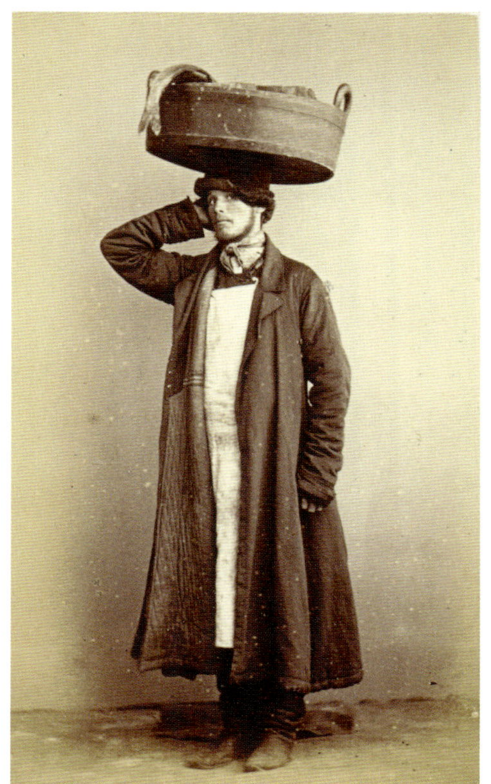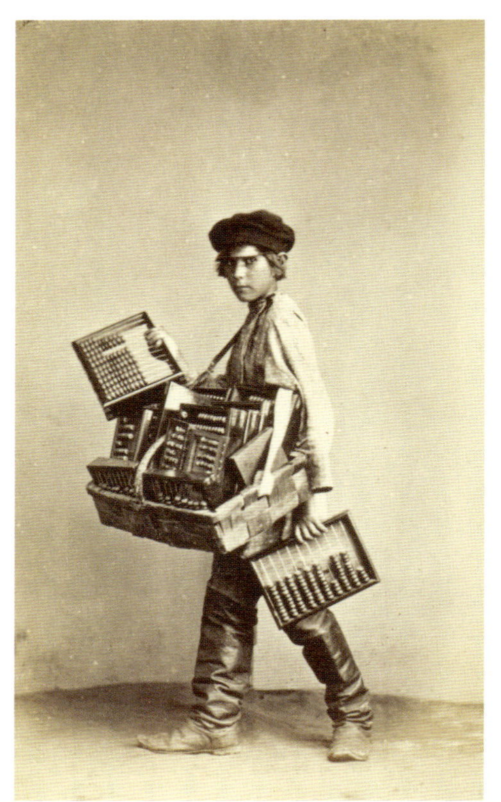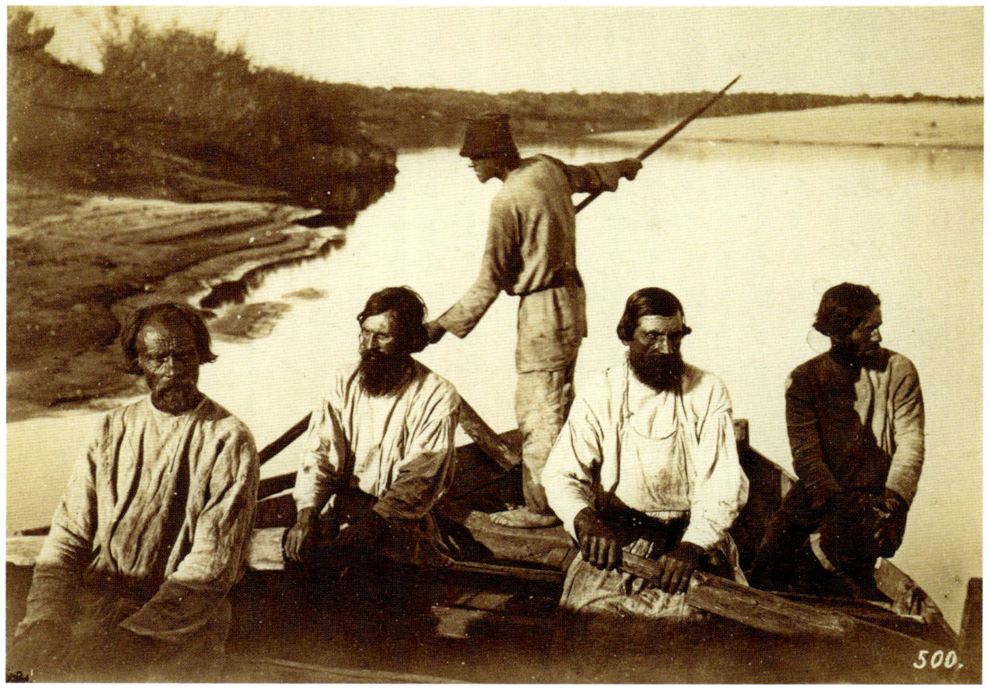

region [Fig. 7.15]. Their host recalled the immense pleasure of the month they spent there, which was only hindered by one 'formalist policeman' stopping the work because they did not have official permission. Sokovnin wrote:

> They worked from sunrise to dawn, without getting weary, without rest, often making up to 25 negatives a day. It is here that the remarkable collection of Russian types and views, types of minorities (Tartarians, Mordovians, Chuvash) that we see in Carrick's portfolios, came together. We travelled all together in a big company, covering a large region, opening new horizons and competing in choosing subjects for photographs. The crown of Carrick's work was several landscapes photographed 100 versts [about 65 miles] away from our homestead, in a century old virgin linden forest and filled with inexpressible wild charm and power. Innumerable studies of horses, cows, still lives were made …. The large and loving Russia was after Carrick's own large and loving heart.[43]

In another translation of this passage, Sokovnin is quoted as saying: 'Carrick's stay of a month with us went by as if it had been a day, and there cannot be a Mordavian, however cowed and humbled by fate, who appeared on one of his photographs, who would not even today, grin when remembering him.'[44]

John MacGregor died suddenly in August 1872. Carrick mourned 'the most sincere and devoted friend that I ever had'.[45] In later expeditions to Simbirsk, he was supported by another good assistant, called Gania, but was haunted by the memory of his friend. In August 1875, he wrote to his mother: 'I walked again along the places that MacGregor and I adored in summer 71, my soul is filled with memories.'[46] In 1878, he gave a large group of photographs to Leon Warnecke for the London Photographic Society's exhibition:

> Mr Carrick … when presenting to me his magnificent gift, imposed only one obligation – that whenever I showed anyone the result of his labour and artistic genius I must couple with his name the name of the late Mr Macgregor who was his assistant and became his instructor and best friend until his lamented death.[47]

Carrick showed the photographs in exhibitions both of painting and anthropology, and they sat happily in both the analytical and aesthetic context. The sense of reality (not by any means a 'given' of photography) is heightened by our sense of familiarity; the Russian Realist painters used the photographs directly and there is an echo of Carrick's work in 20th-century film-making.

Judging by his photographs and affectionate comments of his friends, Carrick was an eminently humane and sociable man, filled with the pleasure of his work. A friend wrote:

> Of athletic build and stature, and remarkably handsome and expressive in countenance, he also possessed an exceptionally kind heart, a generous nature, and an honesty positively ideal. The hard school of life had not shaken his faith in truth, in virtue, or in the high mission of man …. He loved his art for its own sake, and regarded it not as a means, but as an object, of life; and where another of his profession would have made a fortune, this unceasing labourer barely succeeded in making both ends meet.[48]

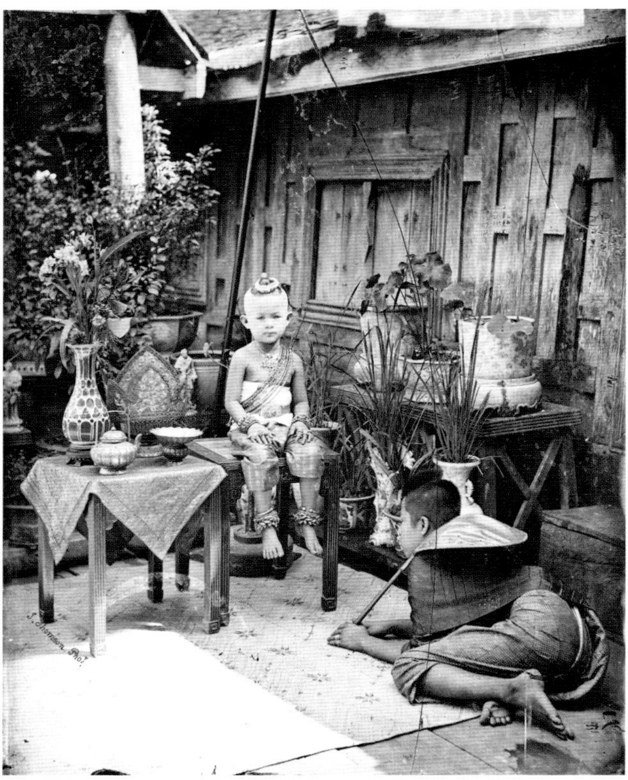

John Thomson, FRGS, in China

In his profession as a photographer, John Thomson (1837–1921) travelled from his native Edinburgh to Singapore (1862); from this base, he moved through the islands and mainland territories of Malaya and Sumatra to Penang, Siam, Cambodia, back for a time to Britain (1866), then out to Vietnam (1867), Hong Kong (1868), along the Pearl River, then up the River Min to Foochow and Formosa, to Peking and up the river Yangtze. He finally returned in 1872.[49]

Thomson was apprenticed in 1844, probably to the Edinburgh instrument maker James M. Bryson, at the time when Bryson had returned from studying advanced lens making in Germany. He worked with the firm until 1862, when he migrated to Singapore to join his brother making and repairing watches and clocks, optical and nautical instruments; he then established a photographic studio. According to Henry Yule, who visited Singapore in September 1863, the majority of the European population 'were evidently, from their tongues, from benorth the Tweed, a circumstance which seems to be true of four-fifths of the Singaporeans. Indeed, if I taught geography, I should be inclined to class Edinburgh, Glasgow, Dundee, and Singapore together as the four chief towns of Scotland.'[50] The decision to go to Singapore was evidently unexceptional. But Thomson's next moves were radical.

His first expedition took him to Siam in 1865, and into Cambodia to record the ruins of Angkor Wat: 'The description given in M. Mouhot's work of the magnificence of the ruined cities which the author found in the heart of the Cambodian forests induced me not only to carry out my resolution of visiting Siam, but to cross the country, and

penetrate to the interior of Cambodia, for the purpose of exploring and photographing its ruins.'[51]

In five months in Siam, he established good relations with the court, photographing the King, and providing the English governess with illustrations for her biographical account of the court (later converted into the musical 'The King and I') [FIG. 7.16].[52] It would have been Thomson's first encounter with the problems of diplomacy, and it was fortunate that the King spoke English:

The portrait was a great success, and his majesty afterwards sat in his court robes, requesting me to place him where and how I pleased. I consulted the Prince, who said – 'Yes, place him, but do not for the life of you lay hands on him, more especially on his thrice-sacred head.'

Here was a difficulty. How to pose an Oriental potentate who has ideas of his own as to propriety in attitude and that, too, without touching a fold of his garments. I told the King, in plain English, what I

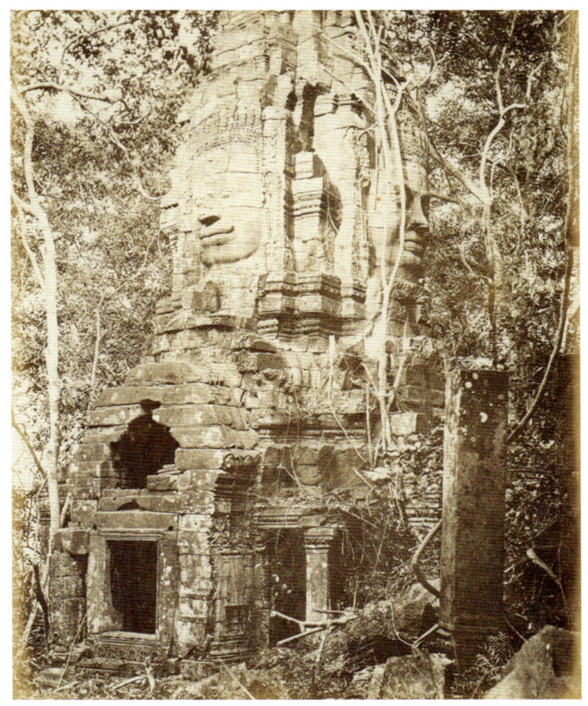

Fig. 7.17: John Thomson, 'One of the towers of the Prea Sat Ling Poun', 1865, from John Thomson, *The Antiquities of Cambodia, A Series of Photographs Taken on the Spot …*, 1867, plate 15, albumen print. (Gernsheim Collection, Harry Ransom Center, University of Texas, Image No. 964_0968_0011)

wanted to do, and he said, 'Mr Town-shun, do what you require for the excellency of your photograph'.[53]

The King of Siam wished to maintain good relations with the British, and identified Thomson as a communicator. The King wanted to underline his rights to the lands of Cambodia, and wrote Thomson a letter, asserting these rights and asking him to 'state everywhere verbally or in books, & newspaper publick papers that those provinces … belonged to Siam … for 84 years'.[54] Thomson, intelligently, fulfilled this promise by photographing the letter and publishing it in his book on Cambodia.

This was his first publication and an impressive start. He was a fluent writer and expressed the fascination of the place and the adventure of travel. Happily, he was accompanied by a young man from the embassy, who took leave to join him, and probably saved his life when he fell ill from fever. He 'engaged two extra carriers specially for taking charge of my chronometer, sextant and other instruments', which helped them find their way and enabled them to make a physical survey of the ruins.[55] He wrote:

> The antiquities of Cambodia, which are now found shrouded in the heart of the dense tropical forests of the country, consist of walled cities of vast extent, exquisitely built stone bridges, spanning with a multitude of arches the streams of the interior; temples more curious and extensive than those of Central America, and approaching in their classical appearance the works of the ancient Greeks or Romans; palaces of the ancient kings, adorned, like the monasteries, with the richest sculpture, artificial lakes surrounded by walls of solid masonry; and the remains of elevated highways, by which

the marshy districts of the country were traversed.[56]

It was evidence of a lost civilisation 'scattered over an area of some fifty miles in diameter', and he found that the living Cambodians 'can tell us nothing. They believe it to have been the work of the gods'. Thomson admired the men who made this city, and determined to map and photograph the extravagancies of the central temple [Fig. 7.17].

> This temple is so much shrouded with forest trees, climbing vines and thorny brushwood, that it was only after a hard day's cutting, with a party of natives, that we succeeded in clearing the tower [an area of 400 to 500 feet] sufficiently to obtain a photograph. Our efforts to produce a plan of the building proved abortive, as we had not sufficient men to make the necessary clearings, and we would have been exposed at every step to the danger of being crushed by falling masses of stone, as some of the blocks seemed to depend for their position upon the vines that were coiled, like a multitude of cables, around them …. The passages beneath, in the

lower storey of the temple, are so numerous and intricate that we frequently found difficulty in extricating
ourselves from the labyrinth, while their dark, damp
interiors were suggestive of the scene of a nightmare.
As we advanced, rifle in hand, every step brought down
flights of shrieking bats that flapped their clammy wings
against our faces.[57]

This is clearly one of the stories that inspired so many
books and films of adventure in the later 19th and 20th
centuries.

Thomson returned to Britain in 1866, to publish and
publicise the work. His reception, held at an elegant soirée
staged by the London Photographic Society, was almost as
implausibly filmic as the experience in the jungle:

Perhaps the most novel and interesting feature of the
evening was the illumination of the refreshment pavilion
by means of magnesium light … an immense pavilion,
forming two crescents, beautifully filled as a winter
garden with beautiful flowers and plants, beautiful
arrangements of rockery, magnificent ferns, artificial
cascades, abundance of varied refreshments, in which
choice fruits formed an important feature – all this with
its living tide of "beauty and chivalry," illuminated by
the brilliant light ….

In this remarkable setting, he read a paper on Cambodia
and the report said:

The photography executed under unusual difficulties
in this remote region in a tropical climate, by the wet
process, was exceedingly perfect, delicate, and soft, as

were also some fine portrait photographs illustrating
ethnological types.[58]

His career was launched.

While in Britain, Thomson established himself as a
journalist writing for the *British Journal of Photography*,
on 'Practical Photography in Tropical Regions'. His text
expresses the lyrical practicality of his work:

The early morning has … many advantages. The temp-
erature is lower, and for an hour or two nature enjoys
the most perfect repose; there is not then a breath of
wind to stir even the restless leaves of the 'people' tree,
and the most delicate stem of long grass bending under
the weight of its feathery flower might be photographed
without a head-rest; in short, morning is the time when
the finest atmospheric effects may be caught. As the
heat of the sun increases, there is the invariable rising
mist of an Indian morning. For the reproduction by the
camera of these dim distances, where the broad lights
on the palm leaves and the deep shadows in the masses
of foliage are softened down to a dreamy indistinctness
by the mist, and where the foreground objects stand
out in well-defined relief, not only is the most delicate
manipulatory skill called into play, but nice artistic
discernment in the operator; so that the picture when
finished may look like nature ….[59]

Filled with energy, John Thomson met his future wife,
Isabel Petrie, finished his book for publication with large
scale albumen prints (including two panoramas), became a
Fellow of the Ethnological Society and Royal Geographical
Society, and lectured with the aid of his photographs, most

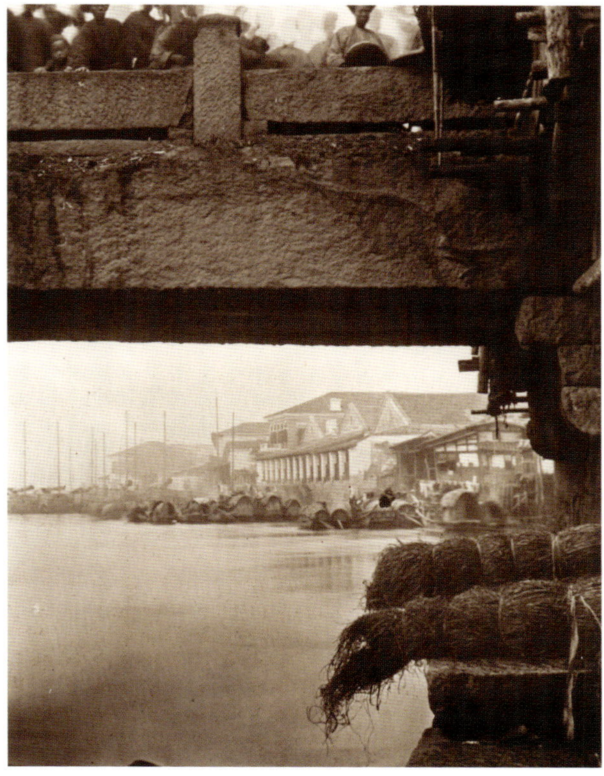

Fig. 7.18: John Thomson, 'The Upper Bridge, Foochow', 1870, carbon print. (Canadian Centre for Architecture, PH1986:1046)

notably to the British Association for the Advancement of Science meeting at Nottingham, but also in Scotland, using the projection of an oxyhydrogen light. He exhibited the work at the Edinburgh Photographic Society's exhibition, with the Glasgow Photographic Association and with the Architectural Institute of Scotland.[60]

He returned east and established a studio in Hong Kong. His success was marked by the arrival of Isabel Petrie, who came out to marry him in 1868. The Thomsons travelled together through Canton, but after the birth of her first child and while she was pregnant with her second, they were anxious that her and her children's health was at risk. They went home in 1870. Thomson put his studio on the market and engaged in a series of journeys into China. He went through the Foochow region from late 1870 to early 1871, up the River Min with the American missionary Reverend Justus Doolittle, author of *Social Life of the Chinese*, and to Amoy and Swatow. He travelled with Dr James Laidlaw Maxwell to Formosa, where they visited the beleaguered Pelopohans. He returned to Hong Kong, visited Shanghai and Peking, then spent three months travelling up the Yangtze river, taking in Ningpo and the Snowy Valley. He then returned to Hong Kong, and left for Britain and his family in mid-1872.[61]

Thomson travelled some 4000 miles through China, and took photographs of landscape, cityscape, antiquities, modern improvements and people – high-powered government officials and beggars; street workers and wealthy merchants; men and women; children and old people. His view of landscape came from a western sense of the picturesque, with an exquisite balance of landscape, water and distance. Some subjects presented themselves, by Chinese design, in an aesthetic beyond a western plan; from time to time, he

set up and treated his subject in an eastern manner, as with the massive granite bridge of great age at Foochow [Fig. 7.18]. He stood on the mud below. The framing, set by the supports of the bridge, pushes the natural subject, the whole reach of the bridge and its life, up into the sky and squares it off as a flat abstract, dwarfing the buildings and the boats beyond.

Thomson presented a wide view of the country and its peoples. He was attempting a visual account of a vast nation, which expressed interest and concern, which criticised, often fiercely, the evils he noted, but also applauded the society and culture. He saw beauty and squalor. He admired the excellence he saw and roundly condemned injustice. He was a compassionate, rather than politically or morally righteous, proposer of reforms.

Thomson's moral judgements were based on western ideas. In common with most western observers of the time (and, indeed, a number of the Chinese in government), he believed that Chinese culture and society were moribund.

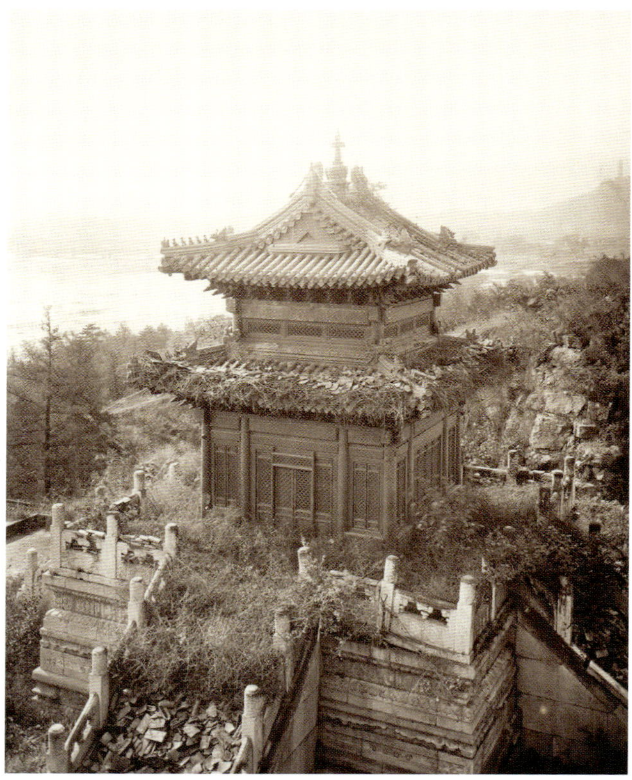

The preface of his 1875 publication said:

> Certain it seems that China cannot much longer lie undisturbed *in statu quo*. Her deeply reverenced policy of inactivity and stagnation has brought floods, famine, pestilence and civil wars in its train; it cannot sink the toiling masses to yet lower depths of misery, or stay the clamours of multitudes wailing for sustenance while the rivers run riot over the fertile plains, and the roads have been converted to watercourses. The rulers meantime, with a blind pride, are arming a beggarly soldiery to fight for nothing that is worth defending ....[62]

This is not objectivity; it expresses passion and concern. His photographs, his subsequent lectures and his books were directed to Europe and the Europeans working in China. He was as concerned to dispel European ignorance as to advocate Chinese progress. And it should be said that he was critical of his own compatriots and appalled by the wanton destruction of the Summer Palace, which he visited in company with Mr Yang, a Chinese friend, and Dr Dudgeon (both photographers) in 1871–72. He saw it as 'a wilderness of ruin and destruction which was piteous to behold', and took one of his most touchingly beautiful photographs of the pagoda outlined against the light and protected by the rubble piled up on its steps [FIG. 7.19].

> It is a pity that redress for a breach of treaty obligations was not sought by some less destructive mode than this .... We might have withdrawn with dignity and left no deep-rooted rankling hatred behind. This hatred will probably manifest itself ere long ... in one desperate concentrated effort to drive the foreigner from Chinese soil.

Thomson was troubled by consideration of Mr Yang, who 'made not a single allusion to the wreck around him. He admired indeed what little was left of the former splendour of the palace; but it was impossible to fathom his real sentiments ...'.[63]

He saw the people in terms of the Scottish principle of the individual and that individual's personal responsibility – a vision all the more striking in dealing with an immense population. The camera could be said to be bound to such individuality, but not necessarily so. For example, it could be subverted by the study of ethnology, requiring 'typical' examples of racial types captured in a standard system of physical measurement, or by a decision to ask amenable people to dress up in clothing relating to a different cultural group.[64]

The subjects of the travelling photographer may be regarded with compassion – perhaps as victims of his obtrusive gaze. Thomson's photography is distinguished by the way his sitters look back at him – at us – sometimes a little

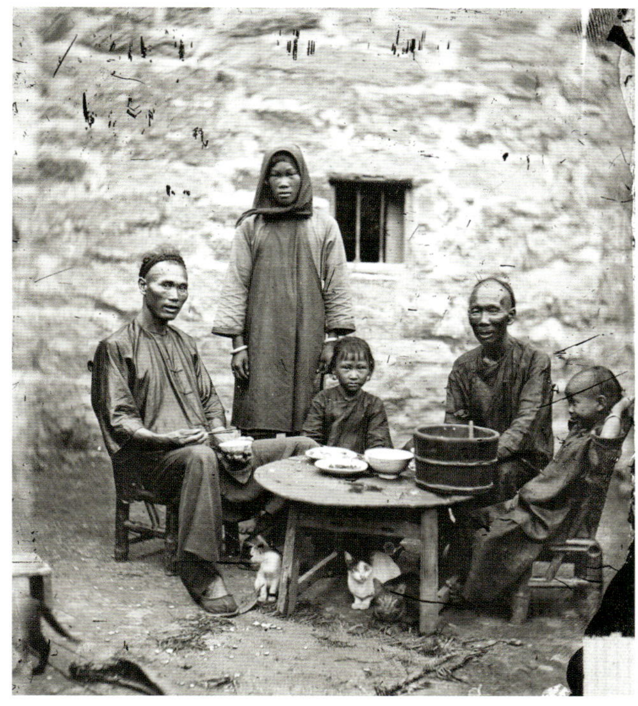

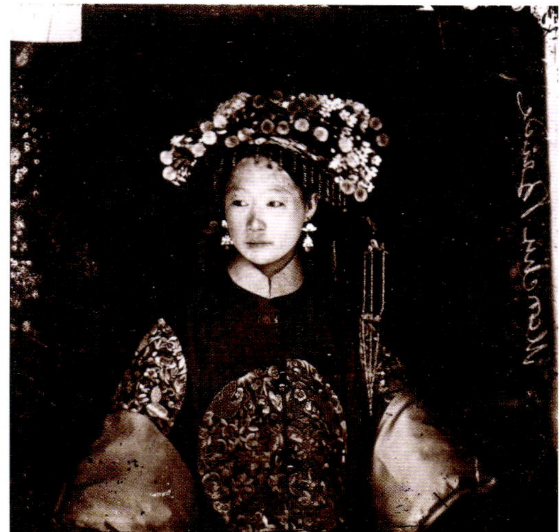

Fig. 7.20 (left): John Thomson, 'Kowloon, Hong Kong, a Chinese family', 1869, digital print from wet collodion negative. (Wellcome Library, 19624i)

Fig. 7.21 (above): John Thomson, 'A Manchu bride in her wedding clothes, Peking', 1869, print from wet collodion negative. (Wellcome Library, 19670i)

nervous, but generally relaxed and sometimes pleased [FIG. 7.20]. We cannot know what they were thinking, but the response seems at least polite and open. Given that he was a western barbarian with no government backing, this is striking. It would be naïve to assume John Thomson was able to take photographs and move freely simply from his own authority, or that the response of his sitters was untroubled by the successful aggression of the west. He was assisted by other westerners – government officials, merchants, clergymen – but that assistance was given as a courtesy, rather than as a right.

Thomson's welcome into private houses is especially notable. He was concerned to photograph the wealthier women [FIG. 7.21], to balance his view of the poorer working women, and he acknowledged the problem of

> … the strong dislike entertained by the people against admitting strangers into the inner courts of their dwellings; for these they hold to be sacred and inviolate. To such an extent, indeed, has this idea of privacy and family isolation been carried, that Chinese homes have

for ages been constructed on all occasions, after a model which seems to aim at perfect family seclusion from relatives even, and friends, no less than strangers.[65]

He explained his access with apparent simplicity:

> I enjoyed exceptional advantages for gleaning information about the inner life of the Chinese wealthy classes, and the arrangements of their households, inasmuch as I never let slip an opportunity of volunteering to take family portraits, in order that while thus engaged I might obtain for myself such groups and interiors ….

Thomson, travelling so far in a comparatively short time, might be hindered in understanding his subject.[66] But he knew more than might be expected. He was acutely aware of his surroundings, and his text fills in a lively sense of how a place looked, felt, smelt or sounded, beyond the pictures. He also knew and worked with men who were long-standing experts.

One of these men was Dr John Dudgeon (1837–1901),

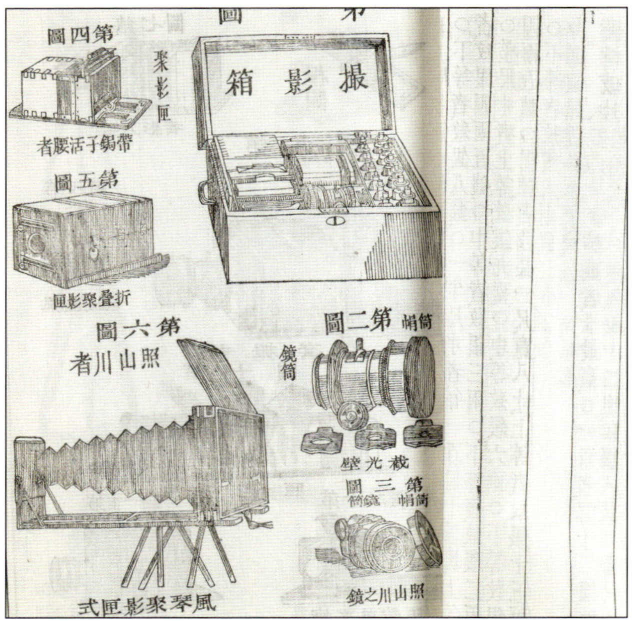

Fig. 7.22: Dr John Dudgeon, illustration from *Tuoyingqiguan*, The Peking Hospital,1873. (National Media Museum / Science & Society Picture Library, Image No. 10676823)

who was born in Galston, Ayrshire, and trained as a surgeon at the University of Glasgow.[67] He went out as a medical missionary to Peking in 1864 and lived there for 31 years, working as a teacher and as a doctor. The medical missionaries had a particular role in influencing the modernisation of China; Dudgeon had patients among the poor, whom he treated free, and within the imperial court, and was able to demonstrate the effectiveness of European medical methods.[68] Among other things, he attempted to find an answer to opium addiction, and set up an experimental refuge in Peking.[69] However, he was ready to learn from Chinese medicine and standards of hygiene – and considered that they were notably better than the prevailing conditions in Britain.[70]

In 1873, he published the first full account of photography in Chinese, and in the text said that he had taken up photography for pleasure about 1853 or 1854 [Fig. 7.22].[71] He made an extensive photographic tour of south China, when suffering from ill-health in 1868. Constance Gordon Cumming, a visitor who stayed with him and his family in the 1870s, was astonished by his workload:

> … it is a source of amazement how Dr Dudgeon gets

through his daily work. To begin with, he must personally prescribe for, on average, 120 hospital patients every morning, besides an extensive outside practice, which includes several of the foreign Legations and involves driving long distances in the blazing heat and in horrible springless carts. Two hours a-day are devoted to translating useful books into Chinese with his students, besides the labour of preparing and delivering his lectures at 'The Government College'.[72]

It is perhaps not surprising that Dudgeon came to believe that the western laborious work ethic, along with its habits of consuming quantities of rich food and drink, was damaging to health, and that the more relaxed and abstemious Chinese approach to work and life was far preferable. How much time he was able to devote to photography is questionable.

Thomson's association with Dudgeon went beyond simple photographic outings together. Dudgeon believed, from his extended knowledge of China, that the British obsession with bad smells, the fear that the corruption which generated the stink inevitably led to disease, was incorrect. He noted that the people who carried the faecal waste, the night soil, from the city into the country were 'among the healthiest and most robust of our population'.[73] Thomson positively admired these women. He wrote:

> The women employed in this and other field work …
> are strong, healthy and many of them attractive-looking.
> Their olive cheeks are warmed with a glow of colour, and
> their glossy black hair is decked with silver ornaments and
> fresh flowers. Their dress is simple and remarkable for
> its bright cleanliness. They never compress their feet,

but rather draw the eye to their natural smallness by wearing prettily embroidered shoes.[74]

Both of these opinions were published in 1873. It may be that Thomson's knowledge of Foochow and his photographs of the women there had reinforced Dudgeon's own observations.

Thomson also shared Dudgeon's view of the evils of city life in Britain – the increasing imbalance of wealth and comfort, flourishing alongside pollution and desperate poverty. When Thomson published *Street Life in London,* in 1877, he concluded his account of the disorganised and risky methods of collecting refuse, 'Flying Dustmen', by comparing them unfavourably with Chinese practice.[75] In the extended series, as a photographer and as a journalist, Thomson criticised London civilisation in terms he had learned in China. It is a pointed comment on his work that the historians Rainer Fabian and Hans Christian Adam could say:

> Had Engels been a photographer, he would have taken these pictures and Karl Marx would have used them to illustrate his *Communist Manifesto.* Thomson's photographs of China and London forecast the revolutions that would finally erupt into the 20th century. They were also the first examples of objective photography.[76]

The parallel sense of reality in Henry Mayhew's *London Labour and the London Poor* and in the novels of Charles Dickens makes Thomson's London work a familiar part of our understanding of the place and time.[77] The three contributions were incorporated into the larger picture of contemporary social and literary concern with the city. His

photography in China is more efficiently isolated, but the sense of familiar humanity may be trusted.

Thomson was inevitably obstructed on occasion. His photographing 'Chao-Chow-Fu Bridge' across the Han river met with overt hostility:

> Seeing my strange instrument pointed cannonwise towards their shaky dwellings, they at once decided that I was practising some outlandish witchcraft …. The market stalls were abandoned [that] the barbarian who had come to brew mischief for them all might be properly pelted. The roughs and market people came heart and soul to the task, armed with mud and missiles, which were soon flying in a shower about my head. I made a plunge for the boat.[78]

He fended the attackers off with the point of his tripod. The glass plate of the photograph cracked across but, with judicious handling, Thomson was able to use it.

Generally speaking, he was capable of defusing such hostility. How remarkable this is may be explained by a comparison of two acts of photography in the same place: one, taken during the Opium War, and the other by Thomson. In 1857, Captain Paul-Emile Berranger photographed the waterside at Canton from his warship, *Mitraille,* shortly before bombarding the city; on the shore a group of Chinese men stand looking at the ship. The image contains its own bloody future.[79]

In 1870, when sailing up the Pearl River in Canton, Thomson reached 'Wong-Tong' village, where the attack was remembered:

> I prepared to take a photograph, and my intention was

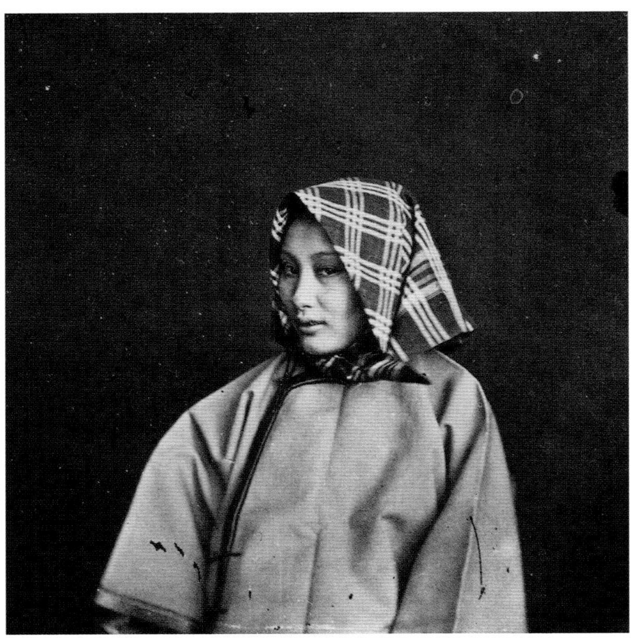

to include a group of old women who were gossiping and drawing water; but when they saw my instrument pointed towards their hamlet, they fled in alarm, and spread abroad the report that the foreigners had returned and were preparing to bombard the settlement. A deputation soon set out from the village, led by a venerable Chinaman, the head man of the clan, and to him we explained that we had come on no hostile errand, but only to take a picture of the place. He gave us a hearty welcome to his house, spreading tea and cake before us. This was one of those many instances of a simple genuine hospitality which I experienced all over the land; and I feel assured that any foreigner knowing enough of the language to make his immediate wants understood, and endowed with a reasonable even temper, would encounter little opposition in travelling over the greater part of China.[80]

The women's reaction was, of course, intelligent, based on a shocking violence committed within memory. Thomson must have offered some convincingly social and unthreatening response that encouraged the Chinese courtesy.

Thomson was particularly sympathetic to the working women of China – in noted contrast to his doubts of the confined women of the wealthier classes, whose painted faces and elaborated hair styles troubled him as a form of disablement.

His photographs of the Cantonese boatwomen [Fig. 7.23] expressed a possibly mutual admiration:

> … these boatwomen are the prettiest and most attractive-looking of their sex to be met with out of doors in this part of China. They never paint [i.e. wear make-up], and are therefore set down by their countrywomen as of doubtful respectability. This is really true of some of them, although in the presence of Europeans who may hire their boats they behave with uniform modesty and decorum. Their boats are the perfection of neatness, and their dress is as simple as it is picturesque. There is a hue of health, too, about their olive cheeks, and sparkling in their lustrous eyes, while the darkness of their raven tresses is charmingly heightened by a crimson flower in the hair. They scull or row with great dexterity, skimming in and out among the crowd of shipping ….[81]

There is an echo, in the admiration of their independence and their beauty, of Hill and Adamson's Newhaven photographs, which is followed through in Thomson's dramatic account of the boatmen's skill on the rapids of the River Min [Fig. 7.24]:

> When I watched the coolness, pluck and daring, with which these poor river navigators will shoot the rapids of the River Min, risking their lives in every voyage – in a country where there are no insurances … and where no higher reward is to be gained from hand-to-mouth

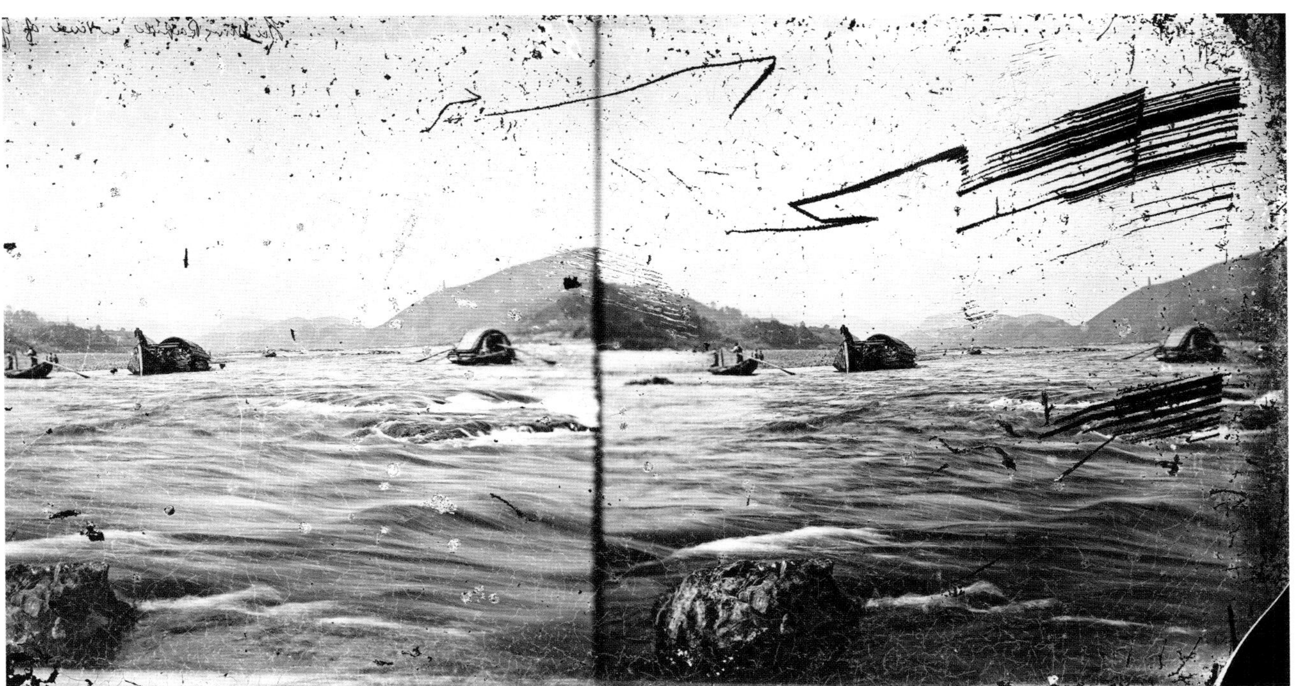

subsistence on the most wretched fare – I began to get a truer insight into the manly and hardy qualities latent in the mis-governed Chinese race .... There he [the helmsman] stood on the bridge, calm and erect, with an iron grasp on the long rudder, impassive until we were just plunging onto the rock; and then, as I prepared to leap for life, he threw his whole weight onto the oar, and brought the boat round with a sweep that cleared the danger by the breadth of a hair. Thus we shot onwards, down! down! down! like a feather tossed to and fro by the caprice of the irresistible waves.[82]

His photographs of people generally show confidence in the sitters, but we cannot know what they were thinking.

However, one of the most extraordinary documents in this history gives us an insight into the way some of Thomson's sitters could respond. He photographed a group of high Chinese dignitaries at the Office of Foreign Affairs in 1871 [Fig. 7.25]. And it is immediately obvious that the three men are relaxed and seated in a way far removed from conventional Chinese portraits, which Thomson made for other sitters. All three men were in favour of change and improvement, and had adopted some western ideas. The picture is remarkable because it shows an amicable collaboration between them and Thomson. The photographs tell us this much. But Bao Yun (1806–91) wrote a poem to mark the occasion, which offers a generous view of Thomson and sets the photograph in a Chinese cultural context:

*Mr Thomson, the visitor from overseas, with his piercing
  eyes, whiskers like a dragon's, and a great forehead,
Uses a lens to capture a man's life. The moonlight reflects
  the imagery of Li Bai.
He arrives unannounced at the Office of Foreign Affairs,
  a nobleman's house by the river, to set up his glittering
  screen.
To make a portrait of the mandarins, Dong, Mao and
  Shen, three figures depicted sitting in a row.
To create a significant portrait, sharing characteristics
  with the benevolent governors of the past.
In an empty courtyard the deep clear colours of a Chinese
  autumn: stamen of chrysanthemum scattered below
  the luxuriant foliage of hidden trees.
In the middle, looking like Wen Lu Gong, our first
  subject sits upright, staring straight ahead, in god-like
  contemplation.*

*Like Zhu Ge in Han times, a flick of his fan can dictate a
  new strategy, or like Tang Shao Ling with the cares of
  the kingdom written in his eyes.
Noble governors of heroic bearing in the court of the
  emperor, facing each other with eyes wide open.
Only Zou and Mei could surpass them, followed by Bao E.
I am just a normal person, like Wang Liang.
I am not a historian; what do history books have to do
  with me?
We write and sing together in harmony, a purple sunset
  in a bright sky,
Walking together to Meihua village.
This handsome portrait hangs at the head of the hall of
  the Office of Foreign Affairs.*[83]

It is remarkable that the photograph should have met with
such a gracious response.

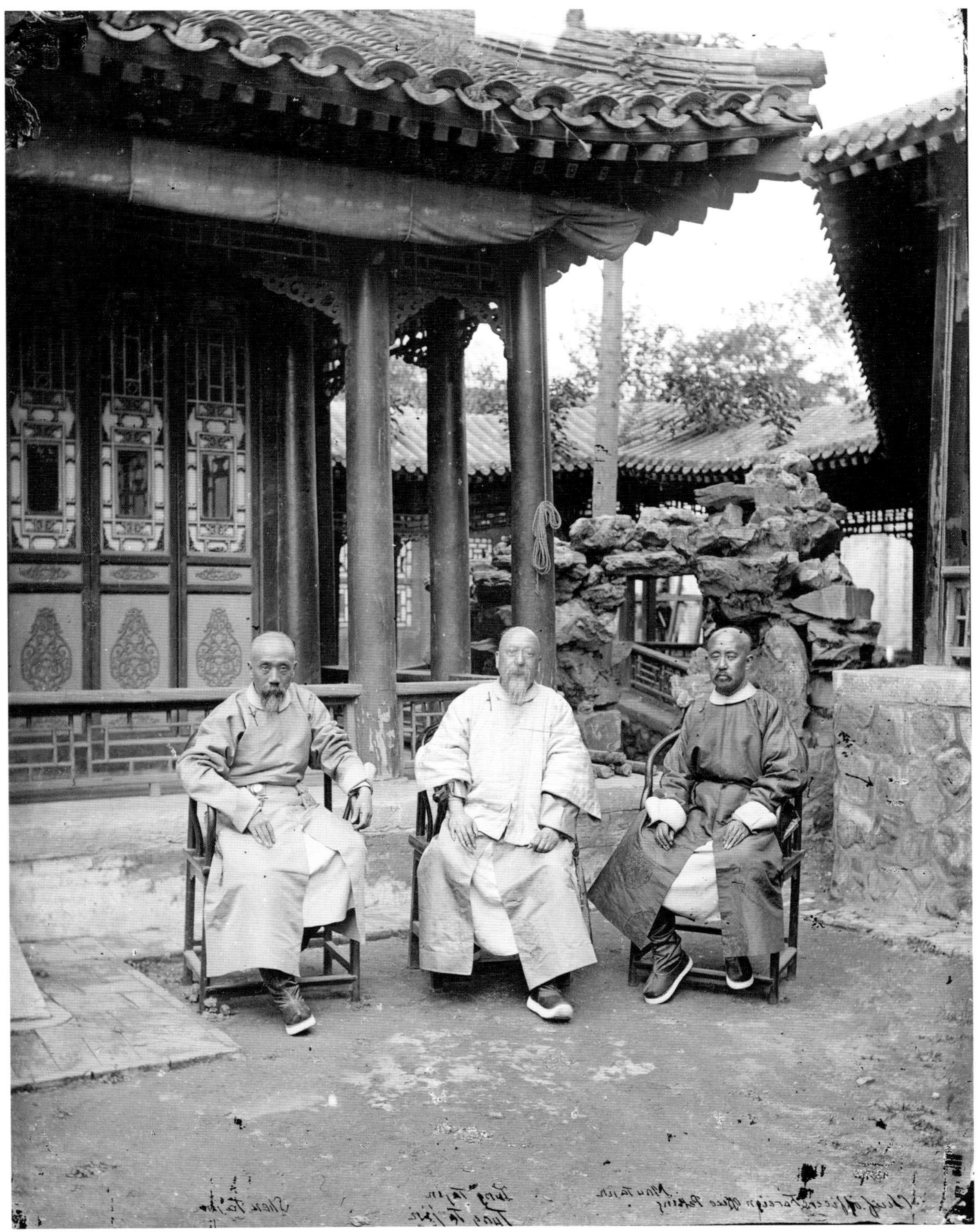

Notes

1. Stevenson 1991.
2. Wilson 1883: 8.
3. Donald McCoo, 'Gardner and his contemporaries: the years in Scotland', in Johnston (ed.) 1991: 13.
4. Although the paper was radical, it was supported by a range of local businessmen, including John Muir Wood, who advertised his concerts regularly in the paper.
5. He advertised and was noticed in the *Dumbarton Herald*, between 27 December 1855 and 3 April 1856.
6. My understanding of Gardner's Civil War work is substantially derived from the excellent exhibition curated by Jennifer Watts, 'A Strange and Fearful Interest: Death, Mourning and Memory in the American Civil War', at the Huntington Art Library, San Marino, in 2012. Unfortunately, this exhibition had no catalogue.
7. Werge 1890: 190.
8. Pinkerton, the original 'private eye', also came from Glasgow.
9. H. Baden Pritchard, 'Photography in connexion with the Abyssinian Expedition', paper given to the Photographic Society of London, 8 December 1868, *Photographic Journal* 10 (15 December 1868): 184.
10. Gardner 1866: vol. 1, pl. 28.
11. Review of the exhibition of the Antietam photographs in New York, *New York Times*, 20 October 1862.
12. Katz 1990: 63. Will Stapp has expressed the contrary opinion, that the public and press were not attracted to such pictures, and most of the photographs copied for the illustrated press of the time were studio portraits, Will Stapp, 'To … Arouse the Conscience and Affect the Heart', in Johnston (ed.) 1991: 24 and 118.
13. Gardner 1866, Introduction.
14. *Ibid.,* pl. 36.
15. *Ibid.,* pl. 4.
16. See, for example, Rosenheim 2013: 8. This sees Gardner's captions as blatantly romantic.
17. Trachtenberg 1989; Sweet 1990; Schantz 2008; Rosenheim 2013.
18. Gardner 1866, pl. 40. Both Gardner's words and the pictures have been pored over and corrected to an extraordinary extent; his text is presented here unmediated.
19. Gardner 1866, pl. 41.
20. Gardner did not sell many copies of his publication, which cost $150. Anne Peterson found 67 sets, and considered this may have been half the number issued: see Anne E. Peterson, 'Alexander Gardner in Review', *History of Photography* 34 (November 2010): 356–67.
21. Miller 1911: 1: 16, Introduction, quoted by Trachtenberg 1989: 79.
22. Miller and Lanier 1911, vol. 9. The disconcerting character of this rewriting of the war was defined by Oscar Handlin: 'Above all, if the war were to bind Americans in national unity, both sides had to seem right', 'The Civil War as Symbol and as Actuality', *Massachusetts Review* 3 (Autumn 1962): 135, quoted by Trachtenberg 1989: 79.
23. Frederic Ray, 'The Case of the Rearranged Corpse', *Civil War Times*, 3(6) (1 October 1961): 19; Frassanito 1975; and Frassanito 1995. It is still a given assumption in, for example, Cushman 1999: 11; Harvey 2012: 85; and Rosenheim 2013.
24. 'He went strong for Leaves of Grass – believed in it, fought for it …', quoted in Traubel 1889/1912, vol. 3: 234.
25. Quoted in Traubel 1889/1912: 346.
26. Barthes (trans. Richard Howard) 2000: 96.
27. De Mallie, quoted in Katz 1990: 245.
28. Katz 1990: 235.
29. Gardner 1869; Sobieszek, 'Conquest by Camera: Alexander Gardner's Across the Continent on the Kansas Pacific Railroad', *Art in America* 60 (March 1972): 80–5.
30. See Jane E. Simonson, 'On Level Ground: Alexander Gardner's Photographs of the Kansa Prairies', in Sayre (ed.) 1999: 61–85.
31. Boime 1991: 21.
32. Wilson 1883: 13.
33. Not the same Joseph Swan who invented the carbon process.
34. First published in 1859, the series was republished on several occasions. See Ray McKenzie, 'A Love Affair with Loch Katrine: Problems of Representation in Early Scottish Landscape', *Scottish Photography Bulletin* 1 (1990): 3–12. Also Simpson 2012: 143–6.
35. See Julie Lawson in Stevenson and Lawson 1986: 116–18; James Lawson, 'The Urban Landscape between Progress and Decay,' *Studies in Photography* (1998): 5–8. Also Antonia Laurence-Allen, 'Class, Consumption and Currency: Commercial Photography

Note: Website addresses checked and correct at the time of going to press.

in Scotland, 1851–1888', unpublished PhD thesis, University of St Andrews, 2012.

36. Octavia Hill, 'Why the Artisans Dwellings Bill was wanted', *Macmillan's Magazine* 15 (June 1874): 181–2.

37. Felicity Ashbee, 'William Carrick: A Scots photographer in St Petersburg, 1827–1878', *History of Photography* 2 (1978): 207–22; Alexey Loginov, 'Carrick, William', in Hannavy (ed.) 2008, vol. 1: 274–6.

38. Smyth 1862: 308–9.

39. *Ibid.*, 168, 362.

40. Barkhatova, Stevenson and Weiss 2010: 45.

41. Quoted from Felicity Ashbee, 'Photograph s MaloyMorskoy', *Yunost'*, 7, (1976), in Barkhatova, Stevenson and Weiss 2010: 45–6.

42. Letters from Mrs Carrick to her son, George, in 1872, and her daughter in 1874, quoted by Julie Lawson, in Ashbee and Lawson 1987: 17.

43. Quoted by Barkhatova, Stevenson and Weiss 2010: 54.

44. Ashbee and Lawson 1987: 10.

45. In a letter to his sister, quoted in Barkhatova, Stevenson and Weiss 2010: 56.

46. Quoted in *ibid*.

47. Leon Warnecke, 'Photographic Notes from Travels in Russia', communication to the Photographic Society of Great Britain, *British Journal of Photography* 25 (29 November 1878): 570.

48. V. Sreznievsky [Secretary of the Photographic Society of St Petersburg], Obituary, *British Journal of Photography* 25 (27 December 1878): 621.

49. On John Thomson, see in particular Ovenden 1997; and Richard Ovenden, 'Thomson, John (1837–1921)', <http://www.oxforddnb.com/view/article/38593>

50. Yule 1921: the third edition has a memoir by his daughter, Amy Frances Yule, Preface.

51. Thomson 1867: 7.

52. Leonowens 1870.

53. Thomson 1875: 94.

54. Thomson 1867, frontispiece.

55. Thomson 1875: 127.

56. *Ibid.*, 9.

57. *Ibid.*, text for pl. 15.

58. Anon., Account of 'The Soirée' of the Photographic Society of London, *Photographic News* 10 (31 August 1866): 412–13.

59. John Thomson, 'Practical Photography in Tropical Regions', *British Journal of Photography* 13 (10 August 1866): 380.

60. Richard Ovenden 1997: 11.

61. *Ibid.*, 13–21.

62. Thomson 1875: vi.

63. *Ibid.*, 526–57.

64. See for example Wu Hung's analysis of the work of Milton Miller, 'in which the ceremonial dress and identities of the various sitters are interchangeable – evidently a picturesque fiction using models': Wu Hung, 'Inventing a Chinese Portrait Style in Early Photography. The Case of Milton Miller', in Cody and Terpak (eds) 2011: 69.

65. Thomson 1873–74, vol. 2, text for pl. 7.

66. See Richard Ovenden's opinion in Ovenden 1997: 14.

67. Pearce 2005; Nick Pearce, 'A Life in Peking: the Peabody Albums', *History of Photography* 32 (2007): 276–87.

68. Gao Xi 2009.

69. See Austin 2007: 245–6.

70. Shang-Jen Li, 'Discovering the Secrets of Long and Healthy Life: John Dudgeon on Chinese Hygiene', *Social History of Medicine* 23 (2009): 21–37.

71. Dudgeon, 1873, unpaginated.

72. Quoted by Shang-Jen Li, 'Discovering the Secrets of Long and Healthy Life: John Dudgeon on Chinese Hygiene', *Social History of Medicine* 23 (2009): 28–9.

73. Quoted by Shang-Jen Li, *ibid.*, 25.

74. Thomson 1873–74, vol. 1, text for pl. 11.

75. Thomson and Smith 1877: text for pl. 35.

76. Fabian and Adam 1983: 252.

77. Discussed, for example, by Richard L. Stein, 'Street Figures: Victorian Urban Iconography', in Christ and Jordan (eds) 1995.

78. Thomson 1873–74: vol. 2, text to pl. 8.

79. Bennett 2009: 91.

80. Thomson 1875: 219.

81. *Ibid.*, 267.

82. *Ibid.*, 394.

83. This poem was published in Mandarin by Ming-chu Fung, 'Decoding John Thomson's Figural Photographs', *National Palace Museum Bulletin*, Taiwan 2011: 107. I am indebted to Yupin Chung who has translated the poem from the original text, *Wenjingong Yiji*, for this publication.

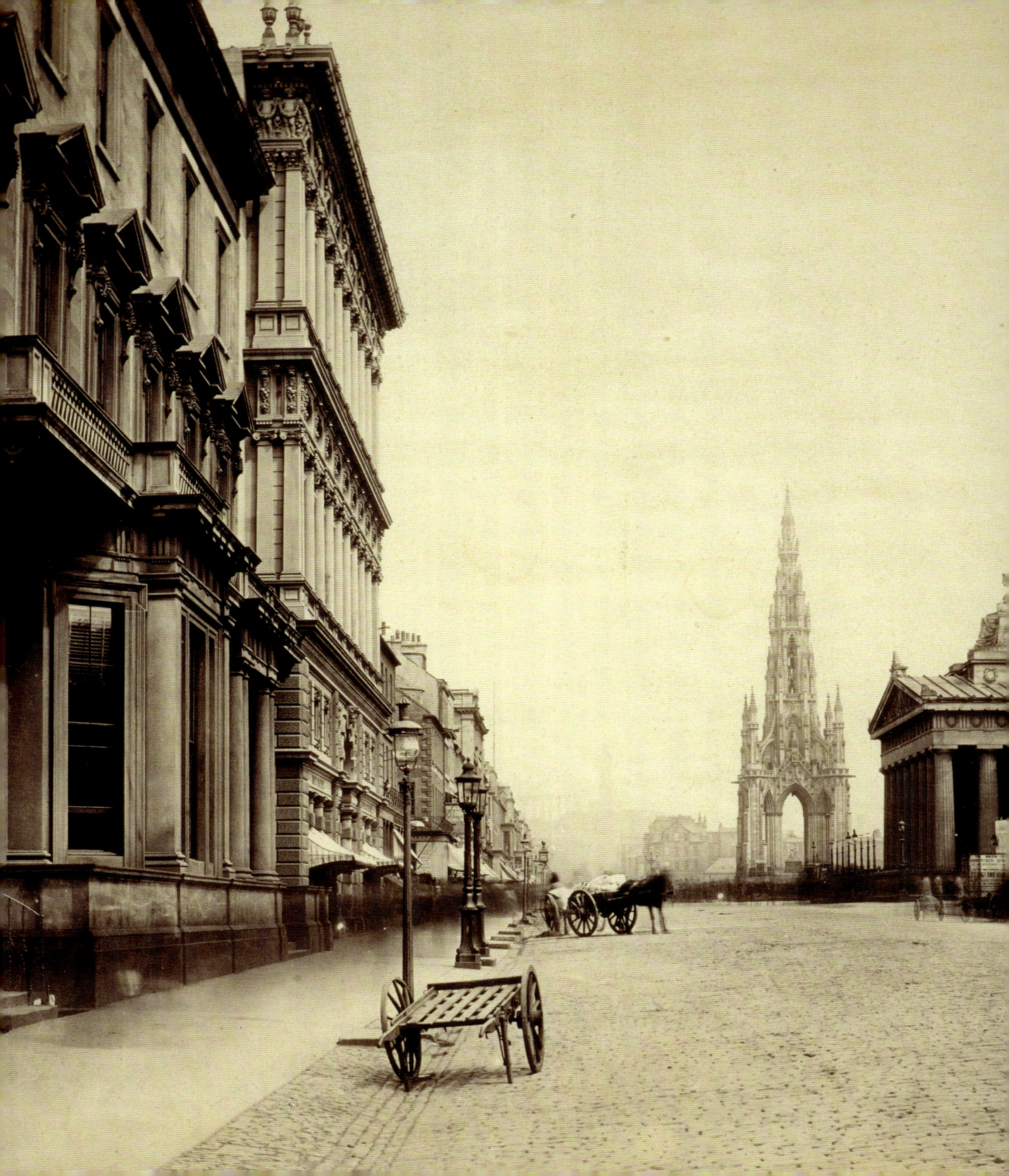

CHAPTER EIGHT

The Nature and Purposes of Photography

When death comes … you can take out these, it may be, wasted,
shadowy, almost vanishing images – how you treasure them
forever, beyond all trim and graceful miniatures by man's hand.

★

Anon. (presumed to be John Brown), Review of the
Photographic Society of Scotland's exhibition, 1862

Criticism of photography

In 1839 Blackwood's *Edinburgh Magazine* published a review of engraving and photography.[1] John Eagles was concerned by the impact of mechanisation on art. He discussed lithography in disparaging terms and turned to photography:

> The phantasmagoria of inventions passes rapidly before us …. Is the hand of man to be altogether stayed in his work? – the wit active – the fingers idle? …. Vanish aquatints and mezzotints – as chimneys that consume their own smoke, devour yourselves. Steel engravers, copper engravers, and etchers, drink up your aquafortis and die! …. The real black art of true magic arises and cries avaunt. All nature shall paint herself …. Here is a revolution in art.[2]

Eagles prophesied the end of topographical painting, amateur sketching and architectural draughtsmanship, animal painting and portraiture; the future identification of criminals, weather recording itself, the waters marking their own tides, and forgery. He ends with this splendid thought:

> Mr Babbage in his … Treatise announces the astounding fact … that every word uttered from the creation of the world has registered itself, and is still speaking, and will speak for ever …. But what too if the great business of the sun be to act registrar likewise, and to give out impressions of our looks, and pictures of our actions … for aught we know of the contrary, other worlds of the system may be peopled and conducted with the images of persons and transactions thrown off from this and each other; the whole universal nature being nothing more than phonetic and photogenic structures.[3]

Opposite, Fig. 8.8 (detail): W. D. Clark, 'Princes Street, Edinburgh', 1858, albumen print.

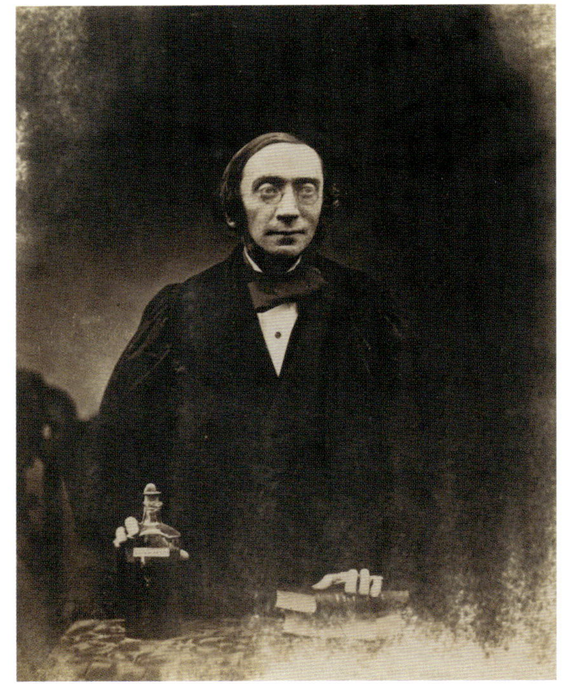

Eagles had not yet seen any photographs, so his proposal of a grand future for photography was largely imaginary. He finished with a question which has since troubled photography and affected our ideas of its importance:

> Do we not despise what is too easily attained? .... People prefer a poor representation of an object made by a human hand to the beauty of the thing itself. They will throw away a leaf, a flower, of exquisite beauty, and treasure up the veriest daub .... There are things so exquisitely beautiful, and at first sight acknowledged to be so by all, that it is surprising they are not in common use. For instance, the camera obscura – how perfectly fascinating it is! Yet how unsatisfied are people with it, because it is not of a human hand, and how seldom do people, even of taste, return, as it might have been expected they would, to the exhibition of it.[4]

The critical possibilities of photography were being mapped out before the art was fully launched. The issues, what photography could do, how it should be developed, and how it related to the arts it challenged, were explored, discovered, denied and enjoyed in the next decades.

George Wilson: the camera's vision *versus* the eye and the mind

When photography was invented, it was assumed that the camera obscura resembled the human eye [Fig. 8.1]; the photographic camera was expected to achieve images conforming to human vision. Dr George Wilson (1818–59) [Fig. 8.2], the first (and only) Professor of Technology at Edin-burgh University and Director of the Industrial Museum of Scotland, published a paper, 'On the Extent to which the received theory of Vision requires us to regard the Eye as a Camera Obscura' in 1855.[5] In this, he challenged the common understanding, and concluded that the eye 'cannot be regarded otherwise than in a limited sense as a camera obscura'.

Wilson asked the chemists, John Spiller and Allan B. Dick, based in London, to undertake some experiments using a bullock's eye to take photographs, both as a lens, supported in the brass mounting of a camera lens and as a camera itself, substituting a piece of curved glass for the retina with sensitive photographic paper behind.[6] They obtained 'very distinct pictures … *of a key* and of a *spotted window curtain*'. Wilson was exploring the phenomenon of colour blindness and the function of the 'yellow spot' or 'macula' on the human retina, which is the point of clearest focus.[7] In laying these photographs on the table, he hinted delicately that anatomists might try a similar experiment with a human eye, and concluded:

> … the views of those who have described visual impressions on the retina, as phenomena of the same kind as photographic impressions on surfaces charged with salts of silver … must fall to the ground if the actinic rays of light are stopped before reaching the optically sensific constituents of the retina. The similar opinion, also, that 'spectral vision,' and other peculiarities of sight, are phenomena of the same kind as the development … of latent photographic images, must … be abandoned.[8]

Wilson was not a practising photographer, but was interested in the camera and in photography. In the 1840s, he had lectured in chemistry to 'hundreds of young ladies … and some two hundred stout fellows'. One of his students recalled that he was 'the greatest favourite and the most efficient teacher' in the School of Arts.[9] He demonstrated the daguerreotype and calotype. The Photographic Society of Scotland noted his early death with sorrow: 'Taking a lively interest in everything connected with the art … Professor Wilson was ever ready to give to the Society the information which he possessed. The communications which

from time to time he made to the Society were of the most valuable and suggestive kind.'[10]

Criticism and the art of photography

In the course of practice, and from their previous knowledge of the camera obscura, early photographers were able to approach photography with this distinction in mind – it was not a direct equivalent of the eye's observation. D. O. Hill made this discovery in working with Robert Adamson: the calotype had a life of its own. The partners' interest in the development of photography was cheered on by artists, such as Clarkson Stanfield the marine painter, who wrote of the photographs of the Newhaven fishermen and women:

> They are indeed most wonderful and I would rather have a set of them than the finest Rembrandts I ever saw.[11]

Benjamin Robert Haydon, the history painter, was 'convinced that Calotype is the greatest thing for Art, since the Elgin Marbles; and I never paint now without one of your heads on my Easil'.[12]

In the 1840s, the principal reviews of photographic practice in Scotland were devoted to Hill and Adamson. They were written by impressive writers: Hugh Miller in 1843, and Elizabeth Rigby (1809–93) and Dr John Brown (1810–82) in 1846.[13] Hill solicited criticism to address the fine art market beyond Edinburgh. The reviews were complimentary and personal; the three critics were friends, but they would not necessarily praise the work – the Scottish enthusiasm for criticism was based on Presbyterian morality laced with a passion for poetry and art. Of these reviewers,

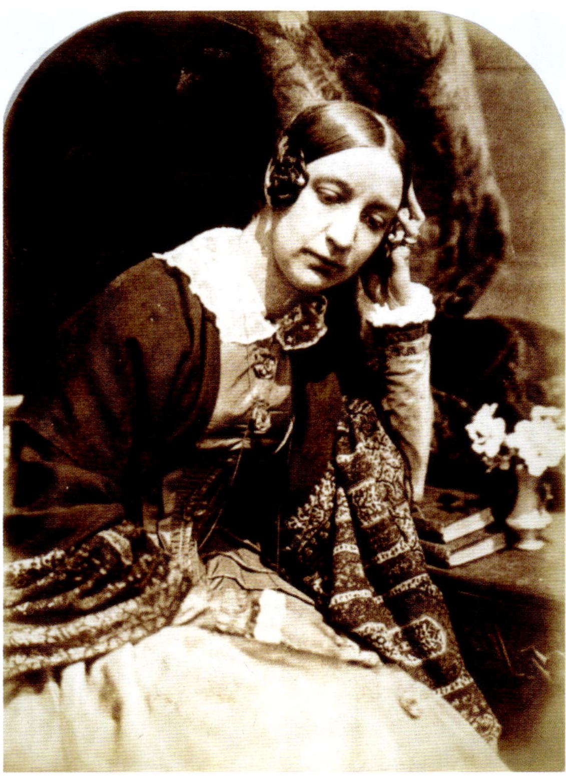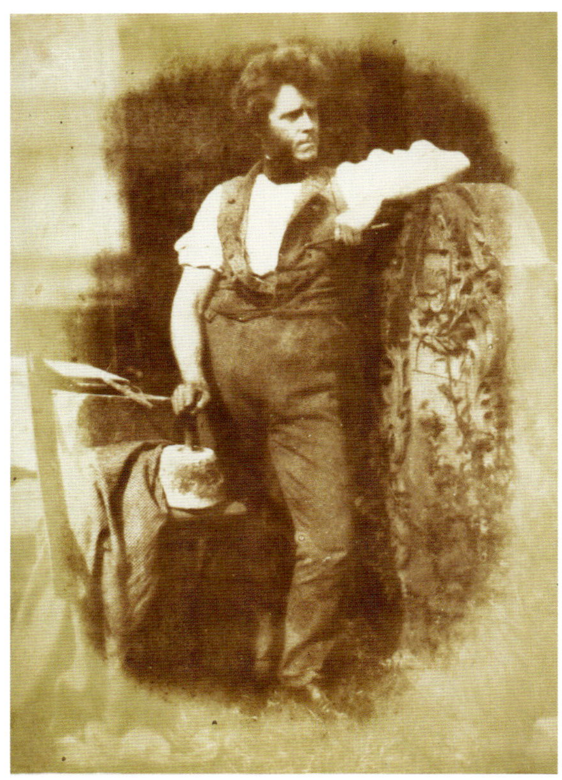

Elizabeth Rigby [Fig. 8.3], an Englishwoman then living in Edinburgh, was unaffected by the Presbyterian ethic and hostile to the Free Churchmen. Her wonderful response to the calotypes was offensively tempered by a footnote referring to 'the fat martyrs of the Free Kirk', and a dismissive remark about Talbot, both of which must have caused Hill serious embarrassment.[14]

Rigby and Miller, and later Brown, were engaged as sitters in a way that suggests collaborative art experiment. The experience of photography gives them authority as critics. Miller used a photograph of himself as a point of abstracted discussion. In this picture, Miller, who was then editor of the *Witness* newspaper, appeared as a stonemason, his earlier profession. He described the picture as a 'well-marked drawing … in which we recognise the capabilities of the art for producing pictures of composition' to be engraved directly as a book illustration.[15] The picture taken in 1843 was evidently important. Hill re-staged it for the large camera in 1844 [Fig. 8.4]. The photographs are true in a broad

sense: they connect Miller's past to the present, establish a biblical parallel (the working man turned evangelist), and show the natural strength of one of the best fighters of the Free Church.

Both Miller and Rigby commented on the relationship between Hill and Adamson's calotypes and the work of painters. Miller found resemblances with the work of the leading portraitists, Henry Raeburn and Thomas Lawrence, and concluded with Joshua Reynolds, '[from] the striking similarity of style that prevails between them, we feel more strongly than at perhaps any former period, that the friend of Johnson and of Burke must have been a consummate master of his art'.[16]

Elizabeth Rigby, who posed for and arranged poses in the Hill and Adamson studio between 1843 and 1847, wrote of 'the beautiful and wonderful Calotype drawings – so precious in every real artist's sight, not only for their own matchless truth of Nature, but as the triumphant proof of all to be most revered as truth in art'.[17]

Fig. 8.3 (opposite left): D. O. Hill and Robert Adamson, 'Miss Rigby', *c.*1845, calotype. (Scottish National Portrait Gallery, PGP HA 286)

Fig. 8.4 (opposite right): D. O. Hill and Robert Adamson, 'Hugh Miller', 1844, calotype. (Scottish National Portrait Gallery, PGP HA 283)

Fig. 8.5 (right): Dr John Adamson, 'Dr John Brown', *c.*1860, albumen print. (National Museums Scotland, T.1942.1.1.126)

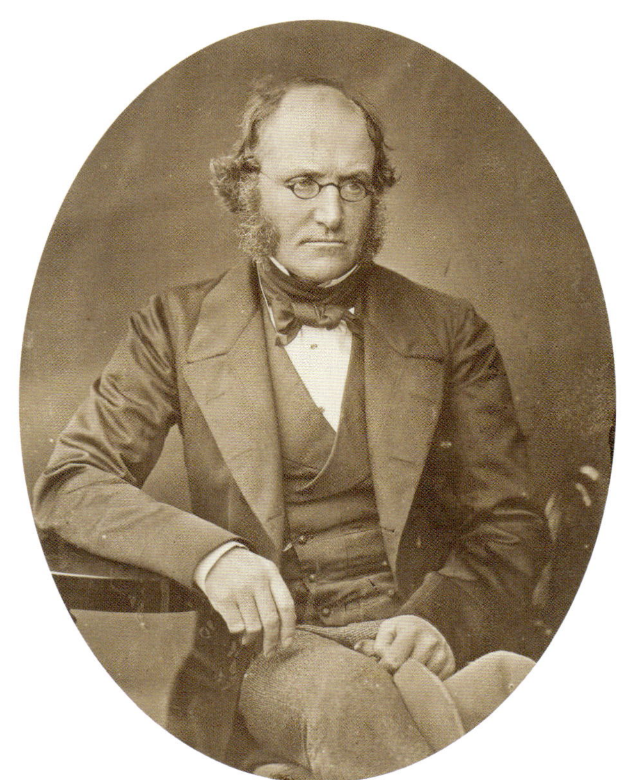

Dr John Brown [Fig. 8.5] wrote a review for the *Witness*, which said of the calotypes: 'They have all the modesty and all the infinite variety of nature, and, to a man with a shaping spirit, are the very stuff from which to body forth his own thoughts.'[18] Brown's review concluded that Hill

> … has humour, which implies, we have always thought, not merely character in its owner, but a power of seeing into the character of others; and he has that thorough human-heartedness and love of his kind, that makes him lay out his affections on them.[19]

Brown could see within the photographs this power of mind and affection. The critical circle engaged with Hill and Adamson's work because it was original. Their calotypes demonstrated photography's potential for a distinct aesthetic in relation to familiar reality.

Dr John Brown's interest in photography grew in the 1850s and 60s. In 1864 a review of the Photographic Society of Scotland exhibition said, cheerfully:

> Of course, there is Dr John Brown. When was there a photographic exhibition or a photographic show case for that matter, without a portrait of *him*? His benevolent countenance appears so frequently that one almost fancies that the photographers practise on it after business hours, as well as during the day, when sitters are few.[20]

Amongst the photographers who took his picture were Dr John Adamson and Thomas Rodger, and he would have discussed photography with them. It may be significant of such a discussion that Adamson sent portraits to the 1861 exhibition with an admonitory note:

> I wish very much that the large heads should be exhibited to advantage as I entertain a hope that they may in some small degree help to turn the public taste from the small 'carte de visite' pictures so fashionable at present and in which I think the photographic art has been progressing backwards – to portraits of a larger size – and a more ambitious aim in the direction of the painters field of operation.[21]

The consistent portrait

The most influential figure amongst the Scottish reviewers was Sir David Brewster. In reviewing photography in January 1843, he stated his view on progress, as divinely-ordained:

… the art of Photography … [is] as great a step in the fine arts, as the steam-engine was in the mechanical arts; and we have no doubt that when its materials have become more sensitive, and its processes more certain, it will take the highest rank among the inventions of the present age.[22]

Much of Brewster's thinking was based on his own experience. He was one of the first to be photographed in Scotland. His portrait appeared prominently in the album the Adamsons sent to Talbot in November 1842.[23] He expressed unease as early as November 1843, when he wrote to Talbot:

I have been very much struck with the *different Calotypes* of the *same person*. In many of them, where the Sitter was steady – the family likeness is scarcely preserved …. Does this arise from the Camera? I have seen among Mr Adamsons Calotypes pictures of Men & Women in one of which the Sitter was decidedly *good looking* and in the other *hideous*.[24]

His eventual complaint was two-fold: the calotype lacked detail and it distorted reality. He published a damaging assessment in these terms, in 1847:

… when it is employed to take portraits, particularly those of children and females, it invariably presents us with unsatisfactory results … it is often a hideous likeness, even when female beauty has submitted to its martyrdom.[25]

Brewster transferred his enthusiasm to the clear albu-men prints taken by Ross and Thomson. From Hill's perspective, the disastrous impact of this was felt at the Great Exhibition in 1851, where Brewster was one of the judges for photography: Ross and Thomson received a Council Medal, while Hill and Adamson's work was given only an Honourable Mention.[26]

Brewster pursued the chimera of resemblance and accuracy through technological improvement – stereoscopic photography and the use of small lenses made of rock crystal. In 1862, he was still in pursuit:

… we look forward to the time when the studio of the photographer shall be so fitted up, that the sitter and the camera have necessarily such fixed positions that the delay and trouble of focusing is entirely avoided, and that portraits can be taken either at such great distances, or with lenses so small, as to remove entirely the two kinds of deformity with which all portraits are affected.[27]

He was proposing that portraiture adopt the practice of ethnology, with the sitters fixed in a measured position. John Francis Campbell of Islay (1821–85), who was interested in the optics and chemistry of photography, shared Brewster's belief that portraits should be taken at a distance.[28] He wrote:

… most photographic portraits are taken with large lenses at very short distances, and generally produce dismay and amazement in the sitter and his friends …. At about 20 yards, figures and groups of figures, though still distorted in a small degree, appear to bear a better proportion to each other and to their own limbs and features … negatives taken with lenses of short focus at

Fig. 8.6: Unknown photographer, 'Robert Louis Stevenson', *c*.1852, daguerreotype. (Scottish National Portrait Gallery, PGP 343)

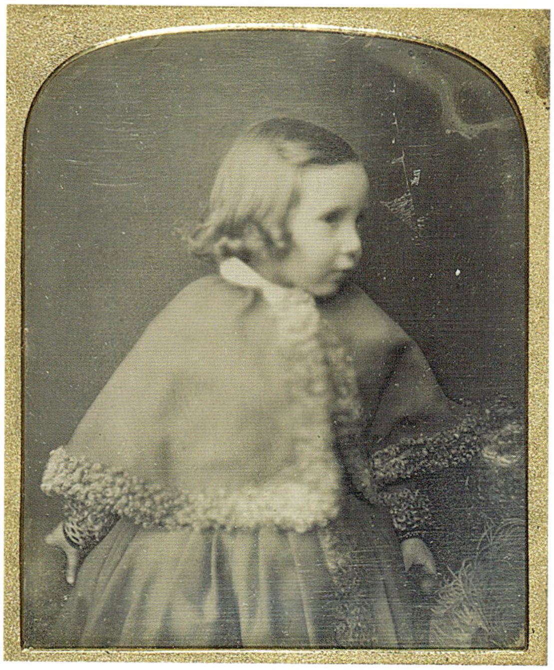

20 yards must be small; but by heating them red-hot, they become positives of great clearness, which can be well seen with a lens.[29]

This distance, which would make his full-length figures visually about two-and-a-half inches high, does not imply a noticeable engagement between Campbell and his sitters. But he had a secondary motive. Like Piazzi Smyth, he was a great traveller, and favoured small cameras. He added:

It is a saving in materials to work with small glasses: an apparatus for taking small negatives can be carried in the hand and costs little, while one for large negatives costs a fortune, is a baggage-train in itself, and is often thrown aside.

Brewster failed to realise that the problem of consistency related to light and expression. Hugh Miller compared the calotypes to engravings of Joshua Reynolds's self-portraits, which showed distinct changes in appearance:

A man at one moment of time, and seen from one particular point of view, may be very unlike himself when seen at another moment of time, and from another point of view. We have at present before us the photographic likenesses of four several individuals – three likenesses of each – and no two in any of the four sets are quite alike. They differ in expression, according to the mood which prevailed in the mind of the original at the moment in which they were imprinted upon the paper. In some respects the physiognomy seems different; and the features appear more or less massy in the degree in which the lights and shadows were more or

less strong, or in which the particular angle they were taken in brought them out in higher or lower relief.[30]

The fact that some people lack a consistent physical appearance – or are 'unphotogenic' – was revealed through photography. This fascinated the author, Robert Louis Stevenson (1850–94). An only child of wealthy parents, he was photographed from an early age. The first photographs of him may be by his uncle David Stevenson [Fig. 8.6], taken when he was two. At the age of 22, he attempted a facetious experiment on the relation of appearance and status, seen through the camera.[31] While staying at Bridge of Allan, near Stirling, with his cousin, he wrote to his mother:

I suppose there are not in Christendom two persons of more nondescript appearance, than yours sincerely Robinson Crusoe and his present Man Friday [Bob Stevenson]. I in a serge coat, jersey, straw-hat, and (if the pavement be quite dry) slippers, may be seen smoking unashamed outside the hotel; but the desperate respectability of Bob's hat and coat – the one green with age, the other simply ragged – is, I flatter myself, much more mean and pitiable. I was so curious to know which looked worse, and whether it was possible to identify either as belonging to any definite class of society, that I hobbled down to the booth of one 'Andw Manson, photographer,' to get this shady couple photographed. Andw Manson proved to be a very gloomy and depressed photographer indeed: he received us with a sort of heart-broken contempt, [and] refused sadly to have anything to do with us.[32]

Stevenson continued to visit photographers, but, like Brewster, he had an unstable relation to portraiture. He promised to send a photograph to a friend, but warned:

> It will not be like me; sometimes I turn out a capital, fresh bank clerk; once I came out the image of Runjeet Singh; again the treacherous sun has fixed me in the character of a travelling evangelist. It's quite a lottery … The truth is I have no appearance; a certain air of disreputability is the one constant character that my face presents; the rest change like water.[33]

Stevenson was interested in these transformations.[34] And since a portrait is a collaboration between photographer and sitter, it is tempting to propose that his self-conscious humour subverted the art as much as enquired into it.

The democratic art

Brewster's proposal for photographs taken at a fixed distance endorsed basic studio practice, producing millions of small photographs by a production-line method. The results generally had little individuality or character. But most customers were happy with this. In the later 1850s, photography shifted into a democratically emotional field. In 1857 Elizabeth Rigby, now Lady Eastlake, expressed this abstraction from art: 'What indeed are nine-tenths of those facial maps called photographic portraits, but accurate landmarks and measurements for loving eyes and memories to deck with beauty and animate with expression, in perfect certainty, that the ground-plan is founded upon fact?'[35]

In 1859 Jane Welsh Carlyle (1801–66), wife of essayist Thomas Carlyle, received a portrait from an Edinburgh friend. She expressed admiration for photography, in terms removed from artifice. For her, as for most of the studio customers of the day (including Queen Victoria), the photograph offered connection. She wrote in her letter of thanks that photography

> … has given more positive pleasure to poor suffering humanity than anything that has 'cast up' in my time or is like to – this art by which even 'the Poor' can possess themselves of tolerable likenesses of their absent dear ones … I have [pictures] … of every place I ever lived at as a *home* – photographs of old *lovers*! old friends, old servants, old *dogs*! – In a day or two, *you*, Dear, will be framed and hung up among the 'friends'. And that bright, kind, indomitable face of yours will not be the least efficacious face there for exorcising my Devil, when I have him![36]

John Brown's 1862 critique of photography distinguished its role in memory and consolation:

> When death comes … you take out these, it may be,

wasted, shadowy, almost vanishing images – how you treasure them for ever, beyond all trim and graceful miniatures by man's hand. That is the very turn of the head, the shape of the bald head, the child's look you so well knew, the restrained smile, the waistcoat, the shawl – the *reality* you can never more forget or see – all are brought back to you, and in that *camera lucida* of your own brain, in that chamber of imagery, from out this poor, imperfect sun-sketch there blooms into life, untouched by time or change, your idea of that face.[37]

All three writers considered the impact of photography outwith the photographer's intention. Photographs could give a fragile hold on the past and absence, of immense significance in a time when people migrated across the world and death was a constant risk. These thoughts (pre-Freud) – and particularly the incidental detail emphasised by Brown – informed the 20th-century philosophers' engagement with photography, and its capacity to reflect poignant and personal observation beyond its time and place.[38]

Time and the landscape

Although people persisted in the idea that the camera did (or should) act like a human eye, even the first results in photography challenged that assumption. The photographic view of time and its relation to solid bodies was one of the first surprises. As John Robison reported of the daguerreotype that included the gentleman and the shoe black, only those parts of the two which had not moved could be clearly seen; the busy street seems empty. The eye and the mind, seeing the street within the time of the

photograph's taking, would have registered the people. We combine our visual knowledge with information from the other senses – particularly touch – and then 'see' or understand solid form in movement; the camera simply registered the effect of light.

J. G. Tunny's photograph of St Mary's Wynd shows a group of people who had been asked to stay still. The crowd gathered in front of Thomas Annan's camera in Glasgow's Saltmarket offers a more disconcerting capture of time – some people understood the need to freeze, others were puzzled and appear more than once, some walked past as a mere blur. The picture contains time and movement, as a kind of condensed movie [Fig. 8.7].

It depended on the inclination of the photographer and viewer, whether they saw this difference as a fault or a character of photography. It had both poetical and practical advantages; the unfocussed or ghostly image of a person, or the absence of people within a city, could de-stabilise the specific sense of time in a photograph. It could, as in Robert Macpherson's photographs of Rome, give the enduring classical ruins for solitary reflection; in Annan's photographs of the slums, it could suggest the threat to life there.

Long exposures enabled the study of architecture, clearing the view of traffic, and the movement of light illuminated details of the buildings [Fig. 8.8]. The Englishman, J. W. G. Gutch, who visited Rosslyn Chapel in 1857, did not photograph the interior: 'the very yellow light of the old glass not promising any possibility of success, though the architecture is strikingly beautiful.'[39] A year later, Alexander Young Herries took this interior with a two and a half hour exposure.[40] The length of time can be seen in the sun's movement, shining through the left window, temporarily blocked by the stonework and then illuminating at a new

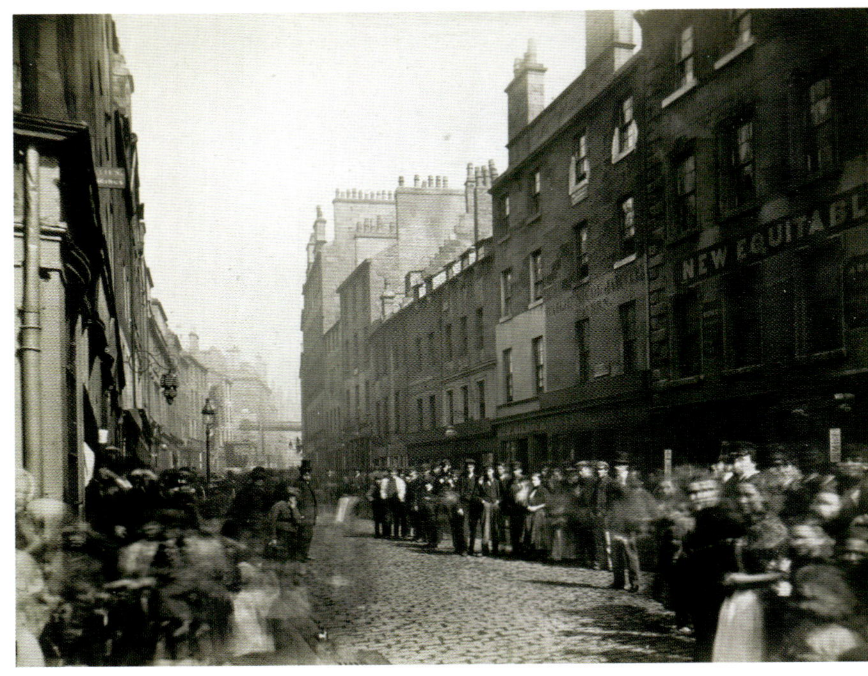

Fig. 8.7 (right): Thomas Annan, 'Saltmarket from Bridgegate, Glasgow', 1868–71, albumen print. (Canadian Centre for Architecture, PH1980:0358:019)

Fig. 8.8 (opposite left): W. D. Clark, 'Princes Street, Edinburgh', 1858, albumen print. (Riddell Collection, Scottish National Portrait Gallery, PGP R 124)

Fig. 8.9 (opposite right): Alexander Young Herries, 'Roslin Chapel', c.1858, albumen print made by John Macgregor, from a waxed paper negative. (Edinburgh Exchange Photographic Club Album, National Media Museum / Science & Society Picture Library, 1990-5131_1_14)

angle from the right [Fig. 8.9]. This, it should be remembered, would have been unacceptable in a painting, which was expected to maintain a fiction of one time of day and one angle of dominant light. Long exposures, and especially the exaggerated, day-long versions, might be defined as aberrations. But however long the exposure, the photograph framed action, life and light. It may be outside our natural experience, but it shows us things that we, tied to our own instant of time, do not see.

In his 1843 article, Hugh Miller assumed that photography would reveal the correct delineation of perspective. One of the strangest things photography 'proved' was that large objects at a distance, such as mountains, appeared unexpectedly small. The painter drew not what the eye saw, but what the mind knew was there, enlarging important aspects of a landscape to achieve that effect. Here, the camera lens necessarily repeated the uncorrected 'error' of the eye, and was generally thought to be wrong. Photographers were caught by such assumptions: for example, while convention in drawing required linear perspective on the flat to show steadily receding lines, vertical perspective was corrected – the upward lines of buildings seen from the

ground were normally shown as parallel. As we have seen, the architect C. G. S. Kinnear devised a camera with a rising back to take photographs to achieve this.

The question of colour balance, especially in copying green, remained a difficulty. In the Scottish landscape this was a perpetual problem. Landscape may seem an unmoving subject, but the wind moves leaves and branches, ruffles water, brings in clouds and fog, and drives in rain. The difference in light levels between the sky and the land meant that capturing the clouds was a difficulty. Photographing trees successfully required long exposure; finding a day with no perceptible breeze was often impractical.[41]

Improved capacity for detail in the 1850s made the photograph's aberrant response more obvious. In 1857, Lady Eastlake wrote:

Far from holding up the mirror to nature, which is an assertion usually as triumphant as it is erroneous, it holds up that which, however beautiful, ingenious, and valuable in powers of reflection, is yet subject to certain distortions and deficiencies for which there is no remedy. The science therefore which has developed the resources

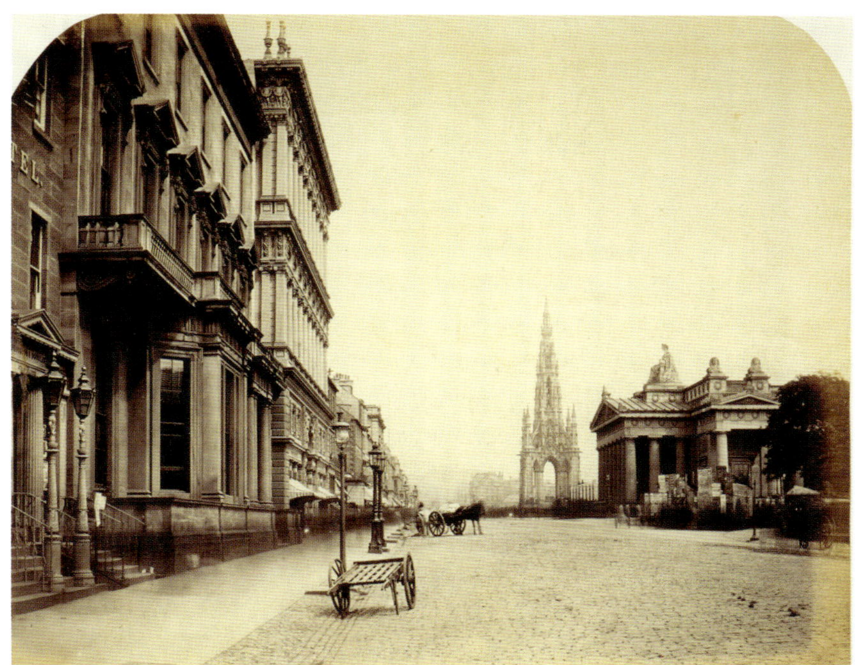

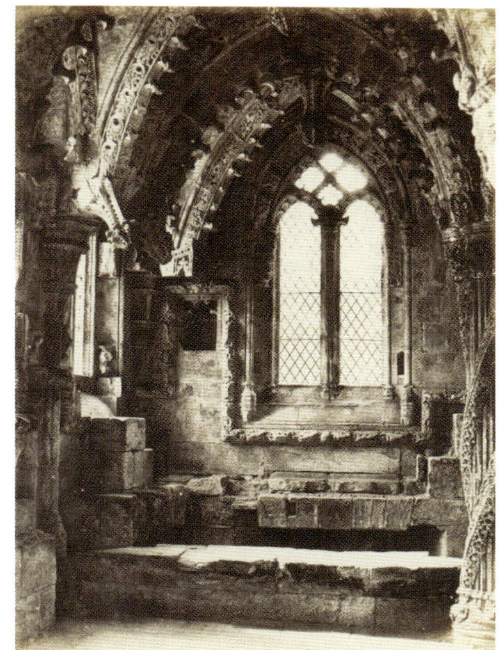

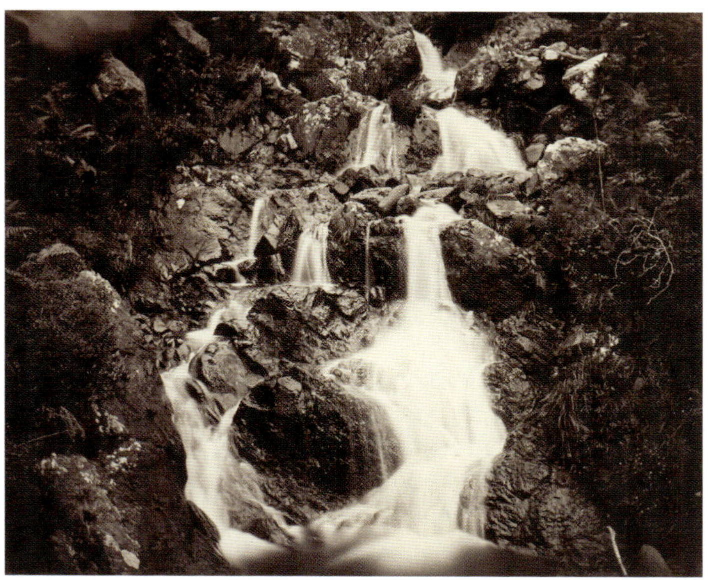

Fig. 8.10: Rev. D. T. K. Drummond, 'Near Loch Earn, Perthshire', *c.*1863. (Wilson Centre for Photography, 84:0656)

of photography, has but more glaringly betrayed its defects.[42]

Nevertheless, there were many beautiful photographs taken under these challenging conditions. A considered and responsive approach enabled a photographic aesthetic. G. W. Wilson's stereo landscapes may relate to an older model of the picturesque, but they were remodelled in three dimensions. The practice of the skilled amateur, the Rev. David Thomas Kerr Drummond (1799–1888), is a further case in point.[43] He used the malt process, a variant of dry plate, which enabled him to process his glass negatives up to ten days before using them, and he found it admirable for architecture and landscape:

> … the malt film has a delicacy of definition peculiar to itself …. A negative which in other processes would be set aside as most unlikely to give anything but a chill print, will in the malt give brilliant pictures.
>
> The advantages of this property are obvious. It makes the development more simple, and a failure less probable, while even in dull weather, prints may be

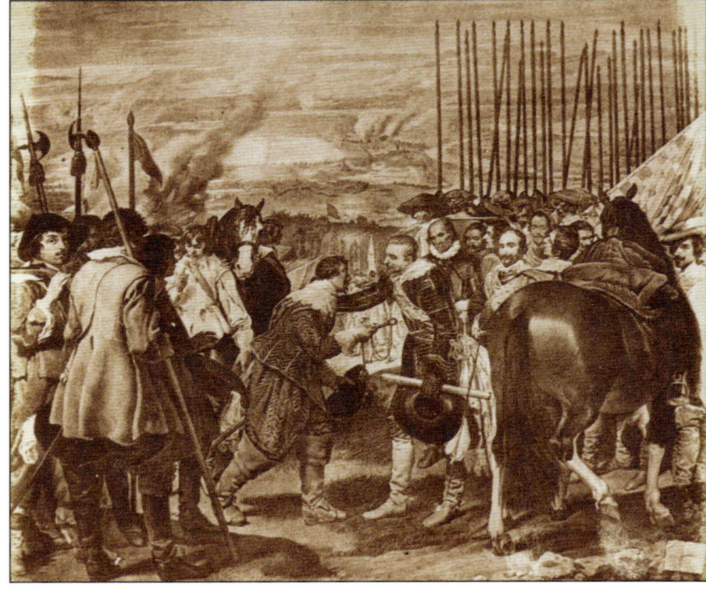

taken from the negative in a wonderfully short time. From about twenty minutes to half an hour is the longest exposure I have ever given, even in very dull weather, to a print under a malt negative.[44]

He was a friend of the botanist John Hutton Balfour, and accompanied him into the Highlands where he took photographs of plants and the landscape of a rich, dark density [FIG. 8.10]. Such strategies enabled landscape photographers to challenge the supremacy of the painters by expressing a distinct rather than imitative aesthetic.

Reproducing and cataloguing art

The original intention behind photography was substantially that it should be a method of reproduction. John Eagles's account in 1839 emphasised that idea in his assumption that the various arts of engraving would be eliminated by the invention. Photography laboured to fulfill that expectation.

In 1848, Sir William Stirling Maxwell of Keir (1818–78) published his ground-breaking history of Spanish art, *Annals of the Artists of Spain*. Here he described the painting 'Las Meninas' as Velásquez's masterpiece: a painting about painting, with the artist and his easel in the picture, Rubens's pictures on the wall and, remarkably, the King and Queen of Spain outside the frame, behind the viewer and only seen in a mirror: 'The perfection of art which conceals art was never better attained than in this picture. Velasquez seems to have anticipated the discovery of Daguerre, and taking a real room and real chance-grouped people, to have fixed them, as it were by magic, for all time on his canvass.'[45]

Stirling Maxwell was assigning a role to photography that it was scarcely capable of at this juncture; it is more than interesting that he read the painting as 'photographic' in our modern sense – partial, immediate and contrary to the formal rules of painting. While preparing his book, Stirling Maxwell decided to publish a supplement with photographs taken from engravings.[46] Hill and Adamson made some of the photographic prints – probably a whole set from 'The Surrender of Breda' [FIG. 8.11] – but Adamson's recurring illness in 1847 stopped the work. The supplement then appeared solely with photographs taken by Nicholaas Henneman at Talbot's Reading establishment.

Photography was an obvious answer to copying artworks – in theory – but there was the immediate problem of colour imbalance; the monochrome reproduction was skewed. So the copying of paintings was only sporadically undertaken, until Thomas Annan took an interest during the 1860s. The Art Unions which promoted Scottish art worked by subscription. Each subscriber was given a fine engraving, along with the chance of winning a painting from the Academies' annual exhibitions. In 1862, the Glasgow Art Union decided to offer three photographs rather than one engraving. They commissioned Annan to photograph work by three painters, J. E. Millais, Joseph Noel Paton and

James Sant.[47] Annan's expertise was remarkable and well-rewarded. The art lotteries were international in their reach, and in 1862 the Glasgow Art Union's profits were hit by the American Civil War. Nevertheless, 3666 people subscribed a guinea, raising the sum of £3849 6s; Thomas Annan printed 10,998 photographs and received £1150 in payment.[48] The reviews were triumphant. The editor of the *Photographic News* wrote:

> … better reproduction, we believe, is impossible to obtain. That of Sant's picture is, perhaps, the most perfect reproduction from a painting we have ever seen, and is so perfect as to have elicited the remark from several clever photographers to whom we have shown it, that the painting must have been painted with a view to the reproduction. It is wonderfully brilliant and yet soft and detailed, rich, deep and transparent in the shadows, without the slightest loss of those delicate greys and demi-tints, upon which perfect modeling, and roundness, and finish, so much depend .... Mr Annan has favoured us with a few particulars of his operations in reproduction, which may interest our readers. The lens was a Dallmeyer's triple achromatic, with an equivalent focus of about thirty inches. In this instance a very small stop could not be used, on account of the loss of light it involved, as the paintings were only about one-third larger than the photograph, and required an extension of the camera to about four feet. A good commercial collodion, bromo-iodized we believe: a strong iron developer with as little acid as possible, and further intensification with pyrogallic acid and silver.[49]

This account does not explain Annan's success; on the contrary, he seems to have compounded his difficulties. His collodion plates were only light sensitive to blue and ultra-violet – both red and green would read as black. The camera extension of four feet would have reduced the density of the light and quadrupled the exposure time, and if he had filtered out the light sensitive blue areas, then the exposure times would have been further increased, possibly to the point where photography failed to work at all. What he may have done to balance the colour remains mysterious.[50]

Annan had not cracked the problem of colour for his professional colleagues. The painter and photographer Norman Macbeth (1821–88) spoke to the Edinburgh Photographic Society five years later and provided a list of colours which developed 'true' and 'untrue'. In the following discussion, James Good Tunny said:

> He had done a great deal in copying, and could say that the difficulties were much greater than anyone who had never tried it could anticipate … [encountering the] evil of different impressibility of the colours, especially the yellows. This he had sometimes helped considerably by dusting them over with colour in powder, such as cobalt blue.[51]

D. O. Hill was responsible for Annan's most demanding art commission [Fig. 8.12]. In 1865, Hill finally finished the painting of the founding of the Free Church, which he had started in 1843 with the help of photography. The picture was nearly twelve feet long, and Hill wanted thousands of copies. Annan first solicited the loan of John Kibble's big camera, and wrote to Hill with his terms for two sizes of print. Characteristically, Hill persuaded Annan to make three sizes – the largest, half the size of the painting and

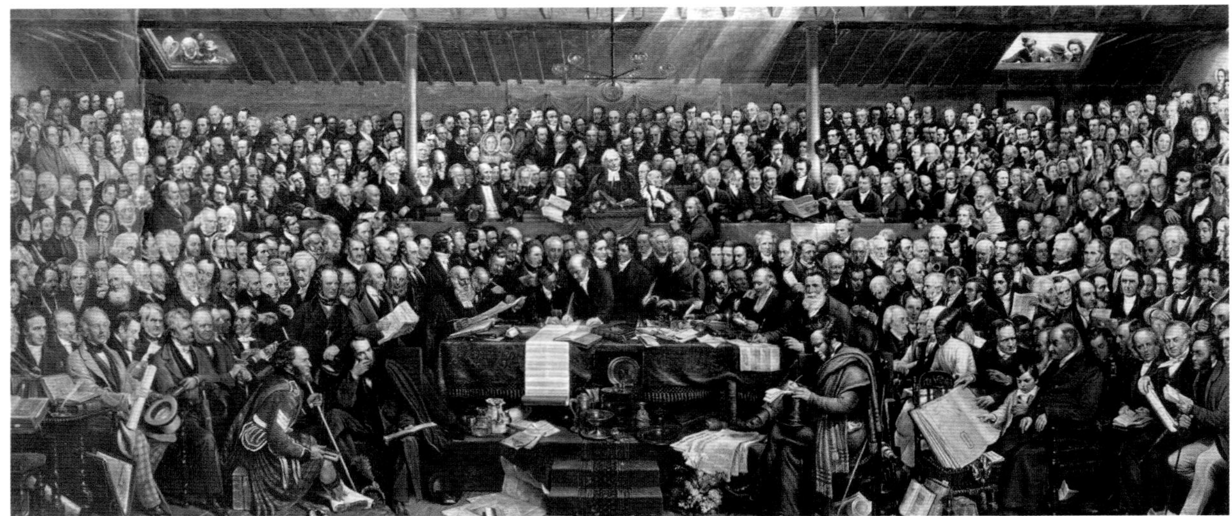

printed in three sections, with the joins carefully cut around the figures. Annan then commissioned from Dallmeyer 'a large Photographic Camera of the latest and most perfect construction'.[52] They decided to print the photographs in the carbon process, which answered the current anxiety about the tendency of silver-based photographs to fade. The carbon image was made in a transparent gelatine relief, hardening at different depths depending on the intensity of the light; the picture was made visible by adding a stable colouring, generally in warm brown or black. Annan negotiated with Joseph Wilson Swan in Newcastle to make the prints. The final work was applauded in the *Photographic News* in June 1866:

> … photography is applied on a more extensive scale for this purpose than on any previous occasion … the picture will become historical … as the first large issue, consisting of photographs of the largest size, ever produced by carbon printing.[53]

Process had been extensively explored in Scotland, by William Blair in Perth, amongst others, and Swan's patents were strongly opposed. Annan, however, recognised the practicality of Swan's method, and took out the rights for Scotland in 1866. He sold or extended these to other photographers, including Thomas Rodger.

Annan 'loved the society of artists, and was never so happy as when endeavouring to faithfully-translate some masterpiece into monochrome through the medium of his camera'.[54] He used the carbon process for publishing books on Scottish art and architecture: *The painted windows of Glasgow Cathedral* (1867), *Illustrated catalogue of the exhibition of portraits on loan in the new Galleries of Art* [in Glasgow](1868), *Selections from the works of Sir George Harvey* (1869) and *The Old Country Houses of the Old Glasgow Gentry* (2nd edition, 1870), with the *Works of Horatio McCulloch* (1872).[55] Regrettably his book on photography, with carbon prints from Hill and Adamson's photographs, was delayed beyond reason by the Edinburgh publisher and not issued until 1928. This, Annan's visual tribute to Hill, and to Hill and Adamson's work, should have been the first ever photographic monograph.[56] However, in the work that he did publish, Annan may well be said to have laid foundations for the study of historic and modern Scottish art.

There is a further, inclusive, story bringing together several threads in this history. An exhibition was held to mark the centenary of Sir Walter Scott's birth in 1871.[57] The organising committee included Sir William Stirling Maxwell, and the history painter, James Drummond. The exhibition of more than six hundred items from 162 lenders was staged within three months; it is thus not

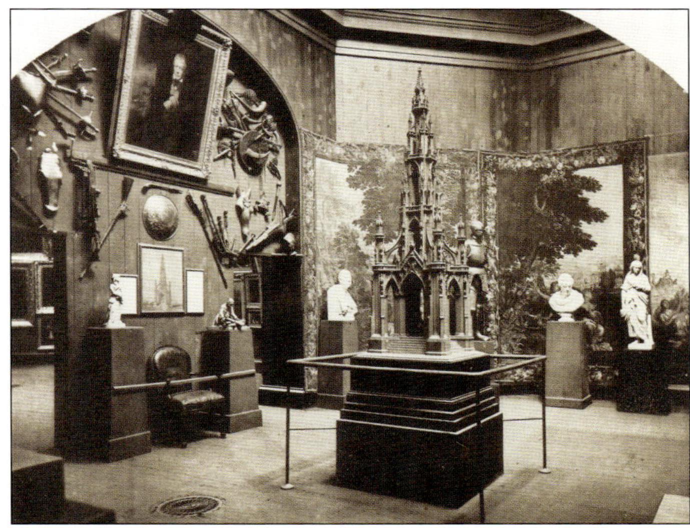

surprising that the catalogues 'were not what the Committee would have wished them to be'.[58] The committee therefore co-opted the exhibition's profit to reprint the catalogue with photo-engravings from the paintings and the manuscripts made by Alexander McGlashon. Stirling Maxwell, Drummond and the antiquary David Laing wrote detailed catalogue entries for the artwork.

Drummond worked with McGlashon to ensure the quality of the prints, and they were issued 'without any attempt to improve them by subsequent touching up of the plates, and thus transmitting the features and expression as given by the pictures, in a way which no engraving could pretend'. In all senses, it was a splendidly professional catalogue [Fig. 8.13].

Ultimately, the illustrations were made by 'a new Process of Photo-Lithography, called Albert-type'.[59] The *British Journal of Photography* observed the work in progress at McGlashon's workshop:

> The Editors, in their notices of visits to various places during the meeting of the British Association in Edinburgh [in August 1871], told us that Mr McGlashon had added 'lichtdruck' to the other departments of his business, and that, although he was doing some good work, he found it difficult to get the necessary kind of men to permit its being carried on as extensively as he wished. That difficulty seems now to be overcome. I saw two presses busy at work turning out prints of great excellence.[60]

'Lichtdruck' was the collotype process patented in France in 1855 and recently perfected by Josef Albert in Munich. It was based on bichromated gelatine, the silver-free substance advocated by Mungo Ponton in 1839, which was spread on plate glass and dried in heat so that it crazed or wrinkled. The edge of the gelatine was more sensitive to light than the sides, which allowed for differential hardening when it was exposed to light under a negative. The dry areas accepted printing ink more readily than the moist. It did not require to be etched and could be printed directly. It was the first printing process to achieve the continuous and dense tones of photography. While the collotype needed careful handling, McGlashon, who had begun with engraving daguerreotypes of George Skene Keith's images of the Holy Land, had at last achieved a fine photographic method of printing.

Natural history

Scotland was the scene of major discoveries in geology, and the first scientific photographs taken from fossils were shown at the British Association meeting in Glasgow in autumn 1840. During the meeting, Sir Roderick Murchison paid tribute to the geological researches of Hugh Miller, and particularly to his investigation of the Old Red Sandstone.[61] The meeting examined fossil fish Miller had originally found near Forres, including one named after him, *Pterischthys Milleri*.[62] The delegates were also able to see

Fig. 8.14 (right): D. O. Hill and Robert Adamson, fossil 'Stagonolepis', 1844, calotype. (Scottish National Portrait Gallery, PGP HA 4471)

Fig. 8.15 (below): Jemima Blackburn, 'A court of owls', from *Illustrations from Scripture by an animal painter*, pl. 13, albumen print from a drawing, published in 1854–55. (Howarth-Loomes Collection at National Museums Scotland, IL.2003.44. 9.299)

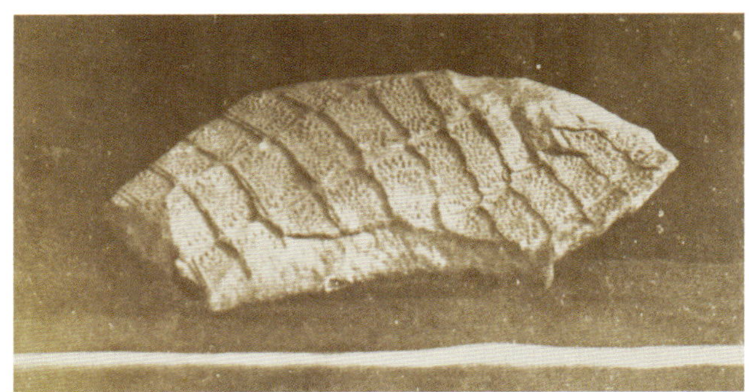

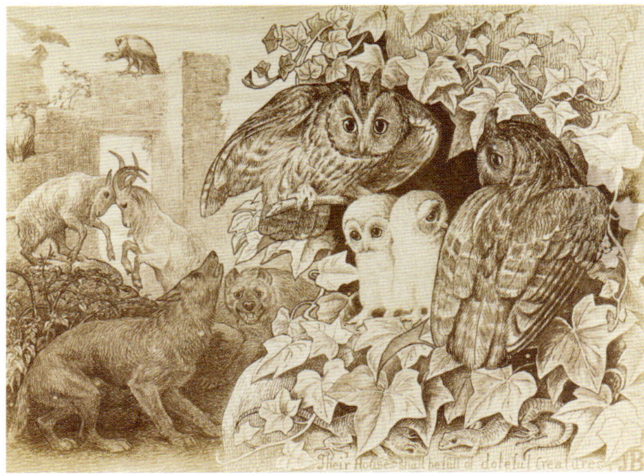

'some of Mr Ibbetson's admirable daguerreotype copies' of the fossils. Ibbetson himself gave a paper, reporting on his success in taking magnified daguerreotypes of fossils [with the 'oxy-hydrogen microscope'].

Miller told the story of a significant fossil fragment, named 'Stagonolepis', which was brought to Patrick Duff, the Town Clerk of Elgin and an interested collector, by a builder of dry-stane walls, or dykes:

> In breaking open a building stone, the diker had found the inside of it … covered over with curiously carved flowers …. The supposed flowers are the sculpturings on the scales of the ichthyolite … the sole representative of an extinct genus …. An Elgin gentleman forwarded to [the expert, Louis Agassiz in] Neufchatel a singularly fine calotype of the fossil, taken by Mr Adamson of Edinburgh, with a full-sized drawing of one of the scales; and from the calotype and the drawing the naturalist has decided that the genus is entirely new ….[63]

The study of fossils was still new and highly-complicated – the 'Stagonolepis' fragment [FIG. 8.14], thought at first to be part of a fish, was later re-identified as part of a reptile. However, the sequence of discovery and expert identification at a distance offered a model of the potential advantage in the use of photography.

One of the earliest publications connected to wildlife and printed photographically was an experiment by Jemima and Hugh Blackburn, assisted by Allan Maconochie in Glasgow.[64] Hugh Blackburn (1823–1909) was Professor of Mathematics at the University. His wife Jemima Blackburn (1823–1909) was an accomplished draughtswoman and a naturalist. She combined these two interests in illustra-

ting a children's book, *The History of Little Downy*,[65] which was sold for the benefit of the Glasgow Ragged School in 1853. Hugh Blackburn sent a copy to the editor of *Notes and Queries*, with a covering explanation. The illustrations used three different methods: two based on the idea of *cliché verre*, being used by Corot and Millet about this time, and the third, straightforward printing from a paper negative – 'a method much more troublesome and tedious than either of the others'.[66] It is characteristic of the explorations of the Blackburns that Hugh photographed her, with her cockatoo on her wrist, and she then painted the scene of him taking the photograph.

In 1854, the Blackburns undertook a second publication with photographs of twenty animal drawings: *Illustrations from Scripture* [FIG. 8.15].[67] These are straightforward albumen prints, printed from glass negatives. W. M. Thackeray thought the book was expensive ('the dreadful fee of two guineas will operate as a barrier between you

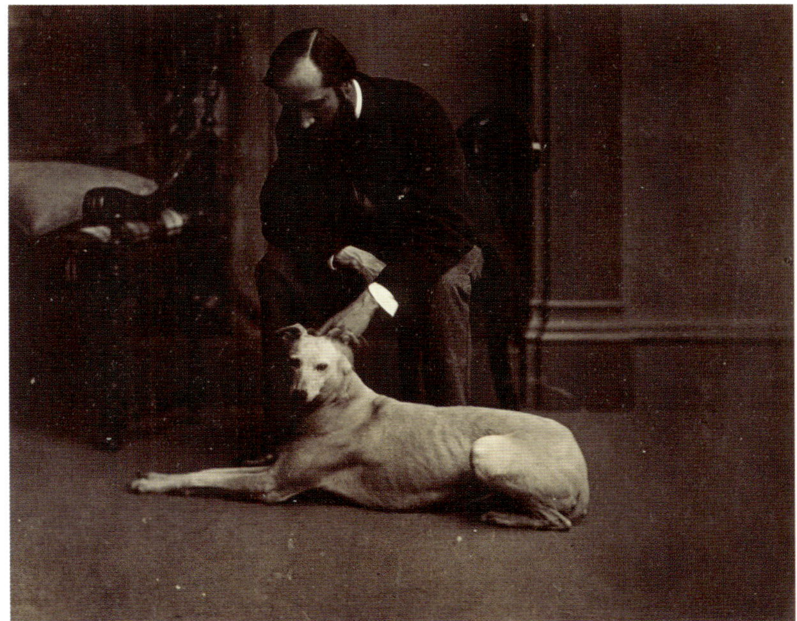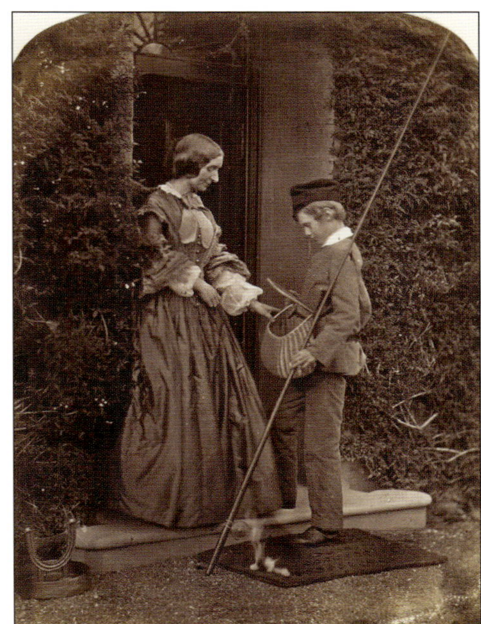

and popularity'), but the sets sold, and went into a second edition.[68]

The Blackburns were an energetic and original pair. Jemima was well-connected; her circle included the Duke of Wellington, her cousin James Clerk Maxwell, Edwin Landseer, John Ruskin, Lady Eastlake and Beatrix Potter (who apparently named Jemima Puddle-Duck in her honour). Her observation resulted in original paintings of animals and birds, and at least one extraordinary discovery: the way a fledgling cuckoo pushes the offspring of the parent birds out of the nest, which she illustrated in her *Birds Drawn from Nature* (1862).

It might be thought that Jemima, who took pride in painting from nature rather than working from the dead animals still used by illustrators, would employ photography extensively. Writing the captions for her book, *Birds from Moidart and Elsewhere*, published in 1895, she explained. Her 'Cormorant' was 'drawn from life in the zoological gardens. A gentleman was trying at the time to photograph them, but they fidgeted too much. It was before the Kodak had come into use. So my drawing was made use of at a meeting of the Zoological Society'.[69] It is a useful reminder that photography never wholly replaced expert

draughtsmanship in studies that required recollection to contribute to the record.

Photographing animals was indeed remarkably difficult. Dr John Adamson, who took an anatomical interest and was responsible for the St Andrews museum in the 1840s, produced calotypes of animal skeletons and prepared specimens. With the faster collodion process, he took live animals. His greyhound Blanche was evidently well-trained to stay still despite her great energy, which may be seen at least in her flickering ears [FIG. 8.16]. His cat, predictably, was rather less amenable. It turned up for the photograph Adamson staged of his nephew returning from fishing [FIG. 8.17], but, bored by the inaction and lack of fish, it wandered off, leaving its cynical trace on the photograph.

The photography of prized animals was assisted by grooms or shepherds, holding the animals still, but the same experts were specific in the picture they wanted to see – like the breeding itself, it required the display of the admired

Fig. 8.16 (left): John Adamson, 'John Adamson's dog, Blanche, with Dr Oswald Home Bell', *c.*1855, albumen print. (Scottish National Portrait Gallery, PGP 178.26)

Fig. 8.17 (right): John Adamson, 'Home from the Burn', *c.*1860, albumen print. (National Museums Scotland, T.1942.1.1.225)

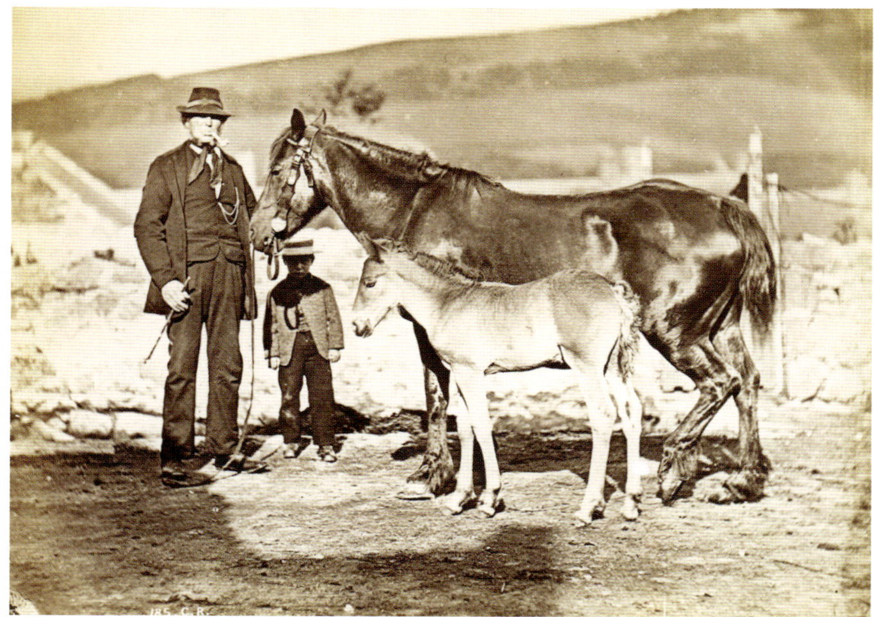

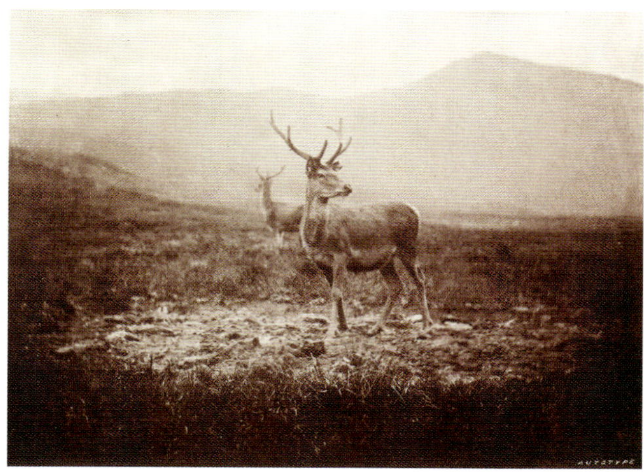

shy subjects have to be allowed sufficient time – perhaps necessitating repeated visits – for them to get familiar with the camera.[70]

His photograph of a pony and foal, with a man and boy in charge, is a perfect balance of human and animal photography – the wide-eyed boy looking out from the shelter of both horse and man [Fig. 8.18].

The photography of wild animals was proportionately difficult and not necessarily helped by advancing technology. Reid and his sons took animal photographs well into the 20th century and still found that deer, startled by the sound, could not be taken by a camera with an instantaneous shutter.[71]

Many of the photographs exhibited by Horatio Ross were concerned with shooting deer; he, his wife and sons were all skilled stalkers. The same skill enabled them to take the photographs of living deer in the wild [Fig. 8.19]. Aged 79, he debated publishing a book showing 'living red deer taken on their "native heath"', with the publisher, William Blackwood'.[72] He added that he had an immense number of negatives, with '… upwards of 300 negatives of living deer & more than 200 of dead ones'.[73]

points of the animal. A certain calm confidence in approach was invaluable, and was a rare professional talent. Charles Reid (1837–1929), based in Wishaw, devoted much of his career to photographing animals, both for farmers and for artists looking for animal studies. He commented:

> … without a lively sympathy with the lower creation no one need approach its members with a camera …. Beasts of a timid disposition must be gently dealt with, the unruly need to be cowed, the slovenly must be roused,

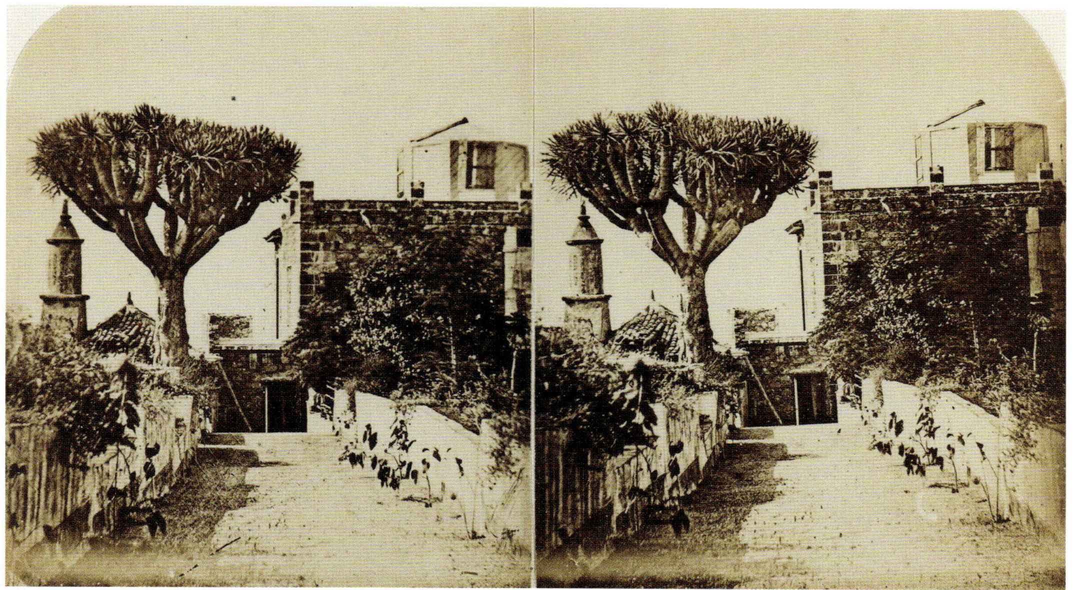

The Rosses can be regarded as among the earliest photographers of wildlife, and under particularly awkward circumstances. Their pony was loaded with equipment and indicates the difficulties in a landscape without roads or even necessarily shelter. They needed the skill developed for hunting the animals to take the photographs; knowing the behaviour of the animals; understanding the impact of the wind and weather; able to approach over open terrain, without being observed. Ross commented:

> As a rule, three or four times as many stalks are spoiled from deer getting the wind of a stalker, as from seeing him. I have sometimes, during the sixty years I have been a stalker, tried experiments as to the power of a deer's sense of smell, and I am sure that I have started them, when there was a pretty strong wind, at the distance of three-quarters of a mile.[74]

The inherent difficulties in approaching close and in taking the photographs without disturbing the animals were in themselves impressive. Ross's claim to priority in taking such photographs in the wild is probably true.

Botany and photogravure

The objective delineation of photography was of importance in copying exotic specimens, because illustrators and their engravers tended to improve or alter what they produced. The test case here was the dragon tree of the Canary Islands. When C. Piazzi Smyth and his wife travelled to Tenerife in 1855, Sir John Herschel recommended that 'he should be provided with apparatus for obtaining photographic impressions of everything worthy of record, *inter alia*, the great Dragon Tree of Orotava (supposed to be the oldest tree in the world)'.[75]

On the Smyths' return to Edinburgh, the professional photographer, André Orange, made transparencies from their photographs. Smyth then gave a talk to the Botanical Society of Edinburgh on the plants of Tenerife, 'optically projected on a screen eight feet square'.[76] In 1858, he spoke to the Royal Scottish Society of Arts, and projected images nine feet square. Smyth discussed the dragon tree [FIG. 8.20] scientifically, challenging the conclusions of such authorities as Baron Humboldt, but he went beyond this. Thanks to a sequence of re-drawn illustrations in authoritative volumes, the tree's natural appearance was unexpected.[77] He wrote:

[Photographs] show the immense debt which the scientific world owes to the inventors of photography … for induction from the facts clearly demonstrates, that even in the simplest feature, man following his fellow-man, diverges inevitably at every step further and further from truth as it is in nature.[78]

In his own photography, Smyth sought precision and the ability to multiply images in serious numbers – necessary for the common experience of data that would enable intelligent progress. He was severely disappointed that the official documentation of his Tenerife survey ignored the many pictures he and his wife produced. Smyth published a popular version of the text as *Teneriffe, An Astronomer's Experiment: or Specialities of a Residence above the Clouds*. This was produced in an edition of two thousand, with twenty stereo photographs, the first book to be so illustrated.[79] The official report to the Admiralty was illustrated with only two photographs, 350 of each printed by Jessica Smyth 'in the course of a very short space of time':

> Duly bearing in mind the burst of enthusiasm with which the birth of photography was hailed by all scientific men, and the prophetic descriptions that were indulged in by the venerable Arago, and a circle of the philosophers of the time … some disappointment must be felt on looking round now; and finding how little has been brought to pass.[80]

The popular book was illustrated with stereo photographs, because the London publisher, Lovell Reeve, wished to address a fashionable market. Reeve was excited by the technological novelty; Smyth wanted scientific illustration.

Smyth also used the dragon tree photograph for a trial of photo-engraving. His lecture to the Botanical Society was to be published and he wrote to the Edinburgh Professor of Botany, John Hutton Balfour, Secretary of the Society, in 1859, to prompt his interest. He suggested that W. H. F. Talbot, who was in Edinburgh for the winter, might make a specimen plate in his 'photoglyphic' process for the Journal, and added that 'the Dragon will never be "laid" until photography is employed in taking his portrait, and printing it in books'.[81]

Talbot and his family spent some time in Scotland in the 1850s and 1860s. The University of Edinburgh awarded him an Honorary Doctorate and the Photographic Society of Scotland presented him with a gold medal for his developments in photography.[82] He also donated photographic engravings to the Photographic Society of Scotland and the Botanical Society of Edinburgh.[83] Talbot explained the process in an article illustrated by the photoglyph of a fern. This too harked back to Mungo Ponton's 1839 proposal:

> [It] consists in covering a plate of steel or copper with a film of gelatine mixed with bichromate of potash, placing the object, in this instance a fern leaf, upon the plate, and exposing it to sunlight for a minute, then removing the object, dusting the plate with finely powdered resin, to give a grain to the engraving, melting the resin, and when the plate is cold brushing it with a camel's-hair brush dipped in perchloride of iron, which speedily penetrates the parts upon which the light has not acted, and effects an etching, while the parts exposed to sunshine are thereby rendered impermeable to the etching liquid. Such a plate (steel), thus prepared, is capable of yielding at least five thousand impressions …. one of

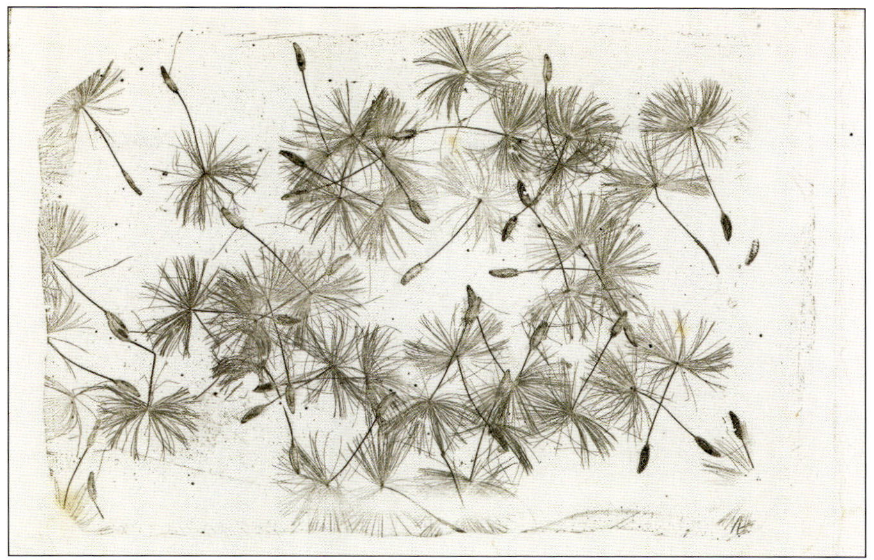

the most curious objects when engraved is the feathery achenes of *Leontodon Taraxacum* (the common dandelion) [FIG. 8.21], which are so well given as sometimes to be almost deceptive .... I wished to have shown a plate of this description to the Botanical Society, but the occurrence of cloudy weather for several days in succession has prevented my doing so on the present occasion.[84]

Talbot was working with Piazzi Smyth on a plate for the government publication on Tenerife. Frustratingly, the Edinburgh engraver, Mr Banks, found the plate of Guajara failing after a hundred prints. Smyth wrote from Edinburgh in July 1863:

I have been to see a Mr Thomas Dick in the old town, a poor, frail old body but an interesting sort of a genius of a man, who engraves, multiplies engraved plates by the electrotype, and sometimes coats them with steel by the same process. So as soon as the next Guajara plate has been proved, lettered, & prepared for printing, I propose to let Mr Dick try if he can put on so thin a coating of steel that Mr Banks shall not complain the engraving is filled up, while the surface shall be so improved in hardness as to bear 400 copies being pulled off without any sensible loss of quality below the first 100.[85]

Talbot thought that the first photoglyph was imperfect because Smyth's photograph was not good. The second, of the fern, was made from a dried specimen and did not show the plant's veins. A desire to show the Society how delightful dandelion seeds were when engraved this way was frustrated by cloudy weather.

With the questionable assistance and encouragement of the Scottish enthusiasts, Talbot was still working on his photo-engraving process after more than ten years.[86] In 1863, he showed photoglyphs in Edinburgh, including one of that risky subject, David Brewster. This was critically approved, but only in part. John Traill Taylor, a man of acerbic disposition, wrote of meeting Talbot in 1863:

In a manner we thought decidedly 'snappish' – and that at our first interview with him – Mr Talbot almost *demanded* our opinion of a photoglyphic portrait of Sir David Brewster he had recently executed, inquiring whether we had ever seen anything finer. We had, many times. 'Do you know,' he almost thundered, 'that Sir David Brewster, Mr Cosmo Innes, and numerous other men capable of judging, have pronounced that to be the very finest engraving I have ever produced?' We replied that we did not care what were the opinions of these men – the picture was not the best that he had produced;

not only so, but it was very, very far from being equal to others of his pictures – that in point of fact it was the worst photoglyph we had ever seen, scarcely reflecting credit upon the advance he had already made. He stared for a moment, as if totally unaccustomed to have his works criticised in such a rough fashion, and, after a few words, he explained that his own opinion entirely coincided with ours; the picture, in *his* estimation, was a very poor one, but we had been the first to have the honesty to say so to his face. And thus was the ice broken.[87]

Traill Taylor was right. Photoglyphic engraving was still not able to accommodate tones and gradations of colour and light. Talbot's dream of placing text and image on the same page had to wait for future developments.

Crime and control

The optimistic early predictions for photography voiced in France and Britain proved hard to achieve, encountering difficulties from inadequate materials to a shortage of sophisticated skills in the supporting staff. The experts who attempted to resolve the inherent problems of the medium could find secondary and tertiary snags and dead ends, requiring yet further exploration and action. Aspects of photography, such as studio portraiture, proved enormously successful. Other issues ran into social inertia. Eagles' proposal of the identification of criminals was only made a legal requirement in Britain in 1871. Earlier activity in the field was, here as elsewhere, dependent on individual initiative.

By mid-century, the unprecedented mobility of the British population had generated social dislocation. For the first time, people did not know their neighbours, and the newly-created police forces often found themselves helpless to identify criminals. 'It frequently happens,' wrote a *Glasgow Herald* reporter in 1854, 'that people, on lodging a complaint of having been robbed in the closes and stair-foots, state that they think they would know the men or women … "if they saw them;" but they cannot give such a description as would put the police on their track'. This statement comes within the report of an attempted theft:

A few days ago, a daguerreotype artist discovered one of those prowling little female pests, of whom we have so many, stealing his gas-pipes. He immediately took the girl into his studio, planted her on a chair, and under the threat of instant annihilation if she stirred, 'took her picture,' when he afterwards sent both original and copy to the Police Office. The portrait is a very strange one, exhibiting pitiable downcast looks, but with a leer of cunning and anger intermixed. … we are glad to learn that it is Captain Smart's intention to daguerreotype all the principal thieves and desperadoes of both sexes with whom this city is infested …. A blackguards' portrait gallery … which Captain Smart contemplates, will freshen the recollection of plundered people, and materially forward the ends of justice.[88]

This article was followed a week later by another news item, under the heading 'The First Police Daguerreotype':

On Saturday, an old man, named Innes Williams, 78 years of age, a native of Wales, was brought before Bailie McGregor, at the Central Police Court, on a charge of

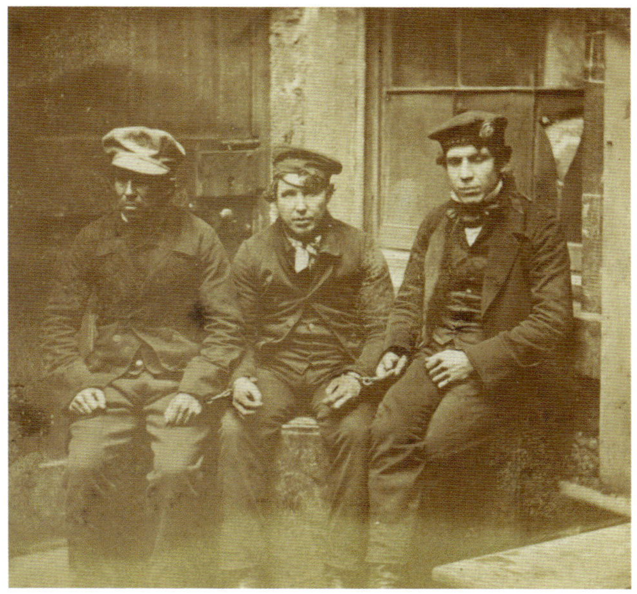

Fig. 8.22: Duncan Brown, 'Two housebreakers and a prison officer', 20 May 1855, albumen print. (Glasgow School of Art, DB_166)

begging. Care was depicted in the old man's countenance; and a silvery beard, which, perhaps for months, had never felt a razor, coupled with possession of a keen eye, ragged clothing, a ponderous wallet, and a sort of knapsack, combined to render him the *beau ideal* of a gaberlunzie man [i.e. licensed beggar]. He had been at Court before; and, on this occasion, on promising to leave town, he got off – not, however, till the artist had transferred his full likeness on glass, in a manner which did him credit. The daguerreotype was used on this occasion to obtain the likeness of a 'character' – not from any suspicion that the old man is likely to do anything in the thieving line.[89]

These two pieces, though appearing in the same newspaper, are distinct in approach and prose style. Possibly the writer could make conventional sense of the portrait of the picturesque vagrant, but was foxed by the picture of the larcenous girl. However, it will be observed that the police interest in photography had netted a young girl and an old man – two easy captures. This attempt to record criminals was, moreover, handicapped by the process. The daguerreotype (or ambrotype) was a single image, not the public method of communication which the police needed. Such photography might be used as a threat, to persuade a wanderer to leave town, but not much more.

The head of the Glasgow police force, Captain James Smart (1804–70), took advantage of photography for a civil case a year later:

Four years ago, when Franconi and his equestrian troupe first visited Glasgow, a young man named Joseph Wilson, relinquished his profession of cloth-lapping, and attached

himself to the staff of Mons. Franconi. Wilson, by good behaviour, secured his master's good opinion, and on the establishment removing from this country to France the young adventurer was included amongst the company.

The story sadly continues that Wilson's father died, leaving his mother destitute. He sent her money from time to time, and also sent her a daguerreotype of himself. By then he was working with a French railway company; but he too fell ill and died. The company had a sick fund and wished to send £10 to his mother, but they could not understand her Glasgow address from the dying man's words. The case was put to Captain Smart and his officers eventually found the widow in one of the wynds. She produced the daguerreotype, which was sent to France and recognised. Joseph Wilson's mother was sent the £10.[90] Without the existence of the photograph, she could never have known of her son's death.

The amateur photographer, Duncan Brown, took a picture of housebreakers in police custody in Glasgow, on 20 May 1855 [Fig. 8.22]. The Government School of Design, where Brown worked, was in Ingram Street, just around the corner from the central police office in Albion Street. Presumably, the police called him in, and the picture may have been taken in the police station yard. In this case, there was a negative and multiple copies could have been made for identification.

In 1856, perhaps as a result of some success attached to Brown's photograph, Captain Smart took direct photographic action:

> On Saturday last the photographs of twenty notorious thieves were taken in the square of the Central Police establishment. The men had been apprehended, not in consequence of being concerned in any robbery or theft, but from being found prowling about the city in suspicious circumstances. By the system now adopted, all suspicious characters although not apprehended for any special offence, will be subjected to the photographic process, and their likenesses preserved. Any person who may have been plundered will, by this means, be enabled to identify any known thief concerned in the robbery by calling at the Police-office. The men whose likenesses were taken sat with great composure, and each was anxious to see if the artist had done him ample justice.[91]

The following is an example of photography being used at this time to establish a man's innocence. Australia had a considerable travelling population – including discharged convicts, the subject of nervous suspicion. The police arrived at John Hunter Kerr's station in Victoria, looking for a murderer. They had the description of a one-eyed man, which resembled a traveller there. Despite the similarity in terms, Kerr felt that this was the wrong man:

> I proposed to take a photograph of his face, and transmit it to the police authorities, keeping him in safe custody during the interval [the traveller and the constables agreed] …. The likenesses, one of his full face, the other a profile, in both of which the unfortunate eye was conspicuously portrayed, were taken and forwarded to the authorities. A few days passed, and we received an intimation that the portraits … were not those of the true offender, who had in the meanwhile been discovered.[92]

The problem of identifying criminals was worse for those policemen who went abroad, who would be strangers in their own jurisdiction. Doubtless as a consequence, one of the earliest uses of photography for police purposes is likely to have taken place in India in 1852 or 1853. Samuel Wauchope (1822–75) went to work in the Bengal Civil Service in 1841. He was responsible for an area to the north of Calcutta, troubled by armed robbers. Wauchope wrote an account of the problem and of an attempt to catch a gang of Dacoits in action in 1850.[93] In the rainy season people took holidays, and the wealthy often travelled hundreds of miles home by river:

> … anchored for the night they would find themselves attacked by a boat load of ruffians who … would beat and otherwise ill use the unhappy travellers, until they disclosed where they had concealed their cash and jewels. It was nearly useless to make any complaint to the local police for the Dakoits have been able in fast boats & in the rainy season when the rivers run like sluices to leave the scene of the robbery many miles behind them before the dawn of day. In scarcely an instance then were the offenders brought to justice & very little was known until a few years ago as to who these Dakoits were.[94]

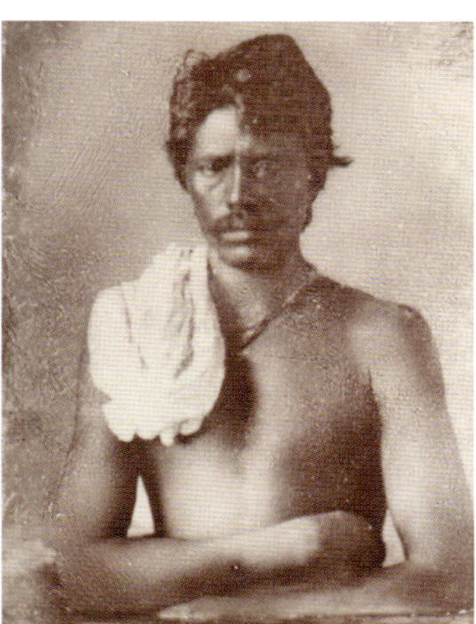 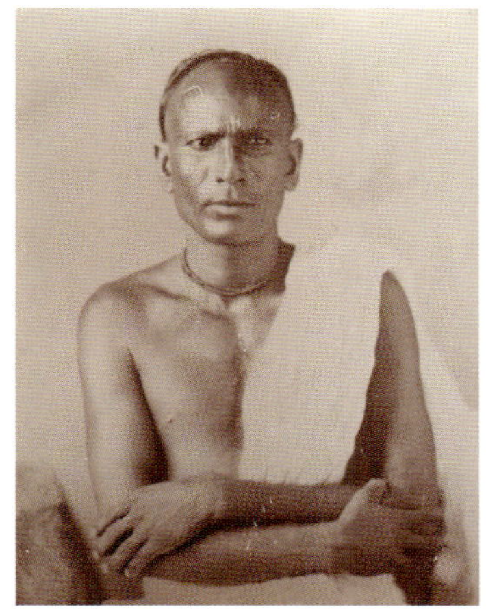 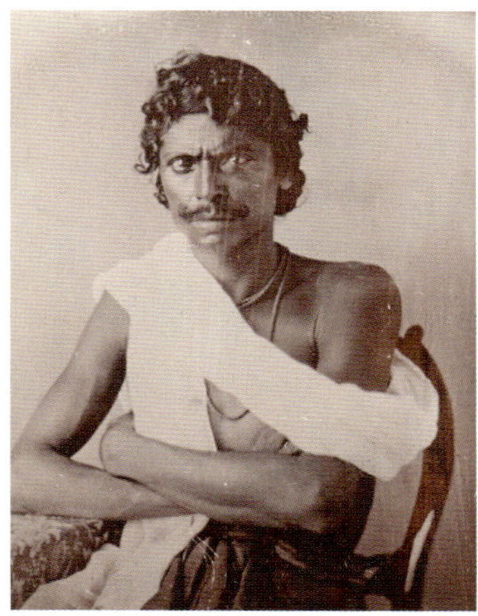 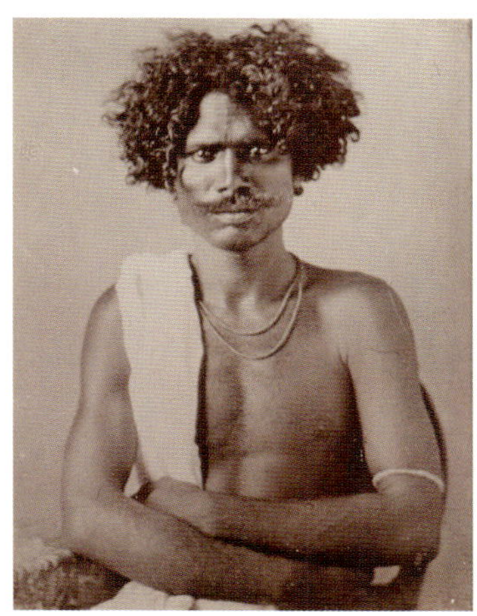

The problem was compounded by the Dacoits intimidating their victims and the gangs' readiness to alibi each other. The legal cases brought against them continually fell apart for lack of evidence.

Wauchope had one advantage: '… a particular facility for recollecting faces once seen.' He discovered the plans for the attack on one particular boat, and he and his men replaced the travelling party. As a consequence, the gang was captured and the ring-leader was convicted and transported. In 1852, Wauchope persuaded the government to give him special powers to engage with the Dacoits.[95] The text of Wauchope's 'adventure with the Bengal Dacoits' is accompanied by seven photographs, and Wauchope described the subjects on their envelopes [FIGS 8.23 a–d]. Three of these men were tried in 1852 and 1853.[96] It is not clear when or why Wauchope took or commissioned the photographs. However, the comments show Wauchope's admiration:

Syndoo Mytee Aged about 38 committed 20 Dacoitees – Carried on a lucrative business of money lending in Calcutta – One of the shrewdest men in this part of the country … Sreenath Dutt alias Cheeroo Kaist – aged about thirty. The most celebrated Dacoit in Bengal – committed about 50 Dacoitees on the river between Calcutta and Dacca in the Soond [illegible] Was never arrested until by me (S.W.) – Always went out on expedition as a respectable Baboo – Is one of the most intelligent energetic & fascinating individuals I ever saw.

Photography would have been very useful to Wauchope, giving him a semblance of control, an objective method of communication. He was promoted to the city of Calcutta as Commissioner of Police and was there during the Indian Mutiny in 1857. Journalist John Kaye wrote admiringly:

… he kept his own counsel, was always cool, never ruffled, reporting what he had to report calmly, and carrying out his orders with tact and discretion …. He was to be seen every morning, riding alone or attended by a police-orderly, in the worst parts of the town, issuing his orders as if no danger were abroad.[97]

Wauchope took photographs in Calcutta, mostly of his colleagues, the British administrators, clerics and soldiers. They are richly-printed images with a good control of light. Amongst them is a relaxed photograph of himself with his two small daughters [FIG. 8.24]. Another group of pictures probably shows the building of sewers in the city; at this period a concern for public health was allocated to the police [FIG. 8.25]. One of these features a group of western engineers and Indian workmen, placed carefully and asked to stand still: both the engineer on the left and the man in the water have fine reflections. Wauchope's album also contains five panoramic photographs from the top of the Ochterlony Monument – the highest structure in Calcutta, and a natural position for photography. One of the photographs from this height shows 'Government House at the

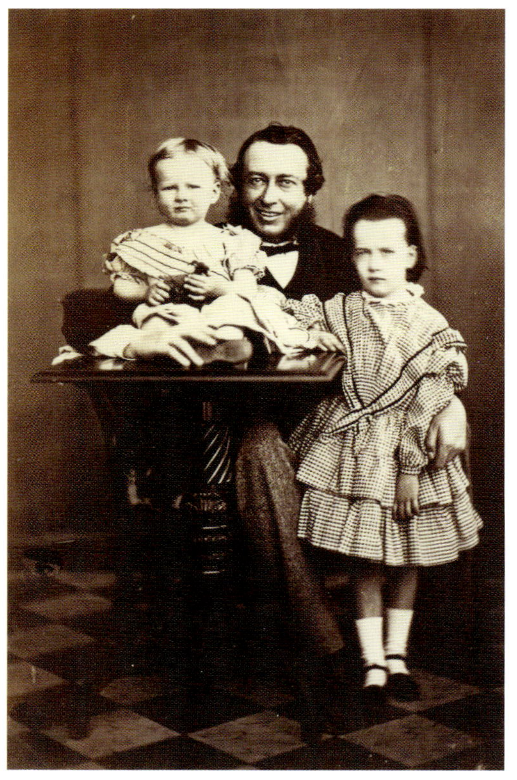

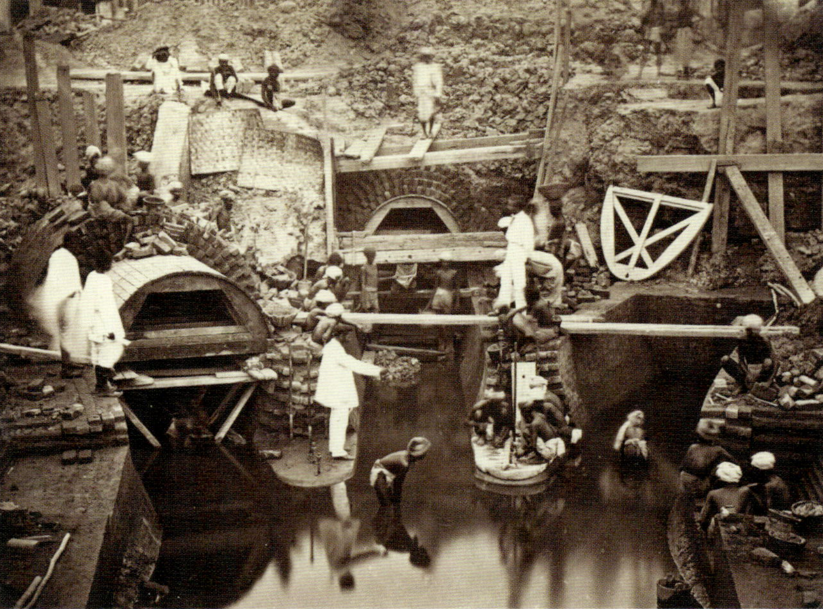

Fig. 8.24 (left): Samuel Wauchope, 'Self portrait with his two daughters, Mary and Helen', *c.*1858, albumen print. (National Library of Scotland, Acc. 10719/121/28)

Fig. 8.25 (above): Samuel Wauchope, 'Building the city sewers, Calcutta', *c.*1858, albumen print. (National Library of Scotland, Acc. 10719/121/18)

Proclamation. 1st November 1858', when the British government formally announced that it was taking control of the subcontinent from the East India Company.

Only in 1871 did British law require the photography of offenders. But by 1866, the photographers were well ahead of that law.[98] According to an article in the *British Quarterly Review*, the gaols took photographs of prisoners if the governors decided to do so. The movement was led in England by J. A. Gardiner, Governor of Bristol gaol. He recommended using photography to identify persistent criminals in a letter to the other governors, because 'the most cunning, the most skilled, and the most daring offenders, are migratory in their habits'.[99] By 1866 Gardiner was accustomed to taking stereoscopic photographs of his prisoners.[100] The gaol in Wick, Caithness, may have followed his recommendation. There is a group of four stereoscopic photographs taken by Alexander Johnston of Wick (*c.*1830–96), apparently in the 1860s, which could be an essay of this kind [FIG. 8.26]. The group includes three men and a boy, and

might be the whole contingent currently within the town's small prison.[101]

The *Review* article commented on Gardiner's photographs: '… there is nothing to suggest the dogged, resisting, vindictive beings, with over-hanging felon brow and sunken cruel eyes, which sensation writers at times attribute to the criminal classes. They are rather examples of God's image degraded and enfeebled by neglect.'[102]

The role of photography in dispelling elementary ideas of the stereotype, and generating a degree of humane sympathy with criminals is an important one. Parliament was keeping a close eye on the prisons at this time.

Photographers might work with the law, but the art of photography proved attractive for many reasons, some dubious. George Mason, the Glasgow photographic supplier, expressed the sudden flood of interest:

A newly discovered gold field could not have called forth more excitement than did photography. Thousands

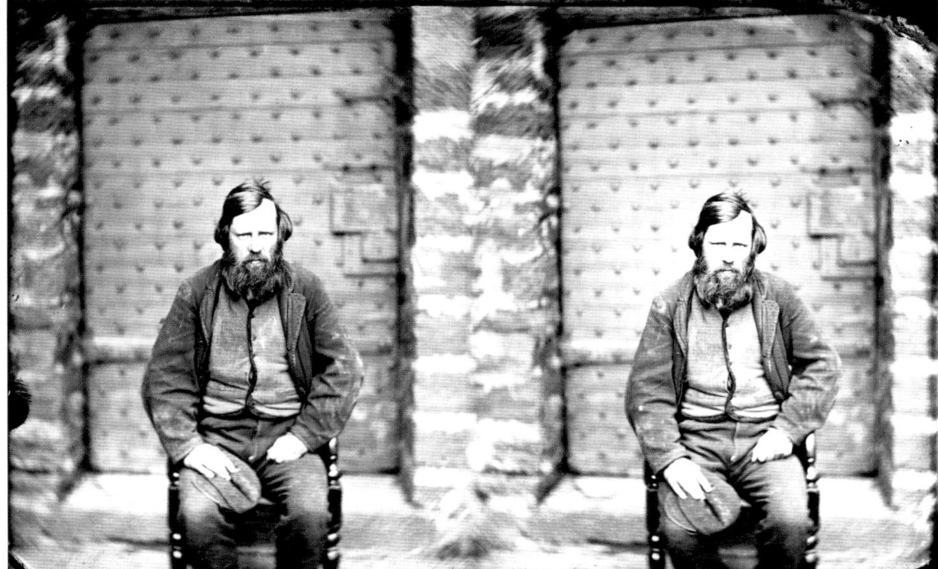

Fig. 8.26: Alexander Johnston, prisoner outside Wick gaol, *c.1865*, modern stereoscopic prints from collodion negative. (Johnston Collection, Wick, JN48737P245)

threw aside their usual employments, tempted by the tales told of fortunes made in no time at this wonderful trade, photography. Like soldiering, love of the art and a desire to excel actuated many; whilst others, like shadows moved on in the trail for plunder and profit only.[103]

Optimism could shade readily into crime. Mason talked of one of his marginal subjects being 'ever ready with a ten-pound secret in a sealed envelope, which he is sure to induce some of his gullible brother photographers to buy'.[104] The huckstering street and fairground photographers could profit from the visual innocence of the public.[105]

But the most tempting criminal proposal came from the photograph's capture of intricate detail. Talbot wrote in 1845 that photography 'will enable us to introduce to our pictures a multitude of minute details which add the truth and reality of the representation, but which no artist would take the trouble to copy faithfully from nature.'[106] Many who were not respectable artists would read such proposals and begin to calculate.

By the mid-19th century the independent Scottish banks were printing an impressive number of banknotes. By 1856 the banks and their customers were seriously worried by the threat of forgery. John Urie in Glasgow took advantage of the growing anxiety. In August 1856, he advertised his own testing solution for detecting photographic forgeries of banknotes, at a shilling a bottle.[107]

The same year the issue was discussed in Scottish photographic societies. At the Dumfries and Galloway Photographic Society, John Traill Taylor read a paper on 'Forgery of Bank Notes by Photography':

Photographers had long been fond of taking positive pictures of bank-notes, to test the fineness and defining accuracy of their lenses; but fraudulent characters had impressed this science into their service to work out their own base ends. Mr Taylor then described the various modes by which paper imitations of bank-notes could be prepared; and he then gave some interesting particulars regarding several processes by which the forged notes – lately detected in Dumfries, and now in the office of Mr Jones, Superintendent of County Constabulary – might have been produced.[108]

Traill Taylor concluded that the banks had more to fear from photographic engraving.

A second paper, given just two months later at the Photographic Society of Scotland, went into greater detail.

J. G. Tunny and James Ross had been consulted by the banks. The map-maker and printer, Thomas Brumby Johnston, addressed the meeting:

> Successful forgery (were it but honest,) fulfils all the expectations of the Alchymists; it is the Philosopher's Stone, converting at once a worthless piece of paper, into it may be, a hundred pieces of pure gold …. I have here a Hundred Pound Note, with the negative and positive copies from it, produced in this way.[109]

Johnston was supervising work for the Edinburgh and Glasgow Bank and advised printing the notes in colour. He was cheerfully waving a hundred pound fake. There was nothing illegal in the act – it was passing the forgery off as the real thing that counted as crime.

In 1866 James Smart, now Chief Constable of Glasgow, offered a reward for information leading to the arrest of a photographer.[110] The detailed description illustrates how beneficial photography would be in a search. It includes the information that the wanted man was

> … about 38 years of age, nearly six feet high – stoutish build, supposed to weigh between 13 and 14 stones – military appearance – gruff voice generally speaks quickly and nervously – English accent – sallow complexion – prominent nose – dark hair, combed over to the right, where it is brushed into a sort of curl – large grey eyes, which he usually opens very wide when speaking.[111]

The man, John Henry Greatrex (1827–76), had arrived in Glasgow in 1861 with his family, and set up a photographic studio in Sauchiehall Street. He joined the Glasgow Photographic Association, and in May 1865 he gave a dull talk on 'an Economic Instrument for Sensitising or Coating Large Surfaces of Paper'.[112] He was a lay preacher and the walls of his studio were lined with religious texts; he displayed a photograph of himself as an upstanding captain in the Volunteers. He was apparently an exemplary figure, but this respectable surface was a veneer. Greatrex had been deported to Australia in 1845 for theft. By 1854 he was back in Britain, setting up a photography studio in Regent Street, London. Although a competent photographer, exhibiting at the London Photographic Society in 1857, bankruptcy caused him to shift his ground to Glasgow.

Like John Traill Taylor, Greatrex tested his camera on bank-notes and, in 1865, he even showed an example to a young bank official, saying that he found it easy to copy a 'passable Scotch note'. However, he knew (perhaps from the report of Traill Taylor's speech) that photography alone could not provide him with efficient forgeries – he needed an engraver. Ironically he seems to have achieved this meeting when he was preaching in the town of Helensburgh in 1866. There he met the brothers, Sewell and Thomas Grimshaw, who joined him in the basement at Sauchiehall Street to undertake covert trials. Sewell had been a die-cutter, making the steel engravings to print elaborate patterns onto calico, and he was a useful ally in crime. Between them they succeeded in creating 1500 photolithographic copies of the Union Bank's one pound note [Fig. 8.27].

Unfortunately (from their perspective), they found difficulty in passing the forgeries. The Grimshaw brothers were captured in Dalkeith. Greatrex had followed his mistress, Jenny Weir, up to Aberdeen. He read the newspaper account of the arrest, and immediately boarded a train for London to take ship for the United States.

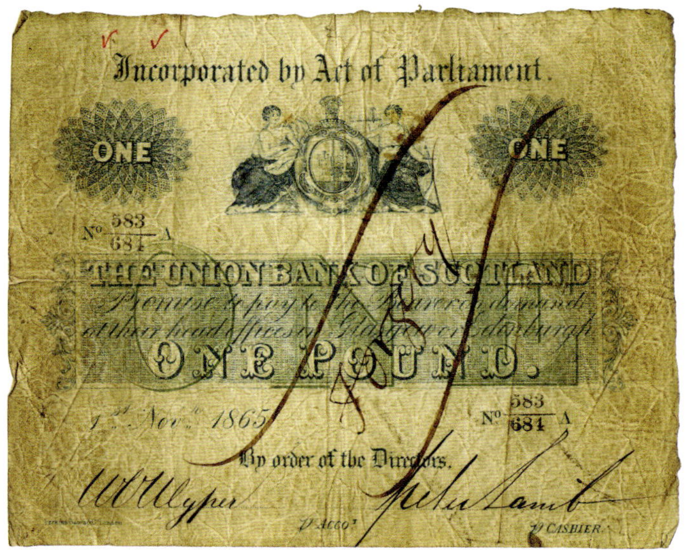

Fig. 8.27: Greatrex and Grimshaw, forged copy of the Union Bank's one pound note, 1866, photolithograph. (HBOS plc Group archives)

The pursuit was led by Detective Superintendent Alexander McCall (d.1888) of the Glasgow police. He followed Greatrex and Jenny Weir across the Atlantic, taking with him the young man from the Union Bank, who had seen Greatrex's copied banknote in 1865. McCall had the photograph of Greatrex from his studio, but had to locate his quarry among the million inhabitants of New York. He succeeded by advertising in the *New York Herald* for a photographer and an experienced receptionist. Jenny Weir, who had been Greatrex's receptionist in Glasgow, answered the advertisement, and the pair were captured. Greatrex was brought back for trial in Edinburgh. Jenny Weir returned as a witness. The case was tried at the High Court in May 1867 in a blaze of public interest. The efficiency of McCall and his colleagues had raised no less than 146 prosecution witnesses, of whom 67 were called during the trial. The judge considered the Grimshaws were less culpable, and sentenced them to fifteen years. Greatrex was sentenced to twenty years' penal servitude and he died in a prison hospital.[113]

The detailed building-up of the evidence for this case gives us a good view of the working of a photographic studio in Glasgow in the 1860s, from the layout of the building to the character of the young staff. The determination McCall put into the pursuit and the construction of the case present a crux in British history, social and legal as well as photographic, where the past merged into a recognisable present. The control of photographic information surrounding the case was here turned into an instrument of the law. In an earlier generation, Greatrex and Jenny Weir would have disappeared in America and rewritten their own history.

A mere four months after this sensational trial, James Proctor, a studio photographer, in Gallowgate, Aberdeen, was in prison to await 'examination on a charge of forgery and uttering' of banknotes on the Aberdeen Town and County Bank.[114] Proctor and his whole family were arrested, but his wife and younger son were released. The *Illustrated Photographer* reported in May 1868:

> James Proctor, senr. and junr. of Aberdeen, who some months ago were committed to take their trial for forging bank-notes by means of photography, have been convicted. The father was sentenced to five years' penal servitude, and the son was released on account of his extreme youth. These forgeries were very clumsily executed, and it seems surprising that any one could have been deceived by them for a moment. Yet several of these forged notes got into circulation.[115]

By contrast with Greatrex's history, this is a sad, domestic tale.

Notes

1. John Eagles, 'New Discovery – Engraving, and Burnet's Cartoons', *Blackwood's Magazine* 45 (1839): 382–91.
2. *Ibid.*, 383.
3. *Ibid.*, 384.
4. *Ibid.*
5. George Wilson, 'On the Extent to which the received theory of Vision requires us to regard the Eye as a Camera Obscura', Paper read to the Royal Society of Edinburgh, 2 April 1855, *Transactions of the Royal Society of Edinburgh* 21 (1857): 327–47. The Industrial Museum is now part of National Museums Scotland; P. J. Hartog, 'Wilson, George (1818–1859)', revised by R. G. W. Anderson, <http://www.oxforddnb.com/view/article/29651> See his sister Jessie Aitken Wilson's biography, Wilson 1860.
6. George Wilson, 'On the Transmission of the Actinic Rays of light through the Eye, and their relation to the Yellow Spot of the Retina', Paper read to the Royal Society of Edinburgh, 7 April 1856, *Proceedings of the Royal Society of Edinburgh* 3 (1850–57): 374–5.
7. His papers on the subject were republished with additions, see Wilson 1855.
8. Wilson 1856: 374–5. The phrase 'spectral vision' refers to the belief that the image of a murderer might be found in the eyes of his victim.
9. Quoted in Wilson 1860: 307–9. Wilson also demonstrated the daguerreotype and calotype: *Scotsman*, 30 October 1852.
10. Note on the Annual General Meeting of the Photographic Society of Scotland, 8 May 1860, *Photographic Journal* 6 (15 May 1860): 237.
11. Quoted in J. M. Gray, 'The Early History of Photography', in Elliot 1928: 6.
12. Letter from Haydon to Hill, 13 April 1846, National Library of Scotland, Acc. 11608.
13. For Hugh Miller, see M. A. Taylor, 'Miller, Hugh (1802–1856)', <http://www.oxforddnb.com/view/article/18723> and Sara Stevenson, 'Hugh Miller in Focus,' in Borley (ed.) 2002: 72–9; for Elizabeth Rigby, see Rosemary Mitchell, 'Eastlake, Elizabeth, Lady Eastlake (1809–1893)', <http://www.oxforddnb.com/view/article/8415> Sheldon (ed.) 2009; and for Dr John Brown, see A. C. Cheyne, 'Brown, John (1810–1882)', <http://www.oxforddnb.com/view/article/3630>
14. [Elizabeth Rigby], Review of books on 'Modern German painting', *Quarterly Review* 78 (1846): 338.
15. Hugh Miller, 'The Calotype', *Witness*, 12 July 1843.
16. *Ibid.*
17. [Elizabeth Rigby], Review of books on 'Modern German painting', *Quarterly Review* 78 (1846): 338. This was ostensibly an attack on the detailed work of German painters.
18. John Brown, Review of the Royal Scottish Academy exhibition, *Witness*, 22 April 1846.
19. *Ibid.*
20. Review of the Photographic Society of Scotland exhibition, *Caledonian Mercury*, 24 December 1864.
21. John Adamson, letter to the Photographic Society of Scotland, sent with his photographs for the exhibition, 29 Nov 1861, National Archives of Scotland, GD3 56/12/71.
22. [David Brewster], 'Photogenic Drawing or Drawing by the Agency of Light', *Edinburgh Review* 76 (1843): 311–2.
23. A. D. Morrison-Low, 'Brewster, Talbot and the Adamsons: the Arrival of Photography in St Andrews', *History of Photography* 25 (2001): 130–41.
24. Document 4898, Brewster to Talbot, 28 November 1843, <http://foxtalbot.dmu.ac.uk/letters/letters.html>
25. [David Brewster], 'Photography,' *North British Review* 14 (1847): 479.
26. *Reports* 1852: 278.
27. [David Brewster], 'Recent Progress of Photographic Art', *North British Review* 36 (1862): 170–203, quote on 189.
28. Obituary, *Scotsman*, 1885, quoted in Thompson 1985: 8.
29. J. F. Campbell, letter written from 'Niddvy [*sic* Niddry] Lodge, Kensington W.', 1 June 1858, 'On the perspective of photography', *Journal of the Photographic Society of London* 5 (22 November 1858): 83–4.
30. Hugh Miller, 'The Calotype', *Witness*, 12 July 1843.
31. S. Stevenson, 'Robert Louis Stevenson and the Portrait Photographers', *History of Photography* 37 (2013): 235–42.
32. Letter from Stevenson to his mother, 30 December 1872, in Booth and Mehew (eds) 1994, vol. 1: 269–70.
33. *Ibid.*, 141, letter to A. Trevor Hadden, 5 July 1883.
34. His thinking may have informed his story, *The Strange Case of*

Note: Website addresses checked and correct at the time of going to press.

Dr Jekyll and Mr Hyde, published in 1886, in which the character's transformation of personality was accompanied by a radical shift in appearance.

35. [Lady Eastlake] 'Photography', *Quarterly Review* 101 (1857): 465.

36. Jane Welsh Carlyle to Mrs Stirling, 21 October 1859, The Carlyle Letters Online: <http://carlyleletters.dukejournals.org/cgi/content/full/35/1/lt-18591021-JWC-SS-01?maxtoshow=&hits=10&RESULTFORMAT=&fulltext=21+October+1859&searchid=1&FIRSTINDEX=0&resourcetype=HWCIT>

37. Anon. [presumed to be John Brown], 'Review of the Photographic Society of Scotland's exhibition', *Scotsman*, 10 February 1862.

38. Bergstein 2010; Barthes 2000 (trans. Richard Howard).

39. John Wheeley Gough Gutch, 'Recollections and Jottings of a Photographic Tour, Undertaken During the Years 1856–7', *Photographic Notes* 3 (15 June 1858): 144.

40. '… from a waxed paper negative, Knight's formula and preparation, exposure time of 2½ hours, and the positives printed by Mr [John] McGregor': Record of the Edinburgh Photographic Exchange Club, National Archives of Scotland, GD356/28.

41. Magnus Jackson, 'Photography outside the studio', a communication to the Dundee and East of Scotland Photographic Association, *British Journal of Photography* 28 (4 February 1881): 56.

42. [Lady Eastlake] 'Photography', *Quarterly Review* 101 (1857): 460.

43. Sara Stevenson, 'The Rev. D. T. K. Drummond 1806–1877', *Scottish Photography Bulletin* 2 (1992): 3–10.

44. Rev. D. T. K. Drummond, Paper read to the Photographic Society of Scotland, 10 November 1863, 'Some Remarks on the Malt Process', *Photographic News* 8 (22 January 1864): 42.

45. Stirling Maxwell 1848: 652.

46. See Hilary Macartney, 'The Reproduction of Spanish Art: Hill and Adamson's Calotypes and Sir William Stirling Maxwell's *Annals of the Artists of Spain* (1848)', *Studies in Photography* (2005): 16–23.

47. Reported in *Glasgow Citizen*, 25 October 1862.

48. From a printed report of the Glasgow Art Union annual meeting for 1862, pasted in Thomas Annan's commonplace book, Mitchell Library, Ms 13/1.

49. G. Wharton Simpson, 'Editorial', *Photographic News* 6 (28 November 1862): 565–6.

50. We are indebted to Michael Gray for analysing this confusion.

51. Norman Macbeth, 'Photographic copying from Paintings and Drawings', *British Journal of Photography* 14 (10 May 1867): 216–7.

52. Anon. [presumed to be D. O. Hill] 1866. See also Roddy Simpson, 'Subscribers to the prints of the Disruption Painting', *Studies in Photography* (2008): 51–7.

53. Anon., 'Large Carbon Reproductions', *Photographic News* 10 (29 June 1866): 304.

54. Obituary of Thomas Annan, *British Journal of Photography* 34 (23 December 1887): 803.

55. Annan took his son, J. Craig Annan to Vienna to learn Karl Klíč's photogravure process in 1883: see Buchanan 1992: 12–13.

56. John M. Gray [probably from information assembled by Dr John Brown], 'Robert Adamson,' in Elliot 1928.

57. Catalogue 1872.

58. Sir William Stirling Maxwell, Preface to *ibid.*, xii.

59. David Laing, note in *ibid.*, 43.

60. Editorial, *British Journal of Photography* 19 (22 November 1872): 596.

61. Miller 1841, first published serially in the *Witness* in 1840.

62. Meeting of Geology Section, *Journal of the Belles Lettres* 1241 (31 October 1840): 703; and *Journal of the Belles Lettres* 1240, 24 October 1840: 689.

63. Miller 2004: 207–8.

64. Fairley (ed.) 1988; and Sara Stevenson, 'The doctor, the lady and the man who printed his own money', *Studies in Photography* (2007): 15–6.

65. Traill 1822.

66. Hugh Blackburn, 'Photographic Engraving', *Notes and Queries* 8 (24 December 1853): 628. *The Little Downy* book does not seem to have survived, perhaps simply because it was well read.

67. [Blackburn] 1854.

68. Letter from Thackeray to Blackburn, 16 February 1855, quoted in Fairley 1988: 42–3.

69. Blackburn 1895: 173.

70. Charles Reid, quoted by C. Lang Neil, 'The Animal Photographs of Charles Reid', *The Studio* 38, no. 162 (1906): 330–1.

71. *Ibid.*, 329.

72. Ross to William Blackwood, 17 May 1880, letter in the National Library of Scotland, Mss 4411, f. 177.

73. Ross to Blackwood, 25 May 1880, letter in the National Library of Scotland, Mss 4411, f. 179.

74. Ross 1880: viii, Introduction.

75. Quoted in Smyth 1858b: 471.

76. Report of a meeting of the Royal Scottish Society of Arts on 11 January, *Scotsman*, 13 January 1858.

77. See Schaaf, 'Piazzi Smyth at Teneriffe: Part 2, Photography and the Disciples of Constable and Harding', *History of Photography* 5 (1981): 27–50.

78. Smyth 1858b: 568–9.

79. Smyth: 1858a.

80. *Ibid.*, 573–4.

81. Letter from Piazzi Smyth to J. H. Balfour, 24 February 1859, manuscript in collection of Royal Botanic Gardens, Edinburgh.

82. See Monica Thorp, 'William Henry Fox Talbot and the Edinburgh Connection, 1855–72', *Studies in Photography* (2005): 24–33.

83. See Arthur Gill, 'Fox Talbot's photoglyphic engraving process', *History of Photography* 2 (1978): 134; Schaaf 2003; Larry J. Schaaf, '"The Caxton of Photography": Talbot's Etchings of Light', in Brusius et al. (eds) 2013: 161–89.

84. Meeting of the Botanical Society of Edinburgh, 11 June 1863, *Transactions and Proceedings of the Botanical Society of Edinburgh* 7 (1863): 568–9.

85. See document 8722, Piazzi Smyth to Talbot, 1 July 1863, <http://foxtalbot.dmu.ac.uk/letters/letters.html>

86. R. E. Lassam, 'Fox Talbot's Original Iron Copper Press', in Collins (ed.) 1990: 15–6. This shows an Edinburgh-made press by D. & J. Greig.

87. John Traill Taylor, 'The Late W. H. Fox Talbot', *British Journal of Photography* 24 (28 September 1877): 460–1. Examples of these, and the steel plate, are at the National Media Museum.

88. *Glasgow Herald*, 19 June 1854.

89. *Glasgow Herald*, 26 June 1854.

90. *Glasgow Herald*, 12 February 1855, 'Singular Incident'.

91. Anon., a letter reporting from Scotland, *The Empire*, Sydney, Australia, 27 October 1856.

92. 'A Resident' [Kerr] 1872; reprinted 1996: 166.

93. For the background to this, see Cassels 2010: 65–6.

94. Samuel Wauchope, 'An adventure with Bengal Dacoits', manuscript in collection of National Library of Scotland, Dundas of Ochtertyre Muniments, Acc. 10654/1.

95. From a Review of John William Kaye, *The Administration of the East India Company: A History of Indian Progress 1853*, in *Calcutta Review* 19 (1853): 373.

96. *Reports of Cases Determined in the court of Nizamut Adawlut from July to December 1853*, 1855, vol. 3, part 2: 126 and 481.

97. Kaye and Malleson (eds) 1898, vol. 6: 23.

98. See Tagg 2007; Finn 2009; Jens Jaeger, 'Police and forensic photography', in Lehman (ed.) 2005: 507–10.

99. J. A. Gardiner, Letter published in *Jurist* [New Series] (13 January 1855): 6.

100. Anon., 'Photography: Its History and Applications', *British Quarterly Review* 44 (1866): 382.

101. At the time of the 1861 census, the prison in Wick held only '5 males and 1 female', *Census of Scotland – 1861. Population Tables and Reports ...* , 1862: 9.

102. Anon., 'Photography: Its History and Applications', *British Quarterly Review* 44 (1866): 382.

103. Mason [1891]: 15.

104. *Ibid*.

105. For an account of the enticing possibilities of sharp practice in photography, see Mayhew 1861–62, vol. 3: 206–10.

106. Talbot 1844–46: 33.

107. Advertisement, *Glasgow Herald*, 15 August 1856.

108. Report on the Dumfries & Galloway Photographic Society meeting on 1 October 1856, *Photographic Notes* 1 (1 November 1856): 217.

109. T. B. Johnston, Paper given to the Photographic Society of Scotland, 9 December 1856, 'Photographic Forgery', *Photographic Notes* 2 (1 January 1857): 4–6.

110. This story is told in Bruce 2013.

111. A copy of the reward notice is among the papers relating to the trial, National Archives for Scotland, AD14/67/284.

112. John Henry Greatrex, 'Remarks on an Economic Instrument for Sensitising or Coating Large Surfaces of Paper &c', *British Journal of Photography* 12 (12 May 1865): 245, 252.

113. Bruce 2013: 172.

114. Anon, 'Forging of Bank Notes by Photography', *British Journal of Photography* 14 (20 September 1867): 453.

115. Anon, 'Bits of Chat', *Illustrated Photographer* 1 (1 May 1868): 159–60.

Fig. 8.17 (detail): John Adamson, 'Home from the Burn', *c.*1860, albumen print.

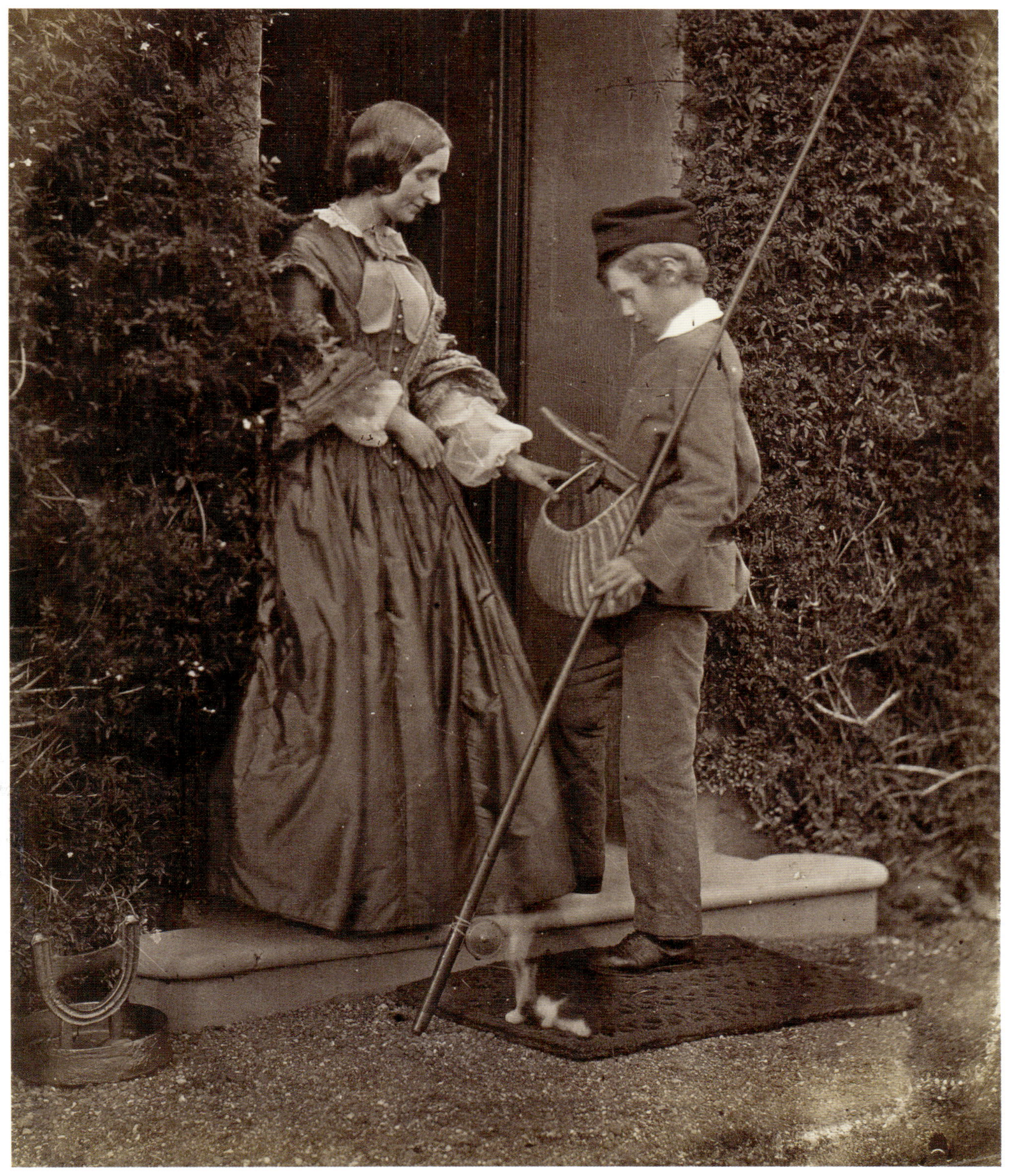

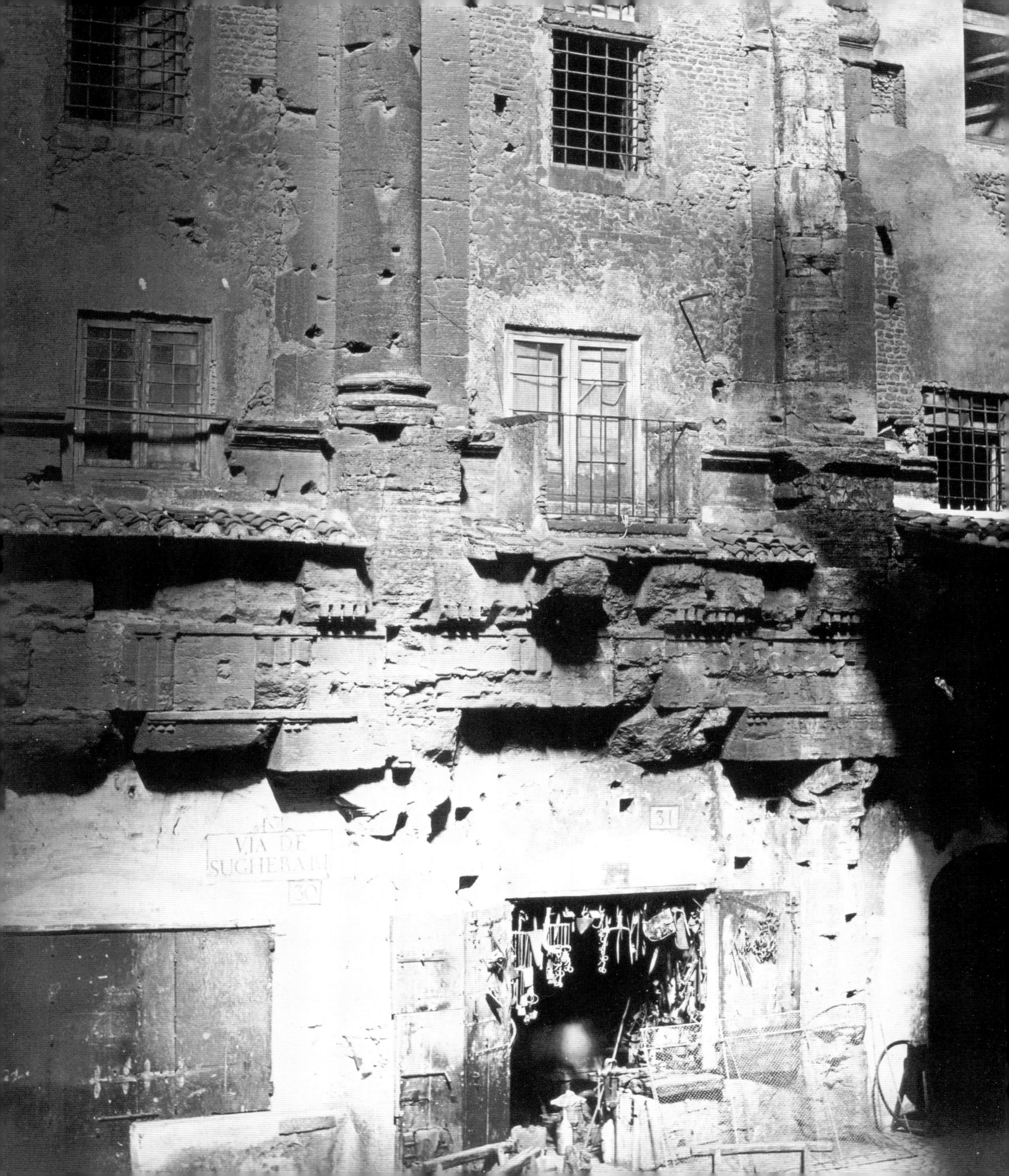
VIA DE
SUGHERARI
30
31

CHAPTER NINE

Travel and Tourism

Dr Brandt kindly brought in a number of soldiers, and they
walked about the stuffed rhinoceroses, and trotted off the preserved
elephants and other such very large deer, until the camera's
ground-glass presented a good picture of the monstrous bones …

✱

C. Piazzi Smyth, writing of the difficulties in photographing a mammoth
in the museum of the St Petersburg Academy, 1858

The 18th-century Grand Tour of Europe was designed so that a gentleman would complete his social education, achieve a good command of languages, and gain sophisticated knowledge of the arts and sciences. While increasingly in the 19th century, the tourist was seeking health and leisure, knowledge continued to be exchanged and spread through Continental and Mediterranean travel.[1]

The Northern Tour

John Muir Wood (1805–92) is first documented as travelling with his camera in 1847.[2] He needed to travel, both within England and on the Continent, in his profession as a musician and later, as an entrepreneur, organising concerts for Glasgow and Edinburgh. In 1847 he kept a journal, which enables us to date his photographs of York to 19 July. He moved rapidly south to London, where he attended the opera and then took a boat for Ostend. In Belgium he visited and photographed in Ghent, Mechelen, Brussels, the battleground of Waterloo, Namur and Liège. Given that he was then close to the German border, this may have been the occasion when he carried the camera to Cologne, Heidelberg, Nuremberg and Munich.[3] The photographs he took exhibit his rich control of chemistry and a pleasing independence in composition. His immediate response to the town of Namur, as 'not interesting', suggests a brisk rejection. Happily, he responded to the challenge and took an effective picture. By including the incidental features of the barges on the river and the poles jutting out over the water, he achieved a pleasing counterchange between the short and long lines of the rooftops and the buildings and the bald strength of the citadel above, complemented by the graceful curve of the quayside [FIGS 9.1].

Opposite, Fig. 9.9 (detail): Robert Macpherson, 'Via Sugherari, the Theatre of Marcellus, Rome', *c*.1858.

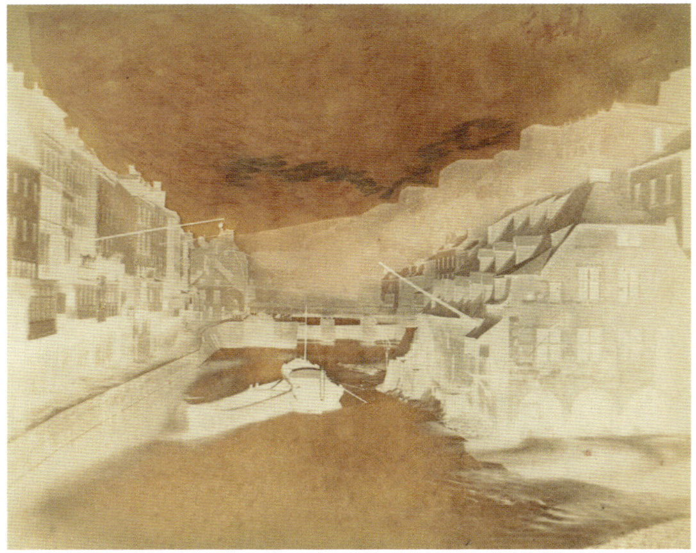 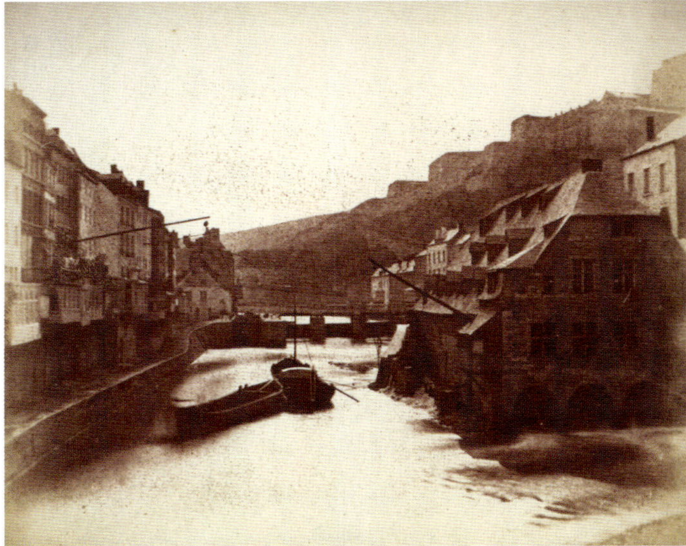

As a lawyer and Professor of History at the University of Edinburgh, Cosmo Innes had the long vacations in which to travel. In 1858, he visited the coast of Spain [Fig. 9.2]. His account to the Photographic Society 'was replete with excellent hints as to hotel accommodation and the quality of the water'.[4] Innes and his family were tolerant travellers, accustomed to cheap hotels. He explained the deficiencies in his work in Valencia: 'I had cause to regret my slow process of working. If I had used collodion, every morning-walk to the market would have filled my glasses with grand men in Roman dress, and the most beautiful women in the most picturesque dress of the mantilla.' But their route gave the paper process a practical advantage:

> The shaking of the diligence was awful. The road was bad and crossed by frequent paved runnels to carry off the mountain streams. Our team of ten mules would come to a standstill, till by kicks and thumps and oaths and adjurations they plunged forward again. Then woe to anything '*fragile!*' I kept my camera on my knee like a baby. I believe no amount of packing would have made glass, of the size of my pictures, safe on that conveyance.[5]

In autumn 1859, Innes travelled through Germany, where he appreciated Heidelberg and Nuremberg, but again encountered difficulties. The Prinz Karl Hotel in Heidelberg was 'badly off for window-shutters; and I, with difficulty, arranged with the house-maid to have a share of her dark closet, where she kept her pails and brushes. It was photography under disadvantages.'[6] The tour continued through Austria, Italy, Switzerland and Paris. Despite his reference to failures, Cosmo Innes was a successful photographer who was working on a large scale; he came home with 'a portfolio of pretty pictures'. The review of the Photographic Society's exhibition in 1859, spoke of his work with pleasure as 'most picturesque scenes in Venice and in the old towns in Germany. They remind us of drawings by Proust [presumably Samuel Prout] in their breadth and effective treatment'.[7]

C. G. H. Kinnear, who heard Innes's talk, made a disconcerting comment, stating 'there was much need of what he would call a photographic "Murray," which would be a guide to the various places of interest on the Continent in a photographic point of view … he often found such places so hemmed in with buildings on every side as to altogether preclude the possibility of reproducing them by means of the camera.'[8] This eminently modern, time-saving idea was perhaps justified by the difficulties of travel – a photographer might go a long distance to be frustrated – but taken literally it would determine the tourists' response and

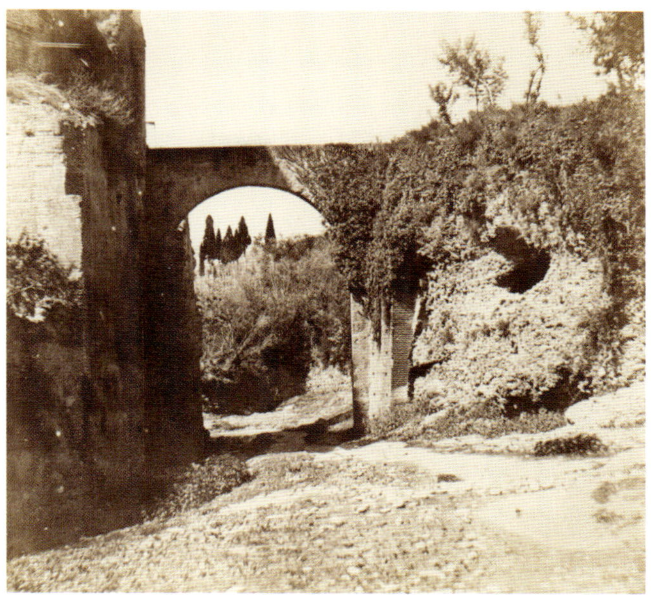

condemn whole towns as unphotographic. When Kinnear, an architect, travelled in northern France with his friends Alexander and James Adam in 1857, his tour was consciously professional, in pursuit of fine historic buildings. He noted in Rouen that 'the photographer … might easily employ himself for a week, taking either the purely architectural subjects, or the equally tempting picturesque bits with which the town abounds', but added,

> he must make up his mind to a good deal of annoyance when he plants his camera in front of any building in the principal streets or squares. The town is more bustling and crowded than almost any other which we visited in our tour, and though cameras must be sights more common in Rouen than in almost any other city in the world, we found they excited a disagreeable amount of sensation in its streets. A French crowd in such a case is always perfectly polite and good-humoured, and will do anything to assist you – except go away.[9]

The eccentric equipment that the photographers constructed, and especially disappearing under a dark cloth so that the operator was no more than a bundle on legs with a tripod, would make them a source of ribald entertainment. Small boys would be there.

Portugal

Scotland has a long-standing connection with Portugal's wine trade – port entered the country through Greenock, Edinburgh and Perth. Joseph James Forrester (1809–61) was a merchant in Portugal, engaged in improving the quality of the wine. He belonged to a long-established firm, which 'purchased not less than one fifteenth part of the whole of the wine of the Douro'.[10] He was 'descended from an old and esteemed family of Perth'.[11] His trading connection with that city is underlined by the gravestone, where he is commemorated, in Greyfriars Churchyard in Perth.[12]

Forrester was involved in photography by the mid-1840s when Hill and Adamson took six large-scale portraits of him in Edinburgh.[13] He studied photography with Dr Hugh Welch Diamond in the early 1850s. In 1855, he contributed two landscapes to the album of the London Photographic Exchange Club, and noted in the printed text: 'This picture is one of 220 views originally intended to illustrate the author's survey of the Douro and they exhibit the bed and margins of the river at all seasons.'[14] At the soirée of the Photographic Society of London in 1856, he showed 'a large stereoscope on a stand, with revolving views of "Douro Scenery".'[15]

He took pictorial photographs of the peasantry, which he sometimes painted [Fig. 9.3]. In 1854, when he was 'about to plant [his] camera amongst the mountain scenery of Portugal', he wrote a letter to the *Journal of the Photographic Society* on 'Waxed Positives'. He preferred salt paper over albumen because colour could be applied more easily;

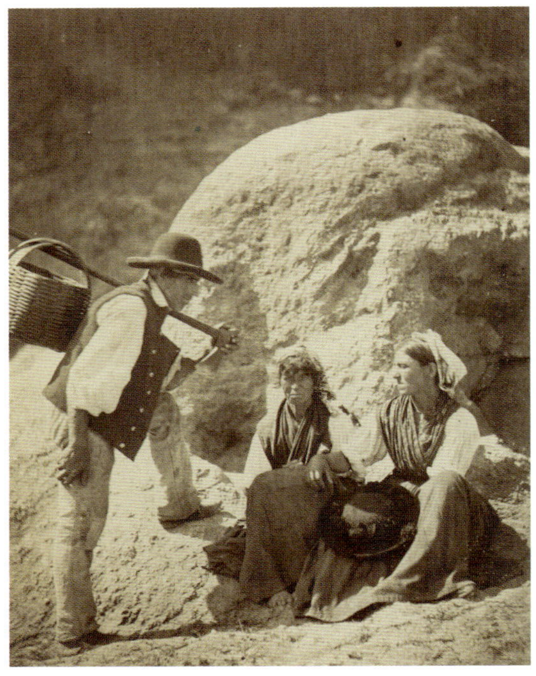

Fig. 9.3: Baron Joseph James Forrester, 'Peasants of the Alto-Douro', 1856. (National Media Museum / Science & Society Picture Library, 2003-5001_2_11415)

tinctly relaxing: 'Every Englishman who has remained some time at Pau, whether ill or well, must confess to a certain degree of self-satisfied dreaminess.'[19] The Scottish enthusiasm for Pau is illustrated by the golf club – the first established on the Continent in 1856, when the Free Church of Scotland opened a place of worship.

John Stewart (1814–87), happily placed as the brother-in-law of John Herschel, took up photography in Pau around 1850 or 1851.[20] In June 1853, Stewart wrote to Herschel:

> I sent you some time ago a few small-sized studies of animals from the life, singly and in flocks, upon collo-dionised glass. The great rapidity of exposition required for such subjects, being but the fraction of a second, together with the very considerable depth and harmony obtained, gave me reason to hope that ere this I should have been able to produce microscopic pictures of animated objects. For the present, I have been interrupted.[21]

He turned his mind to the question of enlarging from small negatives, observing the experiments of Jean-Jacques Heilmann, who succeeded in keeping delicate detail in his enlargements. He wrote also of a method of producing multiple images for the stereoscope. By 1854, he was able to exhibit stereoscopic views 'showing the Waves of the Sea taken instantaneously, &c., &c.' at the Photographic Exhibition in George Street, Edinburgh.[22]

In July, Stewart wrote to the *Journal of the Photographic Society*:

> … since as a solitary labourer two or three years ago I amused myself with photography here, a circle of very active and some distinguished photographers, Mr

when not coloured, 'by waxing them … I have achieved a fine transparent subdued tone'.[16]

Forrester may have encountered another photographer in Portugal, Major Thomas Ross of the 73rd Regiment of Foot.[17] Thomas Sutton, when reminiscing about taking large calotype photographs in Rome, added:

> But what was this to the feats of my friend Colonel Ross at Cintra, with a camera for papers four feet by three, a ream of which was made expressly for him by Messrs. Hollingworth at a cost of £80! *His* was a camera if you like … many a time have I seen the gallant colonel get inside his camera bodily. Fancy what *his* enjoyment must have been, with his six orderlies to carry his apparatus![18]

The Pyrenees

The town of Pau, high in the Pyrenees, was especially attractive to the British as an area promoting good health. In 1842 an English doctor declared that the atmosphere, comparatively dry and good for making the hair curl, was dis-

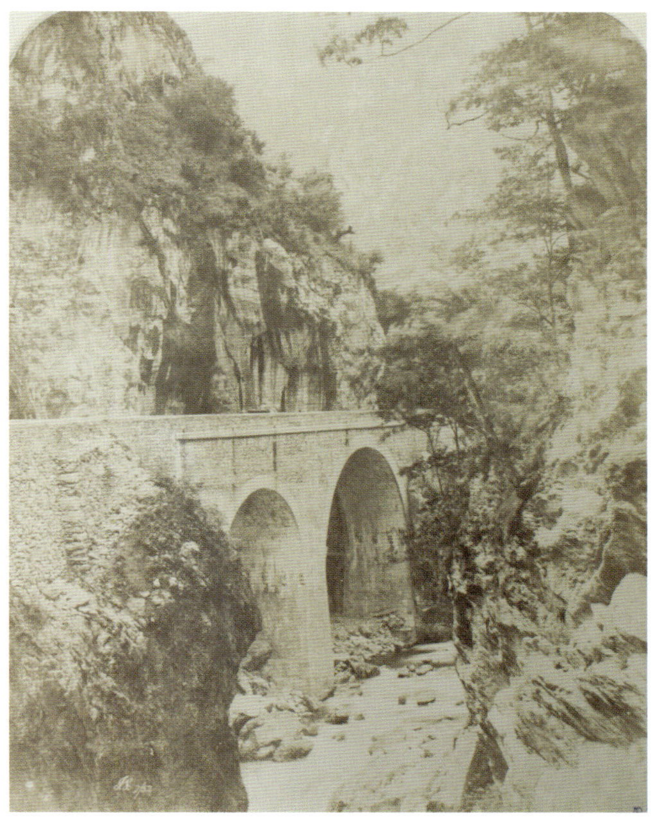

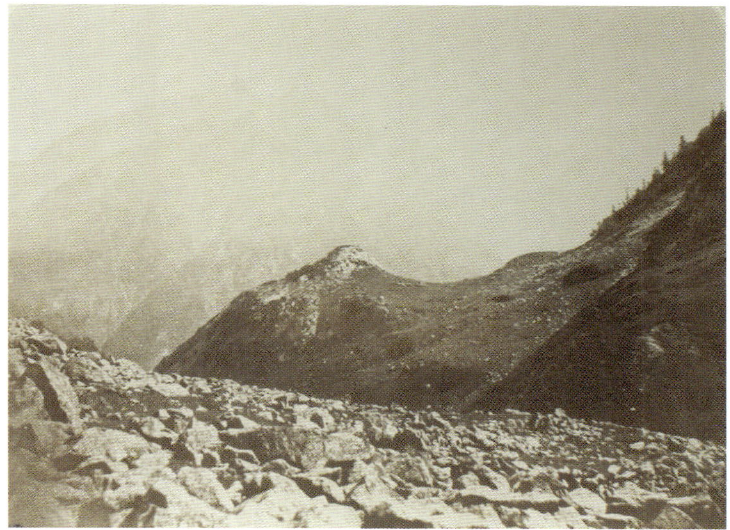

Maxwell Lyte and others has gathered here and given such stimulus to the art, that a Photographic Printing establishment upon a large scale, and which promises to be one of the finest in France, has been established in Pau. The town has also in consequence been endowed with a 'Scientific and Photographic Society' which equally promises to be a great resource to the many strangers that flock hither for the climate .…[23]

Stewart is known as a landscape photographer rather than for microscopic or instantaneous work. Herschel wrote that he was '… singularly successful in his application of that art to the depiction of natural scenery; and whose representations of the superb combinations of rock, mountain, forest and water which abound in the picturesque region of the Pyrenees are among the most exquisite in their finish, and artistic in general effect, of any specimen of that art which I have yet seen'.[24]

This comment leads on to another of Stewart's letters where he stated that the slightly thicker Whatman paper 'gives a minuteness as well as mellowness of detail' to landscape work and, he concluded, 'the preparation of paper here described produces more tone and artistic representation of pure landscape scenes than any other, and I have found it available in conditions of weather and light, or I might also say, absence of light, where every other process I am acquainted with would have failed'.[25]

Stewart's landscape work was broad and generalised in its focus – the opposite of his collodion work. In facing the mountains, roads, rivers and trees around him, he discovered a natural mass and geometry. His 'Gorge de la nouvelle route des Eaux-Chaudes' is a strong, contained image, with the mountain replacing the sky, and the bridge fixing the arbitrary masses of the landscape, but in itself disconcertingly off-kilter – the nearer arch is smaller than the further: engineering creating arbitrary and contradictory planes [FIG. 9.4]. His view of chestnut trees, 'Etudes d'arbres. Châtaigniers', taken from a high angle looking down, has achieved something of the same disconcerting effect. The

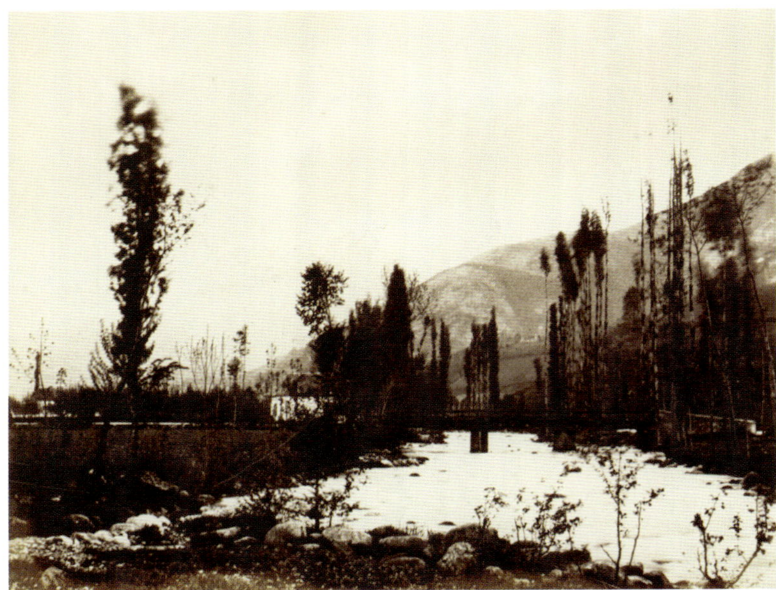

'Vue du col d'Arruns' is a simplified, and extraordinary bleak abstract of rocks and mountains [Fig. 9.5].

Stewart's influence was evidently widespread. He worked with the French, including Louis Désiré Blanquart-Evrard who published his photographs in an album called *Souvenirs des Pyrenees*, and with Henri Victor Regnault who joined him in a photographic expedition to England in 1853.[26] The French historians André Jammes and Eugenia Parry Janis thought that Stewart's landscapes were 'inconceivable without the example of the Frenchman [Regnault]' and that his 'views on the paper negative art [amounted] to a fundamental statement of its aesthetic theory, not unheeded by French artists'.[27]

The circle in Pau drew visitors. One of these was the cleric, Thomas Milville Raven (1828–96).[28] He gave a wordy account of his travels with his family, entitled 'Pau and the Pyrenees, with a slight sketch of a Photographic Tour made to them through the west of France', to the Photographic Society of Scotland in 1858. He showed more than sixty views taken by the waxed paper process, which he adopted after reading Thomas Keith's account. 'I was at that time living in a country parish in Yorkshire and had to fight my way through photographic difficulties and troubles unaided and unadvised by any one. I had been working some little time with various processes before I came to Edinburgh, when I became a member of this Society, where I at once met with kind advice and assistance.'[29]

The skill of Raven's photographs is unquestionable. He was struck by the light and atmosphere in Pau in December:

In no part of any country in which I have been is there such a fine light, with soft broad shadows, as in this part of France. The stillness of the atmosphere is extraordinary, as some negatives I have taken … of Lombardy poplar trees very clearly indicate.[30]

Given the natural twiddling of poplar leaves and the need to extend exposure times up to twenty minutes for the green of trees, Raven's satisfaction with this and his invitation to the members to pick up a magnifying glass and examine the leaves with care, is wholly reasonable.

Raven's two most striking pictures were taken in the Pyrenees. These in the Edinburgh Photographic Exchange Club album which belonged to Horatio Ross, are curiously bleak, black and white images – one of a landscape with a pocket of snow [Fig. 9.6], and the other of a cold swathe of water with reflected trees. When he exhibited them in the London Photographic Society's exhibition in 1859, he encountered a sour critic, who condemned them.[31] But when he showed them in Scotland, they were applauded:

> Probably the first place among the Edinburgh amateurs should be given to the Rev T. Milville Raven, who has contributed a large number of pictures, principally views about Pau and among the Pyrenees. Until we saw these pictures, we were not fully alive to the many excellencies of 'waxed paper,' but in his hands it appears to assert a superiority in many respects over any other process. In no other pictures do we see a similar softness of tone and truthfulness of atmospheric effect. Among his Pyrenean pictures we would particularly point out (216) 'Pierre-fitte,' (214 and 218) 'Bagnères de Bigorre,' (242) 'Pau,' and (491) 'Cauterets.'[32]

Italy

Robert Macpherson (1814–72) was a Highlander and a Jacobite by inclination. Many of his compatriots visited Rome, with their Presbyterian eyes nervously averted from the extravagances of the Roman Catholicism. As a Catholic, Macpherson was involved both in Roman and British society. He originally studied to be a doctor, but found medicine not to his taste. He took up painting and exhibited as Robert Turnbull Macpherson in Scotland in the 1830s. He moved to Rome about 1840, where he acted both as a painter and dealer.[33] A visitor to his studio in the 1840s found him sketching an altarpiece: 'St Peter meeting the vision of our Saviour on the Appian Way.' He showed two figures he had modelled in wax, to 'set in what light or situation I please, so as best to suit my picture'.[34]

Francis Sylvester Mahony, an Irish journalist, gave an account of one of Macpherson's triumphant discoveries in 1846:

> An able artist, as well as a connoisseur, Mr Macpherson has lately had the luck to purchase, at the breaking up of the great storehouse of Cardinal Fesch, an oaken panel, about four feet by five, which is covered with an unfinished painting of Christ borne to the sepulchre, now pronounced by the best judges in Rome, and by Cornelius, to be an undoubted oil picture by [Michelangelo] Buonarotti …. The same gentleman, whose researches in the interesting mine of Stuart antiquities have been rewarded by so many valuable Jacobite treasures … seems to possess a kind of Scottish second sight, by which he instinctively recognises the presence of an old master.[35]

As Ray McKenzie has pointed out, Macpherson's experience in painting, dealing and medicine gave him a unique background for a photographer, combining chemical knowledge with the physical and visual knowledge of picture making.[36] He took up photography in 1851 or 1852, when a friend whom he had known as a medical student, Dr George Sidney Clark (1819–68), came to Rome with photographic equipment. According to his obituary:

> Dr Clark arrived in Rome with a camera. The then new and fascinating art of photography at once attracted Mr Macpherson's attention, and just as his friend, who had little skill, was about giving it up he joined him and speedily overcame the principal difficulties.[37]

Clark may have involved Macpherson deliberately in photography, with the intention of distracting him from grief. Thomas Sutton undertook a tour of Italy for a year from autumn 1851. In 1857, answering a correspondent enquiring if photography was bad for the health, he concluded that photography proved a distraction for Robert Macpherson in bereavement (his three-year-old child had died):

In Photography he speedily found relief from the melancholy which oppressed him, and with a strong will bent to the purpose, mastered in a few weeks the manipulation of the most difficult of all photographic processes, that of Albumen on Glass.[38]

In Rome, Sutton met the French photographer Frédéric Flacheron, as well as Macpherson, and both were free in their communication:

I was greatly interested in Mr Macpherson's operations and in watching his gradual improvement, day by day, in his process, until he achieved that splendid success which raised him to the rank of the first photographer in Rome.[39]

Our knowledge of Macpherson as a man comes from a number of art and literary sources. He married Gerardine Bate, the lively niece of Anna Jameson, the art historian, and through that connection knew the Brownings. The novelist, Mrs Oliphant, encountered the Macphersons in 1859, and she talked about them at length. Her first, published, version was presented in Gerardine Macpherson's *Memoirs of the Life of Anna Jameson* in 1878. Gerardine did

not live to see it through the press, and Mrs Oliphant added a tribute to her last struggles to keep her family after Robert's death. She wrote that Gerardine was

… a pretty, charming and accomplished girl … many people of all classes will remember the pair in their early prosperity and happiness. He was a true Highlander, of good descent … a man of marked and headstrong character, with all the qualities, both good and evil, of his race, little likely to get peaceably or easily through the world, but always warm-hearted, full of kindness and good offices as long as they were in his power, and with much charm of manner and social aptitude …. In this work [photography] he was aided vigorously and successfully by his wife, and his photographs were the first and finest that have ever been executed of Roman scenery and antiquities. Their career was very prosperous for a number of years.[40]

This was a memorial tribute. Mrs Oliphant's *Autobiography* tells a more complicated story. This was not originally designed for publication, and was written to assuage her own distress. In 1859 she was in Florence with her husband Frank, who was seriously ill. Frank insisted on moving to Rome to meet his old friend, Robert Macpherson. Mrs Oliphant had two infants with her, and was pregnant. Her husband told Macpherson, not his wife, that he was dying; she found this hard to forgive. She buried her husband, bore her child and faced debts of thousands of pounds; it is scarcely surprising that she found the energetic and hearty Macpherson hard to bear. Her attempt to rationalise the events of this time was further, and appallingly, exacerbated by a second visit to Rome, urged on her by Gerardine

Macpherson. Mrs Oliphant's only daughter then died in Rome. She wrote the following – most extraordinarily – when her family life had wholly collapsed.[41] The implication is that she was trying to unravel her feelings and, creditably, do justice to Macpherson:

> He had been a long time in Rome, had been there during the bombardment, and I suppose had rendered some services to the papal side, for he was always patronised more or less by the priests … reason had nothing to do with him. He was full of generosities and kindness, full of humour and whim and fun – quarrelling hotly and making up again; a big, bearded, vehement, noisy man, a combination of Highlander and Lowlander, Scotsman and Italian, with the habits of Rome and Edinburgh all rubbed together, and a great knowledge of the world in general and a large acquaintance with individuals in particular to give force to the mixture, and to increase his own interest and largeness as a man. I could not bear him at first, poor Robert – we used to quarrel on almost every subject; but in the end I got to be almost fond of him, as he was, I believe, of me, though we were so absolutely unlike.[42]

Mahony's evidence offers us a man of discriminating intelligence. Macpherson's enthusiasm cloaked a scholar – an art historian, as well as an 18th-century historian and a classicist. He knew the city of Rome, its history and antiquities. However, in photographing Rome, Macpherson had a basic problem. The history of Rome was the subject all educated Westerners would know in depth. Even more than that of Greece (less conventionally a destination of the Grand Tour), it would attract a highly critical audience.

Earlier artists and writers had painted and described not just what they saw, but their emotional response to the great influence on their education and lives – the Roman Empire. An early exponent of photography, Alexander John Ellis, declared that his daguerreotypes would 'draw with unerring correctness', to counterbalance the frivolity of the artists.[43] Ellis was able to quote Joseph Forsyth, a Scots classicist visiting in 1801, who wrote:

> That rage for embellishing, which is implanted in every artist, has thrown so much composition into the engraved views of Rome, has so exaggerated its ruins and architecture, or so expanded the space in which they stand, that a stranger, arriving here with the expectations raised by those prints, will be infallibly disappointed.[44]

The Macphersons' failure to establish a successful business in Rome in the long run was natural enough. Rome, which housed and trained so many artists, was heavily dependent on the wealth of tourists. When political disturbance and disease hit the city in the 1860s, that tourism evaporated. Later explanations of the Macphersons' failure – they were too extravagant, or Macpherson was an inebriate – are gratuitous.[45] It may equally be said that such an idea of failure could be attributed to Macpherson's uncompromising seriousness in his profession – the size and perfection of his prints; his determination to keep business in his own hands, rather than to surrender his negatives to outside printers or dealers; his dispute with the author of the popular Murray's *Guide to Rome* (which recommended other photographers as a consequence).

Macpherson's energy in making and promoting photographs is seen in his approach to sculpture. In Rome, he

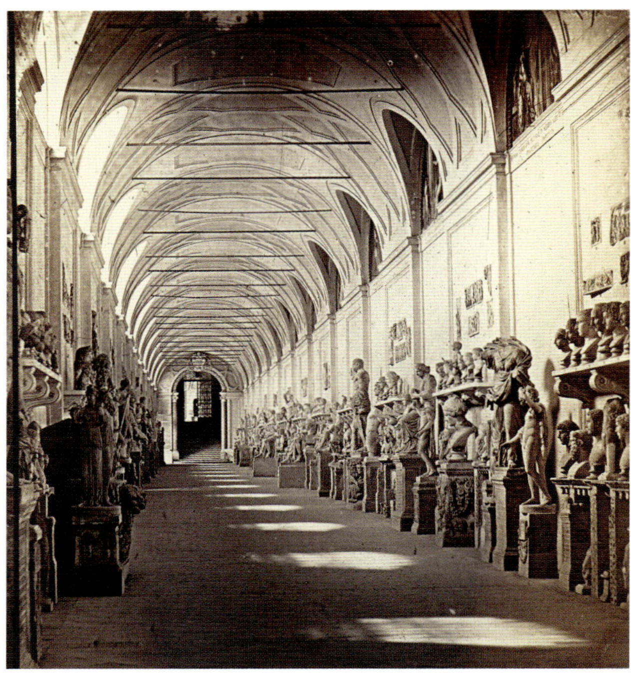
Fig. 9.7: Robert Macpherson, 'Interior of the Museo Chiaramonte', undated, albumen print. (Getty Research Institute, 91-F44)

was in a position to make a photographic record of the finest existing classical sculpture.[46] He had access to 'the cream of the Vatican … the best from the Capitoline & Lateran galleries besides the finest in the private palaces in Rome and villas "Albani" "Ludovici" "Borgese" &c'.[47] Macpherson was offering a privileged view of key classical artworks, crowded together in the galleries [Fig. 9.7]. The *Athenaeum* reviewer, seeing 120 of the photographs exhibited in London in 1862, commented: 'Most of these busts and figures, the admiration and despair of artists, are now photographed for the first time.'[48] Macpherson was given the time to take long exposures by the available interior light ('two hours were often required; and in one or two cases, even exposure of two days was necessary'), which meant that his photographs showed the sculpture as it was lit sequentially by the moving sunlight – a compound experience a visitor would not have seen.[49]

The work took more than ten years. In the 1860s, he sold volumes of *Macpherson's Vatican Sculptures*. In 1860 Macpherson wrote to the artist W. B. Johnstone of a plan for popular lectures on classical sculpture in Scotland and England:

> I have already had proposals from America but I should like first to begin with my own country and that means *Edinburgh* & Glasgow, then Liverpool and Manchester. I have had overtures made to me by those in the interests of a great institution at London but I have a dread of making my debut in the Metropolis of the world and that institution will not have my lectures at all unless I give them there *first*.

The lectures would be accompanied by a simple explana-

tory booklet, illustrated by Gerardine with line engravings – 'carefully traced from the photographs'. He planned to conclude with the photographs enlarged in a magic lantern to 'the size of the originals or even larger'. He added anxiously, given the tendency of magic lanterns to explode:

> My Lantern I suppose is the finest ever made but as yet I have found no portable means of lighting it. Professor Ramsay sent to me from Glasgow an apparatus and [?] of making oxyhydrogen gas with a spirit lamp a blowpipe [?]. But I fear I clearly do not understand it altho' I have gone by the apparently clear & explicit instructions.[50]

Macpherson's extended plan of publication involved him in developing a method of photo-lithography, based on Nicéphore Niépce's original discovery that bitumen became insoluble after exposure to light.[51] He was ultimately frustrated in this by the discovery that in Rome it was difficult to procure lithographic stones and other materials, and the lack of 'a good printer accustomed to fine work in that city'.[52]

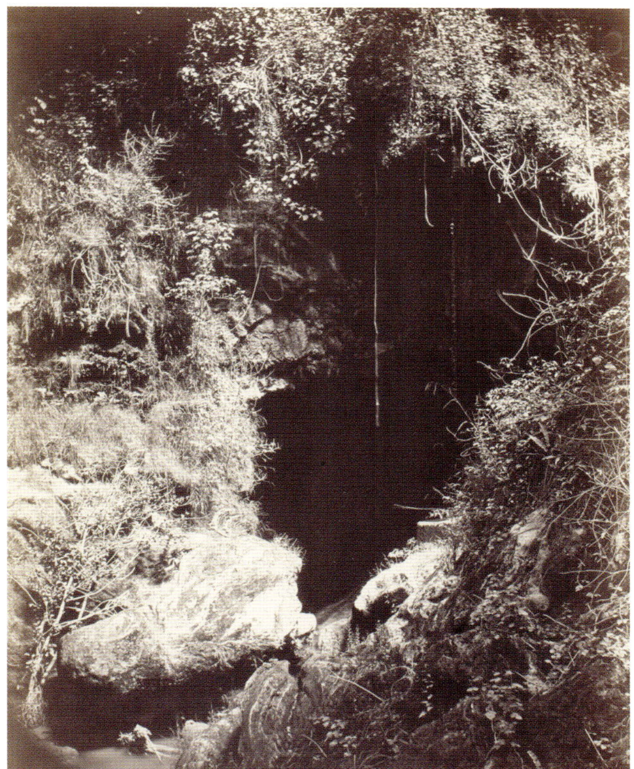

The impact of his architectural and landscape photographs lies substantially in the issue denigrated by a review in 1858:

In this number [124 photographs] there is more diversity in the negatives, and more inequalities in the printing than we ever noticed before in one artist's productions; and not only does this inequality occur in subjects of different classes, such as architecture and landscape, but also in subjects which ought to have been treated alike. There is, besides, on the average, a great want of half tone in these pictures; the blacks and whites are too intense even when the picture is only moderately printed. In some instances, owing apparently to the inferiority of the lens, there is a violation of all received notions of gravitation, and certainly a great want of that which we are always led to expect in architectural drawings – mathematical precision.[53]

In a wide range of pictures, Macpherson achieved both a straightforward and familiar vision of the landscape and subtler and emotionally richer imagery. His picture of the 'Grotto of the Sibyl' [FIG. 9.8] – an image constructed with the minimum of fact – is lush and dark. The detailed plant life in the sun surrounds the central blackness, which is both broken and defined by a couple of hanging strands, marking the cave like plumb lines; the photograph has both delicacy and an appropriately mysterious density. His simply expressed and blurred 'Falls of Terni', set in an oval, offers an echo in lines of a pleasingly cracked egg. One of his photographs of the Temple of the Sibyl, printed in a rich purple grey to black, is almost an exercise in impossibility – an odd opposition between the top and bottom halves of the picture with the sophisticated curve of the temple perched on an arbitrary flattened rock face with two utilitarian windows stamped in. It is evident that Macpherson was using different ways of constructing his pictures – with light and shadow, with focus and with different lenses. A number of exaggerated panoramic views are expressed from differing standpoints and dominated by an idea of space left for the observer, planted on a curve of the paving stones; other pictures show buildings in a crowded perspective, apparently stacked like stage flats.

Some of his photographs offer the familiar print-like imagery of Rome, empty of modern intervention. But Macpherson enjoyed the melancholy and sometimes impertinent detail of modern life: the sense of history, as opposed to archaeological detail, that is conjured up in the Via Sugherari [FIG. 9.9], the grand, ancient building darkly shadowed, with the light falling brightly on the small shop interior set into the wall; or the wide view of the masonry of the Muro Turto, which centres on a drawn or scratched

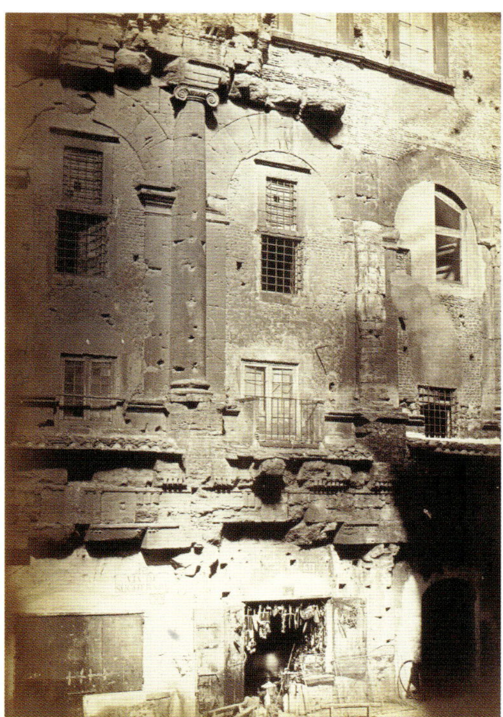

Fig. 9.9 (left): Robert Macpherson, 'Via Sugherari, the Theatre of Marcellus, Rome', *c.*1858, albumen print. (Scottish National Portrait Gallery, PGP 32.3)

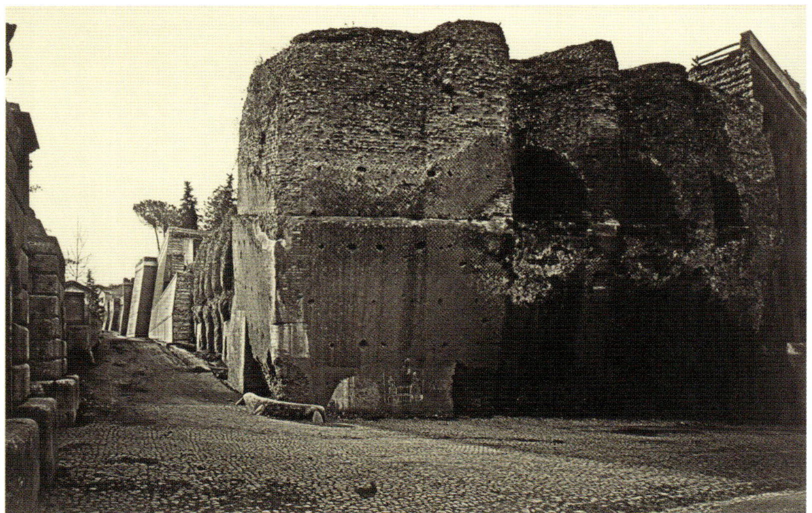

Fig. 9.10 (below): Robert Macpherson, 'Muro Torto, Gate to the Borghese Gardens', before 1871, albumen print. (Princeton University Art Museum, A498003)

Fig. 9.11 (right and detail below): Robert Macpherson, 'Arch of Septimius Severus', *c.*1857, albumen print, and a detail (below) showing the chair which has been moved. (Gernsheim Collection, Harry Ransom Center, University of Texas at Austin, Image No. 964_0041_0044)

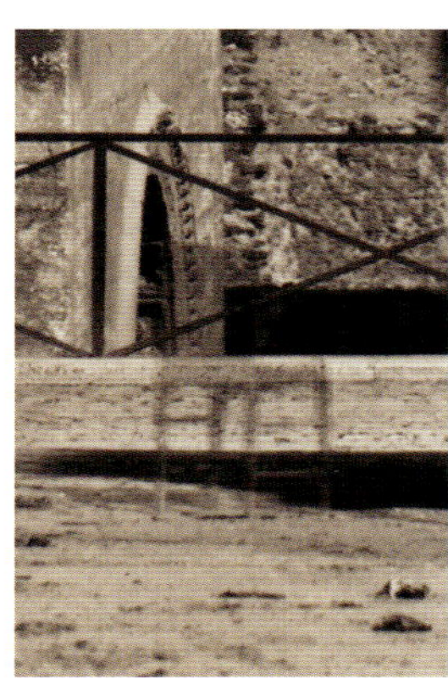

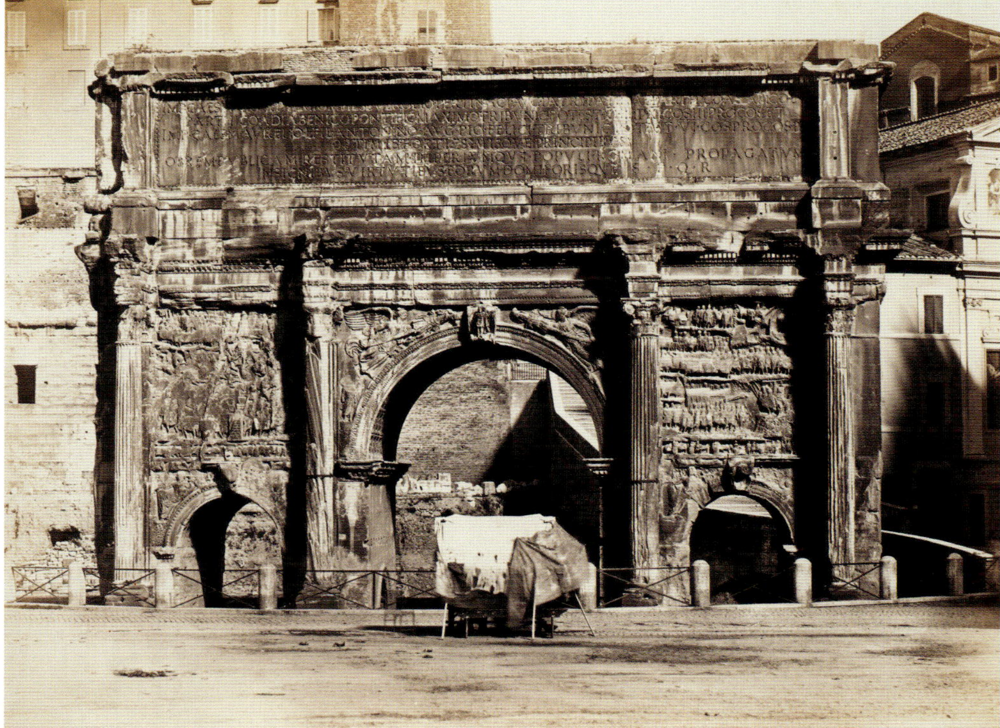

view of the elaborated gate to the Borghese Gardens [Fig. 9.10].[54]

People are generally absent from his images. But their presence is marked by graffiti, torn posters and carts. Arguably the most extraordinary expression of this sense of modern presence offers a kind of haunting in reverse: a trace of ordinary life in the context of a grand monument of the past. Macpherson's picture of the Arch of Septimius Severus [Fig. 9.11] has a strong horizontal composition to show the shape and detail of the arch. The central position, framed in the arch, is occupied by a cart. The cart can be moved and this is a large-scale serious photograph – so it is there for a photographic reason; without the cart, the image would be dull. Roy Flukinger has proposed that this cart is loaded with Macpherson's own photographic equipment and that he put it there himself.[55] If so, this deserves consideration. Painters might place an easel within a landscape, and the convention was followed by photographers in leaving a dark tent or tripod in the view, indicating scale or signalling art within art. But the cart is more forceful: it stands in the centre of the arch; darker cloth, draped over the stained cloth, is there to break its shape, and the folds to collect shadow. There is a further detail. There is no evidence of a person in the picture, but the chair beside the cart has been moved. Someone has walked into the picture and taken it, leaving a transparent chair in the image.

Macpherson had a heightened awareness of the relation between light and time in a long exposure. He said:

> The exposure depended entirely on circumstances:
> for a distant landscape in a good light, five minutes was
> enough; for near objects, ten or twenty minutes.[56]

This photograph is far from an interested tolerance of accident – it is constructed accident. Macpherson was playing with photography and the eccentric way it encompassed time.

Russia and the Near East

In 1853, the Russians invaded lands controlled by Turkey and sank the Ottoman fleet at the Battle of Sinope. The following year Britain joined forces with France, Turkey and Sardinia and embarked for the Crimean peninsula to attack the Russian forces. Ostensibly, the allies were addressing the religious question: who should be the protector of the Christians in the Ottoman Empire (most importantly, in Jerusalem) – France or Russia; in practice they were also moved by the danger to their trade routes to India.

The Crimean War is well-known for its fearful disorganisation: the armies were ill-prepared and badly supplied.[57] The disease that killed men in thousands roused the interest of engineer Isambard Kingdom Brunel, who designed a prefabricated hospital in a healthier position at Renkioi to support the one at Scutari where Florence Nightingale laboured. William Robertson (1818–1882), a physician at the Royal Infirmary, Edinburgh, went out as a Senior Physician. John Kirk (1832–1922) was the youngest of thirty-two medical staff at Renkioi, and had recently qualified in Edinburgh. They found themselves in a strange situation: effectively isolated from the war. The hospital at Scutari had improved, and the flow of patients was not as large as anticipated. This left Robertson and Kirk with time to take photographs: Robertson worked with collodion and Kirk took waxed paper negatives.[58] William Robertson's

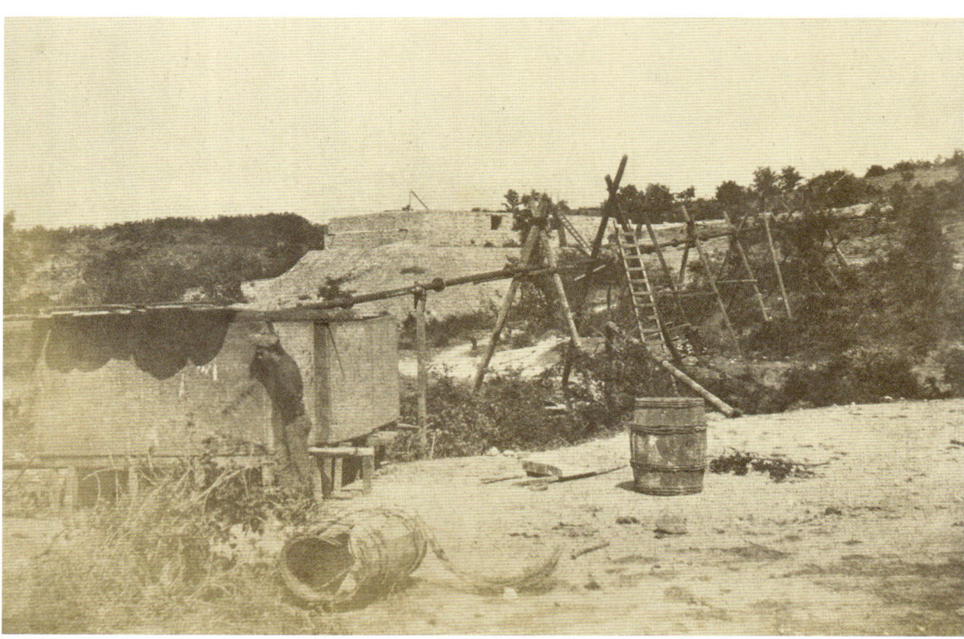

photographs are chiefly portraits of the staff and local people connected to the hospital. Kirk was able to explore the countryside and follow his own interest in botany, in recording trees. He may have been specifically asked to photograph the hospital and its supporting infrastructure – the piling engine for the north pier, the reservoir, the layout and the interior of the hospital [Fig. 9.12].

In the course of his career Charles Piazzi Smyth (1819–1900) developed the idea of the 'peripatetic astronomer', constantly bouncing off his inadequate Edinburgh base. In 1858, he and his wife Jessica went to St Petersburg [Fig. 9.13] to visit Pulkovo Observatory. Given the struggle to publish their first work in Tenerife with photographs, it is not surprising that their book on Russia was illustrated only by Smyth's drawings, but they describe their photographic activities.[59] At the Observatory, 'day after day, so long as any chemical light endured, we hammered away with a couple of stereoscopic cameras, wet collodion and dry'.[60] Nearby they photographed the stone on which Peter the Great sat to contemplate building his great city:

> … our object being, not only to get a verisimilitude of the trees and stones close by, but of the characteristic

Russian flat in the distance, with a road like a straight clean knife-cut dividing it up to its uttermost parts, also – a small aperture was necessary to secure good definition of the near and far; and with that small aperture came many troubles. It entailed for instance, to begin with, long exposures, – a nuisance at any time, and additionally so here when the gusty west winds, ever blowing, blowing, seldom allowed many seconds to pass without wildly waving up and down all the delicate leaves and branches that formed a network of tracery against the sky; and unhappily the exposure had to be even outrageously long, for the heavens were ever heavily clouded and water-laden, while under the trees a dense green shadow almost destroyed photographic action.[61]

They encountered many problems, from the need to acquire an official document to allow photography, to the excessive cost of materials and carriage.[62] In Moscow, they photographed the Kremlin and surrounding cathedrals, in circumstances of technical and social confusion:

> … the sheen of those golden hemispheres in such number and size, and placed just opposite to the sun and to

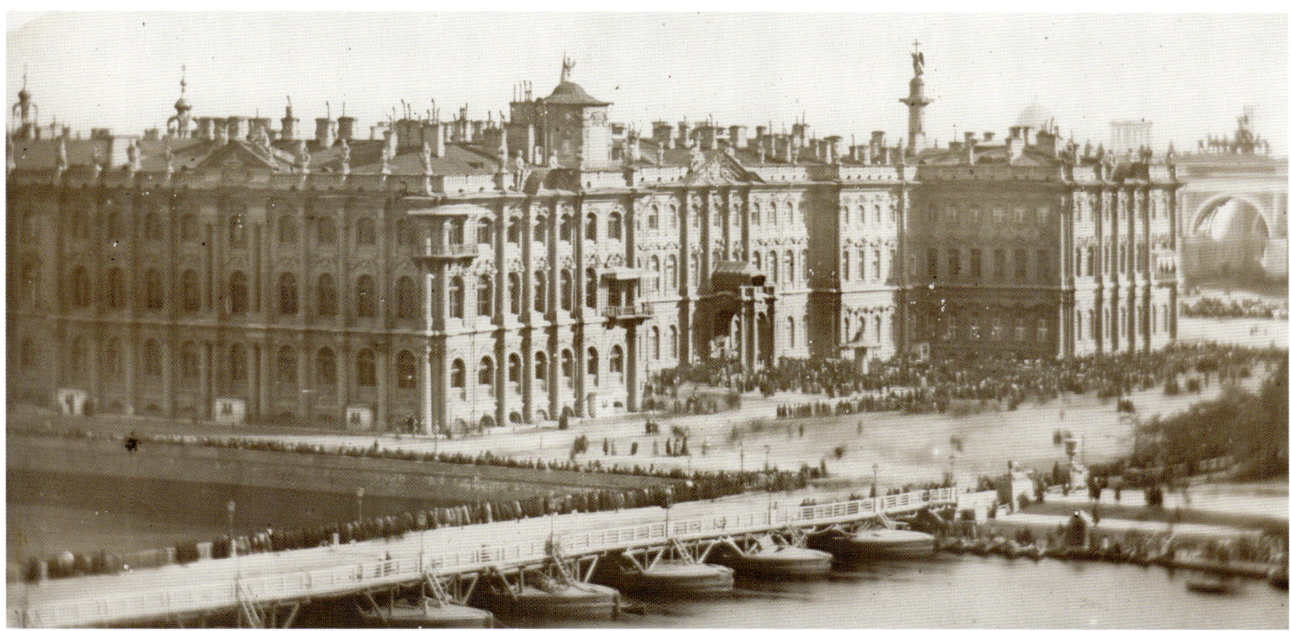

our eyes, struck us as something more truly gorgeous than we had ever expected to behold on earth. In our resulting photograph, as might be anticipated, the metallic surfaces lost much of their effect by a process where the richest yellow tells only as a dull black; but the amount of actual sunshine reflected from them on this occasion went far to overpower their chemically untoward colour, and there is accordingly even in the small stereoscope, a concentrated reflection of light on the various buildings, which at once bespeaks a new effect in architecture .... One of these Kremle churches, with a central large dome of gold, surrounded with four smaller domes of silver, is so photographed … one of the most exquisite things conceivable in the way of expression of the physical nature of surfaces by the pencil of light that we have ever seen; but it requires a compound achromatic microscope, directed on a glass picture, to bring out all the qualities.[63]

They had set up the camera on the open landing place by a bridge, with a constant flow of traffic and an audience of inquisitive peasants. Smyth comments on their decorous behaviour. Such consideration was a key to the Smyths'

success: even operating in sign language, they could express courtesy. They worked well in partnership. He was able to photograph a missal that once belonged to Mary, Queen of Scots, because Jessica Smyth 'made the acquaintance of a Russian lady of exalted sentiment and of infinite spirit [Madame De Lerche]. No sooner had this lady heard of my wish, than she took up the idea most warmly and enthusiastically.' Finding the Hermitage Museum's keeper had declared that no photographs could be taken without the permission of the Emperor, she promptly applied to the Emperor and it was granted: 'On receiving this joyful news we lost not a moment's time, and jumping into a droshky at the door, bade the Ishvostschik, or driver, with a bishop's hat, a sage's beard, and long priestly garment of dark blue cloth, drive us straight to the Hermitage.'[64]

On returning to St Petersburg, they were able to take two radically different photographs. Finding a large gathering to greet the Emperor and his son, they placed themselves on the other side of the River Neva:

… we focused the camera, and in three seconds a couple of pictures were obtained, which gave not only the architecture of the Tsar's abode [the Winter Palace], but the crowd, microscopically minute certainly, of well-booted mouzhiks under his drawing-room windows, as well as others lining all the Neva Quay and the sides of the wooden bridge ….[65]

In the museum of the St Petersburg Academy, where they wished to photograph a mammoth, they had the opposite problem, solved with a generosity unprecedented in the museum world:

> Dr Brandt kindly brought in a number of soldiers, and they walked about the stuffed rhinoceroses, and trotted off the preserved elephants and other such very large deer, until the camera's ground-glass presented a good picture of the monstrous bones ….
>
> There was therefore an abundance worth photography; but when we looked at its prevailing dark-brown tint, and the faint window-light, we were in despair. The air outside was thick and hazy; dingy would express it better … [but] the Doctor bid us not be disturbed by that, for we might leave the camera as long as we pleased. [they asked for 3 days, because the public were due in on the Monday, but the Director said] if a photograph is to be taken, and four days or five are necessary, the door of this room shall be locked for all that time.[66]

The Smyths' photographic practice balanced technological skill with lyrical enthusiasm for the world. They have left a rare and quite remarkable photographic record – certainly impractical and often notionally impossible.

Egypt

In the early 1850s, Robert Murray (1822–93), who had already worked in Malta and Russia, was appointed Chief Engineer to the Viceroy of Egypt.[67] The appointment probably related to the building of the railway between Alexandria and Cairo, undertaken by the engineering business of Robert Stephenson.[68] Murray gave a lecture on 'Egyptian Public Works' when he returned to Britain in 1859, and the tenor of his report suggests that the experience was troubling:

> … he said the labour was, as usual in all government works, forced, parties of soldiers being sent to villages, whence they carried off all the able-bodied men in manacles, for government works, leaving only the old and infirm, the women and children, to till the soil.[69]

Murray may only have been in Egypt for two years, from 1852 to 1854, when the railway was completed. However, his talk also addressed the vexed question of the attempts to control the waters of the Nile by Mehemet Ali ('after an expenditure of upwards of £2,000,000, it gives little hope of ever being completed'), and it may well be that Murray had responsibility for this issue also. His official position would have given him authority and freedom of movement from the coast at Alexandria beyond the first or second cataracts of the Nile into Nubia.

Murray found relief from disagreeable work in turning to photography and the history – 'the durability of Egyptian monuments', rather than the present reality of Egypt. He said later, when showing some of his Egyptian negatives to the Amateur Photographic Association, that

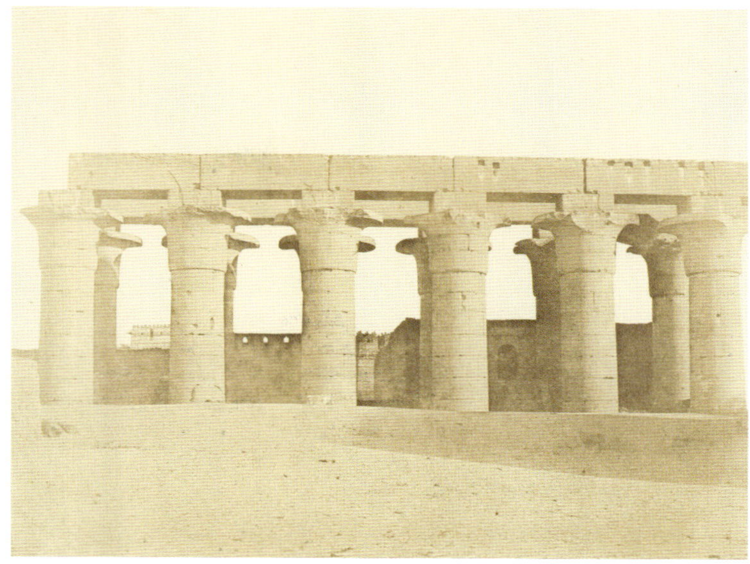

he 'taught himself entirely by a shilling handbook, sent out to him in Egypt, having never seen a negative taken by anyone until after his return to this country'.[70] The leaflet was presumably supplied with the camera.[71] Colin Osman has identified his supplier as Horne and Thornthwaite in London, and suggests he bought their 'No. 2 Calotype Set' at £7. 17. 6d for 9 x 7 inch negatives.[72]

It would be pleasing to think that in his river journeys Murray encountered Félix Teynard, also an engineer, who came to Egypt in 1851–52 and worked in similar territory as a photographer, along the Nile and into Nubia; the impressive French work undertaken at this time could well have inspired him to take photographs.

Murray came back to Britain with a large collection of paper negatives. Twenty-four prints were exhibited at the Photographic Society of Scotland in 1856.[73] Prints from 163 of the negatives were exhibited and sold by Joseph Hogarth as 'a valuable series of views from Malta, Alexandria, Cairo, Thebes, Upper Egypt and Nubia' [FIG. 9.14]. The number varies in the advertisements – in 1857 they were advertised as 'Photographs of Egypt', sold singly at 3s 6d each or at seven for a guinea; fifty selected views in a portfolio for five guineas or the 'complete set of 150 views' for £15.[74] In 1858, there were 168 plates at four shillings each.[75]

The photographs were greeted with fervour by a reviewer in the *Athenaeum*:

All previous photographs of Egypt 'go down' before the large and finely-wrought views published by Robert Murray, late chief engineer to the Viceroy of Egypt …. These views consist of all the best ancient and Saracenic remains of the Valley of the Nile, from Alexandria, to where Osiris sleeps; and even beyond that, into the

Nubia beyond the Cataracts …. The clear, keen, thin air of the hot, bright land is favourable for the chemist-artist. Every year now rubs out some line of hieroglyphic, or cancels some old Pharaoh signature. This Vishnu of art came in due time, and came to save and to record.[76]

This review expresses a fascination with the way photography might open up the cultural world. It celebrates the solemnity and enduring strength of Egyptian sculpture. The reference to Murray as a 'Vishnu' implies the god's character as a truth-teller and preserver.

Murray returned home and took employment as Engineer Surveyor to the Board of Trade. He continued to take photographs when on holiday, and Hogarth issued a set of his photographs of Normandy monuments in 1862. These disappointed the *Athenaeum* reviewer, who wrote flatly: 'Each subject has been carefully studied. If Mr Murray's views in Normandy should appear to be less brilliant than his Nile series, the difference of atmosphere between France and Egypt must be considered.'[77] He joined the Photographic Society of Scotland in 1860 and the Amateur Photographic Association in 1862 – his amateur status apparently not affected by the sales of his photographs – and his pictures achieved prizes [FIG. 9.15].[78]

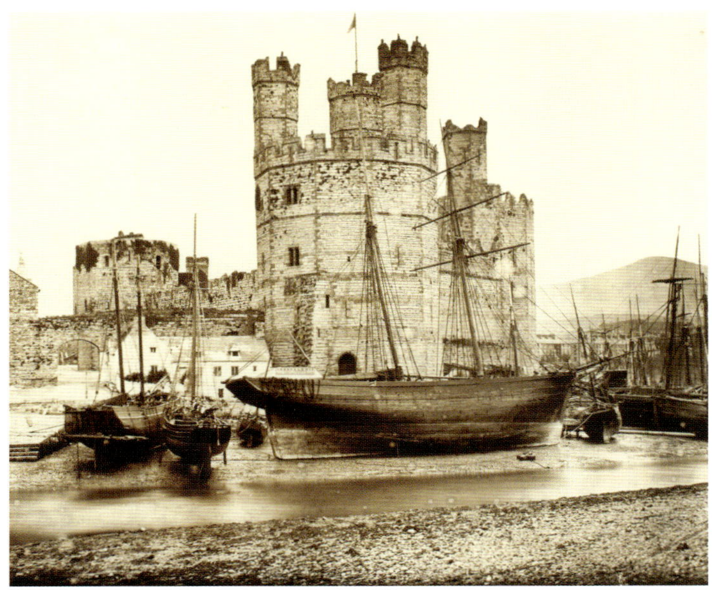

The Smyths' third significant foray into the outside world was of the evangelical kind. By the 1860s Piazzi Smyth had become convinced that the Great Pyramid demonstrated standards of measurement and a relationship to the cosmos of great precision. For example, he thought that the relationship of the base of the pyramid to its height connected to the mathematical concept of *pi*, and that it demonstrated evidence for the classic conundrum of squaring the circle. He thought that the British imperial measurements were divinely ordained, and the inch itself might be connected, by dating the pyramid to the time of the Old Testament, to the Judaic tradition.[79]

The Smyths' visit to Egypt was unofficial. They engaged in meticulous measurement, both inside and outside the Great Pyramid, and photographed the interior by magnesium flare [FIG. 9.16]. Smyth published his conclusions, convinced that he was right. Interest in the pyramid and theories of its covert mysticism are persistent – they are built into Freemasonry and the beliefs of the British Israelites. The Smyths' detailed research, however, presented the idea as a measured and mathematically-based truth, in societies devoted to scientific rigour.[80]

The Edinburgh reception of their argument was, at first, polite, although the surgeon and amateur archaeo-

logist James Young Simpson engaged in detailed destruction of Smyth's work before the Royal Society of Edinburgh. More worryingly, their evidence was undermined by the calculations of Sir Henry James of the Ordnance Survey, who had undertaken the government survey of Egypt.[81] Smyth subsequently found himself in disagreement with another authoritative friend, James Clerk Maxwell.[82] Smyth declared that he was, like Kepler, ahead of his time in his understanding. This did his career little good.

Smyth's exploration of photography did not end here. His further contributions include investigations of the spectrum, and an extended photographic study of cloud formations. His preference for small cameras and lenses was driven by the problem that larger lenses, though they let in more light and could take photographs faster, distorted the image. Smyth devised the first effective anastigmatic lens by 1874, but it failed to convince his contemporaries.[83]

When Jessica died in 1896, she was buried under a small stone pyramid, with a cross on top. The plaque on the tomb says that she

> … was his faithful and sympathetic friend and companion Through 40 years of varied Scientific experiences by land and sea abroad as well as at home at 12000 feet up in the atmosphere on the wind swept peak of Teneriffe as well as underneath and Upon the GREAT PYRAMID OF EGYPT … .[84]

In 1900, he was buried with her. There is a story that they took a camera with them.[85]

In 1861, Dr James Douglas (1800–86), his son James (1837–1918) with his new wife and Miss Mary Macdonald,

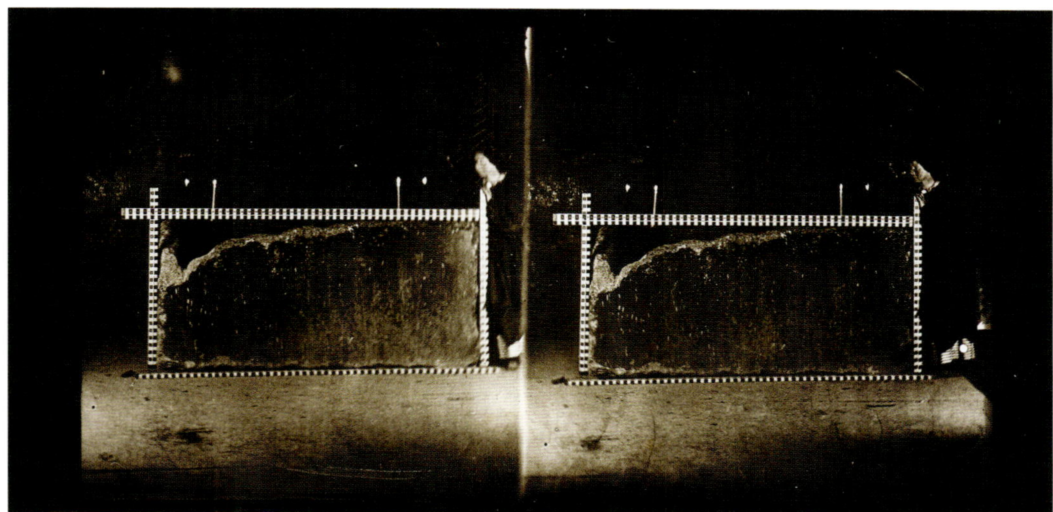

were to be found sailing up the Nile in extreme comfort. By this time, the wealthy tourists were a well-protected species. Dr Douglas wrote:

> To meet the requirements of European travellers, boats, called in Arabic, Dahabiehs, have been built expressly for their use and … travelling in Egypt has been rendered as safe as in England or Canada.[86]

The boat had four rooms, bathroom and closet, was richly carpeted throughout and ornamented by a good French artist: 'nothing is wanting to conduce to that expressive and peculiarly English word – comfort.' Staff included the captain, pilot, thirteen Nubian sailors, a dragoman, cook, waiter, and 'Ramadam, a smart lad [who] makes himself generally useful as assistant photographer and lay figure'.

Dr Douglas was born in Brechin, Angus, in 1800 and was trained by the surgeon, Robert Liston. He arrived in New York State in the 1820s, where he did demonstrations of anatomy. Robert Liston belonged to the generation of Edinburgh anatomists who robbed new graves for dissection, a covert habit that led to the great scandal of the murders committed by Burke and Hare to provide bodies more readily. In New York, the practice of grave-robbing was condoned, as long as the surgeons and their suppliers confined their attentions 'to the bodies of slaves, paupers

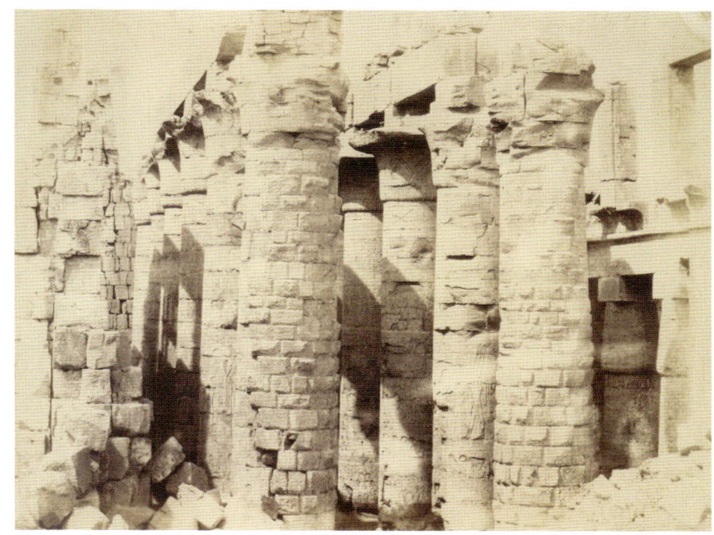

and strangers'.[87] In the winter of 1825, Douglas's contractors confused two recent graves and presented him with the corpse of a substantial citizen, who was recognised on his dissection table. He left town at speed for Quebec, where he improved conditions in the Marine and Emigrant Hospital and subsequently in the care of the insane.[88] In the 1850s, suffering from respiratory illness, he overwintered in the Mediterranean, particularly in Egypt.

His son, James Douglas, trained for the ministry in Edinburgh in 1855, where he met his wife, Naomi. The Douglases' interest in the Egypt was archaeological rather than religious. James Douglas junior offered aesthetic judgements on the architecture, based on James Fergusson's opinions. His photographs of the Grand Hall at Karnac, for example, are accompanied by text criticising the ornamental columns, which, despite their elegance, 'seem never to have supported an architrave nor to have filled any constructive purpose. They are therefore, quite out of place, and are incorrect.'[89] However, in another photograph [Fig. 9.17], his approval is ready: 'the aim of an architect should be so to dispose his masses that the apparent size may be greater than the real; which was undoubtedly attempted here.' The photograph successfully presents a massively packed group.

The Douglases' photographs were mixed in strength. James Douglas junior explained:

> The rapidity with which we moved must account for the defects which are so manifest in many of our pictures. Photography being quite a subordinate object with us, we never left the beaten tract nor did we ever delay an hour for the mere purpose of taking a view. Hence there are wanting to the collection a few interesting monuments and landscapes, which we either visited at night, or to the negatives of which some accident happened after we had passed the spot.

> When some object on the bank attracted our attention and was thought worthy of being taken, I left the *dahabieh* in the small boat with a couple of men, made the picture and had often a long row to overtake the rest of the party, who in the meantime had dropped a mile or two downstream. At other times we pulled for hours in advance of the *dahabieh* in order to gain time for taking a picture before evening set in ....

> We employed the simplest of wax paper processes ... the sensitized sheets keep good for some length of time. We therefore prepared every evening as many papers as we were likely to need next day; put them carefully into a portfolio, and transferred them from the portfolio to the frame in a Tomb or in the dark chamber of a Temple. Thus the only apparatus we required to take with us each day was a folding camera, a tripod stand and the portfolio, all of which one of our sailors easily carried.[90]

The photographs and text were privately published in two handsome volumes; the 'mere purpose' of photography was admired by the photographers despite James Douglas's comments. The text and photographs provide a fascinating account of high-level tourism in 1861, the way cleared by the violent modernisation of Mehmet Ali, and offering singularly luxurious standards. The Douglases' pleasure in the tour is undoubted, and their opinion of the country is aptly enthusiastic. In one remarkably long sentence countering the cynicism of some tourists, they praise

> ... variety of language, of colour, of manners, of the dress, address and no dress of the inhabitants, the abundance and variety of the fruits and vegetables ... the picturesque villages and graceful minarets, in contrast with the grand, sublime and deathlike aspects of the sunburnt hills ... the variety of the numberless monuments ... add to these, a pleasant party of ladies and gentlemen, a good and luxuriously fitted *Dahabieh*, good servants, an excellent cook, and cloudless skies ....[91]

This sounds like a modern tourist brochure – there is an air of unreality in such a sheltered 'experience' – and a feel of the virtual reality, much boosted in photography itself.

The Holy Land

The Holy Land was a place of profound spiritual meaning, especially for evangelical Christians. In their thinking, the real world was a source of divine revelation. Even the collection of data, which took analytical thinking beyond common assumption, might increase faith, and reveal divine intention.

The Rev. Alexander Keith's journeys to the Holy Land were of this kind, and in 1844 his son, Dr George Skene Keith, travelled with him, taking daguerreotypes to demonstrate the truths of prophecy. The Scots Presbyterians were devoted to the study of the Old as well as the New Testament and believed that the conversion of the Jews to Christianity was a key to human progress and perfection. This became a political issue. In 1838, the Ottoman Empire, which ruled Jerusalem, agreed to the establishment of a bishop of Jerusalem and to the setting up of a British Consulate. The Consul and his wife, James and Elizabeth Finn, who arrived in 1846, were Hebrew scholars and archaeologists and sought out biblical sites. In 1849, they were visited by the Rev. George Bridges, who explained his photography to Elizabeth Finn. She promptly sent for photographic equipment.[92]

In 1853, James Graham (1806–1869), a younger son of James Graham of Fereneze, Renfrewshire, arrived in Jerusalem as the Lay Secretary sent by the London Jews Society. Mrs Finn wrote that her friends in England had told James Graham of her photography:

… so he learnt the art and brought with him a fine photographic apparatus, which he used with excellent effect; I have a good many unique photographs of his taking, amongst them one of the great tomb of Hiram, King of Tyre, the friend of King Solomon; it is the finest photograph in existence of that tomb. Mr Graham engaged the help of one of our congregation, of Jewish origin [Mendel Diness], and taught him the art, which he practiced successfully. That was the beginning of photography in Jerusalem.[93]

In his obituary, Graham's motivation was explained:

… he was, like most of his countrymen, well acquainted with the Holy Scriptures. He knew the wonderful history of the chosen people, and he believed in the literal fulfilment of all God's promises to them …. known by the leading Protestants in England and France, he had an immense circle of friends among all ranks in Scotland, England, France, Switzerland and Italy.[94]

His extensive travels, through Europe and in the Holy Land, may have been partly driven by economy, and in later years by poor health. But in Jerusalem he showed energy and generosity. He was practically involved in prayer and religious support for converts, and devoted considerable time to fundraising for the Jews – most importantly during the privations brought on by the Crimean War.

Graham's relations with two pre-Raphaelite painters, Thomas Seddon and William Holman Hunt, are illuminating [FIG. 9.18].[95] Seddon's principal work in the Holy Land was a picture of Jerusalem, which was described by John Ruskin:

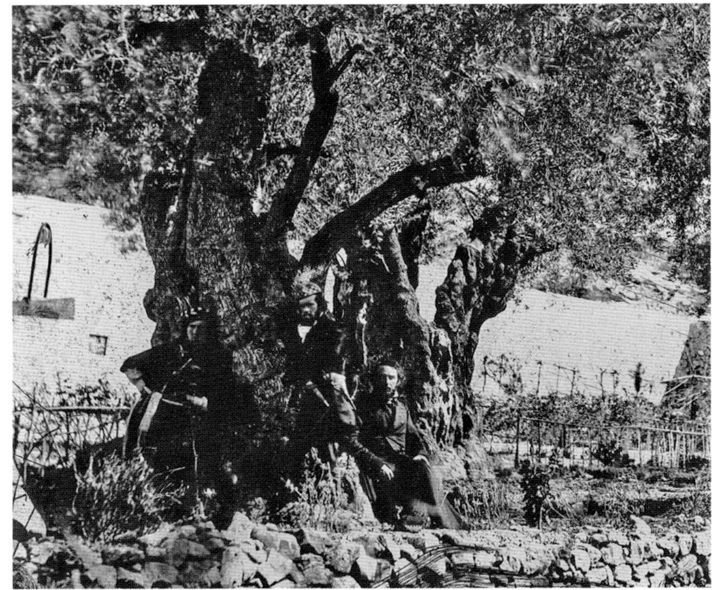

> In Mr Seddon's works, the primal object is to place the spectator, as far as art can do, in the scene represented, and to give him the perfect sensation of its reality, wholly unmodified by the artist's execution.[96]

This modest proposal was supported by Graham's work. Seddon had not completed the picture when he left Jerusalem, and he carried with him a batch of photographs. He wrote:

> I hope to bring some of them to England for him, so that I shall be able to shew them to you and supply my own want of sketches. They are extremely valuable, because perfectly true as far as they go, however they will never supplant the pencil, for there is much in photographs that is false; the greens and yellows become nearly as black as the shadows, so that you often cannot distinguish which is shadow and which grass.[97]

Seddon's reservations, as expressed by many painters, did not prevent him finding the photographs useful – they helped in giving his picture that sense of highly-focussed objectivity, critical to both painters and photographers working in this context. The distinction between his painting of Jerusalem and Graham's photographs lies in the colour – which he painted in an evening saturation of pink-purple light. Seddon explained a problem with the nature of light at mid-day, which was experienced similarly by the photographers:

> In the afternoon, shortly before sunset, the rosy light on it and the mountain range, with the exceedingly blue shadows, gives a beautiful effect, while in the middle of the day it seems colourless and shadowless. It is curious how completely scenes which are lovely by afternoon or early morning light lose all charm in the bright sunshine. The country and buildings are principally mud or sand coloured, while the glare of the sun makes the green trees (and palms especially) look quite grey.[98]

Graham accompanied both Seddon and Hunt into the country, and contributed photographs for Hunt's use. Hunt's stirring account of his painting, 'The Scapegoat', does not acknowledge this: like Seddon, he was concerned to promote his own direct experience. However, one critic observed the photographic effect of his background, and the Consul noted in his diary that the goat had to be found for him and photographed.[99]

Graham occupied a striking feature of the landscape – 'a little square stone tower, like a feudal castle', offering a magnificent view of Jerusalem and the landscape.[100] He entertained friends there. Holman Hunt gave an extended description of the view, which casts a sidelight on Graham:

> On moonlight nights, while my friend read aloud a kind of literature for which I cared little, I could sit at the

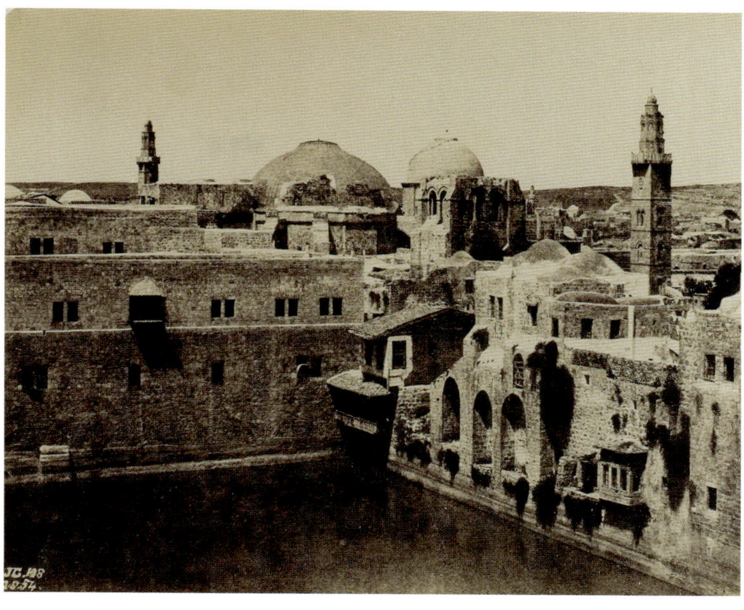

Fig. 9.19: James Graham, 'Church of the Holy Sepulchre and Hezikiah's Pool from the S.W.', 1854, albumen print. (Israel Museum, BO5. 0685/78)

open window resting my brow on its cool lintel, and turn my eyes upon the traces left by the successive masters of the city since the days of Solomon, and upon the land so little changed since its history was first written upon it …

Turning my attention from the window, I heard Graham's enthusiastic droning as before, and when it closed my good friend asked if I had ever heard such an eloquent sermon, and I felt able to say 'Never!'[101]

While it cannot be supposed that Graham was unmoved by this remarkable view, he took a literal approach to the landscape of the Bible [Fig. 9.19]. His negatives were inscribed with quotations from Scripture, which were the motive for the photographs. They were intended to give specific information on the land – places, shown largely empty, for his audience to repopulate with the past and potential future of Israel.

John Cramb (d.1894), who visited Palestine in 1860, was a professional photographer. He was commissioned by the Glasgow publisher, William Collins, who specialised in religious texts, and probably prompted by Francis Frith's handsome publications of the Holy Land, to propose two books and a set of stereoscopic photographs intended for the Christmas market. They were designed for a particular audience: 'A merely fine picture is not … what they care to possess, but a life-likeness of the original Israel. This *desideratum* Photography alone can, with absolute certainty, supply.'[102] William Collins wanted a photographer to go out immediately, and stipulated photographs in a dry process (thinking that this would be more appropriate to the country). Cramb agreed, while admitting that he had no knowledge of the country, climate, political circumstances

or issues of safety. He wrote that 'books of travel had to be gone through at an express-train rate' – they were not unduly helpful.[103] He prepared his albumen negatives in advance, and took twice as many as he thought he would need, 'a rather narrow margin'. He had two stereo cameras and a single, larger camera, which he set up on his stand, 'a considerable distance apart but adjustable, with the large, 8 x 10 camera in the middle'. He set out on 10 April, a mere fortnight after agreeing to the project, with seven packages, weighing in total 435 lbs, but not much in the way of underwear. It is understandable that he had difficulty with the customs in France and in Palestine.

John Cramb's account of the journey was published in the *British Journal of Photography*, in no less than twelve parts between December 1860 and August 1861. He was a nervous and chauvinistic tourist; he distrusted the French and most of the inhabitants of the Holy Land; he had no understanding of the customs or requirements of the countries that he passed through, and he generally preferred Scotland as far better. Fearful of being robbed in the countryside, he stated, 'to one who has roamed over the hills and wild glens of his native Caledonia, the Syrian wady is too narrow, and the hills have neither height, individuality, nor distinction of character'.[104]

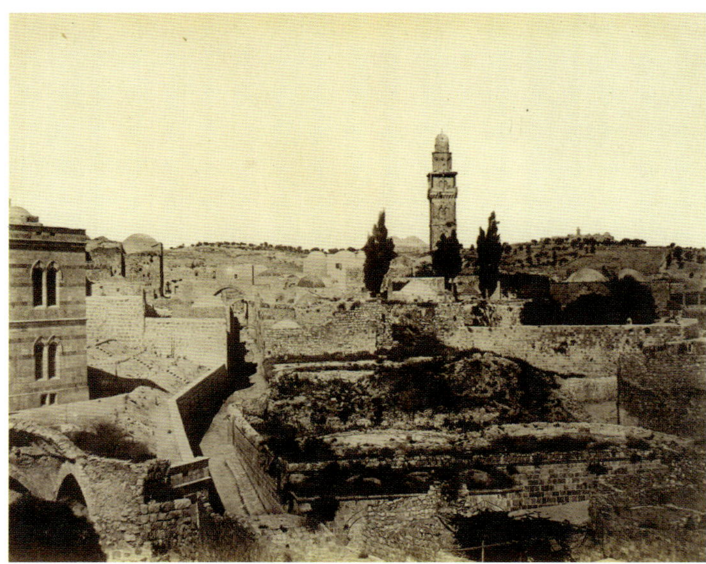

He inadvertently offered an excellent account of the burden of naïve tourism on the consulate. When alone in his hotel in Jerusalem, he decided to take his cameras onto the roof to take an aerial view of the Via Dolorosa. Having set them up, he suddenly found himself joined by an incomprehensibly angry African – he led the man down to his room, so that he could intimidate the stranger in turn with his six-barrelled revolver. They then went to the British consulate where it was explained that he had pointed his camera at a harem garden. When Cramb wanted to join a party travelling to the Dead Sea, the Consul arranged a sheik to accompany them, and persuaded Cramb to leave his gun behind. Cramb nonetheless began by regarding the sheikh with deep suspicion, referring to him as 'Rob Roy'.[105]

Cramb eventually managed to relax and admire, but his photographs exhibit stress. He was working under pressure, at an unfavourable time of year for light and heat. The overall focus of the photographs is poor and they are often overexposed [FIG. 9.20].

He and the publisher bolstered the sale of the photographs with commercial rhetoric. He wrote of pictures of Jerusalem from the Mount of Olives: 'What is actually *to be seen now* I have delineated by the unmatched powers of our wizard-like art, in a manner that no tongue or pen ever could approach – as no eye ever saw, not in fifty visits.' The albumen on these negatives cracked on drying; nevertheless he was confident that they outclassed the magnificent six-volume set of lithographs by the painter, David Roberts.[106]

From October 1864 to June 1865, a group of Royal Engineers undertook a survey of Jerusalem, under the auspices of the Palestine Exploration Fund.[107] Freed to undertake peacetime activity by the end of the Crimean War, they were funded by Baroness Burdett Coutts. The British had been appalled to learn of the condition of Jerusalem, especially the highly polluted wells which was the cause of endemic disease. The survey was intended to address both the biblical archaeology of the city and the problem of the water.

The photographer of the party was one Sergeant James McDonald (1822–85), an experienced and meticulous surveyor, by 1854 regarded as an 'officer of tried ability and indefatigable activity'.[108] The survey was published in three volumes, one devoted to photographs principally by McDonald. It is notable for an army exercise that the individuals in this and the following survey were identified and credited with their work.

In 1868 McDonald was involved in the mapping of the Peninsula of Sinai. This venture was supported by private donations to the Palestine Exploration Fund. The drive was religious and curiously Romantic: the Engineers were mapping out the Book of Exodus. In the introduction, the Rev. George Williams wrote of earlier explorers:

Their statements were at the best the results of very partial information, collected during a hasty journey through the country or a brief sojourn at the [St Katherine's] Convent, of very inadequate observations,

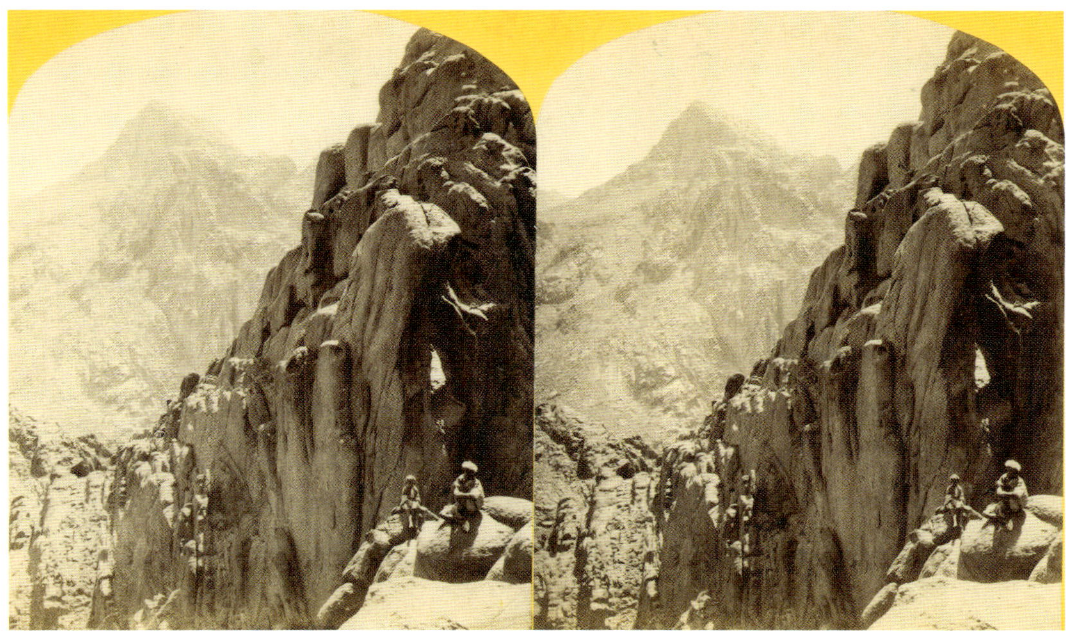

unaided by instruments, and of the merest smattering of the vernacular Arabic, mis-pronounced or mis-interpreted by an illiterate dragoman. There was nothing for it but to bring the material appliances of the Ordnance Survey Office to bear upon the questions at issue, by subjecting the rugged heights of the Peninsula to the unreasoning though logical tests of the theodolite and land-chain, of altitude and azimuth instruments, of the photographic camera, and the unerring evidence of the pole-star and the sun.[109]

He added the underlying terms of the survey:

> The most essential element for the investigation of the various historical questions connected with the Peninsula was a manly unsuspecting trust in the authenticity and authority of the ancient Records.

They were not searching for historical traces but geographical sites, to 'furnish the history with a theatre adequate to the requirements of the stupendous Drama'.

They intended to identify Mount Sinai, from which God had sent down the Ten Commandments to the people of Israel (there were currently no less than five contenders), and the remit was splendidly literal – the mountain required a plain large enough 'to admit of some two or three million spectators being present as the witnesses of the sublime spectacle' and nearby pasturage for the 'flocks and herds of this enormous host'.[110]

The detailed survey concentrated on the two most likely mountains, Jebel Musa and Jebel Serbal, with an overview of the general area and St Katherine's Convent [FIG. 9.21]. The Engineers were surveying a wilderness, a visual landscape unrelated to Western experience:

> It is a desert, certainly, in the fullest sense of the word, but a desert of rock, gravel, and boulder, of gaunt peaks, dreary ridges, and arid valleys and plateaux, the whole forming a scene of stern desolation which fully merits its description as the 'great and terrible wilderness'. So far from there being nothing to survey, the topographer may well shrink from the task of delineating its countless intricacies.[111]

The terrain tested the fitness of the engineers. Captain Palmer, who wrote the report, described, for example, 'hill-

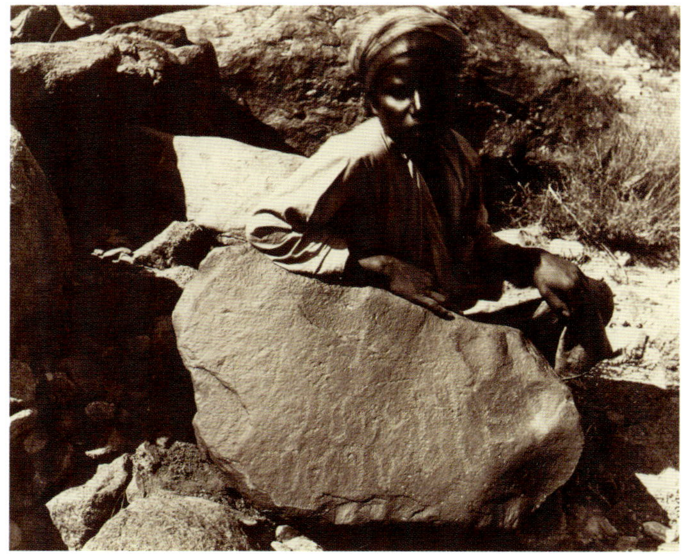

Fig. 9.22 (left): Sergeant J. McDonald, 'Inscription W.[ady] Ajeleh', albumen print, from *Ordnance Survey of the Peninsula of Sinai*, 1869. (National Library of Scotland, Phot. LA.1)

Fig. 9.23 (opposite left): Sergeant J. McDonald, 'The Cypress, Jebel Musa', albumen print, from *Ordnance Survey of the Peninsula of Sinai*, 1869. (National Library of Scotland, Phot. LA.1)

Fig. 9.24 (opposite right): Sergeant J. McDonald, 'Summit of Jebel Musa from Jebel Ed Deir', albumen print, from *Ordnance Survey of the Peninsula of Sinai*, 1869. (National Library of Scotland, Phot. LA.1)

sides, if not as a general rule, so precipitous, were certainly more crumbling and toilsome, and the extremely rugged character of the wadies and ravines offered impedimenta both to travelling and to working which can scarcely be overstated'. While they surveyed Jebel Musa, the weather broke:

> … with a severe gale, accompanied by showers of sleet, which lasted 48 hours. Snow and ice had made their appearance on the higher hill-tops, and in the valleys as well as on the heights the winds were sometimes violent and piercingly cold. At our camp, which was but 4,854 feet above the sea, the temperature had fallen on some nights as low as 22° Fahrenheit, and the inconvenience caused by this degree of cold was aggravated by the extreme scarcity of fuel for camp-fire. It therefore seemed best to leave the hill-sketching until the spring.[112]

They were assisted by Bedouin ibex hunters, who acted as porters for much of their technical luggage. But the terrain still offered difficulties: 'Locomotion in some parts can only be spoken of as a series of leaps from boulder to boulder.'[113]

Evidently there was no concern to maintain the dignity of the British in this expedition – and the mental image of the Engineers bounding from rock to rock is pleasing.

Palmer said that the climbing was not difficult but 'about as steep and laborious as safe climbing can well be'. However:

> After a few days of mountain air, we were busily occupied, almost without intermission, from six in the morning till eleven or twelve at night …. [They had to erect cairns on the triangulation points and whitewash them] as most of them were necessarily placed on the highest and most inaccessible portions, we sometimes found ourselves compelled to clamber up difficult places carrying the white-wash pot between our teeth, an awkward proceeding at best.[114]

In such extreme conditions, where the photographer was standing and how he balanced his camera are particularly edgy questions.

The two photographs that McDonald took of the nine-man party show an army distinction of commissioned and non-commissioned officers, but it was more relaxed than this might suggest. Of the five Westerners with the two Bedouin guides in the first photograph, only two were from the army and they were both captains, Wilson and Palmer. The three civilians in the group were a clergyman (who has charge of the pot of whitewash), a naturalist and orientalist. The second group is dominated by McDonald himself, who probably organised the group through the camera, placing the theodolite as a symbol of his authority, but also as a marker for the location he moved into when the shot

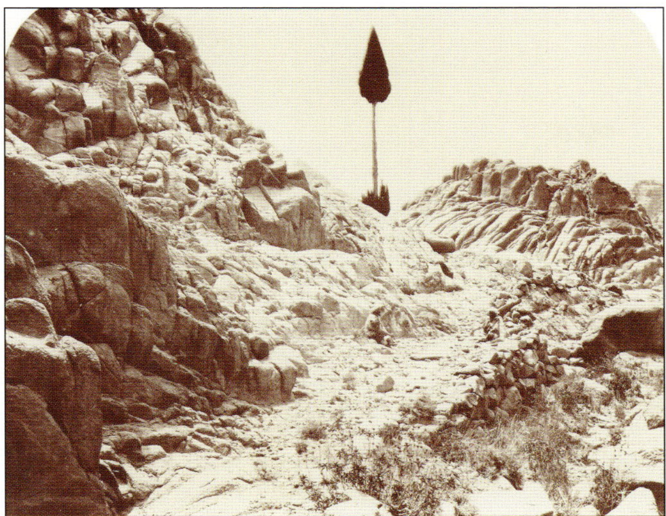 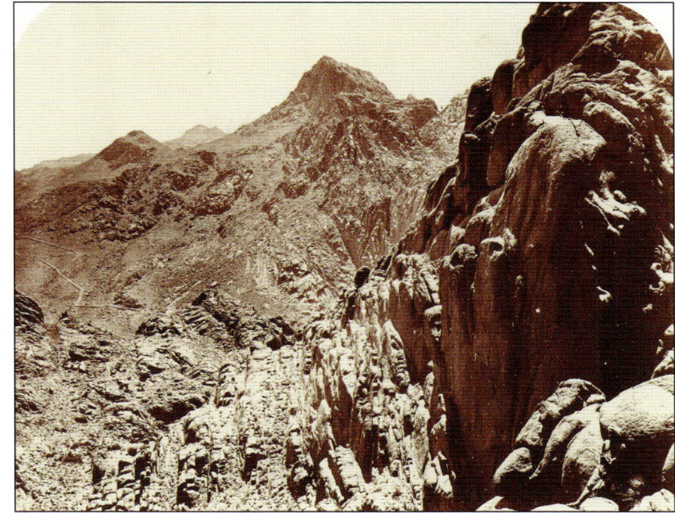

was set up. McDonald is the only one wearing a uniform jacket, and otherwise the group looks similarly at ease. Corporal Brigley is wearing a fez.

McDonald had full command of the detail and delicacy of the collodion process and has communicated the strength and beauty of the light and the region's 'atmosphere of surpassing transparency'.[115] Here his skill addressed a radically new aesthetic – based on a chaos of stone and the desert landscape. His photographs from the hundreds of rock inscriptions in the Wady Mukatteb, add another and extraordinary feature to his work – historic writing on the landscape itself [Fig. 9.22]. The comprehensive nature of the survey gave dimension to the impact of the photographs. The observation from different heights and angles gives an idea of the reality and involves us more effectively in the experience. A simple but notable pair of pictures makes this point. High up and alongside the path up the mountain of Jebel Musa, stands an isolated and distinctive cypress tree – a strange punctuation mark that would have acted as a landmark even more effectively than the features of the rock [Fig. 9.23]. The close photograph of the path through weathered rock shows us the tree standing up proud and significant. He took an additional distant view of the mountain, 'Summit of Jebel Musa from Jebel Ed Deir', which was provided with printed annotations below the summit of the mountain, to the zig-zag line of the

'Pashas' Road'; and on the horizon, the detail, one millimetre high, carefully labelled as 'Cypress Tree' [Fig. 9.24]. The scale of this second picture and the distances the surveyors were coping with becomes immediately clear.

Palmer concluded, with justice: 'As specimens of topographical work, these two special surveys are remarkable, if not wholly unique. Representations so faithful and detailed, tracts of country similarly wild and rugged, with features so stupendous and yet so intricate, have probably never been attempted elsewhere.'[116]

This work was published in a set of handsome volumes, dominated by McDonald's photographs. One hundred and fifty-three of the approximately three hundred that he took were presented in the books, and the Ordnance Survey also offered thirty-six stereoscopic views for sale. The choice of photographs was designed to offer a comprehensive view of

… the natural features of the Peninsula, its geological character and scenery, it antiquities and rock-inscriptions, and the appearance and mode of life of its inhabitants …. These beautiful pictures speak for themselves. Many of them were taken under circumstances of great difficulty; and Serjeant-Major McDonald deserves the highest praise for the superior skill, and indefatigable energy and care, which he has brought to bear upon this important branch of work.[117]

Notes

1. See, for instance, Richardson and Smith (eds) 2001, and Smith 2013.
2. See Stevenson, Lawson and Gray 1988.
3. His journal, held in a private collection, stops at Liège.
4. Account of meeting of the Photographic Society of Scotland, 24 March 1863, *British Journal of Photography* 10 (1 April 1863): 149.
5. Cosmo Innes, 'Short Notes of Photographic Tours', paper read to the Photographic Society of Scotland, 24 March 1863, *Photographic Journal* 8 (15 April 1863): 258.
6. *Ibid.*, 259.
7. Review of Photographic Society of Scotland exhibition, *Scotsman*, 17 December 1859.
8. Account of the meeting of the Photographic Society of Scotland, 24 March 1863, *British Journal of Photography* 10 (1 April 1863): 149.
9. C. G. H. Kinnear, 'Abstract of an Account of an Architectural and Photographic Tour in the North of France', *Journal of the Photographic Society of London* 4 (21 December 1857): 116–21.
10. Forrester 1845: 38.
11. Ian Sumner, 'Baron Joseph James De Forrester', in Hannavy (ed.) 2008, vol. 1: 541. See also Taylor and Schaaf 2007: 315; and Grace Seiberling, 'The Photographs of Joseph James Forrester', *History of Photography* 7 (1983): 51–61.
12. This may indicate a connection with D. O. Hill, who came from Perth and whose first wife, Ann Macdonald, was a member of a wine merchant's family.
13. These are in the collections of the Museum of Modern Art, New York (1), and Glasgow University Library, Special Collections (5).
14. *The photographic album for the year 1855, being contributions from the members of the Photographic Club*, printed for the members of the Photographic Club by Charles Whittingham, [1856]; copy in George Eastman House collection and the British Library. Forrester surveyed and produced a map of the Douro during the 1830s.
15. Anon., 'Proceedings of Societies. Photographic Soirée at King's College', *Chemist: A monthly journal of chemical and physical science* [New Series], 4 (185): 255–6.
16. Forrester, Letter from 24 Crutched Friars, London, 13 July 1854, 'Waxed Positives', *Journal of the Photographic Society* 2 (21 August 1854): 25.
17. *The Amateurs' Photographic Album*, part 4 (published by Thomas Sutton and Blanquart-Evrard) included: '1 The Crucifixion and 2 Doorway of San Geronimo Lisbon, both by Major Ross 73rd Regiment', advertised in *Photographic Notes* 1 (March 1856): 45.
18. Thomas Sutton, 'Landscape Photography for the Artist and the Amateur', *Illustrated Photographer* 1 (28 February 1868): 44.
19. Review of 'Dr Alexander Taylor, On the Curative Influence of the Climate of Pau … with Descriptive Notices of the Geology, Botany, Natural History, Mountain-Sports, Local Antiquities, and Topography of the Pyrenees …', *Edinburgh Medical and Surgical Journal* 59 (1843): 142.
20. See Taylor and Schaaf 2007: 375.
21. John Stewart, 'New Photographic Process', *Athenaeum* 1341 (9 July 1853). It was generally agreed that this was not a new idea, but that Stewart's account gave it currency; it was republished in other journals.
22. Advertisement, *Scotsman*, 1 April 1854.
23. *Journal of the Photographic Society* [*of London*] 1 (21 June 1854): 213.
24. J. F. W. Herschel, Letter, *Athenaeum* 1311 (7 December 1853).
25. 'Mr Stewart on the Paper Process', *Journal of the Photographic Society* 1 (30 June 1854): 225–30.
26. Dahlberg 2005: 35.
27. Jammes and Parry Janis 1983: 93.
28. Taylor and Schaaf 2007: 361–2.
29. Rev. T. M. Raven, 'Pau and the Pyrenees, with a slight sketch of a Photographic Tour made to them through the west of France', *Journal of the Photographic Society* [*of London*] 5 (21 December 1858–21 January 1859): 104–8, 131–2, 155–7.
30. T. M. Raven, Letter to the Editor, *Photographic Notes* 3 (1 February 1858): 45.
31. 'The Exhibition of the Photographic Society', *Photographic News* 1 (21 January 1859): 231.
32. Review of the Photographic Society of Scotland exhibition, *Photographic Journal* 5 (5 February 1859): 180.
33. Alastair Crawford, 'Robert Macpherson 1814–72, the foremost photographer of Rome', *Papers of the British School at Rome* 67 (1999): 353–403.
34. William Gardiner [1847]: 208–9.

Note: Website addresses checked and correct at the time of going to press.

35. [Mahony] 1847: 73–4. The Michelangelo is now in the National Gallery in London.

36. Ray McKenzie, 'The Cradle and the Grave of Empires: Robert Macpherson and the Photography of Nineteenth-Century Rome', in the *Photographic Collector* 4: 2 (Autumn 1983): 215–34.

37. Obituary of Robert Macpherson, *British Journal of Photography* 19 (6 December 1872): 577. On leaving Rome, Dr Clark proceeded to Capri, to open a clinic in 'the sunniest spot' on the island.

38. Thomas Sutton, editorial response to an anonymous letter, 'Is Photography a Healthy Pursuit?', *Photographic Notes* 2 (1 May 1857): 164–5.

39. Thomas Sutton, 'Reminiscences of an Old Photographer', Paper delivered to the Photographic Society of Scotland, *British Journal of Photography* 14 (30 August 1867): 414.

40. Oliphant, in Macpherson 1878: xiii–xiv.

41. This text actually says: 'While I write, October 5, 1894, he [Cecco, the child born in Rome just after his father died], the last, is lying in his coffin in the room next to me – I have been trying to pray by the side of that last bed …. All gone, all gone, and no light to come to this sorrow any more ….', in Coghill (ed.) 1899: 64.

42. *Ibid.*, 58.

43. Alexander John Ellis, introducing a proposed series of engravings from his daguerreotypes of Rome, taken in 1841, quoted by D. B. Thomas in 'Early English Daguerreotypes', *Photography* (July 1962): 38. For Ellis, see also Tom Ruffles, 'Ellis, Alexander John', in Hannavy (ed.) 2008, vol. 1: 480–2. His collection of 158 whole-plate daguerreotypes of Italy is in the National Media Museum, NMSI 1890–56.

44. Forsyth 1824: 166.

45. A descendant of the photographer, James Anderson, who succeeded him in business, told Helmut Gernsheim in the 1950s that Macpherson failed because of his 'very profligate and extravagant lifestyle': quoted by Alistair Crawford, 'Robert Macpherson 1814–72, the foremost photographer of Rome', *Papers of the British School at Rome* 67 (1999): 401.

46. See Elizabeth Anne McCauley, 'Fawning over Marbles: Robert and Gerardine Macpherson's Vatican Sculptures and the Role of Photographs in the Reception of the Antique ', in Bann (ed.) 2011: 91–122.

47. Ms letter from Robert Macpherson to W. B. Johnstone, 20 August 1860, Royal Scottish Academy archive.

48. Anon., 'Our weekly gossip', *Athenaeum* 1815 (9 August 1862): 181.

49. Report of the Photographic Society of Scotland meeting, *Photographic Journal* 7 (15 December 1862): 184.

50. Ms letter from Robert Macpherson, Royal Scottish Academy archive.

51. His photolithographs were shown at the meeting of the British Association in Glasgow in 1855 and described by Professor A. C. Ramsay, 'On a Process for obtaining Lithographs by the Photographic Process', *Notices and Abstracts, Transactions of the British Association for the Advancement of Science; held at Glasgow in September 1855* (1856), Part II: 69–70. Macpherson gave a detailed account of his process, which required very delicate handling, to the Photographic Society of Scotland on 9 December 1856; see the Report of the meeting, *Photographic Notes* 1 (January 1857): 6–8.

52. Report of the meeting of the Photographic Society of Scotland, *Photographic Journal* 7 (15 December 1862): 184.

53. 'Review of the Exhibition of the Architectural Photographic Association', *Photographic News* 1 (24 December 1858): 185–6.

54. Discussed by Smith 2011: 48–9.

55. Flukinger 2011: 134–5.

56. Report of the meeting of the Photographic Society of Scotland, when Macpherson showed a 'very extensive and beautiful collection of photographs of ancient Rome', *Photographic Journal* 8 (15 December 1862): 184.

57. The key British photographers in the Crimea were Roger Fenton, working with Marcus Sparling, and James Robertson, working with Felice Beato. Robertson is often considered to be of Scottish descent, but we have, sadly, found no evidence for this.

58. Julie Lawson, 'Dr John Kirk and Dr William Robertson: Photographers in the Crimea', *History of Photography* 12 (1988): 227–41.

59. The exception is the gold-stamped image of church domes on the cover, which was 'carefully copied from a photograph taken by myself in the Beloi Gorod of Moskva': see Smyth 1862: xii, Preface.

60. *Ibid.*, 166.

61. *Ibid.*, 167.

62. *Ibid.*, 361.

63. *Ibid.*, 428–30.

64. Smith and Smyth 1862: 4.

65. *Ibid.*, 209.

66. *Ibid.*, 217–21.

67. See Colin Osman, 'Robert Murray of Edinburgh (1822–93): the Discovery of Neglected Calotypes of Egypt', *Photoresearcher* 6 (March 1997): 6–11.

68. Murray was involved in a dispute with Stephenson over the tubular bridges over the Conway and the Menai Straits. Stephenson's design was modified by William Fairbairn, assisted by Murray, which Stephenson failed to acknowledge, see Colin Osman, 'Robert Murray of Edinburgh (1822–93): the Discovery of Neglected Calotypes of Egypt', *Photoresearcher* 6 (March 1997): 7.

69. Anon., Account of Lecture, *The Engineers' Journal, Railway, Public Works and Mining Gazette of India and the Colonies* 2, Calcutta (17 June 1859): 224.

70. Robert Murray, 'A few hints to amateur landscape photographers', *British Journal of Photography* 27 (13 February 1880): 77–8.

71. Report of a meeting of the Amateur Photographic Association, when Murray was elected a member, 26 September 1862, *Journal of the Photographic Society* 8 (15 October 1862): 148.

72. See Howe 1992.

73. <http://peib.dmu.ac.uk/itemphotographer.php?photogNo=292&orderby=coverage&photogName=Murray%2C+Robert+%281822-1893%29>

74. Advertisement in Murray 1857.

75. Advertisement from a leaflet published with an album of Dr John Murray's *Photographic Views in Agra and its vicinity*, British Library, India Office collection, Photo 101.

76. Anon., 'Fine-Art Gossip', *Athenaeum* 1597 (5 June 1858): 727.

77. Anon., Report, *Athenaeum* 1815 (9 August 1862): 182.

78. Murray's photographs of Caernarvon, 1868, and Wells Cathedral, 1870, are identified as prize prints in the Amateur Photographic Association collection in George Eastman House.

79. Smyth 1864.

80. See, for instance, Tompkins 1978; Colavito 2012.

81. James Young Simpson, 'Pyramidal Structures in Egypt and elsewhere, and the objects of their erection', *Proceedings of the Royal Society of Edinburgh* 6 (1868–69): 243–68; Sir Henry James published *Notes on the Great Pyramid of Egypt and the Cubits used in its Design* in 1869. He failed to mention Smyth's work. Smyth published *A Poor Man's Photography at the Great Pyramid* in 1870, substantially as an attack on James's work.

82. The story has recently been retold by Simon Schaffer, 'Metrology, Metrication and Victorian values', in Lightfoot (ed.) 1997: 438–74.

83. 'It was duly completely ignored for the advance it represented and the possibility that successful small format photography could have been initiated many decades before the Leica camera': Sidney F. Ray, 'The Applied Photography of Charles Piazzi Smyth', *Photoresearcher* 1 (October 1990): 37; Kingslake 1989: 45. Smyth published his results in 'Optical Help to "Rapido-manie"', *British Journal of Photography Almanac* (1874): 43–7; and 'How to take landscapes with portrait lenses at full aperture', *British Journal of Photography* 22 (1875): 208–9.

84. From the website of St John's Church, Sharow: <http://www.stjohnssharow.org/page7.html>

85. See Larry J. Schaaf, 'Charles Piazzi Smyth's 1865 Conquest of the Great Pyramid', *History of Photography* 3 (1979): 331–54; discussed on 351.

86. Douglas and Douglas [1862]: 2.

87. Langton 1940: 5.

88. See Sylvio Leblond, 'DOUGLAS, JAMES (1800–86)', in the *Dictionary of Canadian Biography*, vol. 11, University of Toronto/Université Laval, 2003: <http://www.biographi.ca/en/bio/douglas_james_1800_86_11E.html>

89. *Ibid.*

90. *Ibid.*, vol. 2: 15.

91. *Ibid.*, 9.

92. See Perez 2007; Crawford, 'Graham, James', in Hannavy (ed.) 2008, vol. 1: 605–6; and James Downs, 'Shadows of the Truth: the photography of James Graham (1808–69)', *Studies in Photography* (2011): 42–59.

93. Finn 1929: 114–5.

94. Anon., 'One who knew him well', 'Mr James Graham', *The Scattered Nation* (1 February 1870): 48

95. Graham took photographs of the 'Lepers' Gate & Village near the Lion Gate Jerusalem' for Thomas Faed. He sent copies to James Young Simpson in June 1857, referred to in a letter in the collection of the Royal College of Surgeons, Edinburgh, Simpson papers, 1760.

96. Seddon 1858: 171.

97. He added: 'In the books on Syria published by the Christian Knowledge Society, very few places are recognizable, and many are entirely false …. I intend, when I return, to write to them, and protest against their pretended 'Christian Knowledge,' which is most unchristian story-telling', *ibid.*, 111.

98. Letter written by Seddon to an unknown recipient from Cairo, January 1854, Seddon 1858: 36.

99. Bartram 1985: 103; Perez 2007: 16–7.

100. Graham entertained Seddon there when he fell ill in September 1854. See Bartram 1985: 119.

101. Holman-Hunt 1913, vol. 2: 16–21.

102. Cramb 1860a, Preface. Collins announced the publication, as 'Unique Christmas & New Year's Presentation Volumes', two books, Palestine … with 24 photographs at 42 shillings and Jerusalem in 1860, with 12 photographs at 21 shillings, and a set of 25 'Stereoscopic Views of the Holy Land … Mounted on Enamelled Boards, with Descriptive Letterpress. Enclosed in a handsome Box' for 21 shillings. See Advertisement in *The Publishers' Circular* (1 December 1860): 640.

103. The sequence of articles: John Cramb, 'Palestine in 1860: or, a Photographer's Journal of a Visit to Jerusalem', *British Journal of Photography* 7 (1 December 1860) and 8 (15 January, 1 February, 1 April, 15 April, 1 July, 15 August, 1 November 1861).

104. John Cramb, 'Palestine in 1860: or, a Photographer's Journal of a Visit to Jerusalem', *British Journal of Photography* 7 (15 April 1861): 146.

105. John Cramb, 'Palestine in 1860: or, a Photographer's Journal of a Visit to Jerusalem', *British Journal of Photography* 7 (1 July 1861): 237.

106. John Cramb, 'Palestine in 1860: or, a Photographer's Journal of a Visit to Jerusalem', *British Journal of Photography* 7 (15 August 1861): 288; Roberts 1842–9.

107. See Kathleen Howe, 'Palestine Exploration Fund', in Lenman (ed.) 2005: 466.

108. Connolly 1855, vol. 2: 213.

109. Williams, Introduction, in Wilson 1869: 5–6.

110. *Ibid.*, 6–7.

111. Captain H. S. Palmer, 'Descriptive Geography', in Wilson 1869: 17.

112. Captain H. S. Palmer, 'Account of the Survey', in Wilson 1869: 35.

113. *Ibid.*, 37.

114. *Ibid.*, 38.

115. *Ibid.*, 25.

116. *Ibid.*, 39.

117. *Ibid.*, 37. McDonald was a Colour-Sergeant during the survey, but was promoted by the time that it was published.

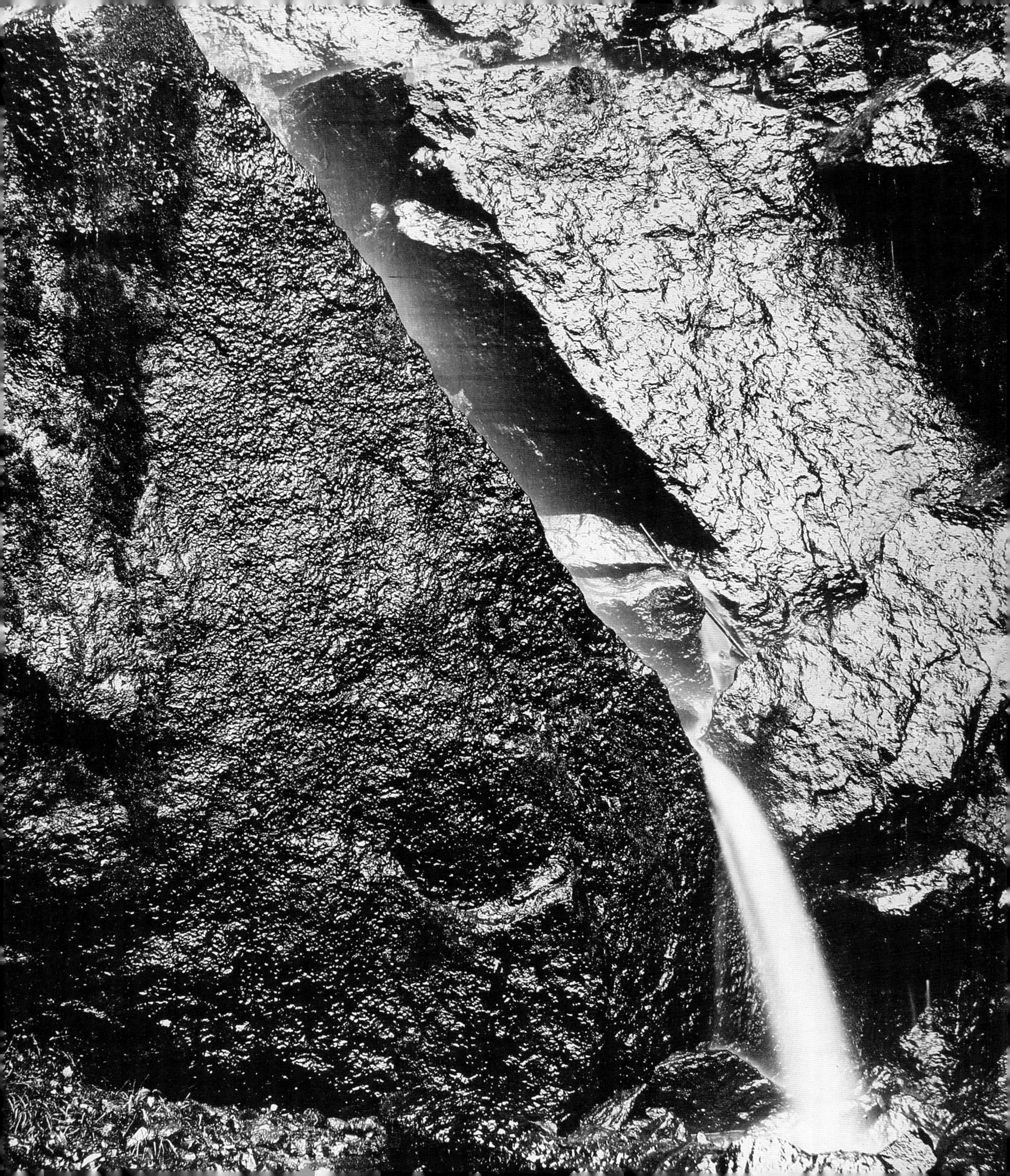

CHAPTER TEN

Migration and Empire

If anything could awaken sympathy for a Railway Company,
pondering of these pictures could hardly fail to do so.

Editor of the *Montreal Witness*, commenting on
Alexander Henderson's photographs of a snow-bound train, 1869

W. H. F. Talbot regarded the calotype as 'a royal road to *Drawing*'.[1] His classically-educated readers would understand this to be the 1500-mile road built by the Persian king, Darius, from Susa to the Aegean Sea, enabling messengers to cover a distance in nine days which previously took three months. Nineteenth-century empire-builders derived much of their understanding from such classical models. In the contemporary context, the importance of communication encompassed surveying, building roads, railways and steam ships, and promoting efficient written (postal services, the telegraph) and visual information (engravings and photographs).

The people who left Scotland to explore or settle elsewhere had a range of motives: trade, missionary work, war or good health. The contrast between life in Scotland and life abroad was by no means a contrast between civilisation and wilderness – Scotland was austere enough to act as a training ground for the fiercest conditions. Photography was an invention of the western Industrial Revolution; taking the cameras and the chemicals out of that context could make it extraordinarily difficult. The successful operators were inventive and skilled in improvisation.

Africa

It is appropriate that Charles Piazzi Smyth, whose enthusiasm for photography runs like a thread through this story, should turn up in this last chapter, at the very beginning of photography and in an unlikely place; Smyth went out to the Royal Observatory at the Cape of Good Hope in 1835. He became interested in photography as early as July 1839, when John Herschel sent notes and examples of his own experiments to the Astronomer Royal there.[2] Smyth asked Robert Hunt to send him supplies, and Herschel wrote to Hunt:

Opposite, Fig. 10.20 (detail): Donald Home Macfarlane, 'Rocks, Darjeeling', *c.*1862, albumen print.

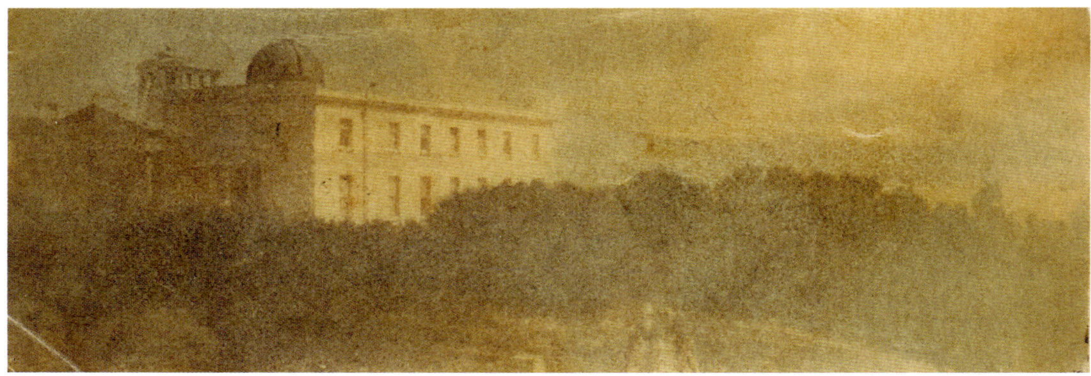

I know Mr Smyth well and you … may be assured he will do justice to the materials sent him, being a young man of great resource & ingenuity. I enclose a specimen of one of his photographic performances being the Diurnal Circle at the Observatory (the room in which it stands is *very imperfectly lighted*) and of course he must have prepared the paper himself from some description of the process and with such materials as could be procured in Cape Town – not a very fertile place in such articles.[3]

As an astronomer, Smyth had expert knowledge of lenses and access to equipment that might be adapted for photography [Figs 10.1]. James Cameron (1800–75), a carpenter, builder and surveyor, was also an astronomer. He came from Dunkeld in Perthshire, and was sent to Madagascar as an evangelist by the London Missionary Society in 1826. When the missionaries were expelled in 1835, he moved to Cape Town. He took calotypes from 1848, photographed the Anti-Convict Riots in 1849, and by 1850 had set up as a professional daguerreotypist.[4]

He returned to Madagascar in 1853, accompanying the Reverend William Ellis, to negotiate on behalf of the Christian converts, and to attempt re-opening the country to trade.[5] James Cameron's skill as a daguerreotypist proved useful in establishing friendly relations. William Ellis reported:

> Mr Cameron and I had shown the natives some photographic pictures which we had taken, and several of the officers … expressed a strong desire to have their likenesses taken before we left; … the apparatus was brought on shore, and the next day, Mr Cameron took a number of daguerreotype likenesses, with which the originals were much delighted.[6]

The negotiations were successful.

Exploration required individuals with a range of talents. While George Berwick studied medicine in Edinburgh, he became the photographic partner of Thomas Annan.[7] When he graduated from the Royal College of Surgeons of Edinburgh in 1856, he was appointed as ship's doctor to an expedition up the River Niger in West Africa. The Glasgow engineer, Robert Napier, recommended him as an expert photographer; but Berwick was not experienced medically. The expedition went spectacularly wrong. The leaders, Alexander Grant, captain of the S.S. *Dayspring*, and Dr William Balfour Baikie, the nominal head of the expedition, quarrelled. The attempts to trade and establish trading stations came to grief. The *Dayspring* struck on the rocks, sinking most of the navigational instruments and stores. Baikie himself died on the way home.

Baikie's report blamed Grant and Berwick for the disaster. He accused Berwick of neglecting a patient who died, and his only, angry, reference to photography relates to the burial:

> Berwick and his friend May, who had kept aloof from all preparations, stood a little way off, taking a photograph of the whole group, wh.[ich] Berwick said would be a very touching memorial to send to Rees' friends – whether it was successful or not, I never knew.[8]

We do not have Berwick's side of the story, and this is the only mention of his photography. Whether Berwick succeeded in taking photographs in conditions of wet tropical gloom and rampant hostility is unknown – his camera and equipment may have sunk with the *Dayspring*. He spent the rest of his career safely land-bound, as a doctor in Sunderland.[9]

Charles Livingstone (1821–73), brother of David Livingstone, the African explorer, was another struggling photographer.[10] When he joined his brother's expedition along the Zambesi river in 1858, the government provided photographic equipment. Henry Peach Robinson commented:

> What he really required, in my opinion, was about thirty pounds weight of apparatus and materials, neatly packed in a small box, or, to be liberal, say another ten pounds for glass – cost: not more than forty or fifty pounds …. What really was provided was contained in several enormous cases weighing nearly a ton, and which cost several hundreds of pounds … I said to the traveller's brother, who was to have been the photographer of the expedition, 'You had better leave this little lot at home, and save yourself the trouble of dropping it into the first jungle you come to'.[11]

John Kirk was appointed as botanist to the expedition, to investigate the medical and commercial possibilities of the plants they found.[12] His private journal was disparaging of Charles Livingstone's efforts. In July 1858, for example, he recorded:

> Mr L. tries the wet collodion process and succeeds to get something having a faint likeness to a picture, but it is a nasty unhealthy work in the dark room in a tropical country and as he has no idea of chemistry or of manipulation, I don't anticipate much to come of the Photography …
>
> Mr L.'s photography came nearer to something today, that is, we can see a white shirt or jacket or the shine of a gunbarrel, but this is dreadful work one minute in a close suffocating tent, quite dark, and steaming of Acetic acid and Colloid, the next out in the bright sunshine, often without a hat.[13]

David Livingstone had asked his brother to take photographs of the tribes in and around Tete. He achieved more

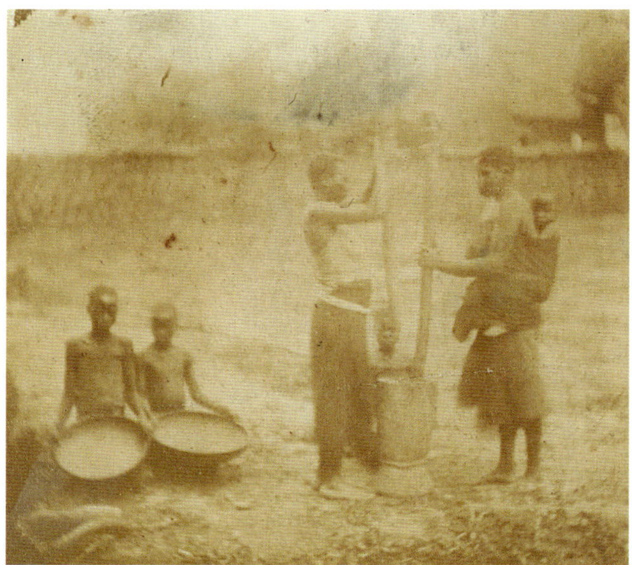

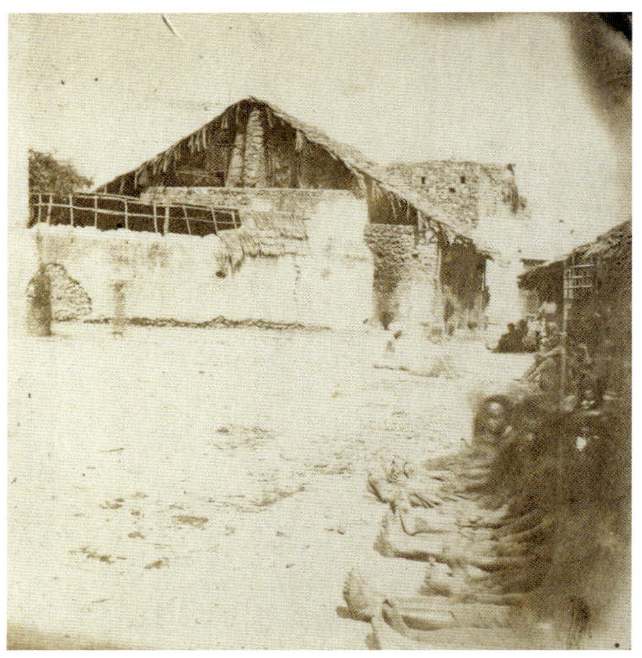

Fig. 10.2 (above): Charles Livingstone, 'African women grinding corn', c.1858, single stereoscopic albumen print. (National Library of Scotland, MS 42440)

Fig. 10.3 (right): Captain James Augustus Grant, 'Slave marketplace, Zanzibar, 28 August 1860', single tereoscopic albumen print. (Royal Geographical Society, S0011716)

than Kirk's sardonic account implies, but only two stereo pictures survive [Fig. 10.2].[14]

The expedition to discover the source of the Nile, undertaken in 1860 by John Hanning Speke and James Augustus Grant (1827–92), a captain in the Bengal Army, also carried stereoscopic equipment.[15] Grant purchased this from Bland and Long in London, who gave him three lessons, which he transcribed into his journal, complete with their aesthetic advice: '… it is thought more *artistic* to have the main object of a view a little to one side.'[16] He paid £60 for the instruments and chemicals, and noted the weight at 276lbs.[17] Whilst considerably less than Robinson's rhetorical estimate of 'nearly a ton', it was heavy – ten times the weight of their medicine chest. Grant's closely written journal indicates that he bought the equipment in advance so that he could practise in Britain, travelling home to Scotland and back. His notes record a distinct struggle then and during the voyage. On the way, he encountered a number of photographers, starting with the

Londoner, J. J. E. Mayall, whose (equally helpful) advice he also wrote down: 'When in Scotland take groups of peasantry, with hills in background, nothing better. In Africa take Ruins, scenery, plants, peasants, animals, water &c, rivers take very well at home.'[18]

On the ship outwards, Grant travelled with a successful photographer, Lieutenant (Lord Charles) Scott, and he worked with a Mr Frost when they landed at Zanzibar. After strenuous efforts over eight months and a sequence of dismal failures, he wrote in September, 'at last I have succeeded. *Hurrah*'.[19] There were set-backs. A week later he was trying out dry plates: 'nearly all failed & no wonder for I never knew it was Sunday': God and contaminated water had intervened.[20] By 22 September, the expedition was about to set off and Grant was constructing a photographic tent. He left the materials for printing behind, taking only the chemicals for the paper process, but seems to have made more drawings than photographs during the trek.[21]

Zanzibar was a notorious slave market. Grant's photograph of the market, taken on 28 August, is a classic example of a picture taken after the subject had shifted out of view; a picture of immense importance, which should have

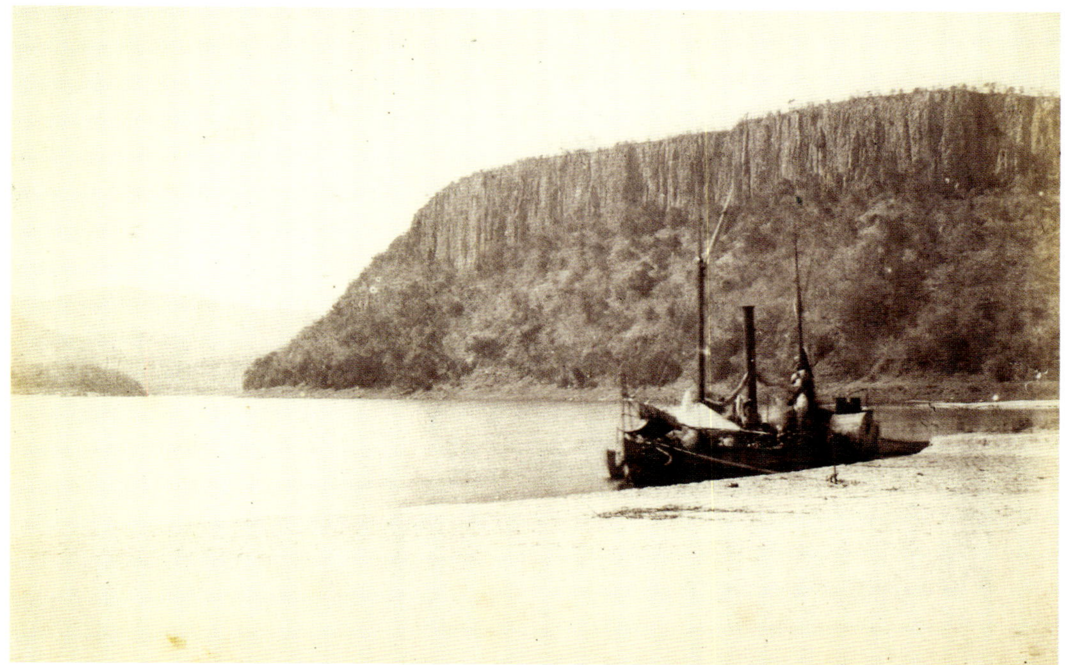

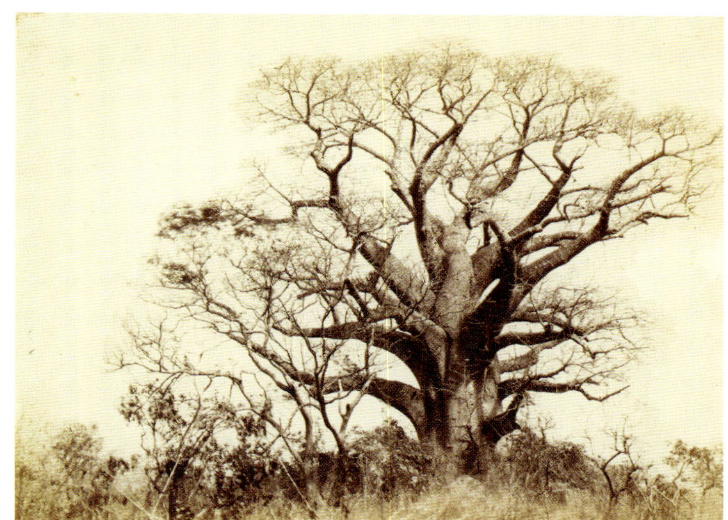

provided serious evidence of the trade [FIG. 10.3]. He was forced to explain the situation, and wrote on the mount:

> – very difficult to take – slaves and arabs keep running away leaving only a line of women slaves whose legs and a face or two may be observed.

In contrast to Charles Livingstone and Grant, John Kirk was an experienced photographer and his work has survived. He preferred the paper process, but took supplies for dry plate photography. On 21 November 1858, Kirk wrote approvingly: 'The Collodion plates of "Dr. Hill Norris" which I brought with me turn out first rate. They are very sensitive and give good negatives'.[22]

Since dry plates were accounted slow, Kirk's experience is interesting – proof of his technical competence, and perhaps the physical conditions for the process were better than in Britain. In March 1859, he commented on two pictures: 'I have fears how they will succeed as they were exposed to a heat about 100° for some time …. At night I developed the Photographs. They came out very well although the heat had been so great.'[23] His readiness to experiment is seen in another entry, which follows references to their 'asthmatic old steam boat', the *Ma Robert* [FIGS 10.4 and 5], navigating the river with increasing difficulty:

> We have [had] a fearful day among the sand banks, hauling her by the anchor chain frequently, the men overboard continually clearing her one way or another.

…. We came up alongside the left bank. I took a photograph of the vegetation. One of the views was with a
paper prepared … substituting citric acid for acetic,
which seems an improvement. The paper is more sensitive and the result in this instance superior. If this success
proves permanent, the substitution will be one of an
essentially practical nature …. The acetic acid is a
nuisance and unhealthy to work among.[24]

He tested this idea on 23 July, when he used the 'citric acid
both for sensitising and developing by the waxed paper
process …. The experiment is completely successful, even
in this first attempt.'[25]

At this point, the boat began to leak alarmingly; the
crew were increasingly disaffected. By January 1860, the
steamboat was disintegrating, and Kirk wrote in his diary:

My specimens, the result of five months … are all wet
and run the risk of utter destruction. The water floods
the floor from the windows, while the roof leaks at every
joint … many a pig lives in a better house than we do.[26]

Kirk's focus on the landscape and the practice of photography is all the more remarkable. His 'Hints to Travellers'
for the Royal Geographical Society, says:

Photography is little suited for distant and wild countries,
yet where it can be employed is of the greatest service
… [I] only mention what I found of use on the lower
Zambesi. My instrument was an ordinary landscape
camera, made by Negretti and Zambra, which, after
travelling or lying about for five years in the tropics,
came home without a joint loose or slip of wood started.

The process adopted was the waxed paper, which for
simplicity of apparatus, and chemicals, and facility in
the transport of negatives, has not been surpassed ….
The negatives, if washed in the bromide of potassium,
need not be fixed for many weeks after, and when finished, if melted together into a cake with bees-wax, may
be taken anywhere without danger, and again separated
and ironed out at home.

The dry collodion process, which I believe will now
supersede almost all others, had not made much progress
when we went out; but in order to test it I took with me
plates, prepared and sensitised in England in January,
1858, which, when tried at various times, continued to
yield pictures up to August, 1863.[27]

Despite the problems, the expedition was deemed a
success. David Livingstone was treated as a hero. John Kirk
was subsequently appointed Vice Consul in Zanzibar, where
he was instrumental in eradicating the slave trade.[28]

China

Photography in China began in the context of the fearsome
violence of the Taiping Rebellion from 1851 to 1864, and the
discreditable western Opium War between 1856 and 1860.
The first identified calotypist in China was Robert George
Sillar (1827–1902), a merchant and dealer in bullion, who
came from Edinburgh, moved to Lancashire and is recorded in Shanghai between 1857 and 1861.[29] There are only a
few of his photographs known – dated between 1857 and
1859 – which show a delicate approach [Fig. 10.6], but his
pictures were taken along the Soochow creek, which was

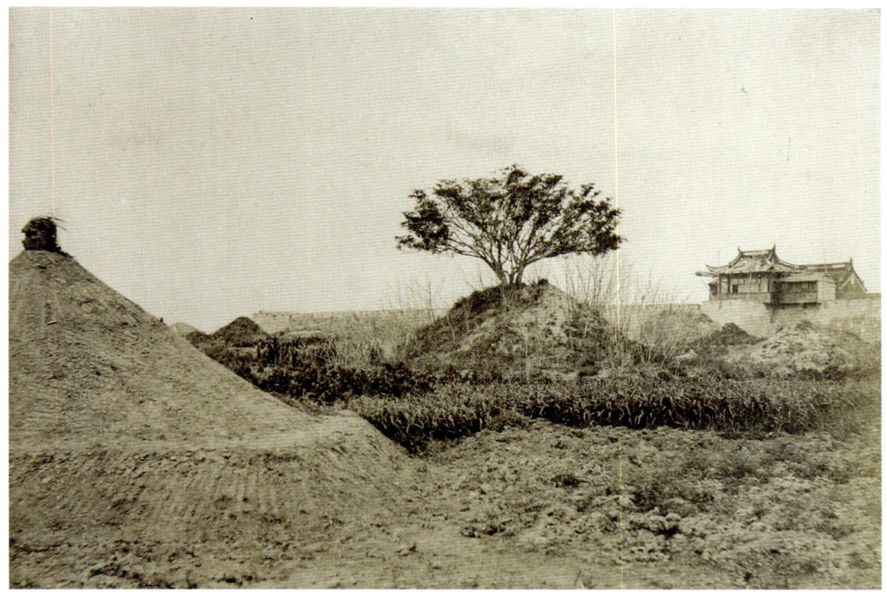

of great strategic importance, leading from Shanghai into the heart of China. The photographs may have assisted in mapping the territory for political and commercial ends. Sillar's photographs were gold-toned, perhaps because he dealt in bullion and had the material to hand.

Corporal John Wotherspoon (1823–89) was born in Airdrie, and joined the Royal Engineers in 1844.[30] In 1848, he was part of the group who surveyed London from the top of the dome of St Paul's Cathedral.[31] Working on a small insecure perch, he and Sergeant James Steel took four months to make 8 to 10,000 observations, fixing 2140 trigonometric points in the City. This highly-controlled exercise is in stark contrast to his photography in China, where he was involved in the attack on Canton.

In the first place, he was not there. The assault was complicated by the Indian Mutiny. By October 1857, the 23rd Company of Royal Engineers being sent out to China was re-routed to Calcutta. Lieutenant-Colonel Lugard wrote a letter to Lieutenant-General Ashburnham underlining 'the very great importance of that Company of men, comprising as they did the whole of the skilled labour to a force destined to carry out operations against a walled city.' He said in his first anxious sentence that they had taken with them to Calcutta, 'the photograph apparatus specially provided for China': the only equipment he mentions.[32] His anxiety was prompted by the recurring problem in contemporary war. The western armies in China had no maps or pictures of the terrain beyond a very narrow area. The Chinese authorities had strictly controlled the movement of westerners, with the result that the military would not know where they were going, or even necessarily where they were. Bizarrely, one report says:

> … the old Jesuit map of China, compiled two centuries ago, is still our only guide, not only for all the interior, but even for those provinces on the seaboard of which our civilians have been so long located. (We believe that this curious and antiquated piece of topography has just been reproduced for the use of our naval and military authorities of China by the topographical department of the War Office.)[33]

Photographs would have been of immense value to the attacking armies, enabling them to grasp some strategic sense of location.

The Engineers arrived in January 1858, a month after Canton fell. Captain Gother Frederick Mann sent nineteen of Wotherspoon's photographs to the Queen, including an

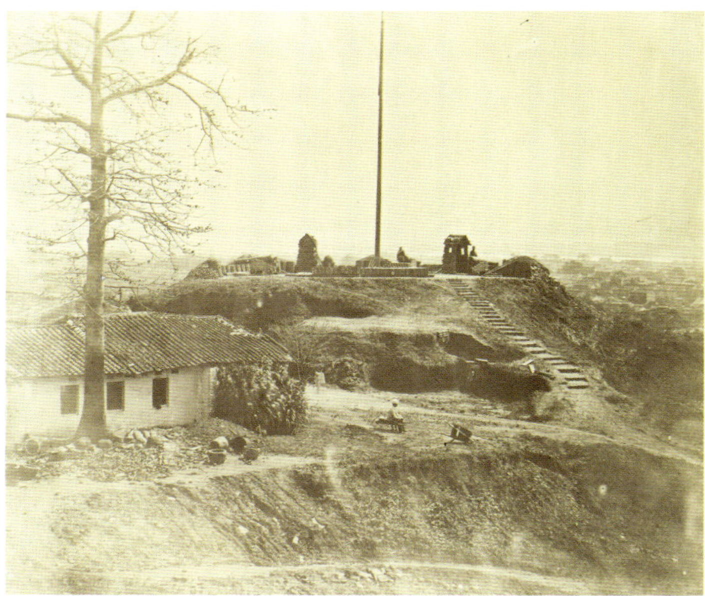

eleven-part panorama of Canton taken from the battery built under Mann's command above the city, and a photograph of the battery itself [FIG. 10.7]. Only seven photographs from this group have been found, and they are principally concerned with the military occupation, with only two photographs of people, one 'The Tartar General in Chief, "Muh" taken by his desire'.[34] Objects of interest noted in the landscape, such as '5 Storied Pagoda', are not clearly seen, being 'partly hidden by a Chinese Fort'. The separate image of a temple is annotated for its usefulness: 'now occupied by 70th Regt. B.N.I.'. The inconsequence of these pictures – taken when they were no longer needed – is an acid comment on the dislocation of war. Only with the declaration of peace was photography a viable proposition.

India

India, colonised by the British through the East India Company's trade, backed by military force, was inevitably a great centre of Scottish migration. Dr John McCosh (1805–85), working with the army in India from the 1830s, described the wide-ranging qualifications necessary to a doctor there, including '… how to grow green-peas and cauliflowers,

how to fatten capons and suckling pigs, how to make jug-soup and tapioca, how to shoot wild-geese, ride a steeple-chase, drive a cabriolet, and sail a cutter'.[35]

His thesis was completed in Edinburgh between 1839 to 1840, and was published in 1841 as *Advice to the Indian Stranger*. His tutor was the surgeon, Robert Christison. McCosh was concerned to dispel the innocence of recruits and to encourage mental health; the soldiers were often dangerously unemployed, and were subject to 'apathy and ennui'.[36] When McCosh retired in 1856, he published a new edition of his book, advocating photography:

I would strongly recommend every assistant-surgeon to make himself master of photography in all its branches, on paper, on plate glass, and on metallic plates. I have practised it for many years, and know of no extra professional pursuit that will more repay him for all the expense and trouble (and both are very considerable) than this fascinating study – especially the new process by Collodion for the stereoscope. During the course of his service in India, he may make such a faithful collection of representations of man and animals, of architecture and landscape, that would be a welcome contribution to any museum. The camera should be made of good substantial mahogany, clamped with brass, made to stand extremes of heat. The flimsy, folding portable cameras, made light for Indian use, soon become useless. It is a great mistake to make things light and portable for Indian use, as if the owner himself had to carry them. Carriage for every piece of apparatus is cheap, safe, and abundant. French paper, Canson frères is the best, and does not get damaged by damp so soon as English paper.[37]

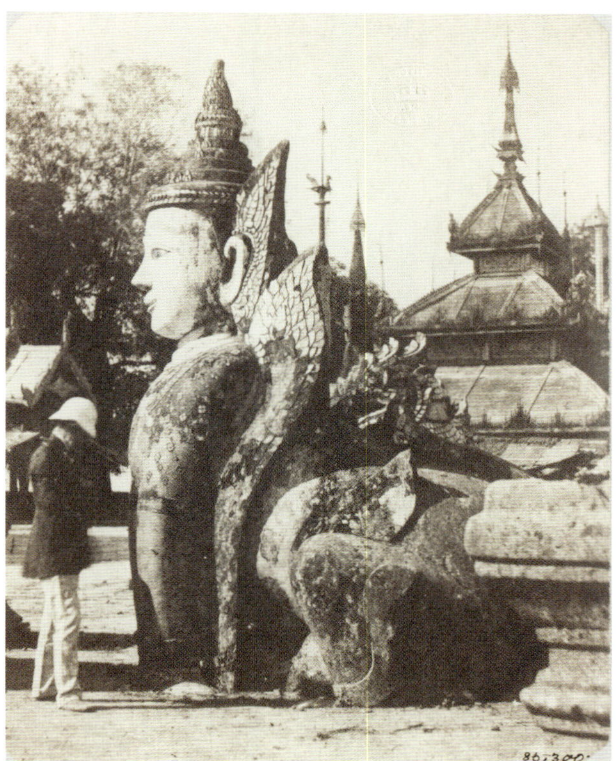

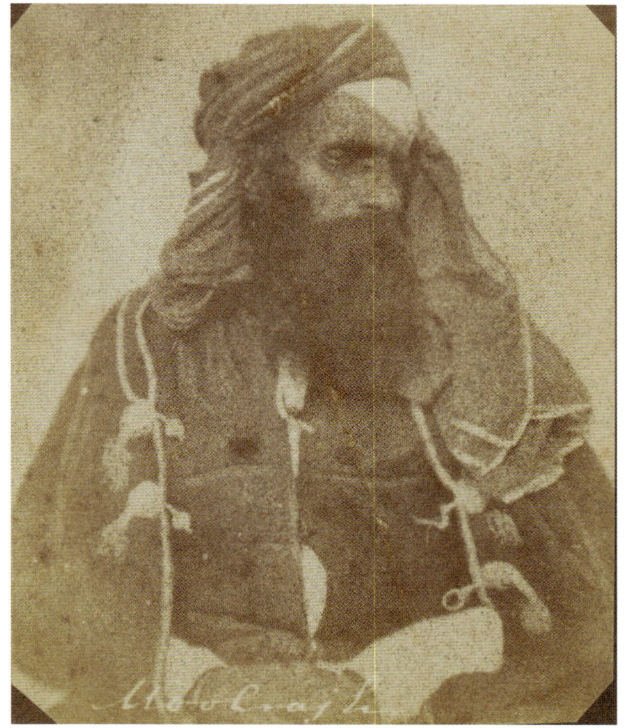

It is not clear when John McCosh first took up photography.[38] He may have begun with the daguerreotype process, as his *Advice* suggests.[39] He introduced the photographs in his surviving album, modestly:

> These photographs have no pretentions to merit. The negatives were taken on paper before the present process of collodion was known.
>
> Their fidelity will however make amends for their many … imperfections.
>
> Like fragile [?] remains of lost ages, their value is enhanced because the originals are no longer forthcoming.[40]

The photographs vary; there is evidence of glass negatives (despite his introduction), gold-toning, and possibly albumen coating of his salt prints after printing [Fig. 10.8]. The quality alters between photographs, indicating, reasonably enough for an army surgeon in the field, that his working conditions and chemicals varied.

After the second Sikh War in 1849, the British took control of the Punjab. Dr John Login was given responsibility for the young Maharajah Dhuleep Singh and his extensive establishment. He noted in a letter to his wife that 'Dr McCosh is anxious to take daguerreotypes here, and begs to be allowed to come tomorrow to take likenesses of all the notabilities collected here . . . . I have told him he cannot take any of the prisoners.'[41]

Login's comment may simply indicate practical reservations. There is a photograph of the Maharajah in McCosh's album, and he succeeded in photographing at least one war prisoner, Mul Raj Diwan, Governor of Multan [Fig. 10.9].

In the Burmese War of 1852–53, McCosh took pictures

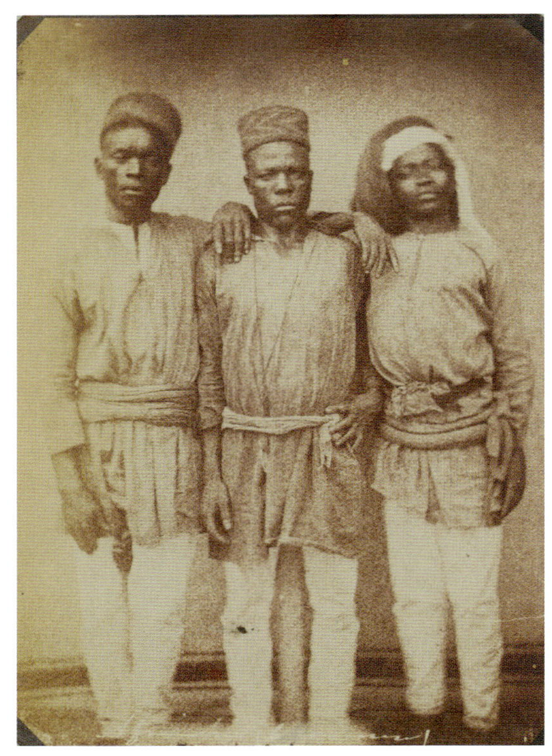

of people and the city of Prome – the focus of that war. A number of significant individuals in the history of warfare figure in his work: General Sir Henry Godwin, who was in command of the British force in Burma; General Sir Charles Napier; Dr William Brydon, who had the melancholy distinction of being 'the only survivor' of a force of 4500 soldiers and 12,000 civilians in the disastrous retreat from Kabul during the first Anglo-Afghan war in 1842; and Major Herbert Clogstoun, who was awarded the Victoria Cross for charging the enemy at Chichumbah in 1859, with only eight men. These were men engaged in a history both bloody and heroic.

McCosh, operating within the army system, gives a broad idea of the history of his time: he photographed and knew personally men and women who were involved in action on and off the battlefield. Many were people whom we might otherwise only encounter in perfunctory records of their movements, appointments, military casualties or fearful murders. Fifty portraits in the album are of women, who are only mentioned in a severely fragmented way in military history. McCosh expressed concern for their position in his *Advice to Officers* – too many soldiers married before they could afford it and lived in debt. He felt the attraction of marriage: 'In no country are the advantages of female society more appreciable than in India, for much time is necessarily spent at home which, without a companion, would be dull and lonely.'[42] It may be that he balanced his own sense of loneliness in the pleasure of mixing with and photographing families.

His album contains portraits of the British, the Indians and Burmese, and visitors to India, including sailors from Africa, particularly Krumen [Fig. 10.10]. The way his sitters are photographed suggests that he allowed them to decide their own pose. The portraits fill the frame of the paper, and McCosh was prepared to work at different heights – accommodating people squatting down as readily as standing up. Despite this unmeasured individuality, the captioning suggests an ethnographic intention behind his 'native' photography.

When he returned to Britain in 1856, McCosh joined the Photographic Society of London and its offshoot, the Photographic Society Club. But before the Club produced its book of members' portraits, 'the absence of Dr McCosh from England … unavoidedly occasioned his retirement' from the group.[43] McCosh travelled throughout his life, presumably taking his camera and, sketchbook with him, and writing fluent, somewhat dire, verse. His remaining photographs are only a trace of his extraordinary life.

Dr George Buist (1805–60) was a combative Tory who edited six newspapers in Perthshire and Fife between 1832 and 1839, when he was appointed editor of the *Bombay Times*. Sir David Brewster wrote him a reference, commending: 'The great extent of his general knowledge, his power

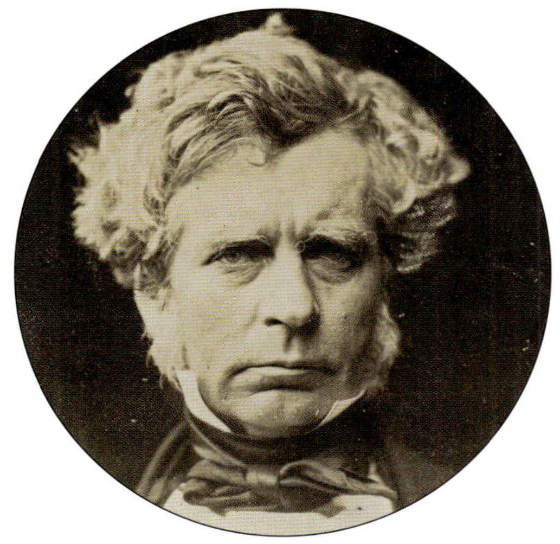

of composition, his acquaintance with various branches of the useful arts, and his familiarity with the sciences of mechanics, meteorology, and geology.'[44] Through his connections with St Andrews and the town of Cupar, with their energetic literary and philosophical societies, he had early knowledge of photography[45] [FIG. 10.11]. He certainly participated in photography when he returned to Britain in 1845, and was photographed by Hill and Adamson.[46]

In 1854, Buist was a founder of the Bombay Photographic Society, and elected Vice-President. He showed portraits and proposed an advanced attempt to photograph plant-life:

> … he had never seen a picture intended to represent a view in that country, which had not a cocoa-nut tree depicted most prominently … as if India could boast of no others; let a few pictures of the exquisite scenery about Bombay be sent home to dispel the fallacy. He advised each member to take a single tree or shrub, and thus, conjointly, make a complete collection.[47]

At the Society's December meeting, he suggested an experiment – a trial of tree photographs to see if any

> … marked actinic difference was shown … [between] plants of slow and very rapid growth, naming the Cassarina tree in which a month's growth is scarcely

perceptible, and the Plantain tree which springs up a foot in 24 hours. He had heard it surmised that plants of rapid growth absorbed greedily the rays which it was supposed produced the most forcible impression upon sensitive surfaces.[48]

Several photographers agreed to experiment with this interesting thought.

While Buist was working in Bombay, Dr Alexander Hunter (1816–*c.*1889) was working in Madras. He founded the first School of Arts in India in 1850, with a School of Industry, to improve the manufacture of 'articles of domestic and daily use'. These schools were given Government support in 1855.[49] Hunter wanted to achieve a balance between Eastern and Western culture. He was responsible for the Madras Exhibition of Raw Products, Arts and Manufacture of South India in 1855, which included a section on Photography, Lithography and Painting: the collection of photographs, he reported, was 'very large and interesting', including work by Captain Linnaeus Tripe, W. E. Cochrane and Dr Andrew Charles Brisbane Neill, who were awarded medals.[50] He started the Madras Photographic Society in 1856 and organised the exhibitions. In the same year he requested a class for photography within the School of Arts, but was told, dismissively, that it could be learned in a few lessons. However, Hunter was allowed to appoint Tripe as the government photographer in Madras, and he was responsible for distributing Tripe's splendid photographs widely.[51] Hunter also promoted his Indian pupils, whose work was bought by the South Kensington Museum in 1871.[52]

Hunter retired to Edinburgh in the 1870s, and joined the Edinburgh Photographic Society: in 1874 he spoke on

'India, Its Scenery, People, Scenery and Antiquities'. In 1879, he gave a paper on 'The Selection of Subjects from Nature suited for Photography', and referred to '32 years of photographic and artistic labours in India'.[53]

The British occupying India in the 18th and 19th centuries were fascinated by its archaeology and architecture. One of the leading figures in this study was James Fergusson (1808–86), who was born in Ayr and went to India as a merchant and set up an indigo factory.[54] He retired in the 1830s to study architecture. In particular, he drew – using a camera lucida – and wrote on, Indian architecture. In the preface to his *History of Architecture* in 1865, he explained its impact:

My faith in the exclusive pre-eminence of mediaeval art was first shaken when I became familiar with the splendid remains of the Mogul and Pathan emperors of Agra and Delhi, and saw how many beauties of even the pointed style had been missed in Europe in the Middle Ages. My confidence was still further weakened when I saw what richness and variety the Hindoo had elaborated not only without pointed arches, but indeed without any arches at all …. I became convinced that no form is in itself better than any other, and that in all instances those are best which are most appropriate to the purposes to which they are applied.[55]

Fergusson maintained that it was essential to record historic Indian architecture, as 'a great stone book, in which every tribe and race has written its annals and recorded its faith … is it possible to overestimate its value to those who wish to know who and what the people are or were, whom we have undertaken to guide and to govern?'[56]

He made a large collection of photographs to assist in his study. His critical writing engaged with photographers and stimulated interest in their work. In 1867, he exhibited his collection at the Paris Universal Exhibition, where it was reviewed with enthusiasm.[57] It included photographs by Andrew Charles Brisbane Neill (1814–91). Neill graduated as an MD from the University of Glasgow in 1837, and joined the Indian Medical Service with the Light Cavalry in Madras, where he served from 1838 to 1858. In his first known expedition with his camera, in December 1854, he travelled with Linnaeus Tripe to Mysore, where they photographed the Hindu and Jain temples at Belloor, Hullabeed and Beejanuggur.[58]

Neill was a master of the waxed paper process, and his work is comparable in quality with Tripe's more celebrated photographs. His pictures have a notable command of architectural texture and detail. In looking at the remarkably clear and contrasted sculpture of the buildings, brought out in Neill's photographs of Hullabeed, Fergusson wrote:

A person standing between the two great Vimánas of the western face of the temple, and looking around him, probably sees a greater amount of skilled labour than was ever exhibited in a like space in any other building in the whole world, and the style of workmanship is of a very high class.[59]

Neill's work is an illustration, even a paradigm, of the claim that photography could copy detail in a way that drawing rarely matched [Fig. 10.12]. The pictures show elaborate sculpture, apparently repetitive but constantly shifting in design; for a western draughtsman, dealing with a culture only partly known, to copy this would be a prohi-

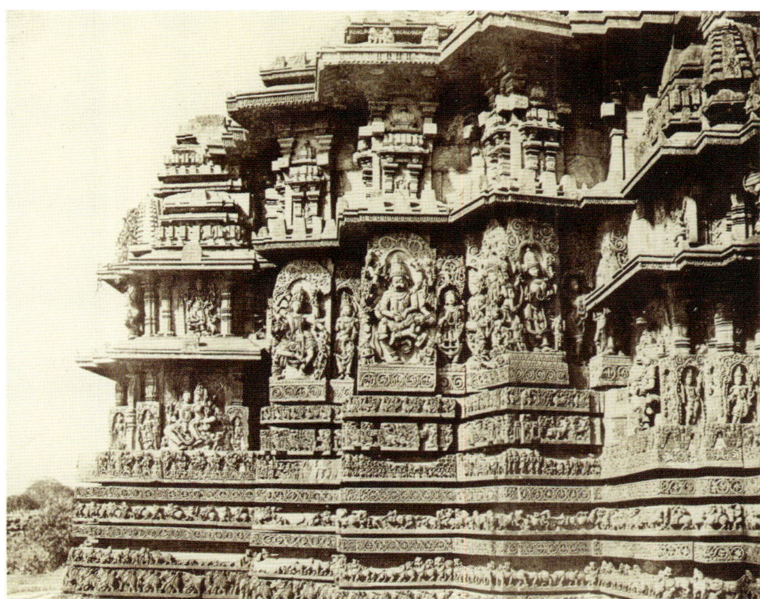

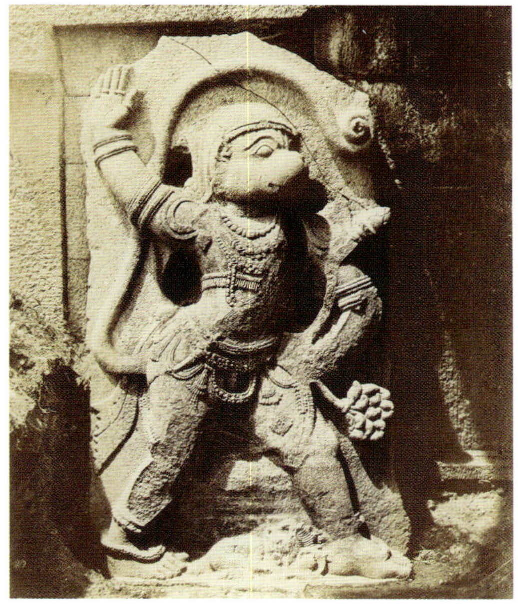

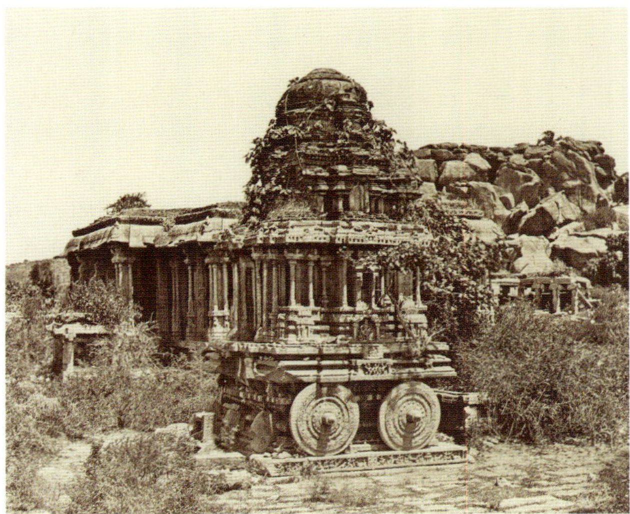

most artistic things ever done …. By the mode adopted of dividing it into masses, and again cutting up these masses into facets at right angles to one another, great play of light and shade is obtained, and a variety of design which could be accomplished by no other known method.[60]

Neill took an interest in sculpture here and at Beejan-uggur, the remains of a vast royal city. His images of 'The Hunooman' – the monkey god – [FIG. 10.13] and the stone chariot have great charm [10.14]. The chariot, 'composed of only one stone, most probably a boulder found on the spot', was photographed against the background of granite rocks – offering both nature and art, the creepers attempting to turn the sculpture back to a natural feature and adding a strange sense that the car has been petrified.

Neill's photographs were published in the 1860s. They appeared in a work called *Architecture in Dhawar and Mysore*, which has an interesting history.[61] The book was published by the Committee of Architectural Antiquities of Western India and handsomely funded by Mr Premchand Roychand. The preface explained the need for startling generosity:

bitively difficult task. Neill achieved accuracy, with genuine relish for his subject:

The basement that runs along the whole of the eastern front, though covered by details as delicate as any jewel-ler's, is still so simple in its outline, that it is as solid and as bold as if it were constructed of rough hewn granite in courses, and the arrangement of the frieze of gods, some 400 feet in length on the west side, is one of the

The expense of producing illustrated works of the

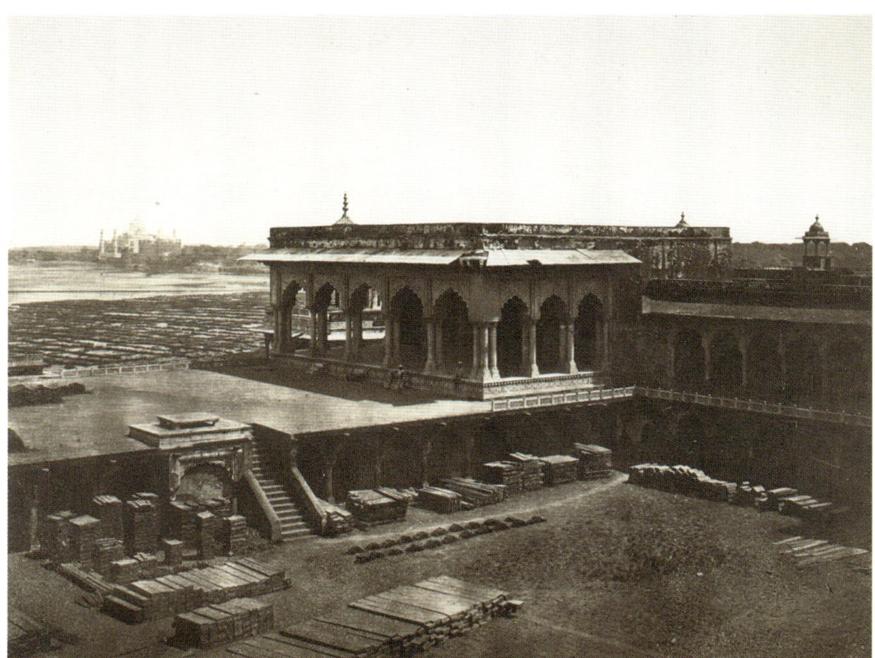

description contemplated being necessarily so heavy that, even if sold at cost price, they would be within the reach of a comparatively small portion of the public, certain native gentlemen volunteered, for the honour of their country and the greater diffusion of an acquaintance with it, each to take one volume under his patronage and contribute £1000 towards its publication.

Dr Pigou and Colonel Biggs were employed to take photographs for the book. The original text was written by Colonel Meadows Taylor. James Fergusson took over after his death and probably added twenty-three of Neill's photographs. With this addition, Fergusson wrote: 'It was found necessary to remodel the whole work, and I then undertook the responsibility.' Neill waived payment for his work.[62] John Murray, the London publisher, sold the book at £12. 12s – presumably below cost price. It would only be bought by wealthy individuals, but it could be purchased for libraries and made available to the public – a heroic publication.

Fergusson's collection included the work of one of the most impressive architectural photographers in India, Dr John Murray (1809–98). He came from Blackhouse, near Peterhead, and studied to be a doctor at Aberdeen, Edinburgh and Paris. In 1833, he joined the East India Company as surgeon to the Horse Artillery.[63]

Murray took up photography about 1849, when he directed the Medical School at Agra, the old Mughal capital. Through the 1850s and 60s, he photographed Mughal architecture in the North-West Provinces, using a large-format camera with the waxed paper process. In the words of John Falconer, Murray produced 'prints that exploit to the full the glowing expressiveness of the salt print …. Returning repeatedly to the same subjects – particularly the Taj Mahal – [he] used the medium to examine the building in minute detail, photographing it from slightly shifting viewpoints'.[64]

This systematic study of the Taj Mahal involved at least sixty-six negatives, and included panoramic joiners. One of the world's most beautiful buildings became a model for technical and aesthetic exploration.

John Murray and his wife, Loveday, returned to Britain in April 1857 with 600 negatives. Joseph Hogarth in London agreed to print and market a selection as *Photographic Views in Agra and its Vicinity* in 1858 and 1859. These were

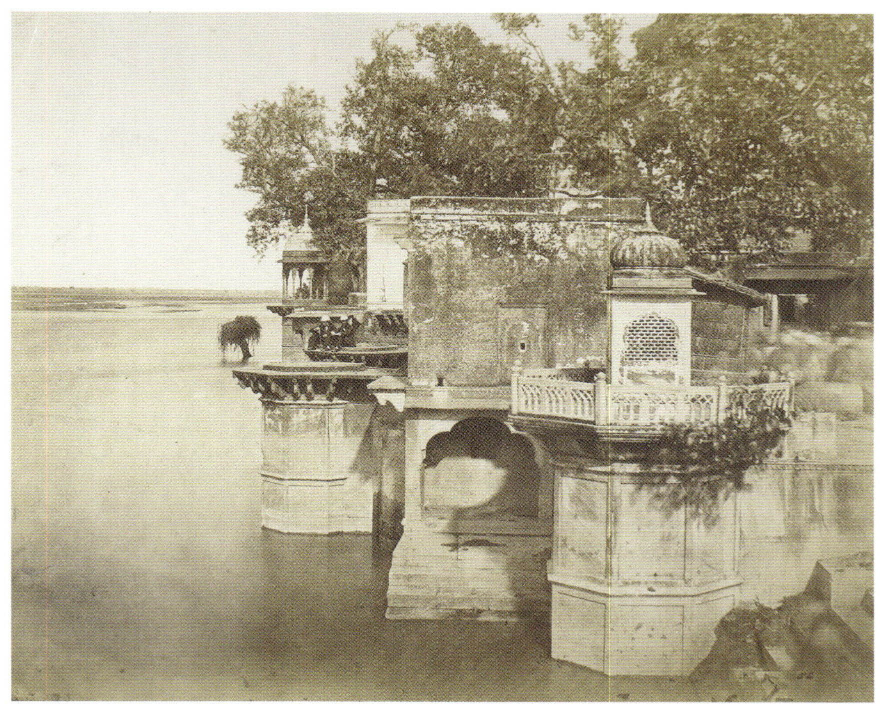

exhibited in Hogarth's gallery and also at the Photographic Society of London. Loveday Murray stayed in London, when John Murray returned to India, and oversaw the publication of the book.

These photographs are strongly framed and detailed. Murray observed the beauty and humour of reality. One of his images, 'The Palace of Shah Jehan' [FIG. 10.15], looks down from a high viewpoint. The camera's position may have been determined by this, and by a wish to frame the Taj Mahal in the centre of the horizon. Arguably he could not avoid the lines of the army stores inside the palace and the squared pattern of the melon beds outside the walls, but these are essential to the picture. A second example from this series shows the Ghaut [bathing place] at Bindrabund. This is a lovely photograph, balancing the building and the water, with one odd detail – the large dish mop sticking out of the water. The text explains that it is an upturned palm tree, uprooted by recent floods. It is well placed to punctuate the bland reach of water, giving a pleasing imbalance to the picture [FIG. 10.16]. A third in the series, of the road from Naini Tal to Bareilly in the Himalayas, is a straight-

forward picturesque image, but the picture is interrupted by a large mushroom shape beside the road. This, the text says, was not 'a jaunty fungus of giant proportions', but a petticoat spread out to dry in the sun – a disconcerting, surrealist interruption to an otherwise orthodox picture. Within three photographs, Murray may be seen to have enjoyed the incidental, the accidental and the surreal possibilities of photography.

While the Murrays were in Britain in May 1857, the Indian Mutiny broke out, adding a painful edge to viewing the pictures. The excitable photography critic in the *Athenaeum* saw them through 'a blood-red haze'.[65] When Murray returned to India in November, Lady Canning, the wife of the Governor of India, wrote to the Queen: 'I think it is possible that Your Majesty has lately seen some photographs of Dr Murray of Agra …. I hope he will be immediately employed to photograph everything to be demolished at Dehli'.[66]

The Royal Collection acquired a set of Murray's photographs. Lord Canning delegated Murray in January of 1858 to photograph the sites of the uprising, in Benares,

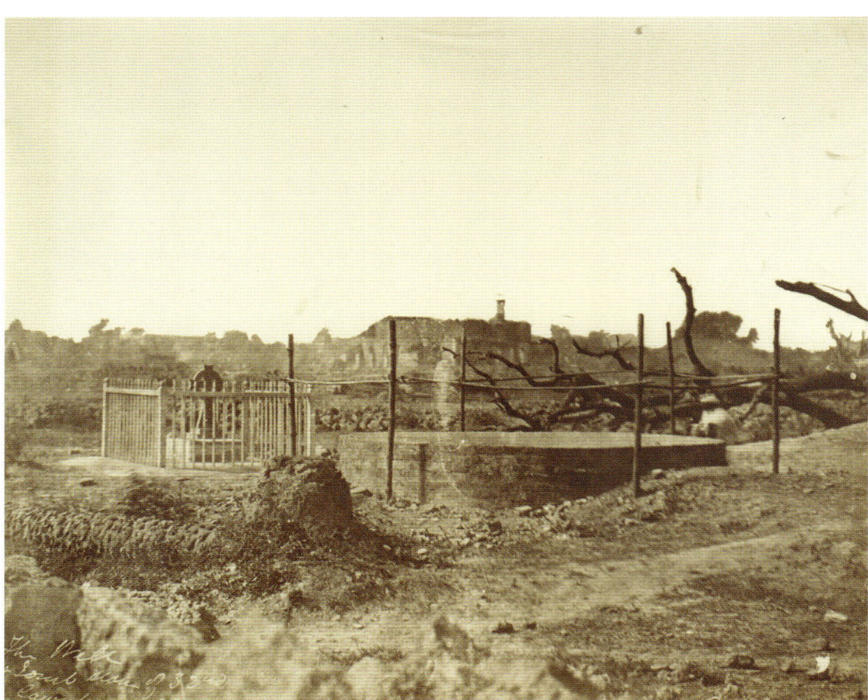

Fig. 10.17: Dr John Murray, 'The Well and Monument, Slaughter House, Cawnpore', 1858, salt print from waxed paper negative. (The British Library Board, India Office Library, Photo. 52/[36])

Allahabad, Cawnpore, Agra and Delhi. Murray was granted 2000 rupees, and assistance in carrying 400lbs of equipment.[67] Canning needed evidence of the moves towards pacification and control of the country, even before the fighting ended. Murray's photographs were designed to offer evidence of the building of barracks and hospitals in the Fort at Allahabad, but they show the aftermath of fighting, and are infused with powerful sorrow. Like McCosh, Murray was directly involved in the war. The photographs relating to the massacres at Cawnpore – the killing of the small, disarmed force evacuating under safe conduct, and the murder of civilian prisoners, including women and children – are unquestionably poignant. Even without a knowledge of this history, Murray's photographs of the landscape with its distressed trees, wrecked buildings and sterile ground are ugly in effect [Fig. 10.17].

Captain Allan Newton Scott (1824–70), who was from Forfar, joined the Madras Artillery in 1840. He was a member of the Madras Photographic Society and a frequent exhibitor in their exhibitions. In 1862, he published his work as *Sketches in India*, and said that he had 'long relieved the monotony of Indian life by the use of his camera', which suggests that he had read McCosh's *Advice to Officers*. In 1859, he sent the editor of the *Photographic Journal*

… some most interesting stereoscopic views, taken in the Deccan …. He says, 'I have about 200 negatives of most interesting subjects …. I hope you will do me the kindness to offer to exchange with any member of the Society [the Photographic Society of London] for similar numbers of their own pictures, so that I may see what progress photography is making in England.'[68]

In 1860, Scott exhibited fifty-four stereograms 'of Native figures, Antiquities, Bazaar scenes, Tombs and Native trades with a few representations of Artillery drill and ordnance'. The Madras committee noted that this was 'unquestionably the best collection of stereograms that has yet been produced in Madras, and possesses the qualities of clear focusing and printing, tasteful selection of subjects and careful manipulation and mounting'. They awarded him first prize in the category. In 1862, the London Photo-

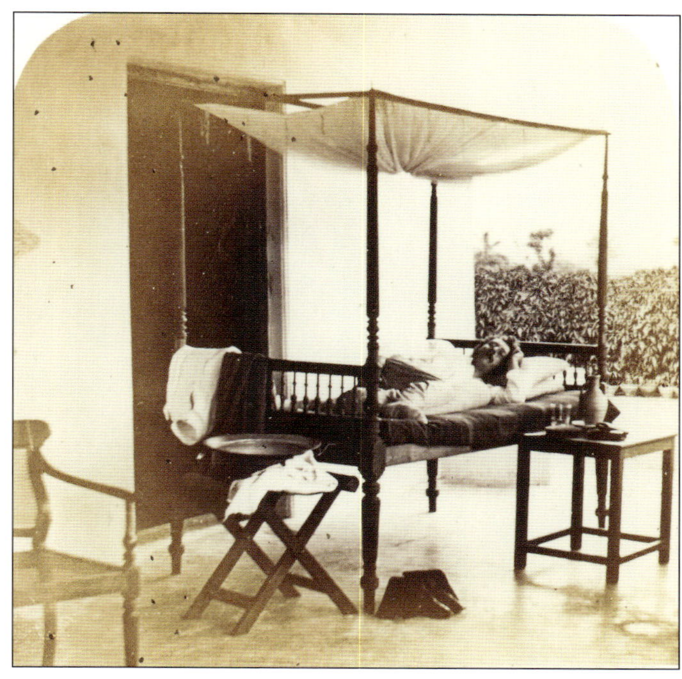

Fig. 10.18: Captain Allan Newton Scott, 'Rest, Warrior, Rest', albumen print, *Sketches of India*, 1862, plate XL. (National Library of Scotland, H.4.d.10)

graphic Society received 'an extensive and most valuable collection of stereoscopic views … illustrating the people of India and their manners and customs … natural scenery and antiquities'.[69]

Captain Scott's *Sketches of India*, published in London that year, contained 100 photographs from stereo halves.[70] The text, presumably written by Scott himself, is comparatively bland, but it gives a fair idea of his range and ability to secure convincing subjects. He illustrates McCosh's idea of the ennui amongst the soldiers, in his 'Rest, Warrior, Rest' [Fig. 10.18]. He photographed artillery stores, but also 'The China Room (in the residence of Nawab Mooktiar ool-Moolk Salar Jung Bahadur, Minister at Hyderabad)', which shows the elaborate 'ornamentation of a room of his residence being produced by China Plates, cups, and saucers, disposed to represent various devices. They are multiplied by numerous mirrors attached to the walls'. He also took street scenes, such as 'A Street in the Bazaar at Secunderabad', and individual portraits of the native population.

Most early Scots photographers in India were officially employed, though their photography was quasi-independent. Donald Horne Macfarlane (1830–1904), a merchant in tea and indigo, was unaffected by political authority.[71] Macfarlane came from Caithness, and went out to Bengal in 1859 as a partner in Begg, Dunlop and Co. He was prominent in the Bengal Photographic Society from November 1860, when he showed a 'very fine collection of views taken in Lucknow, the North West and in and about Calcutta'. His work was praised for 'taste and manipulation … delicate half-tone and just distribution of light and shade'.[72] The Society was much impressed. In 1861, he won the gold medal for the best series of landscapes and the silver medal

for the best single photograph in the exhibition. A reviewer wrote that his contributions were 'chosen with the eye of a true artist …. His prize picture "Creepers" will certainly gladden the heart' [Fig. 10.19].[73] His photographs of this kind are a triumphant, richly dark response to the problem of photographing the plant life expressed by other photographers in India. Macfarlane won first prize again in 1862 with another dense view of plants along a stream, remarkable for detail and a command of distance. In that year, he visited Darjeeling, where his firm had an interest in tea. From this journey comes his 'Rocks, Darjeeling' [Fig. 10.20], a fascinating, curiously flat and dislocated picture, split by the narrow fall of water. His 'Native Huts, Bengal' [Fig. 10.21] further explores the disconcerting possibilities of photographic response, with its reflection giving a different angle on the reality.

Macfarlane became President of the Bengal Society in 1863. After leaving India in 1864, he continued to contribute to their exhibitions, impressing a cynical reviewer in the *Indian Daily News* with English views, 'so charmingly executed that they absolutely tantalize any one who examines them by the fidelity with which they recall "home".'[74]

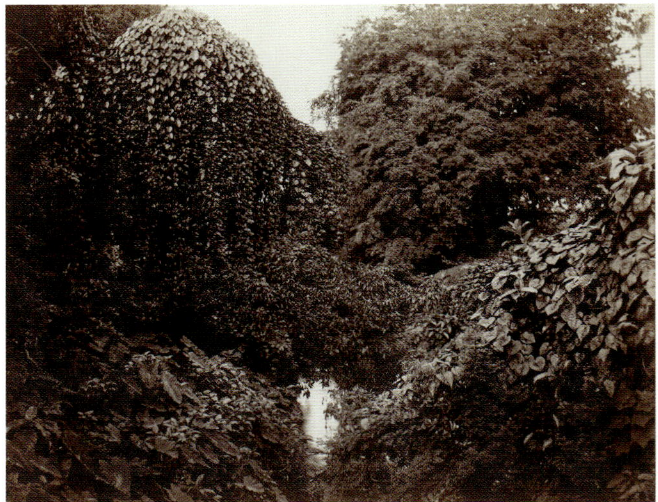

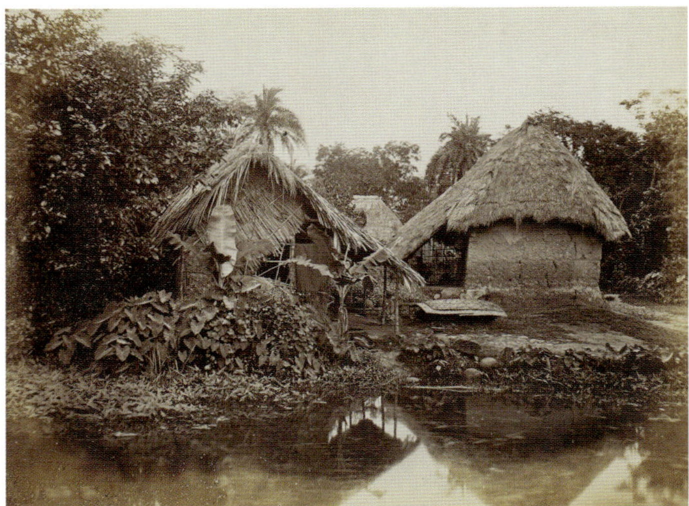

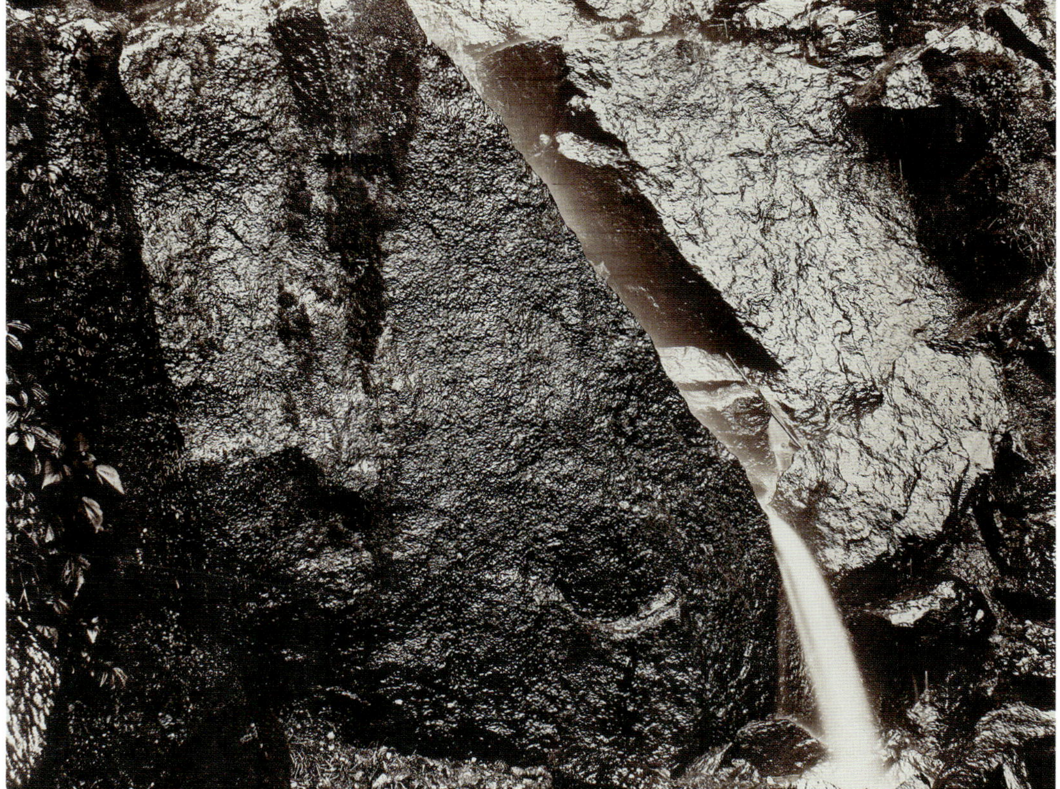

Fig. 10.19 (above left): Donald Horne Macfarlane, 'Creepers', 1860/61, albumen print. (The Collection of Howard and Jane Ricketts, Macfarlane Collection [No. 33])

Fig. 10.20 (left): Donald Horne Macfarlane, 'Rocks, Darjeeling', *c.*1862, albumen print. (The Collection of Howard and Jane Ricketts, Macfarlane Collection [No. 2])

Fig. 10.21 (above right): Donald Horne Macfarlane, 'Native Huts, Bengal', *c.*1862, albumen print. (The Collection of Howard and Jane Ricketts, Macfarlane Collection [No. 56])

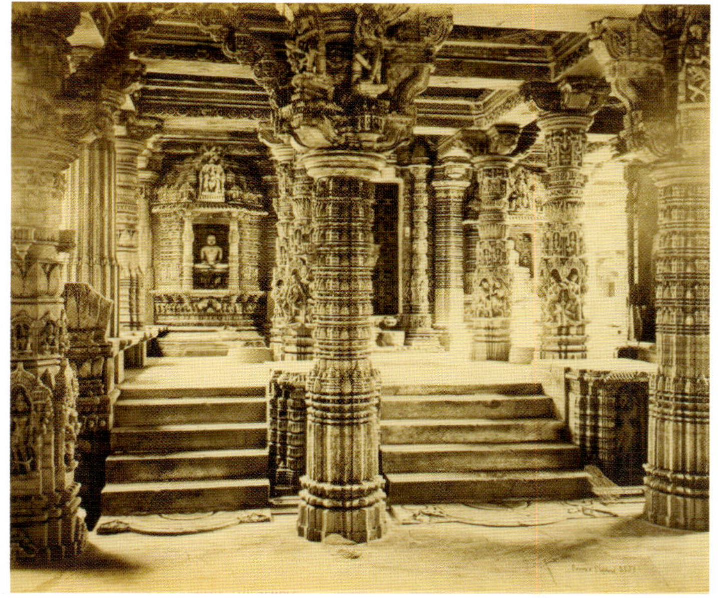

He became a member of the London Photographic Society, and showed his Indian photographs at their exhibitions in 1864 and 1865, when he was awarded another medal. He achieved a bronze medal for 'Views in India' at the Paris exhibition in 1867.[75]

In the 1860s, professional photographers and studios grew within India. The Bengal Photographic Society discovered to its consternation in 1869 that all the chief medals had been awarded to commercial photographers. After anxious discussion, they decided to reserve half the medals for amateurs, which caused the professionals to boycott the exhibition.[76] Photographers of the authority of Samuel Bourne and his partners in business, who included the Scot, Colin Roderick Murray (1840–84), working alongside Indian photographers of the calibre of Lalla Deen Dayall, were now taking the lead in photography, producing photographs of established skill and beauty [FIG. 10.22]. The situation had shifted from amateur to professional.

Colin Murray, who was born on the island of Lewis, migrated to India as a photographer about 1867. In 1870, he succeeded Bourne and followed his standards in work with the same tender delicacy in detail and distance. He inherited Bourne's collection, over two thousand views of the subcontinent and, with his contribution, it formed 'the

model to which the succeeding generations of commercial photographers aspired .... The firm's influence in this respect is difficult to overestimate'.[77]

Murray died of cholera and is buried in Calcutta.

Australasia[78]

One of the earliest mentions of photography in Australia comes from Launceston in Tasmania in April 1844, when the *Launceston Examiner* published a note:

> A gentleman has kindly favoured us with a book of calo-type drawings executed in Scotland, which we will be happy to show to those who take an interest in photo-graphy. The pictures consist of portraits and several well known architectural beauties still remaining at St Andrews.[79]

The pursuit of photography in St Andrews had reached the far side of the world, but whether the example could yet be followed is open to question. The same issue of the news-paper records:

> A deficiency in one of the chemicals used in the Daguer-reotype process, not to be supplied in the colony, has compelled Mr Flavelle to close his establishment earlier than was expected.

In 1846 Captain Stanley, of the naval ship HMS *Rattle-snake*, led an expedition to Australia and New Guinea to make a scientific survey of the Great Barrier Reef and the Torres Strait.[80] He requested the government to supply him with a camera. Dr John Thomson (d.1891/2), from Edinburgh, was the ship's surgeon and already a photographer – he carried with him a photograph he had taken of his new wife, Mary.[81] His junior was the young Thomas Huxley, who gave an account of the survey in his journal and letters.[82] He commented on the ship at the start of their four-year expedition:

> Exploring vessels will be invariably found to be the slowest, clumsiest, and in every respect the most inconvenient ships which wear the pennant. In accordance with the rule such was the Rattlesnake, and to carry out the spirit of the authorities more completely, she was turned out of Plymouth dockyard in such a disgraceful state of unfitness, that her lower deck was continually underwater during the voyage.[83]

Within a few days, the crew were so sick in the Bay of Biscay that they remained in their hammocks, oblivious of their possessions swilling around in the water in the cabins. Three years later, Huxley described the conditions in the area of New Guinea:

> It rains so hard that we have caught seven tons of hot water in one day … the lower and main decks are utterly unventilated: a sort of solution of man in steam fills them from end to end, and surrounds the lights with a lurid halo … my sole amusement consists in watching the cockroaches, which are in a state of intense excitement and happiness ….[84]

This must have made the mere idea of photography (and preserving any paper photographs taken) close to impossible.

Thomson and Huxley had a professional remit beyond medical concerns. Thomson was a botanist and interested in ethnography. Sadly, he found that the captain (who had been warned by the Admiralty not to rouse the hostility of the natives) was so nervous when sailing through the islands of New Guinea, he prevented his men from landing. Given the survey had been substantially prompted by a fearful case of shipwreck, followed by cannibalism, the anxiety was reasonable, but Thomson wrote to his wife in frustration:

> Truly our voyage might have been one of discovery … [but] we have left this great terra incognita after a four months' cruise along its shores without knowing anything more than was known of it before our visit … it makes me sick to think of the opportunities for seeing a country which was unknown ….[85]

Thomson's work from the voyage remains mysterious.[86] He proved, nevertheless, to be a good photographer with a sound understanding of the art.[87] He returned to Edinburgh by 1851 and worked with James Good Tunny for a while. William McCraw wrote later of

> … Mr T., a doctor in the navy, who was then enjoying some leisure time in the neighbourhood of Mr Tunny's studio. The former gentleman devoted days and weeks together in experimenting with the latter, and many a message was sent from home for the errant doctor to come to his dinner. … one day I was invited by Mr Tunny to sit for a portrait, the doctor looking on, and I was presented with a capital negative of myself, developed with iron, the collodion, gun-cotton, and all having been made on the premises.[88]

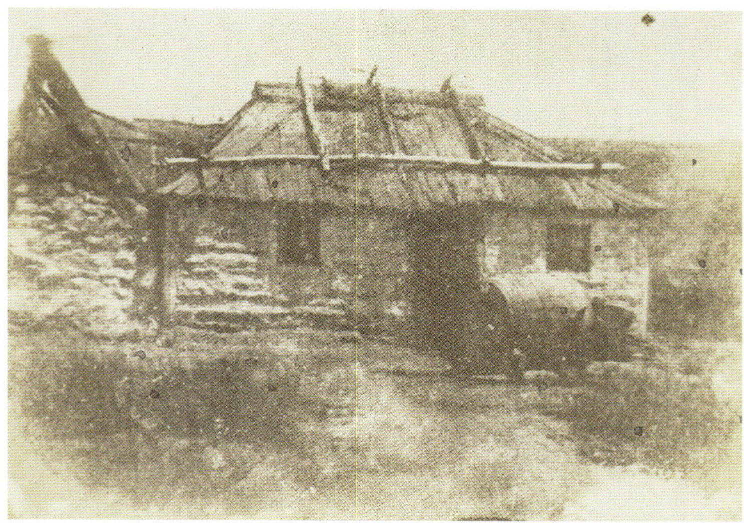

Fig. 10.23: Robert Tennent, 'Kitchen Hut, Gnarkeet Station', Port Phillip, Australia, c.1845, calotype taken with a 'camera made with a cigar box and a telescope lens'. (Scottish National Portrait Gallery, PGP 376.25)

Thomson wrote to Huxley in July, describing his progress:

I have been very busy with my Calotype and have arrived at considerable proficiency. I have nearly discarded paper as the medium of receiving the negative picture and have adopted glass …. When I wish to take portraits I cover the face of the glass plate with collodion having in solution a few drops of Iodide of silver dissolved in a saturated solution of Iodide of Potassium – the hydro Carbon of the Aether seems to play an important part in rendering the surface very sensitive after it has been dipped in a solution of Nitrate of Silver 30 grs to the ounce – 10 to 30 seconds give a good portrait in diffuse day light. When my wish is to take scenery I find if the surface is not rendered very sensitive that the minutest details of the landscape are more clearly developed. I therefore make use of albumen having mixed with it a little of a very strong solution of Iodide of Potassium to coat the surface of the glass – and when this covering is perfectly dry I dip the glass as formerly in to a solution of Nitrate of Silver 30 grs to the ounce. In both cases the pictures are brought out by a mixture of Gallic and Acetic Acid and occasionally are not fully formed until after a lapse of 2 or 3 hours.[89]

Huxley replied to a gift of photographs:

Many thanks for the Calotypes – they are certainly as fine as any I have ever seen. Your own is especially sharp and life-like, and wonderfully like. As for your son's, of course I can't judge of the likeness, but I can quite believe it – as he has all that peculiarly sturdy, *planted*, look – a sort of jolly defiance to the world in general –

which I have heard of as his characteristic. A most indubitable chip! – it makes me laugh whenever I look at him ….[90]

Robert Tennent (1813–90) arrived at Port Phillip, South-eastern Australia in October 1839. He held 75,000 acres in the Portland Bay district from 1841 to 1848, and in partnership nearly 30,000 acres of land at Gnarkeet (with grazing for 50 cattle and 12,000 sheep) from 1844 to 1853.[91] Tennent's photograph, of the 'Kitchen Hut, Gnarkeet Station' [Fig. 10.23], was taken with a 'camera made with a cigar box and a telescope lens', but his brother, Hugh Lyon Tennent, may have sent him better supplies. He took photographs with an efficient camera, including images of the Burra Burra copper mine around 1848, of the landscape and trees, and Port Phillip.

In the 1840s, the area around Melbourne produced a great quantity of meat and wool, generating wealth for the landholders before the gold rush of the 1850s. But the business of farming was subject to slumps like any other trade. As a farmer, John Hunter Kerr (1821–74) veered from prosperity.[92] He arrived on the first emigrant ship to come directly to Port Phillip from Leith, in June 1839. As the ship groped into the harbour, grounding several times on sandbanks, the passengers found 'a group of gentlemen, mostly Scotch, standing on the shore …' waiting for news. 'The colonists', added Kerr 'were few in those days, and the tie of nationality was almost equivalent to that of kinship.'[93] In the mid-1840s, he returned to Edinburgh for two years. It was probably then that he learned photography and acquired a camera, before coming back to Australia in 1849. His first surviving dated photograph belongs to that year. In writing his autobiography, Kerr revealed himself as an observant man, taking pleasure in landscape and birdlife. In the 1840s, the land was sparsely populated. Kerr was much interested in the aboriginal people, and worked well with the Loddon and Jajoweroung tribes, who were closest to his farms. He shared the European view of progress that the future lay with their own culture: 'Though still numerous, it was evident, even then, that the doom of their race was fixed; and that, in obedience to the mysterious decree of Providence, they were passing away to give place to a superior race.'[94]

Kerr set himself to a serious collection of artefacts and study of the people; he established good relations, and the aborigines were prepared to allow him an observer's role in their society.[95] He wrote of the corroboree:

No description can convey any adequate idea of this extraordinary performance. The dark figures, painted in a thousand fantastic and hideous designs – the rustle of the boughs tied round their ankles – the grotesque and savage attitudes, accompanied by a wild monotonous chant rising in fierce chorus – the red glare of the camp-fires … and in strange contrast … the soft, bright beams of the full moon, mingling with the ruddy blaze.[96]

This was, by any definition of the time, unphotographable, but Kerr set about it [Fig. 10.24]:

… the chosen time is at full moon. Being desirous of obtaining photographs of the corroboree I once prevailed on a few of the blacks to dance it by daylight. This was only done for the promise of a considerable present; but no arguments would induce them to allow the lubras [the women] to witness the exhibition at that unusual hour, and to complete my picture I was obliged to content myself with a group of young men, wrapped in their skins, to represent the absent ladies.

He took individual portraits as well as groups:

At first they were a little alarmed at the machinery, but when their first shyness was overcome they were never weary of sitting in any attitude, and laughed with glee at the results. But they rarely expressed surprise before white men, reserving their comments on anything extraordinary and unfamiliar for their privacy.[97]

Kerr's photography incorporated a certain grace in its approach. His subjects were amused by the performance, and he could take advantage of their natural stillness and their dignity. His experience differed from that of Douglas Kilburn, who opened the first professional studio in Melbourne in 1847. He declared his sitters were 'fearful of "some misfortune" in having their portraits made', and took him for a sorcerer.[98] Kerr was working within the landscape familiar to his subjects, without the unnerving paraphernalia of the studio. He was happy, despite his antiquarian gloom, to photograph the aborigines in western dress.

John Smith (1821–85) travelled to Australia as a ship's surgeon. He was born in Peterculter, Aberdeenshire, son of a blacksmith, and was educated at Marischal College,

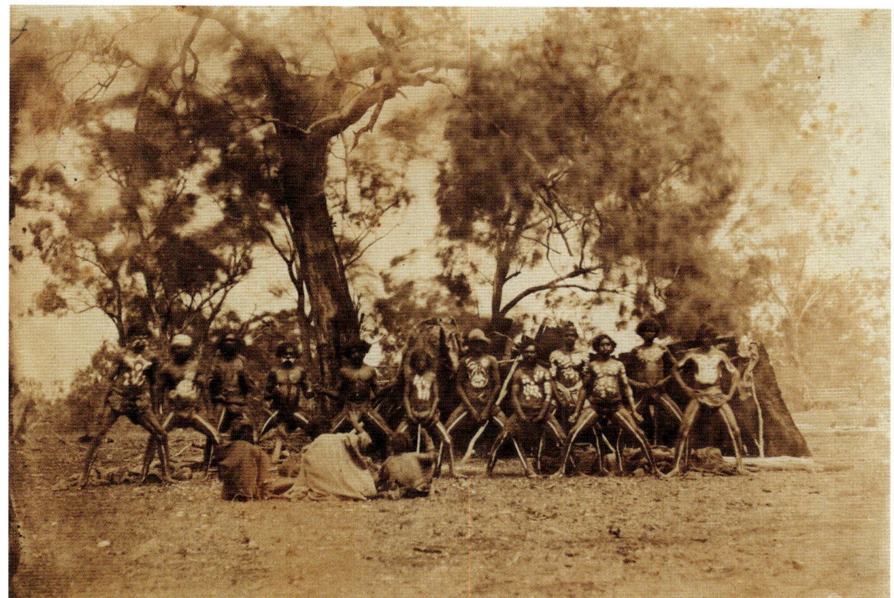

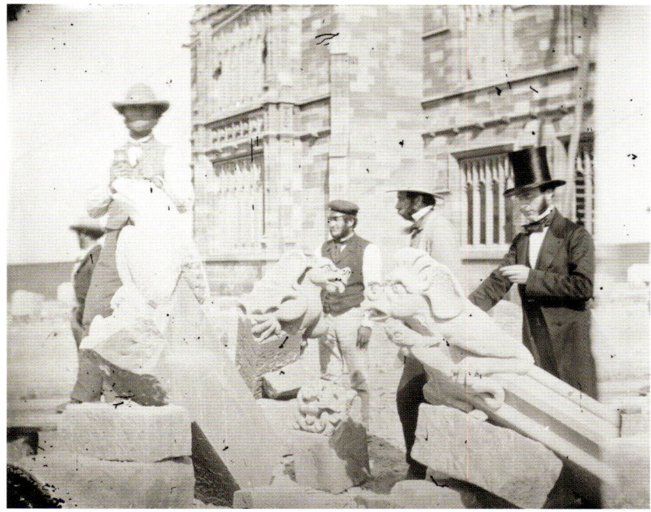

progress [FIG. 10.25]. He photographed family and friends: a stiff group in fashionable dress on an elegant verandah; a tired nurse with a baby in the conservatory. He took his camera out into the country to photograph landscape and geology, and took images of the streets showing the new stone elegance of the developing city.

John Rae (1813–1900) was also born in Aberdeen; he trained in law there, and in Edinburgh. Migrating to Australia in 1839, he became accountant to an investment company. He was the first town clerk of Sydney in 1843, where he joined the School of Arts and took an active interest in education. In 1857, Rae was appointed secretary to railway commissioners, and in 1861 he became under-secretary for public works. He was known as an important, impartial public servant.[101]

Using a camera obscura, he made a series of panoramic drawings of Sydney in 1842, and followed this enthusiasm for his lifetime[102] He built a room-sized camera obscura on top of his house in 1855. In 1883, he exhibited in the Calcutta International Exhibition five panoramas from 1849 onwards, alongside photographs, to show the development of the city within twenty to thirty years – a demonstration of time and change.

Rae gave talks on photography in 1855 [FIG. 10.26],

Aberdeen, where he became lecturer in chemistry and agriculture. He migrated, in 1852, as foundation professor of chemistry and experimental physics at the University of Sydney.[99] Several hundred of his photographs still survive, from a period stretching between 1855 and 1880, using glass negatives and stereoscopic photography.[100] His work was focussed on western advance. In 1859, he photographed the construction of the neogothic University, decorated with large gargoyles, an international signal of intellectual

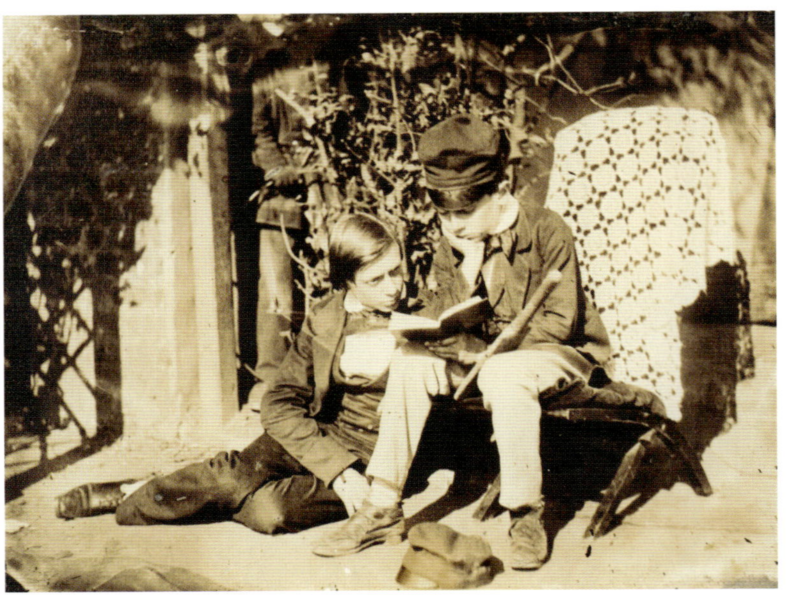

Fig. 10.26 (above): John Rae, 'Two boys', *c.*1855, albumen print. (State Library of New South Wales, P1/2039)

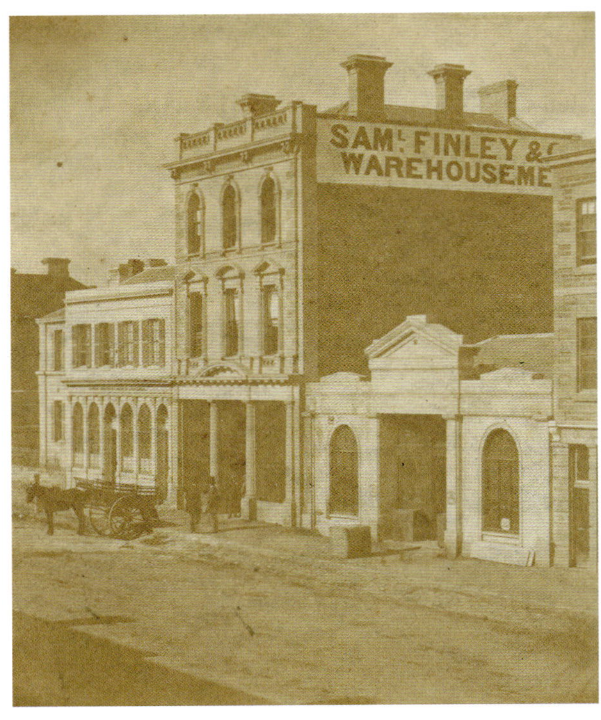

Figs 10.27 (right): Alexander McGlashon, 'Collins Street, Melbourne', 1857, albumen half-stereo image. (Howarth-Loomes Collection at National Museums Scotland, IL.2003.44.6.14.408)

when he said that he had practised for some time, and recommended forming a photographic society

> … [as] the means of disseminating, by means of pictures that could not be accused of exaggeration, a knowledge of this beautiful land throughout the mother country, where the most ridiculous notions are entertained of its barrenness and infertility.
>
> … this beautiful art … is an innocent, delightful, and humanizing recreation; and, I may add from experience, a most enticing and engrossing pursuit ….[103]

In contrast to these settled and successful men, a photographer called McGlashon, or McGlashan, set up in Melbourne in 1856. He advertised modestly, through August:

> Portraits on Glass, from Five Shillings, at McGlashon's photographic gallery, 7 Collins-street east.[104]

By September, his advertisements were even quieter:

> Photographic Portrait Gallery, 7 Collins street east. Portraits taken at this establishment forwarded to England gratis.[105]

This may have been the Alexander McGlashon who worked in Edinburgh, or perhaps a close relative: it was not a common name. In December 1855, a list of unclaimed letters in the South Australian Post Office included 'Alex. McGlashan' from Perthshire.[106] The Photographic Society of Scotland's album contains three photographs by a 'McGlashan': a portrait of Mr Smellie taken in 1854 (perhaps the Edinburgh printer and Alexander McGlashon's father-in-law), and two of Collins Street.[107] Alexander McGlashon took stereoscopic photographs of Scottish scenery; the Australian photographer took at least five stereographs of Collins Street [FIG. 10.27]. Whoever the man was, his practice faced serious competition in Melbourne. He may be visualised, emerging from his studio with a camera to take pictures in the street, with one eye on the studio door-

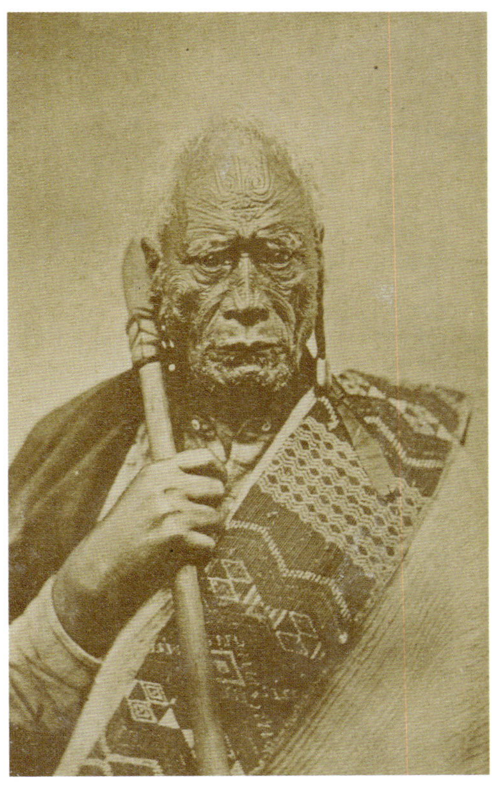

Fig. **10.28**: John Nicol Crombie, 'Taraia Ngakuti Te Tamahuia', 1860–72, albumen print. (Alexander Turnbull Library, National Library of New Zealand, PA2-2820)

the Bank, for the prosecution of the above art in all its details …'.[109]

In 1856 Crombie daguerreotyped twelve Maori chiefs, and sent the pictures to London to be engraved for the *Illustrated London News*. The *Daily Southern Cross* commented: 'The portraits, as a work of art, are very superior, and we trust that the presiding genii of that world renowned publication will avail themselves of a contribution so well calculated to convey a correct impression of the features and character of the aboriginal potentates of this antipodal fraction of the British Empire.' It listed the men in the portraits with notes on their varied character, such as:

> 1 Taraia Ngakuti Te Tamahuia, the principal Chief of the Thames, a great warrior and cannibal [Fig. 10.28] ….
> 12 Tamati Waka Nene – Chief of one of the Ngapuhi tribes at Hokianga, on the West Coast of New Zealand, – a man of deep penetration, firm judgment, and indomitable courage – deservedly respected by all classes of both races.[110]

Crombie promoted himself as the official photographer to the Governor of New Zealand, so his later photographs of the Maori at the Kohimarana Treaty conference in 1860 may have been given political direction. Two hundred chiefs participated, and attempted to achieve an accord.[111] Perhaps the portraiture was linked to the government's move to publish the words of the Maori speakers at the conference – overtly embracing Maori opinion.

In 1862, Crombie returned to Britain, probably to attend the International Exhibition in London.[112] He exhibited a group of photographs, designed to show the progress of the country [Fig. 10.29], including a five-foot panorama

way for potential customers. It may be they did not come. After 1857, his business closed.

McGlashon's failure must have been a common story, which provides a background to the successful photographers, such as John Nic[h]ol Crombie (1827–78), who arrived in Melbourne from Glasgow in 1852. He sought work as an engineer without success, and took employment with the photographic firm of Meade Brothers. He moved to Auckland, New Zealand, in 1855, and set up his studio in Shortland Street. The following year, the *Daily Southern Cross* reported that in his first fifteen months' work, he had taken '1088 persons, of every class in society'. They added, 'His pictures have a roundness and boldness of character, which are frequently found wanting in portraits by the daguerreotype process.'[108]

John Nicol Crombie toured the Southern Provinces of New Zealand in 1856, and the newspapers published good notices of his work. In Nelson in 1858, he advertised his 'fitted apartments in Trafalgar-street, nearly opposite

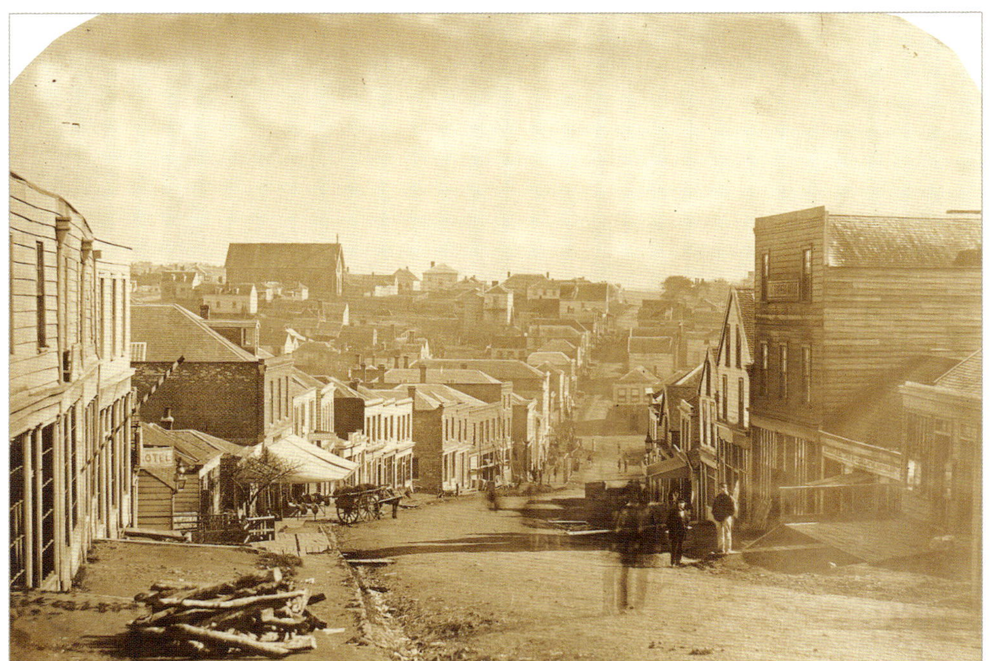

Fig. **10.29:** John Nicol Crombie, 'Shortland Street', n.d., albumenised salt print. (John Leech Gallery, Auckland, New Zealand [from the Collection of Michael-Graham Stewart])

of Auckland, and received an Honourable Mention. 'As a photograph, it is Mr Crombie's very best, and does him infinite credit.' The author of the newspaper report despaired of the ignorance of six million London visitors: 'To hear the different remarks on New Zealand in its court would lead to a supposition … that the natives are still cannibals; that we at Auckland are in a state of fern, and without streets or regular houses, speak a foreign tongue, and are but Maori once removed'.[113]

Canada

In the northern hemisphere, Canada was much-favoured by migrants, especially from the islands and west coast of Scotland. In the mid-19th century, the country was divided by the great distance from east to west. Much of the trade in the east, dependent on hunting, was in the hands of the great trading companies.

James Inglis (1835–1904) trained as a stonemason in Scotland. He migrated in 1856 and learnt photography around 1860 from an itinerant phrenologist and ambro-typist.[114] He set up a toyshop and ambrotype saloon in the village of St Catharines. He then moved to New York and considered going out to Havana. Instead, he went back north to Montreal. He started from nothing, with the loan of 'a one-half size camera and tube, three chairs … a table, the floor uncarpeted, and the walls of the rooms bare'. In two years he changed premises twice and arrived in Great St James Street, the principal thoroughfare of Montreal. By 1871, having started 'with no assistant, doing all his own work, Mr Inglis has so rapidly progressed and advanced that he has now in his employ *twenty* hands, *two* operators, *two* artists and *one* retoucher, which he thinks a pretty good proof that photography is not *quite run out yet*, as so many are endeavoring to persuade themselves'.[115]

Inglis may have initiated the local fashion for composite images. He drew a background in India ink, cut out individual portraits and stuck them onto the design. Re-photographed, they became a group picture. The London *Art-journal* published an admiring comment on his 'large and attractive picture', shown in Montreal in 1870, 'of the joint committee of the Presbyterian Church in the provinces of British North America'.[116]

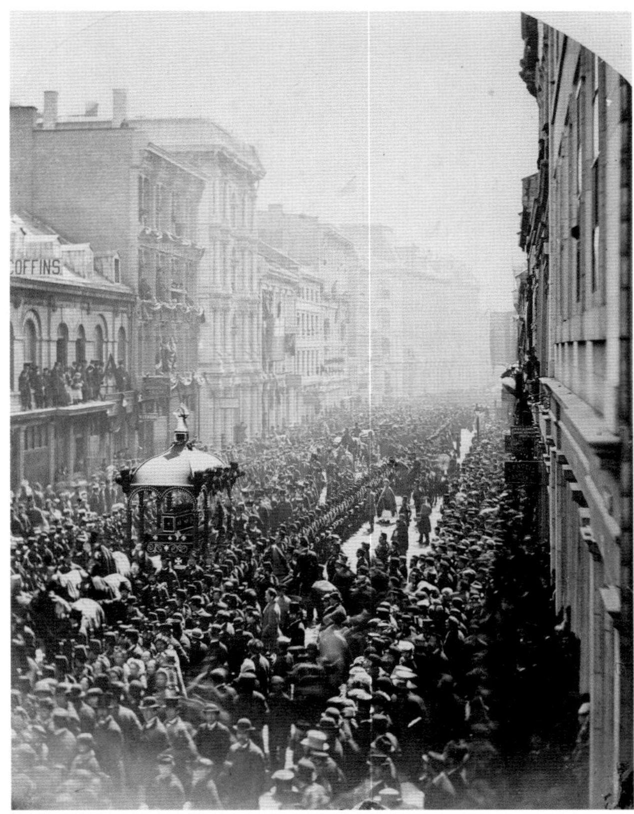

Fig. 10.30: James Inglis, 'Funeral Procession of the late Thomas D'Arcy McGee', 13 April 1868. (Library and Archives Canada, 1975-433, C-083423)

In 1868, Inglis took a remarkable photograph of the funeral of assassinated politician Thomas D'Arcy McGee, instantaneously and with a long focus down the Montreal street [FIG. 10.30]. It was in effect a news photograph, as was his photograph of the lacrosse team of the Mohawk nation, who were Canadian lacrosse champions in 1869. In 1884, Inglis relocated to Chicago, where he manufactured dry plate negatives; he died there while experimenting with magnesium flash photography.[117]

Moose Factory, one of the Hudson's Bay Company's trading posts, was placed on an island in the Moose River, flowing into James Bay, Ontario. An unlikely centre for photography, it became known for a significant group of amateur workers from the 1860s onwards. Charles George Horetzky (1838–1900) was employed by the Company in the 1860s. His father, Felix Horetzky, was a Polish musician, who was dispossessed in 1830 and settled in Edinburgh where he married Sophia Robertson and Charles was born.[118] Charles Horetzky was educated in Aberdeen and Belgium. He emigrated first to the Australian gold fields in 1854. By 1858 he was at Fort William in Canada, as a clerk, and was then promoted as accountant at Moose Factory.

One of the conditions of British Columbia's entry into the Canadian Confederation in 1870, was the building of the Canadian Pacific Railway to link the two sides of the country. In 1871, Charles Horetzky was appointed as the official photographer for Sir Sandford Fleming's survey from Winnipeg to Edmonton, to gather information and take 'views of objects of interest illustrative of the physical features of the country'.[119] The survey team travelled from Fort Garry in Manitoba, more than a thousand miles to the west of Toronto across the South Saskatchewan River to Elbow in Saskatchewan. Horetzky reached Fort Garry

on 20 March with a good group of photographs. Fleming employed Horetzky again in the summer and autumn of 1872, to follow the Peace River, which runs from the Rocky Mountains in British Columbia through Alberta, and consider if a branch line should be sent this way. With the botanist, Dr John Macoun, a miner and a guide, Horetzky undertook a seven-month trek, through swamps and snow. He took a photograph, while detouring up the Wotsonqua River, of an Indian cantilevered bridge of terrifying fragility [FIG. 10.31]. Horetzky saw it as Romantic, 'a suspension bridge across the rocky chasm, through which the waters of the Wotsonqua rush with impetuous haste towards the Skeena .... The bridge is built entirely of wood, fastened together by withies and branches; its height above the roaring waters beneath is fifty feet, and it sways about under the weight of a man, to try even the nerves of a Blondin.'[120] It is was an alarming but elegant design.

They travelled from Fort Edmonton to Fort Simpson

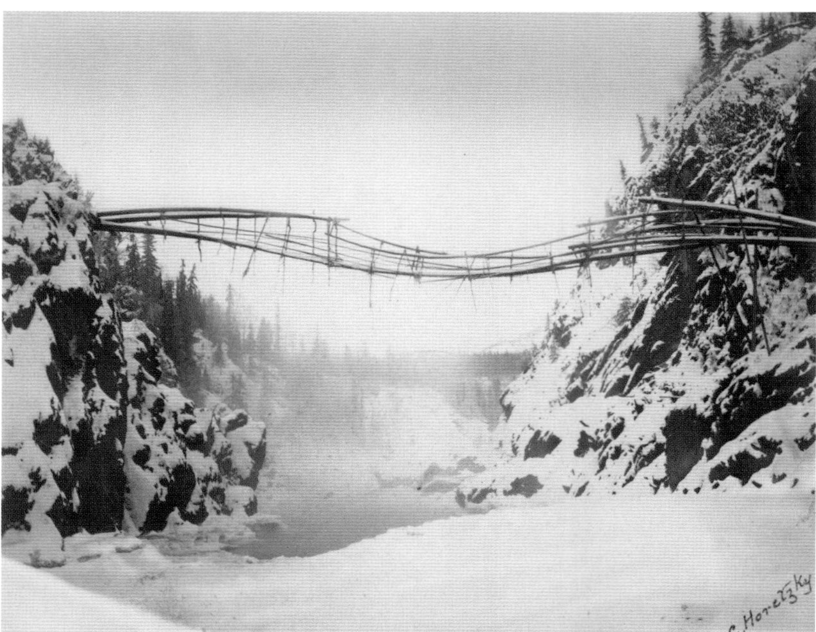

Fig. 10.31: Charles George Horetzky, 'Indian suspension bridge over the Wotsonqua River, 28 Dec. 1872', albumen print. (Library and Archives Canada, 1936-272 [PA-118272])

through the winter, seeking the best route for the railway, in conditions of appalling weather, in which simply arriving at their destination was an achievement without Horetzky's extensive records and fine photographs.[121] He was motivated by a desire, to be treated as an engineer rather than as a photographer. However, he was 'one of a very small group of men in North America to carry the camera into the unexplored parts of the continent ... he could take photographs equal to the best of his day'.[122]

James Laurence Cotter (1839–89) was a son of Colonel George Sackville Cotter and Agnes Kilgour. He too was a second-generation migrant, born in Jalna, India, and brought up by his grandmother in Edinburgh. He moved to Canada in 1857 and joined the Hudson's Bay Company. Arriving at Moose Factory in 1867, he took over from Horetzky, becoming one of the chief traders. Cotter made his own camera, and took 'artistically composed, sharp, clear photographs'. Capturing 'scenes reminiscent of a life which had changed little since the establishment of the fort in 1673... [he] took what are probably the earliest photographs of the Inuit at Little Whale River'.[123] He and his wife, Frances Ironside, set up a darkroom on the ice [Fig. 10.32].

Cotter became interested in the lives of the Inuit while working in the Eastmain District. He wrote later that it was 'a land so inhospitable and so sterile ... [that it is likely] to be pronounced uninteresting', evidently far from an established pattern of the picturesque.[124] This enabled him to make pictures of impressive individuality.

The grandfather and father of Alexander Henderson (1831–1913) were in partnership as 'Eagle & Henderson', seedsmen and florists in Edinburgh.[125] His father, Thomas, inherited Press Castle in East Lothian, south-east of Edinburgh. Thomas Henderson died when Alexander was nine, leaving him to the care of an uncle who introduced him to the outdoor life. He trained, reluctantly, as an accountant, and joined an Edinburgh firm for three years. In 1855, he married Agnes Robertson, and they emigrated to Montreal. Between 1859 and 1863, he was noted in the *Montreal City Directory* as a Commission Merchant. The couple lived a comfortable life, taking both winter and summer holidays.

Henderson began taking photographs in 1857. This emerges in a letter to William Crookes, the editor of the journal *Photographic News*, which reveals something of his unsuccessful attempts with dry collodion processes:

... in two excursions into the woods, where I saw fine

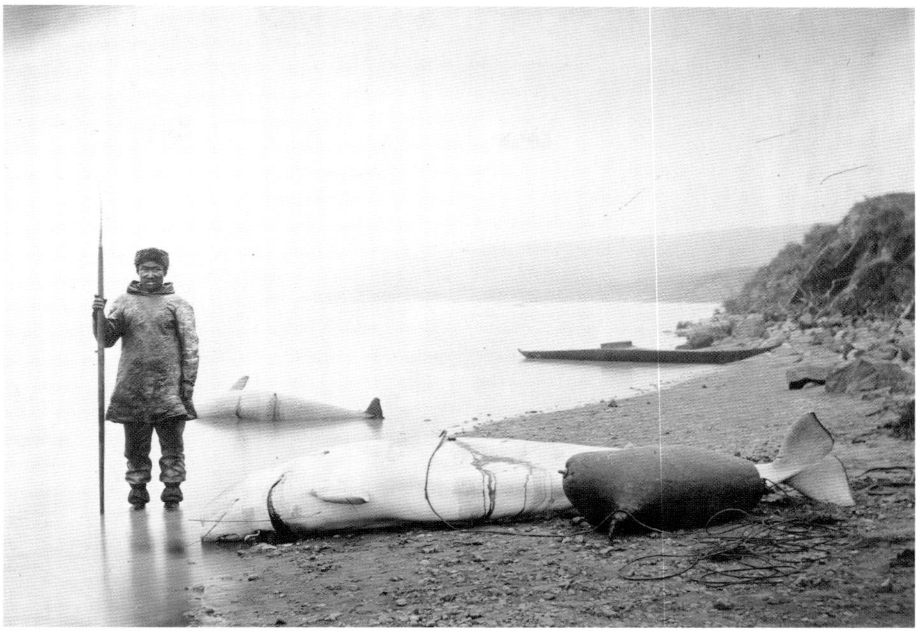

Fig. 10.32: James Laurence Cotter, 'Inuit man with a harpooned whale, 1872', albumen print. (Hudson's Bay Company Archives, HBCA Album 1/62 [N13761])

subjects, and took many, only to find black, dirty glasses on retiring. Now, I have taken a great many negatives with these processes … and am quite satisfied that it was the great heat, often much above 100° in the sun, and as high, once or twice, as 98° in the shade, the same manipulation succeeding in cool weather … After the second excursion, which was up to the 'High Falls,' on the Rivière aux Lièvres … I schemed a developing box, which answers famously …. I came home the other day, after a visit to a place near St Hilaire, C.E., with 24 stereographic negatives, and fifteen turpentine wax paper ditto, 10 x 8. The box is some 20lbs, with everything in it – glasses, water bottles, bath, &c., many of which I carry, or have carried in a fishing basket, if I wish to walk far.[126]

Henderson was the first North American member of the Stereoscopic Exchange Club in 1859. He joined the London Amateur Photographic Association and participated enthusiastically in their exchange scheme.[127] He won a prize from the Association in 1863, of a silver inkstand, for '"The Mountain Maid" (Canadian Steamboat instantaneous)'.[128] His readiness to offer excellent photographs for exchange meant that his circle of influence was international. He must have built up in return a handsome collection of photographs by his fellow photographers, which would have assisted in his own visual development. In 1874, he was elected a member of the Edinburgh Photographic Society, and reinforced his welcome by donating 'a number of very fine prints to the album of the Society'.[129]

Henderson produced an album in 1865, *Canadian Views and Studies* – sold with different pictures, chosen by the buyers from his stock. This may have been his first professional act. In 1866, he opened a studio in Montreal largely devoted to landscape work. In 1872, he undertook photography for the Canadian railways, working first for the Intercolonial Railway, then the Occidental Railway and later the Canadian Pacific Railway.

Henderson's photography took in land and cityscapes of a conventional kind, but it is his fascination with the wild landscape that is most moving. His pleasure in the water is seen in a number of beautiful photographs. 'Spring Inundation, near Montreal, QC', taken before 1865 [Fig. 10.33], offers a pleasing sense of suspension, between water and sky, which is exaggerated by the calm waters of the flood. His photograph called 'Winter harvest fields', taken on the

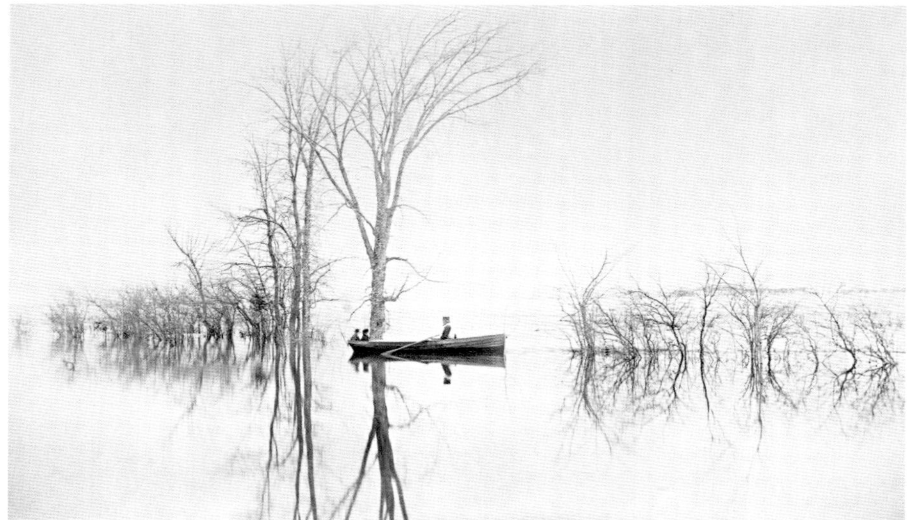

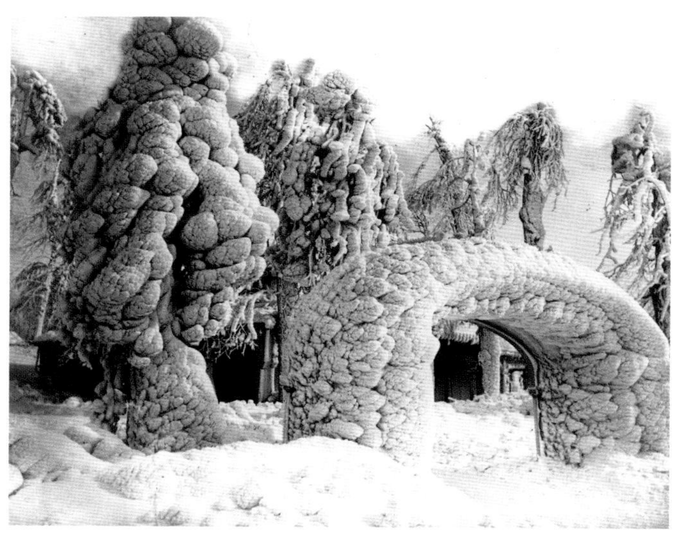

frozen St Lawrence River by Montreal, around 1870, shows the results of cutting ice, a practical business, but visually extraordinary – large, scattered, shining cubes of reflecting light under a lowering sky.[130] His 'Frost on view point, Niagara Falls', taken in 1875, offers the opposite, the appearance of natural, sprouting growth formed by an extravagance of frost [Fig. 10.34] – both images outwith British experience.

Henderson specialised in snow photographs, which allowed him to exploit his pleasure in the winter landscape; he was happy even to photograph during snowstorms. On the night of 22 February 1869, he joined the Grand Trunk Railway at Montreal, travelling to Quebec to take photographs.[131] Ten feet of snow had already built up from the 'severest snow storm experienced for years'.[132] During the night, the storm was driven back in by a north-westerly gale. Three more locomotives and a snow plough were sent out to rescue the train, and shifted it a few miles, but it stuck at Black River for a second night. On 24 February, the storm departed. Henderson had climbed out onto the snow banks to take pictures at intervals during the day [Fig. 10.35]. He took these in to the *Montreal Witness* on 10 March. The editor commented: 'If anything could awaken sympathy for a Railway Company, pondering of these pictures could hardly fail to do so.'[133]

On 4 March, Henderson had advertised, 'Photography in the Snow. – Private residences, &c. photographed; new winter landscapes'.[134] His second album was entitled *Snow and Flood after the Great Storms in 1869*. And only with the third, in 1870, did he engage with the obvious: *Photographs of Montreal*.

Henderson's photographs of Canada, seen both in fierce and changing weather and in contemplative calm, provoke a lyrical response. Stanley Triggs writes of his 'sensual passion for nature and the wilderness'.[135]

William Notman (1826–1891) was born in the west of Scotland, where his father produced Paisley shawls.[136] The

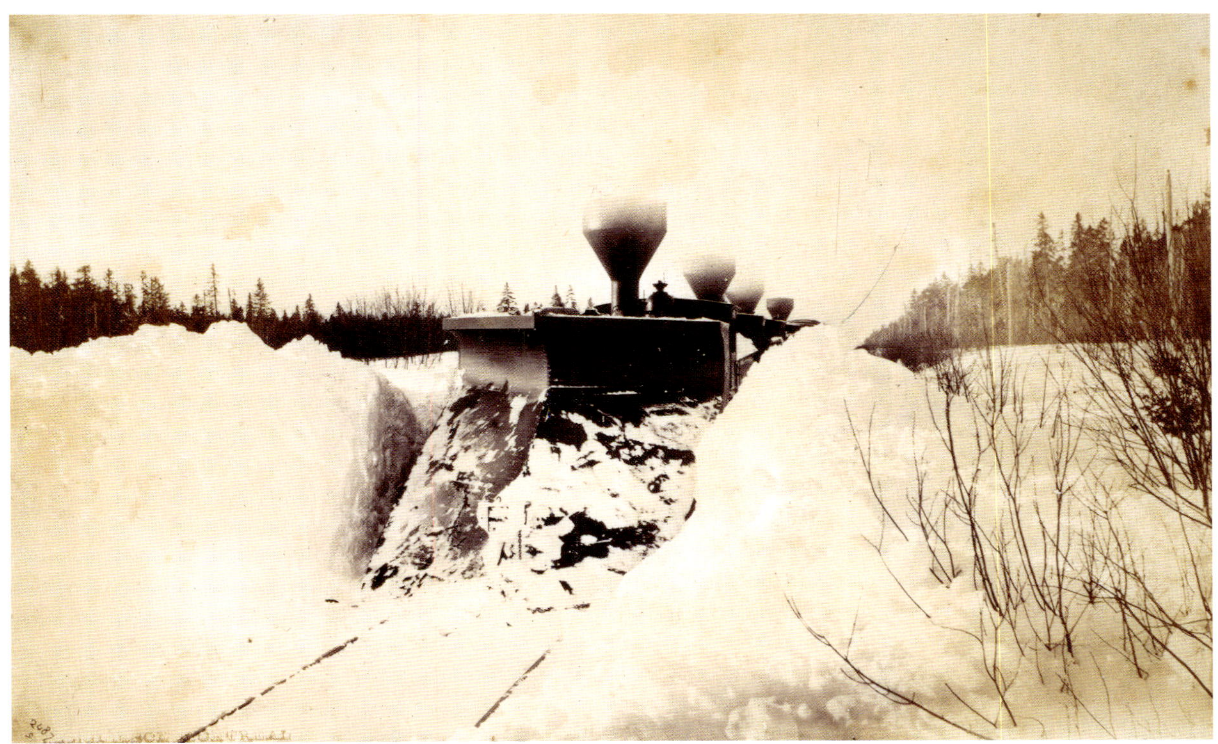

family branched out in Glasgow around 1851; they were variously referred to as 'commission merchants and agents', 'woollen cloth merchants' and 'warehousemen'.[137] But the business went bankrupt.[138] William Notman the younger was fortunate not to be imprisoned, as one of the firm's customers had determined only to supply them with goods which had been specifically ordered: Notman had pretended to have orders which did not exist, on speculation. He needed to leave the country and migrated to Montreal. After a year he set up a photography studio. Within ten years he was employing thirty-five people in the studio, from photographers to printers and painters, with both receptionist and secretary in place. William Notman's family came out to join him – several of the photographers working for the firm were his brothers, and then his sons.[139]

In 1860, Notman's business was drawn to public attention. The Grand Trunk Railway commissioned him to photograph the construction of the Victoria Bridge across the St Lawrence River. He photographed the work in detail; very probably the photographs were used for communi-cation between the railway proprietors and the engineers, Robert Stephenson and Alexander M. Ross. This was the longest railway bridge in the world (about three kilometres), was designed in iron, requiring the import of 9000 tons of iron plates from Britain, and stood on angled stone piers to break the powerful ice flow in winter. It was built for strength and was simple and ugly – an elongated metal box. In these pictures, Notman was working under the visual stress of an awkward and unpicturesque subject. In the composition of 'Piers and Works from the Top of the Tube ...', he achieved a well-filled image, with a pleasing distinction between the hard-edged solidity of the stone, and the unfocussed flow of the river, and the confusion of boats and huts complicated by the foreground movement of men, showing that in this instance the work had not stopped.

A month later, he took a most extraordinary picture, 'Side of Tube with Packings Looking in' [Fig. 10.36], a brutally reduced image where the combination of focussed and unfocussed perspective dramatizes the distance. Notman

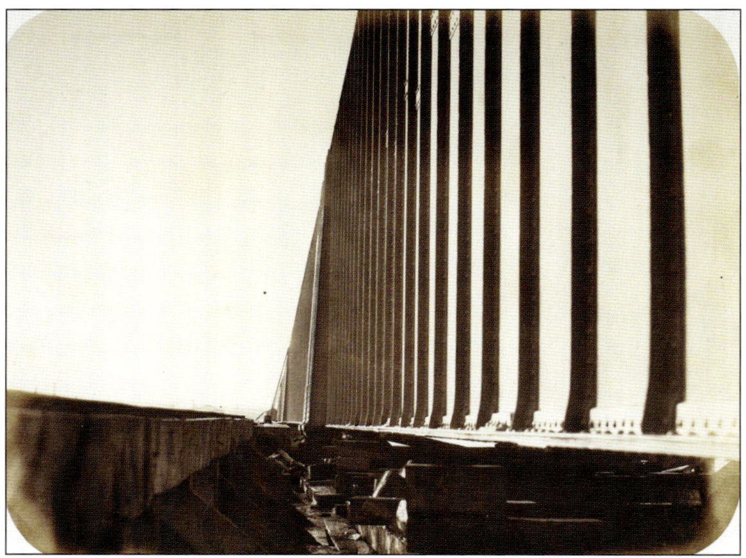

probably took the opportunity to make further work on his own account, using the stereoscopic camera to make images exploiting the astonishing perspective of the bridge.

The inauguration of the Victoria Bridge prompted the first royal visit to Canada. The Prince of Wales arrived to drive in the last rivet in August. The city of Montreal made the most of his visit with triumphal arches, an exhibition of the arts and sciences and a grand ball. Notman constructed two large portfolios of photographs, including his Bridge pictures, with Canadian landscapes and scenes from the royal visit. They were packed in a silver-trimmed maple box, and presented by the Canadian government to the Prince.[140] Notman used the gift to justify his claim to be 'Photographer to the Queen', and carved these fine words over the portico of his studio.[141]

Notman seized the opportunity of the royal visit to make another advance. Henderson and Notman together were responsible for the founding of the Art Association of Montreal on 11 January 1860. The inaugural meeting took place in Notman's studio and was presided over by Henderson. Their first action was to arrange an art exhibition for the visit of the Prince. Uniquely, photographers had initiated an art association rather than a photographic society.

The Victoria Bridge had a stimulating effect on the prosperity of Montreal. Notman was able to tour more freely, taking photographs and making connections, for example, with the editor of the *Philadelphia Photographer* – a vigorous promoter of his work. Between 1865 and 1868, Notman issued a series of *Portraits of British Americans*.[142] The work demonstrates Notman's efficiency. The publication, based on carte-de-visite photographs, was issued in parts, bulked up with a florid text by Fennings Taylor. Each part was accompanied by advertisements, mostly for Notman's own publications and photographs. He sent out the photographs for review, and he quoted favourable commentary.

There is a more remarkable feature to this publication. The series includes Lieutenant Colonel William Rhodes, dressed for hunting, standing in artificial snow with two stuffed caribou heads. Taylor commented:

The dreary country, tortured as it is into wild fantastic shapes of hideous ruin, in which a caribou most commonly abides, or through which he roams, is enough to appal a druid, or make a witch stiffen with fear …. It is no wonder that Colonel Rhodes should be a 'mighty hunter'. Neither is it a wonder that his friends and neighbours should, by common consent, write his name in red letters, and place it conspicuously on the muster-roll of those who may fitly be called the Nimrods of the North.[143]

This was creating a heroic model, based on mythical concepts, newly-associated with a 'gentlemanly' present. The publication was constructing Canadian cultural history.

The idea was explored further in Notman's photographic series of caribou hunting. Rhodes was a farmer,

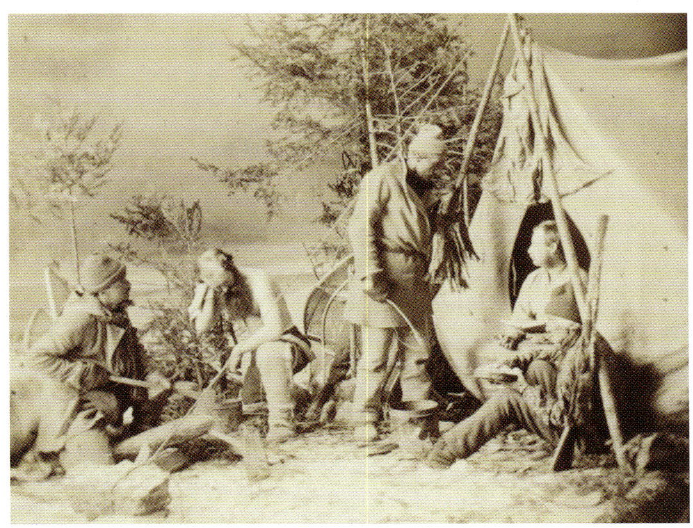

Fig. 10.37: William Notman, 'Sunday in the bush', 1866, albumen print. (McCord Museum, N-0000.57.9)

involved in the prosaic business of the railways, and a member of parliament. He was happy to be pictured in a staging of the caribou hunt, a constructed fiction based on his own life. The moralistic high ground of the pictures is reinforced by the photograph 'Sunday in the bush' [FIG. 10.37], in which one man is holding an open (evidently religious) book; another is stripped to the waist, washing.

This series and two others, depicting moose hunting, and sports and pastimes, were staged in the Notman's studio. They were enthusiastically reviewed in both the *Philadelphia Photographer* and the *British Photographic News*, which noted:

> The effect of wild landscape scenery, with foreground and distance admirably rendered, and the adjuncts of hunting life, trees, tents, thickets, game, &c. – many of these depicted under the varied effects of snow-storm, daylight, and night time, all produced in the studio of the artist – is something as startling in its novelty as it is successful in result.[144]

The studio was set aside for 'winter' photographs, which proved highly popular. In 1867, Notman went so far as to patent his snow effects.[145] His ingenuity was noted with admiration:

> To produce the effect of fallen snow, I have tried many ways, such as carded wool, white furs … but latterly salt, which I find by far the best, as you can throw it on and about stones, rocks, etc … when thrown upon the figure, it adheres to the cloth ….
>
> To represent falling snow: after the negative is dried, and varnished, I take some Chinese white and mix it with water … put it into a phial, introduce one of those perfume-blowers, and blow into the air a shower of liquid ….
>
> To represent ice, I use sheet zinc, over which I have polished plate glass ….[146]

Notman achieved a high point in the absurdity, which flourished in the world's studios in the 1860s – the creation of an indoor 'virtual' world on principles of convenience and comfort. That he should be able to patent snow imitated with sprinkled salt and Chinese white is further evidence of the curious human readiness to admire artifice rather than reality.

Notman, for whom art and artifice were interchangeable, worked extensively with composite photography. Private groups and large public gatherings were photographed from individual figures and attached to elaborate painted backdrops [FIG. 10.38]. The studio employed 'artists' to paint the backgrounds and the surface of the photographs. The result was much applauded for skill and ingenuity; its relation to photography is questionable.

For much of his life and career, William Notman built up his status in Canadian society. His undoubted photographic skill was subsumed by these other concerns. With his family and his staff Notman established a substantial business, working eventually from twenty-six studios in

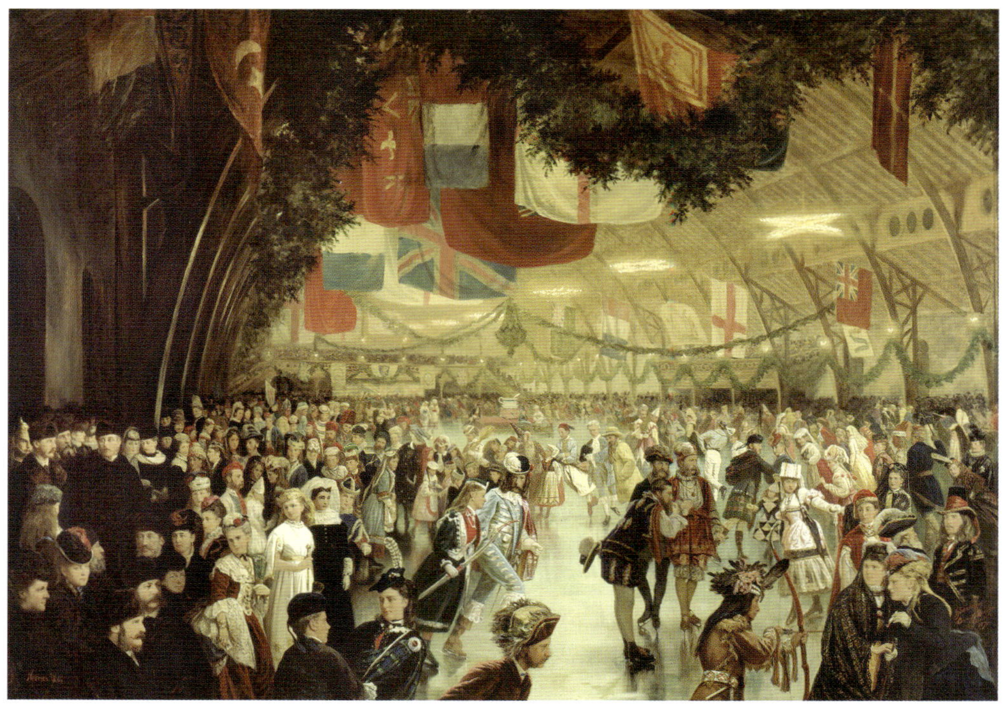

Canada and the United States. It is almost a relief to hear a dissenting voice in the writing of Baroness Brassey, who stopped at Montreal on an extended cruise in 1872. Brassey, herself a photographer, wrote:

> We went to Notman's studio. The owner thereof considers himself THE photographer of the world, and undoubtedly his portraits and groups are excellent; but for *landscapes*, I certainly prefer Henderson, whom we afterwards visited, and from whom we purchased a large collection of photographs.[147]

Nevertheless, she succumbed to the studio's talent for portraiture, and a day later noted, 'At twelve o'clock we all went to have our portraits taken by the great Notman.'[148]

United States of America

Alexander Gardner was the towering figure of Scottish photographers in the United States at this period, and one of a group of expatriate Scots who formed a 'St Andrews Society'.[149] He worked, among others, with his brother, James Gardner (b.1829), David Knox and John Reekie, and later with his own son Lawrence (1847–99). The first three worked in the corps of remarkable photographers operating in the Civil War and joined him when he opened his Washington studio. James Gardner's work is, in itself, excellent, but he disappeared from view after 1865, possibly moving west or joining a partnership as Gilman and Gardner in Boston.[150]

Gardner moved to the United States to escape the moral and political corruption he found in Britain. Others would migrate for less high-flown reasons: generally, to escape poverty or search for health. In distinct contrast to Gardner was Joseph Collier (1836–1910), who began his career as a blacksmith in the town of Elgin, Morayshire. By the 1860s, he had incurred a back injury and he took up photography. He opened a studio in Peterhead, where he photographed the Prince of Wales, and, after five years, moved to Inverness, where he began experimenting with enlargements. His work was critically approved by John Traill Taylor, who wrote of his views that they were '… all of a very large size, and without exception, all of a very high order of merit'.[151]

George Mason described him affectionately:

Joe was a big, strong, powerful-looking man, with a genial, kindly face. To look at him with his wide-awake [wide brimmed hat] pushed back off his brow, and his short pipe in his cheek, one could not help thinking his dark-room performance would be a clumsy arrangement at best. What a deception he was! One of the greatest treats I ever experienced in the way of picture-taking was Joe's dark-room work. In the shady recesses of this secret chamber he had a place for everything …. Not a speck of dust – all was nice, neat, clean, and cool, and his whole manipulation was marked by exactitude and precision …. He was always improving and inventing, not with a patent purpose, but for his own use and the general good …. [152]

Collier left Scotland for the sake of his family's health. They migrated to Central City, Colorado, in 1871, moving in 1878 to Denver. He wrote to his friend, George Washington Wilson, of their improvement:

… although I am some fifty pounds lighter now than when I left Great Britain I have first-rate health, and so have all my family … Our baby, now six or seven months old, is as healthy as a baby can well be; and when I think how often the grim shadow knocked at our door in Scotland, I hope I am thankful.[153]

He wrote to George Mason:

There is splendid scenery everywhere here, and the fact is I could not keep my hands from it …. After getting into order I got up some pictures mostly taken here, and exhibited them at the territorial fair or show at Denver, and got a silver medal. Tintypes are much wanted, but I put a stopper on them at once, and steadily refused to have anything to do with them. Stereoscopic views sell well here. I have only fifteen negatives yet, but I can sell as many as I can print …. I get three or four dollars per dozen wholesale. I can't get patent plate glass here; they tell me that 'crown is the only thing that is used'. Well, I am not going to hunt up these mountains, and have no safer medium to photograph on than crown glass, that's flat. Every photographer that I have spoken to makes his own collodion, and you know what that means; and, worse than all, their whiskey is absolutely undrinkable, so one can't drown his sorrows in the flowing bowl.[154]

In 1874, Collier raised £200 to undertake a photographic trip into the Rocky Mountains [Fig. 10.39], from a cousin, 'a pure Yankee, with some means, and nothing particular to do'.[155] They set off into the mountains with

… three donkeys, one mule, and two capital ponies for riding … [baggage weighing] about 600 pounds, and … provisions for two months, [including] a miniature tool chest and needles, darning needles, thread, worsted, buttons …. We were armed to the teeth with a heavy revolver to each saddle pommel, a large sheath-knife used for all purposes, a rifle packed somewhere handy, and a heavy whip.

It was an exploration of half-known and wild country,

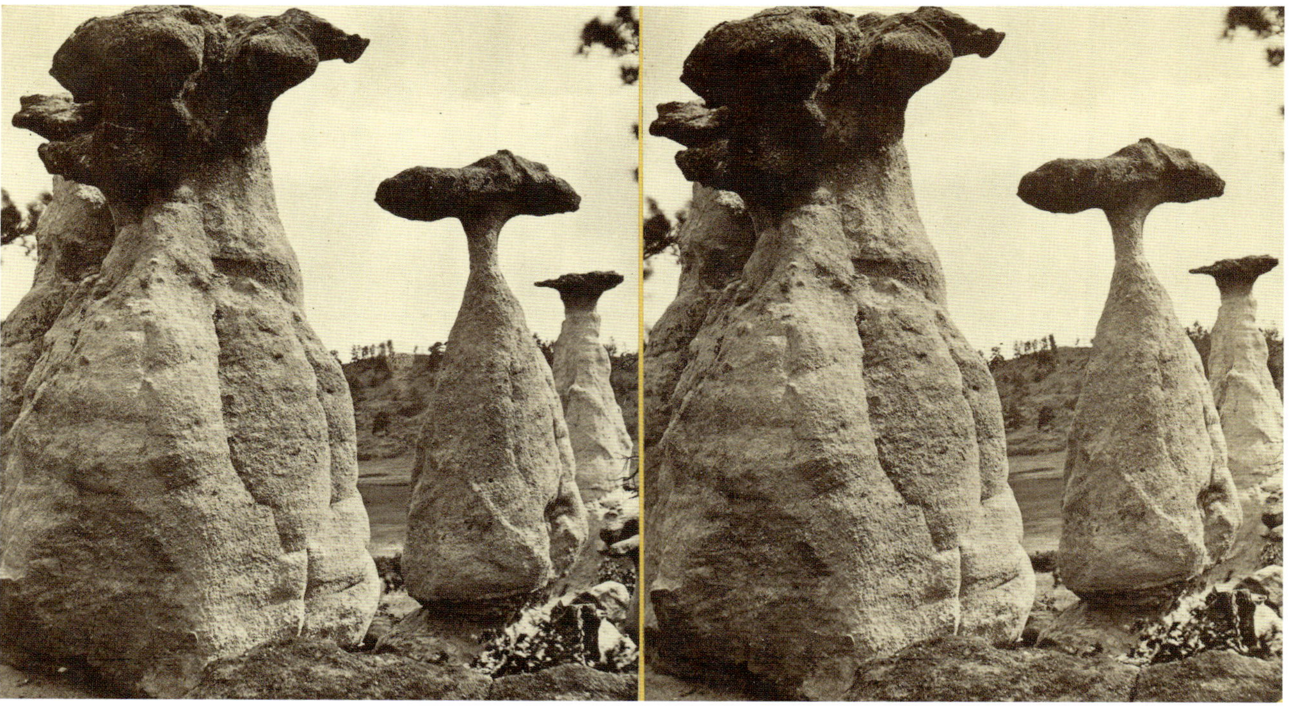

full of animal life – mountain lions, bears, elk, rattlesnake and 'some curious four-legged fishes'. Unnervingly, the Ute Indians were thought to be on the war-path, but they also encountered occasional mines and farms, and met travelling parties, including an unexplained 'wagon containing ladies!'

Collier's experience matched that of other travelling photographers around the world: frustration more often than success; confusing conditions of light; thunder, heavy rain, even snow in August. He described one photographic session in a gorge, where he encountered difficulties with

> … the very clear sunlight, there being no damp atmosphere to diffuse the light, and shadows as black and crisp as possible. I smoked a pipe often while exposing a plate in this place, and the result was still a patchy, ugly thing, and the sun had to be high before it struck any part of the view often, and then the shadows were perpendicular; altogether, taking some twenty-five views in this canyon tried my patience considerably.

Fig. 10.39: Joseph Collier, 'Group of Monuments', 1874, albumen stereoscopic photographs. (J. Paul Getty Museum, 84.XC.870.1065)

At the end of the tour, '… the net results were sixty-three subjects, all duplicate, and a few whole plates'.

> I need not tell you of broken focussing-glasses, or of a camera picked up, after a sudden gust, in three pieces, taking a whole day to mend it with scraps of white iron, old spoons, &c. The tool chest came in handy during that emergency.

With Collier we return to the self-sufficient photographic pioneers who explored the world, working on a small scale and fiercely independent, carefully melting old spoons. The business of photography could still encompass this simplicity alongside the large-scale enterprises, which had grown up. Both worked.

Notes

1. Talbot 1844, caption to pl. XVII, 'Bust of Patroclus'.
2. Discussed by Warner 1983: 115–20; see also Brück 2004, 'Smyth, Charles Piazzi (1819–1900)', <http://www.oxforddnb.com/view/article /25948>; his prints and negatives survive in an album at the Royal Observatory, Edinburgh: see Mary Brück, 'The Piazzi Smyth collection of sketches, photographs and manuscripts at the Royal Observatory, Edinburgh', *Vistas in Astronomy* 32 (1988): 371–408.
3. John Herschel to Robert Hunt, between 1842 and 1844, Ms letter in collection at George Eastman House. In 1846, when Smyth moved to the observatory on Calton Hill in Edinburgh as Astronomer Royal for Scotland, he presumably met Hill and Adamson. There are three of his South African negatives in the collection of Hill/Adamson calotypes in the University of Glasgow, Glasgow University Library, Special Collections, HA0932-4.
4. Taylor and Schaaf 2007: 298.
5. See Ellis 1859; Bell and Denfield 1970: 190–91; and Thompson 2012: 38–49.
6. Ellis 1859: 55–6.
7. Sara Stevenson, 'The doctor, the lady and the man who printed his own money', *Studies in Photography* (2007): 13–5.
8. William Balfour Baikie, manuscript journal, British Library, Add. Ms 32488.
9. In later years, he took up microphotography: see George Berwick, 'Microscopic Photography on Gelatine Plates', *British Journal of Photography* 27 (28 May 1880): 262–3.
10. For Charles Livingstone and James Augustus Grant, see James R. Ryan, 'Photography, Visual Revolutions and Victorian Geography', in Livingstone and Withers (eds) 2005: 199–238.
11. Henry Peach Robinson, 'The Tools we use', *Photographic News* 15 (26 July 1872): 353.
12. David Livingstone wanted 'a man who knows the medicines we now use, to see if they are to be found in that country, who understands about different fibrous substances used in commerce, and also the different dye stuffs', in discussion after 'Reports from the Niger Expedition', 11 January 1858, *Proceedings of the Royal Geographical Society of London* 2 (1858): 101.
13. Foskett (ed.) 1965: 51.
14. The Foreign Office asked for help in printing his photographs. David Livingstone refers to Thomas Baines's drawings, which 'with photographs by Charles Livingstone and Dr Kirk, have materially assisted in the illustrations'. Livingstone and Livingstone 1865 (reprinted 2001): viii, Preface.
15. See Grant 1864; and Koivunen 2009.
16. Grant's manuscript journal, Papers of James Augustus Grant, National Library of Scotland, MS 17915, p. 31.
17. *Ibid.*, 47.
18. *Ibid.*, 33.
19. *Ibid.*, 56
20. Grant was a minister's son from Nairn, so this was a serious admission.
21. Grant's manuscript journal: 60.
22. *Ibid.*, 125. Richard Hill Norris patented his dry-plate process in 1856 and had recently begun the manufacture.
23. *Ibid.*, 172.
24. *Ibid.*, 218, 15 July 1859.
25. *Ibid.*, 222–3.
26. *Ibid.*, 277.
27. 'Hints to Travellers – Extracts from a Letter from John Kirk', *Journal of the Royal Geographical Society* 34 (1864): 290–2.
28. Michael D. McMullen, 'Kirk, Sir John (1832–1922)', <http://www.oxforddnb.com/view/article/34336>
29. His work is in an album belonging to William Vacher, another Shanghai merchant, in the Bath Literary and Historical Society's collection. We are grateful to Michael Gray for drawing this to our attention. See Bennett 2009: 69–75.
30. See *ibid.*, 103–6. Bennett also identifies a group of photographs by Wotherspoon that are in the National Army Museum's collection.
31. Connolly 1855: 82, vol. 2.
32. [Bruce] 1859: 49–50.
33. Anon., 'War and Progress in China', *Blackwood's Edinburgh Magazine* 85 (1860): 579.
34. Dimond and Fenton 1987: 84; see also <http://www.royal collection.org.uk/collection/2934996/photographic-views-of-canton>
35. McCosh 1841: 20–1; Peter R. Russell-Jones, 'John MacCosh's Photographs', *Photographic Journal* 108 (January 1968): 25–7; Ray McKenzie, '"The Laboratory of Mankind": John McCosh and the Beginnings of Photography in British India', *History of*

Note: Website addresses checked and correct at the time of going to press.

Photography 11 (1987): 109–18; and Taylor and Schaaf 2007: 121–4.

36. McCosh 1984: 92–3.

37. McCosh 1856: 7.

38. Ray McKenzie suggests that the annotation, 'massacred at Gwalior', to his portrait of Lieutenant Stewart (169 in the National Army Museum album), relates to a man killed in 1843, although there was also a Lieutenant W Stewart, murdered at Gwalior on 14 May 1857: see Behan 1859: 2250, vol. 2. The issue of dating within the album is confused by identities, written at the time of the photograph's taking in the negative, and the album captions, which were written when the album was assembled.

39. The square format of his photograph of the 'Front of the Great Pagoda Rangoon', in the National Army Museum album, may imply that he had adapted a daguerreotype camera for later use.

40. Manuscript introduction to the album in the collection of the National Army Museum, inv. no. NAM. 1962-04-3.

41. Letter from John Login to his wife, 6 November 1849, quoted in Login 1890: 179.

42. *Ibid.*, 40.

43. Printed in the copy of the Club listing in an album of photographs of the members, in the collection of the Wellcome Museum, London.

44. Quoted in the record of a quarrel, see Buist 1851: 29.

45. *The Bombay Times* published an account of the daguerreotype, 'sufficiently detailed to make practical experimentation a possibility', in December 1839, five months before Buist became editor: see Falconer 2001. Buist provided materials for the St Andrews museum, curated by Dr John Adamson.

46. Dated in the negative, 'Nov 25/45', Glasgow University Special Collections, HA0705.

47. Account of George Buist's talk to the Bombay Photographic Society, *Liverpool Photographic Journal* 1 (14 April 1854): 52.

48. Report of the meeting, 12 December 1854, *Journal of the Photographic Society of Bombay* 1 (January 1855): 11.

49. Murdoch 1862: 144.

50. See G. Thomas, 'The Madras Photographic Society', *History of Photography* 16 (1992): 299.

51. He presented, 'a large series … of the public buildings of Madura, Ryakotta, Seringham, Poodoocotah, Tanjore, &c., and of the Elliot Marbles', to the Industrial Museum of Scotland in

1861. The Director of the Museum noted that Hunter had 'always been a warm friend and most liberal contributor to this Museum'.

52. Sophie Gordon, 'Monumental visions: architectural photography in India, 1840–1901', unpublished PhD thesis [2011], University of London, School of Oriental and African Studies, 248–50. James Fergusson wrote for the official report for the Archaeological Survey of India: 'He has trained some of his pupils to be very expert in the art, and every year sends them out to photograph the most interesting remains. All that is within reach of Madras may safely be left in his charge': see Gordon 2011: 256.

53. Edinburgh Photographic Society, Minute book no. 3 (2 April 1879): 14, and Alexander Hunter, 'On the Selection of Subjects from Nature,' *Photographic Times* 9 (June 1879): 134–6.

54. For an authoritative account of Fergusson's work, see Gordon 2011.

55. Fergusson 1862: I, xiv.

56. James Fergusson, lecture given in 1866, quoted by John Falconer, 'A Passion for Documentation: Architecture and Ethnography', in Deija et al. 2006: 78.

57. Part of his collection is now in Boston Public Library, see Gordon 2011: 50.

58. Dewan 2003: 5.

59. Taylor and Fergusson 1866: 50.

60. *Ibid.*

61. Taylor and Fergusson 1866, Preface. See Gordon 2011: 314–49.

62. *Ibid.*, Preface.

63. Rod Hamilton, 'John Murray (1809–98): Pioneer photographer in India', *Scottish Photography Bulletin* 1 (1993): 3–9.

64. John Falconer, 'A Passion for Documentation: Architecture and Ethnography', in Deija et al. 2006: 75.

65. Anon., Review of the exhibition of the Photographic Society of London, *Athenaeum* (20 February 1858): 246.

66. Letter from Lady Canning to Queen Victoria, 25 November 1857, quoted by Dimond and Taylor 1987: 124.

67. Pinney 2008: 23.

68. 'Answers to Correspondents', *Photographic Journal* 5 (7 May 1859): 288.

69. Report on the Photographic Society of London, *Photographic Journal* 7 (1862): 363.

70. Scott 1862. Stereo versions were published in *Stereoscopic Magazine: A Gallery of Landscape Scenery, Architecture,*

Antiquities, and Natural History, accompanied with descriptive articles by writers of eminence (London: Lovell Reeve 1863 and 1865).

71. Jane Ricketts, 'D. H. Macfarlane, a New Name in Indian Photography', *Photographic Collector* 3 (1982): 86–90.

72. *Ibid.*, 89.

73. *Ibid.*

74. Review quoted in the *Photographic News* 10 (2 March 1866): 108.

75. 'The Award of Prizes at the Paris Exhibition', *Photographic Journal* 11 (16 July 1867): 66.

76. Pinney 2008: 53.

77. Falconer 2001.

78. For the history of Australian photography, see Newton 1988.

79. *Launceston Examiner*, 13 April 1844.

80. Goodman 2006.

81. *Ibid.*, 26 and 42.

82. Huxley (ed.) 1903: 47; Sara Stevenson, 'The Australian Question', *Scottish Photography Bulletin* (Spring 1988): 28–38.

83. Huxley (ed.) 1903: 47.

84. *Ibid.*, 72.

85. Letter from John Thomson to Mrs Thomson, 9 October 1849, quoted by Watters and Koestenbauer 2011: 27–8.

86. My opinion, see Sara Stevenson, 'The Australian Question', *Scottish Photography Bulletin* (Spring 1988), that calotypes of Australia in the Scottish National Portrait Gallery collection could be attributed to Thomson is probably incorrect. They are now attributed to Robert Tennent.

87. Examples of his photographs were donated to the Oxford Museum of Science by his son.

88. William McCraw, 'The True Origin of the Collodion Process in Scotland', *British Journal of Photography* 16 (17 December 1869): 603–4.

89. Letter from John Thomson to Thomas Huxley, 11 July 1851, Huxley Papers 27: 328–9, Imperial College, University of London. According to Mike Ware (pers. com.), Thomson was using the albumen method of Niépce de Saint Victor (1847) the collodion method of Archer (1851), and Furlong's 1843 method of iodising: see Roger Taylor and Mike Ware, 'Pilgrims of the Sun: the Chemical Evolution of the Calotype 1840–1852', *History of Photography* 27 (2003): 308–12.

90. Letter from Huxley to Thomson, 19 December 1851, published in Huxley (ed.) 1935: 361.

91. Wilson, 1849: 19. See also <http://digital.nls.uk/pencilsoflight/

searchDetail.cfm?startRow1&totalRows=1&startRowNext=2& rowsPerPage=1&startRowBack=0&localArea=Melbourne& country=0&photographer=0&keyword=0&highlight=0& talbotype=0&flag=1>

92. 'A Resident' [John Hunter Kerr] 1872/1996; and Madeleine Say, 'John Hunter Kerr: Photographer', *The La Trobe Journal* 76 (2005): 71–6.

93. 'A Resident' [John Hunter Kerr] 1872/1996: 6.

94. *Ibid.*, 11.

95. He made a collection for the Exposition Universelle in Paris in 1863. See Elizabeth Willis, 'Gentlemen Collectors. The Port Phillip District, 1835–1855', in Peterson, Allen and Hamby (eds) 2008: 113–40.

96. 'A Resident' [John Hunter Kerr] 1872/1996: 16.

97. *Ibid.*, 150.

98. Anon., 'Australia Felix', *Illustrated London News*, 26 January 1850: 53, quoted by Warwick Reeder, 'Australia', in Hannavy (ed.) 2008: 1, 98.

99. Michael Hoare and Joan T. Radford, 'Smith, John (1821–1885)', <http://adb.anu.edu.au/biography/smith-john-4608/ text7581>

100. <http://sydney.edu.au/museums/exhibitions-events/virtual-empire.shtml> [Also] <http://sydney.edu.au/medicine/ museum/mwmuseum/index.php/Smith,_The_Hon._John>

101. Nan Phillips, 'Rae, John (1813–1900)', <http://adb.anu.edu.au/ biography/rae-john-4443/text7233>

102. See <http://trove.nla.gov.au/work/11573929?q=+&versionId= 13600956>

103. 'Photography. Being some extracts from a lecture delivered by John Rae, Esq, at the Mechanics' School of Arts' on 11 September, *Sydney Morning Herald*, 14 September 1855.

104. *Argus* [Melbourne], 1–25 August 1856, see: <http://trove.nla.gov.au>

105. *Ibid.*, September and October 1856.

106. 'Unclaimed Letters, December 31, 1855', *South Australia Register*, 11 January 1856. Between 1856 and 1864, the *Edinburgh Post Office Directory* does not record a private address for Alexander McGlashon.

107. Given to T. B. Johnston when the Society terminated: George Eastman House collection, inv. no. 76:0288. See 'Photographs from the Johnston Album', *Image: Journal of Photography of the George Eastman House* 4 (1955): 33–5.

108. *Daily Southern Cross*, 19 September 1856, quoted on website

'Early New Zealand Photographers', <http://canterburyphoto graphy.blogspot.co.uk/2010/09/crombie.html>

109. Advertisement in the *Colonist*, 2 March 1858, quoted on website 'Early New Zealand Photographers'.

110. *Daily Southern Cross*, 20 June 1856, quoted on website 'Early New Zealand Photographers'.

111. Claudia Orange, 'The Covenant of Kohimarama: A Ratification of the Treaty of Waitangi', *New Zealand Journal of History* 14 (1980): 61–82; Lachy Paterson, 'The Kohimarama Conference of 1860: A Contextual Reading', *Journal of New Zealand Studies* [New Series] 12 (2011): 29–46.

112. He gave a diffident talk to the Glasgow Photographic Institution, 'On the Rise and Progress of Photography in New Zealand', *British Journal of Photography* 9 (15 October 1862): 393–4.

113. The London correspondent of the *New Zealander*, quoted in the *Otago Witness*, 20 September 1862; and by Graham-Stewart n.d.

114. Anon., perhaps the editor, 'Sketches of Prominent Photo-graphers. No. 5. James Inglis – Montreal', *The Photographer's Friend: A Practical, Independent Magazine* 1 (1871): 100–1.

115. *Ibid*.

116. Anon., 'Art in Continental States. Montreal', *Art-journal* 33 (January 1871): 8.

117. McCord Museum website: <http://www.mccord-museum.qc.ca/ scripts/explore.php?Lang=1&tableid=1&tablename=artist& elementid=00260__true>

118. W. A. Waiser, 'Horetzky, Charles George' in 'Dictionary of Canadian Biography' <http://www.biographi.ca/en/bio/ horetzky_charles_george_12E.html> See also Hudson's Bay Company Archives: <http://www.gov.mb.ca/chc/archives/hbca/ biographical/h/horetzky_charles-george.pdf>

119. Andrew Birrell, 'Fortunes of a Misfit; Charles Horetzky', *Alberta Historical Review* 19, 1 (1971): 9–25, quote on 10.

120. Horetzky 1874: 104.

121. 'Horetzky's historic hike across Northern BC', *Northword* (December 2008): <http://northword.ca/december-2008/ horetskys-historic-hike-across-northern-bc>

122. Andrew Birrell, 'Fortunes of a Misfit; Charles Horetzky', *Alberta Historical Review* 19, 1 (1971): 25.

123. Shirlee Anne Smith, 'COTTER, JAMES LAURENCE', in 'Dictionary of Canadian Biography' <http://www.biographi.ca/ en/bio/cotter_james_laurence_11E.html>

124. James L. Cotter, 'The Eskimos of Eastmain', *Beaver*, December (1929): 301–2.

125. Louise Guay, 'Alexander Henderson, Photographer', *History of Photography* 13 (1989): 79–94.

126. Alexander Henderson, letter to the editor, 'Notes on Dry Processes', *Photographic News* 1 (21 October 1859): 82–3.

127. The participants each had a number, written in pencil on the back of their prints – Henderson's was 89 – and the images were individually numbered. George Eastman House has loose prints from the Association's collection, and Henderson's have numbers up to 50.

128. This photograph is numbered as '89/1' on the print in Glasgow University Special Collections, Dougan Collection, so this may be his first contribution to the Association.

129. Noted in the *British Journal of Photography* 21 (1874): 503.

130. The McCord Museum Collection, MP-0000.1452.66.

131. John Thompson, 'Alex Henderson's Winter Trip', *Canadian Rail* (January–February 1999): 3–13.

132. *Toronto Globe*, 24 February 1869, quoted in John Thompson, 'Alex Henderson's Winter Trip', *Canadian Rail* (January–February 1999): 3–13.

133. *Toronto Globe*, 11 March 1869, quoted in John Thompson, 'Alex Henderson's Winter Trip', *Canadian Rail* (January–February 1999): 3–13.

134. *Toronto Globe*, 4 March 1869, quoted in John Thompson, 'Alex Henderson's Winter Trip', *Canadian Rail* (January–February 1999): 3–13.

135. Triggs, 'Alexander Henderson: Nineteenth-century Landscape Photographer', *Archivaria* 5 (1977–78): 45–6.

136. Stanley G. Triggs 1985; and Hall, Dodds and Triggs 1993.

137. *Glasgow Post Office Directories* 1851 to 1856.

138. *London Gazette*, 9 July 1855/6, reported in the *Spectator*, 25 June 1856. For an account of William Notman's questionable role in this disaster, and a variant view of his practice, see Lilly Koltun, 'Not the World of William Notman — the World of William Notman: the Nineteenth Century through a Master Lens. Edited by Roger Hall, Gordon Dodds and Stanley Triggs', *Journal of Canadian Studies* 30, 1 (1995): 125–33.

139. A recent assessment of Notman's younger brother can be found in Naves 2013.

140. The firm kept the second portfolio: Colleen Skidmore, 'Notman, William & Sons', in Hannavy (ed.) 2008: 1011–3.

141. The title was self-awarded. See Dimond and Taylor 1987: 211–3.

142. *Portraits of British Americans by Notman with biographical sketches by Fennings Taylor* 1865–68 (3 vols).

143. *Ibid.*, 49–50.
144. 'Canadian Sports in the Camera', review of the Notman series, *Photographic News* 10 (14 September 1866): 434.
145. 'A new and useful Art of taking photographic pictures representing winter scenes, by artificial means, with and without figures Jan 1867', 'Canadian Patents', *Journal of the Board of Arts and Manufactures for Ontario* 7 (September 1867): 229.
146. *Photographic News* in *Annual of Scientific Discovery, or Year-Book of Facts in Science and Art for 1868, exhibiting the Most Important Discoveries and Improvements …* 1868: 146.
147. Brassey 1873: 28.
148. *Ibid.*, 31.
149. The Society's committee, including Gardner, Knox and Reekie, appear in a photograph dated 1865, illustrated in Katz 1990: 231.
150. Discussed by Katz 1990: 270.
151. John Traill Taylor, review of 'Photographic Views in Invernesshire', *British Journal of Photography* 14 (1 February 1867): 54–5.
152. Mason [1888]: 17–18.
153. Joseph Collier, letter to G. W. Wilson, 'Photographic Adventures in Colorado', *British Journal of Photography* 19 (18 September 1874): 450.
154. Mason [1888]: 19–20.
155. This, and the following account of the trip were published: see Joseph Collier, letter to G. W. Wilson, 'Photographic Adventures in Colorado', *British Journal of Photography* 21 (September 1874): 450–1; 464–5; 522–4. See also Robert Collier, 'The Early Years, Photos from the File of Joseph Collier', *Empire Magazine* 40 (October 1977): 10–12; and Kathleen Collier and Mary Collier Ross 1983.

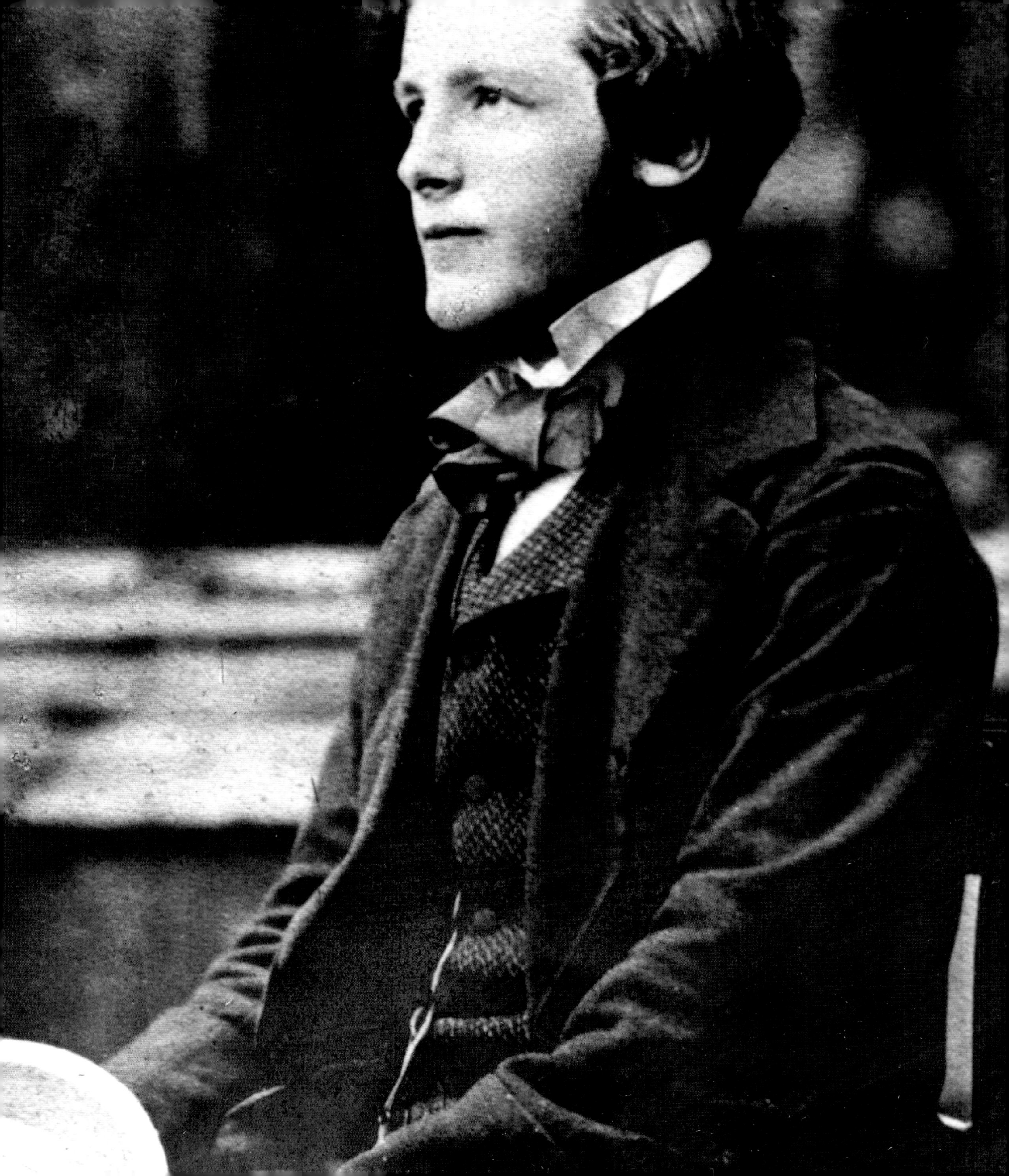

Conclusion

> … photography, in the first hours of its existence, had wished to
> manifest and unfold all its possibilities … had hoped at once to
> approach all but the furthest reaches of the attainable.
>
> ✶
>
> Heinrich Schwarz, writing about D. O. Hill and Robert Adamson in 1932

The first thirty years and their impact

Photography's role as a method of communication was underwritten by the international character of its exploration and development. The nature of Scottish society, religion, education, manufacturing and trade, all combined to connect the Scots directly into that international field, whether as correspondents, travellers or migrants. Scotland has, most happily, a disproportionate role in the international progress of the art.

The initial history of photography depended on individuals, and the curiosity and ambition of social cliques. The 1870s saw a shift from the dominant authority of the 'amateur' to the professional. While the distinction was by no means clear-cut in the early years, the photographers'

behaviour had changed. The need for unprofitable experiment and expenditure of time in its pursuit had receded.

The professionals began to dominate the photographic societies. The change was observed in the *British Journal of Photography* in 1875. A writer, signing himself 'Scotus' and declaring that he was 'an amateur of fully twenty-eight years' standing', wrote gloomily:

Perhaps the principal reason [for the decline of the amateur] is the novelty of the art is gone, and it is now a very commonplace thing to be able to photograph, I do not say 'well and artistically,' but to go through the routine. Besides the art has now become so associated with bagmen and showmen that it is no longer considered a fit occupation for a gentleman's leisure.

I admit this is very unreasonable, but it is, I believe, a very prevailing sentiment with the public; and the reason for the decline is the unfortunate disposition amateurs have of trying every new process and wrinkle,

Opposite, Fig. 1 (detail): Unknown photographer, 'James Clerk Maxwell and his colour wheel'.

and (I speak from my own experience) never attaining very much excellence in any one process practically, however perfect they may be in it theoretically. There is also the constant war at home against the rapidly accumulating impedimenta of lenses, baths and bottles, which soon get antiquated without being able to be got rid of, either from a lingering affection for this and that, or the difficulty of realising. And this reason I feel, in my own experience, is the difficulty with landscapes of getting with the camera any more than a bit [i.e. sketch], while with my palette I can secure a fairly-arranged subject.[1]

Along with so much else, the Victorians had discovered the problem of redundant technological clutter. But the writer, filled with enthusiasm for every new possibility that came his way, was left with a sense of disappointment. His twenty-eight years' experience offers a part explanation. The first generation of photographers had been overtaken; the photographers had changed, and for Scotus the art had lost social cachet. Curiously enough, the 'bag-men' – itinerant photographers – and 'showmen', who had been in the business longer than Scotus allowed, matched his complaint:

> Gone, gone, gone! … All the novelty, hence the profit, is worn out of it. It has descended to the level of an ordinary miserable trade. There is nothing new, and the artist that the people hailed with delight at each fair is really a thing of the past.[2]

These laments are important in this; the emotional balance had shifted. The situation settled, businesses cohered, professionalism was established.

However, the story of the first decades is not an account of stolid progression from comparative innocence or incompetence to business excellence. Photography was a child of the western Industrial Revolution – it was predicated in the underlying actions and productions of that history: chemical, mechanical and optical sophistication. But at the start there was a curious phenomenon at work. The camera and the photographic process failed to achieve industrial simplicity because the results were erratic. There were obvious reasons for this, such as the unpredictability of the rag paper used for the negative / positive processes, or imperfections in the production of chemicals. Light and the behaviour of its colours bedevilled the photographic response. It is perhaps because of these factors that a time-line of photographic proposal and invention is confusing; such achievements as instantaneous photography, flash photography and colour photography were discussed and demonstrated between the 1840s and the 1860s. But they were not effectively practised for decades.

Moreover, for a hundred years, advances in photography were essentially practice-led; the rationale was not determined until the 20th century. The photographers were feeling their way through practical experience and observation. They could discover *what* would happen; *why* often remained mysterious.

There is an interesting case study. In 1861, Professor James Clerk Maxwell and Thomas Sutton demonstrated colour photography. In 1855 Clerk Maxwell had proposed a system for the construction of colour photographs, based on Thomas Young's opinion that colour was observed in the eye by the blending of the three primary colours of light: red, green and violet. Maxwell started from the premise that the three monochrome photographs of a landscape

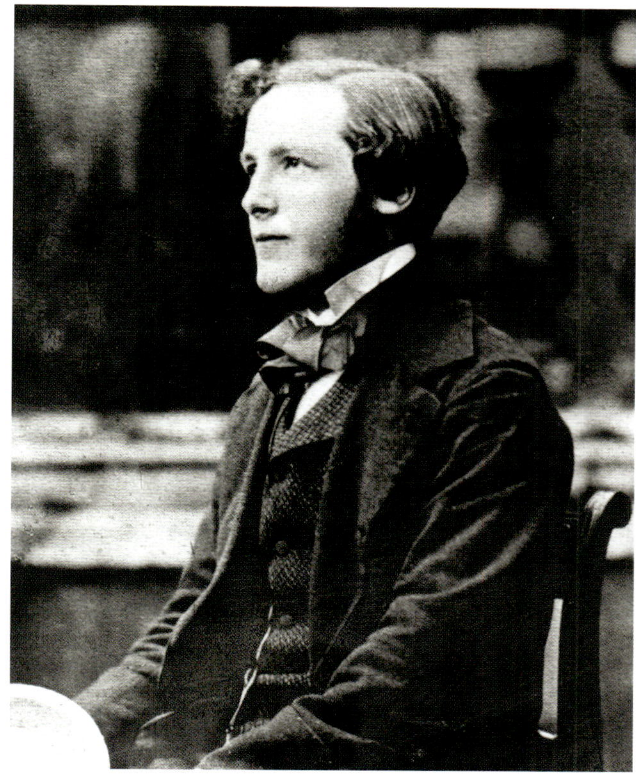

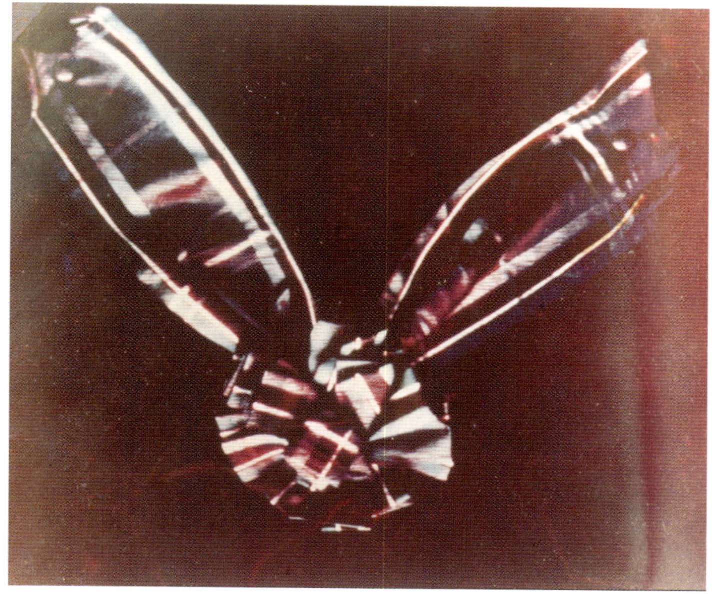

taken through coloured filters should be 'taken on a pre-paration equally sensitive to rays of every colour'.[3] This elementary need was then impractical.

In 1858, Thomas Sutton's *Dictionary of Photography* included the thought:

> It seems probable that different coloured artificial lights, or sunshine transmitted through coloured media, might be successfully employed in illuminating coloured objects to be copied by photography. A variety of highly interesting experiments might be made in this direction.[4]

When Maxwell was appointed a professor at King's College, London, in 1859, he had already presented authoritative, mathematically-analysed experiments on colour [Fig. 1]. At King's he encountered Thomas Sutton as a colleague. They worked together to construct a colour photograph from a tartan rosette [Fig. 2].[5] They demonstrated this to a high-powered audience at the Royal Institution in London, by combining the filtered images from three projectors:

> Three photographs of a coloured ribbon taken through the three coloured solutions [sulphocyanide of iron, chloride of copper, and ammoniated copper] respectively, were introduced into the camera, giving images representing the red, the green, and the blue parts separately. When these were superposed, a coloured image was seen, which, if the red and green images had been as fully photographed as the blue, would have been a truly-coloured image of the ribbon. By finding photographic materials more sensitive to the less frangible rays, the representation of the colours of objects might be greatly improved.[6]

Despite Maxwell's reservations, they succeeded in offering a sufficiently-convincing colour photograph. In the 20th century, the experiment was reproduced from the separations. However, consequent investigation, by Ralph M. Evans of the American Kodak Research laboratory in 1961, suggested that Sutton's photochemistry was still insensitive to red. The photograph is said to have worked because Sutton's red filter 'transmitted ultra violet radiation, to which the wet plate was sensitive. By an extraordinary coincidence, many red dyestuffs also reflect ultra violet radiation, and so the plate "saw" the red portion of the ribbon by invisible radiation which recorded upon the sensitive coating as if it had been responsive to red light'.[7] This would explain why colour photography did not advance immediately from that moment. But it leaves us with another question. Both Sutton and Clerk Maxwell were aware of the underlying difficulty and the need for 'careful experiment'; it would be naïve to suppose that they only took one photograph of this one subject. Sutton knew that his photographic chemistry was not effectively pan-chromatic. The result should have surprised them, but they accepted the demonstration would work. We are left with the questions: Why? What did they think had happened?

In 1845, D. O. Hill reported Robert Adamson as saying mildly that he knew 'some things others do not'.[8] It may be assumed that when Thomas Annan succeeded in taking excellent copies of three paintings in 1862, and offered the press an apparently impractical explanation of his success, that he, like Adamson, was concealing a professional advantage. But these two examples follow a greater mystery: photography was based on a startling principle, which works against reason. The original versions of photography, which required several hours' exposure in bright sunlight, could be understood from long-standing, commonsense scientific principles.[9] However, W. H. F. Talbot's discovery of the latent image in 1840, essential to the effective practice of the art, caused even so knowledgeable a man as John Herschel to surmise that Talbot was dealing with the devil. It took the development of solid state quantum chemistry in the 1930s to deliver an explanation. Larry Slifkin subsequently calculated the likelihood of finding a material capable of forming a latent image. He concluded that the chances of finding a suitable material were only one in a hundred million, while there were only about a hundred thousand suitable materials to explore. The idea is almost impossible, certainly deeply unlikely; and no 20th-century business would have attempted it.[10]

The readiness to persist in the face of radical uncertainty is one of the most impressive aspects of photography in the early decades. Moreover, the odd sense of building on the unknown was not simply a chemical or optical concern. In 1905, J. Craig Annan, son of Thomas Annan, wrote a generous passage on David Octavius Hill's engagement with photography. It began: 'He is indeed a fortunate man who, endowed with talent and courage, finds himself at work in a field where there are no precedents and who must simply follow the guidance of his own instinct.'[11] Heinrich Schwarz followed this in 1932 with a similar rhetorical flourish. He said Hill and Adamson's work offered

> … examples of photography so brilliant that by the side of them everything which has taken place since pales. As though photography, in the first hours of its existence, had wished to manifest and unfold all its possibilities, as though it had hoped at once to approach all but the farthest reaches of the attainable.[12]

Thomas Annan was a knowledgeable photographer, while Heinrich Schwarz was a sophisticated critic. They both convey the sense in which Hill and Adamson rode the crest of a wave. They also, by extension, express the broader excitement in the exploration of photography. This was a time of such enthusiasm that the audience would cheer during a lecture on photography; that impossibilities were proposed and followed through to individual success, which might only become viable decades later, sometimes only in the next century. Mungo Ponton's proposal in 1839 was the basis not just of the carbon process, but of the later process printing techniques and the manufacture of circuit boards. Hill and Adamson invented social documentary photography. Instantaneous photography was demonstrated by Allan Maconochie, John Stewart and George Washington Wilson; David Brewster led the way to three-dimensional photography. An aesthetic for photography, which helped to inform and lead the older arts, was explored by individuals such as James Ross, Thomas Annan, Thomas Keith and Lady Hawarden.

Scotland, and the many individuals who worked with photography in these years, helped to map out a world of frustrations and challenges in chemistry, optics and aesthetics, of implausibility and counter-intuitive procedures, which nevertheless led to the world that we live in and the picture-making we take so lightly.

Notes

1. 'Scotus', Letter to the Editor, *British Journal of Photography* 22 (1875): 71–2.
2. 'Marke Oute' [George Mason] [1888]: 187.
3. Clerk Maxwell, 'Experiments on Colour, as perceived by the Eye, with remarks on Colour-Blindness', Paper read to the Royal Society of Edinburgh, 19 March 1855, Transactions of the Royal Society of Edinburgh 21 (1857): 283.
4. Sutton 1858: 141.
5. See Cat 2013.
6. Clerk Maxwell, 'On the Theory of Three Primary Colours', Paper delivered to the Royal Institution of Great Britain, 17 May 1861, Notices of the Proceedings at the Meetings of the Members of the Royal Institution of Great Britain 3 (1862): 374.
7. Coe 1978: 32; Richard Webb, 'Happy birthday, colour photography' <http://www.newscientist.com/blogs/shortsharp-science/2011/05/happy-birthday-colour.html>
8. Letter from D. O. Hill to David Roberts, 12 March 1845, National Library of Scotland, Acc. 7723.
9. We are indebted to Mike Ware for advice in this; see also his article, 'Photography: The enduring image', *Chemistry World* (August 2007): 62–5.
10. Sutton, 'The Impossibility of Photography', *New Scientist* 112 (25 December–1 January 1987): 40–3.
11. J. Craig Annan, 'David Octavius Hill, R.S.A. 1802-1870,' *Camera Work* 11 (July 1905): 17.
12. Schwarz (trans. Fraenkel) 1932: 18.

Bibliography

Manuscripts

The British Library:
– Add. Ms 32488, William Balfour Baikie, manuscript journal

Fox Talbot Museum, Lacock:
– LA36-58, Letter from Constance Talbot to Lady Elisabeth Feilding, 15 August 1835
– The Fox Talbot letters are available online at http://foxtalbot.dmu.ac.uk/letters/letters.html>
Search for a letter using the document number provided.

George Eastman House, Rochester, NY:
– Letter from John Herschel to Robert Hunt, c.1842–44, Ms Letter in collection

Glasgow Universities Library Special Collections:
– Eph. D/204

Imperial College, University of London:
– Huxley Papers 27 328–29
Letter from John Thomson to Thomas Huxley, 11 July 1851

Jersey Archive:
– J/H/F4/1 and J/H/F4/12

The Mitchell Library, Glasgow
– Ms 13/1, Thomas Annan's commonplace book
– Ms 250, Glasgow Photographic Society/ British Association for the Advancement of Science Exhibition 1855
– Ms250/4, Letter from Dr John Adamson to William Church, 3 September 1855
– Ms 250/34, Charles John Burnett Letter to William Church, 1 September 1855
– Ms 250/159, Account from Wylie and Lochhead, 1855
– TD 1073, Walter Crum Papers

The National Archives, Kew:
– Cust. 119/113,
Case investigated by English Customs and Excise, 1845

National Archives of Scotland:
– AD14/67/284, Trial of John Henry Greatrex and the Grimshaw brothers
– GD 356, Records of the Photographic Society of Scotland
– GD 356/1, 2 and 3, Records of the Photographic Society of Scotland, 1857–62
– GD 356/12/71, Letter from D. O. Hill to the Photographic Society of Scotland, 10 March 1862
– GD 356/15/43, Letter from Mrs Cameron to T. B. Johnston, 24 November 1864
– GD 356/3, Records of the Photographic Society of Scotland: Printed notice, 1 January 1858
– GD 356/12/71, John Adamson, Letter to the Photographic Society of Scotland, sent with his photographs for the exhibition, 29 November 1861
– GD 356/28, Activity of Edinburgh Photograph Exchange Club from 1859

National Army Museum, London:
– NAM album, Manuscript introduction, inv. no. 1962-04-3

National Galleries of Scotland:
– PGP403, Archival material gifted to Scottish National Portrait Gallery with photographs, by Iain and Sandy Clark in memory of Mrs Catherine Clark

National Library of Scotland:
– Acc. 4535, Royal Scottish Society of Arts
– Acc. 5811, W. A. K. Johnston Papers
– Acc. 11608, Letter from Benjamin Robert Haydon to D. O. Hill, 13 April 1846
– Acc. 7723, Letter from D. O. Hill to David Roberts, 25 February 1845
– Acc. 7723, Letters from D. O. Hill to David Roberts, 12 and 14 March 1845, 14 January 1852
– Acc. 10654/1, Dundas of Ochtertyre Muniments
– Acc. 11315, Letters from D. O. Hill to Joseph Noel Paton, 18 January 1848, 23 January 1854
– MS 3815, fols 77–9 and 80, Letter from David Brewster, 15 August 1824
– MS 4411, f. 177, Horatio Ross to William Blackwood, 17 May 1880
– MS 4411, f. 179, Horatio Ross to William Blackwood, 25 May 1880
– MS 17915, Grant's manuscript journal, Papers of James Augustus Grant, 15 July 1859
– MS Acc. 4534, Playfair, 14 February 1842
– Scottish Book Trade Index

Paul Muir Wood:
– Letter in collection; and John Muir Wood's diary

Perth and Kinross County Archives:
– MS 100, Kinnaird Papers
– MS 100/2, Bundle 1154
– MS 100/2, Bundle 665
– MS 100/2, Bundle 668 (John Cumming to Lord Kinnaird, 17 July 1861)
– MS 100/2, Bundle 665 (Miscellaneous correspondence 1859–69: Rodger to Kinnaird, from St Andrews, 25 November 1867)

Royal Archives, Windsor:
– Queen Victoria's Journal, 10 January 1860

Royal Botanic Gardens, Edinburgh:
– Letter from Piazzi Smyth to John Hutton Balfour, 24 February 1859

Royal College of Surgeons, Edinburgh:
– Ms 1760, Simpson Papers Letter from James Graham to J. Y. Simpson, June 1857, including copies of photographs of 'Lepers' Gate & Village near the Lion Gate'

Royal Observatory, Edinburgh:
– Ms Letter James Nasmyth to D. O. Hill, March 1847

Royal Scottish Academy – Archive:
– Letter from C. G. H. Kinnear to D. O. Hill, 12 April 1856
– Letter from D. O. Hill to C. G. H. Kinnear, 14 December 1856
– Letter from Jessie Mann to D. O. Hill, 26 May 1856

– Minute book of the Academy, 1853
– Letter from Robert Macpherson to W. B. Johnstone, 20 August 1860
St Andrews University Library – Special Collections:
– Ms 38081/1, J. D. Forbes Collection, Letter from Forbes to his sister, Lyons, 20 May 1839
– msdep 7/incoming letters 1856/93, J. D. Forbes Papers, Letter from Sir David Brewster to J. D. Forbes, 14 October 1856
– UYUY8525/1, Minutes of Literary and Philosophical Society, 5 April 1841
University of Texas, Austin: Harry Ransom Center:
– Gernsheim Collection
– Ms Letter from J. Craig Annan to Helmut Gernsheim, 21 July 1945

Primary sources: books

A handbook to the watercolours, drawings and engravings in the Art Treasures Exhibition. Being a reprint of critical notices originally published in 'The Manchester Guardian' [n.p.], 1858 (London).

Adamson, John 1857. 'Photography,' in Chambers and Chambers (eds) 1857.

Altick, Richard D. 1978. *The Shows of London* (Cambridge, Massachusetts: The Belknap Press of Harvard University Press).

Amateurs' Photographic Album, The 1856, part 4 (Thomas Sutton and Blanquart-Evrard).

Anderson, Robert 1984. 'Brewster and the Reform of the Scottish Universities', in Morrison-Low and Christie (eds) 1984.

Annual 1868. *Annual of Scientific Discovery, or Year-Book of Facts in Science and Art for 1868, exhibiting the Most Important Discoveries and Improvements …* (Boston: Gould and Lincoln).

Anon. [presumed to be D. O. Hill] 1866. 'The Disruption of the Church of Scotland: An Historical Picture … painted by D. O. Hill, R. S. A.' (Edinburgh: Alexander Hill).

Anon. 1891. 'Messrs. J. Adamson & Son, Photographers, Rothesay', in Stratten 1891.

Ashbee, Felicity and Julie Lawson 1987. *William Carrick 1827–1878* (Edinburgh: National Galleries of Scotland).

Austin, Alvyn 2007. *China's Millions: The China Inland Mission and Late Qing Society 1832–1905* (Grand Rapids: Wm B. Eerdmans).

Baldwin, Gordon, Malcolm Daniel and Sarah Greenough 2004. *All the Mighty World. The Photographs of Roger Fenton 1852–1860* (Newhaven/London: Yale University Press).

Bann, Stephen (ed.) 2011. *Art and the Early Photographic Album* (Washington DC: National Gallery of Art).

Barkhatova, E. V., S. Stevenson and M. Weiss 2010. *William Carrick. Scenes of Russian Life* (St Petersburg: Rosphoto).

Barthes, Roland 2000 (trans. Richard Howard). *Camera Lucida. Reflections on Photography* (London: Vintage).

Bartram, Michael 1985. *The Pre-Raphaelite Camera: Aspects of Victorian Photography* (Boston: New York Graphic Society).

Batchen, Geoff *forthcoming.* 'Beauties and Deformities Alike: Beard, Claudet, and the Business of Photography', in Hellman and Batchen (eds) *forthcoming.*

Beard, Madeleine 1997. *Faith and Fortune* (Leominster: Gracewing).

Behan, T. L. 1859. *Bulletins and Other State Intelligence for the Year 1857*, part 2, July to December (London: London Gazette Office).

Bell, Marjorie and Joseph Denfield 1970. *Secure the Shadow: The Story of Cape Photography from its Beginnings to the End of 1870* (Cape Town: Terence McNally).

Bennett, Terry 2009. *History of Photography in China 1842–1860* (London: Bernard Quaritch).

Bergstein, Mary 2010. *Mirrors of Memory: The Mind's Eye: Freud, Photography and the History of Art* (Ithaca and London: Cornell University Press).

[Blackburn, Jemima, with notes by the naturalist, James Wilson] [1854]. *Illustrations of Scripture by an animal painter* (Edinburgh: Thomas Constable & Co.).

Blackburn, Jemima 1895. *Birds from Moidart and Elsewhere* (Edinburgh: David Douglas).

Boime, Albert 1991. *The Magisterial Gaze: Manifest Destiny and American Landscape Painting c.1830–1865* (Washington DC: Smithsonian Institution).

Bonehill, John and Stephen Daniels (eds) 2009. *Paul Sandby. Picturing Britain* (London: Royal Academy of Arts).

Bonhams Chelsea 1995. *An Important Collection of T. R. Williams Daguerreotypes* [auction catalogue] (6 July 1995).

Booth, Bradford A. and Ernest Mehew (eds) 1994. *The Letters of Robert Louis Stevenson*, 8 vols. (Newhaven and London: Yale University Press), vol. 1.

Borley, Lester (ed.) 2002. *Hugh Miller in Context* (Cromarty and Edinburgh: The Cromarty Arts Trust, The National Trust and National Museums Scotland).

Bowers, Brian 2001. *Sir Charles Wheatstone FRS: 1802–1875* (London: The Institute of Electrical Engineers/Science Museum).

Brassey, Annie, Baroness 1873. *A cruise on the EOTHEN, 1872* (London: printed for private circulation).

Bredon, Miles 2001. *The Pale Abyssinian: a life of James Bruce, African explorer and adventurer* (London: Flamingo).

Brewster, David (ed.) 1806. *Ferguson's Lectures on select subjects … with notes and an appendix,* second edition, 2 vols (Edinburgh: Bell and Bradfute).

Brewster, David (ed.) 1823. *Letters of Euler on different subjects in natural philosophy: addressed to a German Princess, with notes, and a life of Euler,* third edition, 2 vols. (Edinburgh and London: W. & C. Tait, and

Longman, Hurst, Rees, Orme, Brown and Green).

Brewster, David (ed.) 1830. *The Edinburgh Encyclopaedia*, 18 vols (Edinburgh: W. Blackwood).

Brewster, David 1856. *The Stereoscope: its history, theory, and construction* (London: John Murray).

Brock, William 1984. 'Brewster as a Scientific Journalist', in Morrison-Low and Christie (eds) 1984.

Bruce, David 2013. *Greatrex. Forger and photographer* (Edinburgh: Renaissance Press).

Bruce, James 1790. *Travels to discover the source of the Nile, in the years 1768, 1769, 1770, 1771, and 1772*, 5 vols (London: G. G. J. Robinson).

[Bruce, James, 8th Earl of Elgin] 1859. *Correspondence Relative to the Earl of Elgin's Special Missions to China and Japan, 1857–1859* (London: Printed by Harrison & Sons, 1859).

Brusius, M. et al. (eds) 2013. *William Henry Fox Talbot: Beyond Photography* (London and Newhaven: Yale University Press).

Buchanan, William 1992. *The Art of the Photographer, J. Craig Annan* (Edinburgh: National Galleries of Scotland).

Buerger, Janet E. 1989. *French Daguerreotypes* (Chicago and London: University of Chicago Press).

Buist, George 1851. *Some Observations of the "Remarks of Commander Montriou, on the malignant attacks on him by Dr Buist, which have appeared in The Bombay Times, since 1847", by their subject* (Bombay: the Times' Press).

Bukits, Julian 2009. *A Study of James G. Tunny, 1820–1887: Photographer and Political Radical, Edinburgh* (Edinburgh: the author).

Butlin, Martin and Andrew Wilton 1974. *Turner 1775–1851* (London: Tate Gallery).

Campbell, Thomas 1868. *The poetical works of Thomas Campbell with notes by the Rev. W. A. Hill; illustrated by twenty vignette engravings from designs by J. M. W. Turner* (London: Routledge).

Cassels, Nancy Gardner 2010. *Social Legislation of the East India Company: Public Justice versus Public Instruction* (London: Sage Publications).

Cat, Jordi 2013. *Maxwell, Sutton and the Birth of Color Photography* (New York: Palgrave Macmillan).

Catalogue 1840. *Catalogue of the Exhibition of Arts, Manufactures and Practical Science, in the Assembly Rooms, George Street [December 1839–January 1840]* (Edinburgh: Neill & Co.).

Catalogue 1851. *Official Descriptive and Illustrated Catalogue of the Great Exhibition of the Works of Industry of All Nations* (London: Spicer Brothers), 4 vols.

Catalogue 1852. *Catalogue of the Library of the London Institution 1852* (London: privately printed), vol. 4.

Catalogue 1871. *The Scott Exhibition MDCCCLXI. Catalogue of the exhibition held at Edinburgh, in July and August 1871, on the occasion of the commemoration of the centenary of the birth of Sir Walter Scott 1872* (Edinburgh: printed by T. and A. Constable at Edinburgh University Press).

Catalogue 1886. *Catalogue of the Glasgow Photographic Exhibition 1886* (Glasgow: Robert Anderson).

Cavers, Keith 1993. *A Vision of Scotland: the Nation Observed by John Slezer, 1671–1717* (Edinburgh: HMSO for the National Library of Scotland).

Census of Scotland – 1861 [1862]. *Population Tables and Reports …* (Edinburgh: Murray and Gibb).

Chambers, William and Robert Chambers (eds) 1857. *Chambers's Information for the People,* 2 vols (Edinburgh and London: Orr & Smith), vol. 2.

Chance, F. J. 1919. *A History of the Firm of Chance Brothers & Co., Glass and Alkali Manufacturers* (London: Spottiswoode, Ballantyne).

Chandler, Edward 2003. *Photography in Ireland: the Nineteenth Century* (Dublin: Edmund Burke Publisher).

Channing, Norman and Mike Dunn 1996. *British Camera Makers: an A–Z Guide to Companies and Products* (Esher: Parkland Designs).

Chapman, Thomas & Son 1877. *Catalogue of the Collection of the late James Drummond, R.S.A.*

Chiene, John 1908. *Looking Back, 1907–1860* (Edinburgh: Darien Press).

Christ, Carol T. and John O. Jordan (eds) 1995. *Victorian Literature and the Victorian Visual Imagination* (Berkeley: University of California Press).

Clarke, T. N., A. D. Morrison-Low and A. D. C. Simpson 1989. *Brass & Glass: Scottish Scientific Instrument Making Workshops* (Edinburgh: National Museums Scotland).

Claudet, Laura 2008. 'Claudet, Antoine Francois Jean', in John Hannavy (ed.) 2008, vol. 1.

Cockburn, Henry 1889. *Circuit Journeys,* second edition (Edinburgh: D. Douglas).

Cody, Jeffrey W. and Frances Terpak (eds) 2011. *Brush and Shutter. Early Photography in China* (Los Angeles, CA: Getty Research Institute).

Coe, Brian 1978. *Colour Photography. The first hundred years 1840–1940* (London: Ash & Grant).

Coghill, Mrs Harry (ed.) 1974. *Autobiography and Letters of Mrs Margaret Oliphant* (Edinburgh: William Blackwood and Sons, 1899; republished Leicester: Leicester University Press).

Colavito, Jason 2012. *Pyramidiots! Outrageous theories about the Great Pyramid* (Albany, NY: Jason Colavito).

Collier, Kathleen and Mary Collier Ross 1983.

The Photography of Joseph Collier, Colorado: 1871–1910 (Boulder, Colorado: Pruett Publishing Company).

Collins, Kathleen (ed.) 1990. *Shadow and Substance: Essays on the History of Photography in honor of Heinz K. Henisch* (Bloomfield Hills, Michigan: The Amorphous Institute Press).

Comment, Bernard 1999. *The Panorama* (London: Reaktion Books).

Conisbee, Philip, Sarah Faunce and Jeremy Strick 1996. *In the Light of Italy: Corot and Early Open-Air Painting* (Washington DC: National Gallery of Art).

Connolly, T. W. J. 1855. *The history of the corps of Royal Sappers and Miners*, 3 vols (London: Longman, Brown, Green and Longmans).

Conolly, Matthew Forster 1866. *Biographical Dictionary of Eminent Men of Fife of Past and Present Times …* (Cupar-Fife: John C. Orr).

Coope, Rosalys T. and Jane Y. Corbett (eds) 1991, *Bromley House 1752–1991* (Nottingham: Nottingham Subscription Library).

Cox, Julian and Colin Ford 2003. *Julia Margaret Cameron. The complete photographs* (Los Angeles, California: J. Paul Getty Museum).

Cramb, John 1860a. *Palestine in 1860: A series of Photographic Views, Taken Expressly for this Work by John Cramb, Photographer to the Queen with Descriptive letterpress by the Rev. Robert Buchanan D.D.* (Glasgow: Wm Collins).

Cramb, John 1860b. *Jerusalem in 1860: A series of Photographic Views, Taken Expressly for this Work by John Cramb, Photographer to the Queen with Descriptive letterpress by the Rev. Robert Buchanan D.D.* (Glasgow: Wm Collins).

Crary, Jonathan 1990. *Techniques of the observer: on vision and modernity in the nineteenth century* (Boston, MA: Massachusetts Institute of Technology).

Crawford, Alistair 2008. 'Graham, James', in Hannavy (ed.) 2008, vol. 1.

Croucher, J. H. (ed.) [1845]. *Plain Directions for Obtaining Photographic Pictures by the Calotype, Energiatype, and other processes on paper …* (Willats Scientific Manuals, no. 1) (London: T. & R. Willats).

Cushman, Stephen 1999. *Bloody Promenade: Reflections on a Civil War Battle* (Charlottesville, VA and London: University Press of Virginia).

'Cuthbert Bede', pseud. n.d. *c.*1864. *The Visitors' Handbook to Rosslyn and Hawthornden* (Edinburgh: R. Grant).

Daguerre, L. J. M. (J. S. Memes, trans.) 1839. *History and Practice of photogenic drawing on the true principles of the Daguerréotype …* (London and Edinburgh: Smith Elder & Co., and Adam Black).

Dahlberg, Laurie 2005. *Victor Regnault and the Advance of Photography: the Art of Avoiding Errors* (Princeton and Oxford: Princeton University Press).

Dakers, Caroline 1993. *Clouds, The Biography of a Country House* (New Haven and London: Yale University Press).

Daniel, Malcolm (ed.) 2003. *The Dawn of Photography: French Daguerreotypes, 1839–1855* (New York and Newhaven: Metropolitan Museum of Art and Yale University Press).

Davidson, Thomas 1841. *The Art of Daguerreotyping: With Improvements of the Process and Camera* (Edinburgh: [n.p.]).

Deija, Vidya et al. 2006. *India through the Lens. Photography 1840–1911* (Washington DC: Mandala Publishing).

Dewan, Janet 2003. *The Photographs of Linnaeus Tripe: a catalogue raisonné* (Toronto: Art Gallery of Ontario).

Di Bello, Patrizia, Collette Wilson and Shamoom Zamir (eds) 2012. *The Photobook: from Talbot to Ruscha and Beyond* (London and New York: I. B. Tauris & Co.).

Dimond, Frances and Roger Taylor 1987. *Crown & Camera: The Royal Family and Photography 1842–1910* (Harmondsworth: Penguin).

[Douglas, James and James Douglas Jnr] 1862. *Photographic Views taken in Egypt, by James Douglas M.D. and James Douglas junior, During the Winter 1860–1*, vol. 1 (Glenalla [Quebec]: privately printed).

Dudgeon, John 1873. *Tuoyingqiguan* (Beijing: The Peking Hospital).

Edgerton, David 2008. *The Shock of the Old: Technology and Global History since 1900* (London: Profile Books).

Edwards, Steve 2006. *The Making of English Photography: Allegories* (University Park, PA: Pennsylvania State University Press).

Elliot, Andrew 1928. *Calotypes by D. O. Hill and R. Adamson Illustrating an Early Stage in the Development of Photography: Selected from his Collection by Andrew Elliot* (Edinburgh: Andrew Elliot).

Ellis, William 1859. *Three Visits to Madagascar, during the years 1853–1854–1856. Including a Journey to the Capital … illustrated with Woodcuts from Photographs, &c.* (London: John Murray).

Fabian, Rainer and Hans Christian Adam 1983. *Masters of Early Travel Photography* (London: Thames and Hudson).

Fairley, Rob (ed.) 1988. *Jemima: the paintings and memoirs of a Victorian lady* (Edinburgh: Canongate).

Falconer, John 2001. *India: Pioneering Photographers 1850–1900* (London: British Library).

Falconer, John 2006. 'A Passion for Documentation: Architecture and Ethnography', in Deija et al. 2006.

Falconer, John and Louise Hide 2009. *Points of View. Capturing the 19th Century in Photographs* (London: British Library).

Fergusson, James 1862. *A History of Architecture in All Countries*, 3 vols (London: John Murray).

Finberg, A. J. 1961. *The Life of J. M. W. Turner,*

RA, 2nd edition (Oxford: Clarendon Press).

Finn, Elizabeth Anne 1929. *Reminiscences of Mrs Finn* (London: Marshall, Morgan and Scott).

Finn, Jonathan Matthew 2009. *Capturing the Criminal Image: From Mug Shot to Surveillance Society* (Minneapolis: University of Minnesota Press).

Flukinger, Roy 2011. *The Gernsheim Collection* (Austin, Texas: Harry Ransom Center, University of Texas, Austin).

Forrester, Joseph James 1845. *Mr Forrester's Vindication from the Aspersions of the Commercial Association of Oporto …* (Edinburgh: J. Menzies).

Forsyth, Joseph 1824. *Remarks on Antiquities, Arts and Letters, during an excursion in Italy during the years 1802 and 1803*, third edition (Geneva: P. G. Ledouble).

Foskett, Reginald (ed.) 1965. *The Zambesi Journal and Letters of Dr John Kirk 1858–63,* 2 vols (Edinburgh and London: Oliver and Boyd), vol. 1.

Frassanito, William A. 1975. *Gettysburg, A Journey in Time* (New York: Charles Scribner's Sons).

Frassanito, William A. 1995. *Early Photography at Gettysburg* (Gettysburg, PA: Thomas Publications).

Fulhame, Elizabeth 1794. *An Essay on Combustion, with a View to a New Art of Dying and Painting, wherein the Phlogistic and Antiphlogistic Hypotheses are Proved Erroneous* (London: published by the author).

Gage, John 1969. *Colour in Turner: poetry and truth* (London: Studio Vista).

Galassi, Peter 1981. *Before Photography: Painting and the Invention of Photography* (New York: Museum of Modern Art).

Gao Xi 2009. *A Biography of Dudgeon: A British Medical Missionary and the Medical Modernization of the Late Qing Dynasty* (Shanghai: Fudan University Press).

Gardiner, William [1847]. *Sights in Italy: with some account of the present state of music and the sister arts in that country* (London: Longman, Brown, Green and Longmans).

Gardner, Alexander 1866. *Gardner's Photographic Sketchbook of the War,* 2 vols (Washington DC: Philp & Solomons), vol. 1.

Gardner, Alexander 1869. *Across the Continent on the Kansas Pacific Railroad (Route of the 35th Parallel)* (Washington DC: Alexander Gardner).

Garlick, Kenneth and Angus Macintyre (eds) 1979. *The Diary of Joseph Farington,* 16 vols (New Haven and London: Yale University Press), vol. 5.

Gernsheim, Alison 1981. *Victorian and Edwardian Fashion: a Photographic Survey* (New York: Dover Books).

Gernsheim, Helmut 1984. *Incunabula of British Photographic Literature 1839–1875* (London and Berkeley: Scolar Press).

Gernsheim, Helmut and Alison Gernsheim 1968. *L. J. M. Daguerre. The History of the Diorama and the Daguerreotype*, second edition (New York: Dover).

Ginsberg, Madeleine 1982. *Victorian Dress in Photographs* (London: Batsford).

Goodman, Jordan 2006. *The Rattlesnake: A Voyage of Discovery to the Coral Sea* (London: Faber and Faber).

Gordon, M. M. 1870. *The Home Life of Sir David Brewster*, second edition (Edinburgh: Edmonston and Douglas, 1870).

Graham-Stewart, Michael n.d. *Crombie to Burton, Early New Zealand Photography* (Auckland; John Leech Gallery).

Grant, J. A. 1864. *A Walk across Africa: Or Domestic Scenes from my Nile Journal* (Edinburgh and London: William Blackwood and Sons).

Gray, John M. [probably from information assembled by Dr John Brown] 1928. 'Robert Adamson,' in Elliot 1928.

Gray, John Miller 1895. *Memoir and Remains,* 2 vols (Edinburgh: David Douglas), vol. 1.

Guthrie, Thomas 1860. *Seed-time and Harvest of Ragged Schools* (Edinburgh: Adam and Charles Black).

Hall, Basil 1829. *Forty Etchings from Sketches made with the Camera Lucida in North America in 1827 and 1828* (Edinburgh and London: Cadell & Co./Simpkin & Marshall).

Hall, Roger, Gordon Dodds and Stanley Triggs 1993. *The world of William Notman: the nineteenth century through a master lens* (Boston: D. R. Godine).

Hallett, Michael 2008. 'Dancer, John Benjamin', in Hannavy (ed.) 2008, vol. 1.

Hammond, John H. 1981. *The Camera Obscura: A Chronicle* (Bristol: Adam Hilger).

Hannavy, John 1981. *Thomas Keith's Scotland: The Work of a Victorian Amateur Photographer 1852–57* (Edinburgh: Canongate).

Hannavy, John (ed.) 2008. *Encyclopaedia of Nineteenth-Century Photography*, 2 vols. (New York and Abingdon: Routledge).

Hannavy, John 2008. 'Photographic retailing', in Hannavy (ed.) 2008, vol. 2.

Hannavy, John 2008. 'Taylor, John Traill', in Hannavy (ed.) 2008, vol. 2.

Hannavy, John 2015. *The Victorian photography of Dr Thomas Keith and John Forbes White* (Great Cherwell: John Hannavy Publishing).

Harding, Colin 2009. *Classic Cameras* (Lewes: Photographers' Institute Press).

Harvey, Eleanor Jones 2012. *The Civil War and American Art* (New York: Metropolitan Museum).

Heathcote, Bernard and Pauline Heathcote 2002. *A Faithful Likeness: the First Photographic Portrait Studios in the British Isles 1841 to 1855.* (Lowdham: The Authors).

Heathcote, Pauline F. 1991. 'The Photographic Studio', in Coope and Corbett (eds) 1991.

Hellman, Karen and Geoff Batchen (eds), *forthcoming. Sun-Limned Portraits: The Photography of Richard Beard, Antoine Claudet* (London/New Haven: Yale University Press).

Henisch, H. K. 1994. *The Photographic*

Experience 1839–1914: Images and Attitudes (University Park, PA: Penn State Press)

Hewison, Rachel 2011. *Map of a Nation: A Biography of the Ordnance Survey* (London: Granta).

Hill, W. A. 1868. *The poetical works of Thomas Campbell* (London: Edward Moxton), including Thomas Campbell, 'Lochiel's Warning', illustrated by J. M. W. Turner.

Hockney, David 2001. *Secret Knowledge: Rediscovering the Lost Techniques of the Old Masters* (London: Thames and Hudson).

Holman-Hunt, W. 1913. *Pre-Raphaelitism and the Pre-Raphaelite Brotherhood*, 2 vols (London: Chapman and Hall).

Holmes, Nicholas M. McQ. 1988. *Trinity College Church, Hospital and Apse: History and Architecture* (Edinburgh: City of Edinburgh Museums and Art Galleries, 1988).

Horetzky, Charles 1874. *Canada on the Pacific: being an account of a journey from Edmonton to the Pacific by the Peace River valley …* (Montreal: Dawson Bothers).

Howarth-Loomes, B. E. C. 1973. *Victorian Photography: a Collector's Guide* (London: Ward Lock).

Howe, Kathleen 2005. 'Palestine Exploration Fund', in Lenman (ed.) 2005.

Howe, Kathleen Stewart 1992. *Félix Teynard: calotypes of Egypt, a catalogue raisonné* (New York and London: Hans P. Kraus Jnr, Robert Hershkowitz).

Hughes, Stefan 2013. *Catchers of the Light: the Astrophotographers' Family History* (Cyprus: Paphos).

Huhtamo, Erkki 2003. *Illusion in Motion: Media Archaeology of the Moving Panorama and Related Spectacles* (Cambridge, MA and London: MIT Press).

Huneker, James 1900/2008. *Chopin. The Man and His Music* (New York: Charles Scribner's Sons, 1900: reprinted Auckland, NZ: The Floating Press 2008).

Huxley, Julian (ed.) 1935. *T. H. Huxley's Diary of the Voyage of H.M.S.* Rattlesnake (London: Chatto and Windus).

Huxley, Leonard (ed.) 1903. *The Life and Letters of Thomas Huxley* (London: Macmillan).

Hyde, Ralph 1988. *Panoramania! The Art and Entertainment of the 'All-Embracing' View* (London: Trefoil).

Jaeger, Jens 2005. 'Police and forensic photography', in Lenman (ed.) 2005.

James, Sir Henry 1869. *Notes on the Great Pyramid of Egypt and the Cubits used in its Design* (Southampton: Thomas H. Gutch).

Jammes, André and Eugenia Parry Janis 1983. *The Art of the French Calotype. With a critical dictionary of photographers 1845–1870* (Princeton and Oxford: Princeton University Press).

Johnston, Brooks (ed.) 1991. *An Enduring Interest: the photographs of Alexander Gardner* (Norfolk, VA: Chrysler Museum).

Katz, D. Mark 1990. *Witness to an era: the life and photographs of Alexander Gardner* (New York: Viking Studio Books).

Kaye, John and George Malleson (eds) 1898. *Kaye and Malleson's History of the Indian Mutiny of 1857–8*, 6 vols. (London and New York: Longmans, Green, 1898).

Keith, Alexander 1849. *Evidence of the Truth of the Christian Religion: derived from the literal fulfilment of Prophecy; … Thirty-Seventh Edition, much enlarged, with daguerreotype views* (London and Edinburgh: T. Nelson).

Kerr, John Hunter ['A Resident'] 1872/1996. *Glimpses of Life in Victoria* (Edinburgh: Edmonston and Douglas 1872; Carlton, Victoria: Miegunyah Press, 1996), with introduction and notes by Marguerite Hancock.

King James Bible: Judith 13.

Kingslake, Rudolf 1989. *A History of the Photographic Lens* (San Diego and London: Academic Press Inc.).

Kinnaird, George, 9th Lord 1898. *Notes and Reminiscences of Rossie Priory* (Dundee: Printed at the Advertiser Office, Bank Street)

Koivunen, Leila 2009. *Visualizing Africa in Nineteenth-century British Travel Accounts* (New York and Abingdon: Routledge).

Laing, David 1872, note in *The Scott Exhibition* (Catalogue 1871).

Langton, H. H. 1940. *James Douglas. A Memoir* (Toronto: University of Toronto Press).

Lassam, R. E. 1990. 'Fox Talbot's Original Iron Copper Press', in Collins (ed.) 1990.

Lawson, Julie 1990. *William Donaldson Clark 1816–1873* (Edinburgh: National Galleries of Scotland).

Lawson, Julie 1990. 'Iván Szabó: A Hungarian Photographer in Scotland', in Collins (ed.) 1990.

Lawson, Julie 1997. *Women in White: Photographs by Clementina, Lady Hawarden* (Edinburgh: National Galleries of Scotland).

Lawson, Julie, Ray McKenzie and A. D. Morrison-Low (eds) 1993. *Photography 1900: The Edinburgh Symposium* (Edinburgh: National Museums of Scotland and National Galleries of Scotland).

Lenman, Robin (ed.) 2005. *The Oxford Companion to the Photograph* (Oxford: Oxford University Press).

Leonowens, Anna 1870. *The English Governess at the Siamese Court: being recollections of six years in the Royal Palace at Bangkok* (London: Trübner).

Liddy, Brian 2008. 'Wilson, George Washington' in Hannavy (ed.) 2008, vol. 2.

Lightfoot, Bernard (ed.) 1997. *Victorian Science in Context* (Chicago and London: University of Chicago Press).

Livingstone, David and Charles Livingstone 1865 [reprinted 2001]. *Narrative of an Expedition to the Zambesi and its Tributaries 1858–1864* (London: Duckworth).

Livingstone, David N. and Charles W. J. Withers (eds) 2005. *Geography and Revolution* (Chicago: University of Chicago).

Lockhart, J. G. 1819. *Peter's Letters to his Kins-*

folk, 3 vols (Edinburgh and London: W. Blackwood; T. Cadell and W. Davies).

Lockhart, J. G. 1893. *The Life of Sir Walter Scott, Bart.* (London: Adam and Charles Black).

Login, Lady 1890. *Sir John Login and Dhuleep Singh* (London: W. H. Allen and Co.).

Loginov, Alexey 2008. 'Carrick, William', in Hannavy (ed.) 2008, vol. 1.

McCauley, Elizabeth Anne 2011. 'Fawning over Marbles: Robert and Gerardine Macpherson's Vatican Sculptures and the Role of Photographs in the Reception of the Antique', in Bann (ed.) 2011.

McCoo, Donald 1991. 'Gardner and his contemporaries: the years in Scotland', in Johnston (ed.) 1991.

McCosh, John 1841. *Medical Advice to the Indian Stranger* (London: William H. Allen and Co.).

McCosh, John 1856. *Advice to Officers in India* (London: William H. Allen and Co.).

Macdonald, Lindsay W. (ed.) 2009. *Emulous of Light: Turner's Colour Revisited* ([London]: Colour Group [Great Britain]). A lecture given by Dr John Gage, Royal College of Art, London, on 5 February 2009.

McDonald, Sarah 2008. 'London Stereoscopic Company', in Hannavy (ed.) 2008, vol. 2.

McKay, W. D. and Frank Rinder 1917. *The Royal Scottish Academy 1826–1916* (Glasgow: Glasgow University Press).

Macpherson, Gerardine 1878. *Memoirs of the Life of Anna Jameson, by her niece* (London: Longmans Green & Co.).

Macrae, Alexander 1880. *A Handbook of Deer-stalking* (Edinburgh & London: Blackwood).

[Mahony, Francis Sylvester] 1847. *Facts and Figures from Italy, by Don Jeremy Savonarola, Benedictine Monk, addressed during the last two winters to Charles Dickens, Esq., being an appendix to his 'Pictures'* (London: Richard Bentley).

'Mark Oute', pseud. [*see also* Mason, George]

n.d. [1888]. *Pictures in Black and White: or, Photographers Photographed* (London: H. Greenwood & Co.).

Marsden, Richard A. 2014. *Cosmo Innes and the Defence of Scotland's Past, c.1825–1875* (Farnham: Ashgate).

Mason, George ['Mark Oute'] [1891], *Pictures in Black and White, or, Photographers Photographed* (London: H. Greenwood & Co.).

Mayall, John Jabez Edwin 1835. 'Stereoscopic Views of the Great Exhibition', in Measom 1853.

Mayhew, Henry 1861–62. *London Labour and the London Poor*, 4 vols (London: Griffin, Bohn, and Company, Stationers' Hall Court).

Mayhew, Henry 1861–62. 'Statement of a Photographic Man', in Mayhew 1861–62, vol. 3: 206–10.

Measom, George 1853. *The Official Illustrated Guide to the Southeastern Railway* (London: H. G. Collins, C. P. Connelly & W. J. Taylor).

Memoirs and Portraits 1886. *Memoirs and Portraits of One Hundred Glasgow Men Who Have Died During the Past Thirty Years … ,* 2 vols (Glasgow: James Maclehose & Sons, St Vincent Street, publishers to the University)

Miller, Francis Trevelyan Miller and Robert Sampson Lanier 1911. *Photographic History of the Civil War, Poetry and Eloquence of Blue and Gray,* 10 vols (New York: Review of Reviews Company), vol. 9.

Miller, Hugh 1841. *The Old Red Sandstone; or New Walks in an old field* (Edinburgh: John Johnstone). (First published serially in the *Witness*, 1840).

Miller, Hugh [M. A. Taylor (ed.)] 2004. *The Cruise of the Betsey* (facsimile of first edition, 1858: Edinburgh: National Museums Scotland).

Minto, C. S. 1972. *Thomas Keith 1829–1895: surgeon and photographer* (Edinburgh: Edinburgh Corporation [Libraries and Museums Committee]).

Minto, C. S. and Dorothea, Lady Fyfe 1970.

John Forbes White, Miller, Collector, Photographer 1831–1904 (Edinburgh: Edinburgh Libraries and Museums, 1970).

Moffat, John 1989. *John Moffat Pioneer Scottish Photographic Artist, 1819–1894* (Eastbourne: J. S. M. Publishing).

Morrell, J. B. 1984. 'Brewster and the early British Association for the Advancement of Science', in Morrison-Low and Christie (eds) 1984.

Morrison-Low, A. D. 1984. 'Brewster and Scientific Instruments', in Morrison-Low and Christie (eds) 1984.

Morrison-Low, A. D. 1993. 'Dr John Adamson and Thomas Rodger: Amateur and Professional Photography in Nineteenth-century St Andrews', in Lawson, McKenzie and Morrison-Low (eds) 1993.

Morrison-Low, A. D. 2010. 'A Third Dimension', in Reid et al. (eds) 2010: 104–105.

Morrison-Low, A. D. and J. R. R. Christie (eds) 1984. *Martyr of Science: Sir David Brewster 1781–1868* (Edinburgh: Royal Scottish Museum).

Murdoch, John 1862. *Indian Year-Book for 1861. A review of Social, Intellectual, and Religious Progress in India and Ceylon* (London: James Nisbet and Co.).

Murray, Dr John 1857. *Photographic Views in Agra and its vicinity* (British Library, India Office collection).

Murray, John 1857. *Handbook for Travellers in Italy* (London: John Murray).

Napier, James 1851. *A Manual of electro-metallurgy: including the applications of the art to manufacturing processes*, in the series *Encylopaedia Metropolitana* 14 (London: [n.p.]).

Nasmyth, James and James Carpenter 1885. *The Moon considered as a Planet, a World, and as a Satellite* (London: John Murray).

Naves, Elaine Kalman 2013. *Portrait of a Scandal: the Abortion Trial of Robert Notman* (Quebec: Véhicule Press).

Neeley, Kathryn A. 2001. *Mary Somerville: Science, Illumination and the Female Mind* (Cambridge: Cambridge University Press).

Newhall, Beaumont 1967. *Latent Image: the Discovery of Photography* (New York: Doubleday & Co. Inc.).

Newhall, Beaumont (ed.) 1981. *Photography: Essays and Images* (London: Secker & Warburg).

Newton, Gael 1988. *Shades of Light: Photography and Australia 1839–1988* (Canberra: Australian National Museum).

Nicol, John 1898. *The Right Road to Photography: A Course of Instruction in the Theory and Practice of the Art* (New York: G. Gennert [The Gennert Photographic Library]).

Nolte, Vincent 1854. *Fifty Years in Both Hemispheres: or Reminiscences of the Life of a Former Merchant* (New York: Redfield).

Normand, Tom 2007. *Scottish Photography: A History* (Edinburgh: Luath Press).

Odling, Elizabeth Mary (Smee) 1878. *Memoir of Alfred Smee* (London: George Bell and Sons).

Oliphant, Margaret 1878. 'Introduction' to Macpherson 1878.

Onnes-Fruitema, Evelyn, Ton Rombout and Marijnke de Jong 2006. *The Panorama Phenomenon* (Den Haag: Panorama Mesdag).

Ovenden, Richard 1997. *John Thomson (1837–1921). Photographer* (Edinburgh: The Stationery Office).

Oxford Dictionary 2004. *Oxford Dictionary of National Biography*, Oxford University Press, 2004. This is available online at <http://www.oxforddnb.com>

Palmer, Captain H. S. 'Account of the Survey' and 'Descriptive Geography', in Wilson 1869.

Pearce, Nick 2005. *Photographs of Peking, China, 1861–1908. An inventory and description of the Yetts Collection at the University of Durham* (Lampeter: Edward Mellen Press).

Perez, Nissan N. 2007. *Picturing Jerusalem.*

James Graham and Mendel Diness, Photographers (Jerusalem: Israel Museum).

Peterson, Nicholas, Lindy Allen and Louis Hamby (eds) 2008. *The Makers and Making of Indigenous Australian Museum Collections* (Carlton, Victoria: Melbourne University Press).

Pinney, Christopher 2008. *The Coming of Photography in India* (London: British Library).

Pipes, Rosemary J. 1984. *The Colonies of Stockbridge* (Edinburgh: David Flatman Ltd).

Plunkett, John 2008. 'Athenaeum', in Hannavy (ed.) 2008, vol. 1.

Portraits of British Americans by Notman with biographical sketches by Fennings Taylor, 3 vols (Montreal: William Notman, 1865–68).

Pritchard, M. (ed.) 1990. *Technology and Art: the Birth and Early Years of Photography* (Bath: Royal Photographic Society Historical Group).

Reeder, Warwick 2008. 'Australia', in J. Hannavy (ed.) 2008, vol. 1.

Reid, Norman et al. (eds) 2010. *Treasures of St Andrews University Library* (London and St Andrews: TMI and St Andrews University).

Reports 1852. *Exhibition of the Works of Industry of All Nations, 1851: Reports of the Juries on the subjects in the thirty classes into which the exhibition was divided* (London: William Clowes & Sons).

Reports 1855. *Reports of Cases Determined in the court of Nizamut Adawlut from July to December 1853*, 9 vols (Calcutta, Bombay and London: Thacker, Spink & Co.), Bengal, vol. 3, part 2.

Richardson, C. and G. Smith (eds) 2001. *Britannia, Italia, Germania: Taste and Travel in the nineteenth century* (Edinburgh: VARIE).

Richardson, M. (ed.) 2013. *Techniques and principles in three-dimensional imaging: an introductory approach* (Hershey: Information Science Reference/IGI Global).

Richardson, Ruth 1987. *Death, Dissection and the Destitute* (London and New York: Routledge & Kegan Paul).

Roberts, David 1842–49. *The Holy Land: Syria, Idumen, Arabia, Egypt & Nubia, after lithographs by Louis Haghe; from drawings made on the spot by David Roberts*, 6 vols (London: Day & Son).

Robinson, Henry Peach 1897. *Picture-making by Photography* (London: Hazell, Watson & Viney).

Robinson, Henry Peach 1888. *Letters on Landscape Photography* (London: Piper and Carter). (First published as articles in the *Photographic Times* 1887).

Rosenheim, Jeff L. 2013. *Photography and the American Civil War* (New York: Metropolitan Museum of Art).

Ross, Horatio 1880. 'Introduction' to Macrae 1880.

Rosslyn, Helen and Angelo Maggi 2002. *Rosslyn: Country of Painter and Poet* (Edinburgh: National Galleries of Scotland).

Ruffles, Tom 2008. 'Ellis, Alexander John', in Hannavy (ed.) 2008, vol. 1.

Ryan, James 2005. 'Photography, Visual Revolutions and Victorian Geography', in Livingstone and Withers (eds) 2005.

Sambrook, James (ed.) 1981. *The Seasons [James Thomson]* (Oxford: Claredon Press).

Sayre, Robert F. (ed.) 1999. *Recovering the Prairie* (Madison, WI: University of Wisconsin Press).

Schaaf, L. J. 1990. 'The first fifty years of British photography: 1794–1844', in Pritchard (ed.) 1990.

Schaaf, Larry J. 1996. *Records from the Dawn of Photography: Talbot's Notebooks P and Q* (Cambridge: Cambridge University Press).

Schaaf, Larry J. 2003. *Catalogue Twelve: Sun Pictures: Talbot and Photogravure* (New York: Hans P. Kraus, Jr).

Schaaf, Larry J. 2013. '"The Caxton of Photography": Talbot's Etchings of Light', in Brusius et al. (eds.) 2013.

Schaffer, Simon 1997. 'Metrology, Metrication and Victorian values', in Lightfoot (ed.) 1997.

Schantz, Mark S. 2008. *Awaiting the Heavenly Country: The Civil War and America's Culture of Death* (Ithaca, NY: Cornell University Press).

Scharf, Aaron 1968. *Art and Photography* (London: Penguin Books).

Schwarz, Heinrich (trans. Helene Fraenkel) 1932. *David Octavius Hill, Master of Photography* (London: George G. Harrap & Co.).

Schwarz, Heinrich 1985. *Art and Photography: Forerunners and Influences …* (Chicago: University of Chicago Press).

Sclater, P. L. 1872. *Revised List of the Vertebrate Animals now or lately living in the Gardens of the Zoological Society of London* (London: printed for the Society).

Scott, Captain Allan Newton 1862. *Sketches in India* (London: Lovell Reeve).

Scott, Hew (ed.) 1915–61. *Fasti Ecclesiae Scoticanae: the Succession of Ministers in Scotland from the Reformation,* 9 vols (Edinburgh: Oliver and Boyd), vol. III.

Scott, Walter 1833–34. *The poetical works of Sir Walter Scott, Bart,* 12 vols (Edinburgh and London: Robert Cadell and Whitaker and Co.).

Seddon, John Pollard 1858. *Memoir and Letters of the Late Thomas Seddon, Artist, by his Brother* (London: James Nisbet and Co.).

Seiberling, Grace and Carolyn Bloore 1986. *Amateurs, Photography and the mid-Victorian Imagination* (Chicago and London: University of Chicago Press).

Shapin, Steven 1984. 'Brewster and the Edinburgh Career in Science', in Morrison-Low and Christie (eds) 1984.

Sheldon, Julie (ed.) 2009. *The Letters of Elizabeth Rigby, Lady Eastlake* (Liverpool: Liverpool University Press).

Simonson, Jane E. 1999. 'On Level Ground: Alexander Gardner's Photographs of the Kansas Prairies', in Sayre (ed.) 1999.

Simpson, James Young 1856. 'On Modern Advancement of Physics', Presidential address to the Edinburgh Medico-Chirurgical Society, 5 January 1853', in *Physicians and Physic: Three Addresses* (Edinburgh, Adam and Charles Black, 1856).

Simpson, Roddy 2008. 'Ponton, Mungo', in Hannavy (ed.) 2008, vol. 2.

Simpson, Roddy 2012. *The Photography of Victorian Scotland* (Edinburgh: Edinburgh University Press)

Skene, James 1830. 'Painting' in Brewster (ed.) 1830, 15: 226–337.

Skidmore, Colleen 2008. 'Notman, William & Sons', in Hannavy (ed.) 2008, vol. 2.

Smailes, Helen 1992. *Kenneth MacLeay 1802–1878* (Edinburgh: National Galleries of Scotland).

Smiles, Samuel (ed.) 1891. *James Nasmyth, Engineer. An Autobiography* (London: John Murray).

Smith, George Adam 1899. *The Life of Henry Drummond* (London: Hodder & Stoughton).

Smith, Graham 1989. *Sun Pictures in Scotland* (Ann Arbor: University of Michigan Museum of Art).

Smith, Graham 1990a. *Disciples of Light: Photographs in the Brewster Album* (Malibu: The J. Paul Getty Museum).

Smith, Graham 1990b. 'Captain Brewster, Calotypist', in *Photography: Discovery and Invention: Papers delivered at a Symposium Celebrating the Invention of Photography* (Malibu: The J. Paul Getty Museum, 1990).

Smith, Graham 1990. 'James David Forbes and the Early History of Photography', in Collins (ed.) 1990.

Smith, Graham 2012. 'H. Fox Talbot's "Scotch Views" for Sun Pictures in Scotland (1845)', in Di Bello, Wilson and Zamir (eds) 2012.

Smith, Graham 2013. *Photography and Travel* (London: Reaktion Books Ltd).

Smith, Joel 2011. *The Life and Death of Buildings. On Photography and Time* (Princeton, NJ: Princeton University Art Museum).

Smith, R. C. 1975. *Antique Cameras* (Newton Abbot, London and Vancouver: David and Charles).

Smith, R. M. and C. P. Smyth 1862. *Notice of an illuminated vellum manuscript which formerly belonged to Mary Queen of Scots,* republished from *Proceedings of the Antiquarian Society of Scotland,* 3 and 4 (Edinburgh: Neill and Company, 1862).

Smith, Shirlee Anne 1982. 'Cotter, James Laurence,' in *Dictionary of Canadian Biography,* vol. 11 (1881–90), University of Toronto/Université Laval: <http://www.biographi.ca/en/bio/cotter_james_laurence_11E.html>

Smyth, C. Piazzi 1858a. *Teneriffe: An Astronomer's Experiment* (London: Lovell Reeve).

Smyth, C. Piazzi 1858b. *Report on the Teneriffe Astronomical Experiment of 1856, Addressed to the Lords Commissioners of the Admiralty* (London/Edinburgh: Lovell Reeve, Richard Taylor and William Francis, Neill & Co.).

Smyth, Charles Piazzi 1862. *Three Cities in Russia,* 2 vols (London: Lovell Reeve).

Smyth, C. Piazzi 1864. *Our Inheritance in the Great Pyramid* (London: Alexander Strahan and Company).

Smyth, Charles Piazzi 1870. *A Poor Man's Photography at the Great Pyramid* (London: Henry Greenwood).

Stafford, Barbara Maria and Frances Terpak 2002. *Devices of Wonder, from the world in a box to images on a screen* (Los Angeles, CA: Getty Research Institute).

Stapp, Will, 'To … Arouse the Conscience and Affect the Heart', in Johnston (ed.) 1991.

Steadman, Philip 2001. *Vermeer's Camera* (Oxford: Oxford University Press).

Stein, Richard L. 1995. 'Street Figures: Victorian Urban Iconography', in Christ and Jordan (eds) 1995.

Stevenson, Robert Louis 1886. *The Strange Case of Dr Jekyll and Mr Hyde* (London: Longmans, Green & Co.).

Stevenson, Sara 1981. *David Octavius Hill & Robert Adamson: A Catalogue of their calotypes taken between 1843 and 1847 in the collection of the Scottish National Portrait Gallery* (Edinburgh: National Galleries of Scotland).

Stevenson, Sara 1986. 'Robert Adamson and David Octavius Hill', in Ward and Stevenson 1986.

Stevenson, Sara 1990. *Thomas Annan, 1829–1887* (Edinburgh: National Galleries of Scotland).

Stevenson, Sara 1991. *Hill & Adamson's 'The fishermen and women of the Firth of Forth'* (Edinburgh: National Galleries of Scotland).

Stevenson, Sara 2002a. *The Personal Art of D. O. Hill* (New Haven and London: The Paul Mellon Centre for Studies in British Art by Yale University Press).

Stevenson, Sara 2002b. 'Hugh Miller in Focus', in Borley (ed.) 2002.

Stevenson, Sara and Duncan Forbes 2009. *A Companion Guide to Photography in the National Galleries of Scotland*, second edition (Edinburgh: National Galleries of Scotland).

Stevenson, Sara and Helen Bennett 1978. *Van Dyck in Check Trousers* (Edinburgh: Scottish National Portrait Gallery).

Stevenson, Sara and Julie Lawson 1986. *Masterpieces of Photography in the Riddell Collection* (Edinburgh: Scottish National Portrait Gallery).

Stevenson, Sara, Julie Lawson and Michael Gray 1988. *The Photography of John Muir Wood: An Accomplished Amateur 1805–1892* (Edinburgh and London: National Galleries of Scotland and Dirk Nishen).

Stirling Maxwell, William 1848. *Annals of the Artists of Spain*, 3 vols (London: John Ollivier), vol. 2.

Stirling Maxwell, Sir William 1872. Preface to *The Scott Exhibition* [catalogue 1871].

Stratten 1891. *Glasgow and Environs: A Literary, Commercial, and Social View Past and Present; with a description of its leading mercantile houses and commercial enterprises* (London: Stratten & Stratten).

Summerly, Paula 2008. 'Medical Photography', in Hannavy (ed.) 2008, vol. 2.

Sumner, Ian 2008. 'Baron Joseph James De Forrester', in Hannavy (ed.) 2008, vol. 1.

Sutton, Thomas 1858. *A Dictionary of Photography* (London: Sampson Low, Son and Co.).

Sweet, Timothy 1990. *Traces of War: poetry, photography, and the crisis of the Union* (Baltimore, MD: Johns Hopkins University Press).

Tagg, John 2007. *The burden of representation: essays on photographies and histories* (Basingstoke: Palgrave Macmillan).

Talbot, W. H. F. 1844. 'Brief Historical Sketch of the Invention of the Art', in Talbot 1844–46.

Talbot, W. H. F. 1844–46. *The Pencil of Nature* (London: Longman, Brown, Green & Longmans).

Taylor, Col. Meadows and James Fergusson 1866. *Architecture in Dharwar and Mysore Photographed by the late Dr Pigou … A. C. B. Neill, Esq, and Colonel Biggs …, published for the Committee of Architectural Antiquities of Western India* (London: John Murray).

Taylor, Roger 1981. *George Washington Wilson Artist and Photographer (1823–93)* (Aberdeen: Aberdeen University Press).

Taylor, Roger 1987. 'Photographers to Her Majesty', in Dimond and Taylor 1987.

Taylor, Roger unpublished [2009]. 'The Optical Wonder of the Age', in Richardson (ed.) 2013.

Taylor, Roger and Larry J. Schaaf 2007, *Impressed by Light: British Photographs from Paper Negatives, 1840–1860* (New York, New Haven and London: The Metropolitan Museum of Art and Yale University Press).

Thomas, Charles 1988. *Views and Likenesses: Early Photographers and their Work in Cornwall and Scilly 1839–1970* (Falmouth: Royal Institution of Cornwall).

Thomas, D. B. 1969. *The Science Museum Photography Collection* (London: Her Majesty's Stationery Office).

Thompson, Francis 1985. 'J. F. Campbell, Victorian Polymath', in *Lamplighter and Storyteller* (Edinburgh: National Library of Scotland).

Thompson, S. P. 1910. *The Life of Lord Kelvin*, 2 vols (London: Macmillan).

Thompson, T. Jack 2012. *Light on Darkness? Missionary Photography in Africa in the Nineteenth and early Twentieth centuries* (Cambridge and Grand Rapids, MI: Wm B. Eerdmans Publishing Co.).

Thomson, Duncan et al. 1997. *Raeburn: The Art of Sir Henry Raeburn 1756–1823* (Edinburgh: Scottish National Portrait Gallery).

Thomson, John 1867. *The Antiquities of Cambodia, A Series of Photographs Taken on the Spot, With Letterpress Description* (Edinburgh: Edmonston and Douglas).

Thomson, John 1873–74. *Illustrations of China and its Peoples,* 4 vols (London: Sampson Low, Marston, Low and Searle).

Thomson, John 1875. *The Straits of Malacca, Indo-China and China or Ten Years' Travels, Adventures and Residence Abroad* (London: Sampson Low, Marston, Low and Searle).

Thomson, John and Adolphe Smith 1877. *Street Life in London* (London: Sampson Low, Marston, Searle and Rivington).

Thornbury, Walter 1862. *The Life of J. M. W. Turner, RA Founded on Letters and Papers Furnished by his Friends and Fellow Academics,* 2 vols (London: Hurd and Blackett).

Timbs, John 1847. *The Year-book of Facts in Science and Art: Exhibiting the most impor-*

tant discoveries and improvements of the past year (London: David Bogue).

Tompkins, Peter 1978. *Secrets of the Great Pyramid* (Harmondsworth: Penguin Books).

Torrance, D. Richard 2011. *Scottish Studio Photographers to 1914*, 2 vols (Edinburgh: Scottish Record Society).

Trachtenberg, Alan 1989. *Reading American Photographs: Images as History – Mathew Brady to Walker Evans* (New York, NY: Hill and Wang).

Traill, Catherine Parr Strickland 1822. *Little Downy; or, The history of a field-mouse: A moral tale* (London: Printed for A. K. Newman and Co.).

Traill Taylor, J. 1892. *The Optics of Photography and Photographic Lenses* (London: Whittaker).

Traubel, Horace 1912. *With Walt Whitman in Camden: November 1, 1888–January 20, 1889*, 9 vols (New York: Mitchell Kennerley).

Triggs, Stanley 1985. *William Notman: The Stamp of a Studio* ([Toronto]: Art Gallery of Ontario, The Coach House Press).

Turley, Raymond 2008, 'Hughes, Cornelius Jabez', in Hannavy (ed.) 2008, vol. 1.

Urie, John 1908. *Reminiscences of Eighty Years Ago* (Paisley: Alexander Gardner).

Waagen, Gustav Friedrich 1857. *Galleries and Cabinets of Art in Great Britain* (London: John Murray).

Ward, John and Sara Stevenson 1986. *Printed Light: The Scientific Art of William Henry Fox Talbot and David Octavius Hill with Robert Adamson* (Edinburgh: HMSO).

Ware, Mike 1993. 'The Eighth Metal: the Rise of the Platinotype Process', in Lawson, McKenzie and Morrison-Low (eds) 1993.

Ware, Mike 2008. 'Burnett, Charles John', in Hannavy (ed.) 2008, vol. 1.

Ware, Mike 2014. *Cyanomican: History Science and Art of Cyanotype: photographic printing in Prussian blue.* Available online: <http://www.mikeware.co.uk/downloads/Cyanomicon.pdf>

Warner, Brian 1983. *Charles Piazzi Smyth, Astronomer-Artist: His Cape Years 1835–1845* (Cape Town and Rotterdam: A. A. Balkema).

Watters, David and Anna Koestenbauer 2011. *Stitches in Time. Two Centuries of Surgery in Papua New Guinea* (Gordon, New South Wales: Xlibris Corporation) [e-book].

Werge, John 1890. *The Evolution of Photography … Contributions to Photographic Literature, and Personal Reminiscences extending over forty years* (London: Piper & Carter and John Werge).

Weston-Lewis, Aidan et al. 2012. *Expanding Horizons: Giovanni Battista Lusieri and the Panoramic Landscape* (Edinburgh: National Galleries of Scotland).

Williams, Rev George 1869. 'Introduction', *Ordnance Survey of the Peninsula of Sinai* (London: HMSO).

Willis, Elizabeth 2008. 'Gentlemen Collectors. The Port Phillip District, 1835–1855', in Peterson, Allen and Hamby (eds) 2008.

Wilson, [Professor] … and Robert Chambers … 1840. *The Land of Burns, A Series of Landscapes and Portraits, Illustrative of the Life and Writings of the Scottish Poet. The Landscapes from Paintings Made Expressly for the Work, by D. O. Hill, Esq., RSA* (Glasgow: John Blackie).

Wilson, Captain Charles William 1869. *Ordnance Survey of the Peninsula of Sinai* (London: HMSO).

Wilson, Edward 1849. *The Squatters' Directory Containing a List of all the Occupants of Crown Lands in the Intermediate and unsettled Districts of Port Phillip* (Melbourne: Edward Wilson, 1849).

Wilson, George 1855. *Researches on Colour-Blindness* (Edinburgh and London: Sutherland and Knox, Simpkin Marshall & Co.).

Wilson, Jessie Aitken 1860. *Memoir of George Wilson: MD FRSE* (Edinburgh, London and Cambridge: Edmonston and Douglas; Macmillan).

Wilson, Joseph M. 1883. *A Eulogy on the Life and Character of Alexander Gardner, delivered at a Stated Communication of Lebanon Lodge, No. 7 F.A.A.M., January 19, 1883, published by Lebanon Lodge* (Washington DC: H. Beresford).

Wood, J. M. 1879–90. 'Scottish Music', in Grove (ed.) *A Dictionary of Music and Musicians*, 5 vols (London: MacMillan), vol. 3.

Wright, Christopher et al. (eds) 2006. *British and Irish Paintings in Public Collections* (London and New York: Yale University Press).

Wu Hung 2001. 'Inventing a Chinese Portrait Style in Early Photography. The Case of Milton Miller', in Cody and Terpak (eds) 2011.

Xanthakēs, A. X. (J. Solman and G. Cox, trans.) 1988. *History of Greek Photography 1839–1960* (Athens: Hellenic Literary and Historical Archives Society, 1988).

Yule, Henry 1921. *The Book of Ser Marco Polo …* (London: John Murray), third edition with a memoir by Amy Frances Yule, preface.

Unpublished works

Gordon, Sophie 2011. 'Monumental visions: architectural photography in India, 1840–1901', unpublished PhD thesis, University of London, School of Oriental and African Studies.

Heathcote, B. V. and P. F. Heathcote [n.d., unpublished typescript, available at the National Media Museum], Appendix to: 'A Faithful Likeness: The First Photographic Portrait Studios in the British Isles 1841 to 1855' (Lowdham: the authors).

Johnstone, Karen A. 1977. 'Thomas Rodger, 1832–1883', unpublished M.Litt dissertation, University of St Andrews.

Laurence-Allen, Antonia 2012. 'Class, Consumption and Currency: Commercial Photography in Scotland, 1851–1888', unpublished PhD thesis, University of St Andrews.

Syvret, Gareth *forthcoming*. 'Les Îles de la Manche: Photography in the Channel Islands 1840–1870', unpublished PhD thesis, prepared for De Montfort University.

Walker, David W. 2002. 'Peddie and Kinnear, architects', unpublished PhD thesis, University of St Andrews.

Wood, Paul Muir, unpublished research.

List of journals and periodicals
[with abbreviations]

– *Alberta Historical Review*
– *Amateur Photographic Association*
– *American Philosophical Society*
– *Annales des sciences physiques et naturelles, d'agriculture et d'industrie. Publiées par la société royale d'agriculture, d'histoire naturelle et arts utile de Lyon*
– *Archivaria*
– *Art in America*
– *Art-journal*, formerly *Art-union*
– *Athenaeum*
– *Beaver*
– *Blackwood's Edinburgh Magazine/ Blackwood's Magazine*
– *Botanical Society of Edinburgh: Transactions and Proceedings*
– *British Association for the Advancement of Science: Transactions and Notices & Abstracts*
– *British Association for the Advancement of Science (London): Reports*
– *British Journal for the History of Science*
– *British Journal of Photography* [*BJPh*]
– *British Medical Journal*
– *British Quarterly Review*
– *Bulletin of the History of Chemistry*
– *Bulletin of the Scientific Instrument Society*
– *Burlington Magazine*
– *Camera Work*
– *Canadian Rail*
– *Chambers's Edinburgh Journal*
– *Chambers's Information for the People*
– *Chemical News and Journal of Physical Science*
– *Chemist: A monthly journal of chemical and physical science*
– *Chemistry World*
– *Children's Friend*
– *Civil War Times*
– *Colonist*
– *Curtis's Botanical Magazine*
– *Daguerreian Annual*
– *Early Science and Medicine*
– *Edinburgh Medical Journal Edinburgh*, formerly *Medical and Surgical Journal*
– *Edinburgh Monthly Journal*
– *Edinburgh New Philosophical Journal*, formerly *Edinburgh Philosophical Journal*
– *Edinburgh Review*
– *Eliza Cook's Journal*
– *Empire Magazine*
– *Fine Arts Quarterly Review*
– *Freeman's Journal*
– *Gentleman's Magazine*
– *Getty Research Journal*
– *Glasgow Photographic Association: Reports*
– *Hawick Archaeological Society: Transactions*
– *History of Photography* [*HoPh*]
– *Hogg's Weekly Instructor*
– *Humphrey's Journal*
– *Illustrated London News*
– *Illustrated Photographer*
– *Image: The Bulletin of the George Eastman House of Photography*
– *Journal of Canadian Studies*
– *Journal of New Zealand Studies* [New Series]
– *Journal of Stevenson Studies*
– *Journal of the Belles Lettres*
– *Journal of the Board of Arts and Manufactures for Ontario*
– *Journal of the Photographic Society* [*JPhS*]
– *Journal of the Photographic Society* [*of London*] [*JPhSoL*]
– *Journal of the Photographic Society of Bombay*
– *Journal of the Royal Geographical Society*
– *Jurist* [New Series]
– *La Presse*
– *Literary Gazette*
– *Liverpool Photographic Journal*
– *London Literary Journal*
– *London Medical Gazette*
– *London, Edinburgh and Dublin Philosophical Magazine and Journal of Science* [*PhilMag*]
– *Macmillan's Magazine*
– *Macphail's Edinburgh Ecclesiastical Journal and Literary Review*
– *Massachusetts Review*
– *Mercantile Age*
– *Mirror of Literature, Amusement, and Instruction*
– *New Monthly Magazine*
– *New Scientist*
– *New Zealand Journal of History*
– *North British Review*
– *Notes and Queries*
– *Papers of the British School at Rome*
– *Pharmaceutical Journal*
– *Photogram*
– *Photographer's Friend: A Practical, Independent Magazine, The*
– *Photographic Collector*
– *Photographic Journal* [*PhJ*]
– *Photographic News* [*PhNews*]
– *Photographic Notes* [*PhNotes*]
– *Photographic Society of Scotland: Accounts of meetings*
– *Photographic Times*
– *Photography*

– *Photohistorian,* Newsletter of the Royal Photographic Society
– *Photoresearcher*
– *Princeton University Library Chronicle*
– *Quarterly Review*
– *Review of Scottish Culture*
– *Royal Geographical Society of London: Proceedings*
– *Royal Institution of Great Britain: Journal*
– *Royal Institution of Great Britain: Notices of Proceedings*
– *Royal Philosophical Society of Glasgow, Proceedings*
– *Royal Scottish Society of Arts: Transactions (including Proceedings)* [*ProcRSSA*] and [*TRSSA*]
– *Royal Society of Edinburgh* [RSEdin]: *Transactions* and *Proceedings*
– *Royal Society of London, Philosophical Transactions* and *Proceedings*
– *Studies in Photography,* formerly *Scottish Photography Bulletin* [*SPhB*]
– *Social History of Medicine*
– *Stereoscopic Magazine*
– *The Calcutta Review*
– *The Engineers' Journal, Railway, Public Works and Mining Gazette of India and the Colonies*
– *The Illustrated Photographer*
– *The La Trobe Journal*
– *The Publishers' Circular*
– *The Scattered Nation*
– *The Studio*
– *Vistas in Astronomy*
– *Wilson's Photographic Magazine* [New York]
– *Yunost'*

Secondary sources: journals and periodicals

Adie, John, 'The use of brass or copper plates having their surfaces silvered, for producing pictures by the process of daguerreotype', *Edinburgh New Philosophical Journal* 29 (1840): 401.

Annan, J. Craig, 'David Octavius Hill, R.S.A. 1802–1870', *Camera Work* 11 (July 1905): 17.

Archer, Thomas, 'Industrial Museum of Scotland Appendix Y', *Report of the Department of Science and Art of the Committee of Council on Education*, vol. 9 (London, 1862).

Ashbee, Felicity, 'William Carrick: A Scots photographer in St Petersburg, 1827–1878', *HoPh* 2 (1978): 207–22.

Ashbee, F. ,'Photograph s MaloyMorskoy', *Yunost'* no. 7 (1976): 45–6.

Ashbee, Felicity, 'William Carrick: A Scots photographer in St Petersburg, 1827–1878', *HoPh* 2 (1978): 207–22.

Balfour, J. H., 'Notice of the Palm-House in the Royal Botanic Garden at Edinburgh', *Edinburgh New Philosophical Journal* 8 (1858): 283.

Balfour, J. H., 'Description of Nartex Assafoetida, Falconer, at present in flower in the Royal Botanic Garden', *Transactions and Proceedings of the Botanical Society of Edinburgh* 6 (1860): 64–8.

Barfoot, Mike and A. D. Morrison-Low, 'W. C. M'Intosh and A. J. Macfarlan: Early Clinical Photography', *HoPh* 23 (1999): 199–210.

Batchen, Geoffrey, 'Tom Wedgwood and Humphry Davy, "An Account of a Method"', *HoPh* 17 (1993): 172–83.

Berwick, George, 'Microscopic Photography on Gelatine Plates', *BJPh* 27 (28 May 1880): 262–3.

Birrell, Andrew, 'Fortunes of a Misfit; Charles Horetzky', *Alberta Historical Review* 19, 1 (1971): 9–25.

Blackburn, Hugh, 'Photographic Engraving', *Notes and Queries* 8 (24 Dec. 1853): 628.

Bourne, Samuel, 'Photography in the East', *BJPh* 10 (1 July 1863): 268.

Brenni, Paolo, 'Nineteenth-century French scientific instrument makers VII: Paul Gustave Froment [1815–1865]', *Bulletin of the Scientific Instrument Society* 45 (1995): 19–24.

Brenni, Paolo, 'Nineteenth-century French scientific instrument makers XIII: Soleil, Duboscq, and their Successors', *Bulletin of the Scientific Instrument Society* 51 (1996): 7–16.

Brewster, Sir David, 'A Brief Account of the Camera Obscura, and other Apparatus, used in making Daguerreotype Drawings', *Report of the … British Association for the Advancement of Science … 1840* (London: John Murray, 1841), Part II, *Transactions*: 8–9.

[Brewster, David], 'Photogenic Drawing or Drawing by the Agency of Light', *Edinburgh Review* 76 (1843): 309–44.

[Brewster, David], 'Photography', *North British Review* 14 (1847): 465–504.

Brewster, David, 'Notice regarding the recent improvements in photography', *Report of the … British Association for the Advancement of Science; … 1850* (London: John Murray, 1851), Part II, *Transactions*: 6.

Brewster, David, 'The President's Address', *Report of the … British Association for the Advancement of Science; … 1850* (London: John Murray, 1851): xxii–xliv.

[Brewster, David], 'Binocular vision and the Stereoscope', *North British Review* 17 (1851): 165–204.

[Brewster, David], 'Recent Progress of Photographic Art', *North British Review* 36 (1862): 170–203.

Brewster, David, 'Tribute to Skene', *Proceedings of the RSEdin* 6 (1868–69): 243–68.

Brown, Duncan, 'On the Collodion process: its Pursuit under Difficulties', *Humphrey's Journal* 13 (15 June 1861): 54–6.

Brück, Mary T., 'The Piazzi Smyth collection of sketches, photographs and manuscripts at the Royal Observatory, Edinburgh', *Vistas in Astronomy* 32 (1988): 371–408.

Buchanan, William, 'The Annans of Glasgow', *Studies in Photography* (2006): 20–9.

Burnett, C. J., Letter to the Editor from Old Aberdeen, 'A few Remarks on Printing by Carbon and other Pigments by the aid of bichromates and other metallic salts, along with Gelatine, Gum, or other animal and vegetable substances', *JPhS* 5 (22 November 1858): 84–6.

Burnett, C. J., Letter to the Editor, 19 July 1857, 'On Various New Printing Processes', *PhNotes* 2 (1 October 1857): 382–4.

Campbell, J. F. 'On the perspective of photography', *JPhSoL* 5 (22 Nov. 1858): 83–4.

Chambers's Edinburgh Journal 8 (2 November 1839): 327, 328.

Charles Wheatstone, 'Contributions to the Physiology of Vision: Part the First. On Some Remarkable, and hitherto unobserved Phenomena of Binocular Vision', *Philosophical Transactions of the Royal Society of London* 128 (1838): 371–94.

Clark, W. D., 'Notes on the Collodio-Albumen Process', a Paper sent to a Meeting of the Photographic Society of Scotland, *BJPh* 10 (1 May 1863): 194.

Clark W. D., 'Notes on the Collodio-Albumen Process', *JPhSoL* 8 (1864): 281.

Clark W. D., 'On Pictorial and Photographic Representations of Melrose Abbey', Paper read to Photographic Society of Scotland, 8 May 1866, *PhNews* 10 (25 May 1866): 248–50.

Claudet, A.: 'The stereoscopic daguerreotype views of the Great Exhibition, by Mr. Claudet, which have excited the admiration of Her Majesty and Prince Albert, are now exhibited at Mr. Claudet's Photographic Gallery …', *London Literary Journal* (1 Dec. 1851): 581.

Claudet, A., 'On the Practice of the Daguerreotype', *Report of the British Association for the Advancement of Science … 1854* (London: John Murray, 1854), Part II, *Transact.*: 4–5.

Clerk Maxwell, James, 'Experiments on Colour, as perceived by the Eye, with remarks on Colour-Blindness', *Transactions of the RSEdin* 21 (1857): 275–98.

Clerk Maxwell, James, 'On the Theory of Three Primary Colours', *Notices of the Proceedings at the Meetings of the Members of the Royal Institution of Great Britain* 3: (1862): 370–4.

Collie, William, 'Early Calotypes', Letter to the Editor, *PhJ* 6 (15 February 1860): 166.

Collier, Joseph, Letters to G. W. Wilson, 'Photographic Adventures in Colorado', *BJPh* 21 (September 1874): 450–1; 464–65; 522–4.

Collier, Robert, 'The Early Years, Photos from the File of Joseph Collier', *Empire Magazine* 40 (October 1977): 10–2.

Corner, George, 'The Panorama: with Memoirs of its Inventor, Robert Barker, and his son, the late Henry Aston Barker', *Art-journal* [New Series] 3 (1857): 46.

Cotter, James L., 'The Eskimos of Eastmain', *Beaver* (December 1929): 301–6 and (March 1930): 362–5.

Cramb, John, 'Palestine in 1860: Or, a photographer's journal of a visit to Jerusalem', *BJPh* 7 (1 December 1860): 344–5; *BJPh* 8 (15 January–16 December 1861): 32–3, 46–7, 130–1, 146–7, 237–8, 255–6, 287–9, 364–5, 388–9, 425–6, 444–5.

Crawford, Alastair, 'Robert Macpherson 1814–72, the foremost photographer of Rome', *Papers of the British School at Rome* 67 (1999): 353–403.

Crombie, John Nicol, 'On the Rise and Progress of Photography in New Zealand', *BJPh* 9 (15 October 1862): 393–4.

Crum, Walter, 'On the Manner in which Cotton unites with colouring matter', *Proceedings of the Royal Philosophical Society of Glasgow* 1 (1842–3): 98–104.

Cundell, George S. 'On the practice of the Calotype Process of Photography', *PhilMag*, [3rd series], 24 (1844): 321–2.

Cundell, G. S., 'Gallo-Nitrate of Silver and its Action on Iodised Paper', *PhilMag* [3rd series], 29 (1846): 101–3.

Dallmeyer, J. H., 'On the cause of the Central Spot, or "Flare" in Photographic lenses', *BJPh* 14 (21 June 1867): 289.

Davenport, D. A. and K. M. Ireland, 'The Ingenious, Lively and Celebrated Mrs Fulhame and the Dyer's Hand', *Bulletin of the History of Chemistry* 5 (1991): 37–42.

Davidson, Thomas, 'Description and Drawing of a simple but important improvement in the Camera Obscura, in taking portraits and other objects' and 'Description and Diagram of a Method of taking views by Reflection, in the Daguerreotype, or in the common Camera Obscura', *Edinburgh New Philosophical Journal* 31 (1841): 413.

Davidson, Thomas, 'On an Improved Method of Illumination, by a different arrangement of the Lenses, for the Oxyhydrogen Microscope and Magic Lantern', *Edinburgh New Philosophical Journal* 31 (1841): 421.

Davidson, Thomas, 'On some erroneous statements lately made in a paper before the Royal Irish Academy by Dr Robinson of Armagh, regarding the Reflecting Telescopes made by the late James Short and Sir William Herschell [*sic*]', *Edinburgh New Philosophical Journal* 31 (1841): 421.

Davidson, Thomas, 'Description and diagrams of a Compound Achromatic Camera', *TRSSA* 2 (1844), Appendix, 53.

Davidson, Thomas, 'Description of the Process of Daguerreotype, and remarks on the action of light in that process, both in respect to landscape and miniature Portraits', *TRSSA* 2 (1844): 21–5.

Davidson, Thomas, 'The Solar Camera', *PhJ* 6 (1859): 264.

'Dr Keith's Paper on the Waxed Paper Process, given on 10 June 1856', *PhNotes* 1 (17 July 1856): 101–4.

Downs, James, 'Out of the Shadows: Iván

Szabó [1822–58], a forgotten "photographic luminary"', *Studies in Photography* (2008): 28–38.

Downs, James, 'Shadows of the Truth: the photography of James Graham (1808–69)', *Studies in Photography* (2011): 42–59.

Downs Pascal, O. S. B., '"The delight of their existence": the photography of Horatio Ross of Rossie [1801–86]', *Studies in Photography* (2006): 35–43.

Drummond, Rev. D. T. K., 'Some Remarks on the Malt Process', *PhNews* 8 (22 January 1864): 42.

'Dum Spiro Spero', 'Scottish Pioneers in Photography', in *BJPh* 44 (9 July 1897): 442–3.

Dupré, Sven (ed.), Special Issue, 'Optics, Instruments and Painting, 1420–1720. Reflections on the Hockney-Falco Thesis', *Early Science and Medicine* 10, no. 2 (2005): 125–339.

Eagles, John, 'New Discovery – Engraving, and Burnet's Cartoons', *Blackwood's Magazine* 45 (1839): 382–91.

[Eastlake, Lady, formerly Elizabeth Rigby], 'Photography', *Quarterly Review* 101 (April 1857): 442–68, 460, 465.

Eremin, K., J. Tate and J. Berry, 'On the Chemistry of John and Robert Adamson's Salted Paper Prints and Calotype Negatives', *Studies in Photography* (2002–3): 67–74.

Falconer, John, 'Photography and the Royal Engineers', *Photographic Collector* 2 (Autumn, 1981): 33–64.

Forrester, Joseph James, 'Waxed Positives', in *JPhS* 2 (21 August 1854): 25.

Furlonge [*sic*], W. Holland, 'On the Calotype Process', *PhNotes* 1 (1856): 13–6.

Fyfe, Andrew, 'On Daguerreotype', *TRSSA* 1 (1840): 415–20.

Fyfe, Andrew, 'On Photography', *TRSSA* 1 (1840): 319–30.

Fyfe, Andrew, 'Verbal Exposition of Daguerreotype', *Edinburgh New Philosophical Journal* 29 (1840): 397.

Gill, Arthur, 'Fox Talbot's photoglyphic engraving process', *HoPh* 2 (1978): 134.

Graham, Rev. Robert, 'The Early History of Photography', *Good Words* 15 (1874): 450–3; reprinted *HoPh* (1984): 231–5.

Gray, Harry, 'The Johnston Collection, Wick', *Studies in Photography* (2012): 40–7.

Greatrex, John Henry, 'Remarks on an Economic Instrument for Sensitising or Coating Large Surfaces of Paper &c', *BJPh* 12 (12 May 1865): 245, 252.

Guay, Louise, 'Alexander Henderson, Photographer', *HoPh* 13 (1989): 79–94.

Gutch, John Wheeley Gough, 'Recollections and Jottings of a Photographic Tour, Undertaken During the Years 1856–7', *PhNotes* 3 (15 June 1858): 144.

Hallett, Michael, 'Early Magnesium Light Portraits', *HoPh* 10 (1986): 299–301.

Hamilton, Rod, 'John Murray (1809–98): Pioneer photographer in India', *SPhB* 1 (1993): 3–9.

Hannavy, John, 'Richard Beard's Scottish and Irish Patents, and the Development of the Daguerreotype in Those Countries', *Daguerreian Annual* (2007): 88–101.

Hannavy, John, 'Thomas Keith (1827–95) – a Scottish master', *Studies in Photography* (2007): 21–30.

Harvey, George [wrongly published as 'T. W. Harvey'], Letter *BJPh* 9 (1862): 219–20.

Heathcote, B. V. and P. F. Heathcote, 'The Feminine Influence: Aspects of the Role of Women in the Evolution of Photography in the British Isles', *HoPh* 12 (1988): 259–73.

Henderson, Alexander, 'Notes on Dry Processes', *PhNews* 1 (21 October 1859): 82–3.

Herschel, J. F. W., Letter, *Athenaeum* (7 December 1853).

Hill, Octavia, 'Why the Artisans Dwellings Bill was wanted', *Macmillan's Magazine* 15 (June 1874): 181–2.

Hunter, Alexander, 'On the Selection of Sub-jects from Nature', *Photographic Times* 9 (June 1879): 134–6.

Hutton, James, 'Theory of the earth, or, An investigation into the laws observable in the composition, dissolution and restoration of land upon the globe', *Transactions of the RSEdin* 1 (1788): 1–96.

Innes, Cosmo, 'Paper read by Mr Cosmo Innes … ', *PhNotes* 1 (15 September 1856): 169–72.

Innes, Cosmo, 'Short Notes of Photographic Tours', *PhJ* 8 (16 Feb. and 15 April 1863): 231–2 and 258–60.

Jackson, Magnus, 'Photography outside the studio', *BJPh* 28 (4 February 1881): 55–6.

Johnston, T. B., 'Photographic Forgery', *PhNotes* 2 (1 January 1857): 4–6.

Keith, Thomas, Obituary, in *British Medical Journal* 2 (19 October 1895): 1003.

Kinnear, C. G. H., 'Abstract of an Account of an Architectural and Photographic Tour in the North of France', *JPhSoL* 4 (21 December 1857): 116–21.

Kirk, John, 'Hints to Travellers – Extracts from a Letter from John Kirk', *Journal of the Royal Geographical Society* 34 (1864): 290–2.

Koltun, Lilly, 'Not the World of William Notman – [review of] the World of William Notman: the Nineteenth Century through a Master Lens' [Roger Hall, Gordon Dodds and Stanley Triggs (eds) 1993], *Journal of Canadian Studies* 30, 1 (1995): 125–33.

Lawson, James, 'The Urban Landscape between Progress and Decay', in *Studies in Photography* (1998): 5–8.

Lawson, Julie, 'Dr John Kirk and Dr William Robertson: Photographers in the Crimea', in *HoPh* 12 (1988): 227–41.

Lawson, Julie, 'William Walker: an Early Amateur Photographer', in *SPhB* 2 (Autumn 1988): 3–13.

Linkman, Audrey, 'A Roving Scot: Itinerant Photography in the Heart of England in the 1850s', *SPhB* 1 (1992): 3–15.

Lundie, D. Murray, 'Correspondence: The Oldest Studio', *BJPh* 59 (6 December 1912): 947.

Macbeth, Norman, 'Photographic copying from Paintings and Drawings', *BJPh* 14 (10 May 1867): 216–7.

Macartney, Hilary, 'The Reproduction of Spanish Art: Hill and Adamson's Calotypes and Sir William Stirling Maxwell's *Annals of the Artists of Spain* (1848)', *Studies in Photography* (2005): 16–23.

McCoo, Don, 'John Urie Portrait Photographer, 1820–1910', *SPhB* 2 (1989): 3–14.

McCraw, William, 'The True Origin of the Collodion Process in Scotland', *BJPh* 16 (17 December 1869): 603–4.

Macfarlan, A. J., 'Remarks on the Applications of Photography to Botany', *Transactions and Proceedings of the Botanical Society of Edinburgh* 5 (1858): 142–4, 144.

Macfarlan, A. J., 'On the Application of Photography to the Delineation of Disease, with remarks on Stereo-micro-photography', *PhJ* 7 (16 December 1861): 326–9, 329.

McKenzie, Ray, '"The Laboratory of Mankind": John McCosh and the Beginnings of Photography in British India', *HoPh* 11 (1987): 109–18.

McKenzie, Ray, 'The Cradle and the Grave of Empires: Robert Macpherson and the Photography of Nineteenth-Century Rome', *Photographic Collector* 4, 2 (Autumn 1983): 215–34.

McKenzie, Ray, 'A Love Affair with Loch Katrine: Problems of Representation in Early Scottish Landscape', *SPhB* 1 (1990): 3–12.

McKenzie, Ray, 'The Pre-photographic Printmaking Work of D. O. Hill', *Studies in Photography* (2002–3): 34–41.

McNab, Alexander, 'Mr Ribble's [Kibble's] Monster Negatives', *PhNotes* 2 (15 April 1857): 145.

Maconochie, A., 'Normal Collodion and Iodide of Iron', Extracts from Letters to Roger Fenton, *JPhS* 1, no. 7 (21 July 1853): 87–8.

Mactear, Andrew, 'History of Photography in Glasgow', *BJPh* 31 (28 March 1884): 202.

Main, William, 'George Dobson Valentine in New Zealand', *HoPh* 6 (1982): 333–48.

Monteiro, Stephen 2008. 'Veiling the Mechanical Eye: Antoine Claudet and the Spectacle of Photography in Victorian London', *19: Interdisciplinary Studies in the Long Nine-teenth Century* 7 (2008) <www.19.bbk. ac.uk>

Morrell, J. B., 'Thomas Thomson: professor of chemistry and university reformer', *British Journal for the History of Science* 4 (1968–69): 245–65.

Morrison-Low, A. D., 'Sir David Brewster and Photography', in *Review of Scottish Culture* 4 (1988): 63–73.

Morrison-Low, A. D., 'Photography in Edinburgh in 1839: The Royal Scottish Society of Arts, Andrew Fyfe and Mungo Ponton', *SPhB* 2 (1990): 26–35.

Morrison-Low, A. D., 'Robert Adamson 1821–48, in *Studies in Photography* (1998): 2–4.

Morrison-Low, A. D., 'Brewster, Talbot and the Adamsons: the Arrival of Photography in St Andrews', *HoPh* 25 (2001): 130–41.

Morrison-Low, A. D. '"Tripping the Light Fantastic": Henry Talbot and David Brewster', *Studies in Photography* (2002–3): 83–8,

Morrison-Low, A. D., 'Instrument making and Early Photography', *Photohistorian, The Newsletter of the Royal Photographic Society* 149 (January 2007): 29–37.

Murray, Robert, 'A few hints to amateur landscape photographers', *BJPh* 27 (13 February 1880): 77–8.

Myles, Fiona, 'Discovering Thomas Keith's photographs', *Studies in Photography* (2007): 19–20.

Myles, Fiona, 'Dr Thomas Keith: a selective bibliography', *Studies in Photography* (2007): 41.

Neil, C. Lang, 'The Animal Photographs of Charles Reid', in *The Studio* 38, no. 162 (1906): 327–32.

N[ewhall], B. and R. D[oty], 'The Value of Photography to the Artist, 1839', *Image: The Bulletin of the George Eastman House of Photography* 11, no. 6 (1962): 25–8.

Nicol, John, 'Photography in and about the Pyramids: how it was accomplished by Professor C. Piazzi Smyth', *BJPh* 13 (8 June 1864): 268–70.

Nicol, John, 'Notes from the North', *BJPh* 19 (22 November 1872): 54; 23 (25 February 1876): 90–1, 464; 24 (29 December 1877): 309; 25 (27 December 1878): 617; 28 (25 March 1881): 148.

Nicol, John, 'Reminiscences of Thomas Davidson, a Weaver Lad', *BJPh* 26 (15 August 1879): 390–1; (22 August 1879): 399–401.

Nicol, John, '"Which is Older" and "Who of our Readers is Veteran Enough to take up this challenge?"', *Wilson's Photographic Magazine* [New York] 33, no. 470 (February 1896): 81–3.

Niederman, Rob, 'Kinnear Cameras: Large Format in a Smaller Size', *Photogram* 34 (2006): 3–7.

'Old Photo', 'Photography in the Channel Islands', *The Illustrated Photographer* 1 (1868): 456.

Orange, Claudia, 'The Covenant of Kohimarama: A Ratification of the Treaty of Waitangi', *New Zealand Journal of History* 14 (1980): 61–82.

Osman, Colin, 'Robert Murray of Edinburgh [1822–93]: the Discovery of Neglected Calotypes of Egypt', *Photoresearcher* 6 (March 1997): 6–11.

Paterson, Lachy, 'The Kohimarama Conference of 1860: A Contextual Reading', *Journal of New Zealand Studies* [New Series] 12 (2011): 29–46.

Payne, Susan and Paul Adair, 'Magnus Jackson and the Black Art: the happy marriage of old and new technology', *Studies in Photography* (2008): 42–50.

Pearce, Nick, 'A Life in Peking: the Peabody Albums', *HoPh* 32 (2007): 276–87.

Peterson, Anne E., 'Alexander Gardner in Review', in *HoPh* 34 (2010): 356–67.

Ponton, Mungo, 'On the Registry of the Hourly Variations of the Thermometer, by means of Photographic Papers', *Edinburgh New Philosophical Journal* 39 (1845): 270–6.

Pritchard, H. Baden, 'Photography in connexion with the Abyssinian Expedition', *PhJ* 13 (15 December 1868): 184–8.

Ramsay, A. C., 'On a Process for obtaining Lithographs by the Photographic Process', *Transactions of the British Association for the Advancement of Science; held at Glasgow in September 1855* (London: John Murray, 1856): 69–70.

Raven, T. M., Letter to the Editor, *PhNotes* 3 (1 February 1858): 45.

Raven, Rev. T. M., 'Pau and the Pyrenees, with a slight sketch of a Photographic Tour made to them through the west of France', *JPhSoL* 5 (21 Dec 1858–21 Jan 1859): 104–8, 131–2, 155–7.

Ray, Frederic, 'The Case of the Rearranged Corpse', *Civil War Times* 3 (6) (1 October 1961): 19.

Ray, Sidney F., 'The Applied Photography of Charles Piazzi Smyth', *Photoresearcher* 1 (October 1990): 37.

Review of John William Kaye, *The Administration of the East India Company: A History of Indian Progress*, *The Calcutta Review* 19 (1853): 373.

Ricketts, Jane, 'D. H. Macfarlane, a New Name in Indian Photography', *Photographic Collector* 3 (1982): 86–90.

[Rigby, Elizabeth], 'Modern German painting', *Quarterly Review* 77 (March 1846): 323–48.

[Rigby, Elizabeth], 'Planche's *History of Costume*', *Quarterly Review* 79 (March 1847): 372–48.

Robinson, Henry Peach, 'The Tools we use', *PhNews* 15 (26 July 1872): 353.

Robison, Sir John, 'Notes on Daguerre's Photography [1 June 1839]', *Edinburgh New Philosophical Journal* 27 (1839): 155–7.

Robison, Sir John, 'Notice regarding a cheap and easily used Camera Lucida, applicable to the delineation of Flowers and other small objects', *TRSSA* 2 (1844): 85–6.

Rodger, Thomas, 'On Collodion Calotype', *TRSSA* 4 (1856): 292–9.

Rodger, Thomas, 'The Collodion Process', *BJPh* 3 (1856): 256–7.

Ross, Horatio, 'Paper on the comparative merits of different processes of Photography in taking views in mountainous districts', *PhNotes* 2 (15 March 1857): 95–7.

Ross, Horatio, 'On Fading', *BJPh* 22 (1875): 29–30.

Ross, James, 'On Taking and Printing Stereoscopic Pictures', *PhNotes* 2 (15 July 1857): 258–9.

Ross, James, 'On the fading of positives', *PhNotes* 2 (10 October 1857): 361.

Ross, James, Letter defending photography as a fine art, *BJPh* 11 (28 October 1864): 423.

Ross, James, 'A Few Extracts from a Photographer's Old Ledger', *BJPh* 20 (14 February 1873): 75–7.

Russell-Jones, Peter, 'John MacCosh's Photographs of the 2nd Sikh War, 1848–49, and the 2nd Burman War, 1852–53', *PhJ* 108 (January 1968): 25–7.

'S. J .W. Edinburgh', 'Prize Medals', *PhNews* 2 (25 March 1859): 32.

Say, Madeleine, 'John Hunter Kerr: Photographer', *The La Trobe Journal* 76 (2005): 71–6.

Schaaf, Larry J., 'Charles Piazzi Smyth's 1865 Conquest of the Great Pyramid', *HoPh* 3 (1979): 329–41.

Schaaf, Larry, 'Piazzi Smyth at Teneriffe: Part I, The Expedition and the Resulting Book', *HoPh* 4 (1980): 289–307.

Schaaf, Larry, 'Piazzi Smyth at Teneriffe: Part 2, Photography and the Disciples of Constable and Harding', *HoPh* 5 (1981): 27–50.

Schaaf, Larry, 'The First Photograph James Nasmyth Ever Saw', *SPhB* 2 (1990): 15–22.

Schaaf, Larry, '"Splendid Calotypes" and "Hideous Men": Photography in the Diaries of Lady Pauline Trevelyan', *HoPh* 34 (2010): 329–32.

Scott, R. E. 'Hawick's Photographers since 1854', *Transactions of the Hawick Archaeological Society* 1974: 42–7.

Seiberling, Grace, 'The Photographs of Joseph James Forrester', *HoPh* 7 (1983): 51–61.

Shang-Jen Li, 'Discovering the Secrets of Long and Healthy Life: John Dudgeon on Chinese Hygiene', *Social History of Medicine* 23 (2009): 21–37.

Sheldon, Julie, 'Elizabeth Rigby and the calotypes of Hill and Adamson: correspondence from the John Murray Archive, 1843–1880', *Studies in Photography* (2007): 42–8.

Simpson, G. Wharton, 'Editorial', *PhNews* 6 (28 November 1862): 565–6.

Simpson, James Young, 'On solutions of Gun-Cotton, Gutta Percha, and Caoutchouc, as Dressings for wounds &c.', *Pharmaceutical Journal* 8 (1 August 1848): 84–9.

Simpson, James Young, 'Pyramidal Structures in Egypt and elsewhere, and the objects of their erection', *Proceedings of the RSEdin* 5 (1868–69): 243–68.

Simpson, Roddy, 'Stairs and lamp-posts: evidence of location in images by Thomas Keith', *Studies in Photography* (2007): 31–6.

Simpson, Roddy, 'The Artist and the Engineer – the friendship of David Octavius Hill and John Miller', *Studies in Photography* (2007): 49–58.

Simpson, Roddy, 'Archibald Burns – photographer of Old Edinburgh', *Studies in Photography* (2009): 68–77.

Simpson, Roddy, 'Julia Margaret Cameron and

the Photographic Society of Scotland', *HoPh* 28 (2004): 82–7.

Simpson, Roddy, 'Exposing Miss Mann', *Studies in Photography* (2010): 42–8.

Smailes, Helen, 'A Gentleman's Exercise: Ronald Leslie Melville, 11th Earl of Leven, and the Amateur Photographic Association', *Photographic Collector* 3, no. 3 (Winter 1982): 262–93.

Smart, Robert, '"Famous throughout the World": Valentine & Sons Ltd., Dundee', *Review of Scottish Culture* 4 (1988): 75–87.

Smee, Alfred, 'Photogenic Drawing', *Literary Gazette* 12 (18 May 1839): 314–6; (25 May 1839): 332.

Smith, Graham, 'A calotype view of Trinity College Church, Edinburgh, by David Octavius Hill and Robert Adamson', *Burlington Magazine* 126, no. 981 (December 1984): 781–82, 786.

Smith, Graham, 'A Group of Early Scottish Calotypes', *Princeton University Library Chronicle* 46 (1984): 81–94.

Smith, Graham, 'James David Forbes and Thomas Rodger', *SPhB* 2 (Autumn 1987): 14–19.

Smith, Graham, 'Magnesium Light Portraits', *HoPh* 12 (1988): 88–9.

Smyth, C. Piazzi, 'How to take landscapes with portrait lenses at full aperture', *BJPh* 22 (1875): 208–9.

Sobieszek, Robert, 'Conquest by Camera: Alexander Gardner's Across the Continent on the Kansas Pacific Railroad', *Art in America* 60 (March 1972): 80–5

Sreznievsky, V. [Secretary of the Photographic Society of St Petersburg], Obituary of William Carrick, *BJPh* 25 (27 December 1878): 621.

Stereoscopic Magazine: *A Gallery of Landscape Scenery, Architecture, Antiquities, and Natural History, accompanied with descriptive articles by writers of eminence* (London: Lovell Reeve, 1863 and 1865).

Stevenson, Sara, 'The Australian Question', *SPhB* 1 (Spring 1988): 28–38.

Stevenson, Sara, 'The Rev. D. T. K. Drummond 1806–1877', *SPhB* 2 (1992): 3–10.

Stevenson, Sara, 'The Hill View; "The eye unsatisfied and dim with gazing"', *HoPh* 30 (2006): 212–34.

Stevenson, Sara, 'The doctor, the lady and the man who printed his own money', *Studies in Photography* (2007): 15–16.

Stevenson, Sara, 'Seeing in Time. Visual Engagement in Stevenson's idea of Edinburgh, considered in the light of paintings and photographs by David Octavius Hill and Robert Adamson', *Journal of Stevenson Studies* 8 (2011): 264–85.

Stevenson, S., 'Robert Louis Stevenson and the Portrait Photographers', *HoPh* 37 (2013): 235–42.

Stevenson, S., 'Painting in Light and Chemistry: D. O. Hill's The Market Cross, Ayr (1835) and its Relation to His Photographic Work with Robert Adamson, 1843–47', *Getty Research Journal* 6 (2014): 29–46.

Steward, A. A., 'Glasgow's "Broomielaw"', *HoPh* 10 (1986): 70.

Stewart, John, 'New Photographic Process', *Athenaeum* 1341 (9 July 1853): 831.

Stewart, John, 'On the Paper Process', *JPhS* 1 (30 June 1854): 225–30.

Sutton, Christine, 'The Impossibility of Photography', *New Scientist* 112 (25 December–1 January 1987): 40–3.

Sutton, Thomas, editorial response to an anonymous letter, 'Is Photography a Healthy Pursuit?', *PhNotes* 2 (1 May 1857): 164–5.

Sutton, Thomas, Editorial, *PhNotes* 2 (15 July 1857): 257.

Sutton, Thomas, Review, 'Stereoscopic views of Scotch scenery, by G. W. Wilson of Aberdeen', *PhNotes* 2 (15 July 1857): 262.

Sutton, Thomas, 'Reminiscences of an Old Photographer', *BJPh* 14 (30 Aug. 1867): 414.

Sutton, Thomas, 'Landscape Photography for

the Artist and the Amateur', *The Illustrated Photographer* 1 (28 February 1868): 44.

[Taylor, Dr Alexander], Review of Dr Alexander Taylor, On the Curative Influence of the Climate of Pau … with Descriptive Notices of the Geology, Botany, Natural History, Mountain-Sports, Local Antiquities, and Topography of the Pyrenees …, *Edinburgh Medical and Surgical Journal* 59 (1843): 142.

Taylor, Roger and Mike Ware, 'Pilgrims of the Sun: the Chemical Evolution of the Calotype 1840–1852', *HoPh* 27 (2003): 308–19.

'The Daguerreotype', *Chambers's Edinburgh Journal* (29 August 1839): 243–4.

Thomas, D. B. 'Early English Daguerreotypes', *Photography* (July 1962): 36–9.

Thomas, G., 'The Madras Photographic Society 1856–61', *HoPh* 16 (1992): 299–301.

Thompson, John, 'Alex Henderson's Winter Trip', *Canadian Rail* (Jan.–Feb. 1999): 3–13.

Thomson, John, 'Practical Photography in Tropical Regions', *BJPh* 13 (10 August 1866): 380; (17 August 1866): 393; (24 August 1866): 404; (4 September 1866): 436–7; (5 Oct. 1866): 472–3; (12 Oct. 1866): 487.

Thorp, Monica, 'William Henry Fox Talbot and the Edinburgh Connection, 1855–72', *Studies in Photography* (2005): 24–33.

Traill Taylor, John, 'The Optics of Photography and Photographic Lenses. Chapter IX Wide-angle, Non-distorting Lenses', *BJPh* 30 (20 June 1883): 370.

Traill Taylor, John, Letter to the Editor, *Liverpool Photographic Journal* 12 (Jan. 1856): 15.

Traill Taylor, John, 'On the Albumen Process', *JPhS* 3 (21 July 1856): 84.

Traill Taylor, John, 'Discoveries and Rediscoveries in Photography; with an account of the Alabastrine Process', *JPhS* 5 (1859): 151–4.

Traill Taylor, J., Review of the International Exhibition, *BJPh* 9 (15 May 1862): 129.

Traill Taylor, John, Review of 'Photographic Views in Invernesshire', *BJPh* 14 (1 February 1867): 54–5.

Traill Taylor, J., 'The Late W. H. Fox Talbot', *BJPh* 24 (28 September 1877): 460–1.

Triggs, Stanley G., 'Alexander Henderson: Nineteenth-century Landscape Photographer', *Archivaria* 5 (1977–78): 45–59.

Tunny, J. G., 'Early Reminiscences of Photography', *BJPh* 16 (12 November 1869): 546.

Urie, John, 'Pictures from Life: From the Scrap Book of a Photographer', *BJPh* 24 (5 Oct. 1877): 474–5; (12 October 1877): 486–7.

Wall, A. H., 'A Few Thoughts About Photographic Societies', *BJPh* 10 (15 Oct. 1863): 407.

Wallace, Veronica, 'Maria Obscura', *Edinburgh Review* 88 (1992): 101–9.

Ware, Mike, 'Photography: The enduring image', *Chemistry World* (Aug. 2007): 62–5.

Warnecke, Leon, 'Photographic Notes from Travels in Russia', *BJPh* 25 (29 November 1878): 570.

Wedgwood, Thomas and Humphrey Davy, 'An Account of a Method of Copying Paintings Upon Glass and Making Profiles by the Agency of Light Upon Nitrate of Silver', *Journal of the Royal Institution of Great Britain* 1 (1802). Reprinted in Newhall (ed.) 1981.

Wheatstone, Charles, 'Contributions to the Physiology of Vision: Part the First. On Some Remarkable, and hitherto unobserved Phenomena of Binocular Vision', *Philosophical Transactions of the Royal Society of London* 128 (1838): 371–94; see also Bowers 2001: 45–54.

Wilson, G. M., 'Early Photography, Goitre and James Inglis', *British Medical Journal* 4 (May 1973): 104–5.

Wilson, George, 'On the Transmission of the Actinic Rays of light through the Eye, and their relation to the Yellow Spot of the Retina', *Proceedings of the RSEdin* 3 (1850–57): 371–6.

Wilson, George, 'On the Extent to which the received theory of Vision requires us to regard the Eye as a Camera Obscura', *Transactions of the RSEdin* 21 (1857): 327–47.

Wilson, George, 'On dryness, darkness, and colours, and coldness as a means of preserving photographs from fading', *Journal of the Photographic Society* 5 (23 May 1859): 290–3.

Wilson, G. W., 'On developing negatives with iron', *PhNotes* 3 (1 May 1858): 113–14.

Wilson, George Washington, 'A voice from the hills: Mr Wilson at home', *BJPh* 11 (16 Sept. 1864): 352–4; (30 Sept. 1864): 374–5; (7 Oct. 1864): 388; (21 October 1864): 410.

Wood, R. Derek, 'The daguerreotype in England: some primary material relating to Beard's lawsuits', *HoPh* 3 (1979): 305–9.

Wood, R. Derek, 'The Daguerreotype Patent, the British Government, and the Royal Society', *HoPh* 4 (1980): 53–9.

Newspapers

- *Aberdeen Herald*
- *Aberdeen Journal*
- *Argus* [Melbourne]
- *Berwick & Kelso Warder*
- *Bombay Times*
- *Caledonian Mercury*
- *Daily News*
- *Daily Scotsman*
- *Daily Southern Cross*
- *Dumbarton Herald*
- *Dumfries & Galloway Courier*
- *Dundee Advertiser*
- *Dundee Courier*
- [Dundee] *Evening Telegraph*
- *Perth and Cupar Advertiser*
- *Edinburgh Courant*
- *Edinburgh Evening Courant*
- *Elgin Courier*
- *Empire* [Sydney]
- *Exeter & Plymouth Gazette*
- *Fife Herald*
- *Forres, Elgin and Nairn Gazette*
- *Glasgow Advertiser*
- *Glasgow Argus*
- *Glasgow Citizen*
- *Glasgow Examiner*
- *Glasgow Herald*
- *Glasgow Sentinel*
- *Hull Packet and East Riding Times*
- *Inverness Advertiser*
- *Inverness Courier*
- *Inverness Courier & General Advertiser*
- *Inverness Journal*
- *John O'Groat Journal*
- *Launceston Examiner*
- *Liverpool Mercury*
- *London Gazette*
- *London Standard*
- *Manchester Courier*
- *Manchester Times & Gazette*
- *Newcastle Courant*
- *Newcastle Journal*
- *New York Times*
- *New Zealander*
- *Otago Daily Times*
- *Otago Witness*
- *Royal Cornwall Gazette, Falmouth Packet and General Advertiser*
- *Scotsman*
- *South Australia Register*
- *Spectator*
- *Sydney Morning Herald*
- *Toronto Globe*
- *Witness*

Post Office directories 1839–70

Aberdeen; Dundee; Edinburgh; Glasgow; Kilmarnock and Riccarton

Select Index

Adam, Alexander Forsyth (1822–81), W.S. 147, 174, 271

Adam, James (dates unknown), advocate 147, 271

Adams, George (1750–95), scientific instrument maker 235

Adamson, Dr John (1809–70), of St Andrews 45–7, 96, 102, 123, 134, 135, 164–5, 176, 196, 239–40, 251, 311

Adamson, John (*c*.1822–1912), photographer, Glasgow 35, 81–2

Adamson, Robert (1821–48), of St Andrews and Edinburgh 27, 31, 40–1, 45, 46–7, 95–102, 105, 111, 115, 125, 130, 131, 145–6, 176–7, 203–4, 237–40, 246, 248, 250, 271, 311, 343, 346, 347

Adie & Son, scientific instrument makers, Edinburgh 26

Adie, Alexander (1775–1858), scientific instrument maker 26

Adie, John (1805–57), scientific instrument maker 26, 27, 181

Africa
- Abyssinia 5: Magdala 191; Senafé 192; war 191–2
- Egypt 150, 284–9: Alexandria 284–5; Great Pyramid of Giza 150, 286; Karnac, Grand Hall 287–8; Luxor 285; River Nile 284–5, 304
- Krumen 310
- Madagascar 302
- Nubia 285

- River Niger 302–3
- South Africa: Cape Town 302; Cape of Good Hope, Royal Observatory 301–2
- Tete 303
- Zambesi river 303–4
- Zanzibar 304–5

Agassiz, Louis (1807–73), geologist and biologist 250

Albert, Prince Consort (1819–61) 61, 143, 173, 189

Albert Edward (1841–1910), Prince of Wales 189, 192, 332

Albert, Josef (1825–86), improver of the collotype, Munich 249

Alexandra (1844–1925), Princess of Wales 189

Alphonse, M., itinerant daguerreotypist 72

American Civil War 204–10
- Antietam, Battle of 206
- Gettysburg 207–9; Union Cemetery 207–8
- Norfolk Navy Yard 206, 207
- Potomac 205
- Rapidan 205
- Stone Church, Centreville 207

Annan, James Craig (1864–1946), photographer, Glasgow 346

Annan, Thomas (1829–87), photographer, Glasgow 18, 121, 138, 142, 212–6, 243–4, 346, 347

Anthony, E. & H. T., photographic suppliers, New York 204

Arago, François (1786–1853), physicist 23, 41, 48

Archer, Frederick Scott (1813–57),

inventor of the collodion process 81, 83, 135, 163

Astley, Thomas (1809–50), chemist 26

Australia
- Burra Burra copper mine 321
- Corroboree 321–2
- gold fields 321, 327
- Great Barrier Reef 319
- identification of criminals 258
- Jajoweroung 321
- Launceston, Tasmania 319
- Loddon tribe 322
- Melbourne 321–2: Collins Street 324
- Portland Bay 321
- Port Phillip 321
- Sydney 124, 323–4: School of Arts 323; University of 323
- Torres Strait 319

Babbage, Charles (1791–1871), mathematician 235

Baikie, Dr William Balfour (1824–64), explorer 303

Bairds of Gartsherrie, ironmasters 163

Balfour, Prof. John Hutton (1808–84), botanist 183, 246, 254

Balugani, Luigi (1737–71), draughtsman 5

Bao Yun (1806–91), civil servant 229–30

Barker, Robert (1739–06), inventor of the panorama 12

Barnard, George N. (1819–1902), photographer, United States 206

Barratt, John (b.1816), daguerreotypist 67

Barry, Charles (1823–1900), architect 108

Barry, William H. (dates unknown) 108

Bate, Gerardine, *see* Macpherson, Gerardine

Beard, Richard (1801–85), entrepreneur 23, 38, 60, 64, 76

Beattie, John (d. 1883), itinerant photographer 82–3

Belgium 99, 100, 107
- Antwerp 74
- Brussels 269: Ghent 5, 108, 269; Liège 269
- Mechelen 108, 269
- Namur 269–70
- Waterloo 269

Bell, Robert, joiner 146–7, 148

Belletie & Co., daguerreotypists, Glasgow 66–7

Belletie & Henderson, daguerreotypists, Glasgow 66–7

Bernard, J. B., daguerreotypist, Glasgow 64–6, 67, 69

Berranger, Captain Paul-Emile (1815–96), French navy 227

Berwick, Dr George (b.*c*.1829, d.1892/3), photographer 18, 134, 212–3, 302–3

Bible, The: Exodus 292; Judith 187, 189

Biggs, Colonel Thomas (1822–1905) 314

Bishop, Robert, daguerreotypist, Edinburgh 112

Black, Professor Joseph (1728–99), chemist 16

Blackburn, Professor Hugh (1823–1909), mathematician 250–1

Blackburn, Jemima (1823–1909), illustrator 250–1

Blackmore, William (1827–78), investor 210

Blackwood, James (1823–93), carpet manufacturer, Kilmarnock 35

(1826–85), Union Army 205–6
McCosh, Dr John (1805–85),
    surgeon, India 176, 308–10
McCraw, William (1825–c.1883),
    photographer, Edinburgh 133,
    186, 320
McCulloch, Horatio (1805–67),
    painter 163, 175, 248
McDonald, D. (dates unknown),
    daguerreotypist, Aberdeen 40
McDonald, Sergeant James
    (1822– 85), photographer, Royal
    Engineers 292–5
Macfarlan, Dr Alexander John-
    stone (1838–69), physician 183
Macfarlane, Donald Horne (1830–
    1904), merchant in India 317–9
McGee, Thomas D'Arcy (1825–
    68), Canadian politician 327
McGlashon [or McGlashan]
    Alexander (d.1877), photo-
    grapher 172–3, 196, 249, 325
MacGregor, John (d.1872),
    photographer, Edinburgh and
    St Petersburg 216–19
Mackie, Alexander (dates
    unknown), daguerreotypist,
    Huntly 71–2
Maclagan, Dr (later Sir) Andrew
    Douglas (1812–1900), surgeon
    and physician 26–7, 177
MacLeay, Kenneth (1802–78),
    miniature painter and photo-
    grapher 86, 134,
McMillan, Daniel (1805–81),
    photographic supplier, Edin-
    burgh and London 76
McMillan [Daniel] and [John]
    Thomson, daguerreotypists,
    Edinburgh 76, 77
McMillan and Rutherford, pocket-
    book and leather-case makers,
    Edinburgh 76

McNab, Alexander (b.c.1822),
    photographer, Glasgow 166
MacNee, Sir Daniel (1806–82),
    painter 163
Maconochie, Allan Alexander
    (later Maconochie Welwood)
    (1806–85), Professor of Roman
    and Scots Law, Glasgow 33, 167,
    168, 247
Macpherson, Gerardine (née Bate)
    (c.1830–78), photographer,
    Rome 276–8
Macpherson, Robert Turnbull
    (1814–72), photographer, Rome
    169, 170–1, 243, 275–81
Macrae, Justine Henrietta, see
    Ross, Justine Henrietta
Mactear, Andrew (c.1816–96),
    engraver and photographer,
    Glasgow 32, 64–5, 67, 69
Mahony, Francis Sylvester [pseud.
    Don Jeremy Savonarola] (1804–
    66), journalist 6, 275
Mann, Jessie (d.1867), photo-
    graphic assistant, Edinburgh
    98, 102
Manson, Andrew (b.c.1820),
    photographer, Bridge of Allan
    242
Markelova, Alexandra Grigory-
    evna (1835–1916), militant
    nihilist 217
Marx, Karl (1818–83), political
    theorist 227
Mary, Queen of Scots (1542–1587)
    10, 189, 283
Mason, George, FRPS [pseud.
    Mark Oute] (1839–1901),
    photographic supplier, Glasgow
    150–2, 260–2, 335
Matheson, Lady (née Mary Jane
    Perceval) (1821–96), of Storn-
    oway 192

Maxwell, Professor James Clerk
    (1831–79), physicist 186, 251,
    286, 344, 345, 346
Maxwell, Dr James Laidlaw (1836–
    1921), missionary, Formosa 223
Mayall, John Jabez Edwin (1813–
    1901), photographer, London
    11, 65, 67, 122
Mayhew, Henry (1812–87),
    journalist 227
Melville, Ronald Leslie (later 11th
    Earl of Leven and 10th Earl of
    Melville) (1835–1906) 190–2
Memes, John Smith (1795–1858),
    Rector of Ayr Academy 56
Mendelssohn, Felix (1809–46),
    composer 108
Michelangelo Buonarotti (1475–
    1564), artist 275
Middleton, Lady (formerly Mrs
    Willoughby, née Ross) 190–1
Miles, daguerreotypist, Edinburgh
    61
Millais, John Everett (1829–96),
    painter 246
Miller, Hugh (1802–56), journalist
    12, 96–7, 237–8, 241, 249–50
Miller, John (1805–83), railway
    engineer 172
miniature painters 86, 121;
    miniatures 55, 85
missionaries 226, 301–2, 223, 226
Moffat, John (1819–94), photo-
    grapher, Edinburgh 86, 132,
    135–7, 149,
Moir, Sheriff George (1800–70),
    Professor of Scots Law, Edin-
    burgh 162, 169, 174
Montgomery, James Francis
    (1818–97), advocate 162
Montreal, D., daguerreotypist 31
Morton, Thomas (1783–1862),
    carpet manufacturer 9

Mouhot, Henri (1826–61),
    explorer 220
Muh, Tartar General in Chief 308
Mullins, daguerreotypist, Edin-
    burgh 76
Mul Raj Diwan (1814–51),
    Governor of Multan 309
Munby, Giles (1813–76), botanist
    105
Murchison, Sir Roderick Impey, Bt
    (1792–1871), geologist 249
Murray, Colin Roderick (1840–
    84), photographer 319
Murray, Dr David (dates
    unknown), surgeon, Forfar 34
Murray, Dr John (1809–98),
    surgeon 314–6
Murray, Loveday Marian (d.1901)
    314–5
Murray, Robert (1822–93),
    engineer 192, 284–5
Mytee, Syndoo, dacoit 259

Napier, General Sir Charles (1782–
    1853), soldier 310
Napier, Mark (1798–1879),
    advocate 162
Napier, Robert (1791–1876), naval
    engineer 212, 303
Napoleon, Emperor (1769–1821)
    56
Nasmyth, Alexander (1758–1840),
    painter 8
Nasmyth, James (1808–90),
    engineer 8–9, 19, 98, 102,
    105–6
Negretti and Zambra, photo-
    graphic suppliers, London 150
Neil [Neill], daguerreotypist,
    Dundee 75
Neill, Dr Andrew Charles Brisbane
    (1814–91), physician, Madras
    311–4

photography
- animal 250-3
- art 246-9
- botanical 253-5
- composite 213, 326, 333
- documentary 203-4
- forgery 261-3
- instantaneous 167-8, 272, 344
- landscape 137-8, 143-4
- medical 176-83
- micro- 272
- portraiture 139-40, 143
- Royal Warrant 113, 127, 142, 332
- studio snow effects 333
- tourism 269-95
- war 191-2, 205-9, 211, 281, 289, 292, 307-10, 316, 334
phrenology 82
phreno-mesmerism 96-7
Pickering, Edward John (1827-28), daguerreotypist, Glasgow 64-5, 69
Pigou, Dr William Henry (1817-58), Government Photographer, Bombay 314
Pinkerton, Allan (1819-84), detective 205
Pixis, Johann Peter (1788-1874), musician 106
Playfair, Captain George Ranken (1816-85), surgeon 192
Playfair, Major (Sir) Hugh Lyon (1786-1861), Provost of St Andrews 37-8, 45
Playfair, Professor John (1748-1819), mathematician 8
police 256-9, 263
Ponder, Joseph J. (dates unknown), itinerant daguerreotypist 71
Ponton, Mungo (1802-80), photographic inventor 8, 29, 44-5, 249, 254, 347

Popowitz, George (b.1801), daguerreotypist, Edinburgh 83-4
Portugal 271-2
- Cintra 272
- River Douro 271
Potter, Beatrix (1866-1943), author 251
Powell [or Payne], Lewis (1844-65), conspirator 209-10
Pretsch, Paul (1808-73), printer, London 170
Price, William Lake (1810-96), photographer 173
Pringle, Thomas (1832-94), photographer, Edinburgh 78, 130
Pritchard, Dr Edward W. (1825-65), murderer 27, 141-2
Pritchard, Henry Baden (1841-84), editor 205
Proctor, James (dates unknown), photographer, Aberdeen 263
Prome (Pyay), Burma 309-10
Prout, Samuel (1783-1852), painter 270
Prout, Victor Albert (1835-77), photographer, London 189-90

Rae, Alexander (1811-97), photographer 40
Rae, John (1813-1900) public servant, Sydney 323-4
Raeburn, Sir Henry (1756-1823), painter 7-8, 238
Raichund, Prechmund, philanthropist 313-4
railways
- Canadian Pacific Railway 327-9
- Grand Trunk Railway 330-2
- Intercolonial Railway 329
- Occidental Railway 329
- Union Pacific Railway 210-2

Ramsay, William (1806-65), Prof. of Humanity, Glasgow 278
Rangavis, Alexandros (1809-92), writer 84
Raven, Rev. Thomas Milville (1828-96), clergyman 170, 171, 174, 274-5
Reekie, John (dates unknown), photographer, United States 206, 334
Reeve, Lovell (1814-65), publisher 150, 254
regiments
- 70th Regiment, Bengal Native Infantry 308
- 73rd Regiment of Foot 272
- 92nd Gordon Highlanders 94, 101
- Life Guards 187
- Madras Artillery 316
- Royal Engineers 292-5, 307
- Scots Fusilier Guards 193
Regnault, Henri Victor (1810-78), chemist 274
Reid, Charles (1837-1929), photographer 252
Rejlander, Oscar Gustav (1813-75), photographer, Wolverhampton 171, 173, 194
Rembrandt, Harmenszoon van Rijn (1606-69), painter 99, 104, 196
Reynolds, Sir Joshua (1723-92), painter 238, 241
Rhodes, Lt Col. William (1821-92), farmer, Canada 332-3
Rigby, Elizabeth (later Lady Eastlake) (1809-93), critic 103, 237-8, 242, 244, 251
Rimmel, Eugène (1820-87), perfumer 192
Rimmer, Richard (1826-1905) of Marchmount 168

Roberts, David (1796-1864), painter 99, 101, 103-4
Robertson, Dr William (1818-82), physician, Crimea 281-2
Robinson, Henry Peach (1830-1901), photographer, London 173, 196, 303
Robison, Sir John (1778-1843), nabob 25, 34, 56
Rodger, Thomas (1832-83), photographer, St Andrews 47, 121, 133, 134-5, 186-7, 239, 248
Roscoe, Henry (1833-1915), chemist 136
Ross, Andrew (1798-1859), optician, London 145
Ross, Horatio (1801-86) of Rossie 38-40, 147, 168-71, 174, 191, 252-3
Ross, James (1816-95), photographer, Edinburgh 76-9, 80, 84-5, 86, 112-6, 127-30, 169-70, 174, 262, 347
Ross, Justine Henrietta (née Macrae) (1815-94) 39-40, 169
Ross and Pringle, photographers, Edinburgh 78
Ross and Thomson, photographers, Edinburgh 76-9, 80, 112-6, 127-30, 131, 132, 165, 240
Ross, Major Thomas (dates unknown), soldier 272
Roychand, Premchand (1831-1906), philanthropist 313
Ruskin, John (1819-1900), art critic 251
Russia 64, 282-4
- Moscow 282: Kremle churches 282-3; Kremlin 282
- River Volga 217-9
- Simbirsk 217-9

Image Credits

The publisher is grateful to the following sources for permission to use images within this publication. No reproduction of material in copyright is permitted without prior contact with the publisher or the original source.

Ashmolean Museum

© Ashmolean University, University of Oxford
for Figure 1.6

Bath Royal Literary and Scientific Institute

for Figure 10.6

Bayerisches Nationalmuseum Munich

© Bayerisches Nationalmuseum München, Photo Stöckmann, Marianne
for Figure 2.1

The British Library

© The British Library Board
for Figures 6.27b, 9.17, 10.15, 10.16, 10.17, 10.36

Canadian Centre for Architecture

Collection Centre Canadian d'Architecture/ Canadian Centre for Architecture, Montréal
for Figures 6.22, 7.12, 7.13, 7.18, 7.19, 8.7 (detail on p. 234)

City Art Centre, Edinburgh

Edinburgh Museums & Galleries
for Figure 1.11

Edinburgh Central Library

Courtesy of Edinburgh City Libraries and Information Services – Edinburgh Room
for Figures 5.18, 6.21 (detail on p. 160)

George Eastman House, Rochester, NY

Courtesy of George Eastman House International Museum of Photography and Film
for Figures 6.32, 9.8, 9.15

Getty Research Institute

Research Library, Getty Research Institute, Los Angeles
for Figure 9.7

Glasgow Museums

© CSG CIC Glasgow Museums and Libraries Collections
for Figures 1.12, 6.7

Glasgow School of Art

Library Special Collections, Archives and Museum Collections
for Figures 6.5, 8.22

HBOS plc

Courtesy of Lloyds Banking Group PLC Archives
for Figure 8.27

Howard and Jane Ricketts

From the Collection of Howard and Jane Ricketts
for Figures 10.19, 10.20 (and detail on p. 300), 10.21

Hudson's Bay Company

Archives of Manitoba, for Figure 10.32

The Israel Museum

© The Israel Museum, Jerusalem
for Figures 9.18, 9.19

The J. Paul Getty Museum

© The J. Paul Getty Museum, Los Angeles
for Figures 6.10, 6.29, 6.30, 6.31, 6.37, 7.8, 7.9, 9.12, 10.39

John Leech Gallery, Auckland, New Zealand

From the Collection of Michael Graham Stewart
for Figure 10.29

Library and Archives Canada

© Library and Archives of Canada
for Figures 10.30, 10.31

Library of Congress, Washington DC

© Library of Congress
for Figures 7.6, 7.7

McCord Museum, Montreal

© McCord Museum
for Figures 10.33, 10.34, 10.37, 10.38

The Mitchell Library, Glasgow

© The Mitchell Library Special Collections
for Figures 1.16, 5.22, 7.11

National Army Museum, London

Courtesy of the Council of the National Army Museum, London
for Figures 10.9, 10.10

National Galleries of Scotland

© Scottish National Portrait Gallery
for Figures 2.3, 2.9, 3.1, 3.3, 3.8, 3.11, 3.12, 3.13 (detail on p. 54), 3.15, 3.19, 3.20, 4.2, 4.6, 4.8a, 4.8b, 4.9, 4.10, 4.11, 4.12, 4.13, 6.1, 6.12, 6.15, 6.17, 6.19, 6.28, 6.33, 6.34, 7.10, 7.14, 7.15, 8.3, 8.4, 8.6, 8.8, 8.12, 8.14, 8.16, 9.1, 9.9 (detail on p. 268 and back cover), 10.23, 10.35

National Gallery, Ireland

Photography Courtesy of the National Gallery of Ireland
for Figure 1.8

National Gallery, London

Photo © National Gallery, London
for Figure 1.1

National Library of New Zealand

Alexander Turnbull Library
for Figures 3.18, 10.28

National Library of Scotland

Reproduced by kind permission of the
National Library of Scotland
for Figures 1.17, 2.7, 6.2, 6.8, 6.24, 8.19,
8.23 a–d, 8.24, 8.25, 9.20, 9.22, 9.23,
9.24, 10.2, 10.4, 10.5, 10.12, 10.13, 10.14,
10.18

National Museums Scotland

© National Museums Scotland
for Figures 1.2, 1.3, 1.4, 1.5, 1.14, 2.2, 2.5,
2.12, 2.14, 2.15, 3.2, 3.4, 3.5, 3.6, 3.9, 3.10,
3.14, 3.16, 4.1, 4.3, 4.5 (detail on p. 94),
5.1, 5.3, 5.4, 5.5 (detail on p. 120), 5.6,
5.7, 5.8, 5.13a, 5.13b, 5.17a, 5.17b, 5.19,
5.23a 5.23b, 5.25, 5.26, 5.30, 5.31, 6.3, 6.4,
7.1 (detail on p. 202), 8.1, 8.5, 8.11, 8.13,
8.15, 8.17, 8.20, 9.21, 10.11, 10.27

Princeton University, NJ

© Photo SCALA, Florence, Princeton
University Art Museum
for Figure 9.10

Private Collections

Photography Courtesy National Museums
Scotland
for Figures 1.9, 1.15, 5.8, 5.14, 5.27

Private Collections

Photography Courtesy Michael Gray
for Figure 1.10 (detail on p. 2)

Rijksmuseum, Amsterdam

Source Rijksmuseum
for Figure 3.17

Royal College of Surgeons, Edinburgh

© Royal College of Surgeons, Edinburgh
Collections
for Figure 6.18

The Royal Collection

Royal Collection Trust/© Her Majesty Queen
Elizabeth II 2015
for Figures 4.16, 4.17, 4.18, 10.7

**Royal Commission on the Ancient and
Historical Monuments of Scotland**

© Courtesy of RCAHMS.
Licensor www.rcahms.gov.uk
for Figures 5.10, 6.16, 8.18

Royal Geographical Society, London

© Royal Geographical Museum
for Figure 10.3

Royal Observatory, Edinburgh

Photography Courtesy National Museums
Scotland
for Figures 2.4 (detail on p. 22), 9.13, 9.16,
10.1

Royal Scottish Academy

© Royal Scottish Academy
for Figures 5.11, 6.9, 6.20, 6.23, 9.4, 9.5

Science & Society Picture Library

National Media Museum
for Figures, 3.7, 4.4, 4.15, 5.28, 5.29, 6.11,
6.14, 6.25, 7.22, 8.9, 8.21, 9.2, 9.3, 9.6,
Figure 2 (Conclusion)

Royal Photographic Society
for Figures 2.6, 4.14, 5.17c, 6.13

Science Museum
for Figure 1 (Conclusion) (detail on p. 342)

SCRAN

© Perth Museum and Art Gallery.
Licensor www.SCRAN.ac.uk
for Figures 5.20, 5.21

State Library, New South Wales

© State Library of NSW
for Figure 10.26

State Library, Victoria

for Figure 10.24

Universiteit Leiden, The Netherlands

© Leiden University Library
for Figures 5.12, 8.2

University of Glasgow Library

By Permission of University of Glasgow
Library, Special Collections
for Figure 10.22

University of St Andrews

Photography © Lawrence Levy Photographic
Collection. All rights reserved. Images courtesy
of the University of St Andrews Library
for Figures 2.8, 2.13, 5.2, 5.15, 5.16, 5.24,
6.26

University of Sydney

University of Sydney Archives
for Figure 10.25

University of Texas

Harry Ransom Center, The University of Texas,
Austin
for Figures 4.7, 5.9, 6.6, 7.2, 7.3, 7.4a, 7.4b,
7.17, 9.11

Victoria and Albert Museum

© Victoria and Albert Museum, London
for Figures 2.10, 2.11, 6.35, 6.36, 10.8